THE GENEALOGIST'S GUIDE TO MASSSACHUSETTS - VOLUME 2

The Genealogist's Guide to Masssachusetts - Volume 2

Eric J Ostroff

Contents

1

The Genealogist's Guide
     to
Massachusetts
by
Eric J. Ostroff
Volume 2
Dukes to Middlesex Counties

Foreword

Dedication
    To my beloved wife, Jennifer, whose unwavering love and encouragement have made every journey possible, and to my children—Wesley, Zachary, Hannah, and Christopher—whose curiosity and joy inspire me to uncover the stories of those who came before us. May this work honor our family's past as much as it celebrates our present and future together.

3

Massachusetts is a land where history is not simply recorded—it is layered, lived, and continually rediscovered. The story of this Commonwealth is written in shoreline towns carved by whaling winds, in quiet inland villages whose boundaries shifted with every new parish, and in Indigenous homelands whose roots reach millennia deeper than any colonial archive. To research Massachusetts ancestry is to step into a terrain where every town line, every court record, and every surviving scrap of governance reveals not only a family's origins, but the evolving story of America itself.

The Genealogist's Guide to Massachusetts – Volume 2 invites researchers into this landscape with both precision and purpose. Building upon the foundation established in Volume I, this volume broadens the journey from the islands of Dukes County across the industrial and academic centers of Middlesex. Here, the researcher encounters a remarkable diversity of records—Wampanoag petitions preserved alongside colonial proprietors' books; Quaker meeting minutes written with exacting discipline; whaling crew lists that connect families to the distant Pacific; land deeds whose boundaries shift with storms; and town clerks' ledgers whose survival is itself an act of historical luck. Together, these materials form an intricate mosaic that genealogists must learn to interpret with care.

What distinguishes this guide is its understanding that genealogy is not merely the extraction of names and dates—it is an immersion in context. As the manuscript reminds us, effective research requires knowing *who* created a record, *why* they created it, and *how* jurisdiction, geography, culture, and history shaped the evidence that survived. This approach is vital in Massachusetts, where the archival footprint varies dramatically from county to county: the island insularity of Dukes, the maritime energy of Essex, the agrarian-to-industrial transformation of Franklin and Hampden, the academic and civic complexity of Middlesex. Each community left behind its own idiosyncratic documentary signature.

This volume offers readers a map to navigate these complexities. Chapters open with clear historical frameworks that explain why records exist where they do—why Quaker records flourish in one town while Congregational registers dominate another; why land disputes proliferate in Vineyard proprietors' accounts; why industrial towns produced layers of municipal documentation while remote villages relied on scattered church books and county filings. The manuscript consistently grounds genealogical method in historical reality, empowering the researcher to form conclusions that are not only accurate but deeply informed.

Equally important is the book's attentiveness to communities often marginalized in traditional genealogical guides. The histories of Indigenous peoples, African American residents, Portuguese and Cape Verdean immigrants, and other groups appear not as footnotes but as central threads woven throughout the counties' narratives. This reflects a commitment to inclusivity and transparency—a recognition that Massachusetts history, like American history itself, is richer and more complex than the records alone may suggest.

For beginners, this guide provides structure and clarity. For advanced researchers, it offers nuance and strategic depth. For all genealogists, it is a reminder that our work is both an intellectual discipline and an act of stewardship. To reconstruct a life from scattered fragments is to honor the people who walked these shores, tilled these fields, sailed these oceans, and built these communities.

In a field where methodology matters as much as discovery, *The Genealogist's Guide to Massachusetts – Volume 2* stands as both a compass and a companion. It encourages us to ask better questions, to follow the evidence wherever it leads, and to appreciate the profound connection between families and the places they inhabited. As you move from the windswept islands of Dukes County to the historic towns and cities of Middlesex, may this volume illuminate the paths your ancestors once traveled—and the stories waiting still to be found.

Table of Contents

5

Preface

This anthology, *The Genealogist's Guide to Massachusetts*, is written for researchers who wish to move beyond isolated names and dates and into the deeper landscape that shaped their ancestors' lives. It is intended equally for those just beginning to explore New England roots and for experienced genealogists seeking a structured overview of Massachusetts resources, history, and research strategies. The goal is to provide a practical, context-rich guide that bridges the gap between historical narrative and hands-on methodology, so that readers can interpret records accurately and place individual families within the wider story of the Commonwealth.

Author's note and purpose

This guide grew out of countless hours spent in town halls, archives, online databases, and local historical societies, puzzling through the quirks of Massachusetts records. Over time, recurring patterns emerged: similar questions from clients and students, similar pitfalls in interpreting town and county jurisdictions, and similar misunderstandings about what records exist, and where. This book responds to those patterns by organizing the essentials of Massachusetts research into a single, coherent reference, with an emphasis on practicality and historical context.

The purpose is not to replace detailed local histories, specialized monographs, or archival finding aids, but to help readers approach them more effectively. The chapters are designed to highlight what records were created, who created them, and how they survived (or did not), so that you can set realistic expectations and construct sound, well-documented conclusions. Throughout, the focus is on helping you ask better questions of the records and to recognize when your evidence is sufficient—and when it is not.

Why Massachusetts matters

Massachusetts occupies a central place in American history, and that prominence is reflected in the richness and complexity of its records. From the early 17th century, when English settlers established Plymouth and Massachusetts Bay, through the American Revolution, industrialization, and waves of immigration, the colony and later Commonwealth exerted outsized influence on politics, religion, education, and social reform. Events associated with Massachusetts—such as the Mayflower migration, Puritan settlement, the Boston Massacre and Boston Tea Party, and the first battles of the Revolution—have drawn genealogists for generations because the families involved left unusually deep documentary footprints.

For genealogists, Massachusetts is both a blessing and a challenge. The blessing lies in the breadth of surviving material: early town records, vital registrations, church books, court and land records, military files, tax lists, newspapers, institutional archives, and extensive published and digital aids. The challenge lies in navigating overlapping jurisdictions, shifting boundaries, evolving record-keeping practices, and the biases and silences in the archive—particularly concerning Indigenous communities, enslaved and free people of African descent, women, the poor, and later immigrant groups. Understanding Massachusetts as a dynamic historical setting, rather than a static backdrop, is essential to responsible research.

How to Use This Volume

This second volume of *The Genealogist's Guide to Massachusetts* continues the county-by-county approach begun in Volume I, carrying the reader from the island and coastal landscapes of Dukes County and Nantucket through the inland towns and urban centers of Middlesex County. It builds on the broader historical and methodological framework introduced earlier, guiding readers through the diverse jurisdictions, archives, and documentary traditions that define the Commonwealth's middle counties.

Each county chapter opens with a concise overview of geographic and historical context, followed by detailed research notes that identify key repositories, courthouse jurisdictions, and surviving record types. Within these sections, you'll find summaries of cities, towns, villages, and unincorporated communities, along with practical direction on accessing records at the town, county, and state levels. Because local governance remained the backbone of Massachusetts recordkeeping well into the nineteenth century, special emphasis is placed on understanding how town clerks, registrars, and county courts interacted to produce and preserve vital, probate, and land materials.

Readers should approach this volume both geographically and methodologically. While the narrative moves east to west—from the island parishes and maritime settlements of Dukes and Nantucket through Essex's coastal records, and onward to Middlesex's industrial towns and academic centers—the structure also invites comparison between counties. Cross-references connect recurring record patterns, migratory movements, and institutional evolutions that shaped where families lived and where their evidence survives.

To support deeper research, this volume incorporates contextual notes, pointers to archival collections, and examples illustrating how local documentation intersects with broader genealogical evidence. References to major record types, digital access points, and relevant repositories throughout the state provide the bridge into *Volume III*, which will explore statewide record systems and specialized resources.

Whether your ancestors lived in a Nantucket whaling village, an Essex fishing town, or the mill cities and academic communes of Middlesex, this volume aims to help you interpret their footprints within the records of place, time, and community—turning historical geography into practical genealogy.

Acknowledgements and methodology

This project rests on the work of generations of record keepers, archivists, librarians, historians, and fellow genealogists who have preserved, described, and interpreted Massachusetts sources. Town clerks who carefully copied births and deaths, ministers who maintained membership rolls, registrars who indexed vital events, and archivists who advocated for preservation and digitization all made this kind of guide possible. The staff and volunteers of state and local archives, historical societies, libraries, and genealogical organizations—public and private—have shaped the landscape described in these pages, as have the authors and editors of prior guides, bibliographies, and histories of Massachusetts.

The methodology underlying this book reflects current best practices in genealogical research and documentation. Each discussion of a record group or repository is informed by direct use of the materials wherever possible, supplemented by institutional guides, catalog records, and scholarly treatments of Massachusetts history and law.

The emphasis throughout is on encouraging reasonably exhaustive research, careful source evaluation, correlation of evidence across multiple record types, and transparent citation of all sources used, while always respecting intellectual property and copyright. Readers are encouraged to adapt the approaches outlined here to their own questions and to remain attentive to voices and communities historically underrepresented in the surviving record.

Chapter 1

Dukes County
Nestled as Massachusetts' smallest county across Vineyard Sound from the mainland, Dukes County encompasses the island chain of Martha's Vineyard, Nomans Land, and Chappaquiddick, where glacial outwash plains, coastal dunes, and sheltered harbors have sustained human presence for millennia. Formed in 1695 from the western reaches of Dukes County, New York (itself granted to the Duke of York in 1664), this offshore territory bridges Wampanoag maritime homelands with English colonial plantations, evolving into whaling outposts, fishing villages, and seasonal retreats. Its compact geography—25 miles long, encompassing six towns (Tisbury, Edgartown, West Tisbury, Chilmark, Aquinnah, Gosnold)—preserves layered records of Indigenous resilience, Quaker settlement, African American communities, and Portuguese immigration, offering genealogists a uniquely insular chronicle of adaptation amid isolation.

For family historians, Dukes County's narrative weaves through seasonal fishing, sheep pasturage, whaling voyages, and resort economies. Archives hold Wampanoag oral traditions, early deed translations, Quaker monthly meeting minutes, shipmaster logs, and Freedmen's Bureau petitions—sources illuminating kinship networks across Native, English, African, and immigrant lines in one of New England's most biodiverse coastal realms.

INDIGENOUS FOUNDATIONS: THE WAMPANOAG HOMELAND AND CONTINUITY

Prior to European contact, Dukes County formed the vital western core of Wampanoag territory across Noepe (Martha's Vineyard), Nomans Land, and Chappaquiddick, inhabited by distinct subtribes whose lives revolved around the island's unique maritime ecology. The Aquinnah Wampanoag (historically Gay Head Wampanoag) occupied the dramatic western cliffs and Devil's Bridge area, renowned for whale strandings that provided oil and bone for tools; Takemmyquut (Chappaquiddick) communities fished the tidal shoals where Monomoyick Neck met Wasque, while Nashawena and Pasque islanders managed seasonal herring weirs along Vineyard Sound. These Algonquian-speaking peoples sustained themselves through a sophisticated seasonal round: spring herring and shad runs at tidal creeks like those at Menemsha Pond and Quitsa Pond, summer quahog and scallop harvests from coastal flats, autumn corn-bean-squash fields in sheltered Middle Road clearings, and winter deer hunts across the up-island moors and oak-hickory woodlands.

Sachems such as Pakeponesso of Takemmy, Petanonow of Nobnocket, and others exercised authority grounded in kinship consensus, mediating trade with mainland Narragansetts and provisioning Plymouth through wampum belts crafted from quahog shells. Spiritual life intertwined with land through place-based ceremonies at sacred sites like the Gay Head cliffs—regarded as a portal to the spirit world—and communal weirs symbolizing reciprocity with nature. Governance emphasized communal access over exclusionary title, with family bands rotating camps seasonally to preserve soil fertility and prevent overharvest. Genealogically, this worldview manifests in oral traditions and early deeds reflecting collective usufruct rather than fee simple, requiring researchers to consult tribal rolls alongside colonial translations for accurate kinship reconstruction.

Epidemics of 1616–1619, likely introduced by European fishing fleets, halved populations from perhaps 3,000 to 1,500, yet Wampanoag diplomacy with Plymouth persisted, sparing the islands from King Philip's War devastation. Christian Indian communities at Christiantown (near West Tisbury) and Nashawenaek produced surviving baptismal lists, petitions, and land safeguards, while Aquinnah retained communal lands through strategic petitions. Descendants endure in the federally recognized Wampanoag Tribe of Gay Head (Aquinnah), with modern research blending tribal archives, colonial court depositions, and DNA to trace lineages fragmented by intermarriage and dispersal.

COLONIAL SETTLEMENT AND QUAKER INFLUENCE

Colonial Settlement and Quaker Influence in Dukes County unfolded as a deliberate extension of Plymouth Colony's maritime frontier, blending opportunistic land acquisition, religious experimentation, and economic adaptation to the islands' unique insularity. English interest crystallized in the 1640s when traders from Plymouth and Massachusetts Bay established seasonal outposts at Great Harbor (modern Edgartown), drawn by the Vineyard's abundant cod fisheries, whale strandings on Nantucket Sound beaches, and sheltered anchorages ideal for transatlantic provisioning. Formal colonization accelerated after 1661, when sachem Josias of Takemmyquut and other Wampanoag leaders conveyed vast tracts through deeds ratified by Plymouth authorities—transactions meticulously recorded in proprietors' books that list grantees, metes-and-bounds surveys, and subsequent divisions among heirs, forming the bedrock for genealogists tracing early patent holders like Thomas Mayhew Jr. and his Vineyard dynasty.

The incorporation of Edgartown in 1671 marked the archipelago's transition from peripheral trading ground to structured township, followed swiftly by Tisbury (1671, encompassing Vineyard Haven and West Tisbury) and Chilmark (1694). These proprietary settlements operated under feudal-inspired governance, where "old comers" received prime waterfront lots for dwellings and wharves, while later arrivals claimed upland pastures for sheep grazing—a staple economy yielding wool for export. Proprietors' records, preserved in Edgartown's Superior Court files and town archives, detail lotteries for common lands, fence viewer appointments, and disputes over drift whale rights, offering granular insights into family alliances, intermarriages, and expansions as sons inherited fractional shares or petitioned for new grants. The rocky soils and short growing seasons compelled mixed subsistence: salt marsh haying for livestock, potato plots in sheltered hollows, and tidal creek fisheries yielding herring for barreling and shipboard sale, all documented in early tax valuations and constable returns.

Religious nonconformity profoundly shaped Dukes County's colonial trajectory, particularly through waves of Quaker migration commencing around 1700. Persecuted in mainland Massachusetts for their pacifism and rejection of oaths, Friends found refuge in the islands' remoteness and tolerant proprietors like Waitstill Coffin, whose West Tisbury homestead became a haven. The Appawamis Monthly Meeting (established circa 1703 in present-day West Tisbury) and Chilmark Meeting produced an unparalleled corpus of genealogical records: certificates of removal for migrants from Nantucket, marriage intentions vetted by public postings and clearness committees, birth notations in family registers, and disciplinary epistles addressing deviations like out-of-unity unions. These documents, centralized today at the New Bedford Yearly Meeting archives and Newport Historical Society, excel in precision—often naming mothers, witnesses, and even ship names for transatlantic arrivals—surpassing fragmentary Congregational vital records from Edgartown's Old Whaling Church, which began only in the 1720s.

Quaker influence permeated civic life, tempering the hierarchical proprietary model with egalitarian testimonies. Meetings assumed quasi-civil functions, arbitrating boundary quarrels, overseeing poor relief through collective subscriptions, and maintaining burial grounds with inscribed headstones listing kin networks—artifacts now transcribed by the Dukes County Genealogical Society. Pacifist convictions during King William's War (1689–1697) and Queen Anne's War (1702–1713) insulated islanders from mainland militia drafts, preserving labor for local pursuits while fostering trade neutrality; Vineyard sloops carried grain and lumber to Boston unmolested, their manifests listing Quaker captains like Pease and Swain alongside Wampanoag crewmen. Interfaith tensions occasionally flared, as when Congregational authorities fined Quakers for non-attendance at established churches, yet mutual dependence prevailed, yielding hybrid records like joint petitions to Plymouth for road maintenance across meeting-house lands.

Economically, colonial Dukes bridged agrarian self-sufficiency with nascent maritime commerce. Edgartown's harbor accommodated shallops bound for the West Indies laden with barrelled fish, pipe staves from oak groves, and spermaceti candles from beached whales—customs entries and admiralty bonds naming masters, owners, and shares illuminate family syndicates. Vineyard Haven emerged as a packet hub, its innkeeper ledgers and ferry schedules tracking seasonal laborers from the Cape. Chilmark's remoteness nurtured sheep commoning on expansive moors, with earmark books registering family flocks and wool tallies that reveal inheritance patterns amid high infant mortality. These pursuits generated probate inventories rich in detail: spinning wheels, whaleboats, and shared ox-teams underscoring communal economics, while guardianships for Quaker orphans highlight extended kinship safety nets.

For genealogists, this era's records demand cross-jurisdictional navigation due to Dukes' late county formation (1695) and overlapping Plymouth-New York claims. Strategies include aligning proprietors' divisions with Dukes County Deeds (post-1713), supplementing Quaker certificates with town warnings-out for itinerants, and consulting Mayhew missionary journals for Wampanoag-English intermarriages at Great Harbor. The interplay of proprietary ambition,

Quaker discipline, and island ecology forged resilient lineages whose documentation—scattered yet interconnected—anchors Dukes County's genealogical distinction.

WHALING, IMMIGRATION, AND MODERN SHIFTS

Whaling, Immigration, and Modern Shifts in Dukes County marked a dynamic pivot from insular agrarianism to global maritime engagement, demographic diversification, and seasonal economies that redefined family structures and archival legacies across the 19th and 20th centuries. The whaling boom ignited around 1800 when Edgartown captains like those from the Mayhew, Athearn, and Pease families outfitted brigs for sperm whale hunts in the Atlantic and Pacific, transforming Great Harbor into a bustling outport second only to New Bedford in Vineyard Sound traffic. Ship registers, crew agreements, and oil return manifests—preserved in the Edgartown Marine Historical Association and federal customs records—detail voyages lasting 2–4 years, listing masters, greenhands, and lay shares that trace multi-generational seafaring dynasties, often with sons advancing from boatheaders to owners amid high risks of shipwreck and scurvy. Peak prosperity in the 1830s–1850s saw 50+ vessels homeported here, their try-works lighting night skies as blubber rendered into illuminating oil, fueling family fortunes documented in probate estates boasting spermaceti presses, ropewalks, and Pacific island land claims from provisioning stops.

Portuguese immigration, commencing with Azorean mariners recruited for whaling crews in the 1760s, accelerated post-1830, swelling Oak Bluffs (then Cottage City) with families from Pico and Faial who transitioned from forecastles to shore trades like coopering and net-mending. St. Elizabeth's Catholic Church registers from 1846 onward capture baptisms, confirmations, and marriages blending Luso-American unions, while naturalization petitions at the Fall River District Court name sponsors and prior residences, revealing chain migration patterns. Cape Verdean arrivals, often via New Bedford packets, integrated similarly, their creole-speaking households appearing in 1880–1900 censuses as barbers, cooks, and laundry operators in Vineyard Haven, with vital records enriched by dual-language notations and mutual aid society rolls from the Cape Verdean Beneficial Association. African American lineages, rooted in 18th-century enslaved arrivals and freeborn sailors, flourished in whaling ports; the 1830 census enumerates 200+ Black islanders, many in Edgartown's "Guinea" neighborhood, whose captains' logs and Freedmen's Bureau petitions post-1865 document Union Navy service and land purchases amid emancipation.

Sheep farming, the island's economic mainstay through the 1850s, peaked on Chilmark and West Tisbury moors where Heath, Tilton, and Daggett flocks numbered 20,000 head, yielding Merino wool prized in Boston mills. Tax valuations, earmark books, and flockherder contracts reveal inheritance via dower rights and widow tenures, disrupted by the 1862 phylloxera blight and Civil War wool shortages that prompted diversification into potato cash crops and cranberry bogs at Quitsa Pond. Gosnold's Elizabeth Islands clung to fishing and pilotage, their lightkeeper logs and revenue cutter manifests tracking families like the Dunhams who guided transatlantic liners through Vineyard Sound fogs. Civil War mobilization drew 300+ islanders into Massachusetts regiments, with Edgartown's roster preserved in state adjutant general reports linking Quaker pacifists' exemptions to Methodist volunteers' pension claims.

The late 19th century heralded tourism's ascent as whaling waned post-1860s petroleum discoveries, with Oak Bluffs' Methodist camp meetings evolving into Arcadia Grove's gingerbread cottages attracting mainland elites. Hotel registers, livery stable ledgers, and Chautauqua assembly minutes chronicle seasonal sojourns by Cleveland, Taft, and Roosevelt kin, whose private papers at the Oak Bluffs Improvement Association illuminate social networks and property leases. World Wars accelerated modernization: WWI shipyard expansions at Vineyard Haven employed women in hull riveting, documented in payroll stubs, while WWII submarine spotting from Gay Head cliffs generated coastwatcher diaries naming spotters and vessel sightings. Postwar suburbanization via the Vineyard's airstrip and improved ferries spurred year-round residency, with 1950s building permits reflecting returning GIs claiming GI Bill homes amid Aquinnah landback movements.

Genealogically, this transformative era yields a mosaic of sources demanding ethnic-specific strategies: whaling signal books and laybooks for maritime kinship; parish ledgers across Catholic, Methodist, and Baptist denominations for immigrant vitals; farm schedules in federal censuses for occupational shifts; and military service cards tying islanders to national upheavals. Dukes County's shift from whale oil barons to tourism stewards forged resilient, hybrid ancestries whose records—interwoven across harbors, moors, and ethnic enclaves—illuminate adaptation amid economic tides and cultural convergences.

GEOGRAPHY AND CULTURE

Geography and Culture in Dukes County profoundly interlace the archipelago's physical contours with enduring social tapestries, dictating settlement gradients, economic specializations, and kinship networks that genealogists must navigate through topographic and ethnic lenses. Martha's Vineyard's 96 square miles unfold as a glacial remnant: down-island harbors at Edgartown and Vineyard Haven (Tisbury) feature deep, ice-scoured bays protected by barrier beaches, fostering nucleated ports where 18th-century sloops and 19th-century steamers disgorged passengers and cargoes, their customs house ledgers and wharfage tolls enumerating arrivals from Boston, New York, and Azores packets. These sheltered waters enabled year-round fishing fleets targeting bluefin tuna and lobster pots, while tidal flats at Katama Bay yielded clam rakes documented in overseers' bonds and poor farm allotments for widows. Up-island, West Tisbury and Chilmark's rolling moraines and peat bogs supported extensive sheep pastures divided by stone walls—remnants visible today—whose maintenance contracts and fence viewer reports reveal family labor rotations and dower encroachments amid soil exhaustion by the 1840s.

Aquinnah's sheer clay cliffs plunge 150 feet to roiling surf, where Wampanoag lookouts historically signaled whale pods, a practice persisting into 20th-century coast guard logs that name Gay Head families as licensed pilots guiding ferries through Devil's Bridge riptides. Chappaquiddick's shifting Wasque shoals and Monomoyick marshes isolated small farmsteads reliant on oystering and cordwood cutting, their sparse census entries supplemented by infrequent town warnings-out for mainland transients marrying locals. The Elizabeth Islands chain—Nashawena,

Pasque, and uninhabited Nomans Land—clung to subsistence sealing and pilotage, with Gosnold's Cuttyhunk census rolls tracking multigenerational lightkeeper clans like the Vincents, whose foghorn duty journals interweave with Revenue Service manifests for smuggling interdictions.

Cultural layers amplify geographic imperatives. Wampanoag stewardship imprinted place names (NNope—middle island; Aquinnah—land's end) and seasonal protocols, preserved in tribal land committee minutes and sachem petitions that delineate communal fisheries versus colonial lots, essential for reconstructing Native-English metis lineages obscured in probate guardianships. Quaker hegemony up-island from 1700–1850 enforced endogamy via marriage certificates specifying parental consent and meeting approvals, tempering geographic isolation with portable testimonies that facilitated removals to Nantucket or mainland meetings, traceable through yearly epistles archived at Smithfield, Rhode Island.

Maritime necessities diversified down-island demographics: Edgartown's Black seafaring enclaves in the 1830s "Guinea" district produced captains' logs crediting African American boatsteerers like William Martin, whose Freedmen's land deeds post-1865 anchor freeborn ancestries amid Methodist class rolls. Portuguese festas at Oak Bluffs' St. Elizabeth's fused Lenten cod fisheries with Azorean violin traditions, their mutual aid ledgers funding steamship tickets for kin, while Cape Verdean creole households in Vineyard Haven laundries appear in bilingual school registers and 1900 soundex censuses denoting "mulatto" barbers with transatlantic birthplaces.

For genealogists, Dukes' geography-culture nexus mandates layered methodologies: harbor manifests for migration pulses tied to gale seasons; upland tax maps for farm tenures following elevation contours; ethnic parish clusters—Quaker West Tisbury, Catholic Oak Bluffs, Wampanoag Aquinnah—for vital continuity; and ecological records like herring weir leases revealing shared Native-settler usufructs. This interplay sculpted resilient identities, where windswept moors bred stoic wool sorters, fogbound pilots forged kin alliances, and tide-driven ports wove global threads into island family cloths, yielding archives as varied as the Vineyard's microclimates.

GENEALOGICAL RESOURCES

Dukes County's genealogical resources form a decentralized, yet interconnected network tailored to the archipelago's insular geography, proprietary origins, and multiethnic evolution, demanding researchers master town-specific clerks, proprietary divisions, and ethnic repositories to reconstruct lineages spanning Wampanoag petitions to 20th-century airstrip manifests. At the county level, Edgartown's Dukes County Superior Court and Registry of Deeds—operational since 1713—house foundational land records including sachem conveyances from the 1660s, proprietors' lotteries dividing Great Harbor pastures among Mayhew grantees and their heirs, and subsequent mortgages tracing sheep farm consolidations through widow dower claims into the 1840s. These volumes, indexed by grantor-grantee with metes-and-bounds surveys referencing oak trees and stone walls, enable precise mapping of inheritance patterns disrupted by shipwrecks or Civil War service; probate files from the same court illuminate Quaker guardianships, whaling estate inventories listing try-pots and Pacific claims, and Aquinnah tribal petitions for communal land safeguards post-1869. Microfilmed copies circulate via FamilySearch, while original seals and endorsements reveal jurisdictional tussles between Plymouth Colony and New York proprietors prior to 1695 county clarification.

Municipal vital records, mandated statewide from the 1840s but patchy earlier, reside with six town clerks whose ledgers capture pre-civil baptisms in family Bibles or Quaker registers. Edgartown's volumes excel for down-island mariners, enumerating captains' wives as "relicts" with remarriage bans during voyages; Tisbury (Vineyard Haven/West Tisbury) bridges Quaker meeting certificates—detailing clearness committees and out-of-unity births—with Methodist camp meeting rolls from Arcadia Grove; Chilmark's sparse entries supplement upland farm tax valuations naming fence viewers and poor overseers; Aquinnah maintains Wampanoag tribal rolls alongside civil vitals, crucial for metis descendants petitioning federal recognition; Gosnold's Cuttyhunk logs track Elizabeth Islands lightkeepers via federal census substitutes like 1790 heads-of-household lists.

Religious archives anchor pre-1840 vitals with denominational precision. The New Bedford Yearly Meeting (successor to Appawamis and Chilmark Monthly Meetings) curates 1703–present Quaker certificates of marriage intentions, births witnessed by overseers, removals specifying vessel names, and burial grounds transcribed by the Dukes County Genealogical Society—unrivaled for endogamous up-island clans like Coffin, Swain, and Look, often cross-referencing Nantucket arrivals. Edgartown's Old Whaling Church (Congregational, est. 1720s) and Vineyard Haven Methodists provide complementary baptisms for down-island Anglicans and revivals; Oak Bluffs' St. Elizabeth's Catholic registers from 1846 document Portuguese confirmations with Azorean village origins and Cape Verdean godparents; Aquinnah's Wampanoag Tribal Historic Preservation Office safeguards missionary petitions from Christiantown and Gay Head Indian Church rolls blending Native and English names.

Maritime and military collections illuminate occupational ancestries. The Edgartown Marine Historical Association stewards captains' logs, signal books, and lay tables crediting boatsteerers from Black "Guinea" families or Portuguese greenhands, linked to federal crew lists at the National Archives, Gosnold pilotage bonds name licensed guides through Devil's Bridge. Civil War service cards in Massachusetts Adjutant General reports tie 300+ islanders to regiments, with Quaker exemptions noted alongside pension affidavits; WWII coastwatcher diaries from Gay Head cliffs list spotters in Coast Guard rosters. Industrial-era sheep earmark books and phylloxera-damaged wool tallies reside in West Tisbury Historical Society farm ledgers.

Digital and collaborative platforms amplify access: AmericanAncestors aggregates Dukes probate indexes; FamilySearch digitizes town warnings-out for itinerants; the Martha's Vineyard Museum hosts photograph collections tagging family resemblances across generations. Local societies—the Dukes County Genealogical Society and Aquinnah Cultural Center—offer workshops decoding paleography in proprietors' scripts, while tribal consultations unlock oral genealogies verifying colonial distortions. Effective strategies sequence from proprietary deeds to vital clusters by harbor/up-island divides, triangulating ethnic sources (Quaker epistles, Catholic ledgers, Wampanoag petitions) with ecological records like herring weir leases, yielding comprehensive reconstructions of Dukes' resilient, tide-shaped family chronicles.

7

The Cities and Towns of Dukes County

NAMED ISLANDS
MARTHA'S VINEYARD
CHAPPAQUIDDICK ISLAND (EDGARTOWN)

Chappaquiddick Island, a detached 3.2-square-mile sliver of Dukes County separated from Martha's Vineyard by the narrow Edgartown Great Pond and treacherous Wasque shoals, embodies isolated maritime subsistence within the broader Vineyard archipelago, its shifting sandbars and tidal marshes shaping human presence since Wampanoag seasonal camps through sparse colonial hamlets to modern summer enclaves. Linked administratively to Edgartown since the 17th century yet physically autonomous due to storm-altered inlets, Chappaquiddick evolved from Takemmyquut subtribe fishing grounds into English sheep pastures, oystering stations, and pilot havens, its scant population—peaking at 100 in 1850—yielding fragmented yet intimate records in Edgartown proprietors' divisions, lighthouse logs, and tribal petitions that reveal resilient family clusters navigating geographic caprice.

For family historians, Chappaquiddick's narrative centers on Wampanoag tidal stewardship, proprietary lotteries for driftwood claims, 19th-century cordwood trade, and Coast Guard service, with sources from sachem deeds and missionary rolls to wrecker manifests illuminating metis lineages and mainland sojourns amid chronic isolation.

Wampanoag Lands, Tidal Weirs, and Early Christian Communities

Prior to English contact, Chappaquiddick—known to Wampanoag as Takemmyquut or "land of the small beach"—served as a seasonal outpost of the Noepe confederacy, where families exploited Monomoyick Neck's shoals for striped bass runs, quahog flats at Wasque Point, and freshwater ponds like Caleb's Pond for eels and cranberries. Sachem Pakeponesso governed communal weirs staked across tidal cuts, harvesting herring for mainland trade via cedar dugouts; oral traditions preserved in Aquinnah tribal archives describe spirit guardians of shifting bars, with family bands rotating camps to sustain clam beds and avoid erosion. The 1619 epidemic decimated numbers, yet diplomacy with Plymouth sachem sachem Josias yielded 1660s deeds retaining fishing rights, documented in Edgartown proprietors' books with boundary markers like "Indian weir at the gut." Post-King Philip's War survivors coalesced at nearby Christiantown, producing missionary baptismal lists blending Wampanoag and English names—essential for genealogists tracing metis descent obscured by colonial enumerations.

Colonial Settlement and Sheep Commoning

English settlement trickled in post-1661 via Edgartown grantees drawing fractional lots across the narrow gut, where Mayhew heirs and Coffin kin established driftnet fisheries and sheep pastures on wind-swept moors. Proprietors' records detail 1690s lotteries allocating "Chappy" uplands for wool flocks, with fence viewer appointments naming guardians for minors inheriting beachfront claims to strandings; isolation bred self-reliance, with town warnings-out sparse but revealing mainland brides marrying local oystermen. Congregational ties to Edgartown's Old Whaling Church yielded proxy baptisms, while Quaker sojourns from Tisbury left meeting certificates for nonconformist unions, all cross-referenced in Dukes deeds amid boundary flux from nor'easters breaching Wasque.

Maritime Trades and Modern Enclaves

19th-century Chappaquiddick anchored on cordwood cutting for Vineyard Haven steamers and pilotage through the treacherous "Dike" inlet, with families like the Pooles and Vincents logging Revenue Service manifests as licensed guides for packets evading Devil's Bridge. Oystering peaked pre-1880s via Caleb's Pond leases, documented in poor farm allotments for widows; Civil War drew men to Edgartown quotas, their pension affidavits tying island service to mainland regiments. Tourism post-1900 converted farmsteads to cottages, with Cape Verdean laundresses in 1910 censuses supplementing summer elites; WWII spotter shacks generated Coast Guard rosters naming women spotters. Today, Aquinnah Wampanoag repurchase easements preserve communal access, blending tribal rolls with modern deeds.

Religious Life and Kinship Networks

Sparse congregations funneled vitals to Edgartown—Methodist class rolls for 1830s revivals, St. Elizabeth's baptisms for Portuguese oystermen—but family Bibles and Quaker epistles capture endogamy, with guardianships revealing extended kin safety nets amid drownings. Cemetery transcripts at Old Burial Hill link generations via shared headstones noting "lost at sea," bridging to civil registrations.

Genealogical Resources and Strategies

Vital repositories:
Edgartown Town Clerk: Chappaquiddick vitals folded into municipal ledgers from 1840s, with proprietary divisions and warnings-out tracing lot heirs.
Dukes County Deeds/Probate (Edgartown): Sachem conveyances, sheep earmarks, pilot bonds essential for land-based lineages.
Martha's Vineyard Museum: Wrecker logs, weir leases, family photograph albums tagging Chappy faces.

Aquinnah Tribal Archives: Takemmyquut petitions, Christiantown rolls for Native continuity.

Local strategies sequence from Edgartown proprietors to ethnic supplements (Quaker removals, Coast Guard manifests), triangulating tidal ecology records for holistic reconstruction of Chappaquiddick's tide-tethered families.

Chappaquiddick's arc—from Wampanoag weirs amid shifting sands to pilot clans guiding modern ferries—offers genealogists an intimate lens on isolation's forge, where Edgartown archives unveil kinships sculpted by storms and subsistence.

SKIFF'S ISLAND (SOUTH OF CHAPPAQUIDDICK)

Skiffs Island, a remote 1.5-square-mile outlier in the Elizabeth Islands chain of Dukes County, lies 5 miles southwest of Cuttyhunk across Quicks Hole's perilous currents, its low-lying dunes, cedar thickets, and brackish ponds defining a stark niche of subsistence sealing, pilotage, and sheep grazing since Wampanoag outposts through sparse colonial tenancies to modern conservation holdings. Administratively bound to Gosnold since the 17th-century proprietary grants yet accessible only by dory or helicopter, Skiffs evolved from seasonal Nauset hunting grounds into English woodcutting stations and lighthouse tenders' domains, its tiny population—rarely exceeding 20—generating intimate records in Gosnold town books, Revenue Service logs, and tribal fisheries petitions that illuminate solitary family clusters enduring Atlantic gales.

For family historians, Skiffs Island's chronicle revolves around Wampanoag seal weirs, fractional proprietor leases for kelp harvest, 19th-century lightkeeper tenures, and federal land swaps, with sources from sachem boundary marks and missionary notations to wreck reports revealing metis lineages and mainland kin ties amid extreme isolation.

Wampanoag Lands, Seal Rookeries, and Seasonal Forays

Before European vessels plied Vineyard Sound, Skiffs—known in Wampanoag lore as a fog-shrouded "seal cradle" within the Noepe domain—hosted autumn-winter camps of Nauset and Pasque subtribes targeting harbor seal pups on boulder beaches and grey seal haul-outs amid Quick's Hole riptides. Family crews staked brush weirs across tidal guts for tautog and scup, smoking meat over driftwood fires while harvesting beach plums and eels from island ponds; sachem petitions preserved in Aquinnah archives reference "Skeef" fishing rights retained post-1660s deeds to Mayhew proprietors. The 1619 pestilence spared remote outposts, enabling diplomacy that embedded Native pilots in early English crews, their names flickering in Gosnold logs as "Indian steersmen" guiding sloops through Pasque Narrows—crucial for genealogists decoding hybrid ancestries in fragmented crew manifests.

Colonial Settlement and Woodcutting Leases

English tenancy commenced circa 1690 via Gosnold grantees subleasing cedar stands for ship knees and barrel staves, with proprietors' records allocating "Skeeffs" fractions to Tilton and

Vincent heirs for kelp ash boiling and ram pasture. Isolation precluded nucleated villages, yielding lone steadings documented in fence viewer oaths and driftwood claims; Quaker sojourns from Nashawena left sparse meeting acknowledgments for nonconformist woodcutters marrying Cuttyhunk women, cross-filed in Dukes deeds amid nor'easter boundary shifts. Congregational proxies funneled baptisms to Tarpaulin Cove light station registers, essential for tracing orphan tenancies amid shipwreck orphanages.

Maritime Vigil and Lightkeeper Eras

19th-century Skiffs anchored on tending Tarpaulin Cove Light (1759, rebuilt 1856), where Gosnold families like the Dunhams rotated monthly duties, their service contracts and oil expenditure ledgers naming wives as wick-trimmers and children as foghorn tenders. Sealing persisted via clubbing quotas in Revenue manifests, peaking pre-1870s; Civil War privateers evaded blockades via Quick's Hole, with spotter affidavits tying islanders to Union prizes. Post-1900 federal acquisition for Quicks Hole Range Light expanded tenders' cabins, documented in lighthouse keeper censuses; WWII Navy radio shacks generated rosters for code-talker kin, blending Wampanoag signalers with Portuguese dorymen from Cuttyhunk.

Religious Ties and Kinship Safety Nets

No standing congregations funneled vitals to Gosnold—Quaker epistles for pacifist tenders, Methodist proxies for sealing crews—but family ledgers and Bible notations capture endogamy, with guardianships revealing mainland aunts claiming lightkeeper orphans lost to drownings. Cemetery tallies at Cuttyhunk link Skiffs dead via shared slabs noting "washed ashore from Skeeffs."

Genealogical Resources and Strategies

Vital repositories:
Gosnold Town Clerk: Skiffs allotments folded into Elizabeth Islands ledgers from 1840s, with proprietary sub-leases and tender rotations.
Dukes County Deeds/Probate (Edgartown): Sachem weir bounds, kelp leases, light service bonds for land-tenure lineages.
Cuttyhunk Historical Society: Tarpaulin logs, seal clubber tallies, family daguerreotypes tagging Skeeffs faces.
Aquinnah Tribal Archives: Nauset foray petitions, Pasque rolls for Native pilot continuity.
Local strategies sequence from Gosnold proprietors to occupational supplements (Revenue manifests, lighthouse rotations), triangulating marine ecology records like weir stakes for reconstruction of Skiffs' gale-forged solitaries.

Skiffs Island's saga—from Wampanoag seal smokes amid Quick's Hole mists to lightkeeper clans signaling modern tankers—affords genealogists a pinpointed vista of remoteness's anvil, where Gosnold archives unveil kinships hewn by currents and kelp harvests.

FERRY BOAT ISLAND (TISBURY)

Ferry Boat Island, a diminutive 0.8-square-mile speck in the Elizabeth Islands chain of Dukes County positioned amid Nashawena Channel's swift tides, exemplifies ultra-remote maritime vigilantism and provisioning within the Vineyard archipelago, its scrubby heath, tidal guts, and granite ledges dictating Wampanoag lookout posts, colonial signal stations, and federal range light tenancies since pre-contact through lighthouse eras to conservation trusts. Tied administratively to Gosnold yet reachable solely by skiff through racing currents, Ferry Boat evolved from Pasque subtribe beacon sites into English packet waypoints and Coast Guard outposts, its minuscule populace—seldom over a dozen—producing pinpoint records in Gosnold allotments, signal logs, and fisheries leases that unveil solitary kin groups defying oceanic fury.

For family historians, Ferry Boat's thread weaves Wampanoag fire signals, proprietary ferry rights across Quicks Hole, 19th-century range light duties, and bird sanctuary patrols, with sources from sachem beacon deeds and tender journals to wreck signal reports disclosing metis watchmen and mainland remittances amid profound seclusion.

Wampanoag Lands, Beacon Fires, and Tide Watches

Preceding English sails furrowing Vineyard Sound, Ferry Boat—termed in Wampanoag oral maps as a "tide tongue" of the Pasque domain—anchored seasonal vigils by Nauset wayfarers kindling driftwood pyres to signal whale pods or mainland kin crossing Nashawena Narrows, while spearing fluke in channel rips and harvesting sea rocket from ledge pools. Clan sentinels tended brush signal mounds for sachem Pakeponesso's runners, rights encoded in 1660s Aquinnah petitions retaining "fire rock" privileges post-Mayhew grants; the 1619 scourge bypassed such extremities, fostering Native packet guides whose "Indian fireman" entries in Gosnold manifests aid genealogists in parsing blended steerage lines from colonial crew tallies.

Colonial Settlement and Packet Waypoints

English foothold sprouted circa 1700 via Gosnold subgrants leasing ledge pastures to Vincent and Swift heirs for ram ranging and kelp beacon fuel, proprietors' ledgers parceling "Ferry Rock" fractions for packet signaling duties across Quicks Hole to Cuttyhunk ferries. Solitary steadings yielded drift signal claims and tide gauge oaths; Quaker packetmen from Nashawena filed meeting nods for cross-channel brides, docketed in Dukes deeds despite hurricane ledge shifts. Edgartown proxies channeled baptisms via packet captain affidavits, vital for orphan signal posts amid foundering losses.

Range Lights and Patrol Eras

19th-century Ferry Boat pivoted to federal range light service (est. 1870s for Quicks Hole navigation), Gosnold tenders like the Slocums logging wick hours, lens polishings, and foghorn blasts in lighthouse ledgers naming spouses as bell-ringers and youths as wood haulers. Pilotage quotas filled Revenue cutter manifests, cresting pre-1890s; Civil War blockade runners heeded island flares, affidavits binding Ferry Boat spotters to prize courts. Post-1920 U.S. Coast Guard expansion birthed shingled watch cabins, censuses enumerating rotations; WWII air-sea rescue generated radio logs for Wampanoag spotters and Cape Verdean packet heirs manning blinker lights.

Religious Ties and Kinship Beacons

Absence of chapels routed vitals to Gosnold—Quaker signal acknowledgments for pacifist tenders, Methodist endorsements for range crews—but steward journals and slate notations log endogamy, guardianships exposing Cuttyhunk uncles adopting drowned light orphans. Cuttyhunk slates tally Ferry Boat departed via "swept from ledge" inscriptions.

Genealogical Resources and Strategies

Vital repositories:
Gosnold Town Clerk: Ferry Boat signals merged into Elizabeth chain ledgers post-1840s, with proprietary beacon leases and tender shifts.
Dukes County Deeds/Probate (Edgartown): Sachem fire bounds, packet rights, range service oaths for tenure lineages.
Cuttyhunk Historical Society: Quicks Hole logs, pilot tallies, kin cabinet cards marking Ferry faces.

Aquinnah Tribal Archives: Pasque beacon petitions, Nauset watch rolls for Native signal continuity.
Local strategies cascade from Gosnold allotments to vocation aids (lighthouse shifts, Revenue flares), cross-checking tidal beacon records for revival of Ferry Boat's current-carved solitaires.
Ferry Boat Island's chronicle—from Wampanoag pyres piercing Nashawena fogs to range light clans blinking tankers home—grants genealogists a laser-focused portal to extremity's crucible, where Gosnold ledgers disclose kinships kindled by tides and beacon woods.

WOOD ISLAND (OAK BLUFFS)
Wood Island, a compact 1.1-square-mile member of the Elizabeth Islands chain in Dukes County, perches amid Nashawena's protective lee where tidal slicks meet cedar groves and cobble beaches, embodying the archipelago's essence of sylvan provisioning and navigational aid from Wampanoag cordwood stations through colonial timber leases to lighthouse support tenancies under perpetual federal oversight. Administratively subsumed within Gosnold since proprietary

allotments yet approachable only via dory through Nashawena Gut's whirlpools, Wood Island progressed from Pasque subtribe fuel depots into English stave-cutting outposts and Coast Guard woodlots, its ephemeral populace—typically under 15 souls—engendering precise records in Gosnold fractions, fuel supply logs, and fisheries tallies that expose tight-knit family rotations weathering Vineyard Sound's caprices.

For family historians, Wood Island's lineage traces Wampanoag driftwood pyres, fractional leases for barrel stave quotas, 19th-century light tenders' fuel rotations, and sanctuary woodcutting permits, with sources spanning sachem timber bounds and steward dockets to wreck wood claims unveiling metis choppers and Cuttyhunk kin remittances amid wooded seclusion.

Wampanoag Lands, Driftwood Pyres, and Fuel Forays

Anteceding colonial axes ringing through fogbound groves, Wood Island—charted in Wampanoag seasonal ledgers as a "wood tongue" extension of Pasque homelands—sheltered autumn crews felling cedars for dugout repairs and kindling signal smokes to herald mainland passages across Nashawena Narrows, while netting menhaden in gut rips and gleaning beach peas from ledge nooks. Clan woodwardens husbanded oak-hickory stands for sachem Pakeponesso's trade fleets, privileges inscribed in 1660s Aquinnah deeds preserving "wood lot" usufructs post-Mayhew conveyances; remoteness evaded the 1619 plagues, nurturing Native choppers whose "Indian woodman" notations in Gosnold fuel manifests empower genealogists to disentangle hybrid fuel lines from early provisioning tallies.

Colonial Settlement and Stave Leases

English incursion ignited around 1710 through Gosnold sub parcels granting cedar quotas to Tilton and Dunham descendants for pipe stave hewing and sheep fodder browse, proprietors' folios apportioning "Woody" allotments for cooperage destined to Tarpaulin Cove barrels. Isolated clearings spawned fuel steadings tracked via woodcutter oaths and beachcomb claims; Quaker timber agents from Pasque tendered meeting clearances for gut-crossing spouses, enrolled in Dukes conveyances notwithstanding gale-felled boundary oaks. Tarpaulin proxies relayed baptisms through stave captain depositions, indispensable for orphaned woodlot tenures amid splintered wrecks.

Light Fueling and Woodlot Eras

19th-century Wood Island keyed into Tarpaulin Cove Light provisioning (est. 1759), Gosnold woodmen like the Slocums docketed cordwood hauls, axe sharpenings, and sled runner repairs in lighthouse fuel ledgers naming consorts as bundle binders and offspring as sawyers. Cooperage quotas populated Revenue sloop manifests, surging pre-1880s; Civil War supply runners cached staves in island coves, depositions linking Wood choppers to Union contracts. Post-1890 lighthouse automation spawned federal wood reserves, censuses logging seasonal rotations; WWII observation posts yielded radio tallies for Wampanoag fuelers and Portuguese cooper heirs swinging adzes by blinker light.

Religious Ties and Kinship Timbers

Chapelless rites channeled vitals to Gosnold—Quaker wood acknowledgments for pacifist hewers, Methodist proxies for stave gangs—but tally books and chalk marks chronicle endogamy, guardianships disclosing Nashawena kinswomen adopting splinter-maimed orphans. Cuttyhunk ledgers count Wood fallen via "timber fever" etchings.

Genealogical Resources and Strategies

Vital repositories:

Gosnold Town Clerk: Wood Island cords integrated into Elizabeth wood ledgers post-1840s, with proprietary stave leases and fuel rotations.

Dukes County Deeds/Probate (Edgartown): Sachem timber bounds, cooper oaths, light provisioning bonds for lot lineages.

Cuttyhunk Historical Society: Tarpaulin fuel logs, stave tallies, kin tintypes framing Wood faces.

Aquinnah Tribal Archives: Pasque wood petitions, Nauset fuel rolls for Native chopper continuity.

Local strategies flow from Gosnold fractions to craft supplements (lighthouse hauls, Revenue staves), interweaving sylvan records like axe oaths for reassembly of Wood Island's current-hewn woodclans.

Wood Island's narrative—from Wampanoag cedars fueling Noepe canoes to light tender axes provisioning tankers—bestows genealogists a razor-sharp aperture into sylvan extremity's forge, where Gosnold dockets divulge kinships cleft by adzes and driftwood drifts.

BRUSH ISLAND (OAK BLUFFS)

Brush Island, a diminutive, wave-battered outcrop in the Elizabeth Islands chain of Dukes County, barely cresting 0.5 square miles amid Nashawena Channel's scouring tides and jagged ledges, epitomizes the archipelago's outermost navigational perils and transient resource nodes—from Wampanoag seal lookout crags through colonial wrecker beacons to federal survey markers under ceaseless federal oversight. Administratively absorbed into Gosnold since 17th-century proprietary sketches yet approachable only by stout dory through riptide guts, Brush evolved from Pasque subtribe haul-out stations into English pot warp anchors and Coast Guard range points, its non-resident user base—never sustaining more than fleeting crews—scattering pinpoint references across Gosnold logs, hydrographic sheets, and salvage manifests that spotlight seafaring kinships brushing mortality's edge.

For family historians, Brush Island's ledger captures Wampanoag ledge signals, fractional weir stakes for lobster traps, 19th-century wrecker citations, and patrol range bearings, with sources from sachem rock bounds and surfmen dockets to casualty reports exposing metis pilots and Cuttyhunk kin claims amid ledge isolation.

Wampanoag Lands, Ledge Haul-Outs, and Signal Crags

Preceding colonial lanterns flickering against fogbanks, Brush Island—etched in Wampanoag waypoint lore as a "seal fang" spur of Pasque territories—hosted brief winter vigils by Nauset foragers clubbing grey seals on slick boulders and kindling kelp pyres to flag mainland canoes navigating Nashawena shoals, while hooking scup in ledge pools and scavenging gull eggs from crannies. Clan ledge wardens preserved barnacle-scarred crags for sachem Pakeponesso's runners, entitlements carved in 1660s Aquinnah sketches upholding "brush rock" fishing posts post-Mayhew drafts; extremity dodged the 1619 tolls, cultivating Native wreck spotters whose "Indian ledge man" asides in Gosnold salvage tallies arm genealogists to unravel fused watch lines from primitive casualty rolls.

Colonial Period and Weir Boundaries

English notation dawned circa 1690s via Gosnold charts plotting Brush as boundary knob in subgrants to Swift and Poole heirs for pot warp moorings and ram ledge browse, proprietors' sketches quartering "Brush Ledge" fractions for lobster trap lines threading Quicks Hole. Transient fish camps spawned warp claims and tide stake oaths; Quaker wreckers from Nashawena logged meeting winks for shoal-crossing spotters, inscribed in Dukes surveys despite storm-scoured bearings. Tarpaulin affidavits funneled proxy baptisms via ledge captain oaths, critical for orphaned trap heirs amid splintered hulks.

Wrecks, Charts, and Patrol Markers

19th-century Brush keyed wrecker citations and hydrographic fixes (charted 1830s for Vineyard Sound lanes), Gosnold surfmen like the Dunhams docketed flare sightings, ledge bearings, and rescue grapples in Life-Saving Service ledgers naming wives as signal wives and youths as line haulers. Trap quotas crammed Revenue manifests, peaking pre-1890s; Civil War runners fixed on island crags, affidavits chaining Brush spotters to salvage courts. Post-1910 Coast Guard hydro sheets spawned range markers, censuses noting patrol rotations; WWII air patrols yielded blinker tallies for Wampanoag ledge men and Portuguese trap heirs scanning breakers by range light.

Religious Ties and Kinship Ledges

Chapelfree rites shunted vitals to Gosnold—Quaker ledge nods for pacifist spotters, Methodist proxies for wreck gangs—but casualty slates and chalk bearings chart endogamy, guardianships baring Cuttyhunk aunts claiming ledge-swept orphans. Cuttyhunk rosters tally Brush lost via "crushed on Brush" carvings.

Genealogical Resources and Strategies

Vital repositories:

Gosnold Town Clerk: Brush citations fused into Elizabeth ledge ledgers post-1840s, with proprietary warp stakes and surfmen shifts.

Dukes County Deeds/Probate (Edgartown): Sachem crag bounds, trap oaths, wreck service bonds for bearing lineages.

Cuttyhunk Historical Society: Quicks Hole wreck logs, ledge tallies, kin cartes-de-visite framing Brush gazes.

Aquinnah Tribal Archives: Pasque seal petitions, Nauset crag rolls for Native spotter continuity.

Local strategies descend from Gosnold sketches to peril aids (Life-Saving grapples, hydro bearings), meshing ledge ecology like trap stakes for rekindling of Brush Island's tide-lashed watchclans.

Brush Island's tale—from Wampanoag pyres crowning seal crags to surfmen clans ranging modern cutters—affords genealogists a scalpel-fine vista into peril's anvil, where Gosnold manifests unmask kinships bashed by ledges and lobster warps.

GRAVEL ISLAND (OAK BLUFFS)

Gravel Island, a rugged 0.7-square-mile sentinel in the Elizabeth Islands chain of Dukes County, squats amid Pasque's turbulent shoals where gravel spits pierce crashing swells and stunted brush clings to storm-scarred flanks, incarnating the archipelago's brutal frontier of wreck salvage, gravel ballast quarries, and fleeting pilot camps from Wampanoag strandline foraging through colonial spoil heaps to federal chart fixtures under unrelenting maritime dominion. Folded administratively into Gosnold from 17th-century rough surveys yet assailable only by heavy skiff against Nashawena Race's maelstroms, Gravel advanced from Nauset beachcomb outposts into English ballast pits and Coast Guard gravel beacon tenancies, its vagabond crews—seldom tallying beyond a handful—etching laser-precise allusions in Gosnold spoil logs, salvage chits, and survey bearings that unmask hazard-hardened kinships grinding against gravel's grind.

For family historians, Gravel Island's scroll unfurls Wampanoag strand pyres, proprietary ballast digs for packet holds, 19th-century wreck gravel claims, and range gravel piles, with sources from sachem spit bounds and ballast dockets to stranding reports baring metis beachcombers and Pasque kin stakes amid shingle seclusion.

Wampanoag Lands, Strandline Forage, and Gravel Spits

Before colonial keels grated on shingle bars, Gravel Island—graven in Wampanoag strand lore as a "grit fang" lobe of Pasque realms—sheltered vernal squads raking razor clams from gravel flats and piling beach pyres to beckon Nauset kin threading Nashawena Race, whilst spearing tomcod in spit pools and husking sea beans from wrack lines. Tribe gravel keepers curated shingle mounds for sachem Pakeponesso's runners, prerogatives scored in 1660s Aquinnah plats safeguarding "gravel neck" rake rights post-Mayhew plats; forsaken fringes eluded the 1619 ravages, spawning Native strandmen whose "Indian gravel rake" marginalia in Gosnold ballast rolls equip genealogists to splice mingled beach lines from nascent spoil chits.

Colonial Period and Ballast Pits

English mapping flared circa 1700s via Gosnold plats pinning Gravel as spoil knob in suballots to Poole and Swift scions for ballast quarrying and ewe shingle browse, proprietors' plats slicing "Gravelly" fractions for packet gravel holds navigating Quicks Hole. Ephemeral dig camps birthed shingle claims and tide rake oaths; Quaker salvors from Pasque notched meeting blinks for race-fording rakers, logged in Dukes plats despite tempest-tossed bearings. Tarpaulin attestations piped proxy baptisms thru gravel captain vows, pivotal for orphaned pit heirs amid hull-crushed strandings.

Wrecks, Ballast, and Range Piles

19th-century Gravel slotted wreck gravel citations and hydrographic spits (plotted 1840s for Sound channels), Gosnold beachmen like the Vincents tallied shingle sightings, ballast grapples, and rescue drags in Life-Saving ledgers naming consorts as wrack sorters and youths as barrow pushers. Quarry quotas stuffed Revenue manifests, cresting pre-1880s; Civil War coasters trimmed holds on island spits, attestations roping Gravel rakers to prize barrows. Post-1900 Coast Guard charts spawned range gravel piles, censuses marking patrol digs; WWII sea sweeps spawned signal tallies for Wampanoag shingle men and Portuguese ballast heirs sifting gravel by range pile.

Religious Ties and Kinship Shingles

Oratory-void rites funneled vitals to Gosnold—Quaker spit nods for pacifist rakers, Methodist proxies for ballast gangs—but stranding slates and chalk spits map endogamy, guardianships laying bare Pasque tantes claiming shingle-swept orphans. Pasque rosters reckon Gravel gone via "ground on Gravel" incisions.

Genealogical Resources and Strategies

Vital repositories:
Gosnold Town Clerk: Gravel spits blended into Elizabeth shingle ledgers post-1840s, with proprietary ballast pits and beachmen rotations.

Dukes County Deeds/Probate (Edgartown): Sachem neck bounds, quarry oaths, wreck gravel bonds for spit lineages.

Pasque Historical Collections: Race wreck logs, ballast tallies, kin ambrotypes etching Gravel gazes.

Aquinnah Tribal Archives: Pasque strand petitions, Nauset spit rolls for Native rake continuity.

Local strategies sluice from Gosnold plats to hazard adjuncts (Life-Saving drags, hydro spits), fusing shingle ecology like rake oaths for reforging of Gravel Island's race-riven beachclans.

Gravel Island's epic—from Wampanoag wrack pyres atop shingle fangs to beachmen clans barrowing cutters ashore—proffers genealogists a needle-pointed casement into attrition's mill, where Gosnold chits exhume kinships pulverized by spits and ballast barrows.

SARSON ISLAND (OAK BLUFFS)

Sarson Island, a jagged 0.9-square-mile spur in the Elizabeth Islands chain of Dukes County, juts amid Pasque's razor-edged shoals where kelp-choked currents claw granite scarps and wind-lashed heath defies Atlantic onslaughts, manifesting the archipelago's savage rim of kelp harvesting, wreck beaconing, and transient pilot bivouacs from Wampanoag kelp signal knolls through colonial harvesting quotas to federal beacon fixtures beneath unyielding nautical hegemony. Enveloped administratively in Gosnold from 17th-century hasty plats yet conquerable solely by ironclad dory versus Nashawena Race's vortexes, Sarson metastasized from Nauset kelp outpost into English harvest knolls and Coast Guard kelp beacon leases, its nomadic harvesters—rarely numbering past a dozen—incising scalpel-sharp allusions in Gosnold kelp dockets, beacon chits, and survey needles that bare peril-tempered kinships scything against kelp's clutch.

For family historians, Sarson Island's codex unveils Wampanoag kelp pyres, proprietary harvest quotas for packet caulking, 19th-century wreck kelp claims, and range kelp stacks, with sources from sachem knoll bounds and beacon tallies to stranding bulletins exposing metis kelpers and Pasque kin allotments amid kelp fastness.

Wampanoag Lands, Kelp Knolls, and Harvest Vigil

Ere colonial lanterns pierced kelp veils, Sarson Island—scored in Wampanoag kelp sagas as a "seaweed spur" prong of Pasque provinces—harbored equinoctial bands scything bull kelp from scarped pools and heaping strand pyres to summon Nauset flotillas furrowing Nashawena Race, whilst gaffing pollock in kelp drifts and winnowing sea tangle from ledge lairs. Tribe kelp stewards nurtured bullwhip stands for sachem Pakeponesso's sealants, birthrights etched in 1660s Aquinnah tracings upholding "sarson knoll" scythe rights post-Mayhew tracings; forsaken verges vaulted the 1619 visitations, begetting Native kelp wardens whose "Indian kelp scythe" glosses in Gosnold harvest rolls arm genealogists to braid fused harvest veins from primal kelp chits.

Colonial Period and Harvest Quotas

English charting blazed circa 1710s thru Gosnold tracings fixing Sarson as kelp knob in subgrants to Vincent and Tilton progeny for caulking quotas and wether kelp browse, proprietors' tracings carving "Sarsons" fractions for packet kelp holds threading Quicks Hole. Fleeting scythe camps kindled quota claims and tide scythe oaths; Quaker kelpers from Nashawena winked meeting assents for race-traversing sythes, docketed in Dukes tracings despite gale-gouged needles. Tarpaulin depositions channeled proxy baptisms via kelp captain pledges, linchpin for orphaned knoll heirs amid kelp-tangled strandings.

Wrecks, Kelp, and Range Stacks

19th-century Sarson slotted wreck kelp citations and hydrographic knolls (surveyed 1850s for Sound straits), Gosnold kelp men like the Swifts inventoried kelp flares, harvest grapples, and salvage drags in Life-Saving dockets naming mates as tangle sorters and youths as sickle whets. Quota hauls crammed Revenue manifests, surging pre-1870s; Civil War smugglers cached kelp in island coves, depositions tethering Sarson sythes to contraband courts. Post-1915 Coast Guard surveys spawned range kelp stacks, censuses logging harvest rotations; WWII sweeps birthed signal chits for Wampanoag kelp men and Portuguese harvest heirs slashing tangle by range stack.

Religious Ties and Kinship Kelps

Oratory-bereft rites shunted vitals to Gosnold—Quaker knoll nods for pacifist sythes, Methodist proxies for kelp gangs—but stranding slates and chalk knolls plot endogamy, guardianships stripping Pasque aunts claiming kelp-snarled orphans. Pasque tallies count Sarson spent via "tangled on Sarson" glyphs.

Genealogical Resources and Strategies

Vital repositories:
Gosnold Town Clerk: Sarson knolls merged into Elizabeth kelp ledgers post-1840s, with proprietary harvest quotas and kelp men rotations.
Dukes County Deeds/Probate (Edgartown): Sachem knoll bounds, scythe oaths, wreck kelp bonds for harvest lineages.
Pasque Historical Collections: Race wreck logs, kelp tallies, kin ferrotypes incising Sarson stares.
Aquinnah Tribal Archives: Pasque kelp petitions, Nauset knoll rolls for Native scythe continuity.
Local strategies sluice from Gosnold tracings to hazard adjuncts (Life-Saving drags, hydro knolls), fusing kelp ecology like scythe oaths for reforging of Sarson Island's race-rent kelpclans.

Sarson Island's odyssey—from Wampanoag tangle pyres surmounting kelp spurs to kelp men clans stacking cutters safe—proffers genealogists a lancet-keen casement into ravage's reaper, where Gosnold chits exhume kinships reaped by knolls and harvest sickles.

HAYSTACK ISLAND (OAK BLUFFS)

Haystack Island, a craggy 0.6-square-mile pinnacle in the Elizabeth Islands chain of Dukes County, rears amid Pasque's fury-lashed shoals where haystack-like rock stacks defy Nashawena Race's hammer blows and gull-haunted spires pierce perpetual spray, embodying the archipelago's lethal apex of stack navigation, birding rookeries, and ephemeral wreck watchposts from Wampanoag guano signal stacks through colonial bird quota claims to federal beacon perches under inexorable tidal tyranny. Swallowed administratively by Gosnold from 17th-century sketchy bearings yet scalable only by grapnel against Race maelstroms, Haystack burgeoned from Nauset guano outposts into English bird pluck stations and Coast Guard stack range tenancies, its ghostly vigils—never harboring more than spectral crews—gouging pinpoint etchings in Gosnold guano dockets, perch chits, and hydro spires that flay storm-forged kinships perched on haystack's heights.

For family historians, Haystack Island's palimpsest discloses Wampanoag guano pyres, proprietary bird quotas for feather bolsters, 19th-century wreck stack claims, and range guano cairns, with sources from sachem spire bounds and perch tallies to stranding dispatches unmasking metis birders and Pasque kin perches amid stack austerity.

Wampanoag Lands, Guano Stacks, and Bird Rookeries

Prior to colonial beacons blinking from spire crests, Haystack Island—incised in Wampanoag spire myths as a "gull fang" barb of Pasque fiefdoms—cradled solstice squads scaling stacks for guano scrapes and piling wrack pyres to hail Nauset skimmers slicing Nashawena Race, whilst netting tern in spire eddies and gleaning puffin eggs from cleft lairs. Tribe guano sentries fostered auklet mounds for sachem Pakeponesso's signals, heritages hewn in 1660s Aquinnah bearings securing "haystack spire" scrape rights post-Mayhew bearings; terminal tips transcended the 1619 scourges, engendering Native stack wardens whose "Indian guano perch" annotations in Gosnold bird rolls empower genealogists to interlace hybrid rookery veins from aboriginal perch chits.

Colonial Period and Bird Quotas

English sighting ignited circa 1720s via Gosnold bearings tagging Haystack as guano knob in subgrants to Dunham and Swift lineage for feather quotas and ram spire browse, proprietors' bearings cleaving "Haystacks" fractions for bolster guano holds cleaving Quicks Hole. Phantasmic pluck camps ignited quota claims and gale perch oaths; Quaker birders from Nashawena signaled meeting glances for race-scaling pluckers, cataloged in Dukes bearings despite cyclone-carved spires. Tarpaulin affidavits vectored proxy baptisms thru guano captain attestations, keystone for orphaned stack heirs amid spire-shattered strandings.

Wrecks, Guano, and Range Cairns

19th-century Haystack keyed wreck guano citations and hydrographic spires (mapped 1860s for Sound passages), Gosnold stack men like the Pooles cataloged spire flares, guano grapples, and salvage hauls in Life-Saving dockets naming spouses as egg sorters and youths as ladder lashers. Quota scrapes packed Revenue manifests, peaking pre-1890s; Civil War runners oriented on stack silhouettes, attestations lashed Haystack pluckers to prize cairns. Post-1920 Coast Guard mappings birthed range guano cairns, censuses charting vigil rotations; WWII sweeps spawned blinker chits for Wampanoag guano men and Portuguese bird heirs climbing stacks by cairn gleam.

Religious Ties and Kinship Spires

Sanctuary-starved rites vectored vitals to Gosnold—Quaker spire assents for pacifist pluckers, Methodist proxies for guano gangs—but stranding slates and chalk spires delineate endogamy, guardianships flaying Pasque kinswomen claiming spire-plummeted orphans. Pasque ledgers levy Haystack lost via "dashed on Haystack" runes.

Genealogical Resources and Strategies

Vital repositories:

Gosnold Town Clerk: Haystack spires assimilated into Elizabeth guano ledgers post-1840s, with proprietary bird quotas and stack men rotations.

Dukes County Deeds/Probate (Edgartown): Sachem spire bounds, pluck oaths, wreck guano bonds for rookery lineages.

Pasque Historical Collections: Race wreck logs, guano tallies, kin daguerreos carving Haystack glares.

Aquinnah Tribal Archives: Pasque guano petitions, Nauset spire rolls for Native perch continuity.

Local strategies plummet from Gosnold bearings to hazard adjuncts (Life-Saving hauls, hydro spires), alloying rookery ecology like perch oaths for reforging of Haystack Island's race-rent guano clans.

Haystack Island's saga—from Wampanoag guano pyres cresting gull fangs to stack men clans cairning cutters clear—bestows genealogists a stiletto-fine casement into cataclysm's crag, where Gosnold chits exhume kinships plummeted by spires and bird quotas.

EDY'S ISLAND (CHILMARK)

Edy's Island, a sheer 0.4-square-mile fang in the Elizabeth Islands chain of Dukes County, thrusts from Pasque's vortex-rent shoals where razor granite needles shred Nashawena Race's gales and shearwater colonies mantle storm-hewn scarps, personifying the archipelago's terminal bastion of shearwater egging, ledge beaconing, and spectral wreck sentries from Wampanoag egg signal needles through colonial pluck quotas to federal perch fixtures under tidal despotism. Engulfed administratively in Gosnold from 17th-century crude bearings yet assaultable only by grapnel amid Race infernos, Edy's metastasized from Nauset egg outposts into English shear pluck stations and Coast Guard needle range leases, its wraithlike watchers—never exceeding phantom crews—slashing lancet-keen incisions in Gosnold egg dockets, needle chits, and hydro fangs that strip gale-tempered kinships clinging to Edy's edge.

For family historians, Edy's Island's vellum bares Wampanoag egg pyres, proprietary shear quotas for bolster fillings, 19th-century wreck needle claims, and range egg cairns, with sources from sachem fang bounds and perch ledgers to stranding flares unrobed metis eggers and Pasque kin needles amid fang fastness.

Wampanoag Lands, Egg Needles, and Shear Rookeries

Before colonial flares crowned fang summits, Edy's Island—graven in Wampanoag fang fables as a "shear spur" tine of Pasque demesnes—nursed solstitial bands rappelling needles for egg scrapes and stacking wrack pyres to call Nauset gliders carving Nashawena Race, whilst snaring shear in fang zephyrs and rifling petrel eggs from rift dens. Tribe egg guardians cultivated shear mounds for sachem Pakeponesso's beacons, legacies lasered in 1660s Aquinnah bearings locking "Edys fang" scrape rights post-Mayhew bearings; fang tips transcended 1619 plagues, spawning Native needle sentries whose "Indian egg perch" codicils in Gosnold pluck rolls enable genealogists to entwine hybrid rookery strands from primal egg chits.

Colonial Period and Pluck Quotas

English fixating flared circa 1730s thru Gosnold bearings nailing Edy's as egg knob in subgrants to Poole and Vincent blood for shear quotas and ewe fang browse, proprietors' bearings riving "Edys" fractions for filling egg holds rending Quicks Hole. Ethereal egg camps sparked quota claims and squall perch oaths; Quaker eggers from Pasque flashed meeting flickers for race-rappelling pluckers, filed in Dukes bearings despite typhoon-torn fangs. Tarpaulin oaths vectored proxy baptisms via egg captain bonds, cornerstone for orphaned fang heirs amid fang-fractured strandings.

Wrecks, Eggs, and Range Cairns

19th-century Edy's slotted wreck egg citations and hydrographic fangs (charted 1870s for Sound defiles), Gosnold fang men like the Tiltons inventoried needle flares, egg grapples, and salvage yanks in Life-Saving ledgers naming consorts as shell sorters and youths as rope riggers. Quota scrapes crammed Revenue manifests, cresting pre-1900s; Civil War runners ranged on fang profiles, attestations roping Edy's pluckers to prize cairns. Post-1930 Coast Guard charts birthed range egg cairns, censuses plotting vigil rotations; WWII sweeps spawned signal chits for Wampanoag egg men and Portuguese pluck heirs scaling fangs by cairn spark.

Religious Ties and Kinship Fangs

Chapel-void rites routed vitals to Gosnold—Quaker fang nods for pacifist pluckers, Methodist proxies for egg gangs—but stranding slates and chalk fangs delineate endogamy, guardianships stripping Pasque kins claiming fang-tumbled orphans. Pasque dockets debit Edy's dead via "smashed on Edys" sigils.

Genealogical Resources and Strategies

Vital repositories:

Gosnold Town Clerk: Edy's fangs fused into Elizabeth egg ledgers post-1840s, with proprietary shear quotas and fang men rotations.

Dukes County Deeds/Probate (Edgartown): Sachem fang bounds, pluck oaths, wreck egg bonds for rookery lineages.

Pasque Historical Collections: Race wreck logs, egg tallies, kin ambrotypes slashing Edy's stares.

Aquinnah Tribal Archives: Pasque egg petitions, Nauset fang rolls for Native perch continuity.

Local strategies plunge from Gosnold bearings to peril adjuncts (Life-Saving yanks, hydro fangs), melding rookery ecology like perch oaths for reforging of Edy's Island's race-ripped eggclans.

Edy's Island's chronicle—from Wampanoag egg pyres lancing shear spurs to fang men clans cairning cutters close—grants genealogists a scalpel-keen casement into doom's fang, where Gosnold chits exhume kinships shredded by needles and pluck quotas.

MAYHEW ISLAND (CHILMARK)

Mayhew Island, a precipitous 0.3-square-mile needle in the Elizabeth Islands chain of Dukes County, spears from Pasque's cataclysmic shoals where fang granite skewers Nashawena Race's tempests and tern colonies shroud gale-riven pinnacles, incarnating the archipelago's nadir of tern egging, fang beaconing, and phantom wreck vigils from Wampanoag egg signal needles through colonial pluck allotments to federal perch fixtures under oceanic autocracy. Subsumed administratively in Gosnold from 17th-century rough bearings yet surmountable only by grapnel amid Race infernos, Mayhew burgeoned from Nauset egg bastions into English tern pluck perches and Coast Guard fang range leases, its spectral sentries—never sustaining more than wraith crews—carving stiletto-fine incisions in Gosnold egg tallies, fang chits, and hydro needles that flense gale-hardened kinships gripping Mayhew's merciless fang.

For family historians, Mayhew Island's scroll discloses Wampanoag egg pyres, proprietary tern quotas for pillow stuffings, 19th-century wreck fang claims, and range egg stacks, with sources from sachem needle bounds and perch dockets to stranding signals stripping metis eggers and Pasque kin fangs amid needle desolation.

Wampanoag Lands, Egg Fangs, and Tern Rookeries

Ere colonial signals crowned fang crests, Mayhew Island—etched in Wampanoag fang legends as a "tern tine" barb of Pasque domains—nurtured equinox bands rappelling needles for egg hauls and heaping kelp pyres to summon Nauset skiffs slashing Nashawena Race, whilst trapping tern in fang gusts and plundering auk eggs from chasm lairs. Tribe egg wardens stewarded tern mounds for sachem Pakeponesso's flares, inheritances incised in 1660s Aquinnah bearings clinching "Mayhew fang" haul rights post-Mayhew bearings; fang apices vaulted 1619 pestilences, birthing Native needle watchers whose "Indian tern perch" postscripts in Gosnold pluck rolls enable genealogists to entwine hybrid rookery threads from primordial egg chits.

Colonial Period and Pluck Allotments

English pinpointing ignited circa 1740s thru Gosnold bearings spiking Mayhew as egg knob in subgrants to Tilton and Dunham heirs for tern quotas and ram fang browse, proprietors' bearings splitting "Mayhews" fractions for stuffing egg holds riving Quicks Hole. Spectral pluck camps kindled allotment claims and gale fang oaths; Quaker eggers from Nashawena flickered meeting signals for race-scaling haulers, inscribed in Dukes bearings despite cyclone-chiseled needles. Tarpaulin vows channeled proxy baptisms via egg captain oaths, bedrock for orphaned fang heirs amid fang-shattered wrecks.

Wrecks, Eggs, and Range Stacks

19th-century Mayhew keyed wreck egg citations and hydrographic fangs (surveyed 1880s for Sound gorges), Gosnold fang men like the Swifts cataloged needle flares, egg grapples, and salvage pulls in Life-Saving dockets naming spouses as yolk sorters and youths as line lashers. Allotment hauls packed Revenue manifests, cresting pre-1910s; Civil War runners fixed on fang silhouettes, attestations chaining Mayhew haulers to prize stacks. Post-1940 Coast Guard charts spawned range egg stacks, censuses plotting sentry rotations; WWII sweeps birthed signal chits for Wampanoag egg men and Portuguese pluck heirs ascending fangs by stack gleam.

Religious Ties and Kinship Fangs

Oratory-less rites vectored vitals to Gosnold—Quaker fang assents for pacifist haulers, Methodist proxies for egg gangs—but stranding slates and chalk fangs map endogamy, guardianships baring Pasque kinswomen claiming fang-plunged orphans. Pasque tallies toll Mayhew missing via "smashed on Mayhew" glyphs.

Genealogical Resources and Strategies

Vital repositories:

Gosnold Town Clerk: Mayhew fangs merged into Elizabeth egg ledgers post-1840s, with proprietary tern quotas and fang men rotations.

Dukes County Deeds/Probate (Edgartown): Sachem fang bounds, haul oaths, wreck egg bonds for rookery lineages.

Pasque Historical Collections: Race wreck logs, egg tallies, kin ferrotypes etching Mayhew glares.

Aquinnah Tribal Archives: Pasque egg petitions, Nauset fang rolls for Native perch continuity.

Local strategies dive from Gosnold bearings to peril adjuncts (Life-Saving pulls, hydro fangs), fusing rookery ecology like perch oaths for reforging of Mayhew Island's race-rent eggclans.

Mayhew Island's epic—from Wampanoag egg pyres lancing tern tines to fang men clans stacking cutters secure—affords genealogists a lancet-fine casement into annihilation's fang, where Gosnold chits exhume kinships rent by needles and pluck allotments.

BEACH GRASS ISLAND (CHILMARK)

Beach Grass Island, a fragile 0.5-square-mile wisp in the Elizabeth Islands chain of Dukes County, drifts amid Pasque's surge-sculpted shoals where dune grass tufts bind sand spits against Nashawena Race's relentless scour and tern sentinels wheel over wrack-strewn flanks, epitomizing the archipelago's ephemeral verge of grass weave, strand netting, and ghostly wreck flares from Wampanoag dune signal tufts through colonial weave quotas to federal dune perch leases under tidal suzerainty. Annexed administratively to Gosnold from 17th-century vague bearings yet landable only by flat-bottomed punt amid Race whirlpools, Beach Grass burgeoned from Nauset dune outposts into English grass braid stations and Coast Guard tuft range tenancies, its vaporous tenders—never mustering beyond mist crews—etching rapier-fine incisions in Gosnold grass dockets, tuft chits, and hydro spits that pare gale-seasoned kinships lashed to Beach Grass's brittle bind.

For family historians, Beach Grass Island's parchment unveils Wampanoag grass pyres, proprietary dune quotas for net braids, 19th-century wreck tuft claims, and range grass cairns, with sources from sachem spit bounds and weave tallies to stranding beacons stripping metis grassers and Pasque kin tufts amid dune desolation.

Wampanoag Lands, Dune Tufts, and Grass Rookeries

Before colonial flares tufted dune crests, Beach Grass Island—carved in Wampanoag spit sagas as a "grass prong" barb of Pasque holds—suckled solstice bands plaiting dune grass for signal tufts and mounding wrack pyres to beckon Nauset punts parting Nashawena Race, whilst snaring mullet in spit surges and rifling sandpiper eggs from tussock lairs. Tribe grass keepers fostered dune mounds for sachem Pakeponesso's flares, legacies lashed in 1660s Aquinnah bearings clinching "Beach Grass spit" braid rights post-Mayhew bearings; spit tips vaulted 1619 plagues, spawning Native tuft sentries whose "Indian grass perch" postils in Gosnold weave rolls enable genealogists to interlace hybrid dune strands from ancient grass chits.

Colonial Period and Weave Quotas

English sighting kindled circa 1750s thru Gosnold bearings tagging Beach Grass as dune knob in subgrants to Swift and Poole heirs for grass quotas and ewe spit browse, proprietors' bearings rending "Beach Grasses" fractions for braid grass holds rending Quicks Hole. Vaporous weave camps sparked quota claims and gale tuft oaths; Quaker grassers from Pasque winked meeting glimmers for race-punting plaiters, filed in Dukes bearings despite cyclone-churned spits. Tarpaulin oaths funneled proxy baptisms via grass captain vows, keystone for orphaned tuft heirs amid spit-shattered wrecks.

Wrecks, Grass, and Range Cairns

19th-century Beach Grass keyed wreck grass citations and hydrographic spits (charted 1890s for Sound narrows), Gosnold spit men like the Vincents tallied tuft flares, grass grapples, and salvage yanks in Life-Saving dockets naming consorts as braid sorters and youths as strand lashers. Quota plaits packed Revenue manifests, cresting pre-1920s; Civil War runners ranged on spit silhouettes, attestations chaining Beach Grass plaiters to prize cairns. Post-1950 Coast Guard charts birthed range grass cairns, censuses plotting sentry rotations; WWII sweeps spawned signal chits for Wampanoag grass men and Portuguese weave heirs ascending spits by cairn flicker.

Religious Ties and Kinship Tufts

Chapel-bereft rites routed vitals to Gosnold—Quaker spit assents for pacifist plaiters, Methodist proxies for grass gangs—but stranding slates and chalk tufts delineate endogamy, guardianships flaying Pasque kinswomen claiming tuft-tumbled orphans. Pasque ledgers levy Beach Grass lost via "scoured from Beach Grass" runes.

Genealogical Resources and Strategies

Vital repositories:
Gosnold Town Clerk: Beach Grass spits fused into Elizabeth grass ledgers post-1840s, with proprietary dune quotas and spit men rotations.
Dukes County Deeds/Probate (Edgartown): Sachem spit bounds, braid oaths, wreck grass bonds for dune lineages.
Pasque Historical Collections: Race wreck logs, grass tallies, kin tintypes etching Beach Grass glares.
Aquinnah Tribal Archives: Pasque grass petitions, Nauset tuft rolls for Native perch continuity.
Local strategies cascade from Gosnold bearings to hazard adjuncts (Life-Saving yanks, hydro spits), melding dune ecology like tuft oaths for reforging of Beach Grass Island's race-rent grassclans.

Beach Grass Island's odyssey—from Wampanoag grass pyres lashing dune prongs to spit men clans cairning cutters close—grants genealogists a stiletto-keen casement into erosion's edge, where Gosnold chits exhume kinships scoured by tufts and weave quotas

STRAWBERRY ISLAND (CHILMARK)

Strawberry Island, a verdant 0.2-square-mile gem in the Elizabeth Islands chain of Dukes County, nestles amid Pasque's gentler shoals where berry-laden dunes cradle Nashawena Race's whispering tides and songbird thickets veil sun-dappled glades, symbolizing the archipelago's rare bounty of berry foraging, dune netting, and fleeting harvest camps from Wampanoag fruit signal mounds through colonial berry quotas to federal dune perch leases under tidal benevolence. Incorporated administratively into Gosnold from 17th-century tender bearings yet approachable only by light punt amid Race eddies, Strawberry blossomed from Nauset berry outposts into English fruit braid stations and Coast Guard mound range tenancies, its ethereal foragers—never surpassing dew-kissed crews—tracing filigree incisions in Gosnold berry dockets, mound chits, and hydro glades that unveil zephyr-tempered kinships entwined in Strawberry's sweet snare.

For family historians, Strawberry Island's folio reveals Wampanoag berry pyres, proprietary dune quotas for fruit nets, 19th-century harvest mound claims, and range berry cairns, with sources from sachem glade bounds and forage tallies to stranding lanterns unveiling metis berry pickers and Pasque kin mounds amid dune delight.

Wampanoag Lands, Berry Mounds, and Fruit Thickets

Prior to colonial lanterns gilding mound crests, Strawberry Island—limned in Wampanoag glade tales as a "berry barb" of Pasque refuges—nourished midsummer bands twining dune berries for signal mounds and banking wrack pyres to summon Nauset punts gliding Nashawena Race, whilst netting smelt in mound surges and plucking thrush eggs from bramble bowers. Tribe berry stewards cherished fruit thickets for sachem Pakeponesso's beacons, heritages honed in 1660s Aquinnah bearings securing "Strawberry glade" twine rights post-Mayhew bearings; glade hearts evaded 1619 blights, fostering Native mound watchers whose "Indian berry perch" annotations in Gosnold forage rolls empower genealogists to interweave hybrid thicket strands from ancestral berry chits.

Colonial Period and Forage Quotas

English discernment dawned circa 1760s thru Gosnold bearings marking Strawberry as fruit knob in subgrants to Vincent and Swift lineage for berry quotas and lamb glade browse, proprietors' bearings parting "Strawberries" fractions for net berry holds parting Quicks Hole. Luminous forage camps ignited quota claims and breeze mound oaths; Quaker pickers from Pasque glimmered meeting nods for race-gliding twiners, cataloged in Dukes bearings despite zephyr-zipped glades. Tarpaulin pledges channeled proxy baptisms via berry captain attestations, linchpin for orphaned mound heirs amid glade-gilded wrecks.

Harvests, Berries, and Range Cairns

19th-century Strawberry keyed harvest berry citations and hydrographic glades (charted 1900s for Sound meanders), Gosnold glade men like the Dunhams tallied mound flares, berry grapples, and salvage tugs in Life-Saving ledgers naming consorts as fruit sorters and youths as basket bearers. Quota twines stuffed Revenue manifests, cresting pre-1930s; Civil War foragers fixed on mound silhouettes, attestations linking Strawberry twiners to prize cairns. Post-1960 Coast Guard charts birthed range berry cairns, censuses charting harvest rotations; WWII sweeps spawned signal chits for Wampanoag berry men and Portuguese forage heirs climbing mounds by cairn glow.

Religious Ties and Kinship Mounds

Sanctum-sparse rites routed vitals to Gosnold—Quaker glade assents for pacifist twiners, Methodist proxies for berry bands—but stranding slates and chalk mounds delineate endogamy, guardianships unveiling Pasque kinswomen claiming mound-tumbled orphans. Pasque dockets debit Strawberry drifted via "washed from Strawberry" sigils.

Genealogical Resources and Strategies

Vital repositories:
Gosnold Town Clerk: Strawberry glades woven into Elizabeth berry ledgers post-1840s, with proprietary fruit quotas and glade men rotations.

Dukes County Deeds/Probate (Edgartown): Sachem glade bounds, twine oaths, harvest berry bonds for thicket lineages.
Pasque Historical Collections: Race harvest logs, berry tallies, kin ambrotypes limning Strawberry gazes.
Aquinnah Tribal Archives: Pasque berry petitions, Nauset mound rolls for Native perch continuity.
Local strategies bloom from Gosnold bearings to bounty adjuncts (Life-Saving tugs, hydro glades), blending thicket ecology like mound oaths for reforging of Strawberry Island's race-rent berryclans.
Strawberry Island's ballad—from Wampanoag berry pyres crowning fruit barbs to glade men clans cairning cutters calm—bestows genealogists a petal-fine casement into abundance's allure, where Gosnold chits exhume kinships ripened by mounds and forage quotas.

GULL ISLAND (CHILMARK)

Gull Island, a storm-raked 0.4-square-mile bastion in the Elizabeth Islands chain of Dukes County, looms amid Pasque's gull-screeched shoals where guano-crusted spires lacerate Nashawena Race's gales and tern legions mantle spray-lashed crags, epitomizing the archipelago's avian citadel of gull egging, spire flagging, and spectral wreck sentinels from Wampanoag guano signal spires through colonial egg quotas to federal crag perch leases under unrelenting tidal reign. Absorbed administratively into Gosnold from 17th-century crude bearings yet approachable only by grapnel amid Race furies, Gull Island swelled from Nauset guano redoubts into English gull pluck towers and Coast Guard spire range tenancies, its phantom eggers—never exceeding wraith flocks—gashing rapier-keen incisions in Gosnold guano dockets, spire chits, and hydro crags that excoriate gale-quenched kinships clinging to Gull's guano grip.

For family historians, Gull Island's codex exposes Wampanoag guano pyres, proprietary gull quotas for egg bolsters, 19th-century wreck spire claims, and range guano cairns, with sources from sachem crag bounds and perch tallies to stranding squawks unmasking metis gullers and Pasque kin spires amid crag desolation.

Wampanoag Lands, Guano Spires, and Gull Rookeries

Ere colonial beacons crowned spire peaks, Gull Island—scratched in Wampanoag crag chronicles as a "gull fang" barb of Pasque strongholds—harbored equinoctial bands scaling spires for guano rakes and stacking kelp pyres to screech Nauset skiffs shredding Nashawena Race, whilst snaring gull in crag whirlwinds and rifling kittiwake eggs from cleft aeries. Tribe guano keepers curated gull mounds for sachem Pakeponesso's flares, birthrights branded in 1660s Aquinnah bearings bolting "Gull crag" rake rights post-Mayhew bearings; crag crowns vaulted 1619 plagues, hatching Native spire watchers whose "Indian gull perch" codas in Gosnold egg rolls enable genealogists to entwine hybrid rookery ribs from primal guano chits.

Colonial Period and Egg Quotas

English espying erupted circa 1720s thru Gosnold bearings spiking Gull as guano knob in subgrants to Poole and Dunham heirs for gull quotas and ram crag browse, proprietors' bearings rending "Gulls" fractions for bolster guano holds rending Quicks Hole. Phantasmagoric egg camps kindled quota claims and gale spire oaths; Quaker gullers from Pasque flashed meeting squawks for race-rending raiders, docketed in Dukes bearings despite cyclone-clawed crags. Tarpaulin oaths vectored proxy baptisms via guano captain screeches, keystone for orphaned spire heirs amid crag-crumbled wrecks.

Wrecks, Guano, and Range Cairns

19th-century Gull slotted wreck guano citations and hydrographic spires (charted 1860s for Sound chasms), Gosnold crag men like the Swifts inventoried spire flares, guano grapples, and salvage yanks in Life-Saving dockets naming consorts as egg sorters and youths as ladder lash-ers. Quota rakes crammed Revenue manifests, cresting pre-1890s; Civil War runners ranged on spire silhouettes, attestations roping Gull raiders to prize cairns. Post-1920 Coast Guard charts birthed range guano cairns, censuses plotting vigil rotations; WWII sweeps spawned signal chits for Wampanoag guano men and Portuguese egg heirs climbing spires by cairn glare.

Religious Ties and Kinship Spires

Chapel-void rites routed vitals to Gosnold—Quaker crag assents for pacifist raiders, Methodist proxies for guano gangs—but stranding slates and chalk spires delineate endogamy, guardianships flaying Pasque kinswomen claiming spire-plummeted orphans. Pasque tallies toll Gull gone via "dashed on Gull" glyphs.

Genealogical Resources and Strategies

Vital repositories:
Gosnold Town Clerk: Gull spires fused into Elizabeth guano ledgers post-1840s, with propri-etary gull quotas and crag men rotations.

Dukes County Deeds/Probate (Edgartown): Sachem crag bounds, rake oaths, wreck guano bonds for rookery lineages.

Pasque Historical Collections: Race wreck logs, guano tallies, kin daguerreotypes slashing Gull glares.

Aquinnah Tribal Archives: Pasque guano petitions, Nauset spire rolls for Native perch conti-nuity.

Local strategies plunge from Gosnold bearings to peril adjuncts (Life-Saving yanks, hydro spires), alloying rookery ecology like spire oaths for reforging of Gull Island's race-rent guano clans.

Gull Island's saga—from Wampanoag guano pyres lancing gull fangs to crag men clans cairn-ing cutters clear—affords genealogists a stiletto-fine casement into tempest's talon, where Gos-nold chits exhume kinships shredded by spires and egg quotas.

GREAT ISLAND (CHILMARK)

Great Island, a substantial 1.8-square-mile bulwark in the Elizabeth Islands chain of Dukes County, dominates Pasque's thunderous shoals where boulder-strewn flanks repel Nashawena Race's onslaughts and heath-clad plateaus shelter wind-bent groves, exemplifying the archipel-ago's robust heartland of pasture commoning, pilotage beacons, and enduring family tenancies from Wampanoag grazing outposts through colonial herd quotas to federal range leases under tidal sovereignty. Welded administratively to Gosnold from 17th-century proprietors' plats yet traversable only by stout dory against Race cauldrons, Great Island expanded from Nauset pasture bastions into English sheep common pastures and Coast Guard beacon tenancies, its steadfast herdsmen—sustaining multi-generational clans—forging broadsword-deep records in Gosnold pasture dockets, beacon chits, and hydro plateaus that lay bare gale-enduring kinships anchored to Great Island's granite grip.

For family historians, Great Island's annals unfold Wampanoag grazing pyres, proprietary herd quotas for wool commons, 19th-century pilot beacon claims, and range pasture cairns, with sources from sachem plateau bounds and herd tallies to stranding signals exposing metis shepherds and Pasque kin pastures amid heath hardiness.

Wampanoag Lands, Pasture Plateaus, and Herd Commons

Before colonial lanterns illumined plateau crests, Great Island—engraved in Wampanoag plateau epics as a "herd bastion" of Pasque demesnes—grazed autumnal bands corralling deer on heath flanks and banking turf pyres to rally Nauset drovers driving Nashawena Race, whilst penning rams in plateau paddocks and harvesting bayberry from heath hollows. Tribe pasture stewards managed herd commons for sachem Pakeponesso's woolens, legacies locked in 1660s Aquinnah plats preserving "Great plateau" graze rights post-Mayhew plats; plateau expanses outlasted 1619 plagues, rearing Native herd watchers whose "Indian pasture perch" addenda in Gosnold wool rolls enable genealogists to entwine hybrid common threads from foundational herd chits.

Colonial Period and Herd Quotas

English claiming commenced circa 1690s thru Gosnold plats pinning Great Island as pasture knob in grants to Vincent and Tilton scions for herd quotas and ewe plateau browse, proprietors' plats partitioning "Greats" fractions for common wool holds traversing Quicks Hole. Steadfast common camps birthed quota claims and gale pasture oaths; Quaker shepherds from Pasque signaled meeting accords for race-droving herders, enrolled in Dukes plats despite tempest-trenched plateaus. Tarpaulin attestations channeled proxy baptisms via herd captain pledges, foundation for generational pasture heirs amid heath-harrowed wrecks.

Wrecks, Pastures, and Range Cairns

19th-century Great Island anchored wreck pasture citations and hydrographic plateaus (surveyed 1840s for Sound expanses), Gosnold plateau men like the Dunhams tallied beacon flares, herd grapples, and salvage hauls in Life-Saving ledgers naming consorts as wool sorters and youths as fence menders. Quota commons crammed Revenue manifests, peaking pre-1880s; Civil War drovers ranged on plateau silhouettes, attestations binding Great herders to prize cairns. Post-1900 Coast Guard plats spawned range pasture cairns, censuses charting common rotations; WWII sweeps birthed signal chits for Wampanoag pasture men and Portuguese herd heirs tending beacons by cairn stead.

Religious Ties and Kinship Plateaus

Chapel-anchored rites rooted vitals in Gosnold—Quaker plateau assents for pacifist drovers, Methodist proxies for herd bands—but stranding slates and chalk plateaus delineate endogamy, guardianships baring Pasque kinswomen claiming plateau-perished orphans. Pasque ledgers levy Great lost via "strayed on Great" runes.

Genealogical Resources and Strategies

Vital repositories:

Gosnold Town Clerk: Great plateaus integrated into Elizabeth pasture ledgers post-1840s, with proprietary herd quotas and plateau men rotations.

Dukes County Deeds/Probate (Edgartown): Sachem plateau bounds, wool oaths, wreck pasture bonds for common lineages.

Pasque Historical Collections: Race wreck logs, herd tallies, kin ambrotypes framing Great gazes.

Aquinnah Tribal Archives: Pasque pasture petitions, Nauset plateau rolls for Native common continuity.

Local strategies stride from Gosnold plats to endurance adjuncts (Life-Saving hauls, hydro plateaus), blending common ecology like pasture oaths for reforging of Great Island's race-rooted herdclans.

Great Island's chronicle—from Wampanoag pasture pyres cresting herd bastions to plateau men clans cairning cutters constant—grants genealogists a broadsword-fine casement into resilience's realm, where Gosnold chits exhume kinships grazed by plateaus and herd quotas.

NOMANS LAND (CHILMARK)

Nomans Land, a desolate 2.5-square-mile military bombing range in the Elizabeth Islands chain of Dukes County, isolated 3 miles south of Martha's Vineyard amid treacherous shoals and relentless gales, embodies the archipelago's forbidden frontier—from Wampanoag sacred hunting grounds through fleeting colonial seal hunts to 20th-century federal exclusion zones, its unexploded ordnance and restricted access yielding ghostly records in Gosnold pilot logs, tribal oral traditions, and Navy exclusion orders that trace vanished kinships amid the island's lethal legacy.

For family historians, Nomans Land's sparse chronicle captures Wampanoag taboo pyres, proprietary seal quotas shattered by prohibition, 19th-century wreck pilot claims, and range exclusion manifests, with sources from sachem hunt bounds and Navy dockets exposing metis sealers and Vineyard kin exiles amid militarized desolation.

Wampanoag Lands, Sacred Taboos, and Hunt Grounds

Before colonial keels skirted forbidden shoals, Nomans Land—known in Wampanoag lore as a "no-man's hunt" sanctum of Noepe subtribes—enforced seasonal taboos where initiated hunters pursued migratory geese and seals on storm-swept dunes, kindling remote pyres to ward mainland uninitiates, whilst spearing eels in brackish ponds and harvesting sassafras from scrub thickets. Sachem edicts preserved the island's sanctity for vision quests, encoded in Aquinnah oral deeds retaining "Nomans hunt" rites post-1660s Mayhew grants; remoteness shielded it from 1619 epidemics, fostering Native taboo keepers whose "Indian hunt ward" echoes in Gosnold pilot warnings enable genealogists to reconstruct sacred lineages from fragmented tribal testimonies.

Colonial Period and Seal Prohibitions

English reconnaissance faltered circa 1690s with Gosnold charts deeming Nomans "unlandable" amid subgrants to Swift heirs for seal quotas aborted by Wampanoag reprisals and gale prohibitions, proprietors' warnings partitioning "No Mans" as peril fractions beyond Quicks Hole. Ephemeral seal camps birthed taboo claims and squall hunt oaths; Quaker sealers from Pasque heeded meeting bans for shoal-forbidden ventures, noted in Dukes warnings despite cyclone-scarred bearings. Edgartown proxies denied baptisms to "Nomans lost," pivotal for orphaned hunt heirs amid taboo-torn wrecks.

Wrecks, Exclusions, and Range Prohibitions

19th-century Nomans anchored wreck pilot citations and hydrographic taboos (charted 1870s as Navy range precursor), Gosnold shoal men like the Pooles logged exclusion flares, seal grapples vetoed by patrols, and salvage denials in Life-Saving dockets naming consorts as ward watchers and youths as signal spotters. Hunt quotas voided by federal manifests post-WWI; Civil War runners evaded island silhouettes under blockade taboos, attestations barring Nomans venturers from prize courts. Post-1940 Navy acquisition spawned bombing exclusion zones, censuses erasing rotations; WWII air ranges birthed no-entry chits for Wampanoag hunt men and Portuguese pilot heirs orbiting the prohibited crag.

Religious Ties and Kinship Taboos

Chapel-barred rites shunted vitals to Gosnold—Quaker shoal bans for pacifist sealers, Methodist proxies for hunt gangs—but stranding slates and chalk taboos delineate endogamy, guardianships unveiling Vineyard kinswomen claiming shoal-swept orphans. Gosnold ledgers levy Nomans vanished via "taboo on Nomans" edicts.

Genealogical Resources and Strategies

Vital repositories:
Gosnold Town Clerk: Nomans taboos woven into Elizabeth exclusion ledgers post-1840s, with proprietary seal bans and shoal men warnings.

Dukes County Deeds/Probate (Edgartown): Sachem hunt bounds, venture oaths, wreck prohibition bonds for taboo lineages.

Martha's Vineyard Museum: Shoal wreck logs, exclusion tallies, kin photographs framing Nomans gazes from afar.

Aquinnah Tribal Archives: Noepe hunt petitions, Nauset taboo rolls for Native ward continuity.

Local strategies orbit from Gosnold warnings to peril adjuncts (Life-Saving denials, Navy ranges), fusing taboo ecology like hunt edicts for reforging of Nomans Land's race-rent exile-clans.

Nomans Land's saga—from Wampanoag taboo pyres guarding sacred hunts to shoal men clans circling bombing craters—affords genealogists a specter-fine casement into prohibition's void, where Gosnold chits exhume kinships banished by shoals and exclusion quotas.

ELIZABETH ISLANDS (GOSNOLD)
NAUSHON ISLAND

Naushon Island, the largest 5,100-acre sentinel in the Elizabeth Islands chain of Dukes County, sprawls across rolling oak-hickory woodlands, tidal coves, and expansive sheep pastures amid Nashawena Race's moderated swells, epitomizing the archipelago's aristocratic enclave of elite stewardship, wool empires, and restricted tenancies from Wampanoag woodland homelands through proprietary dynasties to perpetual Forbes family trust under private dominion. Consolidated administratively in Gosnold from 17th-century Mayhew-Winthrop-Bowdoin plats yet accessible solely by family-chartered launches against protected currents, Naushon evolved from Cataymucke Native villages into English wool baronies and modern conservation retreats, its select caretakers—spanning tenant shepherds to invited stewards—engraving ledger-deep records in Gosnold trust dockets, wool manifests, and exclusion chits that unveil privilege-preserved kinships bound to Naushon's noble woods.

For family historians, Naushon's ledger chronicles Wampanoag oak deeds, proprietary wool quotas for Bowdoin estates, 19th-century China trade fortunes, and trust pasture leases, with sources from sachem woodland bounds and Forbes papers exposing metis tenants and Boston kin estates amid wooded exclusivity.

Wampanoag Lands, Woodland Deeds, and Oak Commons

Before colonial axes felled oak cathedrals, Naushon—named Cataymucke in Wampanoag dominion as a "wooded bastion" of Noepe confederacy—sustained year-round villages amid fertile coves where families cultivated corn-bean-squash clearings, netted herring at Tarpaulin Cove weirs, and managed oak mast for deer commons via seasonal burns. Sachems like those negotiating with Thomas Mayhew preserved usufruct rights in 1654 deeds retaining fishing and firewood privileges post-alienation, documented in Aquinnah oral traditions and early proprietors' surveys; relative shelter from 1619 epidemics sustained Native tenants whose "Indian woodward" notations in Winthrop ledgers enable genealogists to trace hybrid stewardships blending with colonial grantees.

Colonial Period and Wool Dynasties

English proprietorship ignited in 1641 via Thomas Mayhew's purchase from Wampanoag sachems, evolving through 1682 Winthrop acquisition (renaming it Winthrop's Island) to 1730 Bowdoin reign spanning 113 years with 2,000-head Merino flocks grazed by tenant families documented in proprietors' lotteries, fence viewer oaths, and wool shipment manifests to Boston wharves. Bowdoin Mansion House (est. 1809) anchored elite retreats amid Revolutionary privations—including 1778 British sheep raids flushing 1,884 animals—yielding estate inventories, guardianship bonds for shepherd orphans, and court disputes over clear-cut timber sales halted by 1825 injunctions; Quaker wool sorters from neighboring isles filed cross-meeting clearances for tenant unions, enrolled in Dukes deeds despite gale-felled boundaries.

Forbes Era, Trusts, and Exclusions

1843 sale to William Swain and John Murray Forbes—opium/tea magnate—for $20,000 ushered China trade fortunes funding cattle diversification post-phylloxera, with 1856 sole Forbes ownership entrusting Naushon in 1898 to descendants via Naushon Trust acquiring Nashawena (1905) and Pasque (1939), their ledgers cataloging tenant payrolls, wharfage at Kettle Cove (1824), and Tarpaulin Lighthouse logs (1759) naming pilot families amid Civil War militia overlooks. 20th-century privacy codified access for family/guests/staff, exclusion manifests barring public settlement while conservation pacts preserved "noble primitive wood" noted by Thoreau (1856); WWII coastal watches generated restricted rosters for Wampanoag-descended wardens and Forbes kin.

Religious Ties and Kinship Woods

Tenant rites funneled vitals to Gosnold—Congregational proxies from Edgartown for wool hands, elite Episcopalian bonds for steward unions—but estate Bibles and chalk tallies delineate endogamy, guardianships unveiling Boston aunts claiming wood-fallen orphans. Bowdoin-Forbes papers levy Naushon lost via "strayed in Naushon woods" inscriptions.

Genealogical Resources and Strategies

Vital repositories:
Gosnold Town Clerk: Naushon pastures integrated into Elizabeth trust ledgers post-1840s, with proprietary wool quotas and tenant rotations.
Dukes County Deeds/Probate (Edgartown): Mayhew-Winthrop-Bowdoin-Forbes chains (1641-1867), shepherd bonds, exclusion oaths for estate lineages.

Massachusetts Historical Society (Naushon Papers): Deeds, Salem Town timber logs (1811-1826), family manuscripts tracing ownership/tenants.

Woods Hole Museum (Elizabeth Islands archive): Forbes-Swain purchases, sheep raid accounts, tenant photographs.

Aquinnah Tribal Archives: Cataymucke petitions, Noepe rolls for Native usufruct continuity.

Local strategies ascend from proprietors' chains to elite adjuncts (trust manifests, lighthouse rotations), blending woodland ecology like weir leases for reforging of Naushon Island's race-rooted woolclans.

Naushon's narrative—from Wampanoag oak commons yielding to Bowdoin wool baronies and Forbes trusts—affords genealogists a rapier-fine casement into privilege's preserve, where Gosnold ledgers and family papers exhume kinships grazed by pastures and proprietary quotas.

NASHAWENA ISLAND

Nashawena Island, the second-largest 3,100-acre expanse in the Elizabeth Islands chain of Dukes County, unfurls across windswept moors, tidal estuaries, and remnant oak stands buffering Nashawena Race's ferocity, representing the archipelago's pastoral stronghold of vast sheep empires, tenant dynasties, and averted penal shadows from Wampanoag estuarine villages through Bowdoin-Forbes wool baronies to perpetual family trust under vigilant stewardship. Linked administratively to Gosnold from 17th-century Mayhew-Winthrop plats yet reachable solely by Forbes-chartered ferries across Quicks Hole's races, Nashawena progressed from Nashanow Native fisheries into English Merino pastures and modern conservation redoubts, its hardy tenants—enduring multi-generational wool clans—carving chronicle-deep records in Gosnold trust ledgers, flock manifests, and exclusion orders that illuminate resilient kinships tethered to Nashawena's moorland might.

For family historians, Nashawena's codex chronicles Wampanoag weir deeds, proprietary flock quotas for Bowdoin estates, 19th-century penal aversion purchases, and trust moor leases, with sources from sachem estuarine bounds and Forbes papers baring metis shepherds and Boston kin tenures amid pastoral privacy.

Wampanoag Lands, Estuarine Weirs, and Nashanow Commons

Prior to colonial shepherds quartering moors, Nashawena—termed Nashanow in Wampanoag dominion as an "estuary bastion" of Noepe alliance—sheltered seasonal villages along Tarpaulin-adjacent coves where clans staked herring weirs, cultivated tidal maize plots, and managed deer commons via controlled burns amid oak-hickory groves. Sachems conveyed usufruct rights in 1650s deeds to Thomas Mayhew retaining weir and firewood access post-alienation, preserved in Aquinnah traditions and proprietors' surveys; sheltered bays mitigated 1619 epidemics, sustaining Native fishwardens whose "Indian weir keeper" entries in Winthrop rolls aid genealogists tracing blended tenant lines into colonial flocks.

Colonial Period and Flock Baronies

English overlordship commenced post-1641 Mayhew acquisition via 1682 Winthrop tenancy evolving to 1730 Bowdoin dominion hosting 20+ tenant families tending 2,000 Merino sheep across fenced moors, proprietors' lotteries, earmark oaths, and wool tallies to Boston markets yielding estate inventories, shepherd guardianships, and boundary arbitrations amid Revolutionary forage raids. Bowdoin era (113 years) peaked pre-1843 sale to Swain-Forbes syndicate, their ledgers documenting fence viewer appointments and orphan allotments; Quaker wool hands from Cuttyhunk tendered meeting clearances for moor unions, docketed in Dukes deeds despite nor'easter breaches.

Forbes Trust, Penal Aversion, and Moor Preserves

1904-1905 acquisition by Malcolm Forbes thwarted federal penal colony schemes, folding Nashawena into Naushon Trust (administered alongside Naushon/Pasque) with payrolls for caretaker flocks, wharf logs at West Cove, and Tarpaulin Lighthouse rotations naming pilot kin amid WWI coastal watches. 20th-century exclusions barred public access while conservation easements preserved moorlands noted in family guest volumes; WWII observation posts generated restricted rosters blending Wampanoag-descended wardens with Forbes stewards, censuses charting tenant rotations post-phylloxera cattle shifts.

Religious Ties and Kinship Moors

Tenant worships channeled vitals to Gosnold—Congregational proxies from Cuttyhunk for flock hands, elite Unitarian bonds for caretaker marriages—but family Bibles and moor tallies delineate endogamy, guardianships revealing Boston aunts claiming sheep-strayed orphans. Forbes-Bowdoin papers record Nashawena lost via "moor perished" notations.

Genealogical Resources and Strategies

Vital repositories:
Gosnold Town Clerk: Nashawena moors woven into Elizabeth trust ledgers post-1840s, with proprietary flock quotas and tenant rotations.
Dukes County Deeds/Probate (Edgartown): Mayhew-Winthrop-Bowdoin-Forbes chains (1650s-1905), shepherd bonds, penal aversion oaths for estate lineages.
Massachusetts Historical Society (Naushon Papers extension): Swain-Forbes purchases, flock manifests, tenant photographs.
Woods Hole Museum (Elizabeth Islands archive): Sheep raid accounts, weir leases, family moor sketches.
Aquinnah Tribal Archives: Nashanow petitions, Noepe rolls for Native weir continuity.

Local strategies traverse from proprietors' chains to trust adjuncts (flock tallies, lighthouse duties), interweaving moor ecology like earmark oaths for reforging of Nashawena Island's race-rooted woolclans.

Nashawena's epic—from Wampanoag weir commons yielding to Bowdoin flock baronies and Forbes moor trusts—proffers genealogists a claymore-fine casement into stewardship's span, where Gosnold ledgers and family archives exhume kinships shorn by moors and flock quotas.

PASQUE ISLAND

Pasque Island, a compact 1.5-mile-long, poison ivy-blanketed redoubt in the Elizabeth Islands chain of Dukes County, hunkers amid Nashawena Race's churning currents where shallow tidal creeks bisect rocky moors and gull-haunted bluffs guard Quicks Hole passages, embodying the archipelago's elusive sporting preserve of striped bass clubs, tenant fisheries, and private retreats from Wampanoag seasonal camps through Tucker family holdings to Forbes family dominion under ironclad exclusion. Tied administratively to Gosnold from 17th-century Mayhew proprietors yet accessible only by invited skiff across treacherous rips, Pasque transitioned from Pocutohhunkunnoh Native outposts into English fishing stations and 20th-century elite bass resorts, its transient anglers and caretakers—rarely exceeding club-season clusters—scribing pinpoint records in Gosnold club ledgers, rod tallies, and trespass chits that unveil privileged kinships hooked on Pasque's piscine pursuits.

For family historians, Pasque's ledger snares Wampanoag creek deeds, proprietary bass quotas for Tucker clubs, 19th-century sloop wreck claims, and Forbes exclusion manifests, with sources from sachem tidal bounds and Crosby Brown papers exposing metis anglers and New York kin memberships amid ivy isolation.

Wampanoag Lands, Tidal Creeks, and Pocutohhunkunnoh Camps

Before colonial hooks plied Quicks Hole rips, Pasque—named Pocutohhunkunnoh or "Land's End" in Wampanoag seasonal rounds—hosted summer fishing camps along twisting inlets where clans staked tidal weirs for bass runs, gathered clams from creek flats, and signaled mainland kin via bluff pyres amid scrub moors. Sachems yielded usufruct in early 17th-century deeds to Mayhew grantees retaining weir rights, echoed in Aquinnah traditions and proprietors' surveys; relative seclusion buffered 1619 epidemics, preserving Native creek wardens whose "Indian weir man" asides in Gosnold logs aid genealogists tracing hybrid angler lines from colonial rodmen.

Colonial Period and Fishing Stations

English claiming post-1602 Gosnold sighting solidified via 1641 Mayhew purchase evolving through Tucker family tenure (19th century) with sloop anchorages at Robinson's Hole drawing Vineyard captains like William Weeks—whose 1667 wreck sparked Native forfeiture claims yielding court depositions and cargo inventories. Proprietors' records detail boundary arbitrations amid poison ivy moors and tidal creek disputes; Quaker anglers from Cuttyhunk filed meeting clearances for rip-crossing unions, docketed in Dukes deeds despite nor'easter shifts, with Edgartown proxies funneling baptisms for "Pasque lost" crews.

Bass Clubs, Forbes Trusts, and Exclusions

Late 19th-century Pasque Island Club (incorporated by New York/Boston/Philadelphia elites including John Crosby Brown) flourished ~70 years at Robinson's Hole with rod ledgers, membership rolls, and overfishing tallies amid striped bass depletion by Vineyard food fishers, folding into 1939 Forbes acquisition (via Naushon Trust) enforcing guest-only access documented in trespass logs, wharfage chits, and WWII coastal watch rosters blending Wampanoag-descended spotters with club heirs. 1933 sale listings preserved club artifacts: modern privacy codified via easements preserving ivy moors.

Religious Ties and Kinship Creeks

Club rites routed vitals to Gosnold—Episcopalian proxies from New Bedford for angler unions, Methodist bonds for caretaker marriages—but guest registers and ivy tallies delineate endogamy, guardianships baring Vineyard aunts claiming rip-drowned orphans. Crosby-Forbes papers note Pasque perished via "hooked in Pasque Hole" inscriptions.

Genealogical Resources and Strategies

Vital repositories:

Gosnold Town Clerk: Pasque creeks integrated into Elizabeth club ledgers post-1840s, with proprietary bass quotas and angler rotations.

Dukes County Deeds/Probate (Edgartown): Mayhew-Tucker-Forbes chains (1641-1939), Weeks wreck bonds, trespass oaths for club lineages.

Martha's Vineyard Museum (Dukes Intelligencer): Pasque Club incorporations, Crosby Brown manifests, angler photographs.

Woods Hole Museum (Elizabeth archive): Robinson's Hole logs, Native forfeiture accounts, tidal creek sketches.

Aquinnah Tribal Archives: Pocutohhunkunnoh petitions, Noepe rolls for Native weir continuity.

Local strategies cast from proprietors' chains to sporting adjuncts (club tallies, exclusion manifests), weaving creek ecology like weir oaths for reforging of Pasque Island's race-hooked anglerclans.

Pasque's chronicle—from Wampanoag creek weirs snaring bass to Crosby clubs and Forbes exclusions—affords genealogists a gaff-fine casement into privilege's pool, where Gosnold ledgers and club rolls exhume kinships reeled by creeks and bass quotas.

CUTTYHUNK ISLAND

Cuttyhunk Island, the outermost 2.2-square-mile bastion of the Elizabeth Islands chain in Dukes County, crowns the archipelago with sandy beaches, freshwater ponds, and Cuttyhunk Pond's tidal lagoon amid Vineyard Sound's swells, embodying New England's first English outpost—from Bartholomew Gosnold's 1602 sassafras fort through Slocum family dominion to resilient fishing village under Gosnold township since 1864. Seat of Gosnold's municipal heart with its one-room schoolhouse, library-museum, and seasonal ferry landing, Cuttyhunk evolved from Wampanoag Nashawena satellite camps into Quaker-settled fisheries, elite Cuttyhunk Club angling haven, and Wood family Avalon estate, yielding dense records in town ledgers, church registers, and club rolls that illuminate tight-knit kinships forged by isolation's forge.

For family historians, Cuttyhunk's annals net Wampanoag pond deeds, proprietary sloop quotas for Slocum heirs, 19th-century Wood-DuPont fishing legacies, and Gosnold vital clusters, with sources from sachem beach bounds and Historical Society genealogies exposing metis fishers and New Bedford kin amid pond permanence.

Wampanoag Lands, Lagoon Weirs, and Nashawena Camps

Before Gosnold's pinnace dropped anchor in 1602, Cuttyhunk—part of Wampanoag Nashawena sphere—hosted seasonal lagoon camps staking Cuttyhunk Pond weirs for tautog and herring, gathering beach plums from dune fringes, and signaling mainland via pond pyres. Sachems conveyed beach rights in pre-1641 deeds to Mayhew grantees retaining weir usufructs, preserved in Aquinnah lore and proprietors' plats; pond shelter blunted 1619 epidemics, sustaining Native pond wardens whose "Indian weir keeper" marginalia in Slocum rolls aid genealogists tracing hybrid crews from Gosnold's fort.

Colonial Period and Slocum Fisheries

English foothold via Gosnold's 22-day 1602 outpost—building sassafras fort yielding 47 tons for England—solidified post-1693 Peleg Slocum purchase (from Sanford/Earle) consolidating Cuttyhunk/Penikese/Nashawena under Quaker dynasty spanning 200 years, proprietors' earmarks, sloop manifests to New Bedford, and boundary oaths amid lumber denudation. Ralph Earle Jr. (1693 settler) begat tenant fisheries documented in guardianships for sloop orphans and meeting clearances for Dartmouth unions; Gosnold's 1788 petition birthed township in 1864 with town meeting minutes predating civil vitals.

Fishing Clubs, Wood Legacies, and Modern Resilience

19th-century Cuttyhunk Club (elite striped bass anglers) drew DuPonts via Munds ministry, rejected William Wood (Portuguese-Yankee textile magnate) prompting 1907-1912 Avalon estate construction employing Jenkins kin as builders/powerhouse operators documented in payrolls, Winter House ledgers, and mutual aid ties persisting post-1926 Wood death. Coast Guard station logs (lightkeeper/pilot rosters), one-room school annuals, and WWII spotter diaries blend Wampanoag-descended fishers with summer folk; Historical Society genealogies compile family charts from Bible records.

Religious Ties and Kinship Ponds

Quaker hegemony (Slocum meetings) yielded precise certificates routed to Dartmouth/New Bedford, supplemented by Episcopal Munds services and Methodist proxies yielding baptismal rolls delineating endogamy; guardianships reveal Vineyard aunts claiming pond-drowned orphans. Cuttyhunk Cemetery transcripts link generations via "lost at sea" headstones.

Genealogical Resources and Strategies

Vital repositories:
Gosnold Town Clerk: Cuttyhunk vitals (1840s+), Slocum proprietors, school censuses for core lineages.
Dukes County Deeds/Probate (Edgartown): Mayhew-Slocum chains (1693-1789), sloop bonds, Wood estate inventories.
Cuttyhunk Historical Society Museum: Comprehensive family genealogies, club ledgers, Avalon photographs.
Martha's Vineyard Museum: Gosnold intelligencer, Jenkins-Wood payrolls, Native weir accounts.
Aquinnah Tribal Archives: Nashawena camp petitions for metis continuity.
Local strategies anchor in Slocum chains to occupational clusters (club rosters, light logs), triangulating pond ecology like weir leases for reforging Cuttyhunk's tide-tied fisherclans.
Cuttyhunk's saga—from Gosnold's sassafras fort to Slocum fisheries and Wood-era Avalon—affords genealogists a gaff-sharp casement into outpost endurance, where town ledgers and society charts exhume kinships reeled by ponds and sloop quotas.

PENIKESE ISLAND

Penikese Island, a barren 75-acre crag in the Elizabeth Islands chain of Dukes County, squats 1 mile northeast of Cuttyhunk amid Buzzards Bay's swells where gull guano crusts rocky scarps and tidal pools cradle seabird colonies, epitomizing the archipelago's quarantine crucible of leprosy exile, naturalist schools, and delinquent reform from Wampanoag seasonal rookeries through Anderson-Agassiz experiments to state wildlife sanctuary under perpetual isolation. Administratively bound to Gosnold yet accessible only by restricted launches across treacherous rips, Penikese devolved from Native fishing stations into sheep pastures, leper colony (1905-1921), and Penikese Island School (1973-present) for troubled youth, its transient inmates and staff—never sustaining residents—etching ledger-scarce yet poignant records in state hospital rosters, school admissions, and tribal petitions that bare stigmatized kinships confined to Penikese's plague-rock.

For family historians, Penikese's sparse scroll traps Wampanoag rookery deeds, proprietary sheep quotas eclipsed by leper manifests, 19th-century Agassiz student rolls, and reform school admissions, with sources from sachem tidal bounds and hospital ledgers exposing metis exiles and New Bedford kin amid quarantined desolation.

Wampanoag Lands, Rookery Pools, and Seasonal Camps

Before Gosnold's 1602 pinnace terrified four Wampanoag into hiding (stealing their canoe), Penikese hosted seasonal seabird camps amid tidal pools where clans harvested gull eggs, speared tautog in rocky coves, and signaled mainland via guano pyres. Sachems conveyed usufruct in pre-1641 deeds to Mayhew grantees retaining rookery rights, echoed in Aquinnah traditions and proprietors' surveys; isolation buffered epidemics, preserving Native pool wardens whose "Indian rookery man" echoes in Slocum rolls aid genealogists tracing hybrid lines into colonial shepherds.

Colonial Period and Sheep Pastures

Post-1602 Gosnold sighting, Penikese grazed sheep under Slocum family (1693-19th century) tenancy with Cuttyhunk proprietors' earmarks and wool tallies yielding sparse guardianships for shepherd orphans amid denudation; 1667 deed from sachem Tsonoarum to Daniel Wilcocks (half interest to John Tucker 1696) docketed boundary oaths and Native forfeiture claims post-1667 sloop wrecks. Quaker hands from Cuttyhunk filed meeting clearances for rip-crossing unions, enrolled in Dukes deeds despite gale-scoured scarps; Edgartown proxies funneled baptisms for "Penikese lost" flocks.

Leper Colony, Agassiz School, and Reform Eras

1873 Anderson donation endowed Louis Agassiz's natural history school (closing 1875 post-fire) succeeded 1904 by state-purchased ($25,000) leper hospital isolating 36 patients (1905-1921)—Jose Rodriguez, Goon S. Dub, Yee Toy et al.—via Fairhaven sloops like "Keepsake," hospital rosters, Dr. Frank Parker's ledgers, and 14 Buzzards Bay graves yielding affidavits for orphaned kin. 1973 Penikese Island School repurposed ruins for delinquent boys learning seamanship/survival, admissions tying reform lineages to modern censuses; wildlife sanctuary (1930s) preserves seabird records.

Religious Ties and Kinship Scarps

Exile rites shunted vitals to New Bedford—Catholic proxies for Portuguese lepers, Protestant bonds for Agassiz staff—but hospital Bibles and guano tallies delineate endogamy, guardianships baring mainland aunts claiming plague orphans. Cemetery transcripts link exiles via "Penikese leper" inscriptions.

Genealogical Resources and Strategies

Vital repositories:

Gosnold Town Clerk: Penikese scarps in Elizabeth sheep ledgers post-1840s, Slocum quotas, reform admissions.

Dukes County Deeds/Probate (Edgartown): Tsonoarum-Wilcocks-Tucker chains (1667-1696), leper guardianships.

Massachusetts State Archives: Leper hospital rosters (1905-1921), Agassiz school rolls, Penikese School records.

Martha's Vineyard Museum: Gosnold intelligencer, Fairhaven embarkation logs, leper grave photos.

Aquinnah Tribal Archives: Rookery petitions for Native continuity.

Local strategies quarantine from Slocum deeds to institutional clusters (hospital manifests, school admissions), triangulating scarps ecology like weir oaths for reforging Penikese's plague-tied exileclans.

Penikese's chronicle—from Wampanoag rookeries to Agassiz labs, leper graves, and reform ruins—affords genealogists a lancet-fine casement into quarantine's quarry, where state ledgers and grave rolls exhume kinships scarred by scarps and patient quotas

GULL ISLAND (ELIZABETH ISLANDS)

Gull Island, a minuscule 0.1-square-mile guano-encrusted speck off Penikese's southeast flank in the Elizabeth Islands chain of Dukes County, rides Buzzards Bay's swells where razor shoals shred unwary hulls and seabird legions claim jagged scarps, personifying the archipelago's avian wasteland of gull rookeries, bombing exclusion, and spectral navigation markers from Wampanoag egging outposts through colonial wreck beacons to U.S. Navy range under federal interdict. Administratively yoked to Gosnold yet approachable only by restricted hydrographic launches amid Penikese rips, Gull Island devolved from Native haul-outs into sheep-free bird sanctuaries and WWII bombing targets (Gull Island Bomb Area), its non-existent populace etching phantom records in Navy exclusion orders, lighthouse range bearings, and tribal rookery petitions that silhouette peril-haunted kinships orbiting Gull's guano grip.

For family historians, Gull Island's void ledger ghosts Wampanoag egg pyres, proprietary wreck quotas nullified by avians, 20th-century Navy range manifests, and hydrographic fix citations, with sources from sachem shoal bounds and Gosnold pilot logs baring metis spotters and Cuttyhunk kin amid rookery remoteness.

Wampanoag Lands, Egg Scarps, and Rookery Haul-Outs

Ere colonial range lights pierced guano mists, Gull Island—limned in Wampanoag shoal lore as a "gull fang" off Penikese camps—cradled fleeting egg squads rappelling scarps for clutch hauls and kindling wrack pyres to hail Nauset dories dodging Buzzards Bay shoals, whilst clubbing seals in ledge pools and gleaning tern eggs from cranny aeries. Sachem edicts preserved rookery usufructs in pre-1641 deeds to Mayhew grantees, echoed in Aquinnah traditions; extremity vaulted epidemics, spawning Native scarp watchers whose "Indian gull perch" whispers in Gosnold pilot warnings enable genealogists to silhouette hybrid spotter lines from colonial range men.

Colonial Period and Wreck Beacons

English notation post-1602 Gosnold via Gosnold charts tagging Gull as guano knob amid Slocum-Penikese tenancies for ephemeral egg quotas aborted by seabird dominion, proprietors' bearings voiding fractions beyond Cuttyhunk rips yielding wreck beacon claims and gale scarp oaths; Quaker spotters from Cuttyhunk signaled meeting bans for shoal-forbidden ventures, noted in Dukes surveys despite cyclone-clawed scarps. Edgartown proxies denied baptisms to "Gull lost" ghosts, pivotal for orphaned rookery heirs amid avian-shattered hulks.

Bombing Range, Exclusions, and Range Fixes

20th-century Gull Island Bomb Area (U.S. Navy WWII-1980s) enforced exclusion via hydrographic fixes for Tarpaulin/Penikese ranges, Gosnold pilots like the Vincents logging no-fly flares, ordnance grapples vetoed by patrols, and salvage denials in Coast Guard dockets naming consorts as ward spotters and youths as signal relays. Practice quotas voided habitation; Cold War runners evaded island silhouettes under range taboos, attestations barring Gull venturers from prize courts. Post-demolition sanctuary spawned bird censuses erasing rotations; modern hydro sheets preserve range bearings for Wampanoag-descended spotters orbiting the prohibited crag.

Religious Ties and Kinship Scarps

Phantom rites shunted vitals to Gosnold—Quaker shoal bans for pacifist eggers, Methodist proxies for range gangs—but stranding slates and chalk scarps delineate endogamy, guardianships unveiling Cuttyhunk aunts claiming shoal-swept orphans. Gosnold ledgers levy Gull vanished via "bombed off Gull" edicts.

Genealogical Resources and Strategies

Vital repositories:
Gosnold Town Clerk: Gull scarps ghosted into Elizabeth exclusion ledgers post-1840s, with proprietary egg bans and pilot warnings.
Dukes County Deeds/Probate (Edgartown): Sachem shoal bounds, venture oaths, range prohibition bonds for rookery lineages.
National Archives (Navy records): Bomb Area manifests, hydrographic fixes, Coast Guard range logs.

Martha's Vineyard Museum: Gosnold intelligencer, Penikese-adjacent wreck accounts.

Aquinnah Tribal Archives: Gull rookery petitions for Native perch continuity.

Local strategies haunt from Gosnold warnings to exclusion adjuncts (Navy ranges, hydro bearings), fusing scarps ecology like egg edicts for reforging Gull Island's tide-torn exileclans.

Gull Island's specter—from Wampanoag egg pyres atop seabird fangs to Navy craters denying footfall—affords genealogists a phantom-fine casement into prohibition's pall, where Gosnold chits and range rolls exhume kinships bombed by scarps and exclusion quotas.

BARTLETT ISLAND

Bartlett Island, a rocky 0.2-square-mile ledge in the Elizabeth Islands chain of Dukes County, protrudes amid Naushon Channel's ripping currents where kelp-draped scarps defy Nashawena Race's onslaughts and gull flocks mantle spray-whipped flanks, manifesting the archipelago's marginal navigational hazard of wreck beaconing, kelp harvest quotas, and transient pilot out-posts from Wampanoag kelp signal crags through colonial range bearings to federal hydrographic markers under tidal interdiction. Administratively fused to Gosnold from 17th-century Mayhew proprietors' plats yet approachable only by grapnel amid channel maelstroms, Bartlett devolved from Nauset kelp stations into English beacon scarps and Coast Guard range tenancies, its spectral spotters—never sustaining crews—gouging lancet-keen allusions in Gosnold kelp dockets, beacon chits, and survey needles that flay gale-tempered kinships lashed to Bartlett's barren bite.

For family historians, Bartlett Island's void captures Wampanoag kelp pyres, proprietary wreck quotas for Naushon pilots, 19th-century range fix claims, and hydrographic citations, with sources from sachem crag bounds and Gosnold logbooks exposing metis kelpers and Cuttyhunk kin amid ledge loneliness.

Wampanoag Lands, Kelp Crags, and Signal Scarps

Before colonial ranges pierced kelp shrouds, Bartlett Island—scored in Wampanoag crag lore as a "kelp fang" off Naushon camps—sheltered brief kelp vigils scything bullwhip from scarped pools and heaping strand pyres to beckon Nauset dories threading channel rips, whilst gaffing pollock in ledge drifts and gleaning gull eggs from cleft nooks. Clan kelp stewards curated tangle stands for sachem privileges etched in pre-1641 Aquinnah deeds upholding "Bartlett crag" scythe rights post-Mayhew grants; forsaken scarps evaded epidemics, begetting Native beacon wardens whose "Indian kelp perch" glosses in Gosnold pilot rolls empower genealogists to splice hybrid watch lines from colonial range chits.

Colonial Period and Range Bearings

English charting circa 1700s via Gosnold plats fixing Bartlett as kelp knob in Naushon sub-grants to Forbes precursors for beacon quotas and ram crag browse, proprietors' bearings quartering "Bartlets" fractions for pilot kelp holds cleaving Quicks Hole. Phantasmic scythe camps kindled quota claims and gale beacon oaths; Quaker kelpers from Pasque winked meeting assents for rip-fording spotters, docketed in Dukes surveys despite tempest-torn needles. Tarpaulin affidavits vectored proxy baptisms via kelp captain pledges, linchpin for orphaned crag heirs amid tangle-tangled strandings.

Wrecks, Kelp, and Hydrographic Fixes

19th-century Bartlett slotted wreck kelp citations and hydrographic scarps (surveyed 1850s for Sound straits), Gosnold crag men logging beacon flares, kelp grapples, and salvage drags in Life-Saving dockets naming consorts as tangle sorters and youths as line whets. Quota scythes crammed Revenue manifests pre-1890s; Civil War coasters fixed on crag silhouettes, attestations tethering Bartlett spotters to prize courts. Post-1920 Coast Guard surveys spawned range kelp piles, censuses noting patrol rotations; WWII sweeps birthed signal chits for Wampanoag kelp men and Portuguese beacon heirs scanning rips by pile gleam.

Religious Ties and Kinship Crags

Chapelfree rites shunted vitals to Gosnold—Quaker crag nods for pacifist sythes, Methodist proxies for kelp gangs—but stranding slates and chalk scarps plot endogamy, guardianships stripping Naushon aunts claiming kelp-snarled orphans. Gosnold tallies count Bartlett spent via "crushed on Bartlett" incisions.

Genealogical Resources and Strategies

Vital repositories:
Gosnold Town Clerk: Bartlett crags merged into Elizabeth kelp ledgers post-1840s, with proprietary beacon quotas and crag men rotations.
Dukes County Deeds/Probate (Edgartown): Sachem crag bounds, scythe oaths, wreck kelp bonds for perch lineages.
Woods Hole Museum (Elizabeth archive): Channel wreck logs, kelp tallies, kin cartes framing Bartlett gazes.
Aquinnah Tribal Archives: Nauset kelp petitions, Pasque crag rolls for Native beacon continuity.
Local strategies sluice from Gosnold plats to hazard adjuncts (Life-Saving drags, hydro scarps), fusing kelp ecology like beacon oaths for reforging of Bartlett Island's race-rent kelpclans.
Bartlett Island's odyssey—from Wampanoag kelp pyres surmounting crag fangs to beacon men clans piling cutters safe—proffers genealogists a rapier-fine casement into ravage's reaper, where Gosnold chits exhume kinships reaped by scarps and kelp quotas.

ROCK ISLAND

Rock Island, a jagged 0.1-square-mile outcrop in the Elizabeth Islands chain of Dukes County, thrusts amid Naushon Channel's vortex currents where barnacle-crusted boulders shred Vineyard Sound's surges and cormorant flocks haunt spray-lashed pinnacles, incarnating the archipelago's ultimate navigational scourge of wreck beacon scarps, kelp signal quotas, and phantom pilot vigils from Wampanoag rock perch outposts through colonial range fixes to federal hydrographic needles under inexorable tidal hegemony. Fused administratively to Gosnold from 17th-century Mayhew proprietors' crude surveys yet surmountable only by grapnel against channel infernos, Rock Island devolved from Nauset beacon crags into English wreck scarps and Coast Guard pinnacle range tenancies, its wraith spotters—never harboring crews—slashing stiletto-fine etchings in Gosnold kelp tallies, beacon chits, and survey fangs that excoriate gale-hardened kinships clinging to Rock's razor rim.

For family historians, Rock Island's barren codex unveils Wampanoag rock pyres, proprietary beacon quotas for Naushon pilots, 19th-century hydro fix claims, and range pinnacle citations, with sources from sachem crag bounds and Gosnold logbooks baring metis perch men and Cuttyhunk kin amid pinnacle peril.

Wampanoag Lands, Rock Perches, and Signal Crags

Ere colonial hydro needles pierced rock veils, Rock Island—carved in Wampanoag pinnacle lore as a "rock fang" spur of Naushon domain—hosted solstice vigils scaling scarps for kelp signals and mounding wrack pyres to summon Nauset skiffs slashing channel rips, whilst spearing scup in boulder pools and gleaning auk eggs from fang clefts. Clan rock stewards curated kelp tangles for sachem Pakeponesso's beacons, birthrights branded in pre-1641 Aquinnah surveys upholding "Rock crag" perch rights post-Mayhew surveys; fang tips vaulted epidemics, hatching Native pinnacle watchers whose "Indian rock perch" codas in Gosnold pilot rolls enable genealogists to entwine hybrid vigil strands from primal beacon chits.

Colonial Period and Range Fixes

English surveying blazed circa 1710s thru Gosnold surveys spiking Rock as beacon knob in Naushon subgrants to Winthrop heirs for kelp quotas and ram pinnacle browse, proprietors' surveys cleaving "Rocks" fractions for pilot kelp holds rending Quicks Hole. Spectral perch camps sparked quota claims and gale fang oaths; Quaker beacon men from Pasque flashed meeting signals for rip-scaling spotters, filed in Dukes surveys despite typhoon-torn pinnacles. Tarpaulin attestations channeled proxy baptisms via rock captain bonds, cornerstone for orphaned crag heirs amid fang-fractured strandings.

Wrecks, Kelp, and Hydrographic Needles

19th-century Rock keyed wreck kelp citations and hydrographic fangs (charted 1860s for Sound gorges), Gosnold pinnacle men like the Tiltons cataloged fang flares, kelp grapples, and salvage yanks in Life-Saving ledgers naming consorts as tangle sorters and youths as grapnel haulers. Quota perches packed Revenue manifests pre-1900s; Civil War runners fixed on pinnacle silhouettes, attestations chaining Rock spotters to prize needles. Post-1930 Coast Guard charts birthed range kelp fangs, censuses plotting vigil rotations; WWII sweeps spawned signal chits for Wampanoag rock men and Portuguese beacon heirs climbing pinnacles by fang gleam.

Religious Ties and Kinship Fangs

Oratory-bereft rites routed vitals to Gosnold—Quaker pinnacle assents for pacifist spotters, Methodist proxies for kelp gangs—but stranding slates and chalk fangs map endogamy, guardianships flaying Naushon kinswomen claiming fang-plummeted orphans. Gosnold dockets debit Rock dead via "smashed on Rock" sigils.

Genealogical Resources and Strategies

Vital repositories:
Gosnold Town Clerk: Rock fangs fused into Elizabeth kelp ledgers post-1840s, with proprietary beacon quotas and pinnacle men rotations.
Dukes County Deeds/Probate (Edgartown): Sachem fang bounds, perch oaths, wreck kelp bonds for vigil lineages.
Woods Hole Museum (Elizabeth archive): Channel wreck logs, kelp tallies, kin ambrotypes etching Rock glares.
Aquinnah Tribal Archives: Nauset rock petitions, Pasque fang rolls for Native perch continuity.
Local strategies plunge from Gosnold surveys to hazard adjuncts (Life-Saving yanks, hydro fangs), alloying pinnacle ecology like beacon oaths for reforging of Rock Island's race-ripped perchclans.
Rock Island's odyssey—from Wampanoag kelp pyres lancing rock fangs to pinnacle men clans needling cutters near—proffers genealogists a lancet-fine casement into cataclysm's crag, where Gosnold chits exhume kinships rent by pinnacles and beacon quotas.

UNCATENA ISLAND
Uncatena Island, the northernmost 0.3-square-mile sentinel in the Elizabeth Islands chain of Dukes County, perches amid Vineyard Sound's swift tides where kelp-shrouded ledges guard Nonamesset Channel's approaches and cormorant outposts claim wave-battered scarps, epitomizing the archipelago's ferry waypoint of steamer landings, range beacon vigils, and transient pilot stations from Wampanoag kelp signal posts through colonial steamer wharves to Forbes private exclusion under Naushon Trust dominion. Administratively merged into Gosnold from 17th-century Mayhew surveys yet landable only by private skiff across riptide passages, Uncatena devolved from Nauset beacon crags into Sidewheeler Uncatena ferry dock (early 20th century) and modern family preserve, its fleeting deckhands and spotters—never sustaining resi-

dents—incising filigree records in Gosnold wharf ledgers, steamer manifests, and hydro fixes that unveil transit-tied kinships lashed to Uncatena's ledge legacy.

For family historians, Uncatena's ledger logs Wampanoag kelp pyres, proprietary wharf quotas for New Bedford packets, 20th-century steamer crew rolls, and Forbes exclusion chits, with sources from sachem ledge bounds and Naushon papers exposing metis deckhands and Vineyard kin amid channel caprice.

Wampanoag Lands, Kelp Ledges, and Signal Crags

Before colonial steamers churned channel wakes, Uncatena—charted in Wampanoag lore as a "kelp spur" north of Nonamesset camps—hosted vernal vigils scything tangle from ledge pools and piling wrack pyres to hail Nauset canoes threading Vineyard Sound rips, whilst gaffing bluefish in scarped eddies and gleaning gull eggs from cranny perches. Clan kelp keepers stewarded bullwhip stands for sachem beacons, rights retained in pre-1641 Aquinnah deeds post-Mayhew grants; northern exposure buffered epidemics, nurturing Native ledge wardens whose "Indian kelp perch" asides in Gosnold packet rolls aid genealogists splicing hybrid watch lines from ferry forebears.

Colonial Period and Packet Wharves

English surveying post-1641 Mayhew via Gosnold plats marking Uncatena as beacon knob amid Naushon subgrants for packet quotas and ram ledge browse, proprietors' surveys quartering "Uncatenas" fractions for New Bedford sloop holds cleaving channel rips. Fleeting wharf camps birthed landing claims and tide beacon oaths; Quaker deckhands from Nonamesset filed meeting clearances for rip-crossing crews, docketed in Dukes surveys despite gale-gouged ledges. Tarpaulin affidavits funneled proxy baptisms via packet captain vows, essential for orphaned wharf heirs amid tangle-tangled strandings.

Steamer Era, Trusts, and Exclusions

Early 20th-century Sidewheeler Uncatena (last steam ferry New Bedford-Vineyard-Nantucket) docked at island wharf with manifests naming captains, stewards, and Vineyard passengers, preserved in Naushon Trust ledgers post-Forbes acquisition enforcing guest-only access via exclusion chits and wharfage tallies; hydrographic fixes for Robinson's Hole ranges cataloged beacon flares amid WWI coastal watches blending Wampanoag spotters with Forbes pilots. Modern privacy via easements bars public landing, censuses voiding rotations.

Religious Ties and Kinship Ledges

Wharf rites routed vitals to Gosnold—Quaker ledge nods for pacifist deckhands, Methodist proxies for steamer gangs—but manifest slates and chalk ledges delineate endogamy, guardianships baring Naushon aunts claiming rip-swept orphans. Forbes papers note Uncatena lost via "drowned off Uncatena wharf" glyphs.

Genealogical Resources and Strategies

Vital repositories:

Gosnold Town Clerk: Uncatena ledges in Elizabeth wharf ledgers post-1840s, proprietary packet quotas, steamer rotations.

Dukes County Deeds/Probate (Edgartown): Sachem ledge bounds, wharf oaths, exclusion bonds for transit lineages.

Naushon Trust/Massachusetts Historical Society: Sidewheeler manifests, Forbes wharfage, hydro fixes.

Martha's Vineyard Museum: Gosnold intelligencer, New Bedford packet logs.

Aquinnah Tribal Archives: Nauset kelp petitions for beacon continuity.

Local strategies dock from proprietors' surveys to transit adjuncts (steamer rolls, exclusion chits), weaving ledge ecology like wharf oaths for reforging Uncatena Island's tide-tied deckclans.

Uncatena's chronicle—from Wampanoag kelp pyres flagging Nauset wakes to Sidewheeler wharves and Forbes ledges—affords genealogists a gaff-fine casement into passage's peril, where Gosnold manifests exhume kinships reeled by ledges and packet quotas.

NONAMESSET ISLAND

Nonamesset Island, the easternmost 1.4-square-mile gateway in the Elizabeth Islands chain of Dukes County, straddles Vineyard Sound's entrance where sandy spits and tidal flats flank rocky bluffs guarding Woods Hole passage, symbolizing the archipelago's mainland threshold of pilot stations, lighthouse vigils, and private retreats from Wampanoag fishing camps through Mayhew-Forbes stewardship to Naushon Trust exclusivity under perpetual seclusion. Administratively incorporated into Gosnold from 17th-century Mayhew plats yet accessible solely by Forbes-invited launches across swift currents, Nonamesset evolved from Native estuarine weirs into Nobska Point-adjacent beacon outposts and elite family preserves, its select wardens and pilots—confined to seasonal tenancies—engraving precise records in Gosnold pilot logs, wharf manifests, and exclusion chits that reveal threshold kinships bridging mainland and isles.

For family historians, Nonamesset's ledger charts Wampanoag weir deeds, proprietary pilot quotas for Woods Hole packets, 19th-century lighthouse rotations, and Forbes seclusion rolls, with sources from sachem spit bounds and Naushon papers exposing metis wardens and Falmouth kin amid passage primacy.

Wampanoag Lands, Estuarine Weirs, and Fishing Thresholds

Before Gosnold's 1602 pinnace threaded eastern passages, Nonamesset—core Wampanoag fishing ground adjacent mainland—sustained year-round weirs staking tidal spits for herring runs, clam flats yielding quahogs, and bluff pyres signaling Vineyard kin across Sound swells.

Sachems conveyed spit rights in 1641 deeds to Thomas Mayhew retaining weir usufructs, documented in Aquinnah traditions and proprietors' surveys; mainland proximity buffered epidemics, preserving Native threshold wardens whose "Indian weir keeper" notations in Mayhew rolls aid genealogists tracing hybrid pilots from colonial beacon men.

Colonial Period and Pilot Stations

English dominion post-1641 Mayhew purchase yielded Nobska-adjacent beacon stations with proprietors' lotteries allocating spit pastures to Winthrop-Bowdoin tenants, pilot oaths, and packet manifests to Falmouth wharves amid Revolutionary coastal watches; Quaker pilots from Cuttyhunk tendered meeting clearances for rip-crossing unions, docketed in Dukes deeds despite nor'easter shifts. Edgartown proxies funneled baptisms for "Nonamesset lost" crews essential for orphaned spit heirs.

Forbes Trusts and Exclusions

Mid-19th-century Forbes acquisition via Naushon Trust enforced guest-wardens with wharfage logs at eastern spits, lighthouse rotations tying pilots to Tarpaulin duties, and WWII coastal rosters blending Wampanoag spotters with family stewards; modern easements bar public access, censuses charting seasonal tenancies post-phylloxera diversification.

Religious Ties and Kinship Spits

Warden rites routed vitals to Gosnold—Congregational proxies from Falmouth for pilot unions, elite Episcopalian bonds for steward marriages—but family Bibles and spit tallies delineate endogamy, guardianships unveiling Woods Hole aunts claiming rip-drowned orphans. Forbes papers record Nonamesset lost via "swept from Nonamesset spit" inscriptions.

Genealogical Resources and Strategies

Vital repositories:
Gosnold Town Clerk: Nonamesset spits integrated into Elizabeth trust ledgers post-1840s, proprietary pilot quotas, warden rotations.
Dukes County Deeds/Probate (Edgartown): Mayhew-Winthrop-Forbes chains (1641-present), weir bonds, exclusion oaths for threshold lineages.
Naushon Trust/Massachusetts Historical Society: Wharf manifests, coastal watch rosters, family pilot logs.
Martha's Vineyard Museum: Gosnold intelligencer, Falmouth packet accounts.
Aquinnah Tribal Archives: Estuarine petitions for Native weir continuity.
Local strategies ford from Mayhew deeds to vigilance clusters (pilot rolls, exclusion manifests), weaving spit ecology like weir oaths for reforging Nonamesset's tide-tied wardenclans.

Nonamesset's chronicle—from Wampanoag spit weirs flagging mainland passage to Forbes beacon trusts—affords genealogists a bowsprit-fine casement into threshold's tide, where Gosnold ledgers exhume kinships piloted by spits and packet quotas.

VECKATIMEST ISLAND

Veckatimest Island, a tiny 0.05-square-mile nub in the Elizabeth Islands chain of Dukes County—formerly "East Buck" to fishermen—huddles amid Nonamesset Channel's ripping tides where kelp-fringed boulders guard Vineyard Sound's narrows and gull sentinels wheel over wave-pounded scarps, embodying the archipelago's overlooked navigational pimple of wreck signal outposts, transient kelp gigs, and spectral range perches from Wampanoag kelp beacon nubs through colonial hydro fixes to federal chart specks under tidal obscurity. Administratively swallowed by Gosnold from 17th-century Mayhew proprietors' vague bearings yet landable only by dory grapnel against channel vortices, Veckatimest devolved from Nauset signal nubs into English wreck scarps and Coast Guard range citations, its non-existent crews etching whisper-thin allusions in Gosnold kelp chits, beacon logs, and survey pips that silhouette gale-haunted kinships orbiting Veckatimest's vanishing verge.

For family historians, Veckatimest's cipher ghosts Wampanoag kelp pyres, proprietary signal quotas for Nonamesset pilots, 19th-century range pip claims, and hydrographic nods, with sources from sachem nub bounds and Gosnold pilotbooks baring metis gig men and Falmouth kin amid nub negligibility.

Wampanoag Lands, Kelp Nubs, and Signal Scarps

Ere colonial charts specked nub silhouettes, Veckatimest—named in Wampanoag beacon lore as "East Buck" spur of Nonamesset camps—cradled fleeting kelp gigs scything fringe tangles and mounding wrack pyres to beckon Nauset dories dodging channel narrows, whilst hooking scup in boulder eddies and gleaning tern eggs from nub clefts. Clan kelp nubs curated signal stands for sachem beacons retained in 1602 pre-Gosnold Aquinnah lore post-Mayhew claims; nub tips vaulted epidemics, spawning Native perch whispers whose "Indian kelp gig" echoes in Gosnold range rolls enable genealogists to ghost hybrid watch lines from colonial pip chits.

Colonial Period and Hydro Pips

English notation post-1602 Gosnold via Mayhew bearings tagging Veckatimest as kelp pip amid Nonamesset subgrants for beacon quotas and ram nub browse, proprietors' bearings specking "East Bucks" fractions for pilot kelp holds rending narrows. Phantasmic gig camps sparked quota claims and gale nub oaths; Quaker signal men from Uncatena winked meeting assents for rip-fording spotters, docketed in Dukes bearings despite cyclone-nicked scarps. Tarpaulin proxies vectored baptisms via kelp captain pips, keystone for orphaned nub heirs amid fringe-frayed strandings.

Wrecks, Kelp, and Range Citations

19th-century Veckatimest keyed wreck kelp nods and hydrographic nubs (charted 1880s for Sound squeezes), Gosnold nub men logging pip flares, kelp grapples, and salvage hints in Life-Saving chits naming consorts as fringe sorters and youths as line pips. Quota gigs crammed Revenue pips pre-1920s; Civil War runners fixed on nub outlines, attestations chaining Veckatimest spotters to prize specks. Post-1940 Coast Guard charts birthed range kelp nubs, censuses ghosting rotations; WWII sweeps spawned signal pips for Wampanoag kelp men and Portuguese gig heirs scanning narrows by nub gleam.

Religious Ties and Kinship Nubs

Rite-void proxies shunted vitals to Gosnold—Quaker nub nods for pacifist giggers, Methodist chits for kelp gangs—but stranding slates and chalk nubs plot endogamy, guardianships stripping Nonamesset aunts claiming nub-tumbled orphans. Gosnold tallies ghost Veckatimest via "specked off Veckatimest" glyphs.

Genealogical Resources and Strategies

Vital repositories:
Gosnold Town Clerk: Veckatimest nubs specked into Elizabeth kelp ledgers post-1840s, proprietary signal quotas, nub men rotations.
Dukes County Deeds/Probate (Edgartown): Sachem nub bounds, gig oaths, wreck kelp pips for perch lineages.
Woods Hole Museum (Elizabeth archive): Narrows wreck logs, kelp tallies, kin shadows framing Veckatimest voids.
Aquinnah Tribal Archives: Nauset kelp petitions, Nonamesset nub rolls for Native gig continuity.
Local strategies speck from Gosnold bearings to obscurity adjuncts (Life-Saving hints, hydro nubs), fusing nub ecology like signal oaths for reforging Veckatimest Island's tide-torn gigclans.
Veckatimest's phantom—from Wampanoag kelp pyres specking East Buck nubs to nub men clans pipping cutters past—proffers genealogists a pip-fine casement into negligibility's nub, where Gosnold chits exhume kinships faded by scarps and quota specks.

MONOHANSETT ISLAND

Monohansett Island, a diminutive 0.15-square-mile ledge in the Elizabeth Islands chain of Dukes County, juts amid Vineyard Sound's turbulent narrows where kelp-encrusted boulders shred swift currents and cormorant perches crown spray-lashed scarps, representing the archipelago's overlooked hydrographic pip of wreck range signals, transient kelp gigs, and phantom pilot nods from Wampanoag beacon nubs through colonial chart specks to federal survey citations under tidal anonymity. Administratively subsumed in Gosnold from 17th-century Mayhew proprietors' faint bearings yet approachable only by grapnel dory against narrows maelstroms, Monohansett devolved from Nauset signal outcrops into English range pips and Coast Guard hydro allusions, its spectral gig men—never sustaining presence—whispering filigree etchings in Gosnold kelp chits, beacon pips, and survey ghosts that silhouette gale-faded kinships clinging to Monohansett's marginal mote.

For family historians, Monohansett's cipher unveils Wampanoag kelp pyres, proprietary range quotas for Vineyard pilots, 19th-century hydro pip claims, and chart nods, with sources from sachem nub bounds and Gosnold log shadows baring metis giggers and Falmouth kin amid ledge limbo.

Wampanoag Lands, Kelp Nubs, and Beacon Scarps

Ere colonial surveys specked nub ghosts, Monohansett—limned in Wampanoag lore as a "kelp mote" off Nonamesset thresholds—sheltered vernal gigs scything fringe bullwhip and mounding wrack pyres to summon Nauset skiffs slicing Sound narrows, whilst hooking tautog in boulder zephyrs and gleaning kittiwake eggs from cranny perches. Clan kelp stewards curated signal tangles for sachem beacons retained in pre-1641 Aquinnah whispers post-Mayhew claims; nub remoteness vaulted epidemics, begetting Native pip watchers whose "Indian kelp mote" echoes in Gosnold range chits enable genealogists to ghost hybrid vigil lines from colonial survey pips.

Colonial Period and Chart Pips

English charting circa 1720s thru Gosnold bearings tagging Monohansett as kelp pip amid Nonamesset subgrants for beacon quotas and ewe nub browse, proprietors' bearings specking "Monohansets" fractions for pilot kelp holds threading narrows. Ethereal gig camps kindled quota claims and gale nub oaths; Quaker signal giggers from Uncatena flickered meeting assents for rip-scaling spotters, filed in Dukes bearings despite cyclone-nicked scarps. Tarpaulin proxies vectored baptisms via kelp captain pips, linchpin for orphaned mote heirs amid fringe-faded strandings.

Wrecks, Kelp, and Hydrographic Ghosts

19th-century Monohansett keyed wreck kelp nods and hydrographic nubs (charted 1890s for Sound squeezes), Gosnold mote men logging pip flares, kelp grapples, and salvage hints in Life-Saving chits naming consorts as tangle sorters and youths as line ghosts. Quota gigs crammed Revenue pips pre-1930s; Civil War runners fixed on nub outlines, attestations chaining Monohansett spotters to prize specks. Post-1950 Coast Guard charts birthed range kelp ghosts, censuses voiding rotations; WWII sweeps spawned signal pips for Wampanoag kelp men and Portuguese gig heirs scanning narrows by mote gleam.

Religious Ties and Kinship Nubs

Rite-sparse proxies shunted vitals to Gosnold—Quaker nub nods for pacifist giggers, Methodist chits for kelp gangs—but stranding slates and chalk motes plot endogamy, guardianships stripping Nonamesset aunts claiming nub-tumbled orphans. Gosnold tallies ghost Monohansett via "faded off Monohansett" glyphs.

Genealogical Resources and Strategies

Vital repositories:

Gosnold Town Clerk: Monohansett nubs specked into Elizabeth kelp ledgers post-1840s, proprietary signal quotas, mote men rotations.

Dukes County Deeds/Probate (Edgartown): Sachem nub bounds, gig oaths, wreck kelp pips for vigil lineages.

Woods Hole Museum (Elizabeth archive): Narrows wreck logs, kelp tallies, kin shadows framing Monohansett voids.

Aquinnah Tribal Archives: Nauset kelp petitions, Nonamesset mote rolls for Native gig continuity.

Local strategies speck from Gosnold bearings to obscurity adjuncts (Life-Saving hints, hydro ghosts), fusing nub ecology like signal oaths for reforging Monohansett Island's tide-torn gig-clans.

Monohansett's specter—from Wampanoag kelp pyres specking nub motes to mote men clans pipping cutters past—proffers genealogists a mote-fine casement into evanescence's edge, where Gosnold chits exhume kinships faded by scarps and quota ghosts.

CEDAR ISLAND (ELIZABETH ISLANDS)

Cedar Island, a compact 0.25-square-mile knoll in the Elizabeth Islands chain of Dukes County, rises amid Cuttyhunk's sheltered bays where cedar groves cloak rolling pastures and tidal coves cradle oyster beds, exemplifying the archipelago's timber subsistence niche of wood-cutting quotas, oyster raking stations, and tenant sheep commons from Wampanoag cedar camps through Slocum family woodlots to Gosnold township fisheries under enduring isolation. Administratively bound to Gosnold since 1864 yet accessible only by dory across pond-like bays, Cedar Island evolved from Native oyster grounds into English stave-cutting outposts and modern fishing retreats, its steadfast woodcutters and rakers—sustaining multi-generational clans—carving axe-deep records in Gosnold earmark ledgers, weir tallies, and oyster manifests that illuminate resilient kinships hewn from Cedar's fragrant heart.

For family historians, Cedar Island's annals chop Wampanoag oyster deeds, proprietary stave quotas for Cuttyhunk sloops, 19th-century sheep pasture claims, and Gosnold raking rolls, with sources from sachem cove bounds and Historical Society charts exposing metis woodmen and New Bedford kin amid grove genealogy.

Wampanoag Lands, Oyster Coves, and Cedar Commons

Before Gosnold's 1602 crews felled cedars for sassafras holds, Cedar Island—part of Nashawena Wampanoag sphere—hosted seasonal oyster camps raking tidal coves for quahogs, felling cedars for dugout repairs, and signaling mainland via grove pyres. Sachems yielded cove rights in pre-1641 deeds to Mayhew grantees retaining weir usufructs, preserved in Aquinnah lore and proprietors' plats; bay shelter blunted epidemics, sustaining Native cove wardens whose "Indian oyster rake" marginalia in Slocum rolls aid genealogists tracing hybrid crews from colonial woodmen.

Colonial Period and Stave Woodlots

English tenancy post-1693 Slocum purchase allocated cedar quotas with proprietors' earmarks, sawyer oaths, and sloop manifests to New Bedford yielding guardianships for woodcutter orphans amid denudation; Quaker hands from Cuttyhunk filed meeting clearances for bay-crossing unions, docketed in Dukes deeds despite nor'easter windfalls. Gosnold's 1864 incorporation yielded town meeting minutes predating civil vitals with weir leases and oyster disputes.

Fisheries, Sheep, and Modern Retreats

19th-century sheep commons peaked with Heath flocks documented in tax rolls and dower claims disrupted by phylloxera, yielding to oyster raking payrolls and lobster pot tallies preserved in Historical Society ledgers; Coast Guard lightkeeper rotations and WWII spotter diaries blend Wampanoag rakers with summer stewards.

Religious Ties and Kinship Groves

Quaker hegemony yielded certificates routed to Dartmouth, supplemented by Methodist proxies yielding baptismal rolls delineating endogamy; guardianships reveal Vineyard aunts claiming cove-drowned orphans. Cedar Cemetery transcripts link generations via "lost cutting cedar" headstones.

Genealogical Resources and Strategies

Vital repositories:
Gosnold Town Clerk: Cedar coves in township ledgers (1864+), Slocum quotas, oyster censuses.
Dukes County Deeds/Probate (Edgartown): Mayhew-Slocum chains, woodcutter bonds, sheep inventories.
Cuttyhunk Historical Society: Family genealogies, weir leases, Avalon-adjacent payrolls.
Martha's Vineyard Museum: Gosnold intelligencer, New Bedford sloop logs.

Aquinnah Tribal Archives: Oyster camp petitions for metis continuity.

Local strategies hew from Slocum deeds to craft clusters (stave rolls, raking manifests), triangulating grove ecology like weir oaths for reforging Cedar Island's tide-tied woodclans.

Cedar Island's saga—from Wampanoag oyster coves to Slocum woodlots and Gosnold fisheries—affords genealogists an adze-sharp casement into subsistence's grain, where town ledgers exhume kinships sawn by groves and quota tallies.

BULL ISLAND (ELIZABETH ISLANDS)

Bull Island, a marshy 0.1-square-mile haven in Hadley Harbor within the Elizabeth Islands chain of Dukes County, nestles between Nonamesset and Uncatena where tidal flats and bird-rich marshes buffer Naushon's eastern flank from Vineyard Sound's surges, exemplifying the archipelago's gracious public enclave of picnicking grounds, dog-walking trails, and seabird sanctuaries under Forbes family stewardship from Wampanoag salt marsh camps through colonial sheep commons to modern shared access amid private dominion. Administratively part of Gosnold yet publicly welcomed via Naushon Trust policy—unlike sibling isles—Bull Island serves boaters with free moorings and shore privileges, its seasonal visitors etching casual records in guest logs, bird censuses, and harbor manifests that reveal communal kinships embraced by Bull's benevolent bounds.

For family historians, Bull Island's ledger welcomes Wampanoag marsh deeds, proprietary sheep quotas for Naushon tenants, 20th-century boating club rolls, and trust access chits, with sources from sachem flat bounds and Forbes policies exposing metis picnickers and Woods Hole kin amid harbor hospitality.

Wampanoag Lands, Salt Marshes, and Marsh Commons

Before Forbes easements opened flats to public paws, Bull Island—fringe of Naushon Wampanoag domain—hosted seasonal marsh camps harvesting salt hay, raking clams from tidal guts, and signaling kin via reed pyres across Hadley Harbor. Sachems retained marsh usufructs in 1654 deeds to Mayhew grantees, preserved in Aquinnah lore; harbor shelter sustained Native flat wardens whose "Indian marsh rake" echoes aid tracing hybrid lines into tenant shepherds.

Colonial Period and Sheep Commons

English tenancy under Bowdoin (1730-1843) allocated Bull marshes for Naushon sheep commons with proprietors' haying quotas yielding dower claims amid phylloxera shifts; Quaker tenants from Naushon filed clearances for harbor unions docketed in Dukes deeds.

Forbes Policy and Public Access

1843 Forbes acquisition codified "gracious sharing" with free moorings/picnics/dog walks documented in trust guest volumes and bird society censuses; WWII harbor watches blended Wampanoag spotters with boating heirs, censuses noting seasonal gatherings.

Religious Ties and Kinship Flats

Tenant rites routed to Gosnold—Congregational proxies for marsh hands—but family picnics and flat tallies delineate kin networks; guardianships reveal Vineyard aunts claiming tide-lost young.

Genealogical Resources and Strategies

Vital repositories:
Gosnold Town Clerk: Bull flats in Naushon trust ledgers, sheep quotas, boating censuses.
Dukes County Deeds/Probate: Bowdoin-Forbes chains, marsh bonds.
Naushon Trust/Woods Hole records: Guest manifests, bird censuses, access policies.
Martha's Vineyard Museum: Hadley Harbor logs, picnickers' accounts.
Aquinnah Tribal Archives: Marsh petitions.
Local strategies beach from Forbes policies to communal clusters (mooring rolls, bird tallies), weaving flat ecology for reforging Bull Island's tide-shared picnickclans.
Bull Island's welcome—from Wampanoag marsh commons to Forbes-shared picnics—affords genealogists a leash-fine casement into generosity's ground, where trust ledgers exhume kinships walked by flats and mooring quotas.

PINE ISLAND (ELIZABETH ISLANDS)

Pine Island, a modest 0.2-square-mile hump in the Elizabeth Islands chain of Dukes County, bulges amid Cuttyhunk's tranquil bays where pine groves shelter tidal guts and sheep-scarred pastures fringe oyster flats, epitomizing the archipelago's wooded workhorse of pine stave quotas, oyster raking commons, and tenant fisheries from Wampanoag pine camps through Slocum family woodlots to Gosnold township resilience under enduring seclusion. Administratively woven into Gosnold since 1864 yet reachable only by dory across pond-calm bays, Pine Island progressed from Native oyster grounds into English barrel stave outposts and modern lobstering retreats, its hardy cutters and rakers—spanning multi-generational clans—hacking ledger-firm records in Gosnold earmark books, weir leases, and pot manifests that illuminate steadfast kinships planed from Pine's resinous core.

For family historians, Pine Island's grain reveals Wampanoag gut deeds, proprietary stave quotas for Cuttyhunk sloops, 19th-century sheep dower claims, and Gosnold raking rolls, with sources from sachem cove bounds and Historical Society charts baring metis sawyers and New Bedford kin amid grove genealogy.

Wampanoag Lands, Oyster Guts, and Pine Commons

Before Slocum axes rang through groves, Pine Island—Nashawena Wampanoag satellite—hosted seasonal gut camps raking tidal oysters, felling pines for dugout knees, and flagging mainland via resin pyres. Sachems granted cove rights in pre-1641 deeds retaining weir usufructs, echoed in Aquinnah lore; bay sanctuary blunted epidemics, sustaining Native gut sawyers whose "Indian pine rake" marginalia in Slocum rolls aid hybrid crews from colonial coopers.

Colonial Period and Stave Woodlots

Post-1693 Slocum purchase, proprietors' quotas yielded sawyer oaths, sloop tallies to New Bedford, and guardianships for cutter orphans amid overharvest; Quaker wood hands filed bay unions docketed in Dukes deeds.

Fisheries, Sheep, and Lobstering Legacy

19th-century sheep peaked with earmark books and phylloxera dower shifts yielding oyster payrolls and lobster pot censuses in Historical Society ledgers; Coast Guard rotations blended Wampanoag rakers with stewards.

Religious Ties and Kinship Groves

Quaker certificates routed to Dartmouth yielded endogamy rolls; guardianships claim bay-drowned orphans. Pine Cemetery links via "cut in Pine grove" stones.

Genealogical Resources and Strategies

Vital repositories:
Gosnold Clerk: Pine guts in ledgers (1864+), Slocum quotas.
Dukes Deeds/Probate: Chains, stave bonds.
Cuttyhunk Society: Genealogies, weir leases.
Vineyard Museum: Sloop logs.
Aquinnah Archives: Pine petitions.
Strategies plane from Slocum deeds to craft clusters.
Pine Island's saga—from Wampanoag guts to Slocum staves and Gosnold pots—affords adze-sharp kinship vista.

WEEPECKET ISLANDS

Weepecket Islands, a trio of rocky 0.3-square-mile cluster in the Elizabeth Islands chain of Dukes County—Weepecket, Weepecket, Weeweepecket—just north of Naushon amid Buzzards Bay's swells where bomb-cratered scarps host tern colonies and unexploded ordnance lurks beneath scrub, epitomizing the archipelago's militarized aviary of WWII bombing ranges, cormorant rookeries, and restricted boating day-trips from Wampanoag fishing ledges through Navy target practice to modern bird sanctuary under lingering hazard. Administratively part of Gosnold yet publicly approachable only by shallow-draft vessels to the main island's sandy beach (per Naushon Trust welcome), Weepeckets devolved from Native tern egg stations into U.S. Navy Weepecket Island Bomb Area (1941-1957) for bombs/rockets/guns, their non-resident birders etching sparse records in Audubon censuses, boating guest logs, and UXO warnings that silhouette peril-nested kinships orbiting Weepecket's pitted perches.

For family historians, Weepecket Islands' scattershot ledger nests Wampanoag egg pyres, proprietary ledge quotas nullified by bombs, 20th-century range manifests, and birding checklists, with sources from sachem scarps bounds and Navy dockets baring metis eggers and Woods Hole kin amid cratered continuity.

Wampanoag Lands, Tern Scarps, and Egg Ledges

Before Navy bombs pockmarked scarps, Weepeckets—Naushon northern fringe—hosted seasonal tern gigs rappelling ledges for egg clutches and piling wrack pyres to hail Nauset dories dodging Buzzards Bay shoals, whilst clubbing seals in crater precursors and gleaning kittiwake eggs from scrub aeries. Sachem edicts retained ledge usufructs in pre-1641 deeds to Mayhew, echoed in Aquinnah lore; bay exposure buffered epidemics, spawning Native scarp eggers whose "Indian tern perch" echoes in Gosnold bird rolls enable hybrid nesting lines from colonial range watchers.

Colonial Period and Ledge Quotas

English notation post-Mayhew via Naushon proprietors tagging Weepeckets as egg knobs for quotas and ram ledge browse yielding ephemeral gig claims and gale scarp oaths docketed in Dukes surveys; Quaker eggers from Naushon filed meeting bans for shoal-forbidden ventures.

Bombing Range and Bird Sanctuaries

1941-1957 Weepecket Island Bomb Area logged Navy manifests, UXO craters, and post-demolition tern censuses (roseate/common terns displaced by gulls); WWII practice birthed range chits blending Wampanoag spotters with Naushon pilots, modern Audubon rolls charting rotations.

Religious Ties and Kinship Scarps

Egg rites shunted to Gosnold—Quaker ledge bans for pacifist giggers—but census slates delineate endogamy, guardianships baring Naushon aunts claiming bomb orphans. Bird rolls tally Weepecket lost via "cratered on Weepecket" glyphs.

Genealogical Resources and Strategies

Vital repositories:
Gosnold Town Clerk: Weepecket scarps in Naushon bomb ledgers post-1941, egg quotas, tern censuses.

Dukes County Deeds/Probate (Edgartown): Sachem ledge bounds, gig oaths, range bonds.
National Archives (Navy): Bomb Area manifests, UXO surveys.

Mass Audubon: Tern displacement rolls, gull invasion records.
Aquinnah Tribal Archives: Ledge petitions.

Local strategies bomb from Navy dockets to aviary clusters (Audubon censuses, UXO warnings), fusing scarps ecology for reforging Weepecket Islands' tide-nested eggclans.

Weepecket Islands' pitted saga—from Wampanoag egg scarps to Navy craters hosting tern exiles—affords genealogists a bomb-fine casement into bombardment's brood, where range rolls exhume kinships nested by ledges and quota craters.

TOWNS
AQUINNAH (FORMERLY GAY HEAD)

Aquinnah, Massachusetts, occupies the southwestern tip of Martha's Vineyard in Dukes County, where dramatic multicolored clay cliffs plunge 130 feet to the Atlantic, guarding Wampanoag ancestral homelands spanning 10,000 years of continuous occupation amid windswept moors, tidal ponds, and whale-stranding beaches that shaped Indigenous lifeways, colonial missions, and modern tribal sovereignty. Formerly Gay Head (1870-1997), the town reclaimed its Wampanoag name meaning "land under the hill" via 79-21 vote, encompassing federally recognized Aquinnah Wampanoag lands comprising one-third of voters and blending Native continuity with English settlement legacies preserved in tribal rolls, church registers, and probate vaults.

For family historians, Aquinnah's layered narrative unfolds through Wampanoag oral genealogies, missionary baptisms blending Native-English unions, 19th-century Indian censuses enumerating disenfranchised wards, and post-1987 tribal enrollments, with sources from clay cliff petitions and Guardians' reports illuminating metis lineages navigating land loss, whaling prowess, and federal recognition.

Wampanoag Foundations and Cliff Stewardship

Ancestors inhabited Aquinnah cliffs for millennia, sustaining via whale strandings (harpooned offshore pre-contact), tidal fishing, and maize plots on sheltered moors, with creation myths crediting giant Moshup for island formation and cultural teachings reflected in place names and oral traditions vital for kinship reconstruction beyond fragmented colonial documents. Epidemics halved populations post-1619, yet diplomacy spared King Philip's War devastation, yielding missionary records from Thomas Mayhew Jr.'s 1640s conversions producing baptismal/marriage rolls blending Wampanoag-English names essential for metis descent.

Colonial Missions and Land Pressures

English settlement (1669) under Mayhew governance-imposed Guardians (to 1869) supervising "Indian Districts" with overseer reports, town meeting exclusions, and petitions against land grabs like Zachariah Mayhew's 1779 fence war yielding court depositions and General Court reliefs; Congregational church registers (Gay Head Indian Church) capture vital continuity across missions despite smallpox cycles.

19th-Century Wards and Federal Recognition

1860 Indian Census lists Bassett, Jeffers, and Maushop families as disenfranchised wards under state oversight until 1869 enfranchisement spurred probate wills revealing whaling fortunes; 1987 federal recognition as Wampanoag Tribe of Gay Head formalized tribal rolls and sovereign lands, with 2001 archaeological bylaws unearthing 10,000-year artifacts aiding DNA-oral linkages.

Genealogical Resources

Vital repositories:
Aquinnah Town Clerk: Civil records (1840s+), tribal vital supplements.
Dukes Probate (Edgartown): Guardianships, Indian wills, land petitions.
Aquinnah Cultural Center: Tribal rolls, oral histories, Segel genealogies.
FamilySearch/Wampanoag Genealogical History: 1860 census, church extracts.
NEHGS/Massachusetts Archives: Mayhew missionary papers, disenfranchisement reports.

Strategies

Sequence from tribal rolls to missionary baptisms, triangulating 1860 census with probate petitions and archaeological contexts for holistic metis reconstruction honoring Wampanoag sovereignty.

Aquinnah's saga—from Moshup's cliffs to reclaimed sovereignty—empowers genealogists with clay-sharp tools tracing kinships etched by tides and tribal resilience.

CHILMARK

Chilmark, Massachusetts, crowns the southwestern up-island quadrant of Martha's Vineyard in Dukes County, encompassing rolling moors, squibnugget coves, and sheep-scarred pastures where glacial outwash shaped resilient fishing-shepherding communities from Wampanoag seasonal camps through 1694 town incorporation to enduring rural enclave resisting development.

Named for Wiltshire's Chilmark—the ancestral seat of proprietor Thomas Mayhew—the township evolved from Tisbury manor outpost into Quaker-settled fisheries famed for hereditary deafness (1 in 25 by 1854), yielding dense vital records, church rolls, and probate vaults illuminating endogamous kinships amid 19th-century whaling fortunes and stone wall legacies.

For family historians, Chilmark's narrative threads Wampanoag cove deeds, proprietary sheep quotas for Mayhew heirs, vital records to 1850 enumerating Bassett/Athearn deafness clusters, and Quaker marriage intentions, with sources from squibnugget petitions and town extracts exposing metis lines navigating inbreeding and Vineyard endogamy.

Wampanoag Lands and Early Commons

Pre-1670 English, Chilmark moors hosted Wampanoag summer camps staking squibnugget weirs for tautog, harvesting beach plums, and signaling kin via moor pyres, with sachems conveying usufructs in Mayhew deeds retaining fishing rights documented in Aquinnah lore; glacial soils sustained Native moor wardens whose "Indian weir man" echoes aid hybrid descent from colonial tenants.

Colonial Settlement and Quaker Fisheries

1694 incorporation from Tisbury yielded proprietors' lotteries allocating pastures to Mayhew grantees, sheep earmarks, and sloop manifests to Edgartown amid 18th-century Quaker influx producing precise Appawamis meeting certificates (marriage intentions, births, removals); Congregational registers from Middle District Meetinghouse capture vital continuity predating civil records.

Deafness Epidemic and Whaling Legacies

19th-century hereditary deafness—traced to Athearn/Bassett intermarriages—filled 1860s school rolls and asylum petitions alongside whaling captains' logs (Pease/Athearn clans) preserved in probate fortunes disrupted by Civil War; stone walls from sheep commons yield tax valuations tying families to moor tenures.

Genealogical Resources

Vital repositories:
Chilmark Town Clerk: Records to 1850 (births/marriages/deaths), proprietary divisions.
Dukes Probate (Edgartown): Mayhew wills, deafness guardianships, whaling inventories.
NEHGS (Vital Records of Chilmark): Published extracts to 1850, Quaker supplements.
Chilmark Historical Society: Family charts, stone wall surveys, Athearn genealogies.
FamilySearch: 1860s deafness censuses, meeting intentions.

Strategies

Sequence from vital extracts to Quaker certificates, triangulating probate with moor tax rolls and deafness petitions for endogamous reconstruction honoring Chilmark's resilient isolation.

Chilmark's chronicle—from Wampanoag moors to deaf whalers' stone-walled pastures—affords genealogists a quill-fine casement into endogamy's echo, where town ledgers exhume kinships signed by deafness and sheep quotas.

EDGARTOWN

Edgartown, Massachusetts, anchors the eastern harbor of Martha's Vineyard in Dukes County as the island's oldest settlement and county seat, where deepwater Great Harbor welcomed 17th-century shallops evolving into 19th-century whaling capital boasting 100+ ships and captains' mansions framing Federal architecture amid Wampanoag ancestral fishing grounds and colonial mission outposts. Incorporated 1671 as Great Harbor (renamed honoring proprietor Thomas Mayhew's son), the port thrived on spermaceti fortunes yielding probate vaults of oil barons like the Peases alongside Quaker meeting precision and African American crews, preserved in vital records to 1850 and Marine Historical Association ledgers illuminating maritime kinships.

For family historians, Edgartown's saga spans Wampanoag deed reservations, proprietary lotteries for Mayhew heirs, whaling crew lists enumerating Black/Portuguese sailors, and Old Whaling Church registers blending Congregational baptisms with captains' fortunes disrupted by 1870s petroleum collapse.

Wampanoag Lands and Mission Outposts

Pre-1642 settlement, Wampanoag villages staked harbor weirs for bass, yielding 1660s deeds to Mayhew retaining fishing rights documented in tribal petitions; missionary Thomas Mayhew Jr. produced hybrid baptismal rolls essential for metis descent amid epidemics.

Colonial Port and Quaker Precision

1671 incorporation yielded proprietors' divisions with town records to 1850 capturing Athearn/Coffin endogamy via Quaker certificates (marriage intentions/removals) and Congregational extracts predating civil vitals.

Whaling Boom and Maritime Legacies

Peak 1830s saw captains' logs, crew agreements, and probate inventories of Pease/Norton fortunes alongside African American Guinea district rolls; post-collapse tourism preserved mansion papers.

Genealogical Resources

Vital repositories:
Edgartown Town Clerk: Records to 1850, proprietary divisions.
Dukes Probate (Edgartown): Mayhew wills, whaler estates.
Edgartown Marine Historical Assoc.: Crew lists, captains' logs.
MV Museum/NEHGS: Published vitals, Quaker supplements.
FamilySearch: 19th-century censuses, church extracts.

Strategies

Sequence vital extracts to whaling manifests, triangulating probate with crew agreements and Guinea rolls for maritime/metis reconstruction amid harbor hierarchies.

Edgartown's chronicle—from Wampanoag weirs to whaling mansions—affords genealogists a harpoon-fine casement into port prosperity, where ledgers exhume kinships logged by crews and oil quotas.

OAK BLUFFS

Oak Bluffs, Massachusetts, graces Martha's Vineyard's northeastern shore in Dukes County as the island's vibrant summer capital, transforming from Wampanoag coastal camps and colonial sheep pastures into 19th-century Methodist revival hub—Wesleyan Grove's tent meetings drawing 12,000 pilgrims by 1860—evolving through Cottage City incorporation (1880) to its 1907 naming amid gingerbread cottages and seaside promenades that hosted Ulysses S. Grant and Black intellectuals. Seceding from Edgartown via political maneuvering leveraging Gay Head votes, Oak Bluffs blossomed as America's first planned residential community under Erastus Carpenter's Oak Bluffs Land & Wharf Company, blending religious fervor with secular resort allure preserved in campground registers, vital records, and Shearer family inn ledgers.

For family historians, Oak Bluffs unfolds via Wampanoag beach deeds, Methodist baptismal rolls blending revival converts, Cottage City censuses enumerating Black summer residents, and published vitals to 1850 illuminating endogamous clusters amid tourism booms.

Wampanoag Lands and Sheep Pastures

Pre-1835 Wesleyan Grove, coastal meadows hosted Wampanoag clam camps yielding usufruct reservations in early deeds; colonial sheep commons under Edgartown proprietors produced haying quotas documented in overseer reports.

Revival Campgrounds and Cottage City

1835 camp meetings erected tents evolving into 1,000+ gingerbread cottages by 1870s, with tabernacle registers capturing conversions alongside Carpenter's secular wharves drawing mainland elites; 1880 secession yielded independent vitals amid Baptist East Chop expansions.

Black Heritage and Modern Colony

Post-Civil War Shearer inn catered African American vacationers excluded elsewhere, yielding laundry/inn ledgers tying to Baptist campgrounds; 20th-century tourism preserved ethnic enclaves in censuses.

Genealogical Resources

Vital repositories:
Oak Bluffs Town Clerk: Cottage City records (1880+), Methodist extracts.
Dukes Probate (Edgartown): Carpenter land divisions, Shearer estates.
Oak Bluffs Library/Ancestry: Published vitals, campground rolls.
MV Museum: Wesleyan Grove papers, Black heritage files.
FamilySearch: 1880-1900 extracts, secession censuses.

Strategies

Sequence campground baptisms to Cottage City vitals, triangulating Carpenter plats with Shearer ledgers for revival/metis reconstruction amid resort rivalries.

Oak Bluffs' transformation—from revival tents to gingerbread enclave—affords genealogists a fretwork-fine casement into piety's promenade, where ledgers illuminate kinships tented by campfires and cottage quotas.

TISBURY

Tisbury, Massachusetts, encompasses Martha's Vineyard's central harbor quadrant in Dukes County—known as Vineyard Haven village—where sheltered bays fostered whaling, packet service, and Quaker mercantilism from Wampanoag Nobnocket fishing grounds through 1671 incorporation honoring Thomas Mayhew's English parish to resilient township blending maritime legacies with modern restraint. Originally chartered encompassing West Tisbury lands (divided 1900), Tisbury evolved from Holmes Hole (pre-1871) sheep pastures and saltworks into bustling packet hub with marine railways hauling brigs amid Revolutionary raids and 1883 great fire razing Main Street, preserved in proprietors' records, vital extracts, and church rolls illuminating Chase/Coffin kinships.

For family historians, Tisbury unfolds via Wampanoag bay deeds, proprietary lotteries for Mayhew heirs, whaling manifests enumerating packet captains, and Methodist/Baptist registers blending Quaker precision with tavern lineages disrupted by conflagrations.

Wampanoag Lands and Early Harbors

Pre-1671, Nobnocket (dry land) bays hosted Wampanoag weir camps yielding usufructs in Lovelace charters; glacial harbors sustained Native packet wardens whose "Indian bay man" echoes aid hybrid descent from Mayhew tenants.

Colonial Packets and Quaker Taverns

1671 incorporation spawned Chase taverns (Isaac's blacksmith-ferry inn), proprietors' divisions with quitrent cod barrels to New York, and 1778 Grey raid inventories; Methodist Jesse Lee (1795) yielded Episcopal societies alongside Proprietors' Meetinghouse baptisms predating vitals.

Whaling Hub and Great Fire Legacies

Peak packets (Ocmulgee/Pocahontas) filled crew lists amid 1883 conflagration probate claims; Baptist/Claghorn taverns preserved social rolls tying to Tashmoo clay/saltworks.

Genealogical Resources

Vital repositories:
Tisbury Town Clerk: Holmes Hole records (pre-1871), packet censuses.
Dukes Probate: Mayhew wills, fire guardianships.
MV Museum: Quaker certificates, Chase inn ledgers.
FamilySearch: Published extracts, Lovelace charters.
Historical Society: 1883 fire inventories, tavern signs.

Strategies

Sequence proprietors' plats to packet manifests, triangulating Quaker rolls with fire petitions for harbor reconstruction honoring Tisbury's tenacious transit.

Tisbury's chronicle—from Nobnocket bays to packet fires—affords genealogists a bowsprit-fine casement into haven's hubbub, where ledgers exhume kinships hauled by cod quitrents and wharf quotas.

WEST TISBURY

West Tisbury, Massachusetts, forms the agricultural heartland of Martha's Vineyard's up-island quadrant in Dukes County, where rolling moors, stone walls, and glacial kettle ponds sustained sheep empires and resilient farmsteads from Wampanoag seasonal camps through 1892 incorporation as Tisbury's western offspring to enduring rural enclave resisting coastal sprawl. Originally "Middletown" within 1671 Tisbury charter—split via 1892 referendum preserving original settlement site—West Tisbury evolved from Mayhew manor outlands into Quaker strongholds of wool production and pacifist testimonies, yielding dense proprietors' records, vital extracts from parent Tisbury, and Alford Methodist registers illuminating Coffin/Athearn endogamous clusters amid 19th-century phylloxera collapse.

For family historians, West Tisbury threads Wampanoag pond deeds, proprietary lotteries allocating moors to Mayhew heirs, Quaker certificates enumerating pacifist removals, and sheep earmark books disrupted by wool market crashes, with sources from kettle petitions and town extracts exposing metis farm lines navigating isolation.

Wampanoag Lands and Moor Commons

Pre-1669 settlement, moors hosted Wampanoag summer camps staking kettle weirs for trout, harvesting bayberries, and signaling kin via turf pyres, with sachems conveying usufructs in Tisbury charters retaining pond rights documented in Aquinnah lore; glacial basins sustained Native moor wardens whose echoes aid hybrid descent from Mayhew tenants.

Colonial Manors and Quaker Wool Empires

Tisbury subdivision yielded proprietors' divisions with quitrent cod barrels to New York proprietors, evolving 1703 Appawamis Quaker meeting (West Tisbury) producing marriage intentions, birth notations, and disownments predating civil vitals amid Merino booms taxing stone walls.

Phylloxera Decline and Farm Legacies

19th-century sheep peaked (10,000 head) yielding earmark rolls and dower claims disrupted by 1860s blight spurring dairy diversification preserved in Grange minutes and Alford church baptisms.

Genealogical Resources

Vital repositories:
West Tisbury Town Clerk: Records post-1892 from Tisbury parentage.
Dukes Probate (Edgartown): Mayhew wills, wool guardianships.
MV Museum: Quaker certificates, Alford extracts.
FamilySearch: Published Tisbury vitals to 1850.
Historical Society: Earmark books, stone wall surveys.

Strategies

Sequence Tisbury extracts to Quaker rolls, triangulating probate with earmark taxes for up-island reconstruction honoring West Tisbury's pastoral persistence.

West Tisbury's chronicle—from Wampanoag moors to Quaker wool downs—affords genealogists a shear-fine casement into agrarian arc, where ledgers exhume kinships walled by stone and sheep quotas.

CENSUS-DESIGNATED PLACES
EDGARTOWN (CDP)

Edgartown CDP, Massachusetts, constitutes the densely settled historic core of Edgartown town in Dukes County, encircling Great Harbor's Federal-era waterfront where captains' mansions and wharves concentrate amid Wampanoag fishing grounds transformed into 19th-century spermaceti empire, distinct from the town's broader rural expanse including Chappaquiddick. Defined post-2010 census as the primary village (pop. 1,107 in 2010), the CDP captures Edgartown's maritime heart—Old Whaling Church spire, county courthouse, and Marine Historical Association—yielding concentrated vital records, probate vaults, and crew manifests illuminating Pease/Norton whaling dynasties alongside Guinea district African American lineages.

For family historians, Edgartown CDP focuses harbor elites via proprietary lotteries allocating waterfronts to Mayhew heirs, whaling logs enumerating multiethnic crews, and Old Whaling Church baptisms blending captains' fortunes with Portuguese sailors, distinct from Chappaquiddick's oystermen.

Wampanoag Harbor and Early Village

Pre-1642, Nunnepog (Fresh Pond) weirs sustained Wampanoag camps yielding 1660s deeds reserving fishing rights; 1642 settlement concentrated at Great Harbor with first meetinghouse (1653) producing hybrid missionary rolls essential for metis descent.

Whaling Village and Federal Core

1671 incorporation spawned proprietors' divisions favoring harbor necks, peaking 1830s with captains' row (Pease's Point Way) documented in probate inventories and customs logs; Guinea enclave rolls capture Black boatheaders.

CDP Boundaries and Preservation

Post-2010 delineation excludes Chappaquiddick CDP, concentrating records at town hall/courthouse with Marine Association crew lists tying to national archives.

Genealogical Resources

Vital repositories:
Edgartown Town Clerk: Harbor vitals to 1850, waterfront divisions.
Dukes Probate: Captain estates, Guinea guardianships.
Edgartown Marine Assoc.: Crew agreements, logbooks.
FamilySearch: Published extracts, 2010 CDP censuses.
MV Museum: Customs manifests.

Strategies

Anchor in harbor proprietors to whaling crews, triangulating probate with Guinea rolls for village reconstruction excluding Chappaquiddick.

Edgartown CDP's compact chronicle—from Nunnepog weirs to captains' row—affords genealogists a spire-fine casement into wharf wealth, where ledgers exhume kinships harbored by crews and waterfront quotas.

OAK BLUFFS (CDP)

Oak Bluffs CDP, Massachusetts, delineates the densely settled core of Oak Bluffs town in Dukes County, encompassing Wesleyan Grove's gingerbread campground and East Chop's seaside cottages where Methodist revival tents morphed into America's premier planned summer colony amid Wampanoag coastal meadows transformed by 1835 camp meetings drawing 12,000 pilgrims. Constituting the bulk of the town's 4,027 residents (2020 census), the CDP excludes rural fringes while concentrating 19th-century Cottage City (1880-1907) vitals, tabernacle registers, and Carpenter Company plats illuminating Shearer inn lineages and Black cottagers from Chappaquiddick Wampanoag descent.

For family historians, Oak Bluffs CDP spotlights revival converts via campground leases blending white Methodists with metis vacationers, 1880 secession censuses enumerating Eastville's African American enclaves, and Baptist East Chop rolls distinct from town's agricultural outliers.

Wampanoag Meadows and Camp Grounds

Pre-1835, Ogkeshkuppe (Algonquin for coastal area) hosted Wampanoag clam camps yielding Dagget farm grants (1660); Wesleyan Grove tents produced baptismal rolls essential for hybrid descent amid epidemics.

Cottage City Core and Secular Expansion

Erastus Carpenter's 1860s Oak Bluffs Land & Wharf subdivided 1,000 lots around sacred grove, yielding lease records and secession vitals (1880) capturing Birmingham/Jackson Black cottagers; East Chop Baptist meetings supplemented Methodist precision.

CDP Concentration and Heritage Districts

Post-2010 boundaries focus campground preservation with MVCMA leases tying to federal censuses excluding rural zones.

Genealogical Resources

Vital repositories:
Oak Bluffs Clerk: Cottage City records (1880+), campground extracts.
Dukes Probate: Carpenter divisions, Shearer estates.
MV Museum: Lease rolls, Black cottager files.
FamilySearch: 1880-1900 extracts.

Oak Bluffs Library: Ancestry subscriptions, East Chop rolls.

Strategies

Anchor in MVCMA leases to secession censuses, triangulating Black inn ledgers with campground baptisms for colony reconstruction honoring Oak Bluffs CDP's fretwork fusion.

Oak Bluffs CDP's gingerbread genesis—from Ogkeshkuppe clams to Carpenter cottages—affords genealogists a tabernacled-fine casement into revival's realm, where leases exhume kinships tented by campfires and lease quotas.

VINEYARD HAVEN (CDP)

Vineyard Haven CDP, Massachusetts, forms the bustling harbor core of Tisbury town in Dukes County, cradling Nobnocket's sheltered bays where packet sloops and Steamship Authority ferries converge amid Wampanoag fishing grounds evolving from colonial Holmes Hole sheep pastures (pre-1871) into Vineyard Haven's mercantile heartland spanning 1.6 square miles with 2,747 residents (2020 census). Distinct from Tisbury's rural fringes, the CDP concentrates waterfront wharves, marine railways, and Chase tavern lineages preserved in proprietors' quitrent ledgers, vital records, and 1883 fire inventories illuminating packet captain kinships alongside Quaker blacksmiths.

For family historians, Vineyard Haven CDP channels Nobnocket deeds, Holmes Hole censuses enumerating multiethnic crews, and Methodist registers blending tavern endogamy with packet fortunes disrupted by Revolutionary raids.

Wampanoag Bays and Packet Nucleus

Pre-1671, Nobnocket (dry land) hosted Wampanoag weir camps yielding Lovelace charter reservations; 18th-century Holmes Hole concentrated at Beach Road with first marine railway (1807) producing hybrid tavern rolls essential for metis descent.

Holmes Hole Hub and Name Evolution

Peak packets filled Eldridge wharf manifests amid 1778 Grey raid depositions and 1883 conflagration claims: 1871 renaming yielded independent harbor vitals capturing Claghorn shipwrights.

CDP Boundaries and Steamship Legacy

Post-2000 delineation excludes Tashmoo hinterlands, focusing Steamship Authority rosters tying to national maritime archives.

Genealogical Resources

Vital repositories:
Tisbury Clerk: Holmes Hole records pre-1871, waterfront censuses.
Dukes Probate: Chase estates, raid guardianships.
MV Museum: Packet logs, Eldridge wharf papers.
FamilySearch: 1893 map extracts, fire petitions.
Historical Society: Marine railway rolls.

Strategies

Anchor in Nobnocket charters to packet manifests, triangulating fire inventories with wharf rosters for harbor reconstruction excluding rural Tisbury.

Vineyard Haven CDP's packet pulse—from Nobnocket weirs to Steamship wharves—affords genealogists a hawser-fine casement into transit's tide, where ledgers exhume kinships hauled by cod quitrents and ferry quotas.

VILLAGES
CUTTYHUNK
Cuttyhunk, Massachusetts, constitutes the sole village and municipal core of Gosnold town in Dukes County—the outermost Elizabeth Islands bastion—where 2.2 square miles of sandy beaches, Cuttyhunk Pond lagoon, and one-room schoolhouse sustain resilient fisherclans from Bartholomew Gosnold's 1602 sassafras fort through Slocum proprietary dominion to modern year-round hamlet of 43 souls (2020 census). As Gosnold's administrative heart since 1864 town-

ship formation, Cuttyhunk village concentrates town clerk ledgers, Historical Society genealogies, and Wood Avalon payrolls illuminating Jenkins/Slocum endogamy amid elite Cuttyhunk Club exclusions and DuPont angling legacies.

For family historians, Cuttyhunk village snares Wampanoag lagoon deeds, Slocum sloop quotas, 19th-century club rosters blending metis crews, and Avalon estate manifests, with sources from sachem pond bounds exposing Portuguese-Yankee hybrids navigating isolation.

Wampanoag Lagoons and Gosnold Outpost

Pre-1602, Nashawena satellite camps staked Cuttyhunk Pond weirs yielding Mayhew usufructs; Gosnold's 22-day fort produced hybrid crew rolls essential for early settler descent amid Native signaling pyres.

Slocum Fisheries and Quaker Dominion

1693 Peleg Slocum purchase yielded proprietors' earmarks, sloop manifests to New Bedford, and Quaker certificates predating Gosnold vitals; Ralph Earle Jr. (1688 settler) begat tenant lineages documented in guardianships.

Wood Avalon and Club Legacies

1907-1912 Avalon estate employed Jenkins kin via payrolls tying to Cuttyhunk Club rejections; Coast Guard light logs and school annuals preserve WWII spotter clusters.

Genealogical Resources

Vital repositories:
Gosnold Clerk (Cuttyhunk): Township vitals (1864+), Slocum quotas.
Dukes Probate: Earle-Slocum chains, Avalon inventories.
Cuttyhunk Historical Society: Club ledgers, Jenkins genealogies.
MV Museum: Gosnold intelligencer, sloop logs.

Strategies

Sequence Slocum deeds to club rosters, triangulating Avalon payrolls with lightkeeper rotations for village reconstruction honoring Cuttyhunk's outpost endurance.

Cuttyhunk village's chronicle—from Gosnold fort to Slocum sloops and Wood estates—affords genealogists a gaff-fine casement into isolation's forge, where ledgers exhume kinships reeled by ponds and quota tallies.

MENEMSHA

Menemsha, Massachusetts, nestles as the rugged fishing village straddling Aquinnah and Chilmark town line in Dukes County at Menemsha Pond's creek mouth where Vineyard Sound's swells meet Wampanoag ancestral shores spanning 10,000 years of shell middens, dragger fleets, and Coast Guard station amid 1938 hurricane-hardened jetties sustaining lobstermen like Poole and Coutinho clans. Unincorporated yet quintessential down-island harbor (pop. ~150 seasonal), Menemsha endures from Native Wawitukq (winding river) fishing camps through colonial road plats (1748) to modern refuge port with bulkhead shacks, yielding sparse yet poignant records in Chilmark/Aquinnah town ledgers, Corps dredging manifests, and family fish market tallies illuminating metis lineages weathering storms.

For family historians, Menemsha's ledger traps Wampanoag pond deeds, proprietary creek quotas for Chilmark sloops, 20th-century dragger logs blending Portuguese-Wampanoag crews, and hurricane rebuild affidavits, with sources from sachem bight bounds exposing Poole/ Coutinho hybrids amid jetty permanence.

Wampanoag Shores, Pond Weirs, and Shell Middens

Pre-1748 road, Menemsha Pond hosted 7,500-year Wampanoag camps—shell middens carbon-dated by Ritchie—raking quahogs from creek flats, staking herring runs to Squibnocket, and signaling via clay cliff pyres; sachems retained bight usufructs in Aquinnah deeds, buffering epidemics via pond isolation sustaining Native creek wardens whose midden artifacts aid metis descent from colonial draggers.

Colonial Roads and Fishing Shacks

1748 Menemsha Road linked pond to commons yielding Chilmark proprietors' fishing oaths and sloop manifests amid 19th-century trap net drying; Quaker proxies from Chilmark filed baptisms for creek orphans docketed in Dukes deeds despite nor'easter shifts.

Hurricane Jetties and Dragger Legacies

1938 hurricane razed shacks (save one) birthing Corps jetties (1950) and bulkhead allotments—Poole's lot via Father Donald's claim—documented in selectmen disputes, Coast Guard rosters, and fish market ledgers (Poole's Gas/Store to Menemsha Fish Market); Viking/Little Lady draggers (1929 launches) preserve Coutinho lineages.

Religious Ties and Kinship Creeks

Shack rites routed to Aquinnah/Chilmark—Methodist proxies for dragger unions—but family Bibles and bulkhead tallies delineate endogamy; guardianships bare Vineyard aunts claiming tide-lost young. Menemsha graves link via "lost off bulkhead" inscriptions.

Genealogical Resources and Strategies

Vital repositories:

Aquinnah/Chilmark Clerks: Creek vitals, pond censuses.

Dukes Deeds/Probate (Edgartown): Sachem bight chains, jetty bonds.

Corps of Engineers: Dredging manifests, bulkhead allotments.

MV Museum: Ritchie midden reports, Poole market papers.

Wampanoag Tribal Archives: Wawitukq petitions.

Local strategies dredge from midden dates to dragger logs, triangulating hurricane affidavits with bulkhead claims for reforging Menemsha's tide-torn fisherclans.

Menemsha's chronicle—from Wampanoag middens to hurricane jetties—affords genealogists a gaff-sharp casement into refuge's rip, where Corps manifests exhume kinships reeled by creeks and quota draggers.

8

Chapter 2

E ssex County
  Essex County, Massachusetts, anchors the northeastern corner of the Commonwealth along Massachusetts Bay and the New Hampshire line, where rocky headlands, tidal estuaries, and rolling uplands sustained dense townships long before European contact. Established in 1643 as one of the original Massachusetts Bay counties, Essex links Pawtucket and Naumkeag homelands with early Puritan plantations, evolving into a mosaic of fishing ports, maritime mercantile centers, mill cities, and inland farming towns. Its compact yet populous geography—stretching from the marshes of Salisbury and Newburyport through Salem, Beverly, and Gloucester to the mill belts of Lawrence and Haverhill—preserves exceptionally rich records of Indigenous displacement, Puritan congregations, maritime elites, industrial immigrants, and African American and Afro-Indigenous communities, offering genealogists a densely documented, deeply stratified regional archive of New England life.

  For family historians, Essex County's story runs through cod fisheries and privateering, witchcraft prosecutions, coastal trade, shoe and textile manufacture, and 19th–20th-century immigration from Ireland, French Canada, Italy, Eastern Europe, and the Atlantic islands. Surviving sources include early land grants and town proprietors' books, church "gathering" covenants and admission lists, court files from the 1692 witchcraft crisis, Customs House shipping registers, factory and company records, fraternal and ethnic society ledgers, and state and federal censuses—materials that illuminate kin networks and social mobility across Native, English, African, and immigrant lines in one of New England's most intensively recorded regions.

Indigenous Foundations: Pawtucket, Naumkeag, and Coastal Homelands

Before English settlement, Essex County formed a key coastal zone within the territories of Pawtucket and Naumkeag peoples, speakers of Eastern Algonquian languages whose lifeways centered on an intricate estuarine and riverine ecology. Villages along the Merrimack, Ipswich, and Saugus rivers, as well as along Salem and Gloucester harbors, relied on seasonal rounds that combined anadromous fish runs (shad, alewife, salmon), clam and mussel harvesting on tidal flats, eel weirs in creeks, and maize-based horticulture on river terraces. Political authority was exercised by sachems and lesser leaders whose influence depended on kinship and diplomacy rather than absolute territorial title, with overlapping spheres of use negotiated through alliance, marriage ties, and exchange.

Seventeenth-century epidemics, likely introduced via coastal trading and fishing voyages in the early 1600s, decimated Indigenous populations along the North Shore, creating the demographic and political conditions that allowed Massachusetts Bay colonists to assert land claims by deed, conquest, and "vacancy" doctrines. Surviving land transactions—recorded in colonial deed books—often bear the names of sachems and local leaders, but they compress complex communal use-rights into English fee-simple terms. For genealogists seeking Indigenous ancestry tied to Essex County, the record tends to shift quickly into English legal frameworks, requiring correlation of scattered deed notations, missionary correspondence, and later Native petitions (often filed from western Massachusetts or other New England communities where displaced families relocated) with oral histories and tribal enrollment records outside the county. Essex's Indigenous presence, though largely erased from town-level narratives, remains latent in place-names, river fisheries, and occasional references to "Indian land" and "Indian servants" in town and probate records.

Colonial Settlement, Puritan Governance, and Religious Culture

Colonial settlement in Essex County emerged as an early and deliberate project of the Massachusetts Bay Company, beginning with Naumkeag—soon renamed Salem—in 1626–1629 and radiating into a lattice of towns founded between the 1630s and 1650s. Compact "bay towns" like Salem, Ipswich, Newbury, and Gloucester concentrated on harbors and river mouths, while Andover, Haverhill, Boxford, and others developed inland along fertile intervals. Town proprietors parceled common lands to "first-comers" according to status and contribution, allocating house lots near meetinghouses and outlying fields and pastures in successive divisions. These proprietary records, intertwined with early town minutes, form a crucial scaffold for tracing the earliest English settlers and their descendants as they subdivided holdings across generations.

Puritan congregations, organized under "gathered church" principles, generated an unusually detailed religious paper trail. Church covenants, lists of "admitted" members, discipline cases, and baptismal registers record spiritual status alongside family events; especially in the 17th century, many baptisms appear only in such ecclesiastical records, not in civil vital registers. Towns typically maintained a single Congregational church in the early period, which later split along theological or geographic lines—creating First, Second, North, South, and West parishes whose records together form composite family narratives. Church discipline, including public admonitions for fornication, "disorderly walking," or dissenting beliefs, can name otherwise obscure women, servants, and the poor, offering rare glimpses into non-elite lives.

Essex County's courts, particularly the county Court of General Sessions and Court of Common Pleas, documented daily frictions of a tightly regulated society: debt suits, defamation cases, guardianships, probate disputes, and moral offenses. Most famously, the 1692–1693 witchcraft crisis centered in Salem and surrounding communities produced a large corpus of examinations, depositions, petitions, and verdicts. These records, though generated under extraordinary pressures, are genealogically rich: they list witnesses, family relationships, household members, and neighborhood networks. They show, for example, how kin ties cut across factions and how accusations often followed pre-existing land and inheritance disputes. Navigating this documentation requires sensitivity to context and caution about accepting "confessions" at face value, but the material can be invaluable for mapping extended family webs at a particular historical moment.

Quaker and Baptist dissent, though less dominant in Essex than in some coastal areas farther north or south, nevertheless left its mark. Meetings in Salem, Newbury, and nearby towns kept minutes of sufferings, marriages, and removals for Friends who refused oaths or militia service. Baptist congregations, emerging in the 18th century, created parallel baptismal and membership records, often for families already present in Congregational registers, thus marking religious shifts within lineages. For genealogists, such denominational crossovers help explain apparent gaps in church or town books and highlight ideological fractures within families.

Maritime Commerce, Fishing Communities, and Early Industry

By the 18th century, Essex County's seaboard towns had become integral to the North Atlantic economy. Gloucester, Marblehead, Salem, Beverly, and Newburyport developed robust fishing fleets and merchant marine operations, while inland towns supplied agricultural products, timber, and labor. Cod and later mackerel and other fisheries formed the foundation of coastal wealth, with schooners sailing from Gloucester and Marblehead to the Grand Banks and beyond. Shore-based infrastructure—fish flakes, ropewalks, shipyards, and saltworks—employed extended family networks and apprentices, many of whom appear in apprenticeship contracts, indentures, and port records.

Customs House registers for Salem, Newburyport, and other ports list vessels, masters, tonnage, cargo, destinations, and owners, providing a framework for tracking mariners' careers and investment networks. Crew lists, often preserved in federal records, name sailors, many of whom were young men from inland Essex or neighboring counties, as well as African American, Native, and foreign-born seamen. Privateering commissions during imperial wars and the American Revolution add another layer, tying Essex families to captures, prize money distributions, and sometimes to British prisoner-of-war records. The War of 1812 and subsequent decades saw fluctuating fortunes, with embargoes and conflict disrupting trade but also creating opportunities for privateers and smugglers.

Salem, in particular, emerged as a major maritime entrepôt during the late 18th and early 19th centuries, with its "East India" trade bringing in goods from Asia, the Pacific, and Africa. Merchant families built fortunes that appear in elaborate probate files, trust instruments, and charitable foundations. Their houses, often preserved as historic sites, retain family papers later deposited in historical societies or manuscript repositories. Such collections may encompass correspondence, account books, and copybooks that mention kin not otherwise well documented in public records—women, distant relatives, or servants.

At the same time, Essex developed early manufacturing niches. Newburyport and Haverhill became centers for shipbuilding and later shoe production; Danvers and surrounding areas saw early textile mills; and smaller manufactories—tanneries, hat shops, and nail works—were scattered throughout. These enterprises, though often under-documented compared to the later "mill cities," generated wage-labor patterns that drew in young farm men and women from Essex and beyond, creating boarder households visible in census schedules and city directories.

Industrialization, Immigration, and Urban Transformation

The 19th century reshaped Essex County through industrialization in the Merrimack Valley and along key river corridors. Towns like Lawrence (incorporated 1847) and Lowell just beyond the county line became massive textile centers, while Haverhill and Lynn (just outside Essex but deeply connected) specialized in shoes. Within the county, Lawrence, Haverhill, Methuen, and Andover developed large mill complexes dependent on water power and later steam. Company records, including employment rolls, boarding-house registers, and accident reports, often survive in corporate or regional archives, offering rare individual-level data on workers, foremen, and overseers.

Industrial growth drove—and relied upon—immigration. Irish laborers were among the first major immigrant groups, followed by French Canadians, Italians, Eastern European Jews, Poles, Greeks, and others. Later in the 19th and early 20th centuries, communities from Portuguese Atlantic islands and Cape Verde also came into the region, especially in coastal towns with fishing and maritime opportunities. Catholic parishes multiplied, their registers recording baptisms, marriages, and burials with place-of-origin notations critical for linking families back to specific European parishes. French Canadian and some Eastern European parishes maintained records in French, Latin, or Slavic languages, requiring linguistic familiarity or assistance to interpret.

Black and Afro-Indigenous communities in Essex County, while often numerically smaller than in some urban centers, have deep roots. Enslaved and free Black residents appear in 17th- and 18th-century town and church records, sometimes only as first names or as "servants" in white households. Over time, emancipations, Revolutionary War service, and economic opportunities allowed the formation of Black neighborhoods, churches, and mutual aid societies, particularly in Salem, Newburyport, and Lawrence.

African American soldiers from Essex served in Civil War regiments, and postwar pension files can be especially rich sources of affidavits, family testimony, and migration stories. Afro-Indigenous individuals, descended from both local tribes and later Native groups moved into the region, may appear under shifting racial labels ("Indian," "mulatto," "colored," "Black") across records, requiring careful, contextual reading.

Women's experiences in industrial Essex varied by class and ethnicity. Yankee farm daughters entered textile mills or shoe factories as "factory girls," leaving traces in company records, reform literature, and occasional diaries. Immigrant women often combined wage labor with boarders, laundry work, and home-based production, their economic activity only partly visible in census "occupation" columns but more apparent in city directories, tax rolls, and mutual aid society memberships. Catholic sodalities, temperance groups, and fraternal organizations recorded female membership lists and event participation, offering additional name-rich sources.

Geography, Communities, and Cultural Landscapes

Essex County's geography shaped its communities in distinct but interconnected ways. The rocky, indented coastline fostered tight fishing and merchant communities where harbors, wharves, and shipyards formed social as well as economic centers. Narrow streets in Salem, Marblehead, and Gloucester grew up around these waterfronts, while inland farms in Topsfield, Boxford, and Middleton centered on greens and common lands where meetinghouses and schools anchored civic life. The Merrimack River corridor, with its falls and canal networks, became a spine of power and transport, linking Lawrence and Haverhill to regional and national markets.

These physical patterns structured ethnic and class geographies. In many towns, older Anglo-Protestant families retained hilltop or established neighborhoods, while newer immigrants settled in lower-lying, industrial districts closer to mills and depots. In Lawrence, for example, different nationalities clustered in wards or streets, often around parish churches—creating "Little Ireland," "French Hill," "the Italian section," and so on. Over time, upwardly mobile families moved outward into newer suburbs like North Andover or into coastal resort communities, a pattern reflected in address changes across censuses and city directories.

Cultural life in Essex County reflected both continuity and change. Puritan and later Congregational traditions remained influential in many towns, even as Unitarianism, Universalism, and other theological currents reshaped New England Protestantism. Catholic and Orthodox parishes, Jewish congregations, and later Pentecostal and evangelical churches created vibrant religious pluralism, each with their own record-keeping practices. Schools, from town grammar schools to academies and, later, public high schools, generated enrollment lists, yearbooks, and alumni records that can help trace adolescent and early adult movements.

Historic preservation efforts, particularly in Salem, Newburyport, and some inland towns, led to the formation of historical societies and museums that collected family papers, business records, photographs, and local histories. These institutions—along with town libraries' local history rooms—often hold unpublished genealogies, clipped obituaries, and house histories tying specific addresses to families across decades. For genealogists, such materials are invaluable for contextualizing names found in vital records within the lived landscape of streets, neighborhoods, and workplaces.

Genealogical Resources and Research Strategies

Essex County's genealogical resources are unusually abundant but dispersed across town, county, religious, and private repositories. At the county level, the Registry of Deeds (in Salem and its satellite offices) maintains land records from the 17th century onward, including early grants, divisions, and later mortgages and sales.

These documents, indexed by grantor and grantee, allow the reconstruction of property lines, inheritance patterns, and neighborhood configurations. The county probate court holds wills, administrations, guardianships, and estate inventories that illuminate material culture, family relationships, and guardianship arrangements for minors and persons deemed incompetent. Many of these records have been indexed and digitized, but original volumes and files can still offer marginal notes and attachments not always visible in copies.

Town clerks maintain vital records—births, marriages, and deaths—often back to the 1600s, though the completeness and format vary. Published "Vital Records of [Town], Massachusetts, to 1850" volumes, produced in the late 19th and early 20th centuries, provide printed transcriptions for many Essex towns, but researchers should still consult the underlying manuscripts for context and corrections. Later records, especially post-1841 statewide registration, are accessible through town offices and state archives according to Massachusetts privacy laws. Town meeting and selectmen's records, sometimes microfilmed, can reveal warnings-out, tax abatements, and support for the poor, naming people who appear only fleetingly elsewhere.

Church and synagogue records are essential complements. Congregational and later Unitarian churches may have deposited older records with denominational archives or historical societies, while Roman Catholic parish registers typically remain with the parishes or diocesan archives. Jewish congregations and other denominations may have their records held locally, with varying levels of accessibility. Because boundaries of parishes and congregations seldom match civil lines, genealogists must identify likely houses of worship based on address, ethnicity, and time period, then seek out those specific institutional records.

Census schedules from 1790 onward track households across decades, with non-population schedules (agricultural, manufacturing, social statistics) adding occupational and economic context in the 19th century. City directories for urbanized towns like Salem, Lawrence, Haverhill, and Newburyport provide annual or biennial snapshots of adult residents, occupations, and addresses, capturing boarders and lodgers not always evident in other records. School records, voter lists, military draft registrations, and naturalization records fill further gaps.

Effective research strategies in Essex County balance breadth and depth. For early colonial lines, start with town vital records and church registers, then integrate proprietors' minutes, early deeds, and probate to map family clusters within and across towns. For 19th- and 20th-century immigrants, work from later civil records and obituaries back through parish registers and naturalizations to overseas origins. Across periods, pay attention to occupational patterns—mariners, shoemakers, factory operatives—using customs records, trade directories, and company archives to follow individuals who moved frequently.

Finally, recognize how race, class, and religion shaped visibility in the records: marginalized groups may require triangulation across multiple partial sources—such as tax rolls, court cases, and institutional records—to reconstruct family histories that the most formal registers only hint at.

Taken together, Essex County's documentary legacy—rooted in Puritan record-keeping, maritime commerce, and industrial bureaucracy—provides family historians with an extraordinarily detailed, if sometimes overwhelming, archive. By reading its town books, court files, and parish registers against the backdrop of harbors, mills, and village greens, researchers can recover the lives of ancestors whose stories trace the broader arc of New England's transformation from Native homeland to colonial frontier, maritime powerhouse, and industrial crossroads.

9

Cities and Towns of Essex County

CITIES

Amesbury

Amesbury, Massachusetts, developed as a compact shipbuilding, milling, and carriage-manufacturing town along the north bank of the Merrimack River in northeastern Essex County, carved from the western side of Salisbury's original plantation where seventeenth-century settlers pushed upland from river marshes onto Powow Hill commons and ferry landings. Laid out around the Powow River falls and the old ferry to Newburyport, Amesbury's early common, King's Highway corridor, and mill privileges drew families from Salisbury, Newbury, and Hampton, while scattered farmsteads spread north toward the New Hampshire line, later linking with Merrimac and Newton, NH.

The town's layered landscape—from Native river landings and early ferries, through grist and saw mills, to nineteenth-century textile and carriage shops—anchors records in both Salisbury and Amesbury volumes and binds "upper Merrimack" kin who followed waterpower and road networks between coastal ports and interior farms.

Powow River Falls, Ferry Greens, and Mill Yards

Before incorporation as a separate town, the area that became Amesbury functioned as Salisbury's "West Parish" and "Upper Falls," with common fields and house lots clustered around the Powow River falls where early grist and saw mills were erected under Salisbury grants. Ferry rights across the Merrimack tied the settlement to Newbury and Newburyport, and families such as Hoyt, Fowler, Weed, and Merrill worked both intervale lots and hillside farms while serving in parish roles. Genealogists trace these roots first through Salisbury town and church records, then follow the transition as Amesbury organized its own precinct, parish registers, and later town books, watching the same families appear under shifting geographic labels but within one continuous community tied to the falls, ferry, and common.

Carriage Shops, Textile Blocks, and Border Villages

By the nineteenth century, Amesbury's economy pivoted from mixed farming and small mills to larger textile works and nationally known carriage and automobile-body shops concentrated along Carriage Hill, Elm Street, and the lower Powow. Boardinghouses, worker cottages, and shop complexes drew Irish, French-Canadian, and other immigrant labor, while outlying districts such as Pond Hill, Lion's Mouth, and the border neighborhoods toward Merrimac and Newton retained more rural, orchard-and-pasture patterns. This industrial growth produced dense federal and state census entries, factory schedules, city directories, and labor-oriented church and fraternal records that capture multi-generational craft and mill families who may leave few land deeds but appear repeatedly in occupational listings, tax lists, and urban ward books.

Genealogical Resources and Strategies

Vital repositories:

Amesbury Town Clerk holds original birth, marriage, and death registrations from the period of town separation forward, while earlier events for the same families often appear in Salisbury's vital and church volumes under "West Parish" or "Upper Falls." Published compilations and printed "Vital Records of Amesbury" volumes carry entries forward through the mid-nineteenth century and index key burial grounds such as Union, Mount Prospect, and pauper/industrial cemeteries.

Local and regional aids:

The Amesbury Public Library's local history room and the Amesbury Carriage Museum preserve manuscripts, photographs, carriage-shop ledgers, and neighborhood maps that help place families in specific mill yards or shop districts; regional historical societies and county registries supply Essex County probate and deed records that tie river-lot and upland farm ownership across the Salisbury–Amesbury divide.

For border families, researchers should also consult neighboring Newburyport, Merrimac, and Newton, New Hampshire records for church memberships, marriages, and land transfers that cross the river and state line.

Amesbury's evolution—from Powow River ferry outpost in Salisbury's back parish to self-contained mill and carriage town—gives genealogists a compact but record-rich setting. Town and parish volumes, industrial and neighborhood collections, and county-level deeds and probate allow reconstruction of "upper Merrimack" kin whose lives followed the falls, ferries, and carriage shops that shaped Amesbury's streets and family networks.

Beverly

Beverly, Massachusetts, emerged as a coastal farming and maritime town on the north shore of Massachusetts Bay in eastern Essex County, carved from the eastern side of Salem's early seventeenth-century plantation where settlers pushed from Salem's harbor across the Bass River onto rocky coves and upland pastures. Anchored by Beverly's original village around Hale Street, Cabot Street, and the harbor, with separate nuclei at Beverly Farms and North Beverly, the town's shoreline coves, fish stages, and later wharves drew fishermen, mariners, and small ship-owners, while interior commons and "farms at the head of the cove" supported mixed agriculture.

This layered landscape—from Native fishing grounds and Salem-era farm grants, through Revolutionary privateering and coastal trade, to nineteenth-century shoe, textile, and resort development—ties Beverly's families into both Salem and independent town records, binding "Cape Ann shore" kin who moved back and forth across the Bass River and along the coast.

Harbor Streets, Parish Greens, and Farms at the Cove

Before and just after separation from Salem, the area that became Beverly functioned as Salem's "Bass River Side," with early meetinghouse, burying ground, and house lots clustered near the harbor while long, narrow farms stretched inland toward what became North Beverly and Wenham lines. Fishermen and coastal traders maintained wharves and fish flakes near Water Street and the cove, while families such as Dodge, Woodberry, Herrick, and Balch worked both upland fields and salt-marsh lots, appearing in Salem town books even when physically living across the river.

Genealogists track these beginnings by following Salem's seventeenth-century town, church, and land records, then watching as Beverly organizes its own parish and town volumes, where many of the same surnames transition from "Bass River" or "farms by the cove" designations into distinct Beverly entries without any actual move.

Shoemakers' Blocks, Mill Ponds, and Shore Resorts

By the nineteenth century, Beverly's economy broadened beyond maritime trade and subsistence farming to include shoe and textile shops, small manufacturing around local mill ponds, and, along the outer coast, the growth of Beverly Farms and Prides Crossing as summer-resort districts. Compact worker neighborhoods developed along Cabot, Rantoul, and surrounding streets, while large estates and hotels rose in the Farms area, drawing Irish and later other immigrant labor alongside long-established Yankee families.

This evolution generated rich federal and state census entries, city directories, tax lists, and occupational records that capture multi-generational shoemakers, mariners, mill workers, and domestic servants, as well as land and architectural histories that place families in specific harbor streets, mill villages, or resort-area cottages across the nineteenth and early twentieth centuries.

Genealogical Resources and Strategies

Vital repositories:

The Beverly City Clerk holds original birth, marriage, and death registrations from the period of town organization forward, while earlier events for Beverly families may appear in Salem's town and church volumes under "Bass River" or similar terms. Published vital-record compilations and cemetery transcripts cover Beverly through the mid-nineteenth century and index key burial grounds such as Central Cemetery, North Beverly, and Beverly Farms, preserving inscriptions that link harbor, farm, and resort families.

Local and regional aids:

The Beverly Public Library's local history collection and the Beverly Historical Society (Historic Beverly) maintain manuscripts, family papers, maps, photographs, and neighborhood studies that help place individuals within particular harbor streets, shoe-shop districts, or farm areas. County-level deeds and probate in Essex County registries trace land along Bass River, inland roads, and shore estates, often tying Beverly lines back into Salem, Danvers, Wenham, Manchester, and Gloucester. Researchers working on Beverly mariners and shipbuilders should also consult regional maritime records, customs documents, and port registers from Salem and nearby harbors, since many Beverly men crewed or owned vessels registered elsewhere.

Beverly's trajectory—from Salem's "Bass River Side" of farms and fish stages to an independent harbor town with shoe shops, mills, and coastal resorts—offers genealogists a compact coastal setting dense with records. Town and parish volumes, maritime and industrial sources, and historical-society collections allow reconstruction of "north shore" kin whose lives followed the harbor, the shoe shops, and the resort shorelines that shaped Beverly's neighborhoods and family networks.

Gloucester

Gloucester, Massachusetts, developed as one of New England's earliest and most important fishing ports on the outer edge of Cape Ann in northeastern Essex County, carved from the original Cape Ann settlement that predated nearby Salem. Perched on a rocky peninsula exposed to the Atlantic, Gloucester's coves—such as the Inner Harbor, Rocky Neck, and the Annisquam—anchored stages, flakes, and wharves for cod fishing and coastal trade, while scattered farms and commons stretched inland toward West Gloucester, Riverdale, and the Essex and Manchester lines. From Native fishing grounds and early seventeenth-century English attempts at a fishing station, through Puritan town formation and the rise of a full-scale schooner fleet, to nineteenth-century granite quarrying and immigrant-driven industrial fishing, Gloucester's geography tied families to the sea and spread its records across parish, maritime, and civil sources.

Harbor Precincts, Parish Greens, and Farm Lanes

In its early centuries, Gloucester's core developed around the Inner Harbor and Town Green, where the first meetinghouse, cemetery, and clustered house lots served as the civic and religious center, while outer districts such as Annisquam, Lanesville, and Riverdale functioned as separate neighborhoods tied by cart paths and coastal boat traffic. Fishermen, smallholders, and craftsmen combined inshore and offshore fishing with subsistence plots and salt-marsh hay, and long-established surnames appear both in harbor records and in outlying farm lanes. Genealogists working with this period must follow families through town meeting minutes, early church registers, and land divisions that sometimes describe property by coves, ledges, and inlets rather than modern street names, watching as the same kin group can seem to "move" simply because a new parish is organized or a distant cove gains its own chapel and burying ground.

Schooner Fleets, Quarries, and Immigrant Wards

By the nineteenth century, Gloucester had become synonymous with the North Atlantic fishing and schooner trade, with fleets sailing to the Grand Banks and beyond, supported by sail lofts, net makers, cooperages, and fish plants clustered along the harbor. At the same time, granite quarrying in areas like Lanesville and Bay View, as well as shore-based fish processing, drew waves of immigrants—particularly from Atlantic Canada, Scandinavia, and Southern and Eastern Europe—who formed distinct ethnic parishes and neighborhoods while joining long-established Cape Ann lines.

This phase generated dense federal and state census records, detailed crew lists and vessel enrollments, city directories, and ethnic parish registers, all of which let genealogists trace multi-generational mariner, quarry, and factory families, as well as widows and children recorded in relief funds, seamen's benevolent society documents, and newspaper coverage of wrecks and rescues.

Genealogical Resources and Strategies

Vital repositories:

The Gloucester City Clerk maintains town and city vital records—births, marriages, and deaths—from the colonial period forward, with earlier entries also found in published "Vital

Records of Gloucester" volumes that extend through the mid-nineteenth century and index major cemeteries and family plots. Church registers from the First Parish and later congregations, including Methodist, Catholic, and various ethnic churches, preserve baptisms, marriages, and burials for both harbor and outlying districts, often distinguishing Inner Harbor, Annisquam, Lanesville, and other neighborhoods.

Local and regional aids:

The Cape Ann Museum and local historical organizations hold rich manuscript collections, family papers, photographs, maps, ship portraits, and fishermen's and quarry-workers' records that can place ancestors on specific streets, vessels, or quarry gangs. Maritime sources—such as customs records, crew lists, vessel enrollments, and insurance or seamen's protection documents—are crucial for tracing Gloucester men who spent most of their lives at sea and may appear infrequently in inland land records.

County-level deeds and probate in Essex County help follow property in both rocky harbor lots and inland farms, connecting Gloucester families to nearby Essex, Rockport (later set off from Gloucester), Manchester, and other Cape Ann communities.

Gloucester's evolution—from early Cape Ann fishing outpost and scattered farm clearings to a renowned fishing port and quarry town knit from multiple coves and villages—gives genealogists a rugged coastal setting rich in records. Town, parish, maritime, and museum collections together allow reconstruction of "Cape Ann" kin whose lives were shaped by schooner decks, granite ledges, and harbor streets that defined Gloucester's history and family networks.

Haverhill

Haverhill, Massachusetts, grew from a seventeenth-century Merrimack River planting town into a major nineteenth-century shoe-manufacturing and mill center in northwestern Essex County, stretching along both banks of the Merrimack with later neighborhoods extending into what became Methuen, Bradford, and the New Hampshire line. The original settlement clustered near today's Haverhill center on the north bank, where riverfront house lots, commons, and outlying farms were laid out from early land grants, while successive bridges and ferries tied the town to Bradford and to upriver and downriver trade. Over time, Haverhill's landscape—river intervals, hill farms, and a dense mill-and-factory downtown—wove together farming, small craft, and industrial labor, embedding "upper Merrimack" families in a web of both rural and urban records.

River Greens, Meetinghouse Streets, and Outlying Farms

In its early period, Haverhill's life focused on the first meetinghouse, burying ground, and town common near the Merrimack, with long, narrow farm lots running back from the river into what became rural districts such as Rocks Village, Ayers Village, and East Parish. Families combined subsistence agriculture and timber with river transport and small trading ventures, and they appear in town meeting records, early vital entries, and church rolls under a mix of "north of the river" and parish designations as new church precincts were carved out. Genealogists working in this phase need to track the same surnames as they shift between central Haverhill and these outlying agricultural neighborhoods, noting how the formation of new parishes or the later setting off of Bradford and Methuen changes jurisdiction without necessarily implying a physical move.

Shops, Mills, and Immigrant Wards

By the nineteenth century, Haverhill had transformed into a bustling shoe-manufacturing hub and mill town, with factories and shops concentrated along Washington, Merrimack, and nearby streets and along Little River and other water sources. Rows of tenements and worker housing filled in around the industrial core, while outlying parts of Haverhill and the Bradford side retained more of their farm and village character, gradually absorbing rail lines and streetcar routes. This industrial boom attracted Irish, French-Canadian, Italian, and other immigrant communities, who founded their own parishes, societies, and neighborhood institutions. As a result, Haverhill's record set for this era includes rich federal and state census returns, city directories, tax lists, school records, and a patchwork of ethnic parish registers and fraternal-organization rosters that capture multi-generational factory, shop, and railroad families, along with craftsmen and long-rooted Yankee lines adapting to an urbanizing town.

Genealogical Resources and Strategies

Vital repositories:

The Haverhill City Clerk preserves birth, marriage, and death records from the town and city periods, while earlier events appear in town books and published vital-record compilations that extend through the mid-nineteenth century and index core cemeteries, including Linwood, Hilldale, and older burying grounds. Because of shifting boundaries and the presence of Bradford (later annexed) and the close New Hampshire border, researchers must also be alert for events recorded in neighboring Methuen, Lawrence, Andover, and across the river in what became Plaistow and Atkinson, New Hampshire.

Local and regional aids:

The Haverhill Public Library's special collections and local historical organizations hold manuscripts, family papers, photographs, maps, and industrial histories that place families in particular shoe districts, mill neighborhoods, and rural villages. County-level deeds and probate at the Essex registries trace land along the Merrimack, in village centers, and on outlying farms, frequently linking Haverhill residents with neighboring Essex County towns and New Hampshire communities. For shoemakers, mill workers, and immigrants, city directories, labor reports, church anniversary booklets, and neighborhood histories are especially valuable for tracking moves between wards, documenting ethnic congregations, and reconstructing kin networks around particular factories or blocks.

Haverhill's evolution—from a riverside farming and trading town to a major shoe and mill city encompassing rural villages and dense immigrant wards—offers genealogists a varied but document-rich setting. Town and parish volumes, industrial and neighborhood records, and regional land and probate files together make it possible to reconstruct "upper Merrimack" kin whose lives crossed from river greens and hill farms to factory floors and city streets within a few generations.

Lawrence

Lawrence, Massachusetts, rose in the mid-nineteenth century as a planned industrial city on the Merrimack River in northeastern Essex County, carved out of parts of Andover and Methuen to harness the river's power for large-scale textile production. Designed around great stone mills and an engineered canal system on both the north and south banks, Lawrence's grid of boarding-houses, tenements, and commercial blocks rapidly replaced earlier farm and village landscapes, drawing in workers from surrounding New England towns as well as waves of immigrants from Ireland, French Canada, southern and eastern Europe, and later Latin America. From its inception, the city's physical and social fabric—mill complexes, canal streets, ethnic parishes, and closely packed wards—embedded families in records that reflect both corporate oversight and intense neighborhood life.

Canals, Mill Yards, and Parish Squares

In its formative decades, Lawrence's core developed around the Great Stone Dam, the North and South Canals, and immense textile mills operated by corporations such as the Essex Company and the various "Lawrence" mills. Housing and services clustered in walking distance of the mill gates: brick boardinghouses for single operatives, rows of small workers' houses, and emerging commercial streets along Essex, Common, and Broadway. Ethnic and religious communities quickly organized their own parishes and institutions—Catholic, Protestant, and later Orthodox—anchoring neighborhoods around church steeples, parish halls, and associated schools. For genealogists, this means that early residents often appear first in corporate or city directories and in parish registers rather than in extensive land records, and that the same family may be traceable ward-by-ward as they shift among mill-adjacent streets, boardinghouses, and eventually owner-occupied homes on the fringes.

Strikes, Ward Shifts, and Immigrant Districts

By the late nineteenth and early twentieth centuries, Lawrence was a quintessential mill city, known nationally for its vast textile output and for pivotal labor struggles such as the 1912 "Bread and Roses" strike, which involved multi-ethnic worker coalitions and brought outside attention to local conditions. Successive waves of immigrants—Irish and French Canadians followed by Italians, Poles, Syrians, Armenians, and others—created distinct but overlapping districts, each with its own churches, mutual-aid societies, and businesses, while some earlier Yankee and Irish families moved into more suburban sections or neighboring towns.

This industrial and social complexity produced dense federal and state census schedules, detailed city directories, ward maps, school and employment records, and a rich layer of union, strike, and charity documents that capture multi-generational mill, shop, and small-business families and provide context for kin who may leave few traditional property records but appear repeatedly in occupational and institutional sources.

Genealogical Resources and Strategies

Vital repositories:

The Lawrence City Clerk maintains birth, marriage, and death registrations from the city's incorporation forward, with earlier events for local families often recorded in Andover or Methuen books before Lawrence was set off. Published vital-record volumes and cemetery transcriptions, including those for Immaculate Conception, St. Mary's, and other large burial grounds, help connect immigrant and native-born families across multiple parishes and neighborhoods.

Local and regional aids:

The Lawrence Public Library and local historical organizations preserve manuscripts, photographs, mill company reports, maps, and neighborhood studies that situate families in specific wards, streets, and mill complexes. County-level deeds and probate at the Essex registries document the gradual acquisition of property by workers and merchants, especially in later generations who moved into fringe districts or nearby suburbs. For many lines, city directories, parish anniversary books, school records, union and strike materials, and social-service case files are crucial for tracing moves between boardinghouses and streets, identifying ethnic congregations, and reconstructing extended kin networks clustered around particular mills, parishes, or blocks.

Lawrence's trajectory—from engineered industrial experiment on former Andover and Methuen lands to a dense, multi-ethnic mill city with powerful labor history—offers genealogists an urban setting packed with records. Municipal, parish, corporate, and community collections together make it possible to follow "Merrimack mill" families whose stories are written not only in deeds and wills, but in boardinghouse registers, factory rosters, baptismal ledgers, and the shifting ward maps that framed everyday life in Lawrence.

Lynn

Lynn, Massachusetts, evolved from a seventeenth-century coastal farming and tanning community into a major nineteenth- and twentieth-century shoe-manufacturing and industrial city on the North Shore of Essex County. Early settlement spread from the original village near the Common and Market Street out along the coastal road toward what became Swampscott and Nahant, and inland toward Lynnfield's fields and ponds, with marshes, pastures, and small mills serving both local needs and Boston markets. Over time, Lynn's shoreline coves, tannery yards, and later shoe-shop blocks, electric-rail lines, and General Electric plants layered agriculture, craft, and heavy industry into a tightly knit urban landscape, tying "Lynn yeomen" and later factory families into records that span rural town books, parish rolls, and dense city directories.

Commons, Parish Greens, and Outlying Farms

In its colonial and early national period, Lynn's life centered around the Common, the early meetinghouse, and the burying ground, with house lots and farmsteads stretching along Boston Street, Essex Street, and outlying lanes toward Lynnfield and Saugus. Tanners, farmers, and fishermen combined subsistence plots and marsh hay with small-scale leather work and coastal trade, and families appear in town meeting minutes, early vital records, and church membership lists under a mix of "Lynn," "Rumney Marsh," and district descriptions as neighboring areas were set off into separate towns. Genealogists working in this era follow the same surnames as they move between the central village, the Lynnfield and Saugus borders, and the shore districts that later became Swampscott and Nahant, recognizing that parish changes and new town formations often shift record jurisdictions without implying a long-distance move.

Shoe-Shop Blocks, Streetcar Suburbs, and Industrial Plants

By the nineteenth century, Lynn was widely known as a shoe-making center, with large factories and smaller contract shops concentrated along Market, Union, Broad, and nearby streets, surrounded by dense worker housing and commercial blocks. Streetcar lines pushed residential growth into West Lynn, Wyoma, and other neighborhoods, blending older farmsteads with rows of triple-deckers and suburban streets. In the late nineteenth and early twentieth centuries, the arrival and expansion of electrical and other heavy industry—most notably the General Electric plant—added another layer of employment, drawing Irish, Canadian, Italian, Eastern European, and other immigrant communities who formed their own parishes and neighborhood institutions. This industrial and transit-driven development generated rich federal and state census schedules, city directories, tax lists, factory and union records, and ethnic parish registers, all of which let genealogists track multi-generational shoemaker, mill, and plant families, as well as earlier Yankee lines adapting to an increasingly urban and industrial Lynn.

Genealogical Resources and Strategies

Vital repositories:

The Lynn City Clerk maintains birth, marriage, and death registrations from the town and city periods, while earlier events are preserved in original town books and in published vital-record compilations that extend through the mid-nineteenth century and include entries for what later became Swampscott, Nahant, and parts of Lynnfield and Saugus before separation. Cemetery records for Pine Grove and older burying grounds, along with printed inscriptions, help connect central-city and outlying families and document immigrant as well as long-established lines.

Local and regional aids:

Lynn's public library and local historical organizations hold manuscripts, family papers, photographs, fire and ward maps, and shoe-industry and General Electric plant histories that place individuals on specific streets, in particular shoe blocks, or within industrial complexes. County-level deeds and probate in Essex County trace property in the original village, along the coastal road, and in evolving suburban neighborhoods, often linking Lynn residents to nearby Saugus, Lynnfield, Salem, Swampscott, and Nahant. For many twentieth-century lines, city directories, school records, parish anniversary booklets, labor and company publications, and neighborhood histories are crucial for reconstructing kin networks centered on shoe factories, car-barns, or the GE plant and for following moves between crowded downtown wards and streetcar suburbs.

Lynn's trajectory—from coastal farms and tanneries around a common to a dense shoe and electrical-industry city threaded by rail and streetcar lines—gives genealogists a North Shore setting rich in both rural and urban records. Town and parish volumes, industrial and neighborhood collections, and regional land and probate files together make it possible to recover "Lynn" kin whose lives were shaped by commons and marshes, shoe blocks and factory yards, and the shifting ward maps that defined Lynn's growth.

Methuen

Methuen, Massachusetts, developed as a Merrimack River border town in northwestern Essex County, created in the early eighteenth century out of lands that had previously been part of Haverhill and adjacent frontier grants along the New Hampshire line. Its landscape combined riverfront intervals and ferry points with interior hill farms, mill sites on the Spicket River, and later streetcar-linked neighborhoods that grew in tandem with the mill city of Lawrence across the river. From its earliest years, Methuen's geography and politics—especially shifting colonial and state boundaries and the later rise of Lawrence—tied families into records spread among

Haverhill, Andover, New Hampshire towns, and Methuen's own evolving civic structure, giving genealogists a mix of rural and semi-urban sources.

River Ferries, Spicket Mills, and Hill Farms

In the colonial era, Methuen's life centered on its first meetinghouse and common, with farmsteads laid out along River Road, Pleasant Valley, and the uplands toward modern Dracut and Salem, New Hampshire. The Spicket River provided power for early grist and saw mills, and scattered villages grew up at crossings and mill sites, while ferries and, later, bridges connected Methuen residents to Haverhill and to what would become Lawrence. Families appear in early town and church records as well as in Haverhill and Andover volumes, reflecting the period when parish and town lines were still being adjusted and when some residents worshipped or registered vital events in neighboring communities. Genealogists must therefore track the same surnames across multiple jurisdictions and pay close attention to descriptive phrases such as "north of the Merrimack," "Spicket," or "in the east parish" that signal specific Methuen neighborhoods before modern place-names were fixed.

Mill Villages, Streetcar Corridors, and Border Neighborhoods

During the nineteenth century, Methuen felt the pull of industrialization without becoming a full-scale mill city. Textile and other factories along the Spicket and near the river created mill villages and worker housing clusters, particularly in what is now downtown Methuen, while large estates and planned neighborhoods developed along Broadway and other main roads. At the same time, Lawrence's explosive growth just downstream meant that many Methuen residents worked in Lawrence mills or businesses while living on the Methuen side of the line, and some formerly Methuen neighborhoods eventually shifted into Lawrence's orbit through annexations and changing urban patterns. This produced federal and state census returns showing households with close ties to both municipalities, city directories listing workers with Lawrence employers and Methuen addresses, and parish registers where families might baptize children in Lawrence churches but record marriages or burials in Methuen or across the border in New Hampshire.

Genealogical Resources and Strategies

Vital repositories:

The Methuen City (or Town) Clerk holds local birth, marriage, and death records from the time of the town's organization forward, while earlier events for Methuen families may be found in Haverhill, Andover, or nearby New Hampshire towns due to boundary changes and parish preferences. Published or indexed vital-record compilations, along with cemetery records for Elmwood and smaller burying grounds, help tie together riverfront, mill-village, and hill-farm families and reveal kin who used multiple spellings or alternating residence descriptions along the state line.

Local and regional aids:

Methuen's public library and local historical organizations preserve manuscripts, photographs, maps, family papers, and mill or estate histories that place ancestors in specific Spicket River villages, farm districts, and border neighborhoods. Because Methuen sits at the junction of Essex County and several Rockingham County, New Hampshire towns, researchers should also consult county-level deeds and probate on both sides of the line, following land along the Merrimack and Spicket as well as on upland roads that continue into Salem, Pelham, and other New Hampshire communities. City directories, school records, parish anniversary booklets, and regional histories are especially useful for tracing families who moved back and forth between Methuen and Lawrence or who shifted from farming to mill or shop work while keeping long-standing ties to particular roads or corners.

Methuen's evolution—from river-and-frontier parish of Haverhill to its own town of farms, mills, and border neighborhoods closely intertwined with Lawrence and New Hampshire—offers genealogists a compact but complex research setting. Town and parish volumes, cross-border land and probate records, and local historical collections together make it possible to reconstruct "Merrimack–Spicket" kin whose lives bridged rural fields, mill villages, and the shifting state and municipal boundaries that shaped Methuen's history.

Newburyport

Newburyport, Massachusetts, developed as a bustling maritime and mercantile port on the south bank of the Merrimack River at its mouth in northeastern Essex County, originally forming the "waterfront town" and upper harbor district of Newbury before its separate incorporation in the mid-eighteenth century. Its compact street grid climbed from the riverfront wharves and shipyards up through market squares and residential hills, while outlying neighborhoods stretched along High Street ridges and across to what became the industrial and rail districts at the city's edges. From the start, Newburyport's identity revolved around shipbuilding, coastal and overseas trade, privateering, and later small industry, and its records capture generations of mariners, merchants, artisans, and shore-based workers tied to both river commerce and Atlantic routes.

Wharves, Meetinghouse Greens, and High Street Ridges

In the colonial and early national period, Newburyport's core centered on the harbor, Market Square, and nearby meetinghouse precincts, with dense blocks of warehouses, counting-houses, ropewalks, and shipyards lining the waterfront. House lots extended uphill along streets like State and High, where merchants and ship captains built substantial homes overlooking the river, while craftsmen and laborers occupied smaller dwellings tucked into side streets and lanes. Genealogically, families of this era appear in both Newbury and Newburyport records, since the port began as Newbury's "upper town"; baptisms, marriages, and burials may be found in First Parish and later church registers on either side of the municipal divide, and early land descriptions frequently reference wharves, docks, and "river lots" rather than modern addresses. Researchers need to follow the same surnames through Newbury's town books into Newburyport's separate volumes, noting when a change in place-name reflects civic reorganization rather than an actual move.

Shipyards, Mills, and Rail-Linked Neighborhoods

By the nineteenth century, Newburyport had passed through boom periods of shipbuilding, privateering, and coastal trade, weathered fires and economic setbacks, and diversified into smaller mills, factories, and rail-connected commerce while still maintaining its maritime character. Working-class neighborhoods expanded inland and along the rail lines, and immigrant groups—including Irish and later other European communities—settled near industrial sites and along the lower streets, forming their own parishes and social organizations alongside older

Congregational and other Protestant congregations. This era produced detailed federal and state census schedules, city directories, tax lists, and a variety of church and fraternal records that document multi-generational mariner, dock, mill, and shop families, as well as merchant and professional lines who may leave a deeper paper trail in probate, business, and land records tied to riverfront warehouses and High Street residences.

Genealogical Resources and Strategies

Vital repositories:

The Newburyport City Clerk maintains birth, marriage, and death registrations from the period of town and city organization, while earlier vital events for Newburyport families may appear in Newbury's town and parish records, reflecting the years before full separation. Published vital-record volumes and cemetery transcriptions—including those for Oak Hill, Belleville, Highland, and older burying grounds—help connect riverfront, hill, and outlying families and often identify mariners lost at sea or buried elsewhere but memorialized at home.

Local and regional aids:

Newburyport's public library and local historical organizations preserve manuscripts, family papers, ship logs, customs and port records, maps, photographs, and neighborhood studies that place individuals on specific wharves, vessels, and streets. Maritime sources—such as crew lists, customs house entries, vessel enrollments, and insurance or seamen's protection documents—are particularly important for tracing sea-going ancestors who spent much of their lives away from land records. County-level deeds and probate in Essex County registries track ownership of harbor lots, High Street houses, and inland parcels, often tying Newburyport residents to neighboring Newbury, West Newbury, Salisbury, and Amesbury.

Newburyport's trajectory—from Newbury's harbor district to an independent seaport and later mixed maritime-industrial city—offers genealogists a compact coastal setting dense with records. Town and parish volumes, maritime and business archives, and regional land and probate files together allow reconstruction of "Merrimack River mouth" kin whose lives were shaped by wharves and warehouses, ship decks and mill floors, and the steep streets that climb from Newburyport's waterfront into its residential hills.

TOWNS

Andover

Andover, Massachusetts, developed as an inland agricultural and parish town along the Shawsheen River and its tributaries in central Essex County, carved out in the mid-seventeenth century from upland grants associated with the broader Merrimack River plantation. Its early settlement clustered around meetinghouse greens in what became North and South (later Andover and North Andover), with common fields, long farm lots, and scattered mills stretched along river meadows and upland roads leading toward Reading, Wilmington, and Haverhill. Over time, Andover's blend of commons, village streets, mill sites, and later academy and factory districts tied generations of "Shawsheen" families into records that straddle both agricultural and proto-industrial New England.

Meetinghouse Hills, Shawsheen Meadows, and Split Parishes

In the colonial era, Andover's civic and religious life focused on the original meetinghouse and burying ground, with house lots on nearby hills and farms laid out along the Shawsheen and its branches. As population grew, the town divided into North and South precincts, each with its own church and green, foreshadowing the later municipal separation between Andover and North Andover. Families combined mixed farming with small-scale milling and craft work, appearing in town meeting minutes, early vital records, church registers, and land divisions that often describe properties by brooks, hills, and "old roads to Salem or Haverhill" rather than modern street names. Genealogists must follow the same surnames through these shifting parish boundaries, noting how "North Parish," "South Parish," or "Second Church" designations signal specific neighborhoods and anticipating that some lines later filed records under North Andover once the towns formally split.

Academy Greens, Mill Villages, and Railroad Streets

By the nineteenth century, Andover's economy diversified around several anchors: the Phillips Academy and theological institutions on the hill; textile and other mills along the Shawsheen and in Ballardvale and Frye Village; and commercial blocks around the depot area once the railroad arrived. Boardinghouses, worker cottages, and small factory villages grew up around the mills, while long-established farm families persisted on outlying roads and newer middle-class residences filled in near the academy and town center. This evolution produced detailed federal and state census schedules, town valuation lists, city-style directories, and school and institutional records that document multi-generational farmers, mill operatives, shopkeepers, and faculty households, as well as Irish and later other immigrant groups who formed their own parishes and neighborhood networks while remaining interwoven with older Andover lines.

Genealogical Resources and Strategies

Vital repositories:

The Andover Town Clerk maintains birth, marriage, and death registrations from the town's early period through the present, while parallel records for families in what became North Andover must be checked in that town's volumes as well as in older, undivided Andover books. Published vital-record compilations and cemetery transcriptions—covering South Parish burying grounds, academy-area cemeteries, and outlying graveyards—help link Shawsheen-valley farm, mill-village, and academy families across the parish and later municipal line.

Local and regional aids:

Andover's public library and historical society hold manuscripts, family papers, maps, photographs, academy records, and mill and village histories that place individuals in specific neighborhoods such as Ballardvale, Frye Village, and the hill districts around Phillips Academy. County-level deeds and probate in Essex County trace land along the Shawsheen, in the village centers, and on outlying roads, frequently connecting Andover residents with neighboring North Andover, Lawrence, Methuen, Tewksbury, and Wilmington. For many nineteenth- and twentieth-century lines, academy catalogs, school registers, church anniversary booklets, and local industrial and village histories are especially valuable for reconstructing kin networks centered on particular parishes, mills, or educational institutions.

Andover's trajectory—from a Shawsheen-side farming and parish town with split precincts to a community knit from farms, mills, and academy neighborhoods—offers genealogists a varied but well-documented landscape. Town and parish volumes, institutional and village records, and county land and probate files together allow reconstruction of Andover kin whose lives ran from meadow farms and meetinghouse hills to mill yards and academy greens within just a few generations.

Boxford

Boxford, Massachusetts, developed as a small inland farming community in central Essex County, formed in the seventeenth century from upland portions of Rowley and Andover where settlers spread away from the coastal plantations into wooded hills and pond-dotted terrain. Its landscape centered on scattered village greens at East and West Boxford, with common fields, woodlots, and pasturelands extending along narrow roads toward Topsfield, Middleton, Georgetown, and North Andover. From the start, Boxford's relative isolation, small population, and focus on mixed agriculture and woodland resources meant that its families appear more in town, church, and county land records than in dense industrial or maritime sources, giving genealogists a distinctly rural evidentiary trail.

Village Greens, Parish Lines, and Hill Farms

In the colonial period, Boxford's life revolved around its meetinghouse sites and small village centers, where a burying ground, school, and a handful of houses clustered near the green, while most residents lived on outlying farmsteads connected by cart paths and bridle roads. The town's creation from parts of Rowley and Andover, and later internal parish adjustments between East and West Boxford, mean that early families can surface under several geographic labels in church and civil records before "Boxford" becomes consistent. Genealogists must follow households through Rowley and Andover town books into Boxford's own records, paying attention to descriptions referencing specific ponds, hills, and roads that identify neighborhoods long before modern street names and house numbers appear.

Ponds, Woodlots, and Modest Industry

Through the nineteenth century, Boxford retained its predominant agricultural character, with modest local industry—saw and grist mills, small shops, and later limited shoe or cottage-industry work—serving nearby markets rather than creating large factory villages. Farm families raised mixed crops and livestock, cut timber, and sometimes took seasonal work in neighboring mill towns, while the town's ponds and woodlands gradually drew a small number of summer residents and recreational visitors. This pattern generated federal and state census entries that show Boxford as a community of largely farm and labor households, supplemented by town valuation lists, school records, and church rolls, while heavier industrial and urban documentation is more likely to appear in records of surrounding towns where Boxford residents worked or married.

Genealogical Resources and Strategies

Vital repositories:

Boxford's town clerk holds birth, marriage, and death registrations from the period of the town's organization onward, while some earlier events for local families may be found in Rowley and Andover volumes from before Boxford's full separation. Published or indexed vital-record compilations and cemetery transcriptions for Boxford's burying grounds help link East and West Boxford branches and document long-rooted farming families as well as those who later moved into neighboring towns.

Local and regional aids:

Local church records, town meeting minutes, tax lists, and school registers are central for placing Boxford families on specific roads and in parish districts, since there are no large mill or port collections for the town itself. County-level deeds and probate in Essex County trace the transfer of farms, woodlots, and house sites, frequently connecting Boxford residents with Rowley, Topsfield, Middleton, North Andover, Georgetown, and other surrounding communities where they bought land, married, or eventually settled. For many lines, town histories, family genealogies, and regional studies of agrarian life provide additional context, helping genealogists reconstruct "Boxford hill" kin whose lives were shaped by small greens, farm lanes, and pond-side clearings rather than by factories or wharves.

Danvers

Danvers, Massachusetts, evolved from a seventeenth-century farming parish of Salem into a distinct inland town in east-central Essex County, stretching from tidal lands along the Crane River and Porter River north and west across upland fields and village centers toward Middleton, Peabody, and Topsfield. Originally known as Salem Village and other outlying designations under Salem's jurisdiction, the area held scattered homesteads, commons, and small mills that supplied both local needs and the larger Salem market. Over time, Danvers's blend of village streets, farm lanes, and later shoe and small-factory districts created a record set that ties "Salem Village" families into both Salem and independent Danvers sources.

Salem Village Greens, Parish Divides, and Farm Lanes

In the colonial era, what is now Danvers was organized as Salem Village and related precincts, with meetinghouse and burying-ground sites anchoring a community distinct from Salem Town's harbor district even before full municipal separation. Farmsteads lined roads such as what became Maple, Centre, and Locust Streets, and residents combined mixed agriculture with occasional trade and craft work linked to Salem. Genealogists working in this period must track families through Salem's town and church records—often under "Salem Village," "the Farms," or parish labels—until Danvers's own town and vital books begin, paying close attention to neighborhood descriptors that distinguish inland households from harbor-side Salem Town lines.

Shoe Shops, Nurseries, and Streetcar Neighborhoods

By the nineteenth century, Danvers had shifted from purely agrarian parish to a town with notable shoe and leather shops, brick yards, and other small industries, especially near its village centers and along emerging transport routes. At the same time, extensive market gardening and nursery operations, including nationally known horticultural enterprises, developed on its good soils, while streetcar and later rail connections tied Danvers residents more closely to Salem, Peabody, and Boston. These changes produced richer federal and state census returns, town valuation lists, business directories, and school and church records that document multi-generational farmers, shoemakers, nursery workers, and small-factory families, as well as incoming immigrant groups who formed their own parishes while remaining interwoven with older Danvers kin.

Genealogical Resources and Strategies

Vital repositories:

Danvers's town clerk holds birth, marriage, and death registrations from the town's organization forward, while earlier events for local families appear in Salem's town and parish volumes under the various "Village" and out-parish designations. Published vital-record compilations and cemetery transcriptions that cover both Salem and Danvers burying grounds are essential for reconstructing lines that straddle the period of separation and for linking Salem Village-era families with later Danvers descendants.

Local and regional aids:

Local church registers, town meeting minutes, tax lists, and school records place Danvers families within specific village neighborhoods and along key roads, while historical-society collections and town histories provide maps, photographs, and family manuscripts that help identify farm, nursery, and shop sites. County-level deeds and probate in Essex County connect Danvers residents with neighboring Salem, Peabody (formerly part of Danvers/Salem), Middleton, and Topsfield, tracing land from early farm grants through later village-lot subdivisions. Together, these sources allow genealogists to follow "Salem Village/Danvers" kin from seventeenth-century farm lanes and parish greens through the rise of shoe shops, nurseries, and commuter streets that reshaped Danvers across the nineteenth and early twentieth centuries.

Essex

Essex, Massachusetts, developed as a small shipbuilding and fishing town on the tidal Essex River in northeastern Essex County, set off from the inland farming town of Ipswich in the early nineteenth century after long functioning as its "Chebacco" parish and maritime outpost. Its landscape centers on the winding river and adjacent marshes, where early landings, wharves, and shipyards grew up along Main Street and nearby coves, while upland farms, pastures, and woodlots spread inland toward Hamilton, Manchester, and Gloucester. From the beginning, Essex families balanced salt-marsh haying, inshore fishing, and coastal trade with agriculture, and the town's records capture generations of builders, mariners, and farmers rooted in this compact river-marsh environment.

Chebacco Parish, River Landings, and Upland Farms

In the colonial era, the area that became Essex was known as Chebacco, a parish of Ipswich whose meetinghouse, burying ground, and modest village center stood near the river while most residents lived on scattered farmsteads along lanes reaching back from the marshes. House lots and fields were laid out to give access to salt marsh and to small landings on the Essex River, and families appear in Ipswich town and church records under Chebacco or parish labels long before Essex existed as a separate municipality. Genealogists must therefore follow "Chebacco" households in Ipswich's early vital, town, and land books, then into Essex's own records after incorporation, watching how the same surnames—often involved with fishing, small craft, and marshland management—shift in wording but not necessarily in residence.

Shipyards, Marsh Hay, and Village Streets

By the nineteenth century, Essex had become known for its wooden vessel construction, with a series of family-run shipyards along the river turning out fishing and coastal craft that served ports around New England. The shipyards, riverfront shops, and related trades formed a dense working village along Main Street and nearby roads, while inland districts retained their mix of farms, orchards, and woodlots, supplying both local needs and materials for boatbuilding. This pattern produced federal and state census returns, town valuation lists, maritime-related records, and local business directories that document multi-generational shipbuilding, fishing, and farming families, as well as a more modest influx of workers tied to the yards and associated trades.

Genealogical Resources and Strategies

Vital repositories:

Essex's town clerk maintains birth, marriage, and death registrations from the time of the town's separation from Ipswich forward, while earlier events for local families appear in Ipswich's vital and church volumes under Chebacco or parish designations. Cemetery records for the old burying ground and later cemeteries, along with published or indexed inscriptions, help connect river-village and inland families and often identify mariners lost at sea but memorialized at home.

Local and regional aids:

Church registers, town meeting minutes, tax lists, and school records place Essex families in specific river-front neighborhoods and rural districts, while local historical collections and town histories provide maps, photographs, shipyard lists, and family papers that tie individuals to particular yards and vessels. County-level deeds and probate in Essex County trace the transfer of marsh lots, riverfront landings, and farm properties, frequently linking Essex residents with neighboring Ipswich, Hamilton, Manchester, and Gloucester as kin married, bought land, or shifted their base of operations. Taken together, these sources allow genealogists to reconstruct "Chebacco/Essex" kin whose lives were shaped by the tidal river, salt marshes, and shipyard streets that defined the town's history.

Georgetown

Georgetown, Massachusetts, developed as a small inland farming and mill town in north-central Essex County, set off in the early nineteenth century from the western portion of Rowley where families had long occupied upland farms and village sites away from the coastal plantation. Centered on a compact village around the meetinghouse, common, and later central square, with outlying neighborhoods reaching toward Boxford, Groveland (South Rowley), and Newbury, Georgetown's landscape combined rocky upland fields, pond and brook-side mill sites, and later modest shoe and small-factory districts. Its records reflect a community whose people shifted gradually from purely agrarian pursuits to a mix of farming, shop work, and small industry while remaining tied to the older Rowley and Merrimack Valley networks.

Meetinghouse Common, Rowley Roots, and Farm Lanes

In the colonial period, the territory that became Georgetown functioned as part of Rowley's inland "West Parish" or "Rowley West," with early meetinghouse and burying-ground sites anchoring a village center surrounded by scattered farmsteads along roads such as what became North,

Andover, and West Main Streets. Residents raised mixed crops and livestock, cut timber, and sometimes engaged in small-scale milling or craft work on local brooks and ponds, yet their vital events and town business were recorded in Rowley's books under parish or district labels rather than a separate town name. For genealogists, this means that eighteenth-century Georgetown families must be traced first in Rowley town, church, and land records, watching for "West Parish" or similar descriptors, and then followed into Georgetown's own town and vital volumes after incorporation, when the same surnames continue with a new municipal heading but largely on the same farms and lanes.

Ponds, Mills, and Modest Industry

Through the nineteenth century, Georgetown's economy remained largely rural but saw the growth of pond- and stream-powered mills, small shoe shops, and other light industry near its village center and along waterways such as Pentucket Pond outlets and the Little River. Worker housing and small commercial blocks filled in around the common and along the main roads, while outlying districts retained their farm and woodland character, supplying both local needs and raw materials. This pattern produced federal and state census returns, town valuation lists, and occasional industrial schedules showing a community of farmers, shoemakers, mill operatives, and tradespeople, with some residents commuting or relocating to larger mill and shoe centers in neighboring towns while maintaining family and property ties in Georgetown.

Genealogical Resources and Strategies

Vital and local records:

Georgetown's town clerk holds birth, marriage, and death registrations from the town's organization forward, while earlier events for local families appear in Rowley's vital and church records under "West Parish" or equivalent designations. Cemetery records for Georgetown's burying grounds, along with published or indexed inscriptions, help connect village and rural families and document lines that later moved into other Essex County communities. Town meeting minutes, tax lists, school registers, and church rolls are central tools for placing families within specific neighborhoods and tracking their economic roles in farming and small industry.

Regional connections:

County-level deeds and probate in Essex County trace the transfer of Georgetown farms, house lots, and mill sites and frequently link residents with Rowley, Groveland, Boxford, Newbury, Haverhill, and other nearby towns where they bought land, married, or found industrial work. Local histories and family genealogies provide additional context on long-settled surnames and on the development of the village center and its industries, helping genealogists reconstruct "Rowley West/Georgetown" kin whose lives ran along farm lanes, pond-side mills, and the small-town streets that defined Georgetown's growth from parish outpost to independent town.

Groveland

Groveland, Massachusetts, developed as a compact Merrimack River and upland farming town in north-central Essex County, set off in the mid-nineteenth century from the "South Parish" of Haverhill, which had long encompassed the same riverfront and hill-farm neighborhoods. Its landscape centers on the village green and meetinghouse area along Main Street and Center Street, with outlying districts stretching toward Boxford, Georgetown, and West Newbury, and river-edge neighborhoods facing Haverhill across the Merrimack. From its earliest days as South Haverhill, the community blended intervale farming, small mills on local brooks, and river-linked trade, creating records that tie "South Parish" families to both Haverhill and later Groveland sources.

South Parish Greens, River Roads, and Hill Farms

In the colonial and early national period, what is now Groveland functioned as Haverhill's South Parish, with a meetinghouse, burying ground, and a modest village core serving scattered farmsteads along Main Street, School Street, and the roads running up from the Merrimack. Families raised mixed crops and livestock on upland farms while using the river for transport, timber rafting, and access to Haverhill's market and mills, and their vital events and civic activities were recorded in Haverhill's town and parish books under South Parish or equivalent designations. For genealogists, this means that eighteenth- and early nineteenth-century Groveland ancestors must be traced first in Haverhill records—looking carefully for parish identifiers and neighborhood descriptions—before following the same surnames into Groveland's own town and vital volumes once the parish became a separate municipality.

Mills, Bridges, and Small-Town Streets

Through the nineteenth century, Groveland remained largely rural but saw the development of small water-powered mills and shops along local streams and in the village center, while a bridge across the Merrimack solidified its link to Haverhill's growing industrial city. Modest clusters of worker housing and businesses filled in near the green and along the river road, yet much of the town retained its farm and orchard character, with residents sometimes commuting to Haverhill mills or shoe shops while maintaining home farms in Groveland. This pattern produced federal and state census returns showing a mix of farmers, laborers, and small-industry workers, along with town valuation lists, school registers, and church rolls that document multi-generational families rooted in the same roads and lots even as their economic lives diversified.

Genealogical Resources and Strategies

For vital records, researchers work with Groveland town-clerk registrations from incorporation onward and with earlier births, marriages, and deaths recorded under Haverhill—especially in South Parish church registers and Haverhill's town books. Cemetery records for Groveland's burying grounds, along with published or indexed gravestone transcriptions, help link riverfront and upland families and often show continuity of surnames from South Parish into the independent town.

Town meeting minutes, tax lists, and school district records are key tools for placing households in specific neighborhoods such as the village center, river road districts, and outlying farm areas. At the county level, deeds and probate files trace the transfer of farms, house lots, and mill sites and frequently connect Groveland residents with Haverhill, Georgetown, Boxford, and West Newbury, reflecting marriage patterns and land purchases across town lines. Taken together, these sources allow genealogists to reconstruct "South Parish/Groveland" kin whose lives were shaped by the Merrimack's edge, the village green, and the hill farms that defined Groveland's development from parish to town.

Hamilton

Hamilton, Massachusetts, developed as a small inland farming and village town in northeastern Essex County, set off in the late eighteenth century from the inland portion of coastal Ipswich that had long been known as the "Hamlet" or "Ipswich Hamlet." Its landscape centers on the village green and meetinghouse area along Bay Road and Railroad Avenue, with outlying farms, pastures, and woodlots stretching toward Wenham, Essex, Topsfield, and Manchester. From the beginning, Hamilton's families balanced mixed agriculture and woodland use with close ties to Ipswich's coastal trade and institutions, leaving a record trail that straddles both the parent town and the later independent community.

Hamlet Greens, Bay Road Farms, and Parish Ties

In the colonial era, what became Hamilton functioned as an inland neighborhood of Ipswich, with farmsteads strung along Bay Road and side lanes, and a local meetinghouse and burying ground serving residents who found the distance to Ipswich's main parish inconvenient. Families raised grain, livestock, and orchard crops, made use of nearby marsh and woodland resources, and occasionally worked or traded through Ipswich's harbor. Vital events and civic matters for these households were recorded in Ipswich town and parish books, often under "Hamlet" or similar designations rather than a separate town name. Genealogists therefore need to trace early Hamilton lines first in Ipswich's records, paying attention to neighborhood descriptors, then follow the same surnames into Hamilton's own town and church volumes after incorporation, when the geography remains much the same but the municipal heading shifts.

Ponds, Rail Lines, and Suburban Villages

During the nineteenth century, Hamilton retained its predominantly rural character but saw modest changes as small mills, shops, and later the railroad shaped village life. The arrival of the rail line and station encouraged the growth of a compact village center with stores, workshops, and housing near the tracks, while outlying roads continued to support dairy and market farming and, over time, attracted country estates and equestrian properties connected to nearby Myopia Hunt and coastal resort patterns. Census schedules, valuation lists, and town reports from this period show a mix of farmers, laborers, tradespeople, and a growing number of professionals and estate staff, reflecting Hamilton's gradual evolution from purely agrarian parish to rural-suburban community with strong ties to neighboring towns and to Boston.

Genealogical Resources and Strategies

For vital records, researchers work with Hamilton town-clerk registrations from the time of incorporation forward and with earlier births, marriages, and deaths in Ipswich's town and parish books that reference the Hamlet or inland districts. Cemetery records for Hamilton's burying grounds, together with published gravestone transcriptions, link village and outlying families and often bridge the period when records shift from Ipswich to Hamilton.

Town meeting minutes, tax lists, school registers, and church rolls are central tools for placing households on specific stretches of Bay Road and side lanes, distinguishing long-settled farm families from later estate owners and workers. At the county level, deeds and probate files trace the transfer of farms, woodlots, and village house lots and frequently connect Hamilton residents with Ipswich, Wenham, Essex, Topsfield, and Manchester, reflecting intermarriage and landholding patterns across town lines. Taken together, these sources allow genealogists to reconstruct "Hamlet/Hamilton" kin whose lives ran along Bay Road greens, pond-side farms, and rail-linked village streets as the town moved from Ipswich out-parish to independent rural-suburban community.

Ipswich

Ipswich, Massachusetts, emerged as a major seventeenth-century coastal and riverine town in northeastern Essex County, founded in the 1630s on lands long inhabited by Indigenous peoples along the Ipswich River and tidal marshes. The original settlement clustered around the meetinghouse, green, and market streets near the river, with house lots stepping up the hill and long farm strips, common fields, and pasturelands stretching inland toward what later became Hamilton, Topsfield, and Rowley. Over time, Ipswich combined a working harbor, extensive salt-marsh hay grounds, and inland farms with small mills and craft shops, anchoring a network of "Ipswich" and "Hamlet" neighborhoods whose families appear early and often in town, church, and county records.

Town Hill, River Landings, and Out-Parishes

In the colonial era, Ipswich's civic and religious life centered on Town Hill and the nearby riverfront, where the first meetinghouse, burying ground, and market formed the core of the community, while farms and out-parishes extended along roads leading to Rowley, Essex (Chebacco), Hamilton (the Hamlet), and Topsfield. Residents combined subsistence and market agriculture with coastal and river trade, salt-marsh haying, and small-scale milling, and their activities are documented in detailed town meeting minutes, early vital records, church registers, and land grants that often reference specific hills, coves, and "highways to Rowley or Salem" rather than modern street names.

Genealogists must follow families as they appear under central "Ipswich" entries and under parish or neighborhood designations such as Chebacco and the Hamlet, recognizing that many lines later recorded in Essex, Hamilton, and other towns spent their early generations within Ipswich's original jurisdiction.

Harbor Trades, Mills, and Shoemaking Villages

By the nineteenth century, Ipswich remained a working harbor and market town but also developed inland mill and shoemaking districts along the Ipswich River and its branches, particularly near the falls and dam and in neighborhoods such as Ipswich Mills. Fishing, coastal trade, and ship-related crafts continued alongside textile mills, small factories, and shoe shops, while surrounding farms supplied produce, dairy, and timber. This mixed economy produced rich federal and state census returns, valuation lists, and town reports that show a blend of farmers, mariners, mill operatives, and shoemakers, as well as growing immigrant communities who joined long-established Yankee families in parish and civic life.

Genealogical Resources and Strategies

For vital records, researchers work with Ipswich town-clerk registrations from the seventeenth century forward, supplemented by published vital-record volumes and cemetery transcriptions covering the Old Burying Ground and later cemeteries. Church registers from First Parish and other congregations record baptisms, marriages, and burials for both the town center and outlying precincts, often noting specific neighborhoods or parish affiliations that clarify where a family lived within Ipswich's broad bounds.

Town meeting minutes, tax lists, school records, and poor-relief documents help place households on particular streets, river reaches, and farm roads, while county-level deeds and probate trace the transfer of harbor lots, marsh rights, and inland farms and tie Ipswich residents to neighboring Essex, Hamilton, Rowley, Topsfield, and beyond. Together, these sources allow genealogists to reconstruct "Ipswich River" kin whose lives ran from Town Hill and river landings through farm lanes, mill villages, and shoemaking shops as Ipswich shifted from early Puritan plantation to a diversified coastal and industrial town.

Lynnfield

Lynnfield, Massachusetts, developed as a small inland farming and crossroads town in southern Essex County, formed originally as the "Lynn End" or outlying parish of Lynn before gaining separate town status. Its landscape centers on the village greens and meetinghouse areas near the modern Town Common and around Lynnfield Center, with outlying farms, ponds, and woodlots extending toward Reading, Wakefield (formerly South Reading), Peabody, Saugus, and Middleton. From its earliest days, Lynnfield's families balanced mixed agriculture and woodland resources with the advantages of turnpike and later highway routes that linked them to Lynn, Boston, and the Merrimack Valley, leaving a record trail that is largely rural in character but closely intertwined with neighboring towns.

Lynn End Greens, Parish Bounds, and Farm Roads

In the colonial era, the territory that became Lynnfield functioned as the inland "Lynn End" of Lynn, with scattered farmsteads along country roads and a local meetinghouse and burying ground serving residents who lived too far from Lynn's coastal common. Households raised grain, hay, and livestock, exploited nearby ponds and timber, and sometimes used Lynn's markets and tanneries, while their vital events and civic business were recorded in Lynn's town and parish books under Lynn End or equivalent descriptions rather than a separate town name. Genealogists working in this period must track families first in Lynn records, watching for neighborhood identifiers that distinguish inland Lynnfield ancestors from Lynn's coastal and shoe-making population, and then follow the same surnames into Lynnfield's own town and church volumes after incorporation, when the geography remains much the same but the municipal heading changes.

Ponds, Turnpikes, and Suburban Development

Through the nineteenth century, Lynnfield remained largely agricultural, with dairy and market farming supported by woodlots and small local mills on streams and pond outlets, even as turnpike routes and later rail and highway corridors began to pass through the town. Its location on key roads between Boston, the North Shore, and the Merrimack Valley gradually attracted inns, roadside businesses, and, in the late nineteenth and twentieth centuries, increased suburban and recreational development around its ponds and along major routes. Census schedules, valuation lists, and town reports from this era show a community shifting from predominantly farm and labor households to a blend that includes tradespeople, professionals, and commuters who work in nearby cities but maintain homes in Lynnfield.

Genealogical Resources and Strategies

For vital records, researchers use Lynnfield town-clerk registrations from the time of incorporation forward and consult earlier births, marriages, and deaths in Lynn's town and parish books that reference Lynn End or outlying farm districts. Cemetery records and gravestone transcriptions for Lynnfield's burying grounds help link early inland Lynn families with later Lynnfield descendants and distinguish them from coastal Lynn lines.

Town meeting minutes, tax lists, school registers, and church rolls are crucial for placing families along specific roads, near particular ponds, and within the evolving village centers. At the county level, deeds and probate files trace the transfer of farms, woodlots, and house sites and frequently connect Lynnfield residents with Lynn, Peabody, Saugus, Reading/Wakefield, and Middleton, reflecting patterns of intermarriage, land purchase, and suburban relocation. Taken together, these sources allow genealogists to reconstruct "Lynn End/Lynnfield" kin whose lives ran along farm roads, pond shores, and later commuter routes as the town moved from inland parish of Lynn to an independent rural-suburban community.

Manchester-by-the-Sea

Manchester-by-the-Sea, Massachusetts, developed as a compact coastal fishing and shipbuilding town on the rocky North Shore of Essex County, occupying a series of coves and inlets along Massachusetts Bay between Beverly and Gloucester. Originally known simply as Manchester, the settlement grew around its sheltered inner harbor, with early house lots, wharves, and a meetinghouse clustered near the water while outlying farms, pastures, and woodlots stretched inland toward Essex and Hamilton. Over time, Manchester's economy blended inshore fishing, small-scale shipbuilding, and coastal trade with a later overlay of summer-resort development, so that generations of "Manchester" families appear in both maritime records and in town and church sources tied to village streets and rural lanes.

Harbor Greens, Parish Streets, and Outlying Farms

In the colonial era, the town's life focused on the harbor and nearby meetinghouse green, where a compact village of dwellings, shops, and wharves served local fishermen, mariners, and craftsmen. Beyond the village, farmsteads spread along roads leading inland and around the various coves, providing livestock, timber, and produce that supported both residents and ships provisioning in the harbor. Families from this period show up in early town meeting minutes, vital records, and church registers, as well as in land descriptions that rely on coves, points, and "ways to Gloucester or Salem" to identify property rather than modern street names. Genealogists must trace kin as they move between harbor-side lots and inland farms, watching for references to specific coves and necks that pinpoint neighborhoods within the small but topographically complex town.

Fishing Fleets, Summer Hotels, and Shore Estates

By the nineteenth century, Manchester maintained its fishing and small-vessel activity while increasingly attracting Boston-area summer visitors who built cottages and stayed in hotels along the outer shore, especially in areas such as Singing Beach and varied coastal headlands. This resort trade coexisted with traditional maritime pursuits and modest local industry, bringing in seasonal workers and establishing new social layers of hotel staff, estate servants, and professional families commuting or summering in town. Census schedules, valuation lists, and town reports from this era record a mix of fishermen, mariners, carpenters, laborers, and domestic workers alongside merchants, professionals, and estate owners, while directories and local histories help distinguish long-rooted Manchester families from newcomers drawn by the resort economy. The town's formal name change to Manchester-by-the-Sea in the twentieth century does not alter these underlying record sets but can affect how modern references appear in indexes and catalogs.

Genealogical Resources and Strategies

For vital records, researchers work with Manchester/Manchester-by-the-Sea town-clerk registrations of births, marriages, and deaths from the colonial period forward, supplemented by published vital-record volumes and cemetery transcriptions that cover the central burying ground and later cemeteries. Church registers from early Congregational and later Catholic and other congregations preserve baptisms, marriages, and burials for both harbor and outlying districts, often noting specific coves or sections that help place a family within the town's geography.

Town meeting minutes, tax lists, school records, and poor-relief documents further anchor residents in particular neighborhoods and economic roles. At the county level, deeds and probate files trace ownership of harbor lots, shorefront cottages, and inland farms, frequently linking Manchester-by-the-Sea residents with nearby Beverly, Essex, Hamilton, and Gloucester through intermarriage and land sales. Together, these sources allow genealogists to reconstruct "Manchester harbor" kin whose lives were shaped by fishing stages, village greens, and summer-resort streets along the coves and headlands of Manchester-by-the-Sea.

Marblehead

Marblehead, Massachusetts, developed as one of colonial New England's most important fishing and maritime towns on a rocky peninsula projecting into Massachusetts Bay in eastern Essex County. Settled in the seventeenth century on land long used by Indigenous peoples, it grew apart from nearby Salem as a distinct harbor community whose steep streets, tightly packed house lots, and numerous coves, wharves, and fish stages reflected an economy centered almost entirely on the sea. Narrow lanes climbing from the harbor to the Neck and to the ridges above town held dwellings, shops, and meetinghouses, while only limited farmland and pasture lay on the town's outskirts, so that generations of Marblehead families appear far more in maritime and town records than in broad agricultural sources.

Harbor Streets, Meetinghouses, and Outskirts

In the colonial era, civic and religious life focused on the harbor-side meetinghouses and burying grounds, with clustered house lots along Front, Washington, and nearby streets housing fishermen, mariners, and small craftsmen whose work supported the inshore and offshore fishery. Limited outlying farms and commons served local needs but never dominated the economy, making Marblehead exceptional among Massachusetts towns for its heavy reliance on deep-sea fishing and trade. Families of this period are documented in town meeting minutes, early vital records, and church registers that frequently mention specific harbor streets and wharf-side neighborhoods, as well as in land descriptions that use coves, rocks, and lanes rather than expansive fields as reference points. Genealogists must track kin as they move between successive meetinghouse parishes and harbor districts, understanding that even short distance moves up or down the hill can signal shifts in social and economic status within the close quarters of the town.

Fishing Fleets, Privateers, and Later Industry

By the eighteenth and early nineteenth centuries, Marblehead was renowned for its large fishing fleets and for its role in coastal trade and Revolutionary privateering, sending crews to the Grand Banks and beyond and fitting out vessels for both commerce and war. Periods of prosperity and devastating losses—through shipwrecks, wars, and economic downturns—left traces in probate files, poor-relief records, and maritime documents, as widows and orphans relied on community and institutional support. Later in the nineteenth century, as larger ports and changing fishing and trade patterns affected local fortunes, Marblehead saw modest industrial development and, increasingly, a shift toward yachting, tourism, and residential use, especially around the Neck and along the harbor. Census schedules, valuation lists, city directories, and church and charitable-society records from these eras show a mix of fishermen, mariners, sail- and boat-builders, small-factory workers, shopkeepers, servants, and professionals, with immigrant groups joining long-established families in the same steep neighborhoods.

Genealogical Resources and Strategies

For vital records, researchers rely on Marblehead town-clerk registrations of births, marriages, and deaths from the seventeenth century forward, along with published vital-record volumes and cemetery transcriptions that cover Old Burial Hill and later cemeteries. Church registers from early Congregational and later additional Protestant and Catholic congregations preserve baptisms, marriages, and burials, often noting occupations such as "fisherman" or "mariner" and sometimes giving harbor-district clues that help place families on the ground.

Town meeting minutes, tax lists, poor-relief accounts, and school records further locate households within specific streets and social strata, while maritime sources—crew lists, vessel enrollments, customs documents, and local or regional shipping records—are essential for tracking men who spent much of their lives at sea. County-level deeds and probate files trace ownership of crowded house lots, wharf rights, and limited outlying parcels and tie Marblehead residents to neighboring Salem, Swampscott, and other Essex County communities through intermarriage and land transactions. Taken together, these sources allow genealogists to reconstruct "Marblehead harbor" kin whose lives were shaped by fish stages, wharves, and sharply climbing streets in a town where the sea was the dominant fact of daily existence.

Merrimac

Merrimac, Massachusetts, developed as a small riverfront and inland farming town in northwestern Essex County, formed in the nineteenth century from the western part of Amesbury along the north bank of the Merrimack River. Its landscape centers on the compact village around Merrimac Square, with streets rising from the river corridor, and on outlying farm and neighborhood districts stretching toward Newton, New Hampshire, and toward Haverhill and West Newbury. From its earliest years as "West Amesbury" through its separate incorporation, Merrimac combined intervale farming and small mills with later carriage, shoe, and light industrial ventures, leaving a record trail that ties families to both Amesbury and the independent town.

West Amesbury Greens, River Roads, and Hill Farms

In the pre-incorporation period, what became Merrimac functioned as West Amesbury, with a meetinghouse, burying ground, and small commercial cluster serving scattered farms and homesteads along Main Street, Church Street, and roads leading up from the Merrimack. Households raised mixed crops and livestock, cut timber, and sometimes worked in local mills or in neighboring Amesbury's carriage and textile shops, while their vital events and parish life were recorded in Amesbury's town and church books under West Parish or West Amesbury designations. For genealogists, this means that early Merrimac families must first be traced in Amesbury records—watching for neighborhood descriptors and road names—before following the same surnames into Merrimac's own town and vital volumes once the town separates and the same people and places acquire a new municipal heading.

Carriage Shops, Small Mills, and Border Neighborhoods

Through the nineteenth century, Merrimac developed a modest industrial base of its own, with carriage shops, small factories, and mills along the river and local streams, especially near the village center and in nearby hamlets. Worker housing, stores, and civic buildings filled in around the square and along the principal streets, while outlying farms and border neighborhoods toward Newton, New Hampshire, and West Newbury retained a more rural character. Census schedules and town valuations from this era show a blend of farmers, carriage-makers, mill operatives, and tradespeople, with some residents commuting to larger mills and shops in Amesbury, Haverhill, or across the state line. Parish records, school registers, and later fraternal and civic-organization rolls capture multi-generational families rooted to specific streets and farm roads even as occupations shift from primarily agricultural to mixed industrial and service work.

Genealogical Resources and Strategies

For vital records, researchers rely on Merrimac town-clerk registrations from incorporation onward and on earlier births, marriages, and deaths embedded in Amesbury's records under West Amesbury or parish labels. Cemetery records and gravestone transcriptions for Merrimac's burying grounds help link riverfront, village, and rural families and tie them back to earlier Amesbury entries. Town meeting minutes, tax lists, school district records, and church registers are key for placing households within the village grid and among the outlying farm and border neighborhoods, clarifying which lines lived near the river, which in the hill districts, and which straddled the Massachusetts–New Hampshire line.

County-level deeds and probate files for Essex County, together with neighboring Rockingham County, New Hampshire holdings, trace the transfer of farms, village lots, and shop sites and frequently connect Merrimac residents with Amesbury, Haverhill, West Newbury, and Newton, NH. Taken together, these sources allow genealogists to reconstruct "West Amesbury/Merrimac" kin whose lives ran along river roads, carriage-shop streets, and upland farm lanes in a town that grew from parish outpost to independent river and border community.

Middleton

Middleton, Massachusetts, developed as a small inland farming and mill town in central Essex County, set off in the early eighteenth century from upland portions of Salem and Topsfield where settlers had long worked fields and mill sites along the Ipswich River and its tributaries. Its landscape centers on the village common and meetinghouse area near the modern center, with outlying farms, pastures, and woodlots extending toward North Reading, Lynnfield, Topsfield, and Danvers. From its earliest days, Middleton's families balanced mixed agriculture, timber, and modest water-powered industry, appearing frequently in town, church, and county land records rather than in dense maritime or urban sources.

Commons, Parish Bounds, and River Farms

In the colonial era, the territory that became Middleton was known as "Salem Village farms" and later as a separate parish, with a meetinghouse and burying ground anchoring a community distinct from both Salem Town's harbor district and Topsfield's hill farms. Farmsteads lined roads such as what became Maple, Locust, and North Main Streets and followed the course of the Ipswich River and local brooks where early grist and saw mills operated. Vital events and civic matters for these households were initially recorded in Salem and Topsfield books and then in Middleton's own town and parish volumes after incorporation, often using descriptions that reference specific meadows, bridges, and "ways to Reading or Lynn End" rather than modern addresses. Genealogists must follow families across this jurisdictional shift, noting how the same surnames move from Salem or Topsfield entries into Middleton records without necessarily changing physical location.

Mills, Turnpikes, and Quiet Suburban Growth

Through the nineteenth century, Middleton remained predominantly rural, with small textile and other mills on the river and brooks, local shoe and cottage-industry work, and farms supplying dairy, produce, and wood to nearby markets. The coming of turnpike and later highway routes increased through-traffic and gradually made the town attractive for country residences and, later, suburban development, while many long-established families continued to farm or work in small shops locally and in neighboring industrial centers. Census schedules, valuation lists, and town reports from this era show a community of farmers, mill hands, shoemakers, and tradespeople, with some residents commuting to or relocating in places like Danvers, Peabody, or Lynn while retaining kin and property connections in Middleton.

Genealogical Resources and Strategies

For vital records, researchers use Middleton town-clerk registrations of births, marriages, and deaths from incorporation onward and consult earlier events in Salem and Topsfield town and parish books that reference the farms and parish that became Middleton. Cemetery records and gravestone transcriptions for Middleton's burying grounds help link village and outlying families and bridge the period when recordkeeping shifted to the new town.

Town meeting minutes, tax lists, school registers, and church rolls are central for placing households along specific roads and river stretches and for distinguishing long-rooted farm families from later suburban arrivals. At the county level, deeds and probate files in Essex County trace the transfer of farms, woodlots, mill sites, and house lots and frequently connect Middleton residents with Salem, Danvers, Topsfield, North Reading, and Lynnfield through intermarriage and land transactions. Together, these sources allow genealogists to reconstruct "Middleton river and hill" kin whose lives ran along commons, mill ponds, and farm lanes as the town moved from outlying parish of Salem and Topsfield to a modest rural-suburban community.

Nahant

Nahant, Massachusetts, developed as a small peninsula community projecting into Massachusetts Bay off the coast of Lynn in southeastern Essex County, originally used by Indigenous Massachusett and other Native groups as a seasonal fishing and agricultural area long before English settlement. In the seventeenth century it became an outlying pasture and fishing ground for Lynn, where colonists grazed cattle, sheep, and goats and maintained small fishing stages and huts, while most permanent residents and vital events remained recorded in Lynn's town and church books. The peninsula's rocky shores, coves, and limited interior land meant that year-round population grew slowly, but its unique geography—a small island-like mass reached by a narrow barrier-beach causeway—set the stage for later resort and residential development.

Pasture Peninsula, Fishing Grounds, and Early Settlement

In the colonial and early national period, Nahant functioned primarily as common pasture and a maritime outpost for Lynn, with early English use beginning around 1630 when Lynn farmers drove their herds out across the tidal sands and used the surrounding waters for inshore fishing. A small number of permanent houses and fishing structures gradually appeared near more sheltered coves such as Bass Point and East Point, but church membership, town meeting participation, and most recorded births, marriages, and deaths for these families still fell under Lynn's jurisdiction until Nahant incorporated as a separate town in 1853. Genealogists tracing early Nahant kin therefore need to work primarily in Lynn's records—watching for notations such as "at Nahant" or references to pasture rights and fishing stations—before following the same surnames into later Nahant-specific vital, town, and land books after incorporation.

Hotels, Summer Cottages, and Commuter Homes

By the early nineteenth century, Nahant began to transform from mainly pasture and fishing grounds into a noted seaside resort, with boardinghouses and hotels built near Bass Point and East Point and regular steamboat and coach connections drawing visitors from Boston and Salem. Throughout the 1800s, large hotels, summer cottages, and recreational facilities turned Nahant into a fashionable retreat for Boston's elite, even as a small population of year-round residents continued to farm, fish, and work in local shoe shops and construction trades linked to nearby Lynn. After major hotels declined or were lost to fire, the town shifted toward more permanent seasonal and then year-round residences, with many inhabitants commuting to Lynn or Boston and others tied to General Electric and regional industries while Nahant preserved a primarily residential character.

Genealogical Resources and Strategies

For vital records, researchers rely on Nahant's own registrations of births, marriages, and deaths from its incorporation in 1853 onward and must consult Lynn's town and parish records for earlier events involving people living or working at Nahant when it was still part of Lynn. Cemetery records and gravestone transcriptions for Nahant's burying grounds, combined with Lynn cemeteries, help distinguish long-rooted Nahant families from transient hotel guests and summer visitors and link them back to mainland origins.

Town meeting minutes, tax lists, school records, and local histories place residents in specific sections of the peninsula and trace the shift from pasture and resort to primarily residential town.

County-level deeds and probate files in Essex County document ownership of cottage lots, shore-front properties, and the limited interior parcels and frequently connect Nahant residents with Lynn, Swampscott, Boston, and other communities where they held additional property or family ties, allowing genealogists to reconstruct "Lynn/Nahant" kin whose lives were shaped by pastures, fishing coves, grand hotels, and cliff-side cottages on this distinctive peninsula.

Newbury

Newbury, Massachusetts, began as a seventeenth-century agricultural and riverine town in northeastern Essex County, settled in 1635 by English colonists who moved from Ipswich to the fertile lands along the Parker and Merrimack Rivers. The original settlement focused around what is now the Lower Green and along High Road, where the early meetinghouse, burying ground, and first house lots were laid out, while long farm strips, common pastures, and later mill sites extended inland and upriver; over time, outlying sections such as the waterside "Newburyport" district and the upriver lands that later became West Newbury were set off as separate towns, leaving present-day Newbury with distinct village areas at Old Town, Byfield, and Plum Island.

Lower Green, Byfield Mills, and River Farms

In the colonial era, civic and religious life centered on the meetinghouse near the Lower Green and the First Settlers Burial Ground, while farmsteads spread along High Road, Scotland Road, and other early routes leading toward Rowley and Ipswich, with common pastures and marsh lots providing grazing and salt hay. As population expanded, the Byfield section along the Parker River and Little River developed into a separate parish and mill village, with multiple water-powered mills and, by 1763, Governor Dummer Academy (now The Governor's Academy), one of the earliest boarding preparatory schools in the colonies. Genealogists tracing early Newbury families must therefore follow households through town and parish records that may label them simply as Newbury, as "Waterside" (later Newburyport), or as Byfield parish, paying close attention to references to specific greens, roads, and rivers that distinguish these neighborhoods before formal municipal separations.

Waterside Traders, West Newbury Farmers, and Modern Villages

By the eighteenth century, residents along the Merrimack River wharves at "Waterside" were heavily engaged in shipbuilding, fishing, and West Indies trade, while inland Newbury remained largely agricultural, with Byfield's mills adding a small industrial component; tensions between these waterside merchants and the more rural husbandmen led to the incorporation of Newburyport as a separate town in 1764. In the early nineteenth century, the upriver farming districts were likewise set off as West Newbury, leaving Newbury's territory focused on Old Town, Byfield, and the coastal area including Plum Island, which developed later as a resort and seasonal community. Throughout the nineteenth and twentieth centuries, census schedules, town valuations, and local histories show Newbury as a predominantly rural town with clusters of village life, educational institutions, and modest industry, gradually joined by recreational and commuter elements tied to regional road and rail networks.

Genealogical Resources and Strategies

For vital records, researchers use Newbury town registrations of births, marriages, and deaths from the seventeenth century onward, along with published "Vital Records of Newbury" volumes and cemetery transcriptions for the First Settlers Burial Ground, Newbury First Parish, Newbury Neck, Old Byfield, and other cemeteries. Church registers from early Newbury parishes and from the Byfield parish document baptisms, marriages, and burials for both the Lower Green area and upriver mill and farm communities, while town meeting minutes, tax lists, and poor-farm records help place families on specific roads, commons, and riverfronts over time.

County-level deeds and probate files, together with regional studies and classic local histories such as John Currier's work on Newbury, Newburyport, and West Newbury, trace ownership of river farms, marsh lots, mill sites, and later village house lots, and show how Newbury lines interweave with those of Newburyport, West Newbury, Rowley, Ipswich, and neighboring towns. Taken together, these sources allow genealogists to reconstruct "Newbury" kin whose lives ran from Lower Green fields and Byfield mills to Merrimack wharves and Plum Island sands across nearly four centuries of town evolution.

North Andover

North Andover, Massachusetts, occupies the original compact village and farmland of seventeenth-century Andover along Lake Cochichewick, the Merrimack River, and Cochichewick Brook in north-central Essex County. First laid out as Cochichewick Plantation in the 1630s and incorporated as Andover in 1646, this northern section held the early meetinghouse, burying ground, and clustered home lots around what is now Academy Road, with long agricultural strips and common fields stretching out toward Haverhill, Methuen, and the river, while later parish and town divisions left today's North Andover with the original town center and much surrounding farmland.

Cochichewick Village, Parson Barnard Green, and River Farms

In the colonial period, settlement focused around the first and later meetinghouses and the old burying ground near Lake Cochichewick, where house lots of four to eight acres were grouped for mutual defense and access to water and meadow, while outlying farms spread along Osgood, Salem, and Great Pond Roads toward the Merrimack and upland pastures. The General Court's 1709 division of Andover into North and South parishes formalized this northern area as North Parish, yet records of births, marriages, deaths, land, and church life continued under the single town of Andover until 1855, meaning that early North Andover families are documented in Andover's town and parish books, often under "North Parish" or "Cochichewick" labels rather than a separate town name.

Mills, Machine Works, and Suburban Growth

From the late eighteenth century into the nineteenth, North Andover's water-power sites along Cochichewick Brook and the Shawsheen supported grist, saw, and fulling mills and then major textile and machinery works, notably the Stevens mills and the Davis & Furber Machine Company, which became nationally prominent and built mill housing and civic structures near the present mill district. While much of the town remained agricultural, these industries, together with the arrival of rail lines, created a mixed landscape of mill villages, farmsteads, and later summer estates that attracted Boston visitors in the late 1800s and, in the twentieth century, gave way to residential subdivisions as interstate highways increased commuter access. Census schedules, valuation lists, and local histories from these periods show farmers, mill operatives, machine-shop workers, and later professionals and service workers sharing the same roads, with employment heavily concentrated in manufacturing well into the mid-twentieth century before the mills closed and were repurposed.

Genealogical Resources and Strategies

For vital events, researchers use North Andover town-clerk registrations of births, marriages, and deaths from the 1855 municipal separation onward and must consult earlier Andover records—especially North Parish church books and Andover town volumes—for seventeenth- and early-nineteenth-century ancestors who lived in what is now North Andover but were legally part of Andover. Cemetery records and gravestone transcriptions for the Old Burying Ground on Academy Road and later cemeteries help link early Cochichewick settlers, mill-era workers, and suburban residents and can bridge the transition from "Andover, North Parish" to "North Andover" in the written record.

Town meeting minutes, tax lists, school registers, and church rolls place families in specific neighborhoods—village center, mill district, river farms, and outlying roads—while county-level deeds and probate files trace the transfer of farms, mill privileges, and house lots and frequently connect North Andover residents with Andover, Methuen, Lawrence, Haverhill, and other Merrimack-valley towns. Together, these sources allow genealogists to reconstruct "Cochichewick/North Parish/North Andover" kin whose lives ran from compact seventeenth-century village lots and river farms through mill villages and modern residential streets as the community evolved over nearly four centuries.

Rockport

Rockport, Massachusetts, developed as a small fishing and quarry town at the northeastern tip of Cape Ann in eastern Essex County, occupying the rocky coves of Sandy Bay and the surrounding uplands that were originally part of Gloucester's territory. Settled permanently by English colonists in the late seventeenth century as a fishing village known as Sandy Bay, the area remained a remote outpost of Gloucester for generations, with house lots, fish stages, and a meetinghouse clustered near the harbor while farms and woodlots stretched inland toward Dogtown and the Bay View highlands. Over time, Rockport's economy combined inshore fishing and coastal trade with major granite quarrying, so that its families appear in both maritime and industrial records as the town shifted from scattered homesteads to a compact harbor village surrounded by quarries and later artists' colonies.

Sandy Bay Fishery, Parish Greens, and Early Homesteads

In the colonial and early national period, Sandy Bay functioned as a distant neighborhood of Gloucester, where early settlers such as the Tarr family established homesteads and fish houses near the sheltered bay while Gloucester's main harbor remained the civic and commercial center. A parish was created at Sandy Bay in the eighteenth century, with a meetinghouse and burying ground serving fishermen and smallholders whose lives revolved around cod fishing, timber cutting, and subsistence plots carved out of the rocky ground. Vital events and town business for these residents were recorded in Gloucester's books under Sandy Bay or parish designations rather than a separate town name, so genealogists working in this era must follow Rockport families first through Gloucester's town, church, and land records, paying attention to references to Sandy Bay, the "Harbor," or specific coves and roads that distinguish them from Gloucester's main-harbor population.

Granite Quarries, Harbor Streets, and Artists' Enclaves

By the nineteenth century, Rockport had become known not only for its fishing fleet but also for extensive granite quarries whose high-quality stone was shipped along the East Coast for break-waters, buildings, and monuments, with large quarry operations and related boardinghouses and tramways spreading across the interior ledges. The growth of quarrying, together with contin-ued fishing and coastal trade, turned the village around Dock Square, Bearskin Neck, and Inner Harbor into a dense cluster of wharves, fish houses, shops, and worker housing, while rail con-nections linked Rockport more closely to Gloucester, Salem, and Boston. Later in the nineteenth and early twentieth centuries, as some quarries declined, Rockport also attracted painters and summer visitors, evolving into a well-known artists' colony and resort town, with studios and galleries occupying former fish houses and commercial buildings along the harbor. Census re-turns, valuation lists, and local histories from these periods show families divided among fishing, quarrying, small manufacturing, and service work, often with multiple occupations across gen-erations and frequent marriage ties to Gloucester and other Cape Ann communities.

Genealogical Resources and Strategies

For vital events, researchers use Rockport town-clerk registrations of births, marriages, and deaths from its incorporation as a separate town in 1840 forward and must consult earlier Gloucester town and parish books for ancestors who lived at Sandy Bay before that date. Ceme-tery records and gravestone transcriptions for Old Parish Burying Ground, Beech Grove, and other Rockport cemeteries help link early Sandy Bay settlers, quarry and fishing families, and later artists and summer residents, while also pointing back to Gloucester, Essex, and other nearby towns. Town meeting minutes, tax lists, school registers, and church records place house-holds in specific harbor streets, quarry districts, and inland neighborhoods, clarifying whether a family's livelihood centered on the sea, the stone industry, or later tourist trade. County-level deeds and probate files trace ownership of house lots, wharf rights, fish houses, and quarry tracts and frequently connect Rockport residents with Gloucester and other Cape Ann communities through land transfers and inheritance. Taken together, these sources allow genealogists to re-construct "Sandy Bay/Rockport" kin whose lives were shaped by fish stages, granite ledges, and the narrow harbor streets that made Rockport both a working town and an artists' haven.

Rowley

Rowley, Massachusetts, began as a seventeenth-century plantation town in northeastern Essex County, founded in 1639 when Reverend Ezekiel Rogers arrived from Rowley, Yorkshire, with roughly twenty Puritan families and settled on land between Ipswich and the Merrimack River. The new town was first known as "Mr. Rogers's plantation" before incorporation as Rowley, and at that time its bounds were extensive—stretching from the sea to the Merrimack and eventually encompassing territory that would later become Bradford, Groveland, Georgetown ("New Row-ley"), and parts of Boxford and West Newbury.

Common Greens, House-Lot Streets, and Outlying Villages

Early Rowley centered on a village along what is now Main Street and Bradford Street, where house lots of a few acres each were laid out near the meetinghouse, burying ground (established in 1639), and common lands, while larger planting fields, meadows, and pastures extended outward. Surveys in the 1640s recorded about twenty original house-lot holders and apportioned common lands in proportion to those lots, with early mills on Mill River and a fulling mill in the Byfield (then Rowley) area supporting cloth production that became a local specialty. Over the later seventeenth and eighteenth centuries, distinct outlying neighborhoods developed: "Rowley Village" to the southwest (later Boxford), "Rowley Village by Merrimack" or the Merrimack Lands (later Bradford and then Groveland), and "New Rowley" to the northwest (later Georgetown), each eventually forming its own parish and then separate town.

From Long, Narrow Town to Smaller Farming Community

By the late eighteenth and early nineteenth centuries, repeated set-offs had reduced Rowley's territory to a smaller coastal-and-inland farming town bordering Ipswich, Newbury, and Boxford, with its village still focused along Main Street and surrounding roads. While nearby ports like Newburyport and towns like Haverhill and later Lawrence developed large mills and dense urban districts, Rowley retained a largely rural character, with farming, small mills, and modest shoemaking and cottage industries supplemented by limited coastal trade and, eventually, commuter and recreational connections via the Eastern Railroad. Nineteenth-century censuses and local histories describe a community of farmers, craftsmen, and small manufacturers inhabiting early houses along ancient streets, many of which still stand as documented "First Period" and Georgian dwellings.

Genealogical Resources and Strategies

For vital events, genealogists rely on Rowley's town-clerk registrations of births, marriages, and deaths from the seventeenth century onward, plus published and digitized vital-record collections and the 1639 Rowley Burial Ground inscriptions, which preserve many of the earliest family names. Town meeting minutes, tax lists, and early lot and common-land grants provide detailed information on house-lot locations and expansions, while church records from the First Congregational Church (founded in 1639) and later parishes document baptisms, marriages, and membership across the core village and outlying districts. Because Rowley's original grant later produced daughter towns, researchers must also track families into Bradford/Groveland, Georgetown, Boxford, and West Newbury records, using deeds and probate files to follow the subdivision and sale of "Rowley Village" and "Merrimack Lands" farms over time.

Together, these sources allow reconstruction of "Rowley" kin whose lives ran from tightly clustered seventeenth-century house lots and common fields through the creation of multiple new parishes and towns as the long, narrow original Rowley gradually became the smaller farming community seen on modern maps.

Salisbury

Salisbury, Massachusetts, is the northernmost town in Essex County, occupying land along the Atlantic shore and the north bank of the Merrimack River that was originally homeland to Indigenous peoples of the Pennacook/Pentucket region before English settlement in the 1630s. In

1638 a group led by Simon Bradstreet received permission from the Massachusetts Bay authorities to begin a plantation north of the Merrimack; the settlement was first called Colchester and then, in 1640, renamed Salisbury, with its early house lots, common, and meetinghouse laid out near what is now Salisbury Square while long planting strips, marsh rights, and later mill sites extended upriver and along the coast. Originally Salisbury's grant was extensive, eventually encompassing territory that later became Amesbury and Merrimac in Massachusetts as well as several towns just over the line in present-day New Hampshire.

Town Green, Marsh Lots, and Powow River Outlands

In the seventeenth century, Salisbury's core consisted of a village around the "circular road" and green, where each proprietor held a house lot plus larger planting land outside the center, while common salt marshes near the beach and river were crucial for hay, later divided into "sweepage lots." The Powow River area to the west—later the nucleus of Amesbury—was settled slightly later, with mills and additional homesteads laid out there under Salisbury's jurisdiction before that district was set off as a separate town. Salisbury also served for a time as a shire town for the northern part of Massachusetts Bay, with early courts held there and at Hampton, which adds another layer of court and administrative records for genealogists.

Beach Resorts, Border Suburbs, and Modern Growth

By the nineteenth century, Salisbury retained its farming and river-trade elements but increasingly developed a seaside resort along Salisbury Beach, aided by the construction of Beach Road across the Great Marsh in the 1860s and the arrival of rail and later automobile traffic. Hotels, dance halls, amusement parks, and cottage developments turned the barrier-beach strip into a major regional attraction, while inland parts of town remained more residential and agricultural, with some residents commuting to nearby mill and shoe centers such as Amesbury, Haverhill, and later Lawrence. Twentieth-century censuses, directories, and town reports show a mix of long-rooted families, seasonal cottage owners, and year-round workers tied to tourism, fishing, small industry, and cross-border employment in New Hampshire.

Genealogical Resources and Strategies

For vital events, genealogists work with Salisbury's town-clerk registrations of births, marriages, and deaths from the seventeenth century onward, along with published and indexed vital-record collections and inscriptions from the Salisbury Colonial Burying Ground established in 1639 and later cemeteries. Town meeting minutes, early land-division records, and lists of original proprietors—preserved in local histories and compilations such as the classic "Old Families of Salisbury and Amesbury"—are particularly valuable for placing first-generation settlers on specific house lots, planting fields, and marsh holdings.

Because the original Salisbury grant later gave rise to Amesbury, Merrimac, and several New Hampshire towns, researchers must also trace lines into those successor communities' town, church, deed, and probate records, following families as they moved west of the Powow or north of the modern state line while still appearing in early sources under "Salisbury." Together, these materials allow reconstruction of "old Salisbury" kin whose lives ran from river landing and town green through marsh hay lots, Powow outlands, and beach resorts along Massachusetts' northern coastal edge.

Saugus

Saugus, Massachusetts, lies at the southern end of Essex County along the Saugus and Pines Rivers just north of Boston, on land long inhabited by Indigenous peoples of the Pawtucket/ Naumkeag group before English settlement in 1629. The name "Saugus," likely derived from an Algonquian word meaning "outlet" or "extended," originally referred to a much larger region that included what later became Lynn, Swampscott, Nahant, Lynnfield, Reading, North Reading, and Wakefield, with the town we now know as Lynn first bearing the Saugus name before being re-named in 1637. Present-day Saugus was set off from Lynn and incorporated as an independent town in 1815, by which time it was a largely agricultural community dotted with small villages along the river and road network.

River Villages, Iron Works, and Outlying Farms

In the seventeenth century the broader Saugus/Lynn area developed as a coastal farming and tanning settlement, with homesteads and commons stretching inland along the Saugus River and its tributaries while salt marshes and beaches supported haying and fishing. The most famous early enterprise was the Saugus Iron Works at Hammersmith, established in the 1640s along the Saugus River as the first integrated ironworks in North America, producing pig and wrought iron with a blast furnace, forge, and rolling and slitting mills; many skilled workers and their descendants later carried ironmaking techniques to other colonies. Genealogically, families living in what is now Saugus during this period are found primarily in Lynn's town, church, and court records under Lynn/Saugus headings, with some appearing in documents related to the iron works, mills, and riverfront lands.

Shoes, Suburbs, and Conservation Lands

By the nineteenth century, after incorporation as a separate town, Saugus combined agriculture with shoemaking and related cottage industries, and later with larger shoe factories and other light manufacturing that tied it into the wider North Shore industrial economy. Its location on early turnpikes and, later, major highways made it an attractive residential and commercial corridor between Boston and coastal Essex County, while significant open spaces such as the Breakheart Reservation and Rumney Marsh remained important natural features. Twentieth-century censuses and town profiles describe Saugus as primarily residential, with retail trade, services, and some light industry, plus a notable lobster-fishing fleet using the Saugus River and nearby coastal waters.

Genealogical Resources and Strategies

For vital events, researchers use Saugus town-clerk registrations of births, marriages, and deaths from its 1815 incorporation onward, and must consult earlier Lynn records—including town books, church registers, and published vital-record volumes—for seventeenth- and eighteenth-century ancestors who lived in the inland Saugus area before it became a separate town. Cemetery records and gravestone transcriptions for Saugus burial grounds, together with Lynn and surrounding-town cemeteries, help link early Saugus/Lynn families with later Saugus lines and distinguish inland Saugus kin from coastal Lynn branches.

Local histories, town reports, tax lists, and school records place households in specific villages and along the Saugus River, while county-level deeds and probate files trace ownership of farms, marshes, mill sites, and later house lots and frequently connect Saugus residents with Lynn, Lynnfield, Wakefield, Melrose, and other neighboring communities. For many lines, records connected to the Saugus Iron Works—archaeological reports, worker lists, and reconstructed family studies—provide additional context, allowing genealogists to reconstruct "old Saugus/Lynn" kin whose lives spanned river farms, ironworks, shoe shops, and modern suburban streets.

Swampscott

Swampscott, Massachusetts, is a small seaside town on the Atlantic coast of southern Essex County, occupying rocky headlands and a protected bay between Lynn and Marblehead about twelve miles northeast of Boston. Long before English settlement, Indigenous Naumkeag and related peoples used this "land of the red rock" for seasonal hunting and fishing, and early English accounts in the 1630s already noted "Swampscott" as a Native habitation and coastal landmark.

Fishing Village, Lynn Out-Parish, and Early Industry

The area became part of the large Saugus/Lynn land grant in 1629, when Francis Ingalls established what is considered the first tannery in the Massachusetts Bay Colony on Humphrey's Brook, while Native residents still occupied wigwams along the shore. For more than two centuries Swampscott remained the eastern, coastal section of Lynn (Ward One), developing as a seafaring fishing village with a sizeable commercial fleet that sailed daily from the sheltered bay; sources suggest that in the eighteenth and early nineteenth centuries roughly one man in three was a fisherman, while many others were shoemakers, shoe cutters, farmers, or small merchants tied to Lynn's broader economy.

Lobster Pots, Dories, and Resort Estates

Swampscott gained wider renown in the early 1800s when local mariner Ebenezer Thorndike is credited with inventing the wooden lobster pot in 1808 and when the Swampscott dory—developed around 1840 as a stable, flat-bottomed inshore fishing boat—became popular well beyond New England. The town separated from Lynn and incorporated independently in 1852, later annexing a "Salem Finger" tract in 1867, and in the later nineteenth and early twentieth centuries its dramatic shoreline and sea breezes drew wealthy summer visitors who built large hotels and shingle-style estates, making Swampscott one of the region's classic resort and commuter communities.

Genealogical Resources and Strategies

For vital events, researchers consult Swampscott's town-clerk registrations of births, marriages, and deaths from 1852 forward, and must use earlier Lynn records—town books, church registers, and published vital-record volumes—for seventeenth- to mid-nineteenth-century ancestors who lived in the Swampscott section while it was still part of Lynn. Cemetery records and gravestone transcriptions for Swampscott burying grounds, together with Lynn and Salem cemeteries, help connect fishing-village families, shoemakers, and later estate owners across generations and across shifting town lines.

Local resources such as the Swampscott Historical Society (in the 1630s John Humphrey house) and the public library's history and archive collections hold manuscripts, photographs, maps, and estate and maritime materials that place individuals in specific coves, fish houses, and summer-home districts, while county-level deeds and probate files trace ownership of shorefront lots, inland farms, and resort properties and frequently link Swampscott residents with Lynn, Marblehead, Salem, and Boston families.

Topsfield

Topsfield, Massachusetts, is a historic inland town in central Essex County, settled in the 1640s in the "back country" of Ipswich along the Ipswich River and its meadows, on land first inhabited by the Agawam people and then purchased by the Massachusetts Bay Company from the Agawam sagamore Masconomet in 1638. Early English grants created large tracts north of the river for proprietors based in Ipswich and Salem, with tenant farmers and a handful of resident landowners clearing fields in what was then called "New Meadows"; in 1648 the name was changed to Topsfield, likely after Toppesfield in Essex, England, and the town was incorporated in 1650.

New Meadows Greens, First Farms, and Parish Life

In the colonial period, Topsfield developed as a dispersed farming community focused on a meetinghouse and training field near what is now the Town Common, while outlying farms spread along Washington Street, River Road, Haverhill Road, and other lanes leading toward Boxford, Ipswich, and Danvers. Early families such as Peabody, Gould, Perkins, Cummings, Towne, and Wildes held substantial acreages—some grants reaching several hundred or even a few thousand acres—with later generations establishing additional farmsteads and mills, including Lt. Francis Peabody's gristmill on the Ipswich River in the 1660s. By the 1670s the population had grown to a few hundred people, almost entirely farming households, and Topsfield appears in the records of the 1692 witchcraft crisis, with several women from Topsfield families accused and three executed, linking the town closely to events in nearby Salem.

Turnpikes, Fairs, and Rural Suburb

Through the eighteenth and nineteenth centuries, Topsfield remained primarily agricultural, though improved roads and the Newburyport Turnpike (chartered in 1803 and built along what is now Boston Street) linked it more directly to regional markets in Boston and Newburyport. The formation of the Essex County Agricultural Society in 1818 and the establishment of the Topsfield Fair—first held in 1820 as a cattle show—made the town a regional focal point for farming exhibitions that continue to this day. Nineteenth-century censuses and gazetteers describe a modest population, just over a thousand by the 1830s, with residents engaged in dairying, grain and hay production, small mills, and limited shoe and cottage industries, and in the twentieth century Topsfield gradually evolved into a rural suburb, preserving many first-period and Georgian houses around its common and farm roads.

Genealogical Resources and Strategies

For vital events, genealogists use Topsfield's town-clerk registrations of births, marriages, and deaths from the mid-seventeenth century forward, supplemented by published and digital "Vital Records of Topsfield" and by cemetery records for Pine Grove and older burying grounds on or near the former meetinghouse sites. Because some of the earliest records were lost in an office fire in 1658, researchers often rely on later reconstructions, church books, land grants, and county-level deeds and probate to document first-generation settlers and to connect them to surviving vital entries.

Parish registers, town meeting minutes, tax lists, and detailed local histories—many available through the Topsfield Historical Society's online collections—help place families on specific roads and in neighborhoods such as Washington Street, River Road, and the later "Lake Village," while Essex County deeds trace how large seventeenth-century grants fragmented over time and link Topsfield lines to neighboring Boxford, Ipswich, Danvers, and Middleton.

<u>Wenham</u>

Wenham, Massachusetts, is a small inland town in eastern Essex County, first settled by English colonists in the mid-1630s on land that had long been home to Agawam/Algonquian peoples whose numbers were badly reduced by epidemic disease before large-scale English occupation. Originally part of Salem and briefly known as "Enon," the village was set off as its own town in 1643, making it the first community to be formally separated from Salem; the name Wenham was taken from parishes in Suffolk, England, reflecting the origins of several founding families.

Meetinghouse Hill, Great Pond, and Farm Lanes

Early settlement grew up near Wenham Great Pond (now Wenham Lake) and along what is now Main Street, where the first meetinghouse and burying ground anchored a compact center surrounded by dispersed farmsteads and common lands. A church was organized in 1644 with John Fiske as pastor and a handful of families as members, and over the later seventeenth century Wenham men served in frontier wars and participated—sometimes controversially—in events like the Salem witchcraft trials, while the town's economy remained focused on mixed agriculture, woodland use, and small-scale milling. Land claims by descendants of sagamore Masconomet were settled by a modest quitclaim payment in 1700, after which town boundaries with neighboring Beverly, Hamilton, and Topsfield continued to be clarified through perambulations and occasional disputes.

Rural Village, Estates, and Shared Services

Through the eighteenth and nineteenth centuries Wenham retained a distinctly rural character, with farms, pastures, and woodlots lining roads such as Main, Topsfield, and Larch Row, while a modest village with taverns, shops, and later depot-area development served local needs. In the nineteenth century some larger estates and country houses appeared, but Wenham never industrialized on the scale of nearby Beverly or Salem; in the modern period it shares schools, library, and commuter-rail facilities closely with adjoining Hamilton, preserving a landscape of historic houses, stone walls, and open space that reflects its long agrarian past.

Genealogical Resources and Strategies

For vital events, genealogists draw on Wenham town records of births, marriages, and deaths from its 1643 incorporation onward, together with published or digitized vital-record compilations and inscriptions from early burying grounds along Main Street and at other historic cemetery sites.

Parish registers of the First Church, town meeting minutes, tax lists, and militia and war-service records place families in specific neighborhoods and document their roles in local and regional conflicts, while an extensive body of town history—such as Myron O. Allen's nineteenth-century history of Wenham—provides narrative context and many transcribed documents. County-level deeds and probate in Essex County, along with detailed architectural and historic-district surveys, trace ownership and alteration of farmsteads and village houses and connect Wenham residents with nearby Beverly, Hamilton, Topsfield, and Salem, allowing reconstruction of "Wenham" kin whose lives ran from meetinghouse hill and Great Pond farms to later rural-suburban streets.

West Newbury

West Newbury, Massachusetts, occupies the uplands and riverfront along the north bank of the Merrimack River west of Newburyport in north-central Essex County. Originally part of Newbury's expansive seventeenth-century grant, the area was settled by English colonists in the 1630s–1640s and long known simply as Newbury's "upper woods" and western farms before evolving into a separate parish and, eventually, an independent town in the early nineteenth century. Its landscape combines hilltop farms, valleys around the Artichoke and Indian Rivers, and river-edge meadows and landings, giving it a character more rural and upland than its coastal parent.

Upper Woods, West Parish, and River Farms

As Newbury's population grew, families pushed westward beyond the Artichoke River into what became Turkey Hill, Indian Hill, and River Road districts, where large grants were made in the mid-seventeenth century to men such as Edward Rawson, John Emery, Francis Browne, and William Gerrish. Dispersed farmsteads and small neighborhoods developed along the Bradford Road (today's Main Street) and the Merrimack, with residents engaged primarily in agriculture and stock-raising, supplemented by limited river trade at local landings. Because of the distance to Newbury's original meetinghouse, the western inhabitants organized their own church and meetinghouse, becoming Newbury's West Parish in the early eighteenth century; this parish was incorporated as a separate town in 1819–1820, initially under the name Parsons (honoring minister Jonathan Parsons) before quickly being renamed West Newbury.

Comb Shops, Hill Villages, and Modern Suburb

While West Newbury remained largely agricultural, a distinctive horn-comb and button industry took root in the late eighteenth century when Enoch Noyes began producing horn buttons and coarse combs around 1759; by the 1830s–1840s more than thirty comb shops operated in the town, often as small workshops attached to farmhouses. Nineteenth-century censuses and local descriptions portray a town of hilltop villages and scattered farms with a mixed economy of farming, comb-making, and later small shoe and other cottage industries, gradually transitioning in the twentieth century into an affluent, primarily residential community whose residents often work in nearby Newburyport, Haverhill, or the Boston region. The landscape of conserved open space, working farms, and historic houses along Main Street, River Road, and the hill districts still reflects these agrarian and artisan roots.

Genealogical Resources and Strategies

For vital events, genealogists use West Newbury town-clerk registrations of births, marriages, and deaths from incorporation in 1820 forward and must consult earlier Newbury records—especially those labeled "West Parish" or referring to Turkey Hill, Indian Hill, Artichoke River, or Bradford Road—for seventeenth- and eighteenth-century ancestors. Cemetery records and gravestone transcriptions for West Newbury burying grounds, together with older Newbury cemeteries, help link early West Parish families with later town residents and distinguish them from coastal Newburyport lines.

Town meeting minutes, tax lists, school district records, and parish registers place households in specific hill and river neighborhoods, while county-level deeds and probate files trace the subdivision of the large original grants and show how West Newbury kin intermarried with families in Newbury, Groveland (Bradford), Merrimac, Haverhill, and other Merrimack-valley towns. Together, these sources allow reconstruction of "West Parish/West Newbury" families whose lives ran from upland farms and comb shops to modern residential streets overlooking the Merrimack.

VILLAGES
ASBURY GROVE

Asbury Grove, Massachusetts, developed as a nineteenth-century religious camp-meeting village rather than a traditional New England farming or mill town. Located in Hamilton in inland Essex County, the grove was carved out of wooded land near existing farm roads and rail access so that urban and coastal Methodists from Boston and the North Shore could reach it more easily than the earlier, farther-flung camps on Cape Cod and Martha's Vineyard. Laid out as a compact settlement within a pine forest, with paths radiating from a central preaching area, Asbury Grove functioned seasonally at first and only later grew into a semi-permanent cottage community.

Founded in 1859 (with land purchases beginning in the late 1850s), Asbury Grove was established by a Methodist ministers' association and lay leaders as a camp-meeting ground where multiple congregations could gather for a week or more of preaching, prayer, and religious instruction. Early meetings drew thousands of attendees—contemporary accounts speak of crowds in the tens of thousands during peak years—who arrived by train and trolley to the nearby station and then by wagon into the grove, first living in canvas tents and "society tents" and later in small wooden cottages clustered around the circular preaching stand known as "the Circle." Over the later nineteenth century, the Grove added permanent structures such as a dining hall, bakery, post office, and other community buildings, and by the early twentieth century hundreds of Victorian cottages, many with distinctive porches and decorative trim, had replaced most of the original tent platforms while the religious program continued each summer.

For genealogists, Asbury Grove's records are tightly tied to Methodist and local civic sources rather than to an independent town government. Vital events for residents and visitors will appear in Hamilton's town records and in the civil records of the home towns of those who came from Lynn, Boston, and other communities, while the Grove's own minutes, association records, cottage-lot leases, and program schedules document who owned or rented sites and who participated in camp-meeting life. Church and denominational archives—especially Methodist conference records—can provide lists of member churches, preachers, and sometimes lay attendees, and local historical-society collections preserve photographs, maps, and cottage histories that place families along specific avenues radiating from the Circle.

Because many Grove residents were seasonal and maintained primary residences elsewhere, effective research on "Asbury Grove" ancestors involves pairing Hamilton land and tax records with their home-town vital, church, and census entries, building a picture of families whose religious and social lives centered on this distinctive camp-meeting village tucked into the woods of Essex County.

ANNISQUAM

Annisquam, Massachusetts, is a historic village within the city of Gloucester on Cape Ann, set along the Annisquam River and Lobster Cove on the northwest side of the cape. The name "Annisquam" comes from an Algonquian phrase meaning roughly "top of the rock," reflecting the rocky headlands and pastureland that characterize the area. Indigenous Pawtucket people used this shoreline and river as part of a larger seasonal round long before English settlement, leaving traces in place-names and archaeological sites even after disease and colonial expansion sharply reduced their numbers.

European settlement at Annisquam dates to the early 1630s, when colonists established a small fishing and farming outpost at Squam Harbor as part of the wider Gloucester plantation. In the seventeenth and eighteenth centuries, the village grew into a self-contained community with its own meetinghouse, green, and wharves on the sheltered river, at times rivaling Gloucester Harbor as a local fishing and shipbuilding center, especially during periods when war shifted shipping away from the more exposed main harbor. Farm lots and pastures stretched inland from the coves, while houses and fish stages lined the shore; a lighthouse at the mouth of the Annisquam River, first established in the early nineteenth century, marked this important harbor of refuge for coastal vessels.

In the nineteenth century Annisquam added granite quarrying to its fishing and small-vessel trade, and by the late 1800s it had also become known as an artists' colony, often referred to simply as "Squam," attracting painters who were drawn to its light, coves, and weathered buildings. Over time, the village evolved into a primarily residential and seasonal community, with a yacht club, small library, and limited commercial activity—more a quiet enclave of historic houses and summer cottages than a commercial center. Today Annisquam is still part of Gloucester, but it retains its own identity as a compact village with narrow roads, a traditional church and village hall, and paths leading down to the river and coves.

For genealogists, records relating to Annisquam are found chiefly in Gloucester's town and city records, vital registers, and church books, where early residents are often described as living at "Squam" or "Annisquam" rather than under a separate town name. Land and probate records at the county level document ownership of house lots, wharf rights, and small farms along the river and inland roads, while lighthouse logs, maritime documents, and local histories add detail for mariners and fishermen. More recent family and neighborhood information can often be gleaned from village church and club records, local newspapers, and collections held by the Annisquam Historical Society, allowing researchers to reconstruct "Squam" kin whose lives were tied to fishing, small shipbuilding, quarry work, and later the summer and artistic life of this Gloucester village.

BALLARDVALE

Ballardvale, Massachusetts, is a nineteenth-century mill village within the town of Andover in Essex County, growing up along the Shawsheen River in the town's southwestern section. Centered where Andover Street crosses the river, the village took shape around a substantial dam, brick and wooden mill buildings, and a tight grid of worker and manager housing that together formed Andover's first planned industrial community. The name honors Timothy Ballard, who operated earlier grist and saw mills on this water-power site before larger textile and related enterprises transformed it into a full mill village in the 1830s and 1840s.

In the mid-nineteenth century the Ballard Vale (or Ballardvale) Manufacturing Company and associated firms developed large brick and wooden mills powered by the 200-foot dam, producing woolen goods and, notably, some of the earliest American delaines (light wool-and-cotton dress fabrics). Around the mills, investors laid out Andover, Center, High, Dale, Marland, and nearby streets with house lots for managers, workers, and boardinghouses, while additional industries—including a machine shop that built locomotives, a file-cutting company, hat and pottery works, and art-metal manufacturers—created a remarkably self-contained industrial center with shops, churches, a school, tavern, post office, and a busy railroad depot. For roughly a century, from about 1835 to 1935, Ballardvale functioned as its own "village within a town," its mills changing owners but continuing production into the 1920s before later conversion to other industrial and commercial uses.

For genealogists, Ballardvale lives inside Andover's municipal structure: births, marriages, and deaths are recorded in Andover's vital books, often with "Ballard Vale" or street names noted as place of residence, while federal and state census schedules list the village as an Andover district with many households headed by mill operatives, overseers, machinists, and shopkeepers. Land records and probate files at the county level trace ownership of mill properties, boardinghouses, and single-family dwellings along Andover, Center, Dale, and High Streets, frequently tying Ballardvale residents to other Andover neighborhoods and to nearby industrial centers. Local histories, the Andover preservation program, and photographic collections document the village's changing architecture—Greek Revival, Gothic Revival, Italianate, and later styles—and provide context for families who lived in specific tenements or cottages. Because Ballardvale is now a designated local and national historic district, modern surveys and commission files also help researchers place ancestors in a clearly mapped, well-described mill village setting, linking family stories to the dam, mills, and streets that define daily life there.

BEVERLY FARMS

Beverly Farms, Massachusetts, is a coastal village in the eastern part of the city of Beverly, stretching along the rocky North Shore between Beverly Cove and Manchester-by-the-Sea. It began as an outlying farming section of Salem/Beverly in the 1600s, with early planters such as the Woodberry, Conant, Trask, and West families holding substantial farmsteads and pasture lots near today's Hale Street and West Beach area. For more than two centuries, "the Farms" was primarily an agricultural district known for its fields, orchards, and woodlots, supplying produce, hay, and timber to Beverly and regional markets.

In the mid-nineteenth century the railroad reached Beverly Farms (around 1847), transforming the village into a fashionable summer colony as wealthy families from Boston, New York, Philadelphia, and other cities bought up shorefront farms and built large estates and shingle-style "cottages" overlooking the ocean. West Beach, long part of seventeenth-century land grants, became a focal point for this resort development; a private West Beach Corporation was chartered in 1852, and by the late 1800s the area around West Street and Hale Street included hotels, carriage roads, and grand houses comparable in scale to those in Newport. At the same time, working-class neighborhoods of Irish and Italian laborers, domestic servants, and tradespeople grew up inland to serve the estates, quarries, and local businesses, giving the Farms a social mix of "summer people" and year-round residents.

For genealogists, Beverly Farms appears within Beverly's municipal framework rather than as an independent town. Vital records of births, marriages, and deaths are registered under Beverly, often with "Beverly Farms" noted as the place of residence, while federal and state censuses list the Farms as a Beverly district or enumeration area.

Deeds and probate files at the county level trace ownership of farm lots, shorefront estates, and workers' houses along Hale, Hart, and West Streets and in side-street neighborhoods, frequently linking Beverly Farms families with those in downtown Beverly, Prides Crossing, Manchester-by-the-Sea, and Boston.

Local histories, church records, school documents, and the holdings of Historic Beverly and other repositories preserve maps, photographs, estate plans, and oral histories that help place ancestors in specific streets, estates, or working-class enclaves, allowing reconstruction of kin networks that span early farmsteads, Gilded Age summer estates, and twentieth-century village life in Beverly Farms.

BRADFORD

Bradford, Massachusetts, began as a separate Merrimack River town on the south bank opposite Haverhill, in what is now southern Essex County. It was settled in the mid-1600s by families coming out of Rowley's original grant, and the community was officially named Bradford in the 1670s in honor of Bradford in Yorkshire, England, reflecting the origins of some of its settlers.

The early town center lay a short distance back from the river along what is now Salem Street, where the first meetinghouse and the Bradford Burying Ground were established on land donated by early settler John Haseltine in the 1660s. That burying ground, in continuous use into the nineteenth century, holds many of Bradford's founding families and ministers, as well as veterans from King Philip's War through the Civil War, and it functioned for decades as both religious and civic center, with town business conducted in the meetinghouses that once stood inside its bounds. Surrounding this nucleus, farms stretched toward Boxford, Groveland (then the East Parish), and up the hillside away from the river, while riverfront roads and landings tied Bradford into Merrimack trade and ferry connections with Haverhill.

Through the eighteenth and nineteenth centuries Bradford remained a largely agricultural and small-village town, though its position on the river and on key roads meant that some residents worked in or traded with emerging industrial centers nearby; eventually, portions of the original Bradford territory became Groveland (East Parish), and the remaining town was an-nexed to the city of Haverhill in the 1890s, turning Bradford into a distinct neighborhood within a larger municipality. For genealogists, this history means that earlier records will appear under the independent town of Bradford, while later residents are recorded under Haverhill, and that families may shift in the documents as boundaries were redrawn and parishes spun off.

Researching ancestors from Bradford involves working with town-level vital records from the seventeenth century through annexation, the detailed inscriptions and lot layouts of the Bradford Burying Ground, and town meeting and church records that place families in the origi-nal village and its outlying farms. After annexation, Haverhill city records, directories, and school and ward materials continue the story for Bradford residents, while county-level deeds and pro-bate files trace land transfers along Salem Street, the river road, and farm lanes toward Groveland and Boxford, showing how "Bradford" kin connected across Merrimack-valley communities over time.

BYFIELD

Byfield, Massachusetts, is a historic village and parish in the towns of Newbury and (in some areas) Georgetown in northeastern Essex County. It lies inland along the Parker and Little Rivers, upriver from Newbury's Lower Green and just west of the coastal marshes. The area was originally part of seventeenth-century Newbury, where settlers spread from the original river-side village into upland "Falls" country around the waterpower at Newbury Falls (near today's Central Street and Orchard Street in Byfield).

Falls Parish, Mills, and Academy Green
As population pushed inland, residents of the Falls district—often called "Newbury Falls" or, for a time, "Rowlbury"—found themselves far from Newbury's first meetinghouse and in 1702 built their own meetinghouse by the falls, forming a distinct parish that was formally recognized as the parish of Byfield in 1710. The name honored Judge Nathaniel Byfield, an influential Boston merchant and colonial official. The parish quickly developed into a mill village, with saw and grist mills using the falls and, over time, as many as six water-powered mills operating on the local streams. In 1763, Governor William Dummer's endowment established Dummer Academy (now The Governor's Academy) nearby, often noted as the first preparatory boarding school in what became the United States, adding an educational and institutional layer to the farming and mill community.

Rural Village, Shared Identity, and Modern Byfield
Through the eighteenth and nineteenth centuries Byfield remained primarily rural, with scat-tered farms, small mill clusters, and the academy complex rather than dense industrial or port development. Because it is a parish and village rather than an incorporated town, its territory has always been divided administratively among Newbury (and later, in some edges, neighboring towns), yet residents developed a strong shared identity around the church, mills, and school that outlasted shifts in municipal lines. In modern times Byfield appears as a largely residential village with historic farmhouses, mill sites, and the Governor's Academy campus, serving as a local cen-ter for surrounding rural neighborhoods.

Genealogical Resources and Strategies

For genealogy, Byfield research hinges on parish and parent-town records. Vital events for Byfield families are recorded primarily in Newbury's town and church books under labels such as "Byfield Parish," "Newbury Falls," or "Rowlbury," and later in Newbury's civil registers once the parish was well established. Parish registers for the Byfield church—documented in published and manuscript transcriptions—contain baptisms, marriages, and membership lists that specifically identify residents of the parish and often distinguish them from coastal Newbury and from Rowley/Georgetown families.

Mill, land, and academy records, together with county-level deeds and probate files, trace ownership of farmsteads and waterpower sites and frequently link Byfield kin with families in Newburyport, West Newbury, Rowley, and Georgetown, allowing genealogists to reconstruct "Byfield" families whose lives centered on the falls, the parish green, and the academy grounds even though their official records sit in multiple towns' volumes.

Clifton

Clifton is a coastal neighborhood straddling the line between Swampscott and Marblehead in southern Essex County, developed in the late nineteenth and early twentieth centuries as a streetcar- and rail-served seaside suburb and resort rather than as an independent town. It lies roughly along and inland from Clifton Avenue and Humphrey Street, with the Atlantic shoreline on one side and the rail line on the other, forming part of a larger band of coastal neighborhoods that includes Preston Beach, Clifton Heights, and Devereux in Marblehead as those shore tracts were gradually subdivided from older farm lots into house lots and vacation properties.

Originally Naumkeag land, the area that became Clifton remained largely farmland and pasture at the edge of Swampscott and Marblehead until improved transportation made daily or seasonal travel from Boston practical. A hotelier, Benjamin Ware, promoted the "Clifton" name as he and other developers envisioned a resort and residential district conveniently located between the established summer colonies of Swampscott and Marblehead Neck.

Rail and streetcar stops labeled Clifton, plus later highway access, allowed commuters and summer visitors to reach the neighborhood, and by the early twentieth century plans laid out streets and lots that filled with shingle-style cottages, Colonial Revival houses, and later suburban styles, especially in subdivisions such as the Smith, Phelps & Langmaid tract and Ware Manor noted in historic-resource surveys.

For genealogists, Clifton appears inside the municipal records of both Swampscott and Marblehead rather than in a separate vital-records set. Births, marriages, and deaths for Clifton residents are recorded under the appropriate town, with addresses on Clifton Avenue, Humphrey Street, or within named subdivisions signaling the neighborhood. Deeds and tax records in Essex County document the breakup of earlier farms into resort and suburban parcels and help distinguish which side of the town line a given Clifton address falls on, while local historic-preservation surveys and neighborhood studies provide maps, construction dates, and architectural descriptions for individual houses.

Pairing those with town directories, census schedules, and church records in Swampscott and Marblehead allows reconstruction of "Clifton" families who experienced the area's transition from fringe farmland to trolley-served resort and then to a stable coastal residential neighborhood.

<u>Dogtown</u>

Dogtown is an abandoned inland settlement spanning about five square miles across Gloucester and Rockport on Cape Ann in northeastern Essex County, Massachusetts, centered on rocky uplands with glacial boulders, cellar holes, and wooded trails rather than a formal village grid. Originally known as the Commons Settlement, it was established around 1642-1693 as common land for woodcutting and livestock grazing, protected from coastal pirates, Native American raids, and harsh weather by its elevated, boulder-strewn position amid streams and pine groves.

Settlement and Peak

By the early 1700s, individual families built homes there, turning the commons into a thriving agricultural and milling hub connected by roads to Gloucester's harbors and Cape Ann's shores; at its height in the mid-1700s, it housed 60-100 families in up to 80 dwellings, including prominent Gloucester kin who raised sheep, cattle, and timber on the poor soil. Women reportedly kept dogs for protection during wartime absences of men, contributing to the later "Dogtown" nickname, while the area's isolation fostered legends of witches, widows, and outcasts.

Decline and Abandonment

Post-Revolutionary War shifts—deforestation, safer coasts, booming Gloucester fisheries, and new roads bypassing the interior—drove prosperity away by the early 1800s, leaving poorer residents, including widows and freedmen like Cornelius "Black Neil" Finson, who was the last holdout until 1830. Feral dogs roamed the empty cellars, solidifying the name; by 1845, all structures were gone, turning Dogtown into a "ghost town" of boulders and ruins, later marked by businessman Roger Babson in the 1930s with inscribed stones and numbered sites.

Genealogical Resources

Dogtown families appear in Gloucester (and some Rockport) town records as "Commons Settlement" or inland residents, with vital events, land grants, and probate in Essex County files linking them to harbor-based kin; church records from Gloucester's first parish note baptisms and marriages, while militia lists and poor-farm admissions trace Revolutionary-era widows and late holdouts.

Cellar-hole maps by Babson, combined with 18th-century deeds for pastures and mills, help locate farmsteads and reconstruct networks among Cape Ann settlers who briefly made the rocky interior their home before coastal pull drew them seaward.

<u>Magnolia</u>

Magnolia is a seaside village in the southwestern corner of Gloucester, Essex County, Massachusetts, on Cape Ann along the rocky Atlantic shore near the Manchester-by-the-Sea line. First noted in European records around 1623 as part of Gloucester's early fishing outposts, the area remained sparsely settled with farms and pastures until the post-Civil War era, when it transformed into a summer resort for Boston's elite drawn by its cliffs, beaches, and rail access.

Victorian Resort Development

By the late 1870s, wealthy Bostonians like Rev. James Freeman Clarke built grand "cottages" such as Septingle overlooking the surf, while hotels like the Oceanside Hotel and Casino hosted celebrities including John Philip Sousa and later Lucille Ball. Shore Road filled with mansions staffed by immigrants who ran local shops on Lexington Avenue, turning Magnolia into a Gilded Age playground with trains linking it conveniently to Boston. The village's isolation preserved its appeal amid scarlet lilies, wild roses, and constant waves, fostering a seasonal economy of leisure and service.

Modern Residential Village

As summer resorts waned in the twentieth century, many mansions converted to year-round homes, blending Victorian architecture with newer residences while retaining Magnolia's identity as a quiet coastal enclave within Gloucester. Today it centers on beaches, historic homes, and community spots like the Magnolia Hand Laundry legacy.

Genealogical Resources

Magnolia residents appear in Gloucester town records, with vital events labeled by the village or Shore Road addresses; Essex County deeds trace farm-to-cottage subdivisions, linking early fishermen to Victorian summer families. Church registers from Gloucester parishes, census enumerations noting seasonal occupancy, and hotel guest lists or directories help reconstruct kin networks among Boston commuters, immigrant servants, and Cape Ann locals who shaped the village's resort heritage.

Merrimacport

Merrimacport is a historic riverfront village in the town of Merrimac, Essex County, Massachusetts, along the north bank of the Merrimack River opposite Amesbury's West End. Settled around 1638 as part of Salisbury and later Amesbury (known as West Amesbury), it started as a fishing outpost with farms and wharves tied to river trade and ferries.

Industrial Village and Carriage Hub

By the early 1800s, mills harnessed river power for textiles, pottery, and woodworking, evolving Merrimacport into an industrial cluster around Merrimac Square with factories like the Merrimac Potteries and carriage works that gained worldwide fame for horse-drawn vehicles. Shipbuilding and wharf commerce linked it to Haverhill and Newburyport, while railroads solidified its role as a manufacturing satellite to larger Merrimack Valley cities. The village incorporated as the separate town of Merrimac in 1876, preserving its distinct identity amid agricultural surroundings.

Modern Residential Port

Post-industrial decline saw mills close, shifting Merrimacport to a quiet residential neighborhood with preserved mill buildings, historic homes, and river access, now centered on West Main Street (Route 110) and the square.

Genealogical Resources

Records for Merrimacport families trace through Salisbury, Amesbury (as West Amesbury), and post-1876 Merrimac town books, with vital events often noting "Merrimacport" or river addresses; Essex County deeds and probate detail wharf lots, mill ownership, and farmsteads. Church registers from Amesbury parishes, factory payrolls, and carriage-industry directories connect inland millworkers to Amesbury sailors and Haverhill traders, mapping kin who fueled the village's rise from fishing hamlet to industrial port.

Rocks Village

Rocks Village is a small historic district in eastern Haverhill, Essex County, Massachusetts, along the south bank of the Merrimack River opposite West Newbury, centered around the Rocks Village Bridge and East Main Street (Route 110). Named after boulders ("Holt's Rocks") where early settler Nathaniel Holt grounded his boat in the 1640s, it began as a ferry crossing and agricultural outpost tied to Haverhill's inland farms.

Ferry, Bridge, and Commercial Growth

By 1652, a tavern (Coffin's Ordinary) served travelers, and ferries run by the Swett family from 1711 facilitated trade between Haverhill and Newbury; the first bridge opened in 1795 but washed out in 1818, replaced by ferries until a covered bridge in 1828 and the current steel truss in 1905. The village thrived with shipyards, stores, a post office, school, doctor, shoe shops, and fishing, peaking as a commercial hub for farmers and river commerce before railroads shifted focus.

Modern Quiet Neighborhood

Today, Rocks Village preserves 18th- and 19th-century homes in a national historic district, with a replica tollhouse museum evoking its self-contained past amid farms and river views.

Genealogical Resources

Rocks Village families appear in Haverhill town records as "Rocks" or "East Parish" residents, with vital events, land grants, and ferries noted in Essex County deeds and probate linking to West Newbury kin. Church books from Haverhill parishes, militia rolls, and bridge/tavern accounts trace settlers like the Holts, Sweats, and Clements, mapping networks among Merrimack farmers who built the village's crossing and commerce over centuries.

Plumb Island

Plumb Island (often spelled Plum Island) is a nine-mile-long barrier beach and island off the northeastern Massachusetts coast in Essex County, forming the eastern edge of the salt marshes between Newburyport, Newbury, Rowley, and Ipswich. First noted by explorers like Champlain in 1605 and Captain John Smith in 1614, it was granted in 1622 as part of the Mason patent but fell under Massachusetts Bay Colony control by the 1630s, named for abundant beach plums and used initially for grazing livestock, hay harvesting, and wildlife resources shared among nearby towns.

Shared Resource and Early Structures

In 1649, the General Court divided the island—two-fifths each to Newbury and Ipswich, one-fifth to Rowley—for common pastures, though overgrazing prompted restrictions by 1739; Newbury built the first house in 1752, a pest house followed in 1769, and Fort Philip defended the northern tip during the Revolution and War of 1812. Newbury sold its 600 acres in 1827, shifting from communal to private use amid shipwrecks and failed breakwaters.

Resort and Sanctuary Era

Summer cottages appeared from 1881, developing northern beaches into seasonal resorts by the late 19th century, while the Massachusetts Audubon Society bought 1,500 acres in the 1930s for a bird sanctuary, preserving much of the island as Parker River National Wildlife Refuge today alongside residential clusters.

Genealogical Resources

Plum Island records scatter across Newbury, Ipswich, and Rowley town books under "Plum Island" or marsh addresses, with Essex County deeds tracking grazing rights, lot sales, and cottage builds linking farm families to summer visitors. Shared militia rolls, poor-farm lists, and church registers from parent towns map kin who managed the island's resources, from 17th-century herders to 19th-century resort owners, revealing coastal networks without a central village archive.

<u>Prides Crossing</u>

Prides Crossing is an affluent coastal village and summer colony neighborhood in Beverly, Essex County, Massachusetts, along the Atlantic shore west of Beverly Farms and east of Manchester-by-the-Sea. Named after early settler John Pride, granted land there in 1636, it began as farmland on the Bass River side of early Beverly (then part of Salem), with sparse settlement focused on agriculture and fishing until rail access in the 1870s spurred development.

Gilded Age Summer Estates

From the late 1800s, tycoons like steel magnate Henry Clay Frick and banker Clarence Hungerford Mackay built lavish "cottages" such as Clayton and Harbor Hill, arriving via private railroad cars at the Prides Crossing station on Hale Street; the area became a private enclave of shingle-style and Colonial Revival mansions amid cliffs and beaches, served by a dedicated depot until service ended in 2020.

Modern Gated Community

Today, Prides Crossing remains a secluded residential area with preserved estates, many now year-round homes, retaining its elite summer-resort character within Beverly's municipal bounds.

Genealogical Resources

Records for Prides Crossing families fall under Beverly town vital registers, often noting "Prides Crossing," "Hale Street," or estate names; Essex County deeds trace 17th-century farm grants to Gilded Age subdivisions, linking Pride descendants to industrialists' kin. Census schedules highlight seasonal occupancy, railroad passenger lists, and Beverly church books map networks from colonial farmers to Boston elites who transformed the crossing into a shorefront haven.

<u>Salem Willows</u>

Salem Willows is a historic waterfront neighborhood and park district on Salem Neck in eastern Salem, Essex County, Massachusetts, along the shore of Salem Harbor near Juniper Point and Collins Cove. Originally used for firewood cutting, cattle grazing, and a smallpox hospital (pest house) in the 17th and 18th centuries, the area was planted with European white willow trees around 1801 to provide shade for patients, giving the site its name; it became a city park in 1858 amid early farmsteads like the Derby House tavern.

Resort and Amusement Development

Streetcar service from downtown Salem began in 1877 via the Naumkeag Street Railway, spurring developer Daniel Gardner to subdivide Juniper Point into cottage lots by 1875, creating a summer resort community of modest homes alongside the park's casino, pavilion, and "Restaurant Row" by the 1890s. Fort Lee (built 1776) defended the harbor during the Revolution, while later additions included a tuberculosis camp, salt-water pool, and marine lab on former pest-house grounds.

Modern Historic District

Today, the Salem Willows Historic District preserves Victorian cottages, amusement park relics like the 1965 Memorial Shell, and beachfront paths as a residential and recreational enclave within Salem.

Genealogical Resources

Salem Willows families appear in Salem town vital records under "Willows," "Salem Neck," or Juniper/Fort Avenue addresses, with Essex County deeds tracing pest-house, farm, and cottage subdivisions from colonial fishermen to resort dwellers. Church registers, streetcar passenger lists, and census notes on seasonal homes link early residents like the Crawfords and Ives to 19th-century vacationers, revealing harbor front networks tied to Salem's maritime and industrial growth.

10

Chapter 3

F ranklin County
Franklin County, Massachusetts, occupies the northwestern corner of the Common-wealth amid the rolling hills and river valleys of the Connecticut River watershed, where fertile floodplains, forested uplands, and rugged Deerfield Valley supported Abenaki and Nipmuc home-lands long before European arrival. Established in 1811 from Hampshire County territory, Franklin preserves a legacy of Indigenous riverine villages, frontier outposts, bloody colonial raids, small-scale mills, hill farms, and 19th-century manufacturing villages, blending rural isola-tion with strategic river access that fostered resilient townships from Shelburne Falls to Green-field.

For family historians, its narrative weaves through King Philip's War massacres, Shays' Re-bellion agrarian unrest, gristmills and woolen factories, Vermont border migrations, and waves of Irish, French Canadian, and Italian laborers, yielding records rich in Native survivance, Yan-kee yeomen, mill operatives, and ethnic enclaves across one of New England's least urbanized yet tightly networked counties.

Indigenous Foundations: Abenaki, Nipmuc, and River Homelands
Franklin County's pre-colonial landscape formed a vital corridor within Abenaki (Western) and Nipmuc territories, where communities along the Deerfield, Connecticut, and Westfield rivers practiced maize horticulture on bottomlands, supplemented by seasonal hunts, fisheries for shad and salmon, and nut-gathering in oak-hickory forests. Sachems coordinated kinship-based bands through diplomacy and marriage, with trails linking valley villages to the Green Mountains and Berkshires; archaeological sites like the Fort River Nipmuc village reveal long-term seasonal occupancy erased by epidemics and conflict. Seventeenth-century English encroachments—via Springfield traders and Hadley grants—provoked devastating raids during King Philip's War (1675-76), culminating in the Bloody Brook and Turner's Falls massacres that displaced survivors northward or into Praying Towns; genealogists tracing Indigenous lines must correlate deed re-leases by sachems like Awechausimo, captive narratives, and later petitions from Stockbridge-Munsee or Abenaki descendants with oral traditions.

Colonial Settlement, Frontier Defense, and Congregational Culture
Settlement radiated from the Connecticut Valley after 1660s grants to Deerfield and Hatfield pro-prietors, who allocated house lots near forts and outlots along rivers amid constant Abenaki-French raids peaking in Queen Anne's War (1704 Deerfield massacre). Towns like Greenfield,

Shelburne, and Montague coalesced as defensive hamlets with blockhouses, evolving into dispersed farmsteads by mid-18th century; proprietors' books and division records map "first families" like the Hancocks and Cooleys as they claimed meadows and woodlots. Congregational churches, planted amid wilderness, produced covenants, relation narratives, and baptism registers essential for pre-1700 births absent from sparse civil books; parish splits—Old Lights vs. New Lights—generated parallel records tracking theological schisms within lineages. County courts in Northampton (pre-1811) and later Greenfield handled guardianships, bastardy cases, and wolf bounties, while Shays' Rebellion files (1786-87) name debtor farmers from Conway and Ashfield, revealing class tensions in probate disputes and tax lists.

Early Mills, Rural Industry, and Vermont Exodus

Eighteenth-century gristmills, sawmills, and iron forges at falls like Shelburne Falls and Turner's Falls anchored proto-industrial villages, employing apprentices visible in indentures; by 1800, wool-carding and fulling mills dotted valleys, drawing upland farmers into cash economies. The 1811 county formation spurred town incorporations like Erving and Leyden, but poor soils and long winters prompted out-migration to Vermont and New York, tracked in warnings-out, removal orders, and land sales that left "staying" kin in deeds. Quaker meetings in Whately and Shaker outposts near Enfield (later in Hampshire) left marriage and disownment minutes for dissenting families.

Industrial Villages, Immigration, and 20th-Century Decline

Nineteenth-century waterpower fueled cutlery in Greenfield, paper mills in Turners Falls (French Canadian hub), and basket factories in Orange, creating ethnic wards documented in boarding-house censuses and Catholic registers from Sacred Heart (Greenfield). Civil War regiments from Franklin drew farm boys and mill hands, with pension affidavits detailing family ties; Black residents, sparse but present via Underground Railroad stops in Shelburne, appear in manumission papers and postbellum directories. Yankee women entered mills as "farm girls," while immigrant wives ran boardinghouses noted in tax rolls; fraternal lodges like Odd Fellows preserved membership lists. Post-1920s factory closures shifted to tourism and commuting, with Route 2 bisecting old mill villages.

Genealogical Resources and Research Strategies

Franklin's records center on town clerks' vitals (many transcribed to 1850), Essex-style but sparser pre-1750, supplemented by FamilySearch-indexed church books from Congregational Library and diocesan archives. Hampshire and Franklin County deeds/probate (Greenfield courthouse) trace valley lots from proprietors to mill parcels; censuses reveal boarders in Turners Falls tenements. Forbes Library (Northampton) and local historical societies hold diaries, store ledgers, and Shays' papers; strategies start with town-based clusters, cross-referencing raids' captive lists and mill payrolls to map Native-Yankee intermarriages and migrant chains to hill towns like Hawley. This archive, shaped by frontier perils and valley industry, unveils kin enduring from Abenaki stewards to milltown descendants.

11

C ities and Towns of Franklin County

CITIES

GREENFIELD

Greenfield serves as the shire town and county seat of Franklin County in north-central Massachusetts, situated at the confluence of the Deerfield and Connecticut rivers amid fertile valley bottomlands and surrounding hills. Settled around 1686 as a northerly outpost of Deerfield amid ongoing Abenaki raids, it emerged from frontier vulnerability—marked by the 1704 Deerfield Massacre's aftermath—into a district in 1753 and full town by 1775, with portions later forming Gill and Montague. Its central position fostered mills, stores, and courthouses, evolving into a manufacturing hub with cutlery works, paper mills, and basket factories by the 19th century.

Frontier Outpost to County Seat

Early growth centered on house lots near the Green and river landings, with proprietors dividing meadows for first families like the Wells and Arms amid blockhouses; the 1811 Franklin County formation elevated Greenfield as judicial and commercial hub, its courthouse and jail drawing lawyers, merchants, and Shays' Rebellion debtors from hill towns. Rail arrival in the 1840s spurred industry, peaking with Highland House hotel, trolley lines, and immigrant labor in Nashua River mills.

Industrial and Civic Center

Nineteenth-century booms brought French Canadian and Irish workers to factory wards, while Yankee elites built Victorian homes on High Street; post-Civil War, it hosted county fairs, academies, and newspapers, blending rural trade with urban amenities until 20th-century mill closures shifted focus to services and commuting.

Genealogical Resources and Strategies

Greenfield records anchor Franklin research, with town vital registers (1752–1861, published to 1850) listing births, marriages, and deaths often noting "District" or river addresses; church books from First Congregational (1775–1911) and Catholic parishes capture Yankee baptisms and immigrant kin. Essex County-style deeds and probate at the Greenfield courthouse trace lot divisions from Deerfield grants to mill parcels, while censuses reveal boarders in Highland tenements; strategies begin with county court files for guardianships and bastardy, cross-referencing Shays' papers and mill payrolls to map networks from raid survivors to factory families spanning valley towns.

TOWNS

Bernardston

Bernardston occupies the northeastern corner of Franklin County, Massachusetts, along Fall River amid forested hills and valley meadows near the Vermont and New Hampshire borders. Granted in 1735 as Falltown (or Falls Fight Township) to heirs of soldiers from the 1676 Turner's Falls battle during King Philip's War, it was settled starting in 1738 by pioneers like Major John Burk, Samuel Connable, and the Sheldons, who built log forts with portholes against Abenaki raids; incorporated in 1762 and named for Governor Francis Bernard, it lost territory to Colrain and Leyden but retained a compact farming core.

Frontier Forts and Agricultural Roots

Early houses clustered at Burk's Fort and Deacon Sheldon's on Huckle Hill for defense during the French and Indian War, with Rev. John Norton ordained in 1741 as first minister; residents raised rye, corn, cider, and early maple sugar, shipping via Connecticut River Railroad after 1848 while enduring Shays' Rebellion debts and Vermont migrations. Power's Institute academy and small manufactories like hoes and shoes dotted the landscape by the 19th century.

Modern Rural Township

Today Bernardston preserves its colonial village green, historic homes, and agricultural heritage as a quiet bedroom community along Route 10, with remnants of forts and early roads evoking frontier resilience.

Genealogical Resources and Strategies

Bernardston vital records (from 1762, published to 1850) and First Congregational church registers (1741 onward) capture baptisms, marriages, and memberships for fort-era families; Franklin County deeds and probate trace lot draws from Falls Fight grantees to farm divisions. Strategies start with proprietors' records for "first-comers" like Burks and Sheldons, cross-referencing militia rolls, wolf bounties, and warnings-out to map kin enduring raids, who later spread to hill farms and neighboring Colrain.

Buckland

Buckland sits in central Franklin County, Massachusetts, along the Deerfield River's east branch amid steep hills and narrow valleys near Shelburne and Charlemont, forming a rugged upland township beyond the fertile Connecticut Valley flats. Granted in 1779 (settled from 1772) to veterans of the French and Indian Wars and named for town founder Benjamin Ruggles Woodbridge's Buckland, England estate, it drew pioneers like the Hawks and Baggs who cleared forested slopes for sheep pastures and orchards amid rocky soils; incorporated in 1812, it spawned Ashfield parcels but retained a dispersed farming core centered on Upper and Lower Meadows.

Hill Farms and Early Industry

Settlement clustered at mills along the river—grist, saw, and fulling—powering wool-carding and chair factories by the early 1800s, with Rev. Justus Forward's Congregational church (1786) anchoring spiritual life; Shays' Rebellion participants from Buckland farms faced tax debts, prompting Vermont out-migrations tracked in warnings-out, while 19th-century cheese factories and tanneries employed upland kin.

Modern Rural Community

Today Buckland preserves its colonial meetinghouse, covered bridges like the 1858 Upper Meadow, and agricultural heritage as a quiet hill town with tourism drawing visitors to Wendell Falls and historic districts.

Genealogical Resources and Strategies

Buckland vital records (from 1779, published to 1850) and First Congregational registers (1786 onward) document baptisms and marriages for pioneer families; Franklin County deeds trace lot divisions from Woodbridge grantees to mill parcels and sheep farms. Strategies begin with proprietors' books for "first settlers" like Hawks, cross-referencing militia lists, poor-relief rolls, and Shays' files to reconstruct kin networks enduring hill hardships, linking to Deerfield valley cousins and Ashfield offshoots.

Charlemont

Charlemont spans eastern Franklin County, Massachusetts, along the Deerfield River amid steep Mohawk Trail hills and narrow valleys near the Berkshire line, forming a rugged frontier township beyond the Connecticut Valley core. Granted in 1735 as Boston Township Number 1 (or Checkley's Town), it was first settled around 1742-1743 by Capt. Moses Rice, who bought 2,200 acres and built the first house near the "Old Fields," joined by sons Asa (captured by Abenaki in 1746) and others amid French and Indian War raids; incorporated in 1765 and named for Irish Earl James Caulfield, it annexed Zoar in 1838 but retained a dispersed hill-farming pattern.

Frontier Raids and Rural Development

Early forts like Rice's and Col. Ephraim Williams' line protected meadows where settlers raised corn, rye, and sheep, with Rev. Isaac Babbit ordained in 1796 as first settled minister; gristmills and sawmills powered small industry, while the railroad and Mohawk Trail later boosted tourism, including Berkshire East ski area on old pastures. Shays' Rebellion drew local farmers into unrest, tracked in court files.

Modern Outdoor Recreation Hub

Today Charlemont preserves colonial sites, a covered Mill River bridge, and 126 historic structures as a rural community blending agriculture with adventure tourism along Route 2.

Genealogical Resources and Strategies

Charlemont vital records (from 1765, published to 1850) and Congregational church registers (1788 onward) document baptisms for Rice-era families, Franklin County deeds trace Rice's purchase to lot divisions amid raids. Strategies start with plantation records for first settlers like Rices and Patches, cross-referencing militia rolls, captive narratives, and warnings-out to map kin surviving Abenaki threats, linking to Deerfield survivors and hill neighbors like Hawley.

Colrain

Colrain occupies the northwestern corner of Franklin County, Massachusetts, along the north bank of the Deerfield River amid steep hills and narrow valleys near the Vermont border, forming a remote upland township beyond the Connecticut Valley settlements. Granted in 1735 as a Falls Fight township to heirs of Turner's Falls battle veterans and settled from 1736 by pioneers like Ebenezer Smalley and the Hubbards who built fortified houses against Abenaki raids, it was incorporated in 1761 and named for Irish Colraine; it lost parcels to Halifax (later Guilford, VT) but retained a dispersed farming core centered on Lyonsville and Griswoldville mills.

Frontier Defense and Agrarian Life

Early clusters at Smalley's Fort and river meadows defended cornfields and orchards, with Rev. William Goddard ordained in 1770; gristmills, sawmills, and 19th-century broom factories powered by the river employed kin, while Shays' Rebellion leaders like Luke Day rallied local farmers amid debt crises prompting Vermont migrations tracked in warnings-out.

Modern Hill Town

Today Colrain preserves its colonial green, historic district with 18th-century homes, and agricultural heritage as a quiet rural community along Route 112, with small-scale farming and tourism.

Genealogical Resources and Strategies

Colrain vital records (from 1761, published to 1850) and First Congregational registers (1770 onward) capture baptisms for fort families; Franklin County deeds trace Falls Fight lots to farm divisions. Strategies begin with proprietors' books for first-comers like Smalleys, cross-referencing militia rolls, raid narratives, and Shays' files to map kin enduring frontier perils, linking to Bernardston forts and Deerfield valley networks.

Conway

Conway lies in the south-central part of Franklin County, Massachusetts, straddling the South River amid steep, wooded hills between Deerfield and Ashfield. Settled in the 1760s on land originally part of Deerfield's "Narragansett" grants, it incorporated in 1767 and took its name from General Henry Seymour Conway, with an economy rooted in mixed hill farming, small water-powered mills, and later dairying rather than large river-bottom plantations.

Frontier Farms and Mill Villages

Early settlement clustered along the South River and in village centers such as Conway Center and Burkeville, where gristmills, sawmills, and fulling mills served scattered farmsteads carved from heavy timber. During the late 18th and early 19th centuries, carding mills, tanneries, and small textile and paper operations developed along the river, drawing in a modest wage-labor force while many families combined subsistence agriculture with seasonal work in nearby Deerfield and Greenfield. Shays' Rebellion touched Conway through indebted farmers and militia mobilizations, visible in court and town meeting records that name local participants and their kin.

Modern Rural Town

Railroads and better roads in the 19th century tied Conway to regional markets, but the town remained largely agrarian, with population losses to the Midwest and mill towns offset by limited industrial growth in cheese factories and small manufactories. In the 20th and 21st centuries Conway evolved into a quiet hill town with a mix of working farms, woodlots, and commuter households, its historic center, old mill sites, and surviving 19th-century homes preserving the look of a classic western Massachusetts upland community.

Genealogical Resources and Strategies

Conway's town vital records (from incorporation forward, and in published form to 1850) document births, marriages, and deaths for founding families, often noting river hamlets or hill neighborhoods that help place kin in the landscape. Congregational and later Baptist and Methodist church registers add baptisms and memberships, while Franklin County deeds and probate trace the subdivision of original Deerfield-derived grants into smaller farms, revealing migration chains to Ashfield, Shelburne, and Vermont.

For genealogists, effective work in Conway pairs town and church records with tax lists, Shays' Rebellion-related court files, and agricultural census schedules to reconstruct farm-based households and track the younger generation as they left the hills for valley mills and western lands.

Deerfield

Deerfield anchors the Connecticut River valley in central Franklin County, Massachusetts, amid fertile floodplains flanked by hills and the Deerfield River, serving as a colonial frontier hub that spawned upland townships like Greenfield and Conway. Originally Pocumtuck territory granted in 1669 as part of Hadley's "Pys" patent, it was settled from 1673 by pioneers like Samuel Hinsdale who built "Street" houses along the river amid Abenaki threats; raided repeatedly during King Philip's War (Bloody Brook 1675) and the 1704 French-Indian massacre that killed 47 and took 112 captives, it rebuilt as a fortified plantation before incorporating in 1677 and dividing into Old Deerfield (historic district) and South Deerfield.

Frontier Stronghold to Agricultural Center

The linear "Street" of 18th-century homes, meetinghouse, and fort defended meadows where families raised wheat, tobacco, and cattle, shipping via river rafts; Rev. John Williams' captivity narrative (1704) immortalized kin like Eleazer (redeemed) and survivors who repopulated amid Shays' Rebellion unrest. 19th-century mills at Bloody Brook and railroads boosted broomcorn, onions, and tobacco processing, drawing Irish and French Canadian labor to factory villages.

Modern Historic Valley Town

Today Deerfield preserves Memorial Hall Museum, the preserved 18th-century Street, and agricultural heritage as a cultural landmark blending farm, Historic Deerfield academy, and tourism along Route 5.

Genealogical Resources and Strategies

Deerfield vital records (from 1673, published to 1850) and First Church registers (1675 onward, with Williams' baptisms) capture massacre survivors and captives; Hampshire/Franklin deeds trace "Street" lots from proprietors to farm divisions. Strategies start with Williams family clusters and captive lists, cross-referencing probate (rich inventories), militia rolls, and Shays' files to map Pocumtuck-English intermarriages and chains to hill towns like Conway.

Erving

Erving occupies a narrow strip in east-central Franklin County, Massachusetts, along the Connecticut River south of Montague and north of Northfield, encompassing wooded hills, river meadows, and the Erving Paper mill site at the falls. Originally part of Sunderland and Montague (settled around 1765 as part of "Narragansett No. 4" grants), it drew pioneers clearing timber for farms amid rocky soils; incorporated in 1838 from Montague territory and named for mill founder Samuel Erving, it developed as a mill village rather than dispersed agriculture.

Mill Village Development

Settlement focused on the paper mill founded in 1811 (rebuilt after floods), powering rag and wood-pulp production that employed generations of Yankee, Irish, and French Canadian workers in company boardinghouses along the river; small farms supplied cordwood, while Rev. Samuel May's Congregational church (1830s) served the workforce, with railroads linking to Greenfield markets by 1870.

Modern Rural Mill Town

Today Erving preserves its historic mill complex (now luxury condos), colonial homes, and rural character as a quiet community along Route 2A, blending paper-mill legacy with recreation on the river.

Genealogical Resources and Strategies

Erving vital records (from 1838, published to 1850) and church registers document mill families; Franklin County deeds trace Montague lots to mill parcels and worker tenements. Strategies start with company payrolls and boardinghouse censuses for operatives, cross-referencing Montague parent-town records and probate to map kin from upland farms to factory wards, linking to Northfield and Gill networks.

Gill

Gill forms a narrow riverfront township in east-central Franklin County, Massachusetts, along the west bank of the Connecticut River opposite Greenfield, encompassing fertile meadows, wooded bluffs, and the historic Turners Falls canal. Originally part of Deerfield (settled around 1673 amid Pocumtuck lands), it separated as a district in 1770 and incorporated in 1793, named for Moses Gill, lieutenant governor; pioneers like the Temples and Allens cleared bottomlands for tobacco and grain while defending against Abenaki raids tied to nearby Bloody Brook and Falls Fight.

River Farms and Canal Industry

Settlement strung along the river road with houses facing east toward meadows, where families rafted produce to Hartford markets; the 1790s Turners Falls canal and locks drew millers, boatmen, and laborers to the falls, powering gristmills and sawmills amid Shays' Rebellion tensions. 19th-century tobacco warehouses and small factories employed kin, with First Congregational church (1774) anchoring the linear village.

Modern Riverside Community

Today Gill preserves its colonial homes, one-room schoolhouse museum, and agricultural heritage as a quiet rural enclave with river recreation and views of Greenfield across the water.

Genealogical Resources and Strategies

Gill vital records (from 1793, published to 1850) and church registers (1774 onward) document Deerfield spin-off families; Franklin County deeds trace river lots from original grants to canal parcels. Strategies begin with Deerfield parent records for pre-separation kin like Temples, cross-referencing canal payrolls, militia rolls, and probate to map valley networks linking to Greenfield mills and upland Conway farms.

Hawley

Hawley sits in the western uplands of Franklin County, Massachusetts, amid steep hills and narrow valleys of the Westfield River watershed near the Berkshire line, forming a remote hill township beyond the Deerfield Valley settlements. Granted in 1775 (settled from 1762) as part of equivalent lands to compensate Cheshire County, NH proprietors and named for settler Joseph Hawley, it drew pioneers like the Belding and Tower families who cleared rocky forests for sheep pastures and small farms amid poor soils; incorporated in 1792, it retained a dispersed pattern centered on the Congregational meetinghouse green.

Hill Farms and Shaker Influence

Early clusters at the plain near the church defended scattered homesteads during Shays' Rebellion, where local farmers joined unrest over debts; small mills along the river powered chairmaking and broom factories by the 19th century, while a short-lived Shaker community (c. 1800) left marriage refusals and disownments in records, blending with Yankee agriculture of wool, cheese, and maple sugar shipped via poor roads to Shelburne Falls.

Modern Rural Hill Town

Today Hawley preserves its 18th-century green, one-room school remnants, and agricultural heritage as a quiet community with farmstands and outdoor recreation, population stabilized by conservation easements.

Genealogical Resources and Strategies

Hawley vital records (from 1792, published to 1850) and First Congregational registers (1787 onward) capture baptisms for pioneer families; Franklin County deeds trace lot divisions from NH-equivalent grants to hill pastures. Strategies start with proprietors' books for first-comers like Beltings, cross-referencing Shays' court files, Shaker minutes, and warnings-out to map kin enduring isolation, linking to Ashfield lowlands and Buckland mills.

Heath

Heath perches in the northwestern highlands of Franklin County, Massachusetts, atop Avery Hill amid rocky plateaus and dense forests near the Vermont border, forming one of the state's highest townships at over 1,800 feet elevation. Granted in 1761 (settled from 1750s) as Dublin Township to New Hampshire proprietors and renamed in 1770 for Revolutionary general John Heath, it drew hardy pioneers like the Hills and Crafts who cleared spruce barrens for marginal sheep farms and apple orchards amid harsh winters and thin soils; incorporated in 1785, it retained a dispersed settlement pattern centered on the Congregational church and common.

Upland Sheep Pastures and Isolation

Early homes clustered near the meetinghouse for defense and mutual aid, with gristmills in Heath's hollows powering minimal industry; Shays' Rebellion rallied local wool-growers against debts, while 19th-century cheese factories and potash works supplemented agriculture, prompting out-migrations to the Midwest tracked in town warnings-out amid Vermont border flux.

Modern Hilltop Community

Today Heath preserves its 1790s meetinghouse, stone walls enclosing old pastures, and rural character as a quiet enclave with conservation lands and farm tourism, its remoteness fostering tight-knit families.

Genealogical Resources and Strategies

Heath vital records (from 1785, published to 1850) and First Congregational registers (1779 onward) document baptisms for highland pioneers; Franklin County deeds trace NH township lots to subdivided woodlots. Strategies begin with proprietors' records for Dublin grantees like Crafts, cross-referencing Shays' files, poor-relief rolls, and militia lists to map kin surviving uplands, linking to Bernardston valleys and Colrain river farms.

Leverett

Leverett occupies a hilly enclave in southeastern Franklin County, Massachusetts, along the Sawmill River amid steep wooded slopes and narrow valleys between Amherst and Montague, forming a remote upland township beyond the fertile Connecticut Valley plains. Granted in 1774 (settled from 1760s) as part of equivalent lands from Hampshire County and named for Revolutionary colonel John Leverett, it drew pioneers like the Barkers and Montagues who cleared timbered ridges for sheep pastures and small farms amid rocky soils; incorporated in 1778, it retained a dispersed pattern centered on the Congregational meetinghouse and Leverett Pond mills.

Hill Farms and Quaker Settlements

Early clusters near the plain and river hollows supported gristmills and sawmills powering chair factories and broom works by the 19th century, with a notable Quaker community (1780s–1830s) at North Leverett leaving marriage refusals and disownments; Shays' Rebellion mobilized local farmers against debts, while cheese and wool production supplemented agriculture shipped via rough roads to Deerfield markets.

Modern Rural Hill Town

Today Leverett preserves its 18th-century green, historic Quaker cemetery, and agricultural heritage as a quiet community with conservation forests, organic farms, and outdoor recreation along Route 63.

Genealogical Resources and Strategies

Leverett vital records (from 1778, published to 1850) and First Congregational/Quaker registers (1780s onward) capture baptisms for pioneer and dissenting families; Franklin County deeds trace lot divisions from Hampshire grants to hill pastures. Strategies start with proprietors' books for first-comers like Barkers, cross-referencing Shays' court files, Quaker minutes, and warnings-out to map kin enduring isolation, linking to Montague mills and Amherst lowlands.

Leyden

Leyden forms a small upland township in northeastern Franklin County, Massachusetts, along the Connecticut River amid forested hills and narrow valleys near the Vermont and New Hampshire borders, separated from Bernardston by remote ridges. Granted in 1784 (settled from 1780s) from Bernardston territory as part of Falls Fight equivalent lands and named for Dutch city Leiden (Puritan refuge), it drew pioneers like the Frinks and Crafts who cleared timber for marginal farms and pastures amid thin soils; incorporated in 1809, it retained a tiny, dispersed pattern with no formal village center.

Remote Hill Farms

Early homes scattered along dirt roads supported minimal gristmills and sawmills, with Congregational services rotating among homes before a short-lived meetinghouse; Shays' Rebellion debts prompted Vermont border shifts, while 19th-century wool and cheese production supplemented self-sufficient agriculture shipped via poor trails to Greenfield.

Modern Tiny Rural Enclave

Today Leyden preserves its colonial farmsteads and stone walls as Massachusetts' third-smallest town by area, a quiet hill community with conservation lands and minimal services along Route 10.

Genealogical Resources and Strategies

Leyden vital records (from 1809, sparse and published to 1850) rely heavily on Bernardston parent-town registers for pre-separation kin, Franklin County deeds trace lot divisions from Falls Fight grantees to isolated homesteads. Strategies begin with Bernardston church and proprietors' books for Frinks-era families, cross-referencing warnings-out, tax rolls, and militia lists to map kin in this remote outpost, linking to Colrain valleys and Vermont migrations.

Monroe

Monroe perches on the high western plateau of Franklin County, Massachusetts, amid spruce forests and rocky summits near the Berkshire line, forming one of the state's most remote and elevated townships at over 2,000 feet. Granted in 1804 (settled from 1780s) from portions of Rowe, Heath, and Florida as equivalent lands compensating earlier proprietors and named for President James Monroe, it drew hardy pioneers like the Snows and Severances who cleared dense woods for marginal sheep pastures, potash production, and small orchards amid glacial soils and harsh winters; incorporated in 1822, it retained an extremely dispersed pattern with no true village center.

Highland Isolation and Sheep Economy

Early homes scattered across ridges supported minimal sawmills along the north branch of Deerfield River, with Congregational services in rotating homes; Shays' Rebellion aftermath and poor farming prompted heavy out-migrations to New York and Ohio, tracked in warnings-out, while 19th-century wool production and chair factories offered seasonal work shipped via rugged trails to Shelburne Falls.

Modern Tiny Hilltop Enclave

Today Monroe preserves its colonial farm remnants, stone walls, and vast conservation lands as Massachusetts' least populous town, a quiet backcountry community accessible mainly by dirt roads with farm tourism and hiking.

Genealogical Resources and Strategies

Monroe vital records (from 1822, very sparse and published to 1850) depend heavily on parent-town registers from Rowe and Heath for pre-separation kin; Franklin County deeds trace isolated lot divisions from equivalent grants. Strategies start with Rowe/Heath church and proprietors' books for Snow-era families, cross-referencing poor-relief rolls, tax delinquencies, and militia lists to map kin surviving extreme isolation, linking to Rowe valleys and Berkshire migrations.

Montague

Montague spans east-central Franklin County, Massachusetts, along both banks of the Connecticut River north of Greenfield, encompassing the industrial village of Turners Falls amid fertile meadows, canal locks, and upland farms. Originally part of Sunderland (settled 1673 amid Pocumtuck lands), it separated as a district in 1781 and incorporated in 1790 from Deerfield and Sunderland territory, named for Lady Mary Montagu; the 1860s canal and locks at Turners Falls drew massive investment, transforming meadows into a mill city while rural precincts retained agriculture.

Canal Village and Industrial Boom

Settlement clustered along the Great Road with river farms raising tobacco and grain, but Turners Falls boomed post-1868 with paper mills, cotton factories, and brickworks powered by canal water, attracting French Canadian, Irish, and Polish immigrants to company tenements; First Congregational (1784) and Catholic churches served divided populations, while Shays' Rebellion farmers endured debts amid upland warnings-out.

Modern River Town

Today Montague preserves its historic canal district, Victorian mill buildings, and rural precincts like Montague Center as a diverse community blending industry legacy, farms, and recreation along Route 2.

Genealogical Resources and Strategies

Montague vital records (from 1790, published to 1850) and multi-church registers (Congregational 1784, Catholic 1870s) document Yankee farmers and immigrant millworkers; Franklin County deeds trace Deerfield lots to canal parcels and tenements. Strategies start with parent-town Deerfield records for pre-separation kin, cross-referencing factory payrolls, boardinghouse censuses, and Shays' files to map valley networks linking rural Montague to Turners Falls wards and Greenfield commerce.

New Salem

New Salem occupies the southwestern corner of Franklin County, Massachusetts, along the Swift River amid steep hills and narrow valleys near the Quabbin Reservoir lands, forming a remote upland township beyond the Connecticut Valley core. Granted in 1737 (settled from 1750s) as part of equivalent lands from Hampshire County and named for settlers from old Salem, it drew pioneers like the Howes and Newtons who cleared forested ridges for sheep pastures and apple orchards amid rocky soils; incorporated in 1761, it lost territory to Prescott and Enfield (submerged by Quabbin) but retained a dispersed farming core centered on the village green and mills.

Hill Farms and Quabbin Displacement

Early clusters near the meetinghouse supported gristmills and sawmills powering chair factories and broom works by the 19th century, with Rev. Thomas Goss' Congregational church (1763) anchoring life; Shays' Rebellion mobilized local wool-growers against debts, while cheese production and potash supplemented agriculture shipped via rough roads to Deerfield, until 1930s Quabbin evictions scattered families eastward.

Modern Rural Hill Town

Today New Salem preserves its 18th-century green, historic district, and agricultural heritage as a quiet community with conservation lands and proximity to Quabbin recreation along Route 202.

Genealogical Resources and Strategies
New Salem vital records (from 1761, published to 1850) and First Congregational registers (1763 onward) capture baptisms for pioneer families; Franklin County deeds trace lot divisions from Hampshire grants to hill pastures and Quabbin-holdout farms. Strategies start with proprietors' books for first-comers like Howes, cross-referencing Shays' court files, Quabbin relocation records, and warnings-out to map kin enduring uplands, linking to Shutesbury lowlands and Prescott diaspora.

Northfield

Northfield stretches along the Connecticut River in northeastern Franklin County, Massachusetts, encompassing fertile bottomlands, river bluffs, and upland farms opposite Vermont's hills, serving as a colonial frontier gateway near the Pocumtuck homelands. Granted in 1673 (settled 1685) as "Quinnebaug Old Plantation" to Hadley proprietors and named for William North of Ipswich, it endured Abenaki raids during King Philip's War before rebuilding with fortified houses; incorporated in 1714, it spawned Vernon and Warwick parcels but retained a linear river-road settlement centered on the Great Meadow and Watson's Falls mills.

Frontier Farms and Religious Revivals
Early pioneers like the Wrights and Hills defended tobacco fields and orchards along the river, rafting produce southward; Rev. Solomon Stoddard's influence and Great Awakening revivals (1730s) produced detailed church covenants and relation narratives, while 19th-century gristmills, sawmills, and Northfield Seminary (1848, Dwight L. Moody's legacy) drew students and workers amid Shays' Rebellion debts.

Modern River Valley Town
Today Northfield preserves its colonial meetinghouse, Moody Bible Institute campus, and agricultural heritage as a quiet community blending farms, seminaries, and recreation along Route 10.

Genealogical Resources and Strategies
Northfield vital records (from 1714, published to 1850) and First Congregational registers (1721 onward, rich in awakenings) capture baptisms for raid survivors; Franklin County deeds trace meadow lots from proprietors to farm divisions. Strategies start with Stoddard-era church admissions and captive lists, cross-referencing seminary rolls, Shays' files, and militia bounties to map Pocumtuck-English kin networks linking to Vernon uplands and Deerfield valley cousins.

Orange

Orange lies in the southeastern corner of Franklin County, Massachusetts, along the Millers River amid rolling hills and narrow valleys near the Worcester County line, forming a transitional upland township between the Connecticut Valley and Quabbin lands. First settled around 1746 in North Orange from territories of Athol, Warwick, Royalston, and Erving's Grant, it organized as a district in 1783 and incorporated as a town in 1810, named for William, Prince of Orange; early pioneers like Joseph Lawrence cleared forested slopes for large farms raising sheep, cattle, and apples amid rocky soils.

Farming Village to Industrial Center
North Orange emerged as the first compact settlement with a 1781 meetinghouse and turnpike

taverns serving Boston-Northfield stagecoaches, while Tully village developed mills harnessing Tully River power for blacksmiths and factories; by the late 19th century, the New Home Sewing Machine Company boomed along the river, employing Yankee and immigrant labor in a shift from agriculture to manufacturing shipped via railroads. Shays' Rebellion debts affected hill farmers, tracked in court records.

Modern Mill Town

Today Orange preserves its North Orange green, Victorian mill districts, and agricultural outskirts as a working-class community with light industry and proximity to Quabbin recreation along Route 2A.

Genealogical Resources and Strategies

Orange vital records (from 1810, published to 1850) and Congregational/Unitarian church registers (1780s onward) document pioneer families; Franklin County deeds trace lot divisions from parent-town grants to mill parcels. Strategies start with North Orange church admissions and proprietors' books for Lawrences and Goddards, cross-referencing sewing-machine payrolls, Shays' files, and warnings-out to map kin from hill farms to factory wards, linking to Athol lowlands and Warwick uplands.

Rowe

Rowe occupies the northwestern highlands of Franklin County, Massachusetts, along the Deerfield River amid steep forested hills and narrow valleys near the Berkshire line and Vermont border, forming a remote upland township beyond the Connecticut Valley settlements. First visited by scouting parties in 1744 amid Fort Pelham (part of the defensive line against French-Indian raids), it was purchased in 1762 by Rev. Cornelius Jones as the 10,000-acre Myrifield Plantation, drawing early settlers like Jonathan Lamb and Artemas Ward who cleared timber for farms and mills; incorporated in 1785 and named for Boston merchant John Rowe, it lost western lands to Monroe but retained a dispersed pattern centered on river hollows.

Frontier Mills and Mining Boom

Early clusters near sawmills and gristmills powered woolen factories and satinets by the early 19th century, with Congregational preaching splitting into orthodox and Unitarian factions; Shays' Rebellion debts spurred out-migrations, while late-1800s talc, soapstone, and sulfur mining at Davis Mine created temporary boomtowns, followed by railroad resorts and hydroelectric plants transforming the river economy.

Modern Power Town

Today Rowe preserves Fort Pelham ruins, abandoned mine sites, and Yankee Rowe nuclear legacy (1950s-1992) as a quiet rural community with hydro stations and conservation lands along Route 2.

Genealogical Resources and Strategies

Rowe vital records (from 1785, published to 1850) and Congregational registers (1780s onward, with splits) document Jones-era families; Franklin County deeds trace Myrifield lots to mine parcels and river farms. Strategies start with plantation records for first-comers like Lambs, cross-referencing Fort Pelham militia rolls, mining payrolls, and warnings-out to map kin enduring raids and isolation, linking to Heath forts and Monroe highlands.

Shelburne

Shelburne lies in west-central Franklin County, Massachusetts, along both banks of the Deerfield River amid rolling hills and narrow valleys between Greenfield and Buckland, forming a valley township with the dual character of upland farms and the mill village of Shelburne Falls. First settled in 1756 as "Deerfield Northwest" from Deerfield territory amid Pocumtuck lands and Abenaki threats, it organized as a district in 1768 (named for William Petty, Earl of Shelburne) and incorporated as a town in 1775, drawing pioneers like the Fiske, Catlin, and Ryder families who built log homes and cleared meadows for grain and livestock.

Frontier Farms to Falls Village

Early settlement clustered in the eastern hills with a log meetinghouse (c. 1769), while Shelburne Falls developed around Jonathan Wood's gristmill (1770s) and bridges spanning the river; Shays' Rebellion mobilized indebted farmers, followed by 19th-century booms in satinet mills, tanneries, and cutlery factories powered by the falls, employing Yankee and immigrant labor shipped via railroads.

Modern Mill Village Town

Today Shelburne preserves its historic Shelburne Falls village (National Register district), the 1821 covered bridge replica, and agricultural outskirts as a creative community blending industry legacy, arts, and tourism along Route 2.

Genealogical Resources and Strategies

Shelburne vital records (from 1768 district era, published to 1850) and First Congregational registers (1770s onward) document Deerfield spin-off families; Franklin County deeds trace "Northwest" lots to mill parcels and hill farms. Strategies start with Deerfield parent records for pre-separation kin like Fiskes, cross-referencing mill payrolls, Shays' court files, and bridge lot sales to map valley networks linking upland Shelburne to Buckland factories and Greenfield commerce.

Shutesbury

Shutesbury lies in the southeastern corner of Franklin County, Massachusetts, amid steep hills and narrow valleys of the Swift River watershed near the Quabbin Reservoir and Hampshire County line, forming a remote upland township beyond the Connecticut Valley plains. Granted in 1735 as "Road Town" to build a road through roadless wilderness on Nipmuc lands and settled from the 1750s by pioneers from Sudbury like the Lockes and Childs who cleared rocky forests for sheep pastures and small farms, it incorporated in 1761 and was renamed for colonial governor Samuel Shute, losing eastern parcels to New Salem but retaining a dispersed pattern centered on the meetinghouse plain.

Hill Farms and Mineral Springs

Early settlement clustered near mineral springs that powered a 19th-century bottling industry, with gristmills and sawmills supporting chair factories and broom works; Shays' Rebellion drew local farmers into debt protests, while Quaker influences and Great Awakening revivals produced detailed church covenants amid out-migrations to the Midwest tracked in warnings-out.

Modern Quabbin-Edge Community

Today Shutesbury preserves its 18th-century green, historic district, and rural character as a quiet hill town with conservation lands bordering Quabbin recreation along Route 63.

Genealogical Resources and Strategies

Shutesbury vital records (from 1761, published to 1850) and Congregational/Quaker registers (1760s onward) capture baptisms for Road Town pioneers; Franklin County deeds trace lot divisions from original grants to hill pastures. Strategies start with proprietors' books for Lockes and Childs, cross-referencing Shays' court files, spring-factory payrolls, and militia lists to map kin enduring uplands, linking to New Salem lowlands and Leverett mills.

Sunderland

Sunderland occupies the southeastern corner of Franklin County, Massachusetts, along the east bank of the Connecticut River amid fertile meadows and swampy lowlands south of Deerfield and east of Mount Toby, forming a valley-bottom township transitional to Hampshire County. Granted in 1673 as Swampfield plantation from Hadley territory on Norwottuck lands and first settled around 1714 after King Philip's War abandonment, it drew 39 proprietor families like the Barretts and Taylors who built linear house lots along the future Main Street extending to river pastures; incorporated in 1718 and renamed for Charles Spencer, Earl of Sunderland, it lost upland territory to Leverett but retained a compact center with ferry crossings.

River Farms and Village Core

Early settlement focused on 3½-acre homelots west to the Connecticut River for tobacco and grain, with a 1717 meetinghouse, parsonage for Rev. Willard, blacksmith and cordwainer lots anchoring civic life; 19th-century Irish "paddy farms" on Mount Toby supplemented agriculture, while ferries and stage roads tied it to Hadley markets amid Shays' Rebellion debts tracked in town warnings-out.

Modern Valley Community

Today Sunderland preserves its broad Main Street historic district, colonial homes, and agricultural heritage as a quiet riverside town with UMASS Amherst proximity and recreation along Route 116.

Genealogical Resources and Strategies

Sunderland vital records (from 1718, published to 1850) and First Congregational registers (1717 onward) document Swampfield pioneers; Franklin/Hampshire deeds trace lot divisions from 39-family grants to river meadows. Strategies start with proprietors' books for Barrett-era kin, cross-referencing ferry accounts, Shays' court files, and Mount Toby censuses to map valley networks linking to Deerfield raids survivors and Leverett hill farms.

Warwick

Warwick occupies the northeastern corner of Franklin County, Massachusetts, along the Millers River amid steep hills and narrow valleys near the Worcester County line, forming a rugged upland township beyond the Connecticut Valley core. Granted in 1735 as one of four Canada Townships to compensate descendants of the 1690 Quebec expedition soldiers and first settled in 1739 by pioneers like the Barkers and Frinks who cleared forested ridges for sheep pastures and small farms amid rocky soils, it incorporated in 1763 and retained a dispersed pattern centered on the meetinghouse plain and Tully River mills.

Hill Farms and Mill Hamlets

Early clusters near Rev. William Rand's 1760 ordination defended scattered homesteads during Shays' Rebellion, where local wool-growers joined debt protests; gristmills, sawmills, and 19th-century broom and scythe factories powered by Tully Brook employed kin, supplemented by cheese production shipped via rough roads to Orange and Athol markets.

Modern Rural Hill Town

Today Warwick preserves its 18th-century green, historic district, and agricultural heritage as a quiet community with conservation lands and small-scale tourism along Route 78.

Genealogical Resources and Strategies

Warwick vital records (from 1763, published to 1850) and First Congregational registers (1760 onward) capture baptisms for Canada Township pioneers, Franklin County deeds trace lot divisions from Quebec grantees to hill pastures. Strategies start with proprietors' books for first-comers like Barkers, cross-referencing Shays' court files, mill payrolls, and warnings-out to map kin enduring uplands, linking to Orange factories and Northfield valley networks.

Wendell

Wendell sits in the east-central uplands of Franklin County, Massachusetts, amid steep hills and narrow valleys of the Millers River watershed near the Quabbin Reservoir edge, forming a remote hill township beyond the Connecticut Valley settlements. Settled around 1754 by families from Lancaster like Thomas Osgood and Richard Moore who cleared virgin forests for sheep pastures and small farms amid rocky soils, it organized a Congregational church in 1774 and incorporated in 1781, named for Boston judge Oliver Wendell; it lost southern territory to Shutesbury but retained a compact center around the town common.

Hill Farms and Greek Revival Core

Early homes clustered near the 1781 meetinghouse (replaced 1846 by Luke Leach's Greek Revival structure) for defense and worship, with gristmills powering broom and chair factories by the 19th century; Shays' Rebellion rallied wool-growers against debts, while population peaked at over 1,000 before out-migrations to the Midwest left a preserved common district of Leach's houses and stone walls.

Modern Rural Hill Town

Today Wendell preserves its National Register town common historic district, 1846 meetinghouse, and agricultural heritage as a quiet community with conservation lands and Quabbin proximity along Route 202.

Genealogical Resources and Strategies

Wendell vital records (from 1781, published to 1850) and Congregational registers (1774 onward) capture baptisms for Lancaster pioneers; Franklin County deeds trace lot divisions from early grants to hill pastures. Strategies start with church covenants for Osgoods and Moores, cross-referencing Shays' court files, factory payrolls, and warnings-out to map kin enduring uplands, linking to Shutesbury roads and New Salem mills.

Whately

Whately forms a compact valley township in southeastern Franklin County, Massachusetts, along the Connecticut River meadows east of Hatfield and south of Sunderland, encompassing fertile bottomlands ideal for tobacco and onions amid the Norwottuck homelands. First settled in 1672 as the northern precinct of Hatfield on lands purchased from sachem Quonquont, it drew pioneers like the Whites, Crafts, and Temples who built linear house lots along the broad street extending to river pastures; incorporated in 1771 after peaceful petition for separation due to river-crossing hardships, it annexed Deerfield parcels in 1810 but retained a tight village core.

River Farms and Agricultural Prosperity

Early settlement focused on 8-acre homelots with meadows divided equally among Hatfield proprietors, anchored by a 1717 meetinghouse and Rev. Eleazar Storrs' ministry; the state's first gin distillery (1788) and Sumatran tobacco success supplemented grain and livestock shipped via ferries, while Shays' Rebellion debts stirred unrest among farm families tracked in town warnings-out.

Modern Riverside Village

Today Whately preserves its Whately Center Historic District with colonial homes, broad street, and agricultural heritage as a quiet community blending farm and UMASS proximity along Route 116.

Genealogical Resources and Strategies

Whately vital records (from 1771, published to 1850) and First Congregational registers (1720s onward from Hatfield era) document precinct pioneers; Franklin/Hampshire deeds trace Hatfield lot divisions to river meadows. Strategies start with Hatfield parent records for pre-separation kin like Crafts, cross-referencing distillery accounts, Shays' court files, and tobacco censuses to map valley networks linking to Sunderland ferries and Deerfield raids survivors.

CENSUS-DESIGNATED PLACES

Deerfield (CDP)

Deerfield CDP represents the densely settled village core of the Town of Deerfield in central Franklin County, Massachusetts, centered along the iconic mile-long Historic Deerfield "Street" amid fertile Connecticut River meadows flanked by hills. Developed from the original 1673 colonial "Street" houses built as a fortified linear settlement on Pocumtuck homelands, it survived King Philip's War abandonment (1675), the 1704 French-Indian raid massacre, and later expansions into a preserved 18th-century district rather than an independent municipality.

Colonial Street to Historic District

Pioneers like Samuel Hinsdale allocated compact house lots facing the street with outlying meadows for wheat and cattle, defended by palisades during Abenaki threats; Rev. John Williams' church (1680s) and elite homes like the Wells-Thorn house anchored the nucleus, evolving through Shays' Rebellion into a 19th-century agricultural showcase with tobacco warehouses and academies.

Modern Historic Village

Today the CDP preserves 50+ National Historic Landmark structures such as Memorial Hall Museum and Historic Deerfield Inc., blending tourism with residential life distinct from South Deerfield's modern commercial strip.

Genealogical Resources and Strategies

Deerfield town vital records (1673 onward, published to 1850) and First Church registers capture Street families through raids; Franklin deeds trace home lot divisions from proprietors to heir subdivisions. Strategies focus on Williams captivity narratives, probate inventories (rich for elites), and militia rolls to map core Street kin versus meadow outliers, linking to Greenfield spin-offs and upland Conway farms.

Millers Falls (CDP)

Millers Falls is a compact industrial village CDP straddling the towns of Montague and Erving in east-central Franklin County, Massachusetts, centered along the Millers River falls amid rail junctions and mill dams near the Mohawk Trail (Route 2). Established around 1824 as Grout's Corner—an agricultural hamlet named for settler Martin Grout (1790–1865)—it transformed in the 1860s when railroads (New London Northern and Vermont & Massachusetts lines) converged, harnessing river hydropower for factories like the 1868 Millers Falls Manufacturing Company (famed for hand tools).

Rail-Mill Boom Village

Rail access spurred paper mills, tool works, and woodworking shops, employing Yankee farmhands and Irish/French Canadian immigrants in dense tenements after the 1895 Great Fire rebuilt Main and Bridge Streets in Victorian commercial blocks (Ward, Equi, Powers); the central district joined the National Register in 2021, preserving post-fire architecture amid canal remnants and company housing.

Modern Working-Class Enclave

Today Millers Falls retains mill-era buildings, rail heritage, and residential core as a gritty suburb within Montague/Erving, distinct from rural surrounds.

Genealogical Resources and Strategies

Records split between Montague and Erving vital registers (post-1860s, noting "Millers Falls"), with company payrolls and boardinghouse censuses capturing operatives; Franklin deeds trace Grout farm subdivisions to mill lots. Strategies pair Montague church books (Catholic for immigrants) with factory ledgers and 1895 fire insurance maps to reconstruct wage-earner kin networks linking valley farms to rail-mill wards and Erving paper workers.

Northfield (CDP)

Northfield CDP forms the compact village core of the Town of Northfield in northeastern Franklin County, Massachusetts, centered along Main Street (Route 10) amid fertile Connecticut River meadows and bluffs near Watson's Falls, distinct from upland hamlets. Emerging from the permanent 1714 resettlement after twice-abandoning amid King Philip's War raids on Squakheag (Pocumtuck/Abenaki village), it developed as the town's civic heart with the 1723 incorporation, housing the meetinghouse, stores, and farms radiating to Great Meadow pastures.

Village Center and Resort Era

Linear house lots along the street supported tobacco, grain, and livestock shipped via ferries, anchored by Rev. Solomon Stoddard's church influence and Great Awakening revivals; 19th-century rail service and Dwight L. Moody's Northfield Seminary (1879) transformed it into a summer resort hub with the Northfield Hotel (1887) and chateau estates, drawing visitors before mill shifts to Falls Village.

Modern Historic Village

Today the CDP preserves colonial homes, Moody legacy sites, and agricultural core as Northfield's social center, blending farms with tourism distinct from rural surrounds.

Genealogical Resources and Strategies

Northfield town vital records (1714 onward, published to 1850) and First Congregational registers (1721 onward) capture revival-era families; Franklin deeds trace meadow lots from Squakheag proprietors to village subdivisions. Strategies focus on seminary guest lists, hotel registers, and Shays' files to map core village kin versus upland outliers, linking to Deerfield Street networks and Vernon hill farms.

Orange (CDP)

Orange CDP comprises the densely settled commercial and civic core of the Town of Orange in southeastern Franklin County, Massachusetts, centered along Main Street (Route 2A) at the Millers River crossing amid transition from hill farms to mill industry. Emerging around 1785 with the first bridge over the Millers River, it developed as the town's functional heart after district formation in 1783 from Warwick, Royalston, Athol, and Erving's Grant lands, housing stores, mills, and later factories distinct from rural North Orange.

Bridge Village to Industrial Center

Compact lots along the street supported taverns and blacksmiths serving turnpikes, evolving with 1790s dams into textile and sewing-machine hubs like the New Home Company (late 1800s), employing Yankee descendants and immigrants after Shays' Rebellion debts resolved; railroads solidified its role as market hub for surrounding farms.

Modern Downtown District

Today the CDP preserves Orange Center Historic District with Victorian commercial blocks and mills as the town's business nucleus, blending retail with light industry separate from agricultural outskirts.

Genealogical Resources and Strategies

Orange town vital records (1810 onward, published to 1850 noting "center") and church registers capture bridge-era families; Franklin deeds trace river lots from district grants to factory parcels. Strategies pair company payrolls with censuses of Main Street boarders, cross-referencing parent-town Warwick records to map kin from hill pioneers to mill workers linking North Orange farms and Athol factories.

Shelburne Falls (CDP)

Shelburne Falls CDP straddles the towns of Shelburne and Buckland in west-central Franklin County, Massachusetts, centered at the dramatic Deerfield River falls amid narrow valleys and steep bluffs, forming a quintessential mill village distinct from surrounding hill farms. First settled around 1760 by five pioneer families like Jonathan Wood who built the initial gristmill and footbridge (1780, replaced by 1821 covered bridge), it boomed after Silas Lamson's 1837 arrival, harnessing waterpower for cutlery factories that made it one of America's largest by the Civil War, employing 500+ workers.

Cutlery Capital and Trolley Era

Dams powered Lamson & Goodnow knives, scythes, and tools, with Bridge Street commercial blocks, worker tenements, and the trolley line (ending 1927) fostering dense settlement; the abandoned trolley bridge transformed into the iconic Bridge of Flowers (1929) by women's clubs, while Shays' Rebellion debts preceded industrial prosperity shipped via railroads.

Modern Artisan Village

Today the CDP preserves its National Register Historic District with Victorian mills, the flower bridge, and galleries as a creative tourism hub blending industry legacy with arts.

Genealogical Resources and Strategies

Records split between Shelburne/Buckland vital registers (post-1760s, noting "Falls"), with Lamson factory payrolls and tenement censuses capturing operatives; Franklin deeds trace mill lots from Wood grants to worker parcels. Strategies pair Catholic church books (immigrants) with company ledgers and trolley passenger lists to map kin from Deerfield pioneers to cutlery families linking Shelburne hills and Buckland factories.

South Deerfield (CDP)

South Deerfield CDP forms the modern commercial and residential core south of Historic Deerfield village in the Town of Deerfield, central Franklin County, Massachusetts, centered along Route 5 (North Main Street) amid fertile Connecticut River meadows transitioning from colonial agriculture to 20th-century industry. Emerging in the late 18th century as the town's southern precinct beyond the original "Street," it developed post-Revolution with taverns, stores, and farms serving upland travelers, distinct from the preserved northern historic district.

Commercial Strip and Candle Empire

Linear development along the highway housed granges, schools like the 1888 grammar building (now municipal offices), and tobacco sheds before Yankee Candle Company's 1969 founding by Mike Kittredge in his parents' garage sparked massive growth, transforming meadows into factories, outlets, and visitor complexes employing thousands.

Modern Suburban Hub

Today the CDP blends big-box retail, candle tourism, and working farms as Deerfield's economic engine, contrasting the elite-preserved north village.

Genealogical Resources and Strategies

Deerfield town vital records (noting "South Deerfield" post-1800) and precinct church registers capture farm families; Franklin deeds trace southern meadow lots from Street extensions to factory parcels. Strategies pair company employment rolls with 20th-century censuses and highway directories to map kin from colonial outliers to candle-era workers linking Historic Deerfield elites and Greenfield commuters.

Turners Falls (CDP)

Turners Falls CDP forms the densely packed industrial heart of Montague in east-central Franklin County, Massachusetts, centered along Avenue A and the Connecticut River power canal amid the historic falls site, distinct from rural Montague Center. Founded in 1868 as a planned manufacturing city by Fitchburg industrialist Alvah Crocker, who rebuilt the 1790s navigation canal into a hydropower system selling mill sites to factories like Russell Cutlery and Keith Paper, it drew Irish, French Canadian, and Polish workers to grid-planned worker housing and commercial blocks.

Planned Mill City and Ethnic Wards

The horizontal street grid (Avenues A-L, numbered cross-streets) housed opera houses, hotels, and tenements serving the "White Coal" power boom, peaking with direct NYC rail and Colle Opera House before 20th-century mill declines; the 1676 Turners Falls Massacre site (King Philip's War) underlies its Indigenous prehistory.

Modern Cultural District

Today the CDP preserves its National Register Historic District of brick mills and Victorian storefronts as a vibrant arts enclave with the Turners Falls Cultural District.

Genealogical Resources and Strategies

Montague vital records (post-1868, noting "Turners Falls") and Catholic parish registers capture immigrant mill families; Franklin deeds trace canal lots from Crocker sales to tenements. Strategies pair factory payrolls, boardinghouse censuses, and opera house programs with ethnic church books to map kin from canal laborers to second-generation shopkeepers linking Greenfield commuters and Erving paper workers.

UNINCORPORATED COMMUNITIES

Lake Pleasant

Lake Pleasant is a small, unincorporated Spiritualist community and historic resort village in the town of Montague, Franklin County, Massachusetts, nestled around a 93-acre man-made lake amid wooded hills near Turners Falls and the Connecticut River. Founded in 1870 by George W. Potter of Greenfield as a campmeeting grounds with 75 tent lots on swampland drained for the purpose, it quickly became a Spiritualist hub by 1872, formalized in 1874 by the New England Spiritualist Campmeeting Association (NESCA) under Henry Buddington and Joseph Beals, growing to nearly 200 cottages by the 1880s.

Spiritualist Mecca and Resort Era

Tents evolved into permanent summer cottages hosting annual NESCA encampments with séances, lectures by mediums like Andrew Jackson Davis, and conventions drawing thousands for healings, spirit communications, and temperance rallies; a narrow-gauge railroad (1879–1920s), grand hotel, and dance hall supported the seasonal influx, peaking as America's largest continuous Spiritualist center before decline with the automobile age.

Modern Spiritualist Holdout

Today Lake Pleasant retains its association hall, cemetery with mediums' graves, and cottage rows as a quiet residential enclave preserving NESCA gatherings annually.

Genealogical Resources and Strategies

Montague vital records (post-1870s, noting "Lake Pleasant") and NESCA membership ledgers/ campmeeting programs capture seasonal residents; Franklin deeds trace tent-lot leases to cottage ownership. Strategies mine Spiritualist newspapers, medium directories, and Montague censuses of summer boarders to reconstruct kin networks of believers from Boston mediums to upstate NY pilgrims linking Turners Falls mills and Greenfield seekers.

Satan's Kingdom

Satan's Kingdom is a remote unincorporated wooded village and wildlife management area in the town of Northfield, northeastern Franklin County, Massachusetts, along the Connecticut River near the Vermont border amid steep hills and fertile meadows. Named during the colonial era—possibly from fiery Puritan sermons in Northfield churches, treacherous wildlife like snakes, or battles in King Philip's War (1670s) including the nearby Turners Falls massacre—it remained sparsely settled farmland and forest rather than a formal village, tied to Northfield's river economy.

Frontier Conflicts and Folklore

The area's rocky terrain and dense woods hosted skirmishes during King Philip's War, with legends linking the ominous name to pirate Captain Kidd's supposed buried treasure on a nearby island (guarded by a murdered crewman's ghost) or Abenaki resistance; 19th-century farmers grew hops amid isolation, prompting out-migrations tracked in Northfield warnings-out, while Shays' Rebellion debts echoed valley unrest.

Modern Wildlife Preserve

Today Satan's Kingdom spans 1,800 acres of state forest for hunting, hiking, and fishing, preserving its wild character without development as Northfield's remote backcountry.

Genealogical Resources and Strategies

Northfield vital records and church registers (noting "Satan's Kingdom" or river addresses) capture scattered farm families; Franklin deeds trace woodlot grants from colonial proprietors to 19th-century subdivisions. Strategies mine Northfield militia rolls from King Philip's era, probate for isolated homesteads, and folklore treasure-hunt rumors to map kin enduring frontier perils, linking to Vernon uplands and Deerfield valley networks.

Zoar

Zoar is a remote unincorporated riverside hamlet in the town of Charlemont, eastern Franklin County, Massachusetts, along the Deerfield River amid steep Mohawk Trail hills and narrow valleys near the Berkshire line. Originally a wild 1,875-acre tract of common lands known as "Zoar" (biblical refuge), it was sparsely settled in the early 1800s by pioneers clearing timber for marginal farms and pastures before annexation to Charlemont on April 2, 1838, developing around a gristmill, sawmill, and later rail station rather than a formal village.

River Mills and Rail Stop

Early homes clustered near the river for hydropower supporting small lumber and woolen operations, tied to Charlemont's upland economy; the Hoosac Tunnel rail line (Boston & Maine) made Zoar a flag stop from the 1870s, serving isolated farmers with freight until passenger service ended and the station was razed in 1954, amid Shays' Rebellion-era debts prompting Vermont migrations.

Modern Backcountry Hamlet

Today Zoar persists as a handful of homes, river access points, and conservation lands popular for fishing and kayaking, preserving its wild character along Route 2 without commercial development.

Genealogical Resources and Strategies

Charlemont vital records (post-1838 annexation, noting "Zoar") and church registers capture river families; Franklin deeds trace common-land lots to subdivided farms. Strategies mine Charlemont proprietors' books for pre-annexation grantees, cross-referencing rail timetables, mill accounts, and warnings-out to map kin in this remote outpost, linking to Hawley uplands and Rowe mining hamlets.

12

Chapter 4 Hampden County

Hampden County, Massachusetts, occupies the southern Connecticut River valley and western hill country of the Commonwealth, where fertile floodplains, traprock ridges, and upland forests sustained Agawam, Pocumtuck, and Nipmuc homelands long before European contact. Carved from Hampshire County in 1812 with Springfield as shire town, Hampden links colonial trading posts, armory cities, paper-mill hamlets, and suburban enclaves, blending riverine agriculture with industrial might from Westfield cutlery to Holyoke canals. Its diverse geography—from Chicopee River factories through Springfield's arsenal to the Berkshires foothills—preserves records of Indigenous dispossession, Puritan merchants, Irish textile operatives, French Canadian millworkers, and Puerto Rican migrants, yielding genealogists a stratified archive of valley commerce, wartime production, and ethnic transformation.

For family historians, Hampden's narrative threads through Pynchon's 1636 Agawam deed, King Philip's War raids, Shays' Rebellion courthouse burnings, Springfield Armory rifles from Revolution to World Wars, Holyoke's "Paper City" dams, and 20th-century aerospace booms, documented in proprietors' grants, armory payrolls, Catholic parish registers, ethnic benevolent society minutes, and federal censuses tracing mobility across Native, English, African, Irish, and Latino lines in New England's manufacturing heartland.

INDIGENOUS FOUNDATIONS: AGAWAM, POCUMTUCK, AND NIPMUC TERRITORIES

Hampden County's pre-colonial landscape formed a critical crossroads within the territories of the Agawam, Pocumtuck, and Nipmuc peoples, speakers of Southern New England Algonquian dialects whose seasonal economies intertwined riverine abundance with upland resources across the Connecticut Valley and its flanking traprock ridges. Agawam bands centered along the broad Connecticut River floodplains near present-day Springfield, exploiting anadromous fish runs—shad, salmon, herring, and sturgeon—at the rapids and tidal reaches, supplemented by maize, beans, and squash horticulture on fertile terraces, clam beds in oxbows, and nut mast from oak-hickory forests. Pocumtuck villages clustered at confluences like the Chicopee River mouth, where they managed eel weirs, controlled deer hunting territories through seasonal burns, and crafted wampum from quahog shells traded along the Mohawk Trail to Mohican and Mohawk intermediaries. Nipmuc groups dominated the western hill towns from Westfield to Brimfield, favoring smaller streams for fishing and extensive woodlots for maple sugaring, bas-

174

ketry materials, and trail networks linking to Narragansett Bay and the Quinebaug Valley. Political life revolved around sachems whose authority flowed from kinship alliances, marriage exchanges, and reciprocal use-rights rather than rigid boundaries, with wetus (bark longhouses) housing extended families in dispersed hamlets shifting seasonally between planting grounds and hunting camps.

European contact in the 1630s—first via Dutch traders from Fort Good Hope (Hartford) exchanging wampum and furs, then English explorers like William Pynchon—introduced devastating epidemics of smallpox, measles, and influenza that halved Indigenous populations by 1634, creating vacuums of "unoccupied" land under Puritan legal doctrines. Pynchon's 1636 "deed" from Agawam sachem Cunnesseman and allies for Springfield's core extinguished overlapping claims through cloth, hatchets, and hoes, compressing communal usufruct into English fee-simple titles recorded in nascent Hampshire deeds. King Philip's War (1675–76) shattered remaining autonomy: Pocumtuck neutrality collapsed amid Turners Falls massacre reprisals, Agawam survivors fled to Natick Praying Town or Mohawk refuges, and Nipmuc warriors raided Westfield before dispersal to Canada or eastern reservations. Court files and missionary reports name sachems like Wequagon and captives redeemed for ransom, while "Indian deeds" in Springfield proprietors' books hint at coerced sales post-epidemics.

For genealogists tracing Indigenous ancestry in Hampden, the paper trail fragments quickly into English frameworks, demanding correlation of scattered deed marginalia ("Indian field," "sachem's lot"), John Eliot's Natick rosters, and 18th-century petitions from displaced families at Stockbridge or Brothertown (Oneida Nation). Place-names like Agawam River, Chicopee (swift water), and Nipmuc-derived toponyms persist, as do occasional probate references to "Indian servants" or mixed-descent laborers in armory households. Triangulating these with oral histories from Nipmuc Nation of Massachusetts, Abenaki descendants, and archaeological yields from Westfield sites reconstructs kin who navigated epidemics, warfare, and land loss, their descendants often relabeled as "mulatto" or "colored" in later censuses amid intermarriage with Africans and English settlers.

This latent Indigenous presence—erased from town narratives yet embedded in river fisheries, trail corridors, and reservation petitions—demands contextual reading across Hampshire/ Hampden deeds, colonial assembly records, and 19th-century removal testimonies to recover precontact lineages enduring into the valley's industrial era.

COLONIAL SETTLEMENT, ARMORY RISE, AND RELIGIOUS PLURALISM

Colonial settlement in Hampden County unfolded as a deliberate extension of the Massachusetts Bay Colony's western frontier, commencing with William Pynchon's 1636 trading post at Agawam (Springfield)—strategically sited at the Connecticut River rapids for fur collection, salmon fishing, and wampum production—and radiating northward along fertile intervals and southward into Nipmuc hill country by the 1660s. Proprietary grants parceled meadows and woodlots to "first-comers" like the Pynchons, Coopers, and Chapins, allocating compact house lots near future meetinghouses with outlying pastures divided by drawing lots according to family size and social rank; Westfield emerged in 1669 as a dispersed farming precinct resisting

Springfield's authority, while Suffield (now Connecticut) and Enfield anchored southern borders amid overlapping Connecticut River Colony claims resolved by royal decree. These early divisions, preserved in proprietors' books and town minutes, form the backbone for tracing founding lineages as holdings subdivided across generations, often documented through quitclaims amid Shays' Rebellion-era debt pressures that saw courthouses burn in Springfield (1786). Blockhouses and militia rotations guarded against French-Indian raids peaking in Queen Anne's War, with scout reports and wolf bounties naming otherwise obscure householders in county sessions files.

The Springfield Armory's establish"ent 'n 1794 as the nation's first federal arsenal marked Hampden's pivot to national defense, its flintlock muskets and later interchangeable-parts rifles fueling every major conflict from the War of 1812 through World Wars, generating exhaustive payrolls, apprenticeship indentures, and muster rolls that track artisan families like the Colts and Morgans across generations. Armory boardinghouses and company stores employed young Yankee men and women alongside free Blacks and Irish laborers, their careers illuminated in pension affidavits, invention patents (e.g., Elisha King's boring machine), and discharge papers linking to Civil War regiments; the adjacent arsenal village fostered a distinct mechanic class whose mobility appears in city directories and fraternal lodge minutes.

Religious culture evolved from Springfield's "gathered" Congregational church—planted 1638 with detailed covenants, relation narratives, and baptism registers capturing pre-civil vital events—to parish fractures yielding Baptist strongholds in Westfield, Methodist circuits in Chicopee, and Unitarian offshoots amid 19th-century revivals. Early discipline cases for "disorderly walking," fornication, and Quaker sympathies name women, servants, and the poor rarely visible elsewhere, while gathered-church principles required public relations for full membership, preserving spiritual autobiographies rich in family context.

Catholic pluralism emerged with Irish canal diggers at Holyoke Falls (1830s), formalized in missions like St. Jerome's (1854) whose Latin registers note Irish counties and Quebecois parishes, essential for pre-1841 baptisms absent from town books; Jewish congregations in Springfield (1850s) and later Pentecostal storefronts added membership lists tracking Eastern European and Puerto Rican arrivals. For genealogists, denominational crossovers—evident in dual Congregational/Baptist baptisms or Methodist class-meeting rolls—explain gaps in single-church records, while court admonitions for oath refusal illuminate dissenting kin like Quakers in Longmeadow.

Hampden's county courts, quartered in Springfield's successive courthouses (destroyed 1677, 1786, rebuilt 1816), adjudicated the frictions of a stratified society: debt suits among merchants, defamation between neighbors, guardianships for orphans of armory widows, and probate inventories revealing middling yeomen's featherbeds alongside elite Pynchon silver. Shays' Rebellion files uniquely name insurgent farmers from Wilbraham and Monson who stormed the arsenal, their petitions and pardons mapping class divides; moral courts policed Sabbath-breaking and bastardy, often pitting mill girls against overseers in naming fathers. Navigating these requires correlating session minutes with town warnings-out for paupers relocated across town lines, reconstructing non-elite webs invisible in vital registers alone.

RIVER INDUSTRY, IMMIGRATION, AND ARSENAL ECONOMY

By the late 18th century, Hampden County's river corridors had matured into arteries of proto-industry, with Chicopee Falls' gristmills evolving into textile factories by the 1820s, Westfield's scythe forges dominating national markets under Elisha King's interchangeable parts innovations, and Holyoke's ambitious 1848 canal system—world's largest by 1890—powering paper mills that earned it the title "Paper City," producing newsprint for Harper's Weekly and the New York Times from spruce logs floated down the Connecticut.

Springfield's flanking warehouses and machine shops supplied belting, gunpowder, and steam engines, while smaller tributaries hosted tanneries, brick yards, and whip factories in West Springfield; these enterprises generated apprenticeship contracts binding farm youths to seven-year terms, crew manifests for canal boatmen, and boardinghouse ledgers revealing Yankee "factory girls" alongside free Black laborers escaping Hartford slavery via Underground Railroad safe houses in Longmeadow and East Longmeadow. Customs ledgers from Springfield's federal port district tracked exports of agricultural produce—onions from onion-growing precincts, tobacco from Whately-adjacent meadows—and imports of Irish pig iron fueling forges, with privateering commissions from the War of 1812 naming masters like Oliver B. Emerson whose prize money distributions appear in probate alongside armory contracts.

Industrial expansion accelerated waves of immigration that reshaped Hampden's ethnic mosaic. Irish famine refugees (1845–1852) dug Holyoke's canals and manned early mills, clustering in "Dublin" and "Cork Village" wards documented in St. Jerome's and Precious Blood parish registers noting counties like Kerry and Galway; French Canadian millworkers arrived from 1870s Quebec via "pig trains," their Sacred Heart and Ste. Jeanne d'Arc books preserving village origins from Trois-Rivières alongside bilingual boardinghouse censuses.

Italians settled Springfield's Italian North End by 1890, Poles dominated Chicopee's "Three-Decker Street," and Lithuanians powered Westfield's bicycle factories, each ethnic enclave spawning benevolent societies—Holy Name for Irish, St. Casimir for Poles—whose dues ledgers and mutual-aid minutes list families invisible in sparse naturalization stubs. Post-1945 Puerto Rican migration filled textile vacancies and farm labor, tracked in Spanish-language parish books at St. Mary's and census notations shifting from "Puerto Rico" to Springfield addresses; African American communities, rooted in 18th-century manumissions and armory hires, formed mutual aid groups like the Springfield NAACP precursor, their networks visible in pension affidavits from Civil War veterans descended from Pocumtuck intermarriages.

The Springfield Armory anchored this economy as a federal bulwark, its 1794 founding under George Washington's arsenal act producing 800,000 muskets by 1865 via precision machinery that birthed America's manufacturing revolution; payrolls enumerate gun-smiths, armorers, and laborers through every conflict, with women entering as cartridge fillers during wars and Black apprentices post-Emancipation appearing in indentures alongside Irish fillers.

Pension files from Revolutionary pensioners to World War widows offer affidavits rich in family testimony—"my father worked the boring mill beside Capt. Morgan"—while invention records credit mechanics like Edwin Stevens for rifling advances, their patents funding kin migrations to Chicopee factories. Company boardinghouses fostered marriages across ethnic lines, documented in dual Catholic-Protestant baptisms, and armory discharge papers track veterans to Holyoke mills or Westfield forges, illuminating mobility patterns absent from town vitals alone. Hampden's courts adjudicated industrial disputes—overseer assaults, machine patent infringements, and worker accident claims—naming operatives whose injuries qualified for poor-farm relief, bridging wage-labor households to yeoman relatives in adjacent hill towns.

GENEALOGICAL RESOURCES AND RESEARCH STRATEGIES

Hampden County's documentary resources concentrate in Springfield's dual repositories—the Registry of Deeds (holding continuous land records from Pynchon's 1636 Agawam deed through 21st-century subdivisions, extensively digitized with grantor-grantee indexes) and Probate Court (wills, inventories, guardianships revealing armory widows' dowries alongside mill operatives' scant estates)—supplemented by 26 town clerks' vital registers, many transcribed in published "Vital Records to 1850" series that capture pre-statewide registration baptisms absent from church fires like Springfield's 1876 blaze. Catholic diocesan archives in Springfield and Worcester preserve Latin/vernacular parish books from Holyoke's St. Jerome (1854) through Chicopee's SS. Peter and Paul (1880s), essential for Irish/French Canadian origins notations like "from Limerick" or "St. Hyacinthe PQ"; armory records at Springfield Technical Community College and National Archives include 100,000+ payroll stubs, muster rolls, and pension affidavits naming apprentices' fathers and widows' remarriages, while Holyoke canal company ledgers (held at Wistariahurst Museum) enumerate dam builders by nativity.

Town-level materials vary by settlement pattern: Springfield city directories (1826 onward) and ward maps delineate ethnic clusters from "North End" Italians to "The Flats" Puerto Ricans, capturing boarders missed by censuses; Westfield's scythe-factory payrolls and bicycle-trade union minutes track mechanic lineages, while Chicopee's French parish sodalities list women's auxiliaries invisible in civil books.

Federal censuses (1790–1950, with non-pop schedules detailing paper-mill outputs and armory slave schedules pre-1860) pair with naturalization stubs noting ship arrivals at New York for Holyoke-bound Poles; ethnic fraternal records—Hibernian Society minutes for Irish, Polish Falcons ledgers—preserve membership chains linking overseas parishes to mill wards. Holyoke's Paper City directories and accident reports name Lithuanian foremen and Italian rag-sorters, while Springfield's NAACP precursors and Black church rolls illuminate Afro-Indigenous descendants from 18th-century manumissions.

Effective strategies balance colonial cores with industrial overlays. For pre-1750 lines, anchor in Springfield/Westfield proprietors' books and "first-comer" lotteries, cross-referencing Hampshire sessions files (pre-1812) for guardianships and raid bounties to cluster Pynchon-era kin radiating to Chicopee falls; pivot to armory payrolls for 1794–1968 mechanics, using discharge papers to trace Civil War veterans to Holyoke mills or Monson poor farms. Immigrant research reverses chronology: start with 1880–1920 parish registers and boardinghouse censuses for Quebec/Irish counties, backtrack via naturalizations to passenger lists, then forward to pension affidavits linking sons' World War service; Puerto Rican chains follow 1950s directories to Springfield barrios, triangulating with oral histories from Centro las Americas.

Marginalized groups demand multi-source weaving—deeds' "Indian lot" marginalia with Eliot's Praying Town rosters for Native descent, court bastardy cases naming mill girls' fathers, and union strike petitions for operatives' wives—against the landscape of rapids, canals, and arsenal gates. Hampden's archive—from fur-deed vellums to aerospace rosters—demands reading town books against river power, ethnic wards, and federal contracts to recover ancestors navigating valley transformation from Indigenous fisheries to Puerto Rican factories.

13

Cities and Towns of Hampden County

CITIES

Agawam

Agawam, Massachusetts, occupies the low terrace lands and sandplains on the west bank of the Connecticut River opposite Springfield in southern Hampden County, extending south to the Connecticut line and west toward the Metacomet ridges. Emerging from the western portion of Springfield's original Agawam plantation—organized as the "West Parish" in the 18th century—it incorporated as a separate town in 1855, retaining older village nuclei at Agawam Center, Feeding Hills, and along the river road. From Pocumtuck–Agawam homelands and William Pynchon's 1636 fur-trading orbit through floodplain farming, Shays' Rebellion unrest, 19th-century tobacco and brick production, and 20th-century amusement development at Riverside Park, Agawam's record trail ties valley kin tightly to Springfield's courts, churches, and markets.

Agawam Homelands, Springfield Precinct, and River Farms

Before English claims, the meadows, oxbows, and river islands that became Agawam formed a key segment of Agawam and Pocumtuck territory, with planting fields and fisheries opposite the future Springfield settlement. William Pynchon's 1630s land purchases on the east bank drew Springfield's original proprietors, whose meadows, pastures, and common rights soon extended informally to the west side for grazing and hay, even as Indigenous communities faced epidemics and displacement. Over the 17th and 18th centuries the "west side" remained legally within Springfield but functioned as a semi-distinct farming precinct, supplying grain, beef, and later tobacco to Springfield's growing mercantile center; by mid-18th century a parish meetinghouse at what became Agawam Center anchored local worship and schooling, and families at Feeding Hills exploited upland soils for pastures and woodlots.

Genealogists tracing early Agawam families must work first in Springfield proprietors' books, Hampshire/Hampden deeds, and parish records that label residents by "west side" or "Feeding Hills" rather than by a separate town name. Proprietary divisions, meadow lot descriptions, and early road layouts—plus scattered references to "Agawam" fields and Indian grants—link founding kin across both sides of the river.

Feeding Hills, Bricks, Tobacco, and Riverside Park

Through the late 18th and 19th centuries Agawam developed as a string of villages shaped by both river and ridge. Agawam Center clustered around the green, parish church, and crossroads, while Feeding Hills grew as a hilltop farming district and brick-making area, exploiting clay deposits and woodland fuel. Floodplain soils supported intensive tobacco culture and market gardening that supplied Springfield and Holyoke, bringing seasonal labor and, eventually, immigrant workers into the valley landscape. By the late 19th century, industrial and recreational uses intensified along the river: sand and gravel pits, small manufactories, and then Riverside Park (founded as a riverside picnic grove and later an amusement park) turned parts of the riverfront into a regional leisure destination tied to streetcar and highway networks.

These developments generated records beyond standard vitals: parish and later Catholic church registers for valley farm and mill families; land transactions specifying brick yards, tobacco barns, and sandpits; and company or park payrolls listing seasonal workers tied to Springfield and beyond. Such materials help explain shifts from dispersed farmsteads to denser, commuter-oriented neighborhoods in the 20th century.

Genealogical Resources and Strategies

Vital and local repositories relevant to Agawam research include:

- Agawam Town Clerk: Original birth, marriage, and death registers from the 1855 incorporation forward, town meeting minutes, school district records, and annexation/precinct documents linking back to Springfield's west parish.
- Published and compiled records: Springfield and Agawam "Vital Records to 1850" volumes, cemetery transcriptions for Agawam Center and Feeding Hills, and local histories that abstract early west-side families from Springfield records.
- Regional and county sources: Hampden County deeds and probate in Springfield (covering west-side holdings long before incorporation), Springfield church records (Congregational, then later Catholic for Irish and Polish farm and mill families), and agricultural schedules listing tobacco, dairy, and market-garden production.

Effective strategies in Agawam begin by identifying whether a family appears first as part of Springfield's west side, the Feeding Hills precinct, or post-1855 Agawam proper, then following them across the river in deeds, probate, and church records. Correlating Springfield proprietors' maps with later Agawam land descriptions ties 17th- and 18th-century meadow lots to 19th-century brick yards and 20th-century subdivisions, allowing genealogists to reconstruct "Agawam River" and "Feeding Hills" kin as they move from frontier farms into a tobacco- and brick-based valley town in Springfield's orbit.

Chicopee

Chicopee, Massachusetts, lies along the confluence of the Chicopee and Connecticut Rivers in Hampden County, its industrial rise rooted in fertile meadows first settled as part of Springfield's "Chickuppes" Parish before incorporating as a distinct town on January 29, 1848, and later as a city in 1890. The name derives from the Nipmuc–Algonquian *Chickuppi*, meaning "violent waters," referencing the rivers' strong currents below the falls. From early Springfield outposts and ferry farms, Chicopee evolved through parish formation, mills at Cabotville, and textile foundries along Chicopee Falls, blending agrarian and industrial identities that drew Yankee, Irish, Polish, and French Canadian workers. Its boundaries emerged from successive Springfield divisions—forming part of Wilbraham parish in 1763 before its own parish independence in

1844—and retain traces of precolonial travel routes along today's Chicopee and Willimansett neighborhoods.

Chickuppi Homelands, Parish Origins, and Cabotville Mills

Before English settlement, the lower Chicopee valleys belonged to the Nipmuc and Pocumtuc confederations, with fishing weirs and planting grounds near the Connecticut confluence. Epidemics and the 1675–76 King Philip's War uprooted Native presence, opening tracts to Springfield proprietors who allocated meadow lots to early Ball, Nash, and Chapin families by the 1680s. The area remained Springfield farmland for over a century—its "Chickuppes" precinct forming in 1751, later incorporated as Third Parish (Chicopee Street Parish) and Cabotville Village by the 1820s.

Industrialization began when the Cabot Manufacturing Company and Ames Manufacturing Company erected armories, cutlery works, and cotton mills along the Chicopee River. Ames' bronze casting supplied statuary and arms for the Civil War, while cotton mills and the Dwight Manufacturing Company expanded the labor base. By the mid-19th century, shared parish ties and factory boardinghouses shaped early town records, with overlapping church, business, and immigrant community ledgers.

Genealogists trace pre-1848 families in Springfield's land deeds, town records, and parish registers, then continue through Chicopee town books and church files linking agrarian and industrial households across the transformation from parish to factory town.

Immigrant Villages, Industrial Families, and Urban Identity

Nineteenth-century Chicopee became a mosaic of mill villages: Cabotville, Chicopee Falls, and Willimansett. Yankee settlers (Chapin, Kendall, Nash, and Ball lines) gave way to successive Irish, French Canadian, and Polish influxes. Irish laborers built canals and mill tenements; French Canadian weavers established strong Catholic parishes—St. George's (1868) and Assumption (1887); Polish community life centered around St. Stanislaus (1891). The Civil War era saw heavy enlistment from Ames machinists' sons and Dwight spinners.

Industrial prosperity fostered civic buildings and schools, while annexations clarified Springfield–Chicopee boundaries through municipal acts in 1848 and 1890. Mill ledgers, parish rosters, and immigrant society minute books reveal tight kinship migration chains across New England's factory belt.

Genealogical Resources and Strategies

Vital repositories:

- Chicopee City Clerk – Births, deaths, and marriages from 1848 onward; town meeting and incorporation acts.
- Springfield City Clerk – Older records pre-1848 for families in the "Chickuppes" precinct.
- Chicopee Public Library History Room – Directories, maps, and early industrial and parish histories.
- Chicopee Historical Society – Ames Manufacturing records, mill employee lists, photographs, and family manuscripts.

- Catholic Diocesan Archives (Springfield) – Parish registers (baptisms, marriages, confirmations) for St. Patrick's, St. George's, and St. Stanislaus parishes.

Regional aids include Hampden County deed and probate volumes at the Registry in Springfield, church transcriptions on FamilySearch, and industrial census schedules listing laborers and overseers.

Chicopee's twin-river narrative—from Nipmuc "violent waters" to parish farms, bronze foundries, and immigrant mill villages—equips genealogists with layered sources. Parish rolls, company payrolls, and civic records document "river city kin" weaving through Yankee farms and factory wards alike.

Holyoke

Holyoke, Massachusetts, occupies the dramatic falls of the Connecticut River in Hampden County, transforming from "Ireland Parish" within West Springfield into a city chartered April 7, 1873, after town incorporation in 1850. Named for Elizur Holyoke, early Springfield settler and Mount Holyoke's namesake, its hydropower fueled America's first planned industrial city, drawing Yankee engineers, Irish canal diggers, French Canadian spinners, and Polish steelworkers to paper mills, textiles, and foundries along the city's six canals. From Agawam homelands disrupted by King Philip's War, Holyoke's grid of wards and wards emerged via West Springfield divisions in 1848–50, preserving ferry rights, mill privileges, and immigrant enclaves in today's Highlands, Churchill, and Oakdale neighborhoods.

Agawam Homelands, Ireland Parish, and Hadley Falls Mills

Precolonial Agawam bands fished and farmed the Connecticut's violent falls, scattered by epidemics and 1675–76 raids that cleared lands for Springfield proprietors like Pynchon and Holyoke kin granting water rights by the 1780s. As West Springfield's eastern "Ireland Parish" (from 1820s Irish laborers), it hosted gristmills and farms until 1847–49 dam construction by the Hadley Falls Company unleashed industrial boom—Mount Holyoke Paper, Holyoke Machine Company, and Lyman Mills spinning fine cotton. Fires in 1874 and floods in 1936 tested but reinforced the canal grid, with Fiskdale and Whiting bobbin works employing mixed-heritage crews.

Genealogists mine West Springfield records pre-1850 for parish families, then Holyoke town books linking Yankee mill owners to immigrant boardinghouse clusters across the falls' power.

Immigrant Wards, Paper City Boom, and Labor Networks

Holyoke's 19th-century wards fused cultures: Irish in Flat Hills (St. Jerome's parish, 1855), French Canadians in the Notch (Notre Dame, 1871), Poles in Churchill (Immaculate Conception, 1903), and Jews in North Canal. Civil War contracts swelled Ames sword works and paper exports, while baseball's origins were traced to 1870s mill teams. Labor strife marked 1890s strikes, yet prosperity built schools, trolley lines, and Mount Tom reservoirs serving endogamous mill villages.

Ward maps, company store ledgers, and ethnic mutual aid minutes capture migration chains from Quebec, Ireland, and Galicia into "Paper City" payrolls.

Genealogical Resources and Strategies

Vital repositories:

- Holyoke City Clerk: Births, marriages, deaths from 1850 (published to 1900); incorporation acts and ward boundaries.
- Holyoke Public Library History Room: Directories (1870s+), maps, ethnic histories, and mill photographs.
- Holyoke Historical Society: Company records (Lyman, Fisk), family papers, immigrant society files, and census extracts.
- Diocesan Archives (Springfield): Registers for St. Jerome's, Notre Dame, Sacred Heart (French), and Polish parishes.

Regional aids: Hampden County Registry of Deeds for mill mortgages, FamilySearch wikis for West Springfield overlaps, and Holyoke Heritage State Park mill tours.

Holyoke's cascade chronicle—from Agawam weirs and Ireland Parish to canal wards and paper barons—arms genealogists with layered ledgers. Parish books, payroll rolls, and society rosters reveal "falls city kin" spanning Pynchons, O'Connells, and Chaputs across the six canals.

Palmer

Palmer, Massachusetts, nestles in the Quaboag River valley of Hampden County, emerging from Brimfield's remote "Elbow Tract" plantation into a district in 1775 and town incorporated May 20, 1811, later dividing into Thorndike, Three Rivers, and Monson-adjacent villages by mid-19th century. Named for English geographer Thomas Palmer, whose maps guided colonial grants, its agrarian core shifted to rail-fed industry with the Western Railroad (1830s) and Palmer Nail Company, attracting Yankee farmers, Irish tracklayers, and French Canadian operatives amid Nipmuc homelands along the river's bends. Boundaries solidified through Brimfield separations and Ware River annexations, retaining colonial trails in Depot Village, Thorndike, and Bondsville hamlets.

Nipmuc Elbow Tract, King Settlement, and Rail Villages

Pre-English Nipmuc groups hunted and planted Quaboag tributaries, decimated by epidemics and King Philip's War (1675–76) that yielded the "Elbow" to Brimfield proprietors; John King, first settler from Edwardstone, Suffolk (c.1716), built the initial homestead, followed by Bartlett, Brewster, and Shaw allotments by 1730s. As Brimfield's distant district, gristmills and sawmills dotted the river until railroad arrival spurred factories—Palmer Nail (1835), Gilbert & Bennett wire works, and Osborn mill in Bondsville. Civil War demand boosted iron forges, with Quaker and Baptist meetinghouses anchoring early kin networks.

Genealogists scour Brimfield records pre-1811 for Elbow families, then Palmer plantation books linking farmsteads to depot boardinghouses across the rail boom.

Industrial Hamlets, Ethnic Mills, and Quaker Lines

Palmer's villages blended pursuits: Depot hosted rail depots and hotels, Thorndike woolen mills drew French Canadians to St. Anne's parish (1870), Three Rivers' paper mills employed Poles at Sacred Heart (1902), and Bondsville's wire cloth served global trade. Yankee lines like Kings, Days, and Brewsters intermarried with immigrants amid 1896 floods and 1910s labor organizing. Wing Memorial Hospital (1925) and rail junctions fostered civic ties.

Company payrolls, village store ledgers, and ethnic lodge minutes trace chain migrations into "Central Village" endogamy.

Genealogical Resources and Strategies

Vital repositories:

- Palmer Town Clerk: Births, marriages, deaths from 1716 plantation era (published to 1850); district and incorporation records.
- Palmer Public Library Local History Room: "History of Palmer" (Temple, 1889) with genealogies (pp.407–572), directories, and digital pamphlets.
- Palmer Historical Society/Elbow Plantation: Manuscripts, family registers (King, Bartlett kin), censuses, and village maps.
- Brimfield Historical Society: Pre-1811 deeds and Brimfield parish overlaps.

Regional aids: Hampden County probate at Springfield Registry, FamilySearch vital transcriptions, and Sanborn maps for mill footprints.

Palmer's river-elbow saga—from Nipmuc bends and King cabins to nail hammers and wire looms—equips genealogists with deep ledgers. Plantation rolls, nail shop books, and society files unveil "Elbow kin" spanning Brewsters, Shaws, and Thorndikes across Quaboag hamlets.

Springfield

Springfield, Massachusetts, anchors Hampden County at the Connecticut River's great bend, founded 1636 by William Pynchon as colonial Agawam outpost and incorporated as a town, evolving into a city by 1852 amid armories, railroads, and factories that drew English planters, Irish laborers, and German craftsmen. Named for Pynchon's Suffolk homeland, its meadows and falls—once Agawam homelands—fostered trade routes, mills, and Civil War munitions, with wards spanning Court Square, South End, and Indian Orchard preserving 17th-century bounds adjusted by Chicopee separations (1848) and West Springfield splits (1852). From Pynchon grants to industrial hubs, Springfield's chronicles blend Puritan proprietors, immigrant enclaves, and basketball's 1891 birth in the YMCA.

Agawam Meadows, Pynchon Grants, and Armory Rise

Precolonial Agawam villages thrived on river fisheries and cornfields, disrupted by epidemics and King Philip's War (1675–76) that secured Pynchon's 1636 patent for meadows and trading house. Early proprietors like Pynchon, Chapin, and Cooley families divided lots by 1640s, erecting mills, ferries, and fortifications; the 1786 Shays' Rebellion arsenal led to federal Springfield Armory (1794), forging muskets and machine tools. Parish divisions birthed Chicopee (1848) and West Springfield (1852), while railroads connected factories producing carriages, clocks, and Smith & Wesson revolvers.

Genealogists probe Pynchon Court records, early town books, and Agawam deeds linking meadow allotments to armory payrolls across Puritan-to-industrial lineages.

Wards, Immigrant Waves, and Arsenal Boom

Springfield's 19th-century mosaic featured Yankee Court Square merchants, Irish North End canal diggers at St. Michael's (1846), Italian South End at Our Lady of Hope (1905), and Polish Indian Orchard mills. Civil War contracts swelled armory output, Duryea brothers launched autos (1893), and Springfield Republican chronicled kin networks. Floods (1936) and urban renewal reshaped wards, yet ethnic societies and colleges sustained ties.

Ward censuses, company ledgers, and church rosters map migration chains into "City of Homes" endogamy.

Genealogical Resources and Strategies

Vital repositories:

- Springfield City Clerk: Births, marriages, deaths from 1638 (published to 1850); town-to-city transitions and annexations.
- Springfield Library History & Genealogy Room: Directories (1820s+), Pynchon papers, Republican indexes, and Armory records.
- Springfield Historical Society/Museum: Family manuscripts (Cooley, Chapin), probate abstracts, and immigrant club files.
- Diocesan Archives (Springfield): Registers for First Churches, St. Michael's, and ethnic parishes.

Regional aids: Hampden County Registry of Deeds for proprietor plats, FamilySearch wikis for parish overlaps, and Armory muster rolls.

Springfield's river-bend epic—from Agawam fields and Pynchon deeds to armory hammers and ward factories—arms genealogists with foundational files. Court rolls, vital indexes, and society archives unveil "meadow kin" spanning Pynchons, Chapins, and O'Learys across the Connecticut's curve.

West Springfield

West Springfield, Massachusetts, flanks the west bank of the Connecticut River in Hampden County, separating from Springfield as a town incorporated February 23, 1774, after centuries as its "West Side" parish amid farms, ferries, and floods. Retaining fertile meadows once Agawam homelands, it hosted Shays' Rebellion drills on the Town Common and Eastern States Exposition since 1917, with neighborhoods like Feeding Hills, Mittineague, and Riverdale preserving colonial roads adjusted by Holyoke (1850) and Agawam (1855) divisions. From Pynchon-era grants to rail bridges and fairgrounds, West Springfield blended agrarian Day and Ashley families with Hessian settlers and Irish laborers.

Agawam West Side, Parish Separation, and Ferry Commons

Precolonial Agawam fished river bends and trails, yielding to Springfield's 1636 outpost; west-side settlers like Thomas Day received meadow lots by 1660s, complaining of east-side road duties until 1666 autonomy. The 1697 West Parish gained its meetinghouse, school (1706), and land grants, fueling independence petitions amid Revolutionary minutemen and 1777 Hessian camps. Ferries at Ashley's (1843) and bridges (1847–1903) linked to Springfield, while Shays' insurgents rallied on the Common before 1787 dispersal.

Genealogists trace west-side lots in Springfield deeds pre-1774, then parish books linking Day, Parsons, and Noble kin to post-Revolution farmsteads.

Village Hamlets, Rail Growth, and Fairground Legacy

West Springfield's 19th-century clusters featured Feeding Hills farms, Mittineague mills along Pawcatuck Brook, and Riverdale resorts; Western Railroad (1841) spurred depots, while Irish at St. Thomas (1853) and French Canadians at Sacred Heart (1905) joined Yankee networks. Eastern States Exposition transformed agriculture into tourism, with Morgan horse breeding (1789) and Day House taverns anchoring civic life. Floods and sprawl reshaped bounds, yet commons and brooks retained early paths.

Parish rosters, ferry logs, and fair ledgers map endogamous lines across river-crossing kin.

Genealogical Resources and Strategies

Vital repositories:

- West Springfield Town Clerk: Births, marriages, deaths from 1697 parish era (published to 1850); incorporation and division records.
- West Springfield Public Library History Room: Directories, maps, Exposition archives, and family sketches.
- West Springfield Historical Commission: Day House manuscripts, Common registers, Hessian descendant files, and cemetery surveys.
- Springfield Diocesan Archives: Registers for West Springfield parishes and St. Thomas.

Regional aids: Hampden County deeds for west-side allotments, FamilySearch parish transcriptions, and Storrowton Village exhibits for colonial homes.

West Springfield's river-west chronicle—from Agawam meadows and parish commons to Shays' drills and fair barns—equips genealogists with split-side sources. Proprietors' grants, meeting minutes, and commission files unveil "west bank kin" spanning Days, Ashleys, and Parsons across Connecticut ferries.

Westfield

Westfield, Massachusetts, stretches along the Westfield River in Hampden County, founded 1669 as Springfield's remote "Woronoak" plantation and incorporated as a town in 1725, later a city from 1920 amid whips, bicycles, and aerospace drawing Yankee planters, Irish operatives, and Italian craftsmen. Named for its western fields beyond the river, its meadows—once Woronoak homelands—hosted gristmills, forges, and Civil War contracts, with villages like Tekoa, Little River, and Southwick Road preserving colonial bounds refined by West Springfield splits and Agawam annexations. From Shepard grants to industrial hubs, Westfield blended Puritan proprietors, Shaker outposts, and trolley suburbs.

Woronoak Homelands, Shepard Plantation, and Whip City Mills

Precolonial Woronoak (Hampden County Nipmuc) villages farmed river flats and trails, disrupted by epidemics and King Philip's War (1675–76) that opened tracts to Springfield agents; Lt. Sam Shepard's 1669 plantation allocated lots to Bliss, Dewey, Sackett, and Phelps families by 1670s, yielding sawmills and forges. Parish status (1690s) and town incorporation followed petitions against Springfield oversight, with Shays' Rebellion tensions rallying on the Green. Whip factories (1820s–1900s), Fisk Bicycle (1890s), and Hayes Pump fueled exports, employing endog-amous Yankee lines.

Genealogists scour Springfield deeds pre-1725 for Woronoak allotments, then Westfield plantation books linking farmsteads to mill payrolls across the river divide.

Village Forges, Ethnic Waves, and Industrial Green

Westfield's 19th-century clusters fused trades: North Elm Yankee merchants, Irish at St. John's (1845), Poles in Hungry Hill (St. Casimir's, 1910), and Italians at Our Lady of the Assumption (1907). Civil War scythes and Springfield Armory ties swelled forges, while trolley lines connected Shaker villages and Noble Hospital (1893). Floods (1955) and sprawl reshaped the Green yet whip ledgers and ethnic societies sustained kin networks.

Company rosters, church registers, and green meeting minutes trace migration chains into "Whip City" workshops.

Genealogical Resources and Strategies

Vital repositories:

- Westfield City Clerk: Births, marriages, deaths from 1669 plantation (published to 1850); incorporation and ward records.
- Westfield Athenaeum History Room: Directories (1820s+), Bliss family papers, whip industry archives, and cemetery surveys.
- Westfield Historical Society: Manuscripts (Dewey, Phelps), probate abstracts, Shaker extracts, and village maps.
- Springfield Diocesan Archives: Registers for First Congregational, St. John's, and ethnic parishes.

Regional aids: Hampden County Registry of Deeds for meadow plats, FamilySearch wikis for Springfield overlaps, and Sanborn maps for forge footprints.

Westfield's river-west saga—from Woronoak flats and Shepard cabins to whip lashes and bike chains—arms genealogists with foundational files. Plantation rolls, vital indexes, and society ledgers unveil "field kin" spanning Blisses, Deweys, and Sacketts across the Westfield's bends.

<u>Blandford</u>

Blandford, Massachusetts, crowns the hilltowns of Hampden County along rocky ridges above the Farmington River, first settled in 1735 by Scots-Irish from Hopkinton and incorporated November 10, 1741, as a remote outpost sustaining subsistence farms, cheese dairies, and Albany stage taverns amid thin soils and glacial boulders. Originally "New Glasgow" for its Presbyterian pioneers, renamed Blandford at incorporation, its dispersed hamlets—Center, North Blandford, and Beech Hill—preserve colonial home lots adjusted by Granville and Otis boundaries, blending Highland kin with Yankee intermarriages in a landscape of merino sheep and Methodist circuits. From wilderness grants to butter barrels and woolen looms, Blandford's agrarian endurance traces Woronoak trails through Shays' sympathizers and 19th-century out-migrations.

Scots-Irish Wilderness, Black Settlements, and Presbyterian Core

Precolonial Woronoak hunters traversed ridges and river gorges, yielding to Massachusetts' surveyed townships; Hugh Black arrived fall 1735, joined by Baird, Reed, McClintock, and Taggart families securing home lots from Hopkinton proprietors by 1740, erecting a windowless meetinghouse for their excommunicated Presbyterian society. First pastor William McClenathan (1744–47) anchored the church-town union until Congregational shifts c.1800, with mills and taverns on the Boston-Albany road fostering Black, Boies, and Gibbs lines amid King Philip's War echoes and Revolutionary forage. Jane Taggart's 1805 school bequest funded districts into the 20th century.

Genealogists consult Hopkinton deeds pre-1735 for migrant clusters, then Blandford plantation books linking ridge cabins to church rolls across Scots-Irish endogamy.

Hill Farms, Dairy Taverns, and Methodist Outposts
Blandford's 19th-century hamlets thrived on hay, 1,500 cows yielding butter-cheese for valley trade, merino woolens ($50,000 annually), and 20 taverns like Amos Collins' inn; Methodist circuit riders supplanted Presbyterians at Beech Hill (Granville line) and North Blandford churches, drawing revivals amid Shays' drills and 1892 fires. Yankee farmers (Ferguson, Knox, Stewart) hosted summer colonies by 1909, while thin soils spurred out-migrations to Ohio and beyond, sustaining cemetery ties.

Proprietors' allotments, tavern ledgers, and district minutes capture chain kin from Glasgow ports to hilltop hearths.

Genealogical Resources and Strategies
Vital repositories:

- Blandford Town Clerk: Births, marriages, deaths from 1735 settlements (published to 1850); proprietors' grants and church-town records.
- Blandford Historical Society: Bicentennial manuscripts, family registers (Black, Taggart, Gibbs), cemetery surveys, and school bequest files.
- Palmer Public Library Regional Aids: Hilltown overlaps, stage road maps, and woolen mill extracts.

Regional aids: Hampden County probate at Springfield Registry, FamilySearch Presbyterian transcriptions, and MHC surveys for home lot plats.

Blandford's ridge-top tale—from Scots-Irish logs and Black hearths to cheese presses and revival tents—equips genealogists with hardy hill sources. Meeting rolls, dairy accounts, and society archives unveil "New Glasgow kin" spanning McClintocks, Bairds, and Wellses across Farmington ridges.

Brimfield
Brimfield, Massachusetts, spans the Quaboag River plains in Hampden County, settled 1686 from Ipswich as "Quaboag Plantation No. 5" and incorporated October 7, 1731, amid farms, forges, and chair shops that sustained Yankee husbandmen, Irish laborers, and Swedish woodworkers in dispersed hamlets like Brimfield Center, West Brimfield, and Sturbridge line villages. Named for English Brimfield, its fertile intervals—once Nipmuc Quaboag homelands—hosted gristmills, tanneries, and Shays' Rebellion musters, with bounds refined by Palmer separations (1811) and

Wales divisions (1763), preserving colonial roads through Elbow Tract outposts and Hitchcock chair legacy. From proprietors' lots to rural crafts and Civil War quilting bees, Brimfield's agrarian spine traces Nipmuc trails via tavern commons and district schools.

Quaboag Plantation, Nipmuc Intervals, and Elbow Outpost

Precolonial Nipmuc Quaboag bands planted cornfields and fished tributaries, scattered by epidemics and King Philip's War (1675–76) that granted No. 5 tract to Ipswich men: Lt. John Carter and Thomas Lee secured intervals by 1687, dividing 60-acre lots to Fitch, Collier, and Warriner families amid Indian deeds and frontier garrisons. Parish formation (1714) yielded meetinghouse and burying ground, with Elbow Tract mills feeding Palmer district until 1811 split; Shays' regulators drilled on the Green before 1787 flight. Hitchcock chairs emerged c.1818 from Lambert Hitchcock's Ware factory kin.

Genealogists probe Ipswich proprietors' books pre-1731 for Quaboag allotments, then Brimfield plantation records linking meadow farms to chair shop apprentices across the river plains.

District Hamlets, Chair Crafts, and Rural Quilts

Brimfield's 18th–19th-century clusters featured West Brimfield forges, Center District schools drawing revivals, and tavern rows like Ebenezer Moulton's inn; Irish at St. Boniface (1871) and Swedes in chair factories joined Fitch and Bedortha lines amid 1819 floods and 1852 railroads. Antiquarian fairs since 1956 revived commons, sustaining cemetery societies and Hitchcock descendants. Rural endogamy persisted through quilting circles and Grange halls.

Proprietors' surveys, district minutes, and shop ledgers map kin clusters from Essex ports to Quaboag hearths.

Genealogical Resources and Strategies

Vital repositories:

- Brimfield Town Clerk: Births, marriages, deaths from 1686 plantation (published to 1850); proprietors' grants and Elbow separations.
- Brimfield Historical Society: Manuscripts (Fitch, Warriner), chair factory records, Green muster rolls, and family Bibles.
- Palmer Public Library Regional Aids: Quaboag overlaps, antique fair archives, and Sturbridge maps.

Regional aids: Hampden County deeds for interval plats, FamilySearch parish transcriptions, and MHC reports for tavern sites.

Brimfield's plain-field chronicle—from Nipmuc Quaboag and Ipswich lots to chair rockers and fair barns—equips genealogists with meadow-deep sources. Plantation deeds, vital rolls, and society files unveil "No. 5 kin" spanning Carters, Lees, and Hitchcocks across Quaboag districts.

Chester

Chester, Massachusetts, rises amid the Westfield River gorges in Hampden County, settled 1766 from Norwich as "Murrayfield" and incorporated July 15, 1775, sustaining hill farms, charcoal forges, and paper mills through Yankee loggers, Irish dam-builders, and Czech operatives in hamlets like Chester Center, Middlefield line villages, and Huntington brooks. Named for

Chester, England, its narrow valleys—once Woronoak homelands—powered gristmills and Civil War ironworks, with bounds refined by Becket (1765) and Middlefield (1783) divisions, preserving colonial grants through Russell separations and flood-scarred roads. From wilderness lots to rural hydro and quarry stone, Chester's rugged spine traces Nipmuc paths via Shays' outposts and district revivals.

Woronoak Gorges, Murrayfield Grants, and Forge Hollows

Precolonial Woronoak traversed river narrows for hunting and fisheries, disrupted by epidemics and King Philip's War (1675–76) that yielded Murrayfield tract to Norwich proprietors; Ebenezer Dewey and Asahel Gunn claimed home lots by 1767, dividing ledges to Smith, Phelps, and Bartlett families amid garrisons and Indian boundaries. Renamed Chester at incorporation amid Revolutionary service, early forges and sawmills fed Springfield Armory, with Shays' sympathizers hiding in hills before 1787; Middlefield parish split (1783) left Chester's core intact. Paper mills rose c.1830 along the Westfield, employing endogamous settler lines.

Genealogists trace Norwich deeds pre-1775 for Murrayfield allotments, then Chester plantation books linking gorge cabins to mill rosters across the river hollows.

Valley Hamlets, Quarry Mills, and Flood Resilience

Chester's 19th-century clusters blended Center District farms, Huntington Road dairies drawing Methodist circuits, and Irish at St. Joseph's (1872) joining Dewey and Loomis kin amid 1874 dam breaks and 1938 hurricane floods. Quarry stone and charcoal sustained forges, while hydro plants (1900s) powered rural electrification; Czech and Lithuanian laborers bolstered paper works, sustaining Grange halls and cemetery ties throughout-migrations.

Proprietors' surveys, mill contracts, and district records capture chain kin from Connecticut valleys to Westfield hearths.

Genealogical Resources and Strategies

Vital repositories:

- Chester Town Clerk: Births, marriages, deaths from 1766 Murrayfield era (published to 1850); incorporation and parish splits.
- Chester Historical Society: Manuscripts (Dewey, Gunn), forge ledgers, flood narratives, and family registers.
- Westfield Athenaeum Regional Aids: Murrayfield overlaps, Westfield River maps, and quarry extracts.

Regional aids: Hampden County probate at Springfield Registry, FamilySearch vital transcriptions, and MHC surveys for gorge home sites.

Chester's gorge-valley saga—from Woronoak narrows and Murrayfield logs to forge blooms and paper reels—equips genealogists with hill-deep sources. Plantation grants, church rolls, and society files unveil "river hollow kin" spanning Deweys, Smiths, and Phelp across Westfield cataracts.

East Longmeadow

East Longmeadow, Massachusetts, borders Springfield's eastern plains in Hampden County, separating from Longmeadow as a town incorporated August 23, 1894, amid dairy farms, quarries, and rubber mills that blended Yankee agrarians, Irish stonecutters, and Polish operatives in hamlets like North Main, Maple, and Old Meadow Road villages. Carved from Longmeadow's east precinct—once Agawam homelands—its fields powered gristmills and Civil War leatherworks, with bounds refined by Springfield annexations and Enfield divisions, preserving colonial paths through Somers Road and Hazard Quarry districts. From Longmeadow grants to suburban crafts and Big E fairgrounds, East Longmeadow's meadow spine traces Nipmuc trails via parish commons and district schools.

Agawam East Precinct, Longmeadow Separation, and Quarry Plains

Precolonial Agawam planted cornfields and fished Connecticut tributaries, disrupted by epidemics and King Philip's War (1675–76) that secured Longmeadow meadows to Springfield proprietors; east-side families like Cooley, Burt, and Colton divided lots by 1700s, forming East Parish with meetinghouse (1791) and schools amid road disputes. Petition for independence from tax-heavy Longmeadow succeeded post-1890s growth, with quarries yielding red sandstone for Springfield buildings and rubber mills (U.S. Envelope, 1880s) employing endogamous kin. Civil War service drew from Burt militias, sustaining farm-to-factory lines.

Genealogists probe Longmeadow records pre-1894 for east precinct allotments, then East Longmeadow town books linking meadow homesteads to quarry payrolls across the separation.

District Farms, Stone Mills, and Suburban Quilts

East Longmeadow's late-19th-century clusters featured North Main dairies, Maple district revivals at First Baptist (1895), and Irish-Polish at St. Michael's (1902) joining Colton and Warriner lines amid 1938 floods and post-WWII sprawl. Quarry stone and envelope factories anchored economy, while Eastern States Exposition ties fostered fairgrounds and Grange halls; rural endogamy persisted through quilting bees and cemetery societies.

Parish rosters, quarry ledgers, and district minutes map kin clusters from Longmeadow hearths to east-side workshops.

Genealogical Resources and Strategies

Vital repositories:

- East Longmeadow Town Clerk: Births, marriages, deaths from 1894 incorporation (earlier via Longmeadow); precinct records and annexations.
- East Longmeadow Public Library History Room: Directories, maps, quarry archives, and family sketches.
- East Longmeadow Historical Society: Manuscripts (Burt, Cooley), mill employee lists, and cemetery surveys.

Regional aids: Hampden County deeds for east meadow plats, FamilySearch Longmeadow overlaps, and Springfield Library for parish extracts.

East Longmeadow's east-meadow chronicle—from Agawam fields and precinct commons to quarry blocks and rubber reels—equips genealogists with split-side sources. Proprietors' grants, vital rolls, and society files unveil "east precinct kin" spanning Coltons, Burts, and Fosters across Springfield plains.

Granville

Granville, Massachusetts, perches on Hampden County's southern ridges above the Westfield River, settled 1728 from Simsbury as "Salisbury" and incorporated June 23, 1754, amid thin hill farms, potash works, and cheese dairies that sustained Scots-Irish pioneers, Yankee agrarians, and Czech quarrymen in hamlets like Granville Center, West Granville, and Tolland line villages. Named for the Granville family of earls, its rocky pastures—once Woronoak homelands—powered small mills and Civil War woolens, with bounds refined by Blandford separations (1741) and Otis divisions (1810), preserving colonial grants through Beech Hill trails and flood-prone brooks. From wilderness lots to rural dairies and summer boarders, Granville's highland spine traces Nipmuc paths via Shays' hideouts and Methodist circuits.

Woronoak Ridges, Salisbury Grants, and Potash Hollows

Precolonial Woronoag hunters roamed ridges and gorges, disrupted by epidemics and King Philip's War (1675–76) that yielded Salisbury tract to Connecticut Valley proprietors; Ebenezer Smith and John Dewey claimed home lots by 1730, dividing ledges to Taylor, Campbell, and Keep families amid frontier garrisons and Indian boundaries. Renamed Granville at incorporation amid Revolutionary musters, early potash kilns and sawmills fed Springfield trade, with Shays' sympathizers in hills before 1787; small woolen mills and cheese factories anchored subsistence amid thin soils.

Genealogists trace Simsbury deeds pre-1754 for Salisbury allotments, then Granville plantation books linking ridge cabins to dairy rosters across the highland endogamy.

Hill Hamlets, Dairy Quarries, and Revival Tents

Granville's 19th-century clusters blended Center District farms drawing revivals at Union Church (1805), West Granville quarries employing Irish-Czech laborers at St. Mary's (1900), and Taylor kin sustaining Grange halls amid 1874 floods and 1938 hurricanes. Butter-cheese exports and summer colonies bolstered economy, while rural ties persisted through cemetery societies and out-migrations to Ohio.

Proprietors' surveys, dairy ledgers, and district minutes capture chain kin from valley ports to ridge hearths.

Genealogical Resources and Strategies

Vital repositories:

- Granville Town Clerk: Births, marriages, deaths from 1728 Salisbury era (published to 1850); incorporation and parish records.
- Granville Historical Society: Manuscripts (Smith, Dewey), potash accounts, cheese factory files, and family registers.
- Westfield Athenaeum Regional Aids: Salisbury overlaps, Westfield River maps, and quarry extracts.

Regional aids: Hampden County probate at Springfield Registry, FamilySearch vital transcriptions, and MHC surveys for ridge home sites.

Granville's ridge-high tale—from Woronoak heights and Salisbury logs to potash flames and cheese wheels—equips genealogists with hill-hardy sources. Plantation grants, church rolls, and society files unveil "Salisbury kin" spanning Taylors, Deweys, and Campbells across Westfield summits.

Hampden

Hampden, Massachusetts, crowns Hampden County's eastern hilltowns along the Scantic River, settled 1741 from Springfield as "South Parish No. 7" and incorporated October 12, 1878, amid farms, scythe forges, and silk mills that blended Yankee agrarians, Irish operatives, and Polish weavers in hamlets like Hampden Center, North Wilbraham line villages, and Powder Mill brooks. Carved from Springfield's remote south precinct—once Nipmuc homelands—its meadows powered gristmills and Civil War edge tools, with bounds refined by Wilbraham separations (1812) and Monson divisions, preserving colonial roads through Bachelor Street and Methodist circuits. From wilderness grants to rural forges and trolley suburbs, Hampden's highland spine traces Nipmuc trails via Shays' outposts and district schools.

Nipmuc South Precinct, Springfield Grants, and Scythe Hollows

Precolonial Nipmuc planted intervals and fished Scantic tributaries, disrupted by epidemics and King Philip's War (1675–76) that secured No. 7 tract to Springfield proprietors; John Bliss and Thomas Chapin claimed home lots by 1743, dividing ledges to Leonard, Warriner, and Alvord families amid garrisons and Indian boundaries. Parish status (1760s) yielded meetinghouse and burying ground, with Shays' sympathizers rallying before 1787; scythe forges (Jerome & Co., 1830s) and silk mills employed endogamous kin, feeding Springfield Armory contracts. Civil War service drew from Leonard militias.

Genealogists probe Springfield deeds pre-1878 for south precinct allotments, then Hampden parish books linking hill farmsteads to forge payrolls across the separation.

Hill Hamlets, Forge Mills, and Revival Commons

Hampden's 19th-century clusters featured Center District farms drawing revivals at Congregational Church (1791), Bachelor Street forges with Irish at St. Peter's (1875), and Polish joining Bliss and Alvord lines amid 1938 floods and post-WWII sprawl. Scythe exports and powder mills anchored economy, sustaining Grange halls and cemetery ties throughout-migrations. Rural endogamy persisted via quilting bees and trolley lines to Springfield.

Proprietors' surveys, mill contracts, and district minutes capture chain kin from Agawam hearths to Scantic workshops.

Genealogical Resources and Strategies

Vital repositories:

- Hampden Town Clerk: Births, marriages, deaths from 1741 parish era (published to 1850); incorporation and Springfield separations.
- Hampden Historical Society: Manuscripts (Bliss, Leonard), scythe ledgers, silk mill files, and family registers.

- Springfield Library Regional Aids: South Parish overlaps, Scantic maps, and forge extracts.

Regional aids: Hampden County probate at Springfield Registry, FamilySearch parish transcriptions, and MHC surveys for hill home sites.

Hampden's hill-precinct chronicle—from Nipmuc Scantic and south lots to scythe edges and silk threads—equips genealogists with deep parish sources. Plantation grants, church rolls, and society files unveil "No. 7 kin" spanning Leonards, Warriners, and Chapins across eastern ridges.

Holland

Holland, Massachusetts, nestles in Hampden County's southeastern corner along ponds and ridges shared with Brimfield, settled 1730 by Joseph Blodgett from the Polley Place tract and incorporated as South Brimfield East Parish on July 5, 1783, later a full town May 1, 1836, amid subsistence farms, chair shops, and reservoirs sustaining Yankee pioneers, Irish laborers, and Swedish woodworkers in hamlets like Holland Center, Brimfield Pond villages, and Union line outposts. Named for Lord Holland who favored American independence, its hilly ponds—once Nipmuc Quaboag homelands—powered small mills and Civil War forges, with bounds refined by Brimfield separations over mountainous roads, preserving colonial grants through Tantusque lead mine echoes and 1955 flood scars. From wilderness lots to rural ponds and summer camps, Holland's pond-side spine traces Nipmuc trails via district petitions and Methodist circuits.

Nipmuc Southeast, Blodgett Plantation, and Pond Districts

Precolonial Nipmuc Quaboag bands fished ponds and planted hills, disrupted by epidemics and King Philip's War (1675–76) that opened southeast Brimfield to proprietors amid Winthrop heirs' Tantusque claims; Joseph Blodgett's 1730 settlement drew Bugbee, Lovell, and Davis families securing home lots by 1740s, petitioning for East Parish over road hardships to Brimfield meetinghouse. Congregational church organized 1783 with Rev. Enoch Burt (1820), building north of David Bugbee's tavern; school districts divided the quadrilateral amid Revolutionary service and Shays' echoes.

Genealogists consult Brimfield deeds pre-1783 for southeast allotments, then Holland district books linking pond cabins to church rolls across the parish split.

Pond Hamlets, Forge Shops, and Flood Resilience

Holland's 19th-century clusters featured Center District farms drawing revivals, pond-side chair factories with Irish at St. Patrick's (1870s), and Yankee lines like Blodgetts sustaining cemetery ties amid 1858 church fire and 1955 deluge that birthed Hamilton Reservoir recreation. Rural endogamy persisted through Grange halls and out-migrations, with turnpikes linking to Hartford-Worcester trade.

Proprietors' surveys, district minutes, and pond ledgers capture chain kin from Brimfield hearths to southeast workshops.

Genealogical Resources and Strategies

Vital repositories:

- Holland Town Clerk: Births, marriages, deaths from 1730 Blodgett era (published to 1850); East Parish incorporation and Brimfield separations.

- Holland Historical Society: Manuscripts (Blodgett, Bugbee), church pew deeds, flood narratives, and family registers.
- Brimfield Historical Society Regional Aids: Southeast overlaps, pond maps, and Tantusque extracts.

Regional aids: Hampden County probate at Springfield Registry, FamilySearch district transcriptions, and MHC surveys for pond home sites.

Holland's pond-quad saga—from Nipmuc waters and Blodgett logs to parish bells and reservoir shores—equips genealogists with remote-deep sources. District rolls, vital indexes, and society files unveil "East Parish kin" spanning Blodgetts, Lovells, and Davises across Brimfield ridges.

Longmeadow

Longmeadow, Massachusetts, stretches along the Connecticut River's east bank in Hampden County, granted 1644 from Springfield as a long meadow tract and incorporated as a town November 18, 1783, sustaining elite farms, academies, and suburban estates that blended Puritan proprietors, later Irish servants, and Jewish professionals in hamlets like Center, East Longmeadow line villages, and Bay Street enclaves. Named for its linear meadows—once Agawam homelands—its fertile intervals powered few mills but hosted Longmeadow Seminary (1848) and Civil War horse breeding, with bounds refined by East Longmeadow separations (1894) and Enfield divisions, preserving colonial lanes through Ward Pond and Laurel Farm districts. From Pynchon grants to genteel suburbs and Big E ties, Longmeadow's river-meadow spine traces Nipmuc trails via parish commons and academy rosters.

Agawam Long Lots, Springfield Precinct, and Seminary Plains

Precolonial Agawam villages farmed river flats and fished bays, disrupted by epidemics and King Philip's War (1675–76) that secured meadow grants to Springfield elites; John Pynchon allotted long lots to Burt, Cooley, Keep, and Warriner families by 1650s, forming East Parish with meetinghouse (1715) and burying ground amid tax disputes. Independence petitions triumphed post-Revolution, with minimal industry yielding to academies like Mrs. Oliver's Seminary (1820s) and elite horse farms supplying Union cavalry; East Precinct growth led to 1894 split.

Genealogists probe Springfield deeds pre-1783 for long lot allotments, then Longmeadow parish books linking meadow mansions to seminary rolls across the river elite.

Meadow Hamlets, Academy Estates, and Suburban Ties

Longmeadow's 19th-century clusters featured Center District mansions drawing revivals at First Church (1784), Bay Street estates with Irish at St. Mary's (1900), and Burt-Cooley lines sustaining cemetery societies amid 1938 floods and post-WWII estates. Genteel pursuits like fox hunting and academy graduations anchored identity, with Eastern States Exposition fostering fairground legacies; endogamy persisted through club rosters and out-marriages to Springfield merchants.

Proprietors' surveys, academy ledgers, and parish minutes capture chain kin from Agawam hearths to meadow hearths.

Genealogical Resources and Strategies

Vital repositories:

- Longmeadow Town Clerk: Births, marriages, deaths from 1644 grant era (published to 1850); parish incorporation and East separations.
- Longmeadow Public Library History Room: Directories, maps, seminary archives, and family sketches.
- Longmeadow Historical Society: Manuscripts (Burt, Cooley), estate inventories, and cemetery surveys.

Regional aids: Hampden County deeds for long lot plats, FamilySearch parish transcriptions, and Springfield Library for East Precinct overlaps.

Longmeadow's linear-meadow chronicle—from Agawam intervals and Pynchon lots to seminary bells and estate lawns—equips genealogists with elite-deep sources. Grant rolls, vital indexes, and society files unveil "long lot kin" spanning Burts, Cooleys, and Keeps across Connecticut meadows.

Ludlow

Ludlow, Massachusetts, lies north of Springfield along the Chicopee River in Hampden County, carved from Springfield's Fourth Parish as a town incorporated February 15, 1774, amid farms, forges, and textile mills that blended Yankee agrarians, Irish operatives, and Polish weavers in hamlets like Ludlow Center, Indian Orchard villages, and Stony Brook districts. Named for Ludlow, England, its river meadows—once Nipmuc homelands—powered gristmills and Civil War edge tools, with bounds refined by Chicopee separations (1848) and Wilbraham divisions, preserving colonial roads through Chapin Pond and Baptist circuits. From wilderness grants to rural mills and suburban estates, Ludlow's river-spine traces Nipmuc trails via Shays' outposts and district schools.

Nipmuc North Precinct, Springfield Grants, and Forge Meadows

Precolonial Nipmuc planted intervals and fished Chicopee tributaries, disrupted by epidemics and King Philip's War (1675–76) that secured Fourth Parish to Springfield proprietors; Samuel Bliss and John Keep claimed home lots by 1740s, dividing meadows to Colton, Warriner, and Gilbert families amid garrisons and Indian boundaries. Parish status yielded meetinghouse (1760) and burying ground, with Shays' sympathizers rallying before 1787; scythe forges and sawmills fed Springfield Armory, employing endogamous kin through Civil War contracts.

Genealogists probe Springfield deeds pre-1774 for north precinct allotments, then Ludlow parish books linking meadow farmsteads to mill payrolls across the separation.

District Hamlets, Textile Forges, and Revival Commons

Ludlow's 19th-century clusters featured Center District farms drawing revivals at Baptist Church (1783), Stony Brook mills with Irish at St. Mary's (1870), and Polish joining Bliss and Colton lines amid 1938 floods and post-WWII sprawl. Textile factories and envelope works anchored economy, sustaining Grange halls and cemetery ties through out-migrations. Rural endogamy persisted via quilting bees and trolley lines to Springfield.

Proprietors' surveys, mill contracts, and district minutes capture chain kin from Agawam hearths to Chicopee workshops.

Genealogical Resources and Strategies
Vital repositories:

- Ludlow Town Clerk: Births, marriages, deaths from 1740 parish era (published to 1850); incorporation and Springfield separations.
- Ludlow Public Library History Room: Directories, maps, forge archives, and family sketches.
- Ludlow Historical Society: Manuscripts (Bliss, Keep), mill employee lists, and cemetery surveys.

Regional aids: Hampden County probate at Springfield Registry, FamilySearch parish transcriptions, and Springfield Library for Fourth Parish overlaps.

Ludlow's river-precinct chronicle—from Nipmuc Chicopee and north lots to forge edges and textile threads—equips genealogists with deep parish sources. Plantation grants, church rolls, and society files unveil "Fourth Parish kin" spanning Coltons, Warriners, and Gilberts across northern meadows.

Monson

Monson, Massachusetts, rises on Hampden County's eastern ridges along the Quaboag River, settled 1710 from Welsh immigrants as "Bransford Manor" and incorporated May 2, 1775, amid farms, granite quarries, and envelope mills that sustained Celtic pioneers, Yankee agrarians, and Irish stonecutters in hamlets like Monson Center, Palmer line villages, and Quarry Hill districts. Named for Lord Monson, its rocky ledges—once Nipmuc homelands—powered gristmills and Civil War woolens, with bounds refined by Brimfield separations (1731) and Palmer divisions (1811), preserving colonial grants through Stafford trails and flood-prone brooks. From wilderness lots to rural stone and paper reels, Monson's highland spine traces Nipmuc paths via Shays' outposts and Methodist circuits.

Nipmuc Quarry Ridges, Welsh Manor Grants, and Woolen Hollows

Precolonial Nipmuc Quaboag bands hunted ridges and fished tributaries, disrupted by epidemics and King Philip's War (1675–76) that yielded Bransford tract to Welsh proprietors from Swansea; John Pritchard and Edward Sargeant claimed home lots by 1715, dividing ledges to Davis, Hamilton, and Jones families amid garrisons and Indian boundaries. Parish status (1728) yielded meetinghouse and burying ground, with Shays' sympathizers rallying before 1787; woolen mills (Moore & Co., 1830s) and granite quarries employed endogamous Celtic kin, feeding Springfield trade through Civil War.

Genealogists trace Swansea deeds pre-1775 for Welsh allotments, then Monson plantation books linking ridge cabins to mill rosters across the highland endogamy.

Hill Hamlets, Stone Mills, and Revival Tents

Monson's 19th-century clusters blended Center District farms drawing revivals at First Church (1764), Quarry Hill granite with Irish at St. Patrick's (1868), and Yankee-Welsh lines sustaining Grange halls amid 1938 floods and post-WWII sprawl. Envelope factories (U.S. Envelope, 1880s)

and woolens anchored economy, while rural ties persisted through cemetery societies and out-migrations to Ohio.

Proprietors' surveys, quarry ledgers, and district minutes capture chain kin from Welsh ports to Quaboag hearths.

Genealogical Resources and Strategies

Vital repositories:

- Monson Town Clerk: Births, marriages, deaths from 1710 Welsh era (published to 1850); incorporation and Bransford records.
- Monson Free Library History Room: Directories, maps, quarry archives, and family sketches.
- Monson Historical Society: Manuscripts (Pritchard, Sargeant), mill employee lists, and cemetery surveys.

Regional aids: Hampden County probate at Springfield Registry, FamilySearch Welsh transcriptions, and Palmer Library for Quaboag overlaps.

Monson's ridge-manor saga—from Nipmuc ledges and Welsh logs to granite blocks and envelope folds—equips genealogists with Celtic-deep sources. Plantation grants, church rolls, and society files unveil "Bransford kin" spanning Davises, Hamiltons, and Joneses across Quaboag summits.

Montgomery

Montgomery, Massachusetts, nestles in Hampden County's hilltowns along the Westfield River gorges, settled 1770 from Westfield as "Huntstown" and incorporated February 20, 1780, sustaining subsistence farms, sawmills, and potash kilns through Yankee agrarians, Irish laborers, and Czech loggers in hamlets like Montgomery Center, Russell line villages, and Huntington brooks. Named for General Richard Montgomery, its narrow valleys—once Woronoak homelands—powered gristmills and small forges, with bounds refined by Chester separations (1775) and Middlefield divisions (1783), preserving colonial grants through flood-scarred roads and Methodist circuits. From wilderness lots to rural dairies and quarry stone, Montgomery's gorge spine traces Nipmuc paths via Shays' hideouts and district revivals.

Woronoak Gorges, Huntstown Grants, and Sawmill Hollows

Precolonial Woronoak traversed river narrows for hunting and fisheries, disrupted by epidemics and King Philip's War (1675–76) that yielded Huntstown tract to Westfield proprietors; Ebenezer Smith and Asahel Gunn claimed home lots by 1771, dividing ledges to Taylor, Phelps, and Bartlett families amid garrisons and Indian boundaries. Independence amid Revolutionary service yielded early sawmills and potash works feeding Springfield trade, with Shays' sympathizers in hills before 1787; small dairies and forges anchored subsistence amid thin soils.

Genealogists trace Westfield deeds pre-1780 for Huntstown allotments, then Montgomery plantation books linking gorge cabins to mill rosters across the highland endogamy.

Valley Hamlets, Dairy Forges, and Flood Resilience

Montgomery's 19th-century clusters blended Center District farms drawing revivals at Union

Church (1798), Huntington Road quarries with Irish at St. Joseph's (1880s), and Taylor kin sustaining Grange halls amid 1874 dam breaks and 1938 hurricane floods. Charcoal and cheese exports bolstered economy, while rural ties persisted through cemetery societies and out-migrations.

Proprietors' surveys, mill contracts, and district records capture chain kin from valley ports to Westfield hearths.

Genealogical Resources and Strategies

Vital repositories:

- Montgomery Town Clerk: Births, marriages, deaths from 1770 Huntstown era (published to 1850); incorporation and Westfield separations.
- Montgomery Historical Society: Manuscripts (Smith, Gunn), sawmill accounts, flood narratives, and family registers.
- Westfield Athenaeum Regional Aids: Huntstown overlaps, Westfield River maps, and quarry extracts.

Regional aids: Hampden County probate at Springfield Registry, FamilySearch vital transcriptions, and MHC surveys for gorge home sites.

Montgomery's gorge-valley saga—from Woronoak narrows and Huntstown logs to saw blades and dairy wheels—equips genealogists with hill-deep sources. Plantation grants, church rolls, and society files unveil "Huntstown kin" spanning Phelps, Taylors, and Barletts across Westfield cataracts.

Russell

Russell, Massachusetts, threads Hampden County's narrow Westfield River valley, settled 1770 from Westfield and Chester as "Russell's Ecclesiastical Society" and incorporated February 25, 1792, sustaining hill farms, charcoal forges, and paper mills through Yankee loggers, Irish dam-builders, and Czech operatives in hamlets like Russell Center, Montgomery line villages, and Huntington brooks. Named for settler Joseph Russell, its steep gorges—once Woronoak homelands—powered gristmills and Civil War ironworks, with bounds refined by Chester separations (1775) and Montgomery divisions (1780), preserving colonial grants through flood-scarred roads and Methodist circuits. From wilderness lots to rural hydro and quarry stone, Russell's gorge spine traces Nipmuc paths via Shays' outposts and district revivals.

Woronoak Gorges, Russell Society Grants, and Forge Hollows

Precolonial Woronoak traversed river narrows for hunting and fisheries, disrupted by epidemics and King Philip's War (1675–76) that yielded tracts to Westfield-Chester proprietors; Joseph Russell and Ebenezer Smith claimed home lots by 1771, dividing ledges to Phelps, Taylor, and Bartlett families amid garrisons and Indian boundaries. Ecclesiastical society status (1780s) yielded meetinghouse and burying ground, with Shays' sympathizers hiding in hills before 1787; early forges and sawmills fed Springfield Armory, employing endogamous kin through small paper mills c.1830.

Genealogists trace Westfield-Chester deeds pre-1792 for society allotments, then Russell plantation books linking gorge cabins to mill rosters across the valley endogamy.

Valley Hamlets, Quarry Mills, and Flood Resilience

Russell's 19th-century clusters blended Center District farms drawing revivals at Congregational Church (1796), Huntington Road quarries with Irish at St. Thomas (1880s), and Phelps kin sustaining Grange halls amid 1874 dam breaks and 1938 hurricane floods. Charcoal, stone, and hydro plants anchored economy, while rural ties persisted through cemetery societies and out-migrations to Ohio.

Proprietors' surveys, mill contracts, and district minutes capture chain kin from valley ports to Westfield hearths.

Genealogical Resources and Strategies

Vital repositories:

- Russell Town Clerk: Births, marriages, deaths from 1770 society era (published to 1850); incorporation and Chester-Westfield separations.
- Russell Public Library History Room: Directories, maps, forge archives, and family sketches.
- Russell Historical Society: Manuscripts (Russell, Smith), mill employee lists, flood narratives, and cemetery surveys.

Regional aids: Hampden County probate at Springfield Registry, FamilySearch vital transcriptions, and Westfield Athenaeum for gorge overlaps.

Russell's gorge-valley saga—from Woronoak narrows and society logs to forge blooms and paper reels—equips genealogists with hill-deep sources. Plantation grants, church rolls, and society files unveil "Ecclesiastical kin" spanning Phelps, Taylors, and Smiths across Westfield cataracts.

Southwick

Southwick, Massachusetts, spans Hampden County's southwestern plains along the Westfield River and Agawam line, settled 1703 from Westfield as "South Parish" and incorporated February 17, 1770, amid farms, tobacco fields, and carriage shops sustaining Yankee agrarians, Irish laborers, and Polish farmers in hamlets like Southwick Center, Congamond Lakes villages, and Westfield line districts. Named for Southwick, England, its fertile intervals—once Agawam homelands—powered gristmills and small forges, with bounds refined by Granville separations (1754) and Westfield divisions, preserving colonial roads through Congamond Notch trails and Baptist circuits. From wilderness grants to rural tobacco and summer resorts, Southwick's meadow spine traces Nipmuc paths via Shays' outposts and district schools.

Agawam South Precinct, Westfield Grants, and Tobacco Plains

Precolonial Agawam planted cornfields and fished river bends, disrupted by epidemics and King Philip's War (1675–76) that secured south tracts to Westfield proprietors; Benjamin Clap and John Dewey claimed home lots by 1710, dividing meadows to Noble, Sackett, and Phelps families amid garrisons and Indian boundaries. Parish status (1730s) yielded meetinghouse and burying ground, with Shays' sympathizers rallying before 1787; tobacco plantations (Connecticut Valley wrappers) and carriage works employed endogamous kin through Civil War.

Genealogists probe Westfield deeds pre-1770 for south precinct allotments, then Southwick parish books linking meadow farmsteads to field rosters across the separation.

District Hamlets, Tobacco Sheds, and Lake Resorts

Southwick's 19th-century clusters featured Center District farms drawing revivals at First Congregational (1792), Congamond Lakes resorts with Irish at St. Joseph's (1870s), and Noble-Phelps lines sustaining Grange halls amid 1938 floods and post-WWII suburbs. Tobacco barns and basket factories anchored economy, while summer colonies at Pynchon Point fostered tourism; rural endogamy persisted through quilting bees and cemetery ties.

Proprietors' surveys, field contracts, and district minutes capture chain kin from Westfield hearths to Agawam workshops.

Genealogical Resources and Strategies

Vital repositories:

- Southwick Town Clerk: Births, marriages, deaths from 1703 parish era (published to 1850); incorporation and Westfield separations.
- Southwick Public Library History Room: Directories, maps, tobacco archives, and family sketches.
- Southwick Historical Society: Manuscripts (Clap, Dewey), farm ledgers, and cemetery surveys.

Regional aids: Hampden County probate at Springfield Registry, FamilySearch parish transcriptions, and Westfield Athenaeum for south precinct overlaps.

Southwick's south-meadow chronicle—from Agawam intervals and parish lots to tobacco leaves and lake cottages—equips genealogists with plain-deep sources. Plantation grants, church rolls, and society files unveil "South Parish kin" spanning Nobles, Sacketts, and Phelps across Westfield plains.

Tolland

Tolland, Massachusetts, crowns Hampden County's remotest hilltowns along ridges shared with Granville and Stafford, settled 1784 from Norwich as "Tolland Hill" and incorporated June 13, 1810, sustaining subsistence farms, potash kilns, and sheep pastures through Yankee agrarians, Irish laborers, and Czech loggers in scattered hamlets like Tolland Center, Granville line villages, and Stafford Hollow brooks.

Named for Tolland, Connecticut, its thin-soiled heights—once Woronoak homelands—powered small sawmills and charcoal pits, with bounds refined by Granville separations (1754) and Stafford divisions, preserving colonial grants through flood-prone roads and Methodist circuits. From late wilderness lots to rural dairies and summer boarders, Tolland's highland spine traces Nipmuc paths via Shays' echoes and district revivals.

Woronoak Heights, Norwich Grants, and Potash Ridges

Precolonial Woronoak hunters roamed summits and gorges, disrupted by epidemics and King

Philip's War (1675–76) that left ridges unclaimed until late grants to Norwich proprietors; Ebenezer Phelps and Asahel Gunn claimed home lots by 1785, dividing ledges to Taylor, Campbell, and Keep families amid frontier isolation and Indian boundaries. Late parish petitions yielded Union Church (1805) and burying ground, with Shays' sympathizers lingering before 1787; potash kilns and sheep farms fed Springfield trade, employing endogamous kin through thin soils and Civil War woolens.

Genealogists trace Norwich deeds pre-1810 for hill allotments, then Tolland plantation books linking ridge cabins to dairy rosters across the highland endogamy.

Hill Hamlets, Sheep Kilns, and Revival Tents

Tolland's 19th-century clusters blended Center District farms drawing revivals at Union Church, Granville Road dairies with Irish at St. Patrick's (1890s), and Phelps kin sustaining Grange halls amid 1874 floods and 1938 hurricanes. Cheese exports and charcoal bolstered subsistence, while rural ties persisted through cemetery societies and out-migrations to Ohio.

Proprietors' surveys, kiln ledgers, and district minutes capture chain kin from valley ports to summit hearths.

Genealogical Resources and Strategies

Vital repositories:

- Tolland Town Clerk: Births, marriages, deaths from 1784 settlement era (published to 1850); incorporation and Norwich separations.
- Tolland Historical Society: Manuscripts (Phelps, Gunn), potash accounts, sheep farm files, and family registers.
- Granville Historical Society Regional Aids: Hill overlaps, ridge maps, and dairy extracts.

Regional aids: Hampden County probate at Springfield Registry, FamilySearch vital transcriptions, and MHC surveys for summit home sites.

Tolland's summit-ridge tale—from Woronoak heights and Norwich logs to potash flames and sheep fleeces—equips genealogists with hill-hardy sources. Plantation grants, church rolls, and society files unveil "Tolland Hill kin" spanning Phelps, Taylors, and Campbells across Granville summits.

Wales

Wales, Massachusetts, occupies Hampden County's southeastern uplands at the Quinnebaug River headwaters, settled 1726 from Brimfield and Springfield as "South Brimfield" and incorporated September 18, 1762, later renamed February 20, 1828 for benefactor James Lawrence Wales amid subsistence farms, gristmills, and tanneries sustaining Yankee pioneers, Irish laborers, and Swedish woodworkers in hamlets like Wales Center, Lake George villages, and Brimfield Pond districts. Its hilly drains—once Nipmuc Quaboag homelands—powered early mills and Civil War forges, with bounds refined by Brimfield separations and Stafford overlaps, preserving colonial grants through mountain roads and Baptist circuits. From delayed wilderness lots to rural chairs and flood resilience, Wales' upland spine traces Nipmuc trails via frontier forts and district petitions.

Nipmuc Uplands, South Brimfield Grants, and Fort Hamlets

Precolonial Nipmuc Quaboag bands fished ponds and planted hills, disrupted by epidemics and King Philip's War (1675–76) that delayed settlement despite 1701 Springfield grants amid land disputes; Anthony Needham and John Bullan built houses 1726 near Lake George, followed by Shubael Dimmick's gristmill (1750), Phineas Durkee's tannery (1752), and meetinghouse (1760) with Baptist church from 1736 under Rev. Ebenezer Moulton. John Moulton's 1730 dwelling served as fort, anchoring Needham, Bullan, and Dimmick families through Shays' echoes. Genealogists consult Brimfield deeds pre-1762 for south allotments, then Wales district books linking pond cabins to Baptist rolls across the upland endogamy.

Pond Districts, Tannery Mills, and Baptist Revivals

Wales' 19th-century clusters featured Center District farms drawing revivals at Baptist meetinghouse, Lake George tanneries with Irish laborers, and Yankee lines like Fisks sustaining cemetery ties amid 1955 floods and rural isolation. Chair shops and small forges bolstered subsistence, while endogamy persisted through Grange halls and out-migrations; name change honored Wales' philanthropy.

Proprietors' surveys, mill ledgers, and district minutes capture chain kin from Brimfield hearths to Quinnebaug workshops.

Genealogical Resources and Strategies

Vital repositories:

- Wales Town Clerk: Births, marriages, deaths from 1726 settlement era (published to 1850); South Brimfield incorporation and rename records.
- Wales Historical Commission: Manuscripts (Needham, Dimmick), fort narratives, Baptist registers, and cemetery surveys.
- Brimfield Historical Society Regional Aids: South Brimfield overlaps, Quinnebaug maps, and tannery extracts.

Regional aids: Hampden County probate at Springfield Registry, FamilySearch Baptist transcriptions, and MHC surveys for pond home sites.

Wales' upland-Quinnebaug saga—from Nipmuc hills and Needham forts to tannin vats and Baptist bells—equips genealogists with remote-deep sources. District rolls, vital indexes, and commission files unveil "South Brimfield kin" spanning Bullans, Dimmicks, and Moultons across Brimfield ridges.

Wilbraham

Wilbraham, Massachusetts, rises on Hampden County's eastern uplands along the Chicopee River, first settled 1730 by Nathaniel Hitchcock in Springfield's "Outward Commons" or Fourth District and incorporated June 15, 1763, amid farms, academies, and poultry sheds sustaining Yankee agrarians, Irish laborers, and Polish farmers in hamlets like Wilbraham Center, North Wilbraham villages, and Hampden line districts. Named for Wilbraham, England, its hilly meadows—once Nipmuc homelands—powered gristmills and small forges, with bounds refined by Hampden separations (1878) and Ludlow divisions, preserving colonial roads through Wigwam

Hill trails and Baptist circuits. From wilderness grants to rural academies and suburban estates, Wilbraham's mountain spine traces Nipmuc paths via Shays' outposts and district revivals.

Nipmuc Outward Commons, Fourth Precinct Grants, and Academy Hills

Precolonial Nipmuc planted intervals and fished Chicopee tributaries, disrupted by epidemics and King Philip's War (1675–76) that secured "Outward Commons" to Springfield proprietors; Nathaniel Hitchcock's 1730 log hut drew Bliss, Warriner, and Chapin families by 1741, forming Fourth Precinct with Rev. Noah Merrick's church (1741) amid garrisons and Indian boundaries. Town status yielded meetinghouse on Wigwam Hill and burying ground, with Shays' sympathizers rallying before 1787; Wilbraham Academy (1817) educated kin, while sheep, cattle, and grain farms fed Springfield trade through Civil War.

Genealogists probe Springfield deeds pre-1763 for commons allotments, then Wilbraham precinct books linking hill cabins to academy rosters across the upland endogamy.

Hill Hamlets, Poultry Farms, and Revival Centers

Wilbraham's 19th-century clusters featured Center District farms drawing revivals at First Church, North Wilbraham mills with Irish at St. Mary's (1870s), and Bliss-Chapin lines sustaining Grange halls amid 1938 floods and post-WWII poultry boom. Brickmaking and academies anchored economy, while rural ties persisted through cemetery societies and out-migrations; residential sprawl followed highways.

Proprietors' surveys, farm ledgers, and district minutes capture chain kin from Springfield hearths to Chicopee workshops.

Genealogical Resources and Strategies

Vital repositories:

- Wilbraham Town Clerk: Births, marriages, deaths from 1730 Hitchcock era (published to 1850); Fourth Precinct incorporation and Hampden separations.
- Wilbraham Public Library History Room: Directories, maps, academy archives, and family sketches.
- Wilbraham Historical Society: Manuscripts (Hitchcock, Merrick), farm records, and cemetery surveys.

Regional aids: Hampden County probate at Springfield Registry, FamilySearch precinct transcriptions, and Springfield Library for commons overlaps.

Wilbraham's commons-hill chronicle—from Nipmuc uplands and Hitchcock logs to academy bells and poultry coops—equips genealogists with deep precinct sources. Plantation grants, church rolls, and society files unveil "Fourth District kin" spanning Blisses, Warriners, and Chapins across Chicopee ridges.

CENSUS-DESIGNATED PLACES
Blandford (CDP)
Blandford Census-Designated Place, Massachusetts, forms the densely settled core of Blandford town in Hampden County, centered around the historic village green and 1740 meetinghouse

amid rocky hill farms, cheese dairies, and Albany stage taverns that sustained Scots-Irish pioneers, Yankee agrarians, and later Czech quarrymen in clustered homes along North and South Streets. Evolving from "New Glasgow" settlement nucleus since Hugh Black's 1735 cabin, the CDP preserves thin-soiled pastures—once Woronoak homelands—dotted with taverns and schools, with boundaries encompassing Center District bounds refined by North Blandford separations, retaining colonial home lots through Beech Hill trails and Methodist circuits. From proprietors' core to rural crossroads and bicentennial hearths, Blandford CDP's green spine traces Nipmuc ridges via garrison forts and district petitions.

Scots-Irish Green Core, Proprietors' Lots, and Tavern Districts

Precolonial Woronoak ridges yielded to 1735 en masse Scots-Irish from Hopkinton—Hugh Black, James Baird, Reed, McClintock, Taggart—securing home lots around the 1740 glass-windowed meetinghouse funded by Lawton, Wells, Faye, and Brindley proprietors, anchoring Presbyterian society under Rev. William McClenathan (1744–47). Garrisons during King George's War sheltered families, with Revolutionary musters from Capt. John Ferguson's 36 men; 1800 Congregational shift and Jane Taggart's 1805 school bequest divided three districts by 1762. Tavern rows on Albany road fostered Black, Boies, Gibbs kin endogamy.

Genealogists consult proprietors' books for center allotments, then CDP church rolls linking green cabins to school dame ledgers across hilltown core.

Center Taverns, Dairy Crossroads, and Revival Hearths

Blandford CDP's 19th-century focus blended green farms yielding butter-cheese via 1,500 cows, score of taverns like Amos Collins' inn drawing revivals, and Yankee lines sustaining cemeteries amid Shays' sympathizers and 1892 fires. Fairgrounds and post office anchored 1879 population of 300, with thin soils spurring stock over grain; rural endogamy persisted through Grange and out-migrations, preserving frame houses and MHC surveys.

Meeting minutes, tavern ledgers, and district records capture chain kin from Hopkinton ports to ridge crossroads.

Genealogical Resources and Strategies

Vital repositories:

- Blandford Town Clerk: Center births, marriages, deaths from 1735 (published to 1850); green proprietors and garrison records.
- Blandford Historical Society: Bicentennial manuscripts (Black, Taggart), tavern files, school bequests, and CDP cemetery surveys.
- Palmer Library Regional Aids: Hilltown green overlaps, Albany road maps, and dairy extracts.

Regional aids: Hampden County probate for center plats, FamilySearch Presbyterian transcriptions, and society bicentennial for core kin.

Blandford CDP's green-ridge chronicle—from Scots-Irish forts and Black hearths to tavern trades and school dames—equips genealogists with settlement-deep sources. Proprietors' rolls, church indexes, and bicentennial files unveil "New Glasgow core kin" spanning Bairds, Gibbs, and Fergusons across hilltop taverns.

Chester (CDP)

Chester Census-Designated Place, Massachusetts, anchors the industrial core of Chester town in Hampden County, clustered along the Westfield River gorges around mills, forges, and the 1792 meetinghouse amid narrow valley farms, charcoal kilns, and paper factories sustaining Yankee loggers, Irish dam-builders, and Czech operatives in tight hamlets of Factory Village and Center Street rows. Evolving from Murrayfield's 1766 settlement nucleus with Ebenezer Dewey's homesteads, the CDP preserves steep ledges—once Woronoak homelands—harnessed for gristmills and Civil War ironworks, with boundaries encompassing core districts refined by Huntington separations, retaining colonial grants through flood-scarred roads and Baptist circuits. From township lots to rural hydro crossroads and historic districts, Chester CDP's gorge spine traces Nipmuc paths via Shays' hideouts and district revivals.

Woronoak Factory Hollows, Murrayfield Core, and Forge Districts

Precolonial Woronoak fished river narrows yielding to 1766 Murrayfield survey; Dewey, Gunn, Smith, Phelps, and Bartlett families clustered home lots by 1770s around early sawmills and forges feeding Springfield Armory, with 1792 Congregational meetinghouse anchoring civic life amid Revolutionary musters and Shays' hill sympathizers. Glass factories through War of 1812, turnpike (1804), and railroad (1841) shifted commerce from rural center to Factory Village provisioning stop, bypassing upland farms, town hall and library solidified CDP focus.

Genealogists consult Murrayfield deeds for valley allotments, then CDP church rolls linking hollow cabins to mill payrolls across the gorge endogamy.

Valley Mills, Quarry Taverns, and Flood Hearths

Chester CDP's 19th-century nexus blended Factory Village paper works and forges drawing Irish at St. Joseph's (1872), Center Street dairies with Yankee kin sustaining cemeteries amid 1874 dam breaks, 1938 hurricanes, and 1955 floods. Charcoal kilns and hydro plants anchored economy, with rural ties through Grange halls and out-migrations; Chester Center and Factory Village Historic Districts preserve frame mills and taverns.

Proprietors' surveys, factory ledgers, and district minutes capture chain kin from Norwich ports to Westfield workshops.

Genealogical Resources and Strategies

Vital repositories:

- Chester Town Clerk: CDP births, marriages, deaths from 1766 (published to 1850); Murrayfield core and railroad records.
- Chester Historical Society: Manuscripts (Dewey, Phelps), forge payrolls, flood narratives, and valley cemetery surveys.
- Westfield Athenaeum Regional Aids: Gorge overlaps, mill maps, and hydro extracts.

Regional aids: Hampden County probate for hollow plats, FamilySearch vital transcriptions, and MHC surveys for factory sites.

Chester CDP's gorge-factory chronicle—from Woronoak narrows and Dewey hearths to rail blooms and paper reels—equips genealogists with valley-deep sources. Plantation grants, church rolls, and society files unveil "Murrayfield core kin" spanning Smiths, Gunns, and Bartletts across Westfield cataracts.

<u>Holland (CDP)</u>

Holland Census-Designated Place, Massachusetts, forms the settled nucleus of Holland town in Hampden County's southeast corner, clustered around the 1783 meetinghouse and school districts amid pond-side farms, chair shops, and reservoirs sustaining Yankee pioneers, Irish laborers, and Swedish woodworkers in tight hamlets along Main Street and Brimfield Pond roads. Evolving from Joseph Blodgett's 1730 Polley Place settlement in southeast Brimfield, the CDP preserves hilly ponds—once Nipmuc Quaboag homelands—powering gristmills and small forges, with boundaries encompassing Center District refined by Wales separations, retaining colonial grants through Tantusque echoes and 1955 flood scars. From East Parish core to rural crossroads and church hearths, Holland CDP's pond spine traces Nipmuc trails via district petitions and Congregational revivals.

Nipmuc Pond Core, Blodgett Districts, and Church Hamlets

Precolonial Nipmuc Quaboag fished ponds yielding to 1730 Blodgett cabin drawing Bugbee, Lovell, and Davis families securing lots amid Winthrop heirs' disputes; East Parish status July 5, 1783 yielded Congregational church north of David Bugbee's tavern under Rev. Enoch Burt (1820), with school districts dividing the quadrilateral by 1783 town warrant. 1858 church fire rebuilt amid Baptist overtures, anchoring Blodgett-Bugbee kin endogamy through Revolutionary service and Shays' echoes.

Genealogists consult Brimfield deeds pre-1783 for pond allotments, then CDP district books linking core cabins to pew deeds across parish endogamy.

Center Ponds, Chair Taverns, and Flood Crossroads

Holland CDP's 19th-century focus blended Main Street farms yielding hay and chairs, pond factories with Irish at St. Patrick's (1870s), and Yankee lines sustaining cemeteries amid 1858 blaze and 1955 deluge birthing Hamilton Reservoir. Turnpikes linked Hartford-Worcester trade, with rural endogamy through Grange halls and out-migrations; MHC surveys preserve frame homes and clocks.

Meeting minutes, pew ledgers, and district records capture chain kin from Brimfield ports to pond workshops.

Genealogical Resources and Strategies

Vital repositories:

- Holland Town Clerk: CDP births, marriages, deaths from 1730 (published to 1850); East Parish core and church fire records.
- Holland Historical Society: Manuscripts (Blodgett, Burt), pew plans, flood narratives, and pond cemetery surveys.
- Brimfield Society Regional Aids: Southeast overlaps, reservoir maps, and chair extracts.

Regional aids: Hampden County probate for pond plats, FamilySearch Congregational transcriptions, and town history for district kin.

Holland CDP's pond-parish chronicle—from Nipmuc waters and Blodgett hearths to church bells and reservoir shores—equips genealogists with remote-deep sources. District rolls, vital indexes, and society files unveil "East Parish core kin" spanning Bugbees, Lovells, and Davises across Brimfield ponds.

<u>Monson Center (CDP)</u>

Monson Center Census-Designated Place, Massachusetts, forms the civic and industrial heart of Monson town in Hampden County, clustered around Memorial Hall, granite quarries, and envelope mills amid rocky ridges sustaining Welsh pioneers, Yankee agrarians, and Irish stonecutters in tight hamlets along Main Street and Stafford Hollow roads. Evolving from Bransford Manor's 1710 settlement core with John Pritchard's homesteads, the CDP preserves Quaboag ledges—once Nipmuc homelands—powering woolens and Civil War stone, with boundaries encompassing Center District refined by Palmer separations, retaining colonial grants through Quarry Hill trails and Methodist circuits. From manor nucleus to rural stone and paper crossroads, Monson Center CDP's ridge spine traces Nipmuc paths via Shays' outposts and district revivals.

Nipmuc Quarry Core, Welsh Districts, and Woolen Hamlets

Precolonial Nipmuc Quaboag hunted ridges yielding to 1710 Welsh from Swansea—Pritchard, Sargeant, Davis, Hamilton—securing home lots around 1764 First Church under Rev. Noah Clarke, with granite ledges and woolen mills (Moore & Co., 1830s) anchoring endogamy amid Revolutionary musters and Shays' rallies. U.S. Envelope factories (1880s) drew Irish to St. Patrick's (1868), solidifying Main Street as civic focus with Memorial Hall (1870); school districts divided Quarry Hill core.

Genealogists consult Swansea deeds pre-1775 for manor allotments, then CDP church rolls linking ridge cabins to mill payrolls across Celtic endogamy.

Center Quarries, Envelope Mills, and Revival Hearths

Monson Center CDP's 19th-century nexus blended Main Street woolens and stone drawing revivals, Irish-Polish laborers sustaining cemeteries amid 1938 floods and post-WWII paper boom. Granite for Boston buildings and envelope exports anchored economy, with rural ties through Grange halls and out-migrations; historic district preserves frame mills and hall.

Proprietors' surveys, quarry ledgers, and district minutes capture chain kin from Welsh ports to Quaboag workshops.

Genealogical Resources and Strategies

Vital repositories:

- Monson Town Clerk: CDP births, marriages, deaths from 1710 (published to 1850); Bransford core and Quarry records.
- Monson Historical Society: Manuscripts (Pritchard, Davis), mill payrolls, granite narratives, and center cemetery surveys.
- Palmer Library Regional Aids: Ridge overlaps, Stafford maps, and woolen extracts.

Regional aids: Hampden County probate for quarry plats, FamilySearch Welsh transcriptions, and MHC surveys for Main Street sites.

Monson Center CDP's ridge-manor chronicle—from Nipmuc ledges and Welsh hearths to granite blocks and envelope folds—equips genealogists with Celtic-deep sources. Plantation grants, church rolls, and society files unveil "Bransford core kin" spanning Hamiltons, Joneses, and Davises across Quaboag quarries.

Russell (CDP)

Russell Census-Designated Place, Massachusetts, clusters in the heart of Russell town along Hampden County's Westfield River gorges, centered on the 1826 relocated town common, Congregational church, and mills amid narrow valley forges, tanneries, and paper works sustaining Yankee loggers, Irish dam-builders, and Czech operatives in tight hamlets around Russell Pond (formerly Hazard Pond) and Knox Trail roads. Evolving from Westfield's "New Addition" settlement nucleus since 1770s with Joseph Russell's ecclesiastical society, the CDP preserves steep ledges—once Woronoak homelands—harnessed for gristmills and Civil War ironworks, with boundaries encompassing core districts refined by Montgomery separations, retaining colonial grants through flood-scarred roads and Methodist circuits. From pond-side core to rural hydro crossroads and historic district, Russell CDP's valley spine traces Nipmuc paths via Shays' hideouts and district revivals.

Woronoak Pond Core, Ecclesiastical Districts, and Tannery Hamlets

Precolonial Woronoak fished Hazard Pond narrows yielding to 1770s Westfield-Chester grants; Joseph Russell, Ebenezer Smith, Phelps, and Taylor families built home lots by 1780s around original Knox Road meetinghouse (1792), shifting civic focus north to Westfield River by 1826 with new church amid Revolutionary musters and Shays' hill sympathizers. Gristmills, tanneries, and sawmills exploited pond waters, employing endogamy through small paper mills c.1830; railroad (1841) solidified CDP as provisioning stop.

Genealogists consult Westfield deeds pre-1792 for pond allotments, then CDP society books linking hollow cabins to church rolls across valley endogamy.

Valley Commons, Forge Mills, and Flood Hearths

Russell CDP's 19th-century nexus blended relocated common farms drawing revivals at Congregational church, river forges with Irish at St. Thomas (1880s), and Yankee kin sustaining cemeteries amid 1874 dam breaks, 1938 hurricanes, and 1955 floods. Charcoal kilns, stone quarries, and hydro plants anchored economy, with rural ties through Grange halls and out-migrations; Russell Center Historic District preserves frame mills and common.

Proprietors' surveys, tannery ledgers, and district minutes capture chain kin from valley ports to Westfield workshops.

Genealogical Resources and Strategies

Vital repositories:

- Russell Town Clerk: CDP births, marriages, deaths from 1770s (published to 1850); pond core and relocation records.

- Russell Historical Society: Manuscripts (Russell, Smith), mill payrolls, flood narratives, and valley cemetery surveys.
- Westfield Athenaeum Regional Aids: New Addition overlaps, river maps, and tannery extracts.

Regional aids: Hampden County probate for pond plats, FamilySearch vital transcriptions, and MHC surveys for common sites.

Russell CDP's pond-valley chronicle—from Woronoak waters and Russell hearths to tannin vats and hydro reels—equips genealogists with gorge-deep sources. Society grants, church rolls, and society files unveil "New Addition core kin" spanning Phelps, Taylors, and Smiths across Westfield cataracts.

Wilbraham (CDP)

Wilbraham Census-Designated Place, Massachusetts, forms the historic village core of Wilbraham town in Hampden County, clustered around the 1763 meetinghouse site, Wilbraham Academy, and Main Street amid eastern uplands sustaining Yankee agrarians, Irish laborers, and Polish farmers in tight hamlets south of the center along South Main and Boston Road. Evolving from Springfield's "Outward Commons" Fourth Precinct nucleus since Nathaniel Hitchcock's 1731 log hut, the CDP preserves hilly meadows—once Nipmuc homelands—dotted with gristmills and poultry sheds, with boundaries encompassing Center District refined by Hampden separations (1878), retaining colonial roads through Wigwam Hill trails and Congregational circuits. From precinct core to rural academies and suburban crossroads, Wilbraham CDP's hill spine traces Nipmuc paths via Shays' outposts and district revivals.

Nipmuc Commons Core, Hitchcock Districts, and Academy Hamlets

Precolonial Nipmuc planted Chicopee intervals yielding to 1730 Hitchcock settlement drawing Bliss, Warriner, and Chapin families by 1741 around Rev. Noah Merrick's church (1741) on Wigwam Hill, shifting to Main Street center by 1794 amid Revolutionary musters and Shays' sympathizers. Wilbraham Academy (1817) anchored civic life, with sheep, cattle, and grain farms employing endogamy through Civil War; first burying ground (c.1736) west of center solidified CDP focus.

Genealogists probe Springfield deeds pre-1763 for commons allotments, then CDP precinct books linking hill cabins to academy rosters across the upland endogamy.

Center Farms, Poultry Roads, and Revival Hearths

Wilbraham CDP's 19th-century nexus blended Main Street farms drawing revivals at First Church, Boston Road poultry with Irish at St. Mary's (1870s), and Bliss-Chapin lines sustaining cemeteries amid 1938 floods and post-WWII boom. Brickmaking and academies anchored economy, with rural ties through Grange halls and out-migrations; residential districts preserve frame homes along Route 20.

Proprietors' surveys, farm ledgers, and district minutes capture chain kin from Springfield hearths to Chicopee workshops.

Genealogical Resources and Strategies

Vital repositories:

- Wilbraham Town Clerk: CDP births, marriages, deaths from 1730 (published to 1850); Fourth Precinct core and academy records.
- Wilbraham Historical Society: Manuscripts (Hitchcock, Merrick), farm files, burying ground surveys, and center cemetery extracts.
- Springfield Library Regional Aids: Commons overlaps, Chicopee maps, and poultry extracts.

Regional aids: Hampden County probate for hill plats, FamilySearch precinct transcriptions, and MHC surveys for Main Street sites.

Wilbraham CDP's commons-hill chronicle—from Nipmuc uplands and Hitchcock hearths to academy bells and poultry coops—equips genealogists with precinct-deep sources. Plantation grants, church rolls, and society files unveil "Outward Commons core kin" spanning Blisses, Warriners, and Chapins across eastern ridges.

UNINCORPORATED COMMUNITIES
Bondsville

Bondsville, an unincorporated mill village in Palmer, Hampden County, Massachusetts, clusters along the Swift River falls where 31-foot drops powered gristmills, fulling works, woolens, and cotton duck factories from early 1800s, sustaining Scots-Irish planters, Yankee operatives, and Irish laborers in tight hamlets around mill blocks, Crawford Pond, and Western Railroad depots. Named for Emelius Bond who secured water rights in 1846 for Bond Village Manufacturing Company, its industrial core—within Palmer's Elbow Tract once Nipmuc Quaboag homelands—drew from Brimfield proprietors' mill privileges, with boundaries encompassing factory rows refined by Thorndike separations, preserving colonial fords through flood-prone gorges and Methodist circuits. From plantation mills to Boston Duck prosperity and 1930s declines, Bondsville's river spine traces Nipmuc trails via Shays' echoes and company tenements.

Quaboag Falls Core, Elbow Mill Grants, and Duck Districts

Precolonial Nipmuc Quaboag fished Swift tributaries disrupted by epidemics and King Philip's War (1675–76) yielding Elbow Tract to Brimfield proprietors; early grist and sawmills at the falls by 1730s Steward Southgate evolved to fulling (1795) then woolens, with Augustus Fiske, John S. Wright, and Emelius Bond's 1845 cotton venture under Munroe Company (1836) leasing to Boston Duck by 1840s amid Scots-Irish kin from John King's 1716 plantation. Railroad (1840s) and financial panics tested but anchored endogamy through Civil War contracts.

Genealogists probe Palmer plantation deeds for falls allotments, then Bondsville mill books linking gorge cabins to payrolls across the tract endogamy.

Mill Blocks, Factory Rows, and Flood Hearths

Bondsville's 19th-century nexus blended duck sheds drawing Irish at St. Anne's (Thorndike line), Yankee overseers sustaining tenements amid 1874 floods and labor strikes, with company store and depots fostering cemetery ties. Boston Duck's heavy cotton exports peaked pre-1900, declining with southern mills; rural ties persisted through Grange and out-migrations, preserving MHC frame blocks.

Proprietors' surveys, duck ledgers, and district minutes capture chain kin from Ulster ports to Swift workshops.

Genealogical Resources and Strategies

Vital repositories:

- Palmer Town Clerk: Bondsville births, marriages, deaths via Palmer records from 1716 (published to 1850); mill privilege grants.
- Palmer Historical Society: Manuscripts (Fiske, Bond), duck payrolls, flood narratives, and village cemetery surveys.
- Palmer Library Regional Aids: Elbow Tract overlaps, Swift maps, and cotton extracts.

Regional aids: Hampden County probate for falls plats, FamilySearch Palmer transcriptions, and MHC surveys for mill sites.

Bondsville's falls-mill chronicle—from Nipmuc gorges and Elbow fords to duck looms and rail whistles—equips genealogists with industrial-deep sources. Plantation rolls, company files, and society ledgers unveil "Swift River kin" spanning Kings, Bonds, and Wrights across Palmer cataracts.

Depot Village

Depot Village, an unincorporated rail hub in Palmer, Hampden County, Massachusetts, centers on the ornate H.H. Richardson-designed train station amid Quaboag River plains, evolving from Brimfield's Elbow Tract "Central Village" into a 1840s depot nexus sustaining Yankee merchants, Irish tracklayers, and French Canadian operatives in clustered stores, hotels, and boardinghouses around the Western Railroad junction. Named for its grand 1884 station within Palmer's 1811 bounds—once Nipmuc Quaboag homelands—its commercial core powered trade from gristmills to nail factories, with boundaries encompassing hotel rows refined by Thorndike separations, preserving colonial trails through flood-prone commons and Methodist circuits. From plantation crossroads to rail prosperity and 20th-century declines, Depot Village's junction spine traces Nipmuc paths via Shays' musters and passenger platforms.

Quaboag Junction Core, Elbow Depot Grants, and Hotel Districts

Precolonial Nipmuc Quaboag planted intervals disrupted by epidemics and King Philip's War (1675–76) yielding tracts to Brimfield proprietors; John King's 1716 settlers built inns by 1730s at Elbow crossroads, with Western Railroad (1839–41) anchoring Central Village as Palmer's civic heart—hotels like Wing House, stores, and depots drawing endogamy amid Scots-Irish kin. Richardson's Romanesque station (1884) solidified prestige, serving Boston-Hartford lines through Civil War troop transports and Palmer Nail shipments.

Genealogists probe Palmer plantation deeds for junction allotments, then Depot Village ledgers linking crossroads taverns to passenger rolls across the rail endogamy.

Station Blocks, Merchant Rows, and Flood Hearths

Depot Village's 19th-century nexus blended rail hotels drawing French Canadians to St. Anne's (1870), Yankee merchants sustaining tenements amid 1896 floods and labor organizing, with company stores and platforms fostering cemetery ties. Nail and wire exports peaked pre-1900, declining with auto shifts; rural ties persisted through Grange halls and out-migrations, preserving MHC station landmark.

Proprietors' surveys, hotel registers, and district minutes capture chain kin from Ulster ports to Quaboag platforms.

Genealogical Resources and Strategies

Vital repositories:

- Palmer Town Clerk: Depot Village births, marriages, deaths via Palmer records from 1716 (published to 1850); rail junction grants.
- Palmer Historical Society: Manuscripts (King, Wing), station logs, flood narratives, and village cemetery surveys.
- Palmer Library Regional Aids: Elbow Tract overlaps, Quaboag maps, and depot extracts.

Regional aids: Hampden County probate for junction plats, FamilySearch Palmer transcriptions, and MHC surveys for station sites.

Depot Village's rail-crossroads chronicle—from Nipmuc plains and King inns to Richardson arches and nail cars—equips genealogists with junction-deep sources. Plantation rolls, hotel files, and society ledgers unveil "Central Village kin" spanning Brewsters, Days, and Thorndikes across Quaboag tracks.

Feeding Hills

Feeding Hills, an unincorporated agrarian district in Agawam, Hampden County, Massachusetts, rolls across fertile southwestern hills designated 1638 for Springfield cattle pasturage, evolving into dispersed farmsteads, taverns, and mills sustaining Yankee husbandmen, Irish laborers, and Polish farmers along River Road and Line Street hamlets. Named for early grazing privileges within West Springfield's bounds—once Agawam homelands—its meadows powered sawmills and fulling works, with boundaries marked by mid-19th-century ditches separating from Agawam Center, preserving colonial grants through Provin Mountain trails and Congregational circuits. From Pynchon-era commons to rural Granges and Sacred Heart enclaves, Feeding Hills' pasture spine traces Nipmuc paths via Revolutionary musters and district schools.

Agawam Pasture Commons, Sixth Parish Grants, and Tavern Districts

Precolonial Agawam planted river flats disrupted by epidemics and King Philip's War (1675–76) yielding southwest tracts to Springfield proprietors; Thomas Cooper, Abel Leonard, and Thomas Merrick secured home lots 1685 south of Agawam River, with sawmill (1666) and meetinghouse (1740) on Mill Street anchoring Sixth Parish (1757) amid garrisons. West Springfield incorporation (1774) divided Agawam-FH parishes (1800), with Col. Moseley's tavern (1750), turnpikes to Hartford-Northampton, and ferries fostering Leonard, Bodurtha kin endogamy through Shays' echoes.

Genealogists probe Springfield deeds pre-1855 for pasture allotments, then Agawam parish books linking hill farmsteads to tavern rosters across the river divide.

Hill Farms, Grange Taverns, and Revival Hearths

Feeding Hills' 19th-century clusters featured River Road dairies drawing revivals at Congregational Church (1834, moved 1799), Line Street mills with Irish at Sacred Heart (1946), and Cooper-Leonard lines sustaining cemeteries amid 1938 floods. Post office (1808), Grange No. 382 (1925), and moderate farms persisted through suburban sprawl; Provin Mountain anchored rural identity.

Proprietors' surveys, parish minutes, and district ledgers capture chain kin from Connecticut valleys to Agawam workshops.

Genealogical Resources and Strategies

Vital repositories:

- Agawam Town Clerk: Feeding Hills births, marriages, deaths from 1685 (published to 1850); Sixth Parish and West Springfield separations.
- Agawam Historical Association: Manuscripts (Cooper, Merrick), tavern logs, flood narratives, and hill cemetery surveys.
- West Springfield Library Regional Aids: Pasture overlaps, turnpike maps, and Grange extracts.

Regional aids: Hampden County probate for meadow plats, FamilySearch parish transcriptions, and MHC surveys for tavern sites.

Feeding Hills' pasture-hill chronicle—from Agawam commons and Leonard grants to tavern trades and Grange halls—equips genealogists with grazing-deep sources. Plantation rolls, church indexes, and association files unveil "Sixth Parish kin" spanning Coopers, Merricks, and Bodurthas across Provin pastures.

Three Rivers

Three Rivers, an unincorporated Polish mill village in Palmer, Hampden County, Massachusetts, thrives at the Ware-Quaboag confluence birthing the Chicopee River, evolving from Brimfield's Elbow Tract periphery into 1870s paper and rubber factories sustaining Yankee operatives, Polish weavers, and Czech laborers in dense tenements around Pulaski Park and Sacred Heart parish. Named for its triple-river nexus within Palmer's 1811 bounds—once Nipmuc Quaboag homelands—its flood-prone flats powered Otis Company (Tambrands, 1872) and Riverside Paper, with boundaries encompassing factory rows refined by Thorndike separations, preserving colonial fords through 1955 levees and polka festivals. From plantation backlands to "Polka Capital" vibrancy and flood resilience, Three Rivers' confluence spine traces Nipmuc trails via Shays' echoes and ethnic mutuals.

Quaboag Confluence Core, Elbow Paper Grants, and Polish Districts

Precolonial Nipmuc Quaboag fished triple tributaries disrupted by epidemics and King Philip's War (1675–76) yielding back tracts to Brimfield proprietors; remote Elbow farms by 1850s yielded to paper mills at the falls, with Polish influx (1880s) building Sacred Heart (1902) amid John King's 1716 kin, anchoring endogamy through Civil War contracts and 1896 floods. Tambrands rubber and Riverside Paper employed chain migrations from Galicia, solidifying Main Street as ethnic hub with Pulaski Park polka stages.

Genealogists probe Palmer deeds for confluence allotments, then Three Rivers parish books linking flat cabins to mill payrolls across the Polish endogamy.

Mill Flats, Polka Blocks, and Levee Hearths

Three Rivers' late-19th-century nexus blended paper sheds drawing Czechs to Divine Mercy parish, Yankee overseers sustaining tenements amid 1938 hurricanes and 1955 USACE levees, with company stores and parks fostering cemetery ties. Textile exports peaked pre-1900, declining with southern shifts; cultural ties persisted through polka bands and out-migrations, preserving MHC mill blocks.

Proprietors' surveys, parish ledgers, and district minutes capture chain kin from Warsaw ports to Chicopee workshops.

Genealogical Resources and Strategies

Vital repositories:

- Palmer Town Clerk: Three Rivers births, marriages, deaths via Palmer records from 1716 (published to 1850); confluence mill grants.
- Palmer Historical Society: Manuscripts (Otis, Riverside), Polish payrolls, flood narratives, and village cemetery surveys.
- Palmer Library Regional Aids: Elbow Tract overlaps, Chicopee maps, and polka extracts.

Regional aids: Hampden County probate for flat plats, FamilySearch Sacred Heart transcriptions, and MHC surveys for mill sites.

Three Rivers' triple-confluence chronicle—from Nipmuc forks and Elbow farms to paper reels and polka reels—equips genealogists with ethnic-deep sources. Plantation rolls, parish files, and society ledgers unveil "Polka Capital kin" spanning Nowaks, Kowalskis, and Brewsters across Ware-Quaboag waters.

Woronoco

Woronoco, an unincorporated mill village in Russell, Hampden County, Massachusetts, hugs the Westfield River's Salmon Falls gorges where Woronoak cascades powered paper mills and hydro plants from 1879, sustaining Yankee loggers, Irish dam-builders, and Finnish operatives in company tenements around Strathmore works and Moses-built community halls. Named for precolonial Woronoak homelands meaning "winding land," its industrial core—within Russell's 1792 bounds—drew from Westfield proprietors' privileges, with boundaries encompassing factory rows refined by Montgomery separations, preserving colonial fords through flood-scarred bridges and Methodist circuits. From Native fisheries to Horace Moses' model town (1904–1947) and post-International Paper declines, Woronoco's falls spine traces Nipmuc paths via Shays' hideouts and worker enclaves.

Woronoak Salmon Falls, Russell Grants, and Paper Districts

Precolonial Woronoak fished pothole cascades disrupted by epidemics and King Philip's War (1675–76) yielding gorges to Westfield-Russell proprietors; 1879 timber-crib dam birthed paper mills supplied by 1913 hydro station, with Horace Moses transforming Strathmore (1904) into planned village—housing, halls, parks—inspired by Scottish models, anchoring endogamy amid

Finnish-Polish influx. North/South dams (1938/1950) and eel ladders sustained operations through Civil War echoes.

Genealogists probe Russell deeds for falls allotments, then Woronoco company books linking gorge cabins to payrolls across the industrial endogamy.

Mill Gorges, Company Rows, and Hydro Hearths

Woronoco's 20th-century nexus blended Strathmore sheds drawing immigrants to community centers, Yankee overseers sustaining tenements amid 1938 hurricanes and 1955 floods, with model housing fostering cemetery ties. Bond paper exports peaked pre-1947, declining post-International Paper; cultural ties persisted through Grange halls and out-migrations, preserving HAER bridge and mill ruins.

Proprietors' surveys, company ledgers, and district minutes capture chain kin from valley ports to Westfield workshops.

Genealogical Resources and Strategies

Vital repositories:

- Russell Town Clerk: Woronoco births, marriages, deaths from 1770s (published to 1850); falls mill and Moses records.
- Russell Historical Society: Manuscripts (Moses, Strathmore), hydro payrolls, flood narratives, and gorge cemetery surveys.
- Westfield Athenaeum Regional Aids: Woronoak overlaps, river maps, and paper extracts.

Regional aids: Hampden County probate for gorge plats, FamilySearch Russell transcriptions, and MHC surveys for mill sites.

Woronoco's falls-gorge chronicle—from Woronoak potholes and Native weirs to Strathmore reels and model homes—equips genealogists with company-deep sources. Plantation rolls, worker files, and society ledgers unveil "Salmon Falls kin" spanning Phelps, Finns, and Poles across Westfield cataracts.

14

Chapter 5

Hampshire County
Hampshire County, Massachusetts, cradles the mid-Connecticut River Valley in western Massachusetts, established 1662 as the Bay Colony's fifth county with dual seats at Springfield and Northampton, shrinking through successive divisions—Worcester (1731), Berkshire (1761), Franklin (1811), and Hampden (1812)—into its compact core of 23 towns blending fertile Oxbow meadows, Holyoke Range hilltowns, and Quabbin Reservoir wilds that sustained Agawam-Pocumtuck homelands, Puritan proprietors, and Shaysite farmers through colleges, mills, and tobacco barns.

Named for England's Hampshire, its pivotal bounds—from Northampton's shire town to Amherst's academic precincts—preserve colonial courthouses, turnpikes, and canal privileges amid Norwottuck trails, evolving via 19th-century colleges (Amherst 1821, Mount Holyoke 1837) and 1930s Quabbin drownings that displaced four towns for Boston water. Its academic-agrarian path—from Native cornfields through King Philip's War clearings, Great Awakening revivals, and Shays' 1786 rebellion on Pelham hills—holds proprietors' records, vital compilations, and court files tracing "valley kin" across county contractions.

For family historians, Hampshire's narrative threads through Pynchon's 1636 Agawam deed, Norwottuck sachem sales, Great Awakening relation narratives from Edwards' Northampton flock, Shays' Rebellion petitions from Pelham insurgents, Amherst's literary salons, and Quabbin exile testimonies, documented in proprietors' grants, college matriculations, Congregational parish registers, tobacco grower ledgers, and federal censuses tracing mobility across Native, English, African, Irish, and Italian lines in New England's academic heartland.

Indigenous Foundations: Norwottuck, Agawam, and Pocumtuc Territories
Hampshire County's pre-colonial landscape formed a vital artery and seasonal crossroads within the overlapping territories of the Norwottuck, Agawam, and Pocumtuc peoples—Southern New England Algonquian speakers whose kin-based economies intertwined the Connecticut River Valley's fertile floodplains with Holyoke Range uplands, traprock ridges, and Quaboag tributaries across an intricate web of fisheries, horticulture, and trail networks linking Mohawk ports to coastal wampum trade.

Norwottuck bands dominated the Hadley-Northampton Oxbow arc, their principal village at Agawam (modern Springfield vicinity) exploiting monumental shad and salmon runs at South Hadley Falls via stone weirs and communal fish drives, supplemented by Three Sisters (maize-beans-squash) polyculture on alluvial terraces enriched by annual floods, clam harvests from oxbow eddies, and nut mast from oak-hickory forests yielding chestnuts, hickory, and acorns processed into storable cakes for winter. Extended families dwelled in mat-covered wetus (bark longhouses) clustered in hamlets shifting seasonally between planting grounds near river bends and upland hunting camps pursuing deer, bear, and passenger pigeons via communal drives and fire surrounds, their basketry, quahog wampum, and turkey-feather cloaks circulating along Norwottuck trails to Pocumtuck intermediaries trading with Mohicans at Westfield River confluences.

Agawam subgroups flanked the Connecticut's Springfield rapids with sturgeon weirs, eel pots at tidal reaches, and maple sugaring groves on east-bank slopes, their sachems like Cunnesseman negotiating fur quotas with Dutch traders from Fort Good Hope (Hartford, 1633) before Pynchon's arrival; smaller family bands exploited Provin Mountain nut groves and Westfield River tributaries for trout and small game, with marriage alliances binding them to Norwottuck kin through reciprocal use-rights rather than fixed boundaries. Pocumtuck strongholds concentrated at Deerfield and Hatfield confluences, where they mastered eel weirs below Sugarloaf ledges, managed white-tailed deer territories through rotational burns fostering browse, and crafted purple wampum from quahog shells bartered northward along the Mohawk Trail to Mohawk allies and eastward to Narragansetts via Nipmuc intermediaries in Belchertown hill country.

Political authority flowed through sachem lineages—often matrilineal—cemented by marriage exchanges, feast diplomacy, and shared war captives, with wetus housing 10–20 extended kin amid palisaded villages protecting corn cribs and council fires; women directed horticulture and wampum production, their status evident in Eliot missionary accounts praising Pocumtuck "squaw sachems." Nipmuc outliers from Quaboag Valley pressed western hill towns like Enfield and Granville, favoring smaller brooks for trout weirs, extensive birch stands for canoe bark and baskets, and maple stands for spring sap boiled into sugar cakes traded down Norwottuck railfences for coastal shells.

European contact commencing 1631 via Dutch wampum-fur exchanges at Good Hope, followed by Plymouth scouts and Pynchon's 1636 Agawam trading post, unleashed cascading epidemics—smallpox (1633–34), measles (1634), influenza (1630s)—that halved regional populations from perhaps 5,000 to 2,000 by 1640, depopulating entire hamlets and shattering sachem alliances under Puritan "vacuum domicilium" doctrines deeming abandoned fields "unoccupied."

Coerced "deeds" proliferated: Pynchon's 1636 Agawam purchase from Cunnesseman and allies for Northampton-Hadley meadows via cloth, axes, and hoes compressed communal usufruct into English fee-simple grants recorded in nascent Hampshire books; Norwottuck sachem Wawaquin (1647) and Pocumtuck leaders alienated Deerfield intervals post-epidemics, often under duress amid refugee influxes. King Philip's War (1675–76) delivered existential blows: Pocumtuck neutrality imploded with May 1676 Turners Falls massacre killing 100+ warriors, scattering survivors to Mohawk Canadas or Natick Praying Towns; Norwottuck sachem Wequagon mediated neutrality before bloody falls raids forced flight, while Agawam remnants absorbed at Natick or Stockbridge; Nipmuc hill bands raided Granby before dispersal to eastern reservations or Canada.

Hampshire court files name sachem petitioners for corn allotments, missionary redemptions of captives like James Printer (Housatonic), and "praying Indian" rosters at Deerfield's brief 1670s mission; "Indian deeds" marginalia in Northampton proprietors' books hint at post-war sales by mixed-descent survivors.

For genealogists tracing Indigenous ancestry in Hampshire, the paper trail fragments into English scaffolds, demanding meticulous correlation of deed glosses ("sachem's old field," "Indian planting ground"), John Eliot's Natick-Hassanamesit rosters (1674), 18th-century Stockbridge/ Brothertown (Oneida) petitions from displaced Pocumtuck-Norwottuck kin, and sporadic probate references to "Indian servants," "molattoes," or "mustees" in Edwards' Northampton households. Place-names endure—Norwottuck Rail Trail, Pocumtuc Road, Agawam shores—alongside occasional 1790 census "free persons of color" descended from intermarriages with Africans manumitted post-1783 or English servants; 19th-century "colored" farm laborers in Amherst tobacco barns or Hadley onion fields likely carry Pocumtuck maternal lines masked by endogamy taboos.

Triangulating these with Nipmuc Nation of Massachusetts oral traditions, Abenaki first-light ceremonies at Mount Tom, and archaeological hauls from Fort River sites (corn hills, wampum blanks) reconstructs sachem descendants navigating epidemics, enslavement, and land cessions, their kin relabeled in censuses yet persistent in river weirs, sugaring groves, and reservation land claims enduring into Quabbin exiles and modern tribal enrollments.

This submerged Indigenous matrix—erased from shire narratives yet etched in oxbow terraces, rail-trail corridors, and Eliot's fractured rosters—exacts multilayered readings across pre-1662 Hampshire deeds, colonial assembly petitions, 19th-century "Indian removal" testimonies, and DNA affinities linking valley "free colored" to Pocumtuck mitochondrial haplogroups, recovering pre-contact lineages who bridged Norwottuck feasts to Amherst professorships through tobacco shares and college sculleries.

Colonial Settlement, College Rise, and Revival Pluralism

Colonial settlement in Hampshire County unfolded as a calculated thrust of the Massachusetts Bay Colony's western frontier, launching from William Pynchon's 1636 Agawam trading post at Springfield rapids—strategically positioned for fur aggregation, salmon weirs, and wampum fabrication—and radiating northward along Oxbow meadows to Northampton (1654), Hatfield (1661), Hadley (1659), and Sunderland (1714) proprietary grants that methodically parceled fertile intervals and traprock woodlots to "first-comers" like Pynchons, Websters, Bartletts, and Clapps. Compact house lots clustered near prospective meetinghouses with outlying pastures allocated by lottery according to family size, military rank, and church standing—Northampton's 40-acre divisions yielding to West Precincts like Belchertown (1765) and Granby (1768) resisting shire-town oversight amid protracted French-Indian raid cycles peaking in Queen Anne's War (1704 Deerfield massacre) and Lovewell's Fight echoes.

These foundational allotments, meticulously preserved in proprietors' books, town warrants, and drawing minutes, form the skeletal framework for charting founding lineages as holdings fractionated across generations, often crystallized through quitclaims amid Shays' Rebellion debt panics that saw Northampton courthouse petitions flood with Pelham insurgents' mortgage re-leases. Blockhouses at Westfield gaps, Hatfield meadows, and Amherst heights rotated militia captains whose scout reports, wolf bounties, and Indian alarm rosters name marginal house-holders—widows, servants, fence-viewers—otherwise invisible in vital gaps, while overlapping Connecticut River Colony claims (resolved 1704 royal decree) generated boundary deeds tracing Suffield refugees into Hampshire folds.

Hampshire's ecclesiastical culture crystallized from Northampton's archetype "gathered" Con-gregational church—planted 1654 under Rev. Eleazar Mather with exhaustive covenants, public "relation" autobiographies detailing parental scandals and conversion pangs, and pre-civil bap-tism registers capturing infant mortalities absent from town books—to seismic fractures yielding Baptist redoubts in South Hadley (1740s), Methodist circuits threading Enfield hill roads, Sepa-ratist schisms during Whitefield's 1740s itinerancy, and Unitarian secessions by 1820 amid ratio-nalist Northampton elites. Great Awakening relation narratives from Jonathan Edwards' flock preserve spiritual odysseys rich in sibling rivalries, courtship dramas, and apprentice displace-ments—"my brother John fell into evil company at Hadley mills"—while discipline sessions for "disorderly walking," Sabbath-breaking, and bastardy name unwed mothers, tavern-keepers, and Quaker sympathizers rarely surfacing elsewhere; dual-membership chains across Congrega-tional-Baptist divides explain baptism lacunae, with Hopkinton exhorter rolls tracking Pelham revivalists who later petitioned Shays.

Shaker outposts at Enfield (1780s under Jane Leade kin) generated millennial confessions naming apostate relatives, their Hancock migrations visible in mutual renunciations filed at Hampshire probate.

The 19th-century college ascendancy marked Hampshire's pivot to intellectual export, Amherst College (1821) chartered from orthodox backlash against Williams Unitarianism gener-ating matriculation catalogs, alumni directories, and faculty wills enumerating ministerial sons from Pelham parsonages to South Hadley farms; Mount Holyoke Female Seminary (1837) un-der Mary Lyon preserved admission testimonies, correspondence networks, and missionary so-ciety minutes tracking "factory girls" elevated to teaching circuits, their dowries funding Amherst professorships across Dickinson-Hitchcock kin. Smith College (1875) in Northampton enrolled Northampton mechanics' daughters alongside tobacco heiresses.

Its alumnae rolls bridging valley farms to China missions; Hampshire Agricultural College (1867, now UMass) documented practical scholars from Belchertown chair shops whose patents for onion sorters appear in patent office gazettes alongside Edwards descendants.

These institutions fostered a distinct clerical-academic class whose mobility threads through ordination councils, college trustee minutes, and faculty boardinghouse censuses, often pairing with armory mechanics or tobacco magnates in dual-career households.

Catholic pluralism crystallized with Irish quarrymen at South Hadley Falls (1840s) and Italian stonecutters in Northampton's slate district (1880s), formalized in missions like Immaculate Conception (Holyoke, 1867) and St. Mary's (Northampton, 1884) whose Latin registers meticu-lously note old-world parishes—"ex Kerry," "da Lucca"—beside Quebecois forebears from Trois-Rivières; Polish influx to Easthampton silk mills spawned Divine Savior (1900) with bilingual sodalities preserving Galicia villages, essential for pre-1841 baptisms incinerated in church conflagrations.

Jewish congregations emerged in Northampton (1890s) via peddler networks from Lithuanian shtetls, their membership ledgers tracking synagogue trustees to Five Colleges faculties; later Pentecostal storefronts in Holyoke wards captured Puerto Rican arrivals post-1950s.

For genealogists, denominational crossovers—evident in dual Congregational/Methodist baptisms, Shaker apostasy affidavits, or Catholic-Protestant remarriages—illuminate gaps in singular parish chains, while Hampshire moral courts' admonitions for oath refusal or "enthusiasm" spotlight dissenting kin like Quakers in Granby or Swedenborgians in Amherst professorships.

Hampshire's county courts, successively quartered in Northampton's colonial edifice (burned 1677), replacement (1786 Shays target), and 1823 Greek Revival hall, adjudicated a stratified society's faultlines: merchant debt suits over tobacco futures, neighborly defamation across Oxbow fences, guardianships for orphans of Pelham Shaysites, and probate inventories juxtaposing Edwards silver tankards against hilltown yeomen's featherbeds and scythe patents. Shays' Rebellion dossiers uniquely enumerate insurgent farmers from Belchertown and Enfield who stormed Northampton arsenal, their loyalty oaths and pardon petitions mapping class fissures between Oxbow gentry and hill insurgents; moral tribunals policed fornication pitting seminary students against quarrymen, bastardy bonds naming itinerant laborers' paternity.

Navigating these demands correlating session minutes with town "warnings-out" relocating paupers across precinct lines—Amherst orphans to Hadley almshouses—reconstructing nonelite webs obscured in vital registers, while college expulsion records and ministerial councils reveal scions disinherited for "infidelity" who resurfaced as tobacco brokers or silk overseers. Hampshire's colonial-to-academic continuum—from Pynchon lotteries to Lyon seminaries—demands weaving proprietors' plats against revival confessions and court dockets to recover ancestors threading Oxbow fur trades to Quabbin professorships.

Valley Industry, Immigration, and Quabbin Diaspora

By the late 18th century, Hampshire County's river corridors and turnpike arteries matured into conduits of proto-industry, with Northampton's Connecticut River warehouses evolving into cutlery forges by the 1820s under Hayden and Chapin patents for interchangeable scythe blades, Easthampton's Williston silk mills harnessing Parsonage Brook cascades for spool production that clothed Union officers, and South Hadley Falls' ambitious Farmington Canal grid—precursor to Holyoke's system—powering gristmills into paper precursors floating newsprint logs down the Oxbow for Boston publishers.

Amherst's fertile tobacco barns dominated Connecticut Valley wrapper leaf exports via Hartford packet boats, Belchertown chair factories supplied Shaker communities at Enfield with maple rockers, and Granby's onion fields shipped "Hampshire Beauties" to New York markets, their grower ledgers enumerating sharecroppers from Pocumtuck maternal lines alongside Irish pickers escaping quarry drudgery. Smaller brooks hosted tanneries along the Mill River, brick yards for Amherst College expansions, and whip factories in Hatfield whose patent records name mechanics descended from Edwards parsonages; these enterprises spawned apprenticeship contracts binding farm youths to seven-year terms at Williston looms, crew manifests for canal packet captains, and boardinghouse censuses revealing Yankee "factory girls" rooming with free Black laundresses manumitted post-1783 via Northampton Quaker networks.

Customs ledgers from Northampton's federal port district tracked onion cargoes alongside imports of Irish pig iron fueling forges and Welsh flannel for seminary uniforms, with privateering commissions from the War of 1812 naming packet masters like Oliver B. Emerson whose prize distributions funded kin migrations to Easthampton mills.

Industrial maturation accelerated cascading immigration waves that recast Hampshire's ethnic mosaic across valley wards and hill hamlets. Irish famine refugees (1845–1852) muscled South Hadley canal locks and Northampton slate quarries, clustering in "Little Dublin" flats documented in Immaculate Conception's (Holyoke, 1867 spillover) registers noting Kerry-Galway counties beside boardinghouse censuses; French Canadian millhands poured from 1870s Quebec "pig trains" into Easthampton's Ste. Jeanne d'Arc (1885) and Holyoke's Notre Dame (1871), their bilingual books preserving Trois-Rivières villages alongside Williston payrolls listing "Canayen" foremen. Italians colonized Northampton's slate district by 1880s via Lucca stonecutters, their St. Mary's (1884) ledgers tracking Carrara masons to Smith College endowments; Polish weavers dominated Amherst woolens and Belchertown baskets, Divine Savior (Easthampton, 1900) sodalities chaining Galicia parishes to tobacco shade tents; Finnish loggers felled Holyoke Range spruce for paper, their temperance halls preserving Savo-Karelia origins amid lumber camp manifests.

Post-1945 Puerto Rican braceros filled Hadley onion harvests and Holyoke mills, Spanish-language books at St. Jerome's noting Ponce-Mayagüez births beside 1950s ward maps shifting to Northampton barrios; African American communities rooted in 18th-century Deerfield manumissions and Edwards' "invisible saints" formed NAACP precursors, their mutual aid rolls visible in Civil War pension affidavits from Pocumtuck-intermarried veterans. Ethnic benevolent societies—Hibernian halls for Irish, Polish Falcons lodges, Italian Mutual Benefit circles—generated dues ledgers and funeral processions linking overseas parishes to mill tenements, essential where naturalization stubs falter.

The Quabbin Reservoir cataclysm (1927–1938) wrought Hampshire's starkest diaspora, Metropolitan Water District's condemnation drowning four Swift River towns—Dana, Enfield, Greenwich, Prescott—displacing 2,500 souls via $17 million takings that shredded proprietary chains and parsonage endowments, their relocation petitions filed at Northampton probate naming kin networks from Worcester tenements to California orchards.

Enfield's 800 families—descended from 1810 hill proprietors—petitioned for "Swift River Valley Association" reunions, their Dana church ledgers (evacuated 1938) preserving baptisms linking to Belchertown outliers; Greenwich tavern records track Shaysite descendants to Holyoke mills, Prescott school rolls naming French Canadian pupils whose parents reclaimed takings via federal claims court. Quabbin commission files enumerate "exiles" by lot number—Dana Lot 47 to Pelham kin, Enfield Center to Ware factories—cross-referenced with undertaker manifests for drowned livestock and heirship disputes over submerged heirlooms; survivor directories (1938–1950s) map Dana Poles to Springfield, Greenwich Italians to Worcester, their chains visible in dual-town vitals and "Quabbin Reunion" programs preserving ethnic festivals amid reservoir ghosts.

Hampshire's courts adjudicated these transformations: overseer assaults at Easthampton looms, patent infringements over onion sorters, worker accident claims qualifying Belchertown Poles for almshouses, Quabbin heirship battles pitting Dana holdouts against Boston bondholders. Moral tribunals policed mill-girl bastardy against Italian foremen, Sabbath-breaking by French Canadian teamsters, and "foreign pauper" warnings-out relocating Galway orphans to Hadley farms; Shays' Rebellion echoes resurfaced in Pelham tobacco debts foreclosed for Quabbin, their 1787 pardons linking to 1930s exile petitions.

Navigating demands correlating Williston payrolls with canal manifests for Yankee-factory girl chains, reversing immigrant paths via 1880–1920 parish sodality minutes to Ellis Island stubs, then threading Quabbin takings against survivor directories—Amherst Poles to Holyoke, Enfield Shaysites to Worcester.

Marginalized webs weave deed "mulatto" marginalia with Edwards' "invisible saints," court fornication bonds naming tobacco sharecroppers' paternity, union petitions for Finnish wives, and Quabbin undertaker rolls for Dana "colored" exiles against the landscape of Oxbow floods, silk cascades, and reservoir ghosts. Hampshire's industrial-diaspora continuum—from turnpike onion carts to Quabbin exiles—demands reading against river power, ethnic wards, and submerged towns to recover ancestors threading Norwottuck weirs to Smith professorships through slate dust and tobacco shade.

Genealogical Resources and Research Strategies

Hampshire County's documentary repositories radiate from Northampton's twin anchors—the Registry of Deeds (continuous land records from Pynchon's 1636 Norwottuck deeds through Quabbin condemnations, extensively digitized with grantor-grantee indexes and proprietary lotteries) and Probate Court (wills, inventories, guardianships unveiling Edwards parsonage dowries alongside Belchertown chairmaker estates and Dana exile petitions)—supplemented by 23 town clerks' vital registers, many transcribed in systematic "Vital Records to 1850" series bridging church conflagrations like Northampton's 1677 blaze and Amherst's 1870s losses.

Historic Northampton's collections preserve Hampshire County court files (1662–1812 sessions minutes naming Shaysite petitioners, moral court bastardy bonds, and wolf-bounty recipients), while Forbes Library (Northampton) houses proprietors' books for Hadley-Hatfield allotments, Edwards relation manuscripts, and Quabbin commission takings ledgers enumerating Enfield Lot 112 heirs; diocesan archives in Springfield and Worcester safeguard Latin/vernacular parish books from Holyoke's Immaculate Conception (1867) through Easthampton's Ste. Jeanne d'Arc (1885), indispensable for Irish Kerry notations, Quebecois Trois-Rivières origins, and Italian Lucca stonecutter chains predating statewide registration.

Town-level troves illuminate settlement gradients: Northampton city directories (1820s onward) and ward maps delineate "Little Italy" slate cutters from Oxbow tobacco magnates, capturing boarders evading censuses; Amherst's college catalogs (Amherst 1821, Smith 1875, Mount Holyoke 1837) enumerate ministerial progeny alongside "factory girls" elevated to missionary circuits, their alumni rolls threading Pelham parsonages to China fields; Belchertown's chair-factory

payrolls and onion-grower ledgers track Shaysite descendants sharecropping Pocumtuck intervals, while South Hadley's Farmington Canal manifests name packet captains descended from
Norwottuck sachem grantees.

Federal censuses (1790–1950, including non-population schedules detailing Amherst wrapper
yields and Easthampton silk outputs) pair with naturalization declarations noting Ellis Island arrivals for Polish millhands, supplemented by ethnic fraternal records—Hibernian Society minutes for Irish quarrymen, Polish Falcons dues ledgers for Belchertown weavers, Italian Mutual
Benefit funeral rolls—preserving overseas parish chains invisible in sparse stubs. Quabbin-spe-
cific hauls include Metropolitan District Commission relocation directories (1938–1950s) mapping Dana Poles to Worcester factories, Enfield Congregational rosters (evacuated to Athol), and
Greenwich tavern ledgers tracking Shaysite kin to Holyoke paper mills; undertaker manifests for
drowned livestock and heirship disputes over Prescott heirlooms bridge submerged lots to survivor petitions.

Academic overlays demand specialized dives: Amherst-Smith-Mount Holyoke alumni directories and faculty wills reveal Dickinson-Hitchcock professorial networks funding seminary expansions, cross-referenced with ordination councils naming apostate sons resurfacing as tobacco
brokers; Hampshire Agricultural College (1867 UMass precursor) patent gazettes credit onion
sorters to Granby mechanics whose scythe innovations appear in Westfield overlaps.

Marginalized communities surface in layered sources: deed marginalia ("sachem's old field,"
"Indian planting ground") correlated with Eliot's Natick rosters for Pocumtuck maternal lines,
Northampton Quaker manumission bonds for 1783 free Blacks in Edwards households, and 19th-
century "colored" tobacco sharecroppers in Hadley censuses likely carrying Norwottuck mtDNA
masked by endogamy.

Effective strategies orchestrate colonial cores against academic-industrial overlays. Pre-1700
anchoring deploys Northampton-Hadley proprietors' lotteries cross-referenced with 1662–1812
Hampshire sessions for guardianship chains radiating from Oxbow gentry to Pelham insurgents,
pivoting to Edwards relation autobiographies for spiritual kin webs.

19th-century mobility threads college matriculations to Williston payrolls, using seminary
testimonies to trace "factory girls" to South Hadley canals. Immigrant research reverses chronology: commence 1880–1920 parish sodalities and boardinghouse censuses for Lucca-Galicia counties, backtrack via naturalizations to passenger manifests, forward-track to Quabbin exiles via
Dana directories; Puerto Rican chains follow 1950s Holyoke ward maps to Northampton barrios,
triangulated with Centro las Americas oral histories.

Quabbin diaspora weaves condemnation notices (lot-by-lot takings) against Enfield church
rosters and survivor reunions, mapping Greenwich Italians to Worcester alongside Prescott
Shaysites to Ware factories. Marginalized reconstructions demand multi-register fusion—deed
"mulatto" glosses with Quaker manumissions for Afro-Norwottuck descent, moral court fornication cases naming seminary students' paternity, Finnish temperance rolls for lumber widows, and
Quabbin undertaker ledgers for "colored" Dana exiles—against the topography of Oxbow floods,
silk cascades, college quadrangles, and reservoir specters. Hampshire's archive—from vellum
Norwottuck deeds to Quabbin exile affidavits—exacts panoramic reading across riverine propri-

etors, revival confessions, canal manifests, and academic rosters to resurrect ancestors navigating Pocumtuck weirs to Smith professorships through slate quarries, tobacco shade, and submerged town bells.

15

Cities and Towns of Hampshire County

CITIES

Amherst

Amherst, Massachusetts, sits in the heart of Hampshire County east of the Connecticut River, rising from Norwottuck–Pocumtuc planting grounds and Northampton's "East Precinct" into an incorporated town in 1759 and, later, a three-college center anchored by Amherst College (1821), UMass Amherst (1863 as Massachusetts Agricultural College), and Hampshire College (1970). Its mixed landscape of Fort River lowlands, Pelham-facing hills, and town-center commons sustained Yankee farmers, Congregational divines, Irish and French Canadian laborers, and later global students and faculty in village clusters around North, South, and East Amherst, as well as the college hill. From frontier parish and Shays' mustering ground to academic hub and anti-slavery hotbed, Amherst's valley-hill spine traces Indigenous trails through revival-era farmsteads into a layered campus town.

Norwottuck Intervals, Northampton Precinct, and College Hill

Before English settlement, Norwottuck and related Pocumtuc communities farmed the rich intervales along what became the Fort River and Hop Brook, rotating between cornfields, fishing places, and upland hunting grounds. In the 18th century, Northampton proprietors extended their holdings eastward, granting lots in what was then the "Third Precinct" to families such as Kellogg, Boltwood, Cowls, and Dickinson, who cleared farms and established a meetinghouse by mid-century; Amherst separated as a town in 1759. The town became an intellectual and religious center when conservative Congregationalists founded Amherst College in the 1820s as a training ground for ministers and missionaries, planting dormitories, faculty homes, and academy buildings on College Hill and drawing students from throughout New England and beyond.

Genealogists follow early Amherst lines first in Northampton proprietors' records and church registers, then in Amherst town meeting minutes, vital books, and college-related archives that link outlying farm lots to village houses and academic careers.

Village Hamlets, Shays' Musters, and Academic Villages

Nineteenth-century Amherst developed into several recognizable hamlets: the Main Street village around the common and churches; North Amherst, with its farms, mills, and later factory sites; South Amherst's mixed agriculture and brickmaking; and East Amherst's smaller crossroads. In the 1780s, Shays' Rebellion drew discontented farmers from Amherst and neighboring Pelham into protests over taxes and debts, leaving a paper trail in town meeting debates, militia lists, and court actions. As Amherst and, later, Massachusetts Agricultural College and Hampshire College matured, faculty subdivisions, boardinghouses, and student neighborhoods grew up around the campuses, and waves of Irish, French Canadian, Eastern European, and later Caribbean, African, and Asian migrants entered as farm workers, domestic servants, and campus staff before appearing as students and professionals in their own right.

Directories, tax lists, campus catalogues, alumni registers, and church and cemetery records show how "town and gown" families intermarried and moved between farms, boardinghouses, and faculty homes over generations.

Genealogical Resources and Strategies

Vital repositories:

Amherst Town Clerk: Births, marriages, and deaths from the mid-18th century; town and precinct meeting minutes; Shays' era records; cemetery and road-laying files.

Jones Library (Amherst) special collections: Town and regional histories, maps, local newspapers, photographs, family manuscripts (including Dickinson and allied families), and vertical files on neighborhoods and institutions.

Amherst College Archives & Special Collections and the UMass/SCUA repositories: Student and alumni files, faculty and trustee records, catalogs, yearbooks, and institutional correspondence that situate individuals within academic, civic, and missionary networks.

Regional aids include Northampton's earlier proprietors' and church records for pre-1759 families, Hampshire County deeds and probate volumes, denominational archives for Congregational, Baptist, Catholic, and other churches serving Amherst and its hamlets, and historic resource surveys that document farmsteads, mill sites, and campus buildings. Amherst's Fort River–campus narrative—from Norwottuck fields and Northampton precinct lots to Shays' petitions, Emily Dickinson's parlor, and modern lecture halls—gives genealogists deeply layered sources; land plats, parish records, college archives, and local-history collections together illuminate "college-town kin" linking farm families, divinity students, and global migrants across village greens and academic hillsides.

Easthampton

Easthampton, Massachusetts, lies at the southern edge of Hampshire County along the Manhan River and western flank of the Mount Tom Range, emerging from Northampton's south precinct into a separately incorporated town in 1809 and an industrial-arts city by the late 19th century. Once Norwottuck–Pocumtuc homelands of river meadows and beaver ponds, its landscape shifted from scattered Yankee farms to a planned mill village as the Williston family's textile and button enterprises harnessed the Manhan's falls, drawing Irish laborers, French Canadian operatives, and later Polish and Lithuanian workers into tight neighborhoods around Cottage Street and the mill ponds. From meadow lots and parish roads through canal-fed factories and 20th-century arts mills, Easthampton's valley spine traces Indigenous trails into a "small-city" blend of brick mill blocks, pond-front streets, and hilltown gateways.

Norwottuck Meadows, Northampton Precinct, and Williston Mills

Precolonial Norwottuck and related Pocumtuc groups planted corn along the Manhan's intervals and fished its shallows before epidemics and King Philip's War (1675–76) cleared the way for Northampton proprietors to extend their holdings south into what became Easthampton's home lots. By the early 18th century, families such as Clapp, Bartlett, and Strong held meadow and upland tracts as part of Northampton's "East and West Farms," worshipping at the mother church until Easthampton gained its own parish and meetinghouse in 1780. In the 1840s–1850s, Samuel Williston turned a small button shop into a major textile and elastic webbing enterprise, reshaping the village with brick mills, mill ponds, and worker housing strung along the Manhan—records of which capture the transition from agrarian Clapp–Strong kin networks into a mill-centered economy.

Genealogists track early Easthampton lines first in Northampton proprietors' books and church records, then follow them into Easthampton town books and corporate archives, where deeds and employment lists tie meadow farms to loom floors, boardinghouses, and shopfronts.

Mill Village Hamlets, Immigrant Wards, and Arts-Mill Revivals
Nineteenth-century Easthampton coalesced into linked hamlets: the central mill village around the ponds and Cottage Street, New City and Precinct areas near outlying roads, and hill-edge farms spreading toward Southampton and Westhampton. Irish immigrants arrived first as canal and mill laborers, followed by French Canadians in textile rooms and later Poles and Lithuanians in rubber, elastic, and wire works, forming Catholic parishes that kept Old World place names alive in sacramental registers. As the 20th century brought industrial decline, Easthampton's brick mills gradually refilled with light manufacturing, studios, and arts spaces, while former mill neighborhoods persisted as tight-knit enclaves where intermarried Yankee and immigrant families maintained cemetery lots and veterans' posts.

Company payrolls, city directories, parish rosters, and lodge minutes together reveal how "mill village kin" moved between farms, factory floors, and, later, arts-driven rehabs of the same brick blocks.

Genealogical Resources and Strategies
Vital repositories:

- Easthampton City/Town Clerk: Births, marriages, and deaths from incorporation in 1809 forward, plus town meeting minutes, annexation and precinct-change records, and cemetery filings.
- Easthampton Public Library (local history room): City directories, Sanborn and other fire maps, mill and business histories, high school yearbooks, and photograph collections documenting neighborhoods and mills.
- Easthampton Historical Society: Manuscripts and family papers (Clapp, Strong, Williston and associated partners), mill and company ephemera, veterans' records, and church or cemetery transcriptions.

Regional aids include Northampton's earlier land and church records for pre-1809 families, Hampshire County deeds and probate at the county level, Catholic and other denominational archives for parish registers, and state historic surveys for mill complexes and worker housing. Easthampton's Manhan-side narrative—from Norwottuck plots and Northampton precinct farms to Williston mills and arts lofts—equips genealogists with layered sources; proprietors' plats, industrial archives, and society files illuminate "mill pond kin" spanning Clapps, Willistons, and Franco-Polish mill families across the valley's evolving factory village.

Northampton

Northampton, Massachusetts, anchors Hampshire County's northern Connecticut River Oxbow as the historic shire town, founded 1654 from Hartford planters on Norwottuck homelands and incorporating as a proprietary plantation amid fertile meadows, traprock ridges, and Mill River forges sustaining Puritan divines, Yankee merchants, Irish quarrymen, and Italian stone-cutters in wards from downtown commons to Smith's Ferry villages and Mount Tom gateways. Named for Northamptonshire, England, its pivotal bounds—preserving colonial courthouses amid 1786 Shays' scorchings—evolved from Edwards' revival hearth through 19th-century cutlery-to-calico mills and Smith College academic rise, blending Oxbow agriculture with industrial wards refined by Hatfield separations and Williamsburg hill divisions. From Norwuttuck deeds to tobacco mansions and co-ed colleges, Northampton's valley spine traces Indigenous trails via Great Awakening confessions and Quabbin-echo diasporas.

Norwottuck Oxbow, Hartford Grants, and Edwards Precincts

Precolonial Norwottuck sachems like Wawaquin exploited Oxbow shad runs and corn terraces before epidemics and King Philip's War (1675–76) yielded meadows to Hartford proprietors; William Holton and Henry Burt drew lots by 1655 around Rev. Eleazar Mathers' meetinghouse, dividing intervals to Strong, Lyman, and Clapp families amid palisades and Pocumtuck raids. Parish fractures birthed West Farms (Easthampton line) and King's River precincts, with Jonathan Edwards' 1729 pastorate yielding exhaustive relation narratives; Shays' insurgents torched the 1786 jail before Northampton pardons. Early forges and tanneries fed trade, anchoring endogamy through Civil War contracts.

Genealogists scour Hartford deeds pre-1654 for Oxbow allotments, then Northampton proprietors' books linking meadow cabins to Edwards church rolls across the revival endogamy.

Ward Commons, Calico Mills, and College Hearths

Northampton's 19th-century wards fused downtown merchants drawing revivals at First Church, Smith's Ferry tobacco with Irish at St. Mary's (1884), and Italian slate cutters joining Lyman-Strong lines amid 1938 floods. Williston Seminary (1841) and Smith College (1875) elevated mechanics' daughters, while calico printworks and cutlery employed Yankee overseers; rural ties persisted through cemetery societies sustaining Shaysite kin.

Proprietors' surveys, college ledgers, and ward minutes capture chain kin from Thames ports to Oxbow workshops.

Genealogical Resources and Strategies

Vital repositories:

- Northampton City Clerk: Births, marriages, deaths from 1654 (published to 1850); proprietors' grants, Shays' pardons, and ward records.
- Forbes Library History Room: Directories (1820s+), Edwards papers, Smith College archives, and Quabbin regional extracts.

- Historic Northampton: Court files (1662–1812), family manuscripts (Strong, Lyman), probate abstracts, and Italian parish overlaps.
- Springfield Diocesan Archives: Registers for St. Mary's and ethnic missions.

Regional aids: Hampshire County Registry of Deeds for Oxbow plats, FamilySearch Edwards transcriptions, and MHC surveys for common sites.

Northampton's Oxbow-shire chronicle—from Norwottuck weirs and Holton lots to Edwards confessions and Smith quadrangles—equips genealogists with foundational files. Plantation rolls, vital indexes, and society ledgers unveil "shire town kin" spanning Strongs, Lymans, and Italian masons across Connecticut meadows.

TOWNS

Belchertown

Belchertown, Massachusetts, stretches over the uplands east of the Connecticut River in eastern Hampshire County, first laid out as Cold Spring (1731) from Springfield–Hadley domains and incorporated as Belchertown in 1761 after local petitioners honored Jonathan Belcher, colonial governor. Its broad plains and ridges—once part of Norwottuck and Quaboag homelands—supported mixed grain-and-livestock farms, sawmills, and small chair shops that linked Yankee households to Palmer and Ware markets, later shading into 19th-century onion, tobacco, and dairy production along the Swift River and Jabish Brook valleys. From a far precinct on the county's eastern frontier through Shays' Rebellion discontent, stage-and-turnpike crossroads, and 20th-century bedroom-community growth, Belchertown's "East Bay" of Hampshire County traces Indigenous trails into a town green framed by Congregational, Baptist, and Catholic institutions.

Cold Spring Grants, Shire-Town Frontier, and Shays' Echoes

Before English occupation, Native families planted and hunted along the Swift River and Quabbin-side brooks, moving seasonally between stream valleys and upland ridges. In the early 18th century, Cold Spring Plantation took shape as proprietors from Hadley, Northampton, and Brookfield drew lots in a gridded plan, with families such as Smith, Dwight, Clapp, and Bardwell clearing farms and erecting a meetinghouse near the common while still looking westward to Hampshire's shire towns for courts, markets, and ministers. Revolutionary-era debt, poor soil in some hill sections, and heavy tax burdens fed into the agrarian discontent that helped fuel Shays' Rebellion; Belchertown farmers appear in petitions, militia lists, and court papers that tie them to insurgent activity in nearby Pelham and Northampton.

For genealogists, early Belchertown families are tracked first through proprietors' records for Cold Spring lot assignments and then through the town's vital, land, and church books, which show how frontier farms consolidated, subdivided, or were lost under the pressures of war and post-war debt.

Hill Hamlets, Chair Shops, and Swift Valley Farms

Nineteenth-century Belchertown developed a loose constellation of hamlets: the common-centered village with its green, taverns, and shops; East Village and Bondsville-side neighborhoods oriented toward the Swift River mills; and outlying road districts near Ware, Palmer, and Pelham. Small chair and carriage shops, sawmills, and later modest textile and paper interests drew sons and daughters off the land, while onion and later tobacco plots in the better intervals tied Belchertown to the broader Connecticut Valley crop economy. Irish laborers arrived with roads and railroads, French Canadians and later Polish and other Eastern European families followed industrial work in nearby towns but often lived or married into Belchertown lines, filling pews at Catholic missions and appearing in school and cemetery records alongside older Yankee surnames.

Local maps, tax lists, industrial directories, and church registers—paired with federal censuses—reveal how "hill-and-valley kin" moved between village trades, tenant farms, and mill jobs in adjoining towns over the course of the 19th and early 20th centuries.

Genealogical Resources and Strategies

Vital repositories:

- Belchertown Town Clerk: Births, marriages, and deaths from the mid-18th century onward; town meeting records; road layouts; Shays' era votes and militia rolls; cemetery filings.
- Belchertown public library or historical collections: Printed town histories, family genealogies, local newspapers, historic maps and atlases, school records, and photograph collections that document village streetscapes and outlying districts.
- Belchertown Historical Society (or equivalent local body): Manuscript family papers (Smith, Dwight, Clapp, Bardwell and others), business and farm account books, church and cemetery transcriptions, and materials relating to Shays' Rebellion and 19th-century industries.

Researchers should also consult county-level land and probate records, neighboring towns' archives (especially Palmer, Ware, Granby, and Pelham) for families straddling town lines, and denominational repositories holding Congregational, Baptist, Methodist, and Catholic registers that served Belchertown residents. Belchertown's Cold Spring–to–Swift River story—from Norwottuck ground and rectilinear lots to onion fields, chair shops, and commuter roads—offers a rich paper trail; proprietors' plats, vital books, church rolls, and local manuscripts together illuminate "Cold Spring kin" weaving through common, crossroads, and valley farms.

Chesterfield

Chesterfield, Massachusetts, occupies the hill country of western Hampshire County along the Westfield River and its upland branches, settled in the mid-18th century from Northampton and Hatfield domains and incorporated in 1762 as a small farming town on lands long used by Native hunters. Its rocky pastures, wooded ridges, and scattered intervals supported mixed husbandry, sawmills, and small-scale crafts that tied Yankee households to nearby market centers in Northampton, Williamsburg, and Worthington. From a remote upland parish through the Revolutionary and Shays' Rebellion years into a 19th-century pattern of out-migration, seasonal dairying, and modest industry, Chesterfield's hill-ridge story traces older Native trails into a town green framed by Congregational, Methodist, and later Catholic connections.

Hill Grants, River Gorges, and Parish Beginnings

Before English settlement, Native families hunted and traveled along the Westfield River's branches and across what became Chesterfield's ridges, using small streams and beaver meadows seasonally. In the 1700s, proprietors from older river towns laid out lots here, granting farms to families who cleared land, built early roads, and established a meetinghouse and burying ground that made Chesterfield a distinct parish rather than an appendage of Northampton. These first-comer families—working in grain, stock, and woodland products—left their marks in early town meeting records, proprietors' books, and church rolls that anchor genealogical work.

Researchers tracing early Chesterfield kin typically begin with those proprietors' records and town vital books, following how initial grants were subdivided, mortgaged, or passed to heirs as younger generations sought opportunities elsewhere in New England and beyond.

Ridge Hamlets, Small Mills, and Out-Migration

By the 19th century, Chesterfield had developed a pattern of small hamlets and districts: farms clustered around the hilltop center and church; homesteads and modest mills along the river and brooks; and outlying neighborhoods near the borders of Williamsburg, Worthington, and Goshen. Waterpower on the streams turned sawmills, gristmills, and a few small manufactories, but thin soils and limited industrial base meant many sons and daughters left for valley factories, western states, or city positions, while others remained on increasingly dairy-focused farms. Irish and other immigrant workers appeared in limited numbers, often tied to road work, mills, or neighboring towns, marrying into established families or leaving traces in church and cemetery records.

Local maps, tax assessments, school district lists, and state and federal censuses help show how "ridge-and-river" families moved between hamlets, mills, and neighboring towns during this period, and which surnames persisted on the land.

Genealogical Resources and Strategies

Vital repositories:

- Chesterfield Town Clerk: Birth, marriage, and death records from the town's incorporation era onward; town meeting minutes; records of road layouts and school districts; burial and cemetery filings.
- Local library or historical collections in Chesterfield: Town and regional histories, family compilations, old photographs, maps and atlases, and possibly school, church, or civic group records.
- Any Chesterfield historical or preservation society: Manuscript family papers, farm and mill account books, transcribed cemetery stones, and materials relating to military service, fraternal groups, or notable events such as local responses to Shays' Rebellion or the Civil War.

Researchers will also want to consult Hampshire County land and probate records, since deeds and wills can connect Chesterfield residents to relatives in Northampton, Williamsburg, Worthington, and other towns. Denominational archives may hold Congregational and Methodist registers that include baptisms, marriages, and membership lists. Taken together, these sources—proprietors' plats, vital books, church records, probate files, and local manuscripts—allow genealogists to reconstruct "hilltown kin" whose lives ran along Chesterfield's ridges, brooks, and crossroads.

<u>Cummington</u>

Cummington, Massachusetts, lies along the upper Westfield River in the northwestern hill country of Hampshire County, carved from Northampton and surrounding proprietors' lands and incorporated in 1779 as a compact farming town amid rocky uplands, narrow intervals, and wooded ridges long traversed by Native hunters. Its landscape of river flats, drumlins, and high pastures supported mixed subsistence and market farming, sawmills, and small shops that tied Yankee households to regional centers in Northampton, Pittsfield, and the Berkshires, while the later presence of poet William Cullen Bryant and modest 19th-century industry left a literary and cultural imprint out of proportion to the town's size. From frontier parish to "hilltown" of out-migrating farm families, Cummington's river-and-ridge story traces older Indigenous paths into a green-framed village center, scattered school districts, and church-anchored hamlets.

Westfield Headwaters, Proprietor Grants, and Parish Center

Before English settlement, Native people hunted, fished, and traveled along the headwaters of the Westfield River and its branches, using the valleys and ridges seasonally. In the mid-18th century, proprietors from older valley towns laid out lots here, granting farms to early families who cleared land, opened roads, and established a meetinghouse and burying ground that made Cummington a distinct parish rather than a distant outpost of Northampton. These first-comer households built grist and sawmills on the river and brooks, and appear early in town meeting minutes, vital records, and church rolls that form the backbone of genealogical work in Cummington.

Researchers typically start with these proprietors' records and town books to follow how original grants were divided among heirs, sold, or abandoned as soils proved marginal and younger generations left for better land or wage work elsewhere in New England and the interior.

Hill Hamlets, Small Industry, and Literary Legacy

By the 19th century, Cummington comprised a central village on the high ground near the meetinghouse and several small neighborhoods along the Westfield and its tributaries, where waterpower supported sawmills, carding mills, and other small enterprises. Farm families combined grain, hay, and stock raising with seasonal work in these mills or in trades such as blacksmithing and carpentry, while some residents were drawn westward in the eras of canal, railroad, and western migration. Limited numbers of Irish and other immigrant workers appeared as road builders, mill hands, or farm laborers, sometimes marrying into older Yankee lines. The town also gained a wider reputation through the life and writings of William Cullen Bryant, whose family ties and later commemorations have generated biographical and local-historical records useful to genealogists.

Censuses, tax lists, maps, and school district records—combined with church and cemetery data—show how "river-and-ridge kin" moved between the center village, outlying farms, and neighboring hilltowns across the 19th and early 20th centuries.

Genealogical Resources and Strategies

Vital repositories:

- Cummington Town Clerk: Birth, marriage, and death records from the incorporation era onward; town meeting minutes; road and school district descriptions; burial and cemetery filings.
- Local library or historical collections in Cummington: Town and regional histories, family genealogies, historic maps and atlases, school or church programs, local newspapers if any, and photograph collections documenting farms, mills, and village scenes.
- Any Cummington historical society or museum: Manuscript family papers, farm and business account books, transcribed gravestones, church records or copies, and materials on notable residents such as Bryant, as well as veterans' and civic-organization records.

Beyond the town, Hampshire County land and probate records connect Cummington residents to kin in Northampton, Worthington, Goshen, and other valley or hilltown communities, while denominational archives may hold original Congregational, Methodist, or other church registers that include Cummington families. Taken together, proprietors' plats, vital books, church rolls, probate files, and local manuscripts enable reconstruction of "hilltown kin" whose lives followed Cummington's pattern of upland farms, river mills, and outward migration.

Goshen

Goshen, Massachusetts, perches in the northern hill country of Hampshire County astride the Westfield River's upper reaches and its tributary brooks, settled mid-18th century from Northampton and Hatfield proprietors as "Goshen Gore" and incorporated 1782 amid rocky pastures, narrow intervals, and forested ridges long used by Native hunters for seasonal forays. Its upland terrain supported subsistence grain-and-stock farms, sawmills, and potash works linking Yankee households to Northampton markets and Pittsfield trade, evolving through Shays' Rebellion debt pressures into 19th-century dairying and out-migration hamlets like Goshen Center, Upper Highlands, and Williamsburg-line villages. Named biblically for its "land of plenty," Goshen's hill-river spine traces Pocumtuc trails via parish meetinghouses and Methodist circuits into a compact green preserving colonial grants amid thin soils and flood-prone fords.

Pocumtuc Highlands, Northampton Grants, and Parish Ridges

Precolonial Pocumtuc traversed Westfield headwaters for fishing weirs and deer hunts before epidemics and King Philip's War (1675–76) yielded gores to valley proprietors; mid-1700s lotteries granted ledges to families like Bartlett, Phelps, and Lyman clearing farms and erecting a 1760s meetinghouse amid garrisons and Indian boundaries. Parish independence yielded Congregational church and burying ground, with Shays' sympathizers petitioning Northampton courts before 1787 pardons; small sawmills and potash kilns fed trade, employing endogamy through Civil War woolens.

Genealogists trace Northampton deeds pre-1782 for gore allotments, then Goshen plantation books linking ridge cabins to church rolls across highland endogamy.

Valley Hamlets, Dairy Mills, and Revival Commons

Goshen's 19th-century clusters blended Center District farms drawing revivals at Union Church, river mills with Irish laborers at St. Joseph's missions (late 1800s), and Bartlett kin sustaining Grange halls amid 1874 floods and 1938 hurricanes. Cheese exports and charcoal bolstered subsistence, rural ties persisting through cemetery societies and Ohio migrations.

Proprietors' surveys, mill ledgers, and district minutes capture chain kin from valley ports to summit hearths.

Genealogical Resources and Strategies

Vital repositories:

- Goshen Town Clerk: Births, marriages, deaths from 1760s parish era (published to 1850); incorporation and Northampton separations.
- Goshen Historical Society: Manuscripts (Bartlett, Phelps), potash accounts, dairy files, and family registers.
- Northampton Library Regional Aids: Gore overlaps, Westfield maps, and mill extracts.

Regional aids: Hampshire County probate at Northampton Registry, FamilySearch vital transcriptions, and MHC surveys for ridge home sites.

Goshen's gore-ridge tale—from Pocumtuc heights and Northampton logs to potash flames and dairy wheels—equips genealogists with hill-hardy sources. Plantation grants, church rolls, and society files unveil "Goshen Gore kin" spanning Lymans, Phelps, and Bartletts across Westfield summits.

Granby

Granby, Massachusetts, spans the eastern uplands of Hampshire County between the Connecticut River valley and the Quaboag hills, laid out as "New Grant No. 4" from Hadley and Northampton proprietors in 1735 and incorporated December 28, 1754, sustaining dispersed farms, gristmills, and chair shops amid rocky pastures and Swift River brooks that linked Yankee agrarians, Irish road-builders, and Polish laborers in hamlets like Granby Center, West Granby villages, and Ludlow-line outposts. Named for John Manners, Marquess of Granby, its thin-soiled ridges—once Norwottuck homelands—powered small sawmills and forges, with bounds refined by South Hadley separations (1753) and Belchertown divisions (1761), preserving colonial grants through Shays' musters and flood-prone roads. From frontier precinct to rural crossroads and Grange halls, Granby's hill-plain spine traces Nipmuc trails via Methodist circuits and district schools.

Norwottuck New Grant, Hadley Lots, and Chair Districts

Precolonial Norwottuck planted intervals and fished Swift tributaries, disrupted by epidemics and King Philip's War (1675–76) that yielded No. 4 tract to Hadley proprietors; Lt. David Root and Samuel Dickinson claimed home lots by 1739, dividing ledges to Bartlett, Phelps, and Porter families amid garrisons and Indian boundaries. Parish status (1749) yielded meetinghouse and burying ground, with Shays' sympathizers rallying before 1787; chair factories and gristmills employed endogamous kin through Civil War contracts.

Genealogists trace Hadley deeds pre-1754 for grant allotments, then Granby plantation books linking ridge cabins to mill rosters across the upland endogamy.

Plain Hamlets, Forge Shops, and Revival Commons

Granby's 19th-century clusters featured Center District farms drawing revivals at Congregational Church (1754), West Granby mills with Irish at St. Hyacinth's missions (1880s), and Bartlett kin sustaining Grange halls amid 1938 floods. Onion fields and chair exports anchored economy, rural ties persisting through cemetery societies and out-migrations.

Proprietors' surveys, mill contracts, and district minutes capture chain kin from valley ports to Swift workshops.

Genealogical Resources and Strategies

Vital repositories:

- Granby Town Clerk: Births, marriages, deaths from 1735 grant era (published to 1850); incorporation and Hadley separations.
- Granby Historical Society: Manuscripts (Root, Dickinson), chair ledgers, flood narratives, and family registers.
- Hadley Historical Society Regional Aids: New Grant overlaps, Swift maps, and mill extracts.

Regional aids: Hampshire County probate at Northampton Registry, FamilySearch vital transcriptions, and MHC surveys for ridge home sites.

Granby's grant-plain saga—from Norwottuck brooks and Hadley logs to chair rockers and onion rows—equips genealogists with hill-deep sources. Plantation grants, church rolls, and society files unveil "No. 4 kin" spanning Porters, Phelps, and Bartletts across Quaboag ridges.

Hadley

Hadley, Massachusetts, flanks the Connecticut River's western Oxbow in central Hampshire County, planted 1659 from Hartford and Wethersfield migrants on Norwottuck homelands and incorporated amid fertile meadows, traprock ridges, and Fort River mills sustaining Puritan planters, Yankee agrarians, Irish laborers, and Polish onion growers in wards from the town common to Mount Warner slopes and South Hadley Falls precincts. Named for Hadleigh, Suffolk, its linear bounds—preserving 1661 proprietary grants refined by Hatfield separations (1661) and Amherst divisions (1759)—evolved from Edwards revival hearth through 19th-century asparagus-to-onion empires and apple orchards, blending alluvial agriculture with small forges and chair shops. From Norwuttuck deeds to Shays' musters and Polish parish enclaves, Hadley's Oxbow spine traces Indigenous trails via Great Awakening confessions and district schools.

Norwuttuck Oxbow, Hartford Lots, and Revival Precincts

Precolonial Norwuttuck sachems exploited Oxbow shad runs and corn terraces before epidemics and King Philip's War (1675–76) yielded meadows to Hartford proprietors; John Webster and Andrew Bacon drew 40-acre lots by 1660 around Rev. John Russell's meetinghouse, dividing intervals to Porter, Smith, and Dickinson families amid palisades and Pocumtuck raids. Parish fractures birthed Hatfield and Sunderland precincts, with Jonathan Edwards preaching at nearby Northampton; Shays' insurgents rallied before 1787 pardons, early forges feeding trade.

Genealogists scour Hartford deeds pre-1659 for Oxbow allotments, then Hadley proprietors' books linking meadow cabins to church rolls across revival endogamy.

Common Wards, Onion Fields, and Polish Hearths

Hadley's 19th-century wards fused town common merchants drawing revivals at First Church (1696), Fort River onion plots with Irish at St. Bridget's (1903), and Porter-Smith lines sustaining Grange halls amid 1938 floods. Asparagus carts and apple exports anchored economy, rural ties persisting through cemetery societies.

Proprietors' surveys, grower ledgers, and ward minutes capture chain kin from Thames ports to Oxbow workshops.

Genealogical Resources and Strategies

Vital repositories:

- Hadley Town Clerk: Births, marriages, deaths from 1659 (published to 1850); proprietors' grants, Shays' petitions, and ward records.
- Hadley Historical Society: Manuscripts (Webster, Porter), farm ledgers, church extracts, and onion industry files.
- Forbes Library Regional Aids: Northampton overlaps, Oxbow maps, and revival extracts.

Regional aids: Hampshire County Registry of Deeds for interval plats, FamilySearch Edwards transcriptions, and MHC surveys for common sites.

Hadley's Oxbow-common chronicle—from Norwuttuck weirs and Webster lots to onion empires and Polish parishes—equips genealogists with meadow-deep sources. Plantation rolls, vital indexes, and society files unveil "Oxbow kin" spanning Porters, Smiths, and onion growers across Connecticut intervals.

Hatfield

Hatfield, Massachusetts, occupies the Connecticut River's eastern flats in central Hampshire County, settled 1661 from Hadley proprietors on Pocumtuck meadows and incorporated 1670 amid alluvial intervals, traprock bluffs, and Mill River mills sustaining Puritan defenders, Yankee agrarians, Irish laborers, and Polish onion growers in wards from the town common to Potatuck ridges and Williamsburg-line uplands. Named for Hatfield, Hertfordshire, its compact bounds—preserving 1661 grants refined by Whately separations (1771) and Williamsburg divisions (1810)—evolved from frontier garrison through Shays' musters and 19th-century tobacco-to-onion empires, blending river agriculture with chair shops and distilleries. From Pocumtuck cornfields to Polish parishes and Grange halls, Hatfield's meadow spine traces Indigenous trails via Capt. Moseley's raids and district schools.

Pocumtuck Intervals, Hadley Lots, and Garrison Commons

Precolonial Pocumtuck sachems cultivated rich intervals and shad fisheries before epidemics and King Philip's War (1675–76) yielded flats to Hadley proprietors; Samuel Partridge and John Dickinson drew home lots by 1663 around fortified meetinghouse, dividing meadows to Allis, Belden, and Field families amid stockades and Turners Falls raids. Precinct fractures birthed Whately and Williamsburg parishes, with Capt. Turner mustering defenders; Shays' sympathizers petitioned before 1787 pardons, early distilleries feeding trade.

Genealogists trace Hadley deeds pre-1670 for interval allotments, then Hatfield proprietors' books linking bluff cabins to garrison rolls across meadow endogamy.

Common Wards, Tobacco Fields, and Polish Hearths

Hatfield's 19th-century wards integrated town common farms drawing revivals at First Church (1683), Mill River tobacco sheds with Irish at St. Joseph's (1890s), and Allis-Belden lines sustaining Grange halls amid 1938 floods. Onion carts and chair exports anchored economy, rural ties persisting through cemetery societies and urban migrations.

Proprietors' surveys, grower ledgers, and ward minutes capture chain kin from Thames ports to interval workshops.

Genealogical Resources and Strategies

Vital repositories:

- Hatfield Town Clerk: Births, marriages, deaths from 1661 (published to 1850); garrison rolls, proprietors' grants, and Shays' petitions.
- Hatfield Historical Society: Manuscripts (Partridge, Allis), tobacco ledgers, church extracts, and family registers.
- Forbes Library Regional Aids: Hadley overlaps, Mill River maps, and garrison narratives.

Regional aids: Hampshire County probate at Northampton Registry, FamilySearch vital transcriptions, and MHC surveys for common sites.

Hatfield's interval-garrison chronicle—from Pocumtuck weirs and Partridge lots to tobacco empires and Polish parishes—equips genealogists with meadow-deep sources. Plantation rolls, vital indexes, and society files unveil "Pocumtuck kin" spanning Allis, Beldens, and onion growers across Connecticut flats.

Huntington

Huntington, Massachusetts, rises in the hilly western reaches of Hampshire County along the Westfield River's middle gorge and Chestnut Hill ridges, laid out as "District of Murrayfield South Precinct" from Norwich, Connecticut proprietors in 1767 and incorporated 1801 amid steep pastures, hemlock forests, and mill brooks sustaining frontier loggers, Yankee farmers, Irish sawyers, and Italian laborers in hamlets like Huntington Center, Chester-line villages, and Gossville outposts. Named for Jedediah Huntington, its rugged bounds—preserving 1760s grants refined by Norwich separations and Middlefield divisions (1810)—evolved from Shays' Rebellion strongholds through 19th-century tanneries and chair shops, blending upland dairying with charcoal and potash trades. From Nipmuc hunting grounds to Grange halls and flood-scarred roads, Huntington's gorge-ridge spine traces Indigenous trails via Methodist circuits and district schools.

Nipmuc Gorges, Norwich Lots, and Shays' Strongholds

Precolonial Nipmuc traversed Westfield gorges for trout weirs and bear hunts before epidemics and King Philip's War (1675–76) yielded uplands to Norwich proprietors; Ebenezer Cornish and Asahel Gunn drew home lots by 1770 around log meetinghouse, dividing ledges to Bagg, Phelps, and Bartlett families amid garrisons and Indian boundaries. Precinct status (1779) yielded burying ground and muster fields, with Shays' insurgents drilling before 1787; sawmills and potash kilns fed Pittsfield trade through endogamous kin.

Genealogists trace Norwich deeds pre-1801 for gorge allotments, then Huntington plantation books linking ridge cabins to militia rolls across highland endogamy.

Center Hamlets, Tannery Mills, and Italian Hearths

Huntington's 19th-century clusters featured Center District farms drawing revivals at Congregational Church (1810), river tanneries with Irish at St. Anthony's missions (1890s), and Bagg-Phelps lines sustaining Grange halls amid 1874 floods and 1938 hurricanes. Chair exports and dairy cheese anchored economy, rural ties persisting through cemetery societies and urban migrations.

Proprietors' surveys, mill ledgers, and district minutes capture chain kin from Norwich ports to gorge workshops.

Genealogical Resources and Strategies

Vital repositories:

- Huntington Town Clerk: Births, marriages, deaths from 1767 precinct era (published to 1850); Shays' musters, proprietors' grants, and flood records.
- Huntington Historical Society: Manuscripts (Cornish, Gunn), tannery accounts, church extracts, and family registers.
- Chester Historical Society Regional Aids: Murrayfield overlaps, Westfield maps, and mill narratives.

Regional aids: Hampshire County probate at Northampton Registry, FamilySearch vital transcriptions, and MHC surveys for ridge home sites.

Huntington's gorge-Shays' chronicle—from Nipmuc weirs and Norwich logs to tannery flames and dairy ridges—equips genealogists with hill-forged sources. Plantation grants, militia rolls, and society files unveil "Murrayfield kin" spanning Baggs, Phelps, and Bartletts across Westfield heights.

Middlefield

Middlefield, Massachusetts, crowns the hilly central spine of Hampshire County amid the Westfield River's upper tributaries and Chester Bowl ridges, laid out as "District No. 3" from Norwich, Connecticut proprietors in 1775 and incorporated October 20, 1816, sustaining rocky pastures, hemlock forests, and brook mills for Yankee loggers, subsistence farmers, Irish sawyers, and Italian laborers in hamlets like Middlefield Center, Bancroft villages, and Chester-line outposts.

Named for its medial position between Northampton and Pittsfield grants, its steep bounds—preserving 1770s lots refined by Huntington separations (1801) and Worthington divisions—evolved from Shays' Rebellion outposts through 19th-century potash works and chair shops, blending upland dairying with charcoal trades and flood-prone fords. From Nipmuc hunting grounds to Grange halls and rural circuits, Middlefield's bowl-ridge spine traces Indigenous trails via Methodist meetinghouses and district schools.

Nipmuc Bowls, Norwich Lots, and Shays' Outposts

Precolonial Nipmuc roamed Chester Bowl for seasonal hunts and trout weirs before epidemics and King Philip's War (1675–76) yielded uplands to Norwich proprietors; Asahel Gunn and Ebenezer Cornish drew home lots by 1778 around log precinct house, dividing ledges to Bagg, Phelps, and Bartlett families amid garrisons and Indian boundaries. District status (1783) yielded burying ground and muster fields, with Shays' sympathizers rallying before 1787 pardons; potash kilns and sawmills fed Pittsfield trade through endogamous kin.

Genealogists trace Norwich deeds pre-1816 for bowl allotments, then Middlefield plantation books linking ridge cabins to militia rolls across highland endogamy.

Center Hamlets, Potash Mills, and Italian Hearths

Middlefield's 19th-century clusters featured Center District farms drawing revivals at Union Church (1820), brook potash works with Irish at St. Mary's missions (1890s), and Bagg-Phelps lines sustaining Grange halls amid 1874 floods and 1938 hurricanes. Chair exports and dairy cheese anchored economy, rural ties persisting through cemetery societies and urban migrations. Proprietors' surveys, mill ledgers, and district minutes capture chain kin from Norwich ports to bowl workshops.

Genealogical Resources and Strategies

Vital repositories:

- Middlefield Town Clerk: Births, marriages, deaths from 1775 district era (published to 1850); Shays' musters, proprietors' grants, and flood records.
- Middlefield Historical Society: Manuscripts (Gunn, Cornish), potash accounts, church extracts, and family registers.
- Worthington Historical Society Regional Aids: Norwich overlaps, Westfield maps, and mill narratives.

Regional aids: Hampshire County probate at Northampton Registry, FamilySearch vital transcriptions, and MHC surveys for ridge home sites.

Middlefield's bowl-Shays' chronicle—from Nipmuc heights and Norwich logs to potash flames and dairy ridges—equips genealogists with hill-forged sources. Plantation grants, militia rolls, and society files unveil "District No. 3 kin" spanning Baggs, Phelps, and Bartletts across Chester Bowl summits.

Pelham

Pelham, Massachusetts, occupies the eastern uplands of Hampshire County amid the Quaboag River headwaters and Mounts Toby-Lincoln ridges, laid out as "New Grant No. 5" from

Northampton and Hadley proprietors in 1739 and incorporated 1742 amid rocky pastures, pine forests, and brook mills sustaining frontier loggers, Yankee farmers, Irish sawyers, and Italian laborers in hamlets like Pelham Center, North Prescott villages, and Amherst-line outposts. Named for Thomas Pelham-Holles, Duke of Newcastle, its steep bounds—preserving 1730s grants refined by Prescott separations (1760) and Belchertown divisions—evolved from Shays' Rebellion heartlands through 19th-century potash works and chair shops, blending upland dairying with charcoal trades and flood-prone hollows. From Nipmuc hunting grounds to Grange halls and rural circuits, Pelham's ridge-Quaboag spine traces Indigenous trails via Congregational meetinghouses and district schools.

Nipmuc Ridges, Northampton Lots, and Shays' Heartlands

Precolonial Nipmuc traversed Quaboag headwaters for deer hunts and trout weirs before epidemics and King Philip's War (1675–76) yielded uplands to Northampton proprietors; Samuel Dickinson and David Root drew home lots by 1741 around log meetinghouse, dividing ledges to Bartlett, Phelps, and Porter families amid garrisons and Indian boundaries. Parish status yielded Congregational church and burying ground, with Shays' insurgents mustering captains like Daniel Shays himself before 1787; sawmills and potash kilns fed Springfield trade through endogamous kin.

Genealogists trace Northampton deeds pre-1742 for ridge allotments, then Pelham plantation books linking hollow cabins to militia rolls across highland endogamy.

Center Hamlets, Potash Mills, and Italian Hearths

Pelham's 19th-century clusters featured Center District farms drawing revivals at First Church (1743), brook potash works with Irish at St. Theresa's missions (1890s), and Bartlett-Phelps lines sustaining Grange halls amid 1874 floods and 1938 hurricanes. Chair exports and dairy cheese anchored economy, rural ties persisting through cemetery societies and urban migrations.

Proprietors' surveys, mill ledgers, and district minutes capture chain kin from Northampton ports to ridge workshops.

Genealogical Resources and Strategies

Vital repositories:

- Pelham Town Clerk: Births, marriages, deaths from 1739 grant era (published to 1850); Shays' musters, proprietors' grants, and flood records.
- Pelham Historical Society: Manuscripts (Dickinson, Root), potash accounts, church extracts, and family registers.
- Amherst Historical Society Regional Aids: New Grant overlaps, Quaboag maps, and mill narratives.

Regional aids: Hampshire County probate at Northampton Registry, FamilySearch vital transcriptions, and MHC surveys for ridge home sites.

Pelham's ridge-Shays' chronicle—from Nipmuc heights and Northampton logs to potash flames and dairy summits—equips genealogists with hill-forged sources. Plantation grants, militia rolls, and society files unveil "No. 5 kin" spanning Bartletts, Phelps, and Porters across Quaboag ridges.

<u>Plainfield</u>

Plainfield, Massachusetts, spans the northeastern uplands of Hampshire County along the Swift River's middle reaches and Cummington ridges, laid out as "District of Plainfield" from Northampton and Hatfield proprietors in 1774 and incorporated 1807 amid rocky pastures, pine forests, and brook mills sustaining frontier loggers, Yankee farmers, Irish sawyers, and Italian laborers in hamlets like Plainfield Center, Moores Corners villages, and Hawley-line outposts. Named for its level plain amid hills, its steep bounds—preserving 1770s grants refined by Cummington separations and Williamsburg divisions—evolved from Shays' Rebellion outposts through 19th-century potash works and chair shops, blending upland dairying with charcoal trades and flood-prone hollows. From Nipmuc hunting grounds to Grange halls and rural circuits, Plainfield's plain-ridge spine traces Indigenous trails via Congregational meetinghouses and district schools.

Nipmuc Plains, Northampton Lots, and Shays' Outposts

Precolonial Nipmuc roamed Swift River plains for seasonal hunts and trout weirs before epidemics and King Philip's War (1675–76) yielded uplands to Northampton proprietors; Ebenezer Bagg and Asahel Phelps drew home lots by 1776 around log precinct house, dividing ledges to Bartlett, Phelps, and Porter families amid garrisons and Indian boundaries. District status (1780) yielded burying ground and muster fields, with Shays' sympathizers rallying before 1787 pardons; potash kilns and sawmills fed Northampton trade through endogamous kin.

Genealogists trace Northampton deeds pre-1807 for plain allotments, then Plainfield plantation books linking ridge cabins to militia rolls across highland endogamy.

Center Hamlets, Potash Mills, and Italian Hearths

Plainfield's 19th-century clusters featured Center District farms drawing revivals at Union Church (1810), brook potash works with Irish at St. John's missions (1890s), and Bagg-Phelps lines sustaining Grange halls amid 1874 floods and 1938 hurricanes. Chair exports and dairy cheese anchored economy, rural ties persisting through cemetery societies and urban migrations. Proprietors' surveys, mill ledgers, and district minutes capture chain kin from Northampton ports to plain workshops.

Genealogical Resources and Strategies

Vital repositories:

- Plainfield Town Clerk: Births, marriages, deaths from 1774 district era (published to 1850); Shays' musters, proprietors' grants, and flood records.
- Plainfield Historical Society: Manuscripts (Bagg, Phelps), potash accounts, church extracts, and family registers.
- Cummington Historical Society Regional Aids: Northampton overlaps, Swift maps, and mill narratives.

Regional aids: Hampshire County probate at Northampton Registry, FamilySearch vital transcriptions, and MHC surveys for ridge home sites.

Plainfield's plain-Shays' chronicle—from Nipmuc heights and Northampton logs to potash
flames and dairy ridges—equips genealogists with hill-forged sources. Plantation grants, militia
rolls, and society files unveil "District kin" spanning Baggs, Phelps, and Bartletts across Swift
River summits.

South Hadley

South Hadley, Massachusetts, lies along the Connecticut River's eastern falls in central Hampshire County, settled from 1721 in the unsettled southern portion of Hadley on Pocumtuck homelands and incorporated 1775 after precinct status in 1732 and district in 1753, amid fertile terraces,
Mount Holyoke ridges, and canal-powered mills sustaining Puritan planters, Yankee agrarians, Irish laborers, and Polish growers in wards from the town common to Falls precincts and
Granby-line uplands. Named for its position south of Hadley, its bounds—preserving early grants
refined by Granby separations (1754)—evolved from frontier outposts through Shays' courthouse protests and 19th-century factories, blending river agriculture with the nation's first nav-
igable canal (1795) and Mount Holyoke College (1837). From Pocumtuck cornfields to Polish
parishes and academic enclaves, South Hadley's falls-terrace spine traces Indigenous trails via
Bloody Brook echoes and district schools.

Pocumtuck Falls, Hadley Grants, and Precinct Commons
Precolonial Pocumtuck exploited river falls for shad fisheries and corn terraces before epidemics
and King Philip's War (1675–76), including Bloody Brook ambushes, yielded lands to Hadley proprietors; individual grants from 1675 spurred settlement delayed by raids until 1725, with families
like Porter and Dickinson claiming lots by 1730s around meetinghouse amid garrisons. Precinct
and district status yielded church and burying ground, with Shays' sympathizers joining 1786
Northampton courthouse shutdowns before 1787 pardons; early mills fed trade through endogamous kin.

Genealogists trace Hadley deeds pre-1775 for precinct allotments, then South Hadley town
books linking terrace cabins to church rolls across valley endogamy.

Common Wards, Canal Mills, and College Hearths
South Hadley's 19th-century wards fused town common farms drawing revivals at First Church,
canal factories with Irish laborers at missions, and Porter-Dickinson lines sustaining societies
amid 1938 floods. Textile and paper mills anchored economy post-canal, rural ties persisting
through cemetery groups and urban shifts, later enriched by Mount Holyoke.

Proprietors' surveys, mill ledgers, and ward minutes capture chain kin from Hadley ports to falls
workshops.

Genealogical Resources and Strategies
Vital repositories:

- South Hadley Town Clerk (116 Main St, Room 107): Births, marriages, deaths from 1730
  (microfiche to 1890); precinct records and incorporations.

- South Hadley Historical Society: Manuscripts (Hadley grants), canal accounts, church extracts, and family registers.
- Hadley Historical Society Regional Aids: Precinct overlaps, falls maps, and mill narratives.

Regional aids: Hampshire County probate at Northampton Registry, FamilySearch vital transcriptions (1841–1910 statewide), and MHC surveys for terrace sites.

South Hadley's falls-precinct chronicle—from Pocumtuck ambushes and Hadley grants to canal waters and college halls—equips genealogists with valley-deep sources. Plantation rolls, vital indexes, and society files unveil "South Hadley kin" spanning Porters, Dickinsons, and canal workers across Connecticut terraces.

Southampton

Southampton, Massachusetts, flanks the Manhan River's lower valley in western Hampshire County, settled from the 1680s on Nonotuck/Pocumtuck homelands, established as a precinct in 1730 and district in 1753, then incorporated 1778 amid fertile meadows, Pomeroy ridges, and brook mills sustaining Puritan fur traders, Yankee agrarians, Irish laborers, and Polish growers in wards from Bank Row to Hampton Ponds and Westhampton-line uplands. Named likely for Southampton, England, its bounds—preserving early grants refined by Westfield annexes (1749), Murrayfield separations (1765), and Westhampton divisions (1778)—evolved from frontier trading posts through Shays' debt protests and 19th-century dairying and chair shops. From Nonotuck fur grounds to Grange halls and flood-prone roads, Southampton's meadow-ridge spine traces Indigenous trails via garrison circuits and district schools.

Nonotuck Valleys, Northampton Grants, and Precinct Commons

Precolonial Nonotuck/Pocumtuck pursued fur trades and shad fisheries along Manhan before epidemics and King Philip's War (1675–76) yielded meadows to Northampton proprietors; Caleb Pomeroy petitioned grants in 1680, with families drawing lots by 1730 around meetinghouse amid garrisons and raids. Precinct and district status yielded church and burying ground, with Shays' sympathizers facing taxes amid post-war recession before 1787 pardons; sawmills and forges fed trade through endogamous kin.

Genealogists trace Northampton deeds pre-1778 for valley allotments, then Southampton town books linking ridge cabins to precinct rolls across meadow endogamy.

Bank Row Wards, Dairy Farms, and Polish Hearths

Southampton's 19th-century wards integrated Bank Row farms drawing revivals at Congregational Church, Manhan mills with Irish laborers at missions, and Pomeroy lines sustaining Grange halls amid 1938 floods. Dairying, chair exports, and meadows anchored economy, rural ties persisting through cemetery societies and migrations.

Proprietors' surveys, farm ledgers, and ward minutes capture chain kin from Northampton ports to valley workshops.

Genealogical Resources and Strategies

Vital repositories:

- Southampton Town Clerk: Births, marriages, deaths from 1730 precinct era (1865–1900 published); district records and incorporations.
- Southampton Historical Society: Manuscripts (Pomeroy grants), fur trade accounts, church extracts, and family registers.
- Northampton Historical Society Regional Aids: Precinct overlaps, Manhan maps, and mill narratives.

Regional aids: Hampshire County probate at Northampton Registry, FamilySearch vital transcriptions (1841–1910), and MHC surveys for meadow sites.

Southampton's valley-precinct chronicle—from Nonotuck trades and Pomeroy grants to dairy meadows and Shays' echoes—equips genealogists with hill-deep sources. Plantation rolls, vital indexes, and society files unveil "Manhan kin" spanning Pomeroy, Allis, and dairy lines across Pomeroy ridges.

Ware

Ware, Massachusetts, straddles the Swift and Ware Rivers' confluence in eastern Hampshire County, granted 1713 as "Equivalent Lands" to Narragansett fighters on Nipmuc homelands, settled from 1729 by Jacob Olmstead and John Read tenants, and incorporated 1761 amid rocky vales, pine forests, and river falls sustaining dispersed farmers, Yankee agrarians, Irish millworkers, and Polish laborers in nodes from Ware Center to village mills, Enfield-line lowlands, and Palmer uplands. Named for the Ware River, its irregular bounds—preserving military grants refined by Palmer (1752), Hardwick separations, and Warren annexes (1823)—evolved from manor-like leases through Shays' tax protests and 19th-century textile booms via Ware Manufacturing Company (1821), blending agriculture with cotton mills and chair shops. From Nipmuc fishing weirs to factory villages and Quabbin shadows, Ware's river-vale spine traces Indigenous trails via precinct meetinghouses and district schools.

Nipmuc Confluences, Equivalent Grants, and Precinct Nodes

Precolonial Nipmuc established spring fishing camps at Ware falls and Swift intervals before epidemics and King Philip's War (1675–76) yielded tracts to Narragansett soldiers; John Read bought cheaply in 1713, leasing to Olmstead (1729 Great House) and settlers by 1730s around dispersed mills amid garrisons. Precinct (1742) and district yielded meetinghouse (1748) and burying ground, with Shays' sympathizers facing debts before 1787; potash and sawmills fed Springfield trade through endogamous kin.

Genealogists trace Equivalent deeds pre-1761 for river allotments, then Ware plantation books linking vale cabins to church rolls across upland endogamy.

Village Mills, Textile Hubs, and Polish Hearths

Ware's 19th-century shifts fused Center farms drawing revivals at churches (1757 onward), river factories with Irish at St. Mary's (1855), and Olmstead-Read lines sustaining societies amid Quabbin takings (1930s). Cotton spindles (6,544 by 1837) and village commons anchored economy, rural ties persisting through cemetery groups.

Proprietors' leases, mill payrolls, and ward minutes capture chain kin from Boston ports to falls workshops.

Genealogical Resources and Strategies

Vital repositories:

- Ware Town Clerk: Births, marriages, deaths from 1750 precinct era (to 1850 published); Equivalent grants and mill records.
- Ware Historical Society: Manuscripts (Olmstead, Read), textile ledgers, church extracts, and family registers.
- Palmer Historical Society Regional Aids: River overlaps, Swift maps, and factory narratives.

Regional aids: Hampshire County probate at Northampton Registry, FamilySearch vital transcriptions, and MHC surveys for vale sites.

Ware's river-precinct chronicle—from Nipmuc weirs and Equivalent leases to textile spindles and Quabbin echoes—equips genealogists with mill-deep sources. Plantation rolls, vital indexes, and society files unveil "Ware River kin" spanning Olmsteads, Reads, and mill hands across Swift confluences.

<u>Westhampton</u>

Westhampton, Massachusetts, rises in the western uplands of Hampshire County along Manhan River branches and Pomeroy ridges, first settled around 1762 as the "Long" or "West" Division of Northampton on Nonotuck/Pocumtuck homelands and incorporated September 29, 1778, amid rocky pastures, apple orchards, and brook mills sustaining Yankee agrarians, subsistence farmers, Irish laborers, and Italian hands in hamlets from Westhampton Center to Bank Row villages and Southampton-line lowlands. Named for its position west of Northampton, its compact bounds—preserving 1760s grants refined by Southampton separations (1778)—evolved from frontier divisions through Shays' debt protests and 19th-century woolens and chair shops, blending upland dairying with maple sugar and beef trades. From Nonotuck hunting grounds to Grange halls and rural circuits, Westhampton's ridge-Manhan spine traces Indigenous trails via Congregational meetinghouses and district schools.

Nonotuck Divisions, Northampton Lots, and Church Commons

Precolonial Nonotuck/Pocumtuck roamed Manhan ridges for deer hunts and trout weirs before epidemics and King Philip's War (1675–76) yielded uplands to Northampton proprietors; Pomeroy kin like Pliny and Timothy drew home lots by 1767 around log precinct house, dividing ledges to Bartlett, Phelps, and Hale families amid garrisons and boundaries. Incorporation yielded Congregational Church (1779) with Rev. Enoch Hale and burying ground, with Shays' sympathizers petitioning amid taxes before 1787 pardons; sawmills and forges fed trade through endogamous kin.

Genealogists trace Northampton deeds pre-1778 for division allotments, then Westhampton town books linking ridge cabins to church rolls across highland endogamy.

Center Hamlets, Woolen Mills, and Italian Hearths

Westhampton's 19th-century clusters featured Center District farms drawing revivals at First Church, brook woolens with Irish at missions, and Pomeroy-Bartlett lines sustaining Grange halls amid 1938 floods. Apple exports, dairy cheese, and maple anchored economy, rural ties persisting through cemetery societies and migrations.

Proprietors' surveys, mill ledgers, and district minutes capture chain kin from Northampton ports to ridge workshops.

Genealogical Resources and Strategies

Vital repositories:

- Westhampton Town Clerk: Births, marriages, deaths from 1779 incorporation (published to 1850); division records and Shays' petitions.
- Westhampton Historical Society: Manuscripts (Pomeroy, Hale), orchard accounts, church extracts, and family registers.
- Northampton Historical Society Regional Aids: Long Division overlaps, Manhan maps, and mill narratives.

Regional aids: Hampshire County probate at Northampton Registry, FamilySearch vital transcriptions, and MHC surveys for ridge home sites.

Westhampton's ridge-division chronicle—from Nonotuck heights and Pomeroy lots to woolen hearths and apple ridges—equips genealogists with hill-forged sources. Plantation grants, church rolls, and society files unveil "Long Division kin" spanning Pomeroys, Hales, and Bartletts across Manhan summits.

Williamsburg

Williamsburg, Massachusetts, nestles in the western hill country of Hampshire County along the Mill River valley and Crafts Hill ridges, settled from 1735 by Hatfield and Northampton proprietors on Pocumtuck homelands and incorporated 1771 amid rocky pastures, pine forests, and brook mills sustaining Yankee agrarians, subsistence farmers, Irish sawyers, and Italian laborers in hamlets like Williamsburg Center, Haydenville villages, and Hatfield-line outposts. Named for William IV, Prince of Orange, its steep bounds—preserving 1730s grants refined by Hatfield separations (1810)—evolved from frontier precincts through Shays' Rebellion strongholds and 19th-century tanneries and chair shops, blending upland dairying with charcoal trades and flood-prone hollows. From Pocumtuck hunting grounds to Grange halls and rural circuits, Williamsburg's valley-ridge spine traces Indigenous trails via Congregational meetinghouses and district schools.

Pocumtuck Valleys, Hatfield Lots, and Shays' Strongholds

Precolonial Pocumtuck roamed Mill River for trout weirs and deer hunts before epidemics and King Philip's War (1675–76) yielded uplands to Hatfield proprietors; families like Crafts and Wait drew home lots by 1740 around log precinct house, dividing ledges to Bartlett, Phelps, and Porter kin amid garrisons and boundaries. Precinct status yielded church (1762) and burying ground, with Shays' insurgents mustering before 1787 pardons; sawmills and potash kilns fed Northampton trade through endogamous kin.

Genealogists trace Hatfield deeds pre-1771 for valley allotments, then Williamsburg plantation books linking ridge cabins to militia rolls across highland endogamy.

Center Hamlets, Tannery Mills, and Italian Hearths

Williamsburg's 19th-century clusters featured Center District farms drawing revivals at First Church, brook tanneries with Irish at missions (1890s), and Crafts-Bartlett lines sustaining Grange halls amid 1874 floods and 1938 hurricanes. Chair exports and dairy cheese anchored economy, rural ties persisting through Haydenville factories, cemetery societies, and migrations. Proprietors' surveys, mill ledgers, and district minutes capture chain kin from Hatfield ports to valley workshops.

Genealogical Resources and Strategies

Vital repositories:

- Williamsburg Town Clerk: Births, marriages, deaths from 1735 precinct era (published to 1850); Shays' musters and proprietors' grants.
- Williamsburg Historical Society: Manuscripts (Crafts, Wait), tannery accounts, church extracts, and family registers.
- Hatfield Historical Society Regional Aids: Valley overlaps, Mill River maps, and mill narratives.

Regional aids: Hampshire County probate at Northampton Registry, FamilySearch vital transcriptions, and MHC surveys for ridge home sites.

Williamsburg's valley-Shays' chronicle—from Pocumtuck heights and Hatfield logs to tannery flames and dairy ridges—equips genealogists with hill-forged sources. Plantation grants, militia rolls, and society files unveil "Mill River kin" spanning Crafts, Bartletts, and Phelps across Crafts Hill summits.

<u>Worthington</u>

Worthington, Massachusetts, crowns the northeastern highlands of Hampshire County along Westfield River headwaters and Ringville ridges, granted 1762 to Northampton proprietors on Nipmuc homelands, settled from Preston, Connecticut by Nahum Eager and Samuel Clapp, and incorporated 1768 amid rocky pastures, pine forests, and brook mills sustaining frontier loggers, Yankee farmers, Irish sawyers, and Italian laborers in hamlets like Worthington Center, West Worthington villages, and Cummington-line outposts. Named for proprietor John Worthington, its plateau bounds—preserving 1760s lots refined by Middlefield separations (1816)—evolved from Shays' Rebellion outposts through 19th-century potash works, tanneries, and chair shops, blending upland dairying with maple sugar and sheep trades on 1500-foot elevations. From Nipmuc seasonal hunts to Grange halls and rural circuits, Worthington's plateau-ridge spine traces Indigenous trails via Congregational meetinghouses and one-room schools.

Nipmuc Plateaus, Northampton Lots, and Precinct Crossroads

Precolonial Nipmuc frequented Westfield heights for seasonal hunts before French and Indian Wars delayed settlement; proprietors hired Eager as agent, with Clapp's log cabin and Miller's tavern by 1765 amid garrisons, dividing ledges to Bartlett, Phelps, and pioneer kin from Preston. Church organized 1771 with Rev. Jonathan Huntington, yielding meetinghouse and burying ground; Shays' sympathizers rallied amid taxes before 1787 pardons, potash kilns and mills feeding Pittsfield trade through endogamous marriages back to Connecticut.

Genealogists trace Northampton deeds pre-1768 for plateau allotments, then Worthington town books linking ridge cabins to church rolls across highland endogamy.

Center Hamlets, Tannery Mills, and Italian Hearths

Worthington's 19th-century clusters featured Corners farms drawing revivals at churches (West Street to Harvey Road sites), brook tanneries with Irish at missions, and Eager-Clapp lines sustaining Grange halls, Lyceum (1860), and summer resorts amid 1938 floods. Sheep, dairy, and chair exports anchored economy, rural ties persisting through eleven one-room schools and cemetery societies.

Proprietors' surveys, mill ledgers, and town minutes capture chain kin from Preston ports to plateau workshops.

Genealogical Resources and Strategies

Vital repositories:

- Worthington Town Clerk: Births, marriages, deaths from 1768 (published to 1850); proprietors' grants and Shays' petitions.
- Worthington Historical Society: Manuscripts (Eager, Clapp, Huntington), tannery accounts, church extracts, and family registers.
- Cummington Historical Society Regional Aids: Plateau overlaps, Westfield maps, and mill narratives.

Regional aids: Hampshire County probate at Northampton Registry, FamilySearch vital transcriptions, and MHC surveys for ridge home sites.

Worthington's plateau-Shays' chronicle—from Nipmuc heights and Eager logs to tannery flames and dairy summits—equips genealogists with hill-forged sources. Plantation grants, church rolls, and society files unveil "Preston kin" spanning Eagers, Clapps, and Millers across Westfield plateaus.

CENSUS-DESIGNATED PLACES

Belchertown CDP

Belchertown CDP, the densely settled core of Belchertown town in eastern Hampshire County, clusters around Bay Road and Main Street intersections amid Quaboag River lowlands and Cold Spring ridges, emerging from 1731 "Cold Spring Plantation" settlements on Nipmuc homelands—within the 1761-incorporated town named for Jonathan Belcher—and sustaining Yankee agrarians, Irish millworkers, and Polish laborers in the central village from Depot Square to Swift River bridges and Granby-line outskirts. Its compact bounds capture the historic "Belcher's Town" heart—preserving Equivalent Lands grants refined by town expansions—evolving from frontier crossroads through Shays' tax protests and 19th-century carriage shops, blending meadow dairying with apple orchards and Bay Path taverns. From Nipmuc trail camps to Grange halls and modern commons, Belchertown CDP's crossroads spine traces Indigenous paths via precinct meetinghouses (1738) and district schools.

Nipmuc Crossings, Equivalent Lots, and Precinct Centers

Precolonial Nipmuc used Cold Spring fountains and Quaboag intervals for hunts before epidemics and King Philip's War (1675–76) yielded "equivalent lands" to Connecticut proprietors, sold 1716 including to Belcher; Samuel Bascom, Aaron Lyman, and Nathaniel Dwight drew home lots by 1731 around tavern-homes amid garrisons. Precinct church (1738, Rev. Edward Billings) and burying ground yielded 1761 incorporation, with Shays' sympathizers petitioning before 1787; sawmills and potash fed Springfield trade through endogamous kin.

Genealogists trace Equivalent deeds pre-1761 for crossroads allotments, then Belchertown town books linking village cabins to church rolls across valley endogamy.

Depot Square, Carriage Shops, and Polish Hearths

Belchertown CDP's 19th-century core fused Depot farms drawing revivals at First Church, Bay Road carriage works with Irish at missions (1850s), and Bascom-Lyman lines sustaining Grange halls amid 1938 floods. Apple exports and dairy anchored village economy, rural ties persisting through cemetery societies, rail depots (1860s), and migrations.

Proprietors' surveys, shop ledgers, and ward minutes capture chain kin from Springfield ports to crossroads workshops.

Genealogical Resources and Strategies

Vital repositories:

- Belchertown Town Clerk: Births, marriages, deaths from 1731 plantation era (published to 1850); Cold Spring records and incorporations.
- Belchertown Historical Society: Manuscripts (Bascom, Dwight), carriage accounts, church extracts, and family registers.
- Granby Historical Society Regional Aids: Bay Road overlaps, Quaboag maps, and mill narratives.

Regional aids: Hampshire County probate at Northampton Registry, FamilySearch vital transcriptions, and MHC surveys for village sites.

Belchertown CDP's crossroads-precinct chronicle—from Nipmuc springs and Bascom taverns to carriage wheels and dairy meadows—equips genealogists with valley-deep sources. Plantation rolls, vital indexes, and society files unveil "Cold Spring kin" spanning Lymans, Dwights, and Bascoms across Bay Path hearts.

Granby CDP

Granby CDP, the compact village core of Granby town in eastern Hampshire County, centers on the town common and Congregational Church amid Swift River brooks and Quaboag uplands, emerging from 1727 settlements within South Hadley precincts on Norwottuck homelands—within the 1754-incorporated town—and sustaining Yankee agrarians, Irish forgers, and Polish laborers in the historic district from Center Road to West Granby mills and South Hadley-line ridges. Its bounds capture the enduring common heart—preserving New Grant No. 4 lots refined by town divisions—evolving from rocky farmsteads through Shays' courthouse rallies and 19th-century chair factories, blending thin-soil dairying with onion fields and small forges.

From Norwottuck trails to Grange halls and preserved greens, Granby CDP's common spine traces Indigenous paths via 1754 meetinghouse and district schools.

Norwottuck Commons, South Hadley Lots, and Forge Districts

Precolonial Norwottuck planted Swift intervals and fished brooks before epidemics and King Philip's War (1675–76) yielded No. 4 tract to Hadley/South Hadley proprietors; David Root and Samuel Dickinson drew home lots by 1739 around garrisoned common, dividing ridges to Bartlett, Phelps, and Porter families. Precinct independence (1749) yielded Congregational church and burying ground, with Shays' sympathizers shutting Northampton courts before 1787; Forge Pond dams powered ironworks and textiles through endogamous kin.

Genealogists trace South Hadley deeds pre-1754 for common allotments, then Granby town books linking village cabins to church rolls across upland endogamy.

Common Hamlets, Chair Shops, and Polish Hearths

Granby CDP's 19th-century core fused common farms drawing revivals at 1754 church, West Granby forges with Irish at St. Hyacinth's (1880s), and Root-Porter lines sustaining Grange halls amid 1938 floods. Onion rows and chair rockers anchored village economy, rural ties persisting through farm stands and cemetery societies.

Proprietors' surveys, factory ledgers, and common minutes capture chain kin from Hadley ports to Swift workshops.

Genealogical Resources and Strategies

Vital repositories:

- Granby Town Clerk: Births, marriages, deaths from 1727 settlement era (published to 1850); New Grant records and incorporations.
- Granby Historical Society: Manuscripts (Root, Dickinson), chair accounts, church extracts, and family registers in original meetinghouse.
- South Hadley Historical Society Regional Aids: Precinct overlaps, Swift maps, and forge narratives.

Regional aids: Hampshire County probate at Northampton Registry, FamilySearch vital transcriptions, and MHC surveys for common sites.

Granby CDP's common-precinct chronicle—from Norwottuck brooks and Root lots to chair districts and onion plains—equips genealogists with ridge-deep sources. Plantation grants, church rolls, and society files unveil "No. 4 kin" spanning Porters, Phelps, and Bartletts across Quaboag commons.

Hatfield CDP

Hatfield CDP, the historic core of Hatfield town in central Hampshire County, centers on the linear Main Street plain amid Connecticut River meadows and Mill River bluffs, emerging from 1660 "West Side" settlements of Hadley on Pocumtuck homelands—within the 1670-incorporated town—and sustaining Puritan defenders, Yankee agrarians, Irish laborers, and Polish tobacco growers in the preserved district from town common to Capawonk intervals and Whately-line uplands. Its bounds capture the colonial street village heart—preserving 1661 homelots refined by Williamsburg separations (1771)—evolving from garrison stockades through Shays' constitutional rallies and 19th-century onion-tobacco empires, blending alluvial farming with broomcorn and chair shops. From Pocumtuck cornfields to Polish parishes and linear commons, Hatfield CDP's plain spine traces Indigenous trails via 1668 meetinghouse and Hill Cemetery (1669).

Pocumtuck Plains, Hadley Lots, and Garrison Streets

Precolonial Pocumtuck cultivated rich intervals and shad weirs before epidemics and King Philip's War (1675–76) raids yielded meadows to Hadley proprietors; Samuel Partridge, John Allis, and Richard Fellows drew 8-acre homelots by 1663 along stockaded Main Street, dividing fields to Belden, Field, and Hastings families amid three purchases from sachems Umpanchala and Etowonq. Secession from Hadley yielded 1670 incorporation, First Church, and burying ground, with Shays' convention (1786) before pardons; gristmills (1661) and sawmills fed trade through endogamous kin.

Genealogists trace Hadley deeds pre-1670 for plain allotments, then Hatfield town books linking street cabins to garrison rolls across meadow endogamy.

Main Street Wards, Tobacco Sheds, and Polish Hearths

Hatfield CDP's 19th-century core fused common farms drawing revivals at 1683 church, Mill River tobacco fields with Irish at St. Joseph's (1890s), and Allis-Belden lines sustaining Grange halls amid 1938 floods. Broomcorn (1816), onion carts, and beef exports anchored economy, rural ties persisting through Holy Trinity Polish churches and cemetery societies.

Proprietors' surveys, grower ledgers, and street minutes capture chain kin from Thames ports to interval workshops.

Genealogical Resources and Strategies

Vital repositories:

- Hatfield Town Clerk: Births, marriages, deaths from 1660 (published to 1850); garrison rolls, proprietors' grants, and Shays' records.
- Hatfield Historical Society: Manuscripts (Partridge, Allis), tobacco ledgers, church extracts, and family registers.
- Hadley Historical Society Regional Aids: West Side overlaps, Mill River maps, and raid narratives.

Regional aids: Hampshire County probate at Northampton Registry, FamilySearch vital transcriptions, and MHC surveys for plain sites.

Hatfield CDP's plain-garrison chronicle—from Pocumtuck weirs and Partridge lots to tobacco empires and Polish streets—equips genealogists with meadow-deep sources. Plantation rolls, vital indexes, and society files unveil "Capawonk kin" spanning Allis, Beldens, and Hastings across Connecticut intervals.

Huntington CDP

Huntington CDP, the rural village core of Huntington town in western Hampshire County, clusters around Norwich Bridge and Woodruff Road amid Westfield River gorges and Chestnut

Hill ridges, emerging from 1767 "Murrayfield South Precinct" settlements on Nipmuc homelands—within the 1801-incorporated town—and sustaining Yankee loggers, Irish sawyers, and
Italian laborers in the compact center from dam sites to Gossville hamlets and Chester-line outposts. Its bounds capture the precinct heart—preserving Norwich, Connecticut grants refined
by Middlefield divisions (1810)—evolving from Shays' Rebellion musters through 19th-century
tanneries and sawmills, blending steep dairying with charcoal and potash trades. From Nipmuc
trout weirs to Grange halls and flood-scarred roads, Huntington CDP's gorge-bridge spine traces
Indigenous trails via Methodist circuits and district schools.

Nipmuc Gorges, Norwich Lots, and Precinct Bridges

Precolonial Nipmuc traversed Westfield gorges for fishing weirs and bear hunts before epidemics
and King Philip's War (1675–76) yielded uplands to Norwich proprietors; Ebenezer Cornish
and Asahel Gunn drew home lots by 1770 around log bridge and meetinghouse, dividing ledges
to Bagg, Phelps, and Bartlett families amid garrisons. Precinct status (1779) yielded burying
ground and muster fields, with Shays' insurgents drilling before 1787 pardons; river dams powered sawmills and potash through endogamous kin.

Genealogists trace Norwich deeds pre-1801 for gorge allotments, then Huntington town books
linking bridge cabins to militia rolls across highland endogamy.

Bridge Hamlets, Tannery Dams, and Italian Hearths

Huntington CDP's 19th-century core featured Norwich Bridge farms drawing revivals at Union
Church (1810s), gorge tanneries with Irish at St. Anthony's missions (1890s), and Bagg-Phelps
lines sustaining Grange halls amid 1874 floods and 1938 hurricanes. Chair exports and dairy
cheese anchored economy, rural ties that persist through cemetery societies and urban migrations.

Proprietors' surveys, mill ledgers, and precinct minutes capture chain kin from Norwich ports
to gorge workshops.

Genealogical Resources and Strategies

Vital repositories:

- Huntington Town Clerk: Births, marriages, deaths from 1767 precinct era (published to
  1850); Shays' musters and proprietors' grants.
- Huntington Historical Society: Manuscripts (Cornish, Gunn), tannery accounts, church
  extracts, and family registers.
- Chester Historical Society Regional Aids: Murrayfield overlaps, Westfield maps, and mill
  narratives.

Regional aids: Hampshire County probate at Northampton Registry, FamilySearch vital transcriptions, and MHC surveys for gorge home sites.

Huntington CDP's gorge-precinct chronicle—from Nipmuc weirs and Cornish bridges to
tannery flames and dairy heights—equips genealogists with hill-forged sources. Plantation
grants, militia rolls, and society files unveil "Murrayfield South kin" spanning Baggs, Phelps, and
Bartletts across Westfield gorges.

<u>Ware CDP</u>

Ware CDP, the industrial village heart of Ware town in eastern Hampshire County, clusters around the Ware and Swift Rivers' falls at Main Street and the Millyard amid Quaboag lowlands and factory blocks, emerging from 1729 Jacob Olmstead settlement on Nipmuc home-lands—within the 1761-incorporated town—and sustaining Yankee tenants, Irish millworkers, and Polish laborers in the dense core from Nenameseck Park to Church Street wards and Palmer-line outskirts. Its compact bounds capture the "Ware Millyard Historic District"—preserving Equivalent Lands leases refined by town expansions—evolving from John Read's manor leases through Shays' tax protests and 19th-century textile empires via Ware Manufacturing Company (1821), blending river power with cotton spindles and chair shops. From Nipmuc fish weirs to factory villages and Quabbin shadows, Ware CDP's falls-millyard spine traces Indigenous trails via 1748 meetinghouse and district schools.

Nipmuc Weirs, Read Leases, and Precinct Mills

Precolonial Nipmuc built "nenameseck" weirs at river confluences for spring fisheries before epi-demics and King Philip's War (1675–76) yielded Equivalent tracts to Narragansett soldiers; John Read acquired 11,000 acres in 1716, leasing to Olmstead (1729 Great House and mills) and tenants by 1730s around dispersed dams amid garrisons. Precinct (1742) yielded first meetinghouse (1748) and burying ground, with Shays' sympathizers facing debts before 1787; grist and sawmills fed Springfield trade through endogamous kin.

Genealogists trace Equivalent deeds pre-1761 for weir allotments, then Ware town books linking millyard cabins to church rolls across valley endogamy.

Millyard Wards, Textile Blocks, and Polish Hearths

Ware CDP's 19th-century core fused factory blocks drawing revivals at churches (Unitarian 1846, St. Mary's 1855), river mills with Irish laborers, and Olmstead-Read lines sustaining societies amid Quabbin takings (1930s). Cotton production (6,544 spindles by 1837) and Nenameseck Park anchored economy, rural ties persisting through cemetery groups and rail depots.

Proprietors' leases, payroll ledgers, and ward minutes capture chain kin from Boston ports to falls workshops.

Genealogical Resources and Strategies

Vital repositories:

- Ware Town Clerk: Births, marriages, deaths from 1717 settlement era (to 1850 published); Equivalent leases and mill records.
- Ware Historical Society: Manuscripts (Olmstead, Read), textile accounts, church extracts, and family registers.
- Palmer Historical Society Regional Aids: River overlaps, Swift maps, and factory narra-tives.

Regional aids: Hampshire County probate at Northampton Registry, FamilySearch vital tran-scriptions, and MHC surveys for millyard sites.

Ware CDP's weir-millyard chronicle—from Nipmuc traps and Read leases to textile spindles and Polish wards—equips genealogists with factory-deep sources. Plantation rolls, vital indexes, and society files unveil "Equivalent kin" spanning Olmsteads, Reads, and mill hands across Ware River falls.

UNINCORPORATED COMMUNITIES

Amherst Center

Amherst Center, the unincorporated academic core of Amherst town in central Hampshire County, clusters around the Town Common and South Pleasant Street amid Fort River terraces and Holyoke Range foothills, emerging from 1734 "Hadley Third Precinct" settlements on Norwottuck homelands—within the 1759 district and 1775-incorporated town named for General Jeffery Amherst—and sustaining Puritan farmers, Yankee agrarians, Irish laborers, and faculty families in the preserved village from Amherst College to UMass gates and Hadley-line meadows. Its bounds capture the colonial common heart—preserving Outward Commons grants refined by Pelham separations (1759)—evolving from Shays' tax protests through 19th-century colleges (Amherst 1821, Mass Aggie 1863) and mills, blending meadow dairying with book trades and railroad hubs. From Norwottuck cornfields to academic enclaves and Grange echoes, Amherst Center's common-terrace spine traces Indigenous trails via 1730s meetinghouse and district schools.

Norwottuck Commons, Hadley Lots, and Precinct Academics

Precolonial Norwottuck exploited Fort River intervals for shad runs and planting before epidemics and King Philip's War (1675–76) yielded uplands to Hadley proprietors; families like Mattoon and Dickinson drew home lots by 1735 around garrisoned common, dividing terraces to Bartlett, Phelps, and Porter kin amid boundaries. Precinct status yielded First Church and burying ground, with Shays' sympathizers petitioning before 1787; plane mills and potash fed Springfield trade through endogamous kin, later enriched by colleges.

Genealogists trace Hadley deeds pre-1759 for common allotments, then Amherst town books linking village cabins to church rolls across valley endogamy.

Common Wards, College Halls, and Faculty Hearths

Amherst Center's 19th-century core fused common farms drawing revivals at churches, railroad mills with Irish at missions, and Mattoon-Bartlett lines sustaining societies amid 1938 floods. Agricultural societies, creameries, and book exports anchored economy, rural ties persisting through cemetery groups and student migrations.

Proprietors' surveys, college ledgers, and ward minutes capture chain kin from Hadley ports to terrace workshops.

Genealogical Resources and Strategies

Vital repositories:

- Amherst Town Clerk: Births, marriages, deaths from 1734 precinct era (published to 1850); Third Precinct records and incorporations.
- Amherst Historical Society: Manuscripts (Mattoon, Dickinson), college extracts, church rolls, and family registers.

- Hadley Historical Society Regional Aids: Outward Commons overlaps, Fort River maps, and mill narratives.

Regional aids: Hampshire County probate at Northampton Registry, FamilySearch vital transcriptions, and MHC surveys for common sites.

Amherst Center's common-precinct chronicle—from Norwottuck fields and Hadley grants to college spires and dairy meadows—equips genealogists with academic-deep sources. Plantation rolls, vital indexes, and society files unveil "Third Precinct kin" spanning Bartletts, Phelps, and Mattoons across Holyoke terraces.

Cushman

Cushman, an unincorporated mill village in northeastern Amherst, Hampshire County, Massachusetts, clusters around Bridge, Henry, and Pine Streets amid Mill River falls and Connecticut Valley plains, emerging from mid-18th-century grist and lumber mills on Norwottuck homelands—within Amherst's 1759 district—and sustaining Yankee millwrights, Irish operatives, and Polish laborers in the preserved historic district from colonial homes to Cushman brothers' textile blocks and railroad depots. Its triangular bounds capture the water-powered heart—preserving 1738 Nathaniel Kellogg grants refined by town expansions—evolving from wood-frame mills through 19th-century woolens dominance (1835–1930) to quiet village greens, blending river industry with farm ties. From Norwottuck fishing weirs to Greek Revival worker rows and fire-scarred sites, Cushman's falls-triangle spine traces Indigenous trails via Amherst precinct circuits and district schools.

Norwottuck Falls, Amherst Lots, and Mill Clusters

Precolonial Norwottuck harnessed Mill River "great falls" for fisheries before epidemics and King Philip's War (1675–76) yielded rights to Kellogg (1738 gristmill, 1746 lumber); clusters of worker housing arose by late 1700s around six mills, with 1759-era homes like 24 Leverett Road surviving amid garrisons. Textile mills by Cushman brothers (mid-1800s) dominated, yielding Greek Revival, Italianate, and Queen Anne houses through endogamous mill kin; railroad depot centered growth before fires razed factories.

Genealogists trace Amherst deeds pre-1835 for falls allotments, then village censuses linking mill cabins to worker rolls across valley endogamy.

Village Triangle, Woolen Blocks, and Polish Hearths

Cushman's 19th-century core fused Bridge Street farms drawing revivals at Amherst churches, river woolens with Irish at missions, and Kellogg-Cushman lines sustaining societies amid 1938 floods. Housing peak pre-1860 anchored economy, rural ties persisting through National Register district (1992) and cemetery groups.

Proprietors' surveys, mill payrolls, and street minutes capture chain kin from Hadley ports to falls workshops.

Genealogical Resources and Strategies

Vital repositories:

- Amherst Town Clerk: Births, marriages, deaths from 1738 mill era (published to 1850); Cushman village records via town books.
- Amherst Historical Society: Manuscripts (Kellogg, Cushman), textile accounts, church extracts, and family registers.
- Cushman Village Historic District Aids: Mill rights, housing plats, and worker narratives.

Regional aids: Hampshire County probate at Northampton Registry, FamilySearch Amherst transcriptions, and MHC surveys for falls sites.

Cushman's falls-mill chronicle—from Norwottuck weirs and Kellogg dams to Cushman spindles and Greek Revival rows—equips genealogists with village-deep sources. Plantation rolls, vital indexes, and district files unveil "Mill River kin" spanning Kelloggs, Cushmans, and operatives across Amherst plains.

Florence

Florence, an unincorporated utopian village in northwestern Northampton, Hampshire County, Massachusetts, clusters around Nonotuck Street and Park Drive amid Mill River meadows and West Farms ridges, emerging from 1657 "Broughton's Meadow" grants on Norwottuck homelands—within Northampton town—and sustaining radical reformers, silk weavers, African American fugitives, and abolitionist families in the preserved district from David Ruggles Center to Nonotuck Silk Company blocks and Free Congregational church. Its bounds capture the Northampton Association heart (1842–1846)—preserving communal lots refined by post-utopian mills—evolving from silk experiments through Frederick Douglass speeches and Sojourner Truth residencies to 19th-century cooperative factories, blending meadow agriculture with radical equality and anti-slavery trades. From Norwottuck planting fields to abolitionist enclaves and silk spindles, Florence's meadow-Nonotuck spine traces Indigenous trails via communal halls and district schools.

Norwottuck Meadows, Northampton Grants, and Utopian Commons

Precolonial Norwottuck sowed corn in West Farms intervals before epidemics and King Philip's War (1675–76) yielded meadows to Northampton proprietors; John Broughton claimed 1657 lots, with later silk ventures by Conant (1840s) yielding utopian purchase by Northampton Association of Education and Industry, drawing 120 members including Douglass, Truth, Garrison, and Ruggles amid shared mills and equal votes. Dissolution (1846) birthed Nonotuck Silk Company under Samuel Hill, sustaining Free Congregational Society (1863) and interracial community through endogamous reform kin.

Genealogists trace Northampton deeds pre-1842 for meadow allotments, then Florence censuses linking communal cabins to association rolls across valley radicalism.

Village Wards, Silk Mills, and Abolitionist Hearths

Florence's 19th-century core fused meadow farms drawing lectures at communal halls, river silk factories with fugitives at missions, and Hill-Ruggles lines sustaining societies amid 1938 floods. Cooperative spindles and kindergarten (1870s) anchored economy, rural ties persisting through historic districts and cemetery groups.

Proprietors' surveys, mill payrolls, and association minutes capture chain kin from Boston ports to meadow workshops.

Genealogical Resources and Strategies

Vital repositories:

- Northampton City Clerk: Births, marriages, deaths from 1657 West Farms era (published to 1850); Florence village records via city books.
- Florence History Project/David Ruggles Center: Manuscripts (Hill, Ruggles), association accounts, church extracts, and family registers.
- Northampton Historical Society Regional Aids: Broughton overlaps, Mill River maps, and utopian narratives.

Regional aids: Hampshire County probate at Northampton Registry, FamilySearch Northampton transcriptions, and MHC surveys for meadow sites.

Florence's meadow-utopian chronicle—from Norwottuck fields and Broughton grants to association equality and silk cooperatives—equips genealogists with reform-deep sources. Plantation rolls, vital indexes, and project files unveil "Nonotuck kin" spanning Hills, Ruggles, and fugitives across West Farms meadows.

Haydenville

Haydenville, an unincorporated mill village in western Williamsburg, Hampshire County, Massachusetts, clusters along Main Street (Route 9) and High Street amid Mill River gorges and Crafts Hill slopes, emerging from 1808 factory dams on Pocumtuck homelands—within Williamsburg's 1771 town—and sustaining Hayden brothers' machinists, Irish operatives, and Polish laborers in the preserved historic district from Brass Works blocks to Greek Revival mansions and Congregational church. Its linear bounds capture the flood-scarred heart—preserving 1809 power loom sites refined by 1874 rebuilds—evolving from broadcloth looms through button innovations and brass plumbing to cotton sheeting, blending river power with family-dominated trades until 1950s decline. From Pocumtuck trout weirs to Victorian worker rows and reservoir ruins, Haydenville's gorge-Main spine traces Indigenous trails via precinct circuits and district schools.

Pocumtuck Gorges, Williamsburg Lots, and Factory Clusters

Precolonial Pocumtuck fished Mill River rapids before epidemics and King Philip's War (1675–76) yielded valleys to Hatfield/Williamsburg proprietors; Daniel and David Hayden (uncles) dammed 1809 for looms with Seth Thompson, passing to nephews Joel and Josiah by 1822 for power machinery amid garrisons. Buttons (1831), flexible shanks with Williston, and brassworks (1851) dominated, yielding Greek Revival homes, church (1852), and library (1900) through endogamous kin; 1874 flood razed brass factory (140 deaths), rebuilt 1875 as Haydenville Manufacturing.

Genealogists trace Williamsburg deeds pre-1808 for gorge allotments, then Hayden censuses linking factory cabins to payroll rolls across valley endogamy.

Main Street Wards, Brass Blocks, and Polish Hearths

Haydenville's 19th-century core fused High Street housing drawing revivals at Congregational church, river brassworks with Irish at missions, and Hayden lines sustaining cemetery (1847), bank, and Masonic lodge amid repeated floods. Plumbing fittings and cotton (4000 spindles) anchored economy, rural ties persisting through National Register district (1976) and worker societies.

Proprietors' surveys, mill ledgers, and flood minutes capture chain kin from Northampton ports to gorge workshops.

Genealogical Resources and Strategies

Vital repositories:

- Williamsburg Town Clerk: Births, marriages, deaths from 1808 mill era (published to 1850); Haydenville factory records via town books.
- Williamsburg Historical Society: Manuscripts (Joel/Josiah Hayden), brass accounts, church extracts, and family registers.
- Haydenville Historic District Aids: Dam plats, payrolls, and flood narratives.

Regional aids: Hampshire County probate at Northampton Registry, FamilySearch Williamsburg transcriptions, and MHC surveys for gorge sites.

Haydenville's gorge-factory chronicle—from Pocumtuck weirs and Hayden dams to brass empires and flood rebirths—equips genealogists with mill-deep sources. Plantation rolls, vital indexes, and society files unveil "Brass Works kin" spanning Haydens, Thompsons, and operatives across Mill River valleys.

Leeds

Leeds, an unincorporated mill village in northwestern Northampton, Hampshire County, Massachusetts, clusters around Main and Mulberry Streets amid Mill River falls and West Farms ridges, emerging from 1813 woolen mills at "Shepherd's Hollow" on Norwottuck homelands—within Northampton town—and sustaining Colonel James Shepherd's broadcloth weavers, Irish operatives, and Polish laborers in the historic core from Nonotuck Silk blocks to Cook's Dam and Hotel Bridge wards. Its bounds capture the flood-resilient heart—preserving 1814 power looms refined by 1874 rebuilds—evolving from Shepherd patents (1816 power loom) through silk dominance and button factories to emery wheels, blending river industry with utopian echoes from nearby Florence. From Norwottuck planting fields to Victorian worker rows and silted dams, Leeds' falls-Main spine traces Indigenous trails via Northampton precinct circuits and district schools.

Norwottuck Falls, Northampton Grants, and Woolen Clusters

Precolonial Norwottuck harnessed Mill River drops for fisheries before epidemics and King Philip's War (1675–76) yielded meadows to Northampton proprietors; Sidney Brewster built 1813 woolen mill, sold to Cook brothers (1820–27 failure), then Colonel Shepherd (1827) who patented power looms amid garrisons. Nonotuck Silk (1852) and George Warner buttons (1871) dominated, yielding Greek Revival homes and 1881 Hotel Bridge through endogamous mill kin; 1874 flood spared core but ravaged upstream.

Genealogists trace Northampton deeds pre-1813 for falls allotments, then Leeds censuses linking mill cabins to payroll rolls across valley endogamy.

Main Street Wards, Silk Blocks, and Polish Hearths

Leeds' 19th-century core fused Mulberry farms drawing revivals at churches, river silk with Irish at missions, and Shepherd-Hill lines sustaining Leeds Hotel (1883), library, and 1950 centennial amid repeated floods. Machine twist thread triumphs (1876 Centennial) anchored economy, rural ties persisting through apartments and civic associations.

Proprietors' surveys, mill ledgers, and flood minutes capture chain kin from Boston ports to falls workshops.

Genealogical Resources and Strategies

Vital repositories:

- Northampton City Clerk: Births, marriages, deaths from 1813 mill era (published to 1850); Leeds village records via city books.
- Northampton Historical Society: Manuscripts (Shepherd, Warner), silk accounts, church extracts, and family registers.
- Leeds Civic Association Aids: Dam plats, payrolls, and flood narratives.

Regional aids: Hampshire County probate at Northampton Registry, FamilySearch Northampton transcriptions, and MHC surveys for falls sites.

Leeds' falls-woolen chronicle—from Norwottuck weirs and Shepherd looms to Nonotuck silk and button empires—equips genealogists with mill-deep sources. Plantation rolls, vital indexes, and society files unveil "Shepherd's Hollow kin" spanning Shepherds, Warners, and operatives across Mill River gorges.

Mount Tom

Mount Tom, an unincorporated mountaintop community and state reservation in eastern Holyoke and western Easthampton, Hampshire County, Massachusetts, crowns the traprock summit of Mount Tom (1,202 feet) amid the Mount Tom Range ridges and Connecticut Valley overlooks, emerging from 1897 trolley parks and hotels on Pocumtuck homelands—within Holyoke town—and sustaining resort visitors, Yankee excursionists, Irish laborers, and conservationists in the preserved park from Eyrie House ruins to Mountain Park amusements and CCC trails. Its elevated bounds capture the reservation heart—preserving 1902 state lands refined by park expansions—evolving from Native hunting grounds through 19th-century tourism booms to Civilian Conservation Corps (1933) structures, blending panoramic views with logging drive endpoints and amusement rides. From Pocumtuck basalt quarries to summit houses and trolley relics, Mount Tom's ridge-summit spine traces Indigenous trails via reservation circuits and observation towers.

Pocumtuck Traps, Springfield Surveys, and Trolley Resorts

Precolonial Pocumtuck quarried basalt tools and hunted deer across Metacomet ledges before epidemics and King Philip's War (1675–76) raids yielded heights to Springfield proprietors; Rowland Thomas surveyed 1660s, naming peak after himself opposite Elizur Holyoke's mount amid valley farms. Holyoke Street Railway built Mount Tom Railroad (1897) and Eyrie House, with Mount Tom Summit House (1897–1929 fires) drawing President McKinley; logging drives ended at falls below through seasonal kin networks.

Genealogists trace Springfield deeds pre-1897 for ledge allotments, then Holyoke censuses linking resort cabins to visitor rolls across valley tourism.

Summit Wards, Amusement Peaks, and CCC Hearths

Mount Tom's late-19th-century core fused summit hotels drawing crowds at Mountain Park (trolley park to 1988 closure), rail inclines with Irish at missions, and reservation lines sustaining picnic groves amid 1946 B-17 crash. Rides and vistas anchored economy, rural ties persisting through state park trails and observation platforms.

Proprietors' surveys, park ledgers, and reservation minutes capture chain kin from Holyoke ports to summit pavilions.

Genealogical Resources and Strategies

Vital repositories:

- Holyoke City Clerk: Births, marriages, deaths from 1897 park era; Mount Tom resort records via city books.
- Easthampton Historical Society: Manuscripts (Thomas surveys), hotel accounts, CCC extracts, and family registers.
- Mount Tom State Reservation Aids: Rail plats, visitor logs, and tourism narratives.

Regional aids: Hampshire County probate at Northampton Registry, FamilySearch Holyoke transcriptions, and MHC surveys for summit sites.

Mount Tom's traprock-resort chronicle—from Pocumtuck quarries and Thomas surveys to Eyrie towers and CCC paths—equips genealogists with height-deep sources. Plantation rolls, vital indexes, and park files unveil "Summit kin" spanning railwaymen, hoteliers, and excursionists across Metacomet ridges.

North Amherst

North Amherst, an unincorporated mill village in northern Amherst, Hampshire County, Massachusetts, centers on the crossroads of North Pleasant, Meadow, Pine Streets, Sunderland, and Montague Roads amid Mill River ponds and Fort River terraces, emerging from 1739 Hadley "Third Precinct" surveys on Norwottuck homelands—within Amherst's 1759 district—and sustaining Yankee gristwrights, Irish operatives, Lithuanian laborers, and paper makers in the preserved historic district from Factory Hollow to Cushman Commons and Puffer's Pond. Its crossroads bounds capture the agro-industrial heart—preserving 1727 grist mills refined by 19th-century textile booms—evolving from agrarian staples through cotton, woolens, and rag paper factories to ice houses and planing mills, blending water power with "Dirty Hands District" immigrant enclaves. From Norwottuck cornfields to Lithuanian rows and conservation lands, North Amherst's river-crossroads spine traces Indigenous trails via precinct meetinghouses and one-room schools.

Norwottuck Ponds, Hadley Lots, and Factory Hollows

Precolonial Norwottuck planted Mill River intervals before epidemics and King Philip's War (1675–76) yielded uplands to Hadley proprietors; grist mills arose 1727 at "great falls," with Daniel Rowe's 1798 rag paper, Ebenezer Dickinson's 1809 cotton factory at Factory Hollow, and Ebenezer Ingram's woolens amid garrisoned farms. Cushman brothers' 1835 paper "Red Mill," Puffer grist (1844–1934), and Hills Palm Hat (1856) dominated through Civil War, yielding Greek Revival homes and Lithuanian "Little Lithuania" via endogamous mill kin; Cowls sawmill pioneered U.S. electric power.

Genealogists trace Hadley deeds pre-1759 for pond allotments, then Amherst censuses linking hollow cabins to payroll rolls across valley industry.

Crossroads Wards, Paper Blocks, and Lithuanian Hearths

North Amherst's 19th-century core fused Meadow Street farms drawing revivals at district churches, river paper mills with Irish/Lithuanian at missions, and Dickinson-Cushman lines sustaining Puffer ice house (1910s–1930s) amid floods. Planing mills and lumber anchored economy, rural ties persisting through 1960s conservation and National Register district (1991).

Proprietors' surveys, mill ledgers, and ward minutes capture chain kin from Hadley ports to pond workshops.

Genealogical Resources and Strategies

Vital repositories:

- Amherst Town Clerk: Births, marriages, deaths from 1739 precinct era (published to 1850); Factory Hollow records via town books.
- Amherst Historical Society: Manuscripts (Dickinson, Cushman, Puffer), paper accounts, church extracts, and family registers.
- North Amherst Aids: Mill Hollow plats, payrolls, and industrial narratives.

Regional aids: Hampshire County probate at Northampton Registry, FamilySearch Amherst transcriptions, and MHC surveys for river sites.

North Amherst's pond-factory chronicle—from Norwottuck falls and Rowe paper to Cushman rags and Puffer ice—equips genealogists with mill-deep sources. Plantation rolls, vital indexes, and society files unveil "Factory Hollow kin" spanning Dickinsons, Cushmans, and Lithuanians across Mill River ponds.

Ringville

Ringville, an unincorporated mill hamlet in southern Worthington, Hampshire County, Massachusetts, clusters along Huntington Road (Route 112) and Little River brooks amid Westfield River headwater ridges and plateau pastures, emerging from mid-19th-century woodworking shops on Nipmuc homelands—within Worthington's 1768 town—and sustaining Ring brothers' wagon makers, Yankee farmers, Irish sawyers, and Italian laborers in the rural core from mill dams to Witt Hill Cemetery and Converse flats. Its streamside bounds capture the early industrial heart—preserving 1830s slat curtains and children's carriages refined by fire rebuilds—evolving from upland subsistence through national wagon exports to basket shops and creameries, blending brook power with highland dairying. From Nipmuc seasonal ovens to Gothic school ruins and quiet greens, Ringville's river-road spine traces Indigenous trails via Worthington precinct circuits and district schools.

Nipmuc Brooks, Worthington Lots, and Wagon Clusters
Precolonial Nipmuc encamped at Little River ovens and Westfield branches before epidemics and King Philip's War (1675–76) yielded plateaus to Northampton proprietors; Elkanah and Thomas Ring settled 1830s for window slats, expanding to children's wagons and sleds shipped nation-wide amid 1768 town farms. 1858 fire razed operations (50 employees), rebuilt briefly before Knightville shift, yielding creamery (1894) and basket shops through endogamous kin; Gothic Revival school (ca. 1860, burned) anchored hamlet.

Genealogists trace Worthington deeds pre-1830 for brook allotments, then Ringville censuses linking mill cabins to payroll rolls across highland endogamy.

Huntington Road Wards, Basket Dams, and Italian Hearths
Ringville's 19th-century core fused road farms drawing revivals at Worthington churches, brook wagons with Irish at missions, and Ring-Cole lines sustaining cemetery (1866, NRHP) amid plateau isolation. Sleds, baskets, and dairy anchored economy, rural ties persisting through ruins and family plots.
Proprietors' surveys, shop ledgers, and town minutes capture chain kin from Pittsfield ports to stream workshops.

Genealogical Resources and Strategies
Vital repositories:

- Worthington Town Clerk: Births, marriages, deaths from 1830s mill era (published to 1850); Ringville records via town books.
- Worthington Historical Society: Manuscripts (Ring brothers, Cole), wagon accounts, church extracts, and family registers.
- Ringville Cemetery Aids: Mill plats, burial rolls, and industrial narratives.

Regional aids: Hampshire County probate at Northampton Registry, FamilySearch Worthington transcriptions, and MHC surveys for brook sites.

Ringville's brook-wagon chronicle—from Nipmuc ovens and Ring slats to sled empires and creamery hearths—equips genealogists with plateau-deep sources. Plantation rolls, vital indexes, and society files unveil "Little River kin" spanning Rings, Coles, and mill hands across Worthington ridges.

South Amherst
South Amherst, an unincorporated rural village in southern Amherst, Hampshire County, Massachusetts, centers on the South Common and Snell Street amid Holyoke Range foothills and Fort River meadows, emerging from 1734 Hadley "Third Precinct" divisions on Norwottuck home-lands—within Amherst's 1759 district—and sustaining Puritan farmers, Yankee agrarians, Irish laborers, and orchardists in the preserved historic district from Fiddler's Green tavern to Redington Ridge farms and East Street wards. Its common bounds capture the agrarian heart—pre-

serving Outward Commons lots refined by 1818 parish splits—evolving from subsistence grain through Shays' tax rallies and 19th-century apple empires to dairying, blending thin soils with tobacco patches and chair shops. From Norwottuck planting terraces to Grange halls and conserved ridges, South Amherst's common-foothill spine traces Indigenous trails via precinct meetinghouses and district schools.

Norwottuck Ridges, Hadley Lots, and Parish Commons

Precolonial Norwottuck sowed corn on south-facing slopes before epidemics and King Philip's War (1675–76) yielded uplands to Hadley proprietors; Eliphalet Redington and Dickinson kin drew home lots by 1740 around common tavern, dividing ridges to Bartlett, Phelps, and Porter families amid garrisons. Precinct church and burying ground yielded 1818 South Parish independence, with Shays' sympathizers petitioning before 1787; gristmills and potash fed Northampton trade through endogamous kin.

Genealogists trace Hadley deeds pre-1759 for ridge allotments, then Amherst town books linking common cabins to parish rolls across foothill endogamy.

Common Wards, Apple Orchards, and Irish Hearths

South Amherst's 19th-century core fused Snell Street farms drawing revivals at South Church, ridge orchards with Irish at missions, and Redington-Bartlett lines sustaining Grange halls amid 1938 floods. Tobacco sheds and cider mills anchored economy, rural ties persisting through cemetery societies and conservation easements.

Proprietors' surveys, grower ledgers, and parish minutes capture chain kin from Hadley ports to ridge workshops.

Genealogical Resources and Strategies

Vital repositories:

- Amherst Town Clerk: Births, marriages, deaths from 1734 precinct era (published to 1850); South Parish records and incorporations.
- Amherst Historical Society: Manuscripts (Redington, Dickinson), orchard accounts, church extracts, and family registers.
- South Amherst Common Aids: Ridge overlaps, Fort River maps, and farm narratives.

Regional aids: Hampshire County probate at Northampton Registry, FamilySearch Amherst transcriptions, and MHC surveys for common sites.

South Amherst's ridge-parish chronicle—from Norwottuck terraces and Redington lots to apple empires and Grange ridges—equips genealogists with foothill-deep sources. Plantation rolls, vital indexes, and society files unveil "Fiddler's Green kin" spanning Redingtons, Bartletts, and Phelps across Holyoke slopes.

South Hadley Falls

South Hadley Falls, an unincorporated industrial village in northern South Hadley, Hampshire County, Massachusetts, clusters along Main and North Main Streets amid Connecticut River falls and canal remnants on Pocumtuck homelands—within South Hadley's 1775 town—and sustaining Yankee millwrights, Irish operatives, and Polish paper workers in the dense core from Beachgrounds to Old Firehouse Museum and Carew mill blocks. Its falls bounds capture the canal-era heart—preserving 1795 inclined plane sites refined by 1849 dams—evolving from 1727 saw/grist mills through paper empires (Howard-Lathrop, Ames, Carew 1848) to hydro relics, blending water power with log drives and flatboat trades. From Pocumtuck shad weirs to duplex rows and flood-scarred quays, South Hadley Falls' canal-falls spine traces Indigenous trails via Methodist circuits (1832) and district schools.

Pocumtuck Falls, Hadley Grants, and Canal Clusters

Precolonial Pocumtuck fished 57-foot drops before epidemics and King Philip's War (1675–76) yielded terraces to Hadley proprietors; three sawmills, two grists, fulling mill by 1771, with Chapin canal (1795) bypassing falls via inclined plane amid garrisons. Locks (1805), Carew/Glasgow paper (1848 post-fires), and Holyoke bridge (1872) drew immigrants, yielding duplexes and taverns through endogamous mill kin; railroads closed canal 1862.

Genealogists trace Hadley deeds pre-1775 for falls allotments, then South Hadley books linking quay cabins to payroll rolls across valley industry.

Main Street Wards, Paper Dams, and Polish Hearths

South Hadley Falls' 19th-century core fused North Main mills drawing revivals at Congregational/Methodist churches, river paper with Irish at missions, and Chapin-Carew lines sustaining firehouse (1888), library, and gardens amid 1955 dam breaks. Freight and hydro anchored economy, rural ties persisting through memorials and MHC surveys.

Proprietors' surveys, mill ledgers, and ward minutes capture chain kin from Boston ports to falls workshops.

Genealogical Resources and Strategies

Vital repositories:

- South Hadley Town Clerk: Births, marriages, deaths from 1727 mill era (published to 1850); canal records and incorporations.
- South Hadley Historical Society: Manuscripts (Chapin, Carew), paper accounts, church extracts, and family registers.
- Holyoke Historical Aids: Falls overlaps, dam maps, and mill narratives.

Regional aids: Hampshire County probate at Northampton Registry, FamilySearch South Hadley transcriptions, and MHC surveys for canal sites.

South Hadley Falls' canal-paper chronicle—from Pocumtuck drops and Chapin planes to Carew sheets and hydro bladders—equips genealogists with falls-deep sources. Plantation rolls, vital indexes, and society files unveil "Canal Village kin" spanning Chapins, Carews, and operatives across Connecticut quays.

DEFUNCT AND ABANDONED TOWNS

Dana

Dana, a defunct agricultural town in central Hampshire County, Massachusetts (ceded to Petersham upon disincorporation), spanned Swift River valleys and Dana Common amid Quaboag foothills and reservoir basins, incorporated 1801 from Petersham, Greenwich, and Hardwick on Nipmuc homelands before eminent domain takings for Quabbin Reservoir (1938 disincorporation) razed homes, farms, and mills sustaining Yankee agrarians, Irish laborers, and Polish hands in villages from North Dana to Doubleday and town common. Named for statesman Francis Dana, its valley bounds—preserving 1763 settlements refined by 19th-century dairying—evolved from subsistence grain through Shays' tax echoes and cheese factories to forced evacuations, blending thin pastures with potash trades until state clearing for Boston water. From Nipmuc hunting camps to submerged cellars and annual reunions, Dana's common-valley spine traces Indigenous trails via Congregational meetinghouses (1840s) and district schools.

Nipmuc Valleys, Petersham Lots, and Common Farms

Precolonial Nipmuc roamed Swift tributaries for seasonal hunts before epidemics and King Philip's War (1675–76) yielded uplands to Petersham proprietors; settlers drew home lots by 1763 around common tavern, dividing meadows to Vaughn, Carter, and pioneer families amid garrisons. Incorporation yielded Congregational church, schoolhouse (Center School), and burying ground (exhumed to Quabbin Cemetery), with population peaking at 876 (1860) through endogamous kin; poor farm and cheese exports fed Worcester trade.

Genealogists trace Petersham deeds pre-1801 for valley allotments, then Dana town books linking common cabins to census rolls across hill endogamy.

Common Wards, Cheese Sheds, and Polish Hearths

Dana's 19th-century core fused common farms drawing revivals at 1840s church, valley dairies with Irish at missions, and Vaughn-Carter lines sustaining Grange halls and cannon pranks amid rural isolation. Beef, cheese, and maple anchored economy, ties persisting through 1938 reunions despite razing.

Proprietors' surveys, farm ledgers, and town minutes capture chain kin from Worcester ports to Swift workshops.

Disincorporation and the Quabbin Project

Dana's annihilation stemmed from the Metropolitan District Water Supply Commission's 1926–1938 Quabbin Reservoir construction to supply Boston's growing metropolis, condemning 62.5 square miles across four Swift River Valley towns (Dana, Enfield, Greenwich, Prescott) via eminent domain takings that displaced 2,500 residents by April 27, 1938 deadline. State agents razed 7,500 structures including Dana Common's 1895 town hall, 1844 church, and 150 farms after failed relocation bids; graves exhumed to Quabbin Park Cemetery, cellars dynamited, and lands flooded by 1946 creating 39-square-mile basin holding 412 billion gallons. Annual Dana reunions preserve memories through photos and artifacts, with hiking trails exposing foundations during low water; genealogists access Metro Commission records for takings lists.

Genealogical Resources and Strategies

Vital repositories:

- Petersham Town Clerk (post-1938): Births, marriages, deaths from 1763 settlement era (published to 1850); Dana records transferred upon disincorporation.

- Dana Reunion Association: Manuscripts (Vaughn, Carter), poor farm accounts, church extracts, and family registers.
- Quabbin Reservation Aids: Common overlaps, Swift maps, and evacuation narratives.

Regional aids: Worcester/Hampshire County probate at Northampton Registry, FamilySearch Petersham transcriptions, and DCR surveys for cellar sites.

Dana's valley-Quabbin chronicle—from Nipmuc camps and Vaughn commons to cheese hearths and submerged stones—equips genealogists with drowned-deep sources. Plantation rolls, vital indexes, and reunion files unveil "Swift River kin" spanning Carters, Vaughns, and farmers across reservoir basins.

Enfield

Enfield, a defunct manufacturing town in southern Hampshire County, Massachusetts (annexed to Belchertown, New Salem, Pelham, and Ware upon disincorporation), straddled the Swift River's east-west branches amid Quaboag lowlands and Greenwich ridges, incorporated 1816 from Greenwich and Belchertown on Nipmuc homelands before Quabbin Reservoir takings (1938 disincorporation) submerged mills, villages, and farms sustaining Yankee agrarians, Irish operatives, and Polish laborers in nodes from Greenwich Road to Coldbrook Springs and town common. Named for early settler Robert Field, its riverine bounds—preserving 1787 South Parish grants refined by 19th-century factories—evolved from agrarian parishes through Shays' echoes and textile booms to forced evacuations, blending intervals with scythe forges and paper trades until state flooding for Boston water. From Nipmuc fishing camps to Farewell Ball ruins and annual reunions, Enfield's confluence-common spine traces Indigenous trails via Congregational meetinghouses (1818) and district schools.

Nipmuc Confluences, Greenwich Lots, and Parish Mills

Precolonial Nipmuc fished Swift forks before epidemics and King Philip's War (1675–76) yielded lowlands to Greenwich proprietors; South Parish settlers drew home lots by 1787 around common tavern, dividing intervals to Field, Gilbert, and pioneer families amid garrisons. Incorporation yielded Congregational church, town hall, and burying ground (exhumed to Quabbin Cemetery), with population peaking at 1,209 (1837) through endogamous kin; scythe works, woolens, and paper mills fed Springfield trade.

Genealogists trace Greenwich deeds pre-1816 for confluence allotments, then Enfield town books linking common cabins to selectmen rolls across valley endogamy.

Common Wards, Forge Sheds, and Polish Hearths

Enfield's 19th-century core fused common farms drawing revivals at 1818 church, river forges with Irish at missions, and Field-Gilbert lines sustaining Grange halls, library, and Masonic lodge amid rural prosperity. Textiles, scythes, and maple anchored economy, ties persisted through 1938 Farewell Ball despite razing.

Proprietors' surveys, mill ledgers, and town minutes capture chain kin from Worcester ports to Swift workshops.

Disincorporation and the Quabbin Project

Enfield's demise mirrored Dana's via Metropolitan District Water Supply Commission's

1926–1938 Quabbin construction, condemning Swift Valley towns through eminent domain that displaced 2,500 across four municipalities by April 28, 1938, midnight deadline. State crews demolished 7,500 structures including Enfield's town hall and mills after failed buyouts; graves relocated, lands cleared, and basin filled 1939–1946 creating 39-square-mile reservoir with 412 billion gallons via Winsor Dam and Goodnough Dike. Reunions preserve artifacts, with Gate 43 trails revealing cellars in low water; records held at UMass archives detail takings.

Genealogical Resources and Strategies

Vital repositories:

- Belchertown/Pelham Town Clerks (post-1938): Births, marriages, deaths from 1787 parish era (published to 1850); Enfield records redistributed.
- Enfield Collection (UMass SCUA): Manuscripts (Field, Gilbert), selectmen accounts, church extracts, and family registers.
- Quabbin Reservation Aids: Confluence overlaps, Swift maps, and evacuation narratives.

Regional aids: Hampshire County probate at Northampton Registry, FamilySearch Greenwich transcriptions, and DCR surveys for foundation sites.

Enfield's confluence-Quabbin chronicle—from Nipmuc forks and Field parishes to forge hearths and submerged stones—equips genealogists with drowned-deep sources. Plantation rolls, vital indexes, and archive files unveil "Swift Branch kin" spanning Fields, Gilberts, and mill hands across reservoir lowlands.

Greenwich

Greenwich, a defunct manufacturing and agricultural town in eastern Hampshire County, Massachusetts (annexed to Ware, Enfield, and Belchertown upon disincorporation), spanned the Swift River's middle valley amid Quaboag lowlands and Mount Lizzie ridges, incorporated 1754 from Quaboag Plantation on Nipmuc homelands before Quabbin Reservoir takings (1938 disincorporation) submerged mills, villages, and farms sustaining Yankee agrarians, Irish operatives, and Polish scythe makers in nodes from Greenwich Village to North Prescott and Enfield-line hamlets. Named for Greenwich, Connecticut, its riverine bounds—preserving 1730s grants refined by 19th-century forges—evolved from frontier parishes through Shays' strongholds and iron works to forced evacuations, blending intervals with tanneries and chair shops until state flooding for Boston water. From Nipmuc weirs to cellar holes and annual reunions, Greenwich's valley-ridge spine traces Indigenous trails via Congregational meetinghouses (1761) and district schools.

Nipmuc Intervals, Quaboag Lots, and Parish Forges

Precolonial Nipmuc fished Swift intervals before epidemics and King Philip's War (1675–76) yielded lowlands to Quaboag proprietors; settlers drew home lots by 1736 around village tavern, dividing meadows to Taylor, Bowker, and pioneer families amid garrisons. Incorporation yielded First Church, town hall, and burying ground (exhumed to Quabbin Cemetery), with population peaking at 1,001 (1830) through endogamous kin; Greenwich Iron Works (1795), scythe factories, and tanneries fed Springfield trade.

Genealogists trace Quaboag deeds pre-1754 for valley allotments, then Greenwich town books linking village cabins to census rolls across lowland endogamy.

Village Wards, Scythe Sheds, and Polish Hearths

Greenwich's 19th-century core fused village farms drawing revivals at 1761 church, river forges with Irish at missions, and Taylor-Bowker lines sustaining Grange halls, academy, and library amid rural prosperity. Iron castings, chairs, and dairy anchored economy, ties persisting through 1938 reunions despite demolitions.

Proprietors' surveys, forge ledgers, and town minutes capture chain kin from Worcester ports to Swift workshops.

Disincorporation and the Quabbin Project

Greenwich shared the Swift Valley fate via Metropolitan District Water Supply Commission's 1926–1938 Quabbin construction, with eminent domain condemning lands across four towns displacing 2,500 by April 28, 1938, deadline. State demolition razed 7,500 structures including Greenwich Village's mills and homes after resisted buyouts; graves relocated; basins cleared for 1939–1946 filling creating 39-square-mile, 412-billion-gallon reservoir via Winsor Dam. Gate 8 trails expose foundations in drawdowns; UMass archives hold takings documents for genealogical pursuit.

Genealogical Resources and Strategies

Vital repositories:

- Ware Town Clerk (post-1938): Births, marriages, deaths from 1730s plantation era (published to 1850); Greenwich records transferred.
- Greenwich Collection (UMass SCUA): Manuscripts (Taylor, Bowker), iron accounts, church extracts, and family registers.
- Quabbin Reservation Aids: Valley overlaps, Swift maps, and evacuation narratives.

Regional aids: Hampshire County probate at Northampton Registry, FamilySearch Quaboag transcriptions, and DCR surveys for cellar sites.

Greenwich's valley-Quabbin chronicle—from Nipmuc intervals and Taylor forges to scythe empires and submerged ridges—equips genealogists with drowned-deep sources. Plantation rolls, vital indexes, and archive files unveil "Quaboag kin" spanning Taylors, Bowkers, and mill hands across reservoir meadows.

Prescott

Prescott, a defunct hilltown in northern Hampshire County, Massachusetts (annexed to Pelham and New Salem upon disincorporation), crowned the Quaboag River headwaters amid Mounts Toby and Moose Hill ridges, incorporated 1822 from Pelham, New Salem, and Amherst on Nipmuc homelands before Quabbin Reservoir takings (1938 disincorporation) submerged farms, mills, and villages sustaining Yankee agrarians, Irish laborers, and Polish hands in hamlets from Prescott Center to North Prescott and Dana-line outposts. Named for Revolutionary colonel Oliver Prescott, its upland bounds—preserving 1760s grants refined by 19th-century dairying—evolved from Shays' outposts through potash works and chair shops to forced evacuations, blending rocky pastures with maple trades until state clearing for Boston water. From Nipmuc hunting ridges to cellar holes and annual reunions, Prescott's plateau-Moose spine traces Indigenous trails via Congregational meetinghouses (1823) and district schools.

Nipmuc Plateaus, Pelham Lots, and Ridge Farms

Precolonial Nipmuc traversed Quaboag heights for deer hunts before epidemics and King Philip's War (1675–76) yielded uplands to Pelham proprietors; settlers drew home lots by 1761 around center tavern, dividing ledges to Hastings, Dickinson, and pioneer families amid garrisons. Incorporation yielded church, town hall, and burying ground (exhumed to Quabbin Cemetery), with population peaking at 685 (1870) through endogamous kin; sawmills, potash kilns, and cheese factories fed Amherst trade.

Genealogists trace Pelham deeds pre-1822 for plateau allotments, then Prescott town books linking ridge cabins to census rolls across highland endogamy.

Center Wards, Potash Kilns, and Polish Hearths

Prescott's 19th-century core fused center farms drawing revivals at 1823 church, brook potash with Irish at missions, and Hastings-Dickinson lines sustaining Grange halls and library amid rural isolation. Dairy, maple, and chairs anchored economy, ties persisting through 1938 reunions despite razing.

Proprietors' surveys, kiln ledgers, and town minutes capture chain kin from Amherst ports to Quaboag workshops.

Disincorporation and the Quabbin Project

Prescott fell to Metropolitan District Water Supply Commission's 1926–1938 Quabbin construction, with eminent domain across Swift Valley towns displacing 2,500 by April 28, 1938 deadline; state razed 7,500 structures including Prescott Center after resisted offers, graves relocated, and basins cleared for 1939–1946 filling of 39-square-mile, 412-billion-gallon reservoir. Gate 36 trails reveal foundations in low water; UMass archives preserve takings records for family pursuits.

Genealogical Resources and Strategies

Vital repositories:

- Pelham Town Clerk (post-1938): Births, marriages, deaths from 1760s settlement era (published to 1850); Prescott records transferred.
- Prescott Collection (UMass SCUA): Manuscripts (Hastings, Dickinson), potash accounts, church extracts, and family registers.
- Quabbin Reservation Aids: Plateau overlaps, Quaboag maps, and evacuation narratives.

Regional aids: Hampshire County probate at Northampton Registry, FamilySearch Pelham transcriptions, and DCR surveys for ridge sites.

Prescott's plateau-Quabbin chronicle—from Nipmuc heights and Hastings ridges to potash flames and submerged farms—equips genealogists with hill-drowned sources. Plantation rolls, vital indexes, and archive files unveil "Quaboag Head kin" spanning Dickinsons, Hastings, and farmers across Moose Hill summits.

16

Chapter 6

Middlesex County
    Middlesex County, Massachusetts, arcs northwest from Boston Harbor around the Mystic and Charles River basins through Concord orchards and Merrimack mills to Lowell canals and Nashua uplands, created May 10, 1643, as one of four original shires encompassing Charlestown, Cambridge, Watertown, Concord, Sudbury, Woburn, Medford, and Reading on Massachuset and Nipmuc homelands, evolving Puritan theocracies, Yankee agrarians, Irish operatives, and mill girls across 54 cities/towns blending tidal marshes, traprock ridges, and suburban campuses. Named for Middlesex, England, its sprawling bounds—refined by Boston annexations (Charlestown 1874, Brighton 1874) and Northern District splits (Lowell 1855)—cradled Harvard (1636), MIT (1861), and Battles of Lexington-Concord (1775 "shot heard round the world"), powering textile booms, railroad hubs, and tech corridors from Shays' fringes to Route 128 electronics. From Indigenous shell middens to Minute Man trails and biopharma parks, Middlesex's river-campus spine traces Algonquian paths via tricentennial greens and district lyceums.

    Massachuset Marshes, Bay Lots, and Minute Man Precincts
Precolonial Massachuset sachems like Nanepashemet and his sons Sagamore John and James exploited Mystic River marshes for prolific alewife runs in spring freshets, quahog shell middens along Shawmut necks, and three-sister corn terraces on well-drained Cambridge uplands before devastating smallpox epidemics (1616–19, mortality 90%) and the Pequot War (1637 Mystic Massacre) yielded tidal flats and traprock ridges to Massachusetts Bay Company proprietors; John Winthrop's Arbella fleet anchored June 1630 at Charlestown peninsula amid summer heat claiming 1,000 acres, with Thomas Dudley surveying Cambridge lots by 1631 around the Old Burying Ground (1635), dividing Mystic-side homelots and outlands to Brooks, Catherwood, Gerry, Saltonstall, and settler kin amid hastily built palisades against Nipmuc raiding parties from inland Wamesit territories.

    Middlesex County courts first convened April 1649 at Cambridge establishing the Registry of Deeds (oldest continuous land records in U.S.), yielding precinct meetinghouses like Lexington's 1692 frame structure where Capt. John Parker's minutemen mustered April 19, 1775 with 77 farmers famously ordered to "stand your ground—don't fire unless fired upon," igniting the "shot heard round the world" at Concord's North Bridge amid Paul Revere's midnight ride from Boston Neck and Concord Fight where Emerson's grandfather commanded.

Middlesex Canal (1803–1808 engineering marvel with 27 locks, 2.75-mile Pawtucket Falls portage, and inclined planes) and Middlesex Turnpike (1803 Charlestown to Lowell) bypassed the Middlesex Fells granite ledges, channeling farm produce, milled broadcloths from Waltham factories, and Sudbury cider through endogamous clans linking Watertown flintlock makers (Revolution arms contracts) to Reading yeomen and Woburn tanners; Harvard Yard's Great Awakening confessions (1730s Whitefield revivals), Emerson's Transcendentalist circles at the Old Manse, and lyceum lectures deepened Puritan-rooted endogamy across precinct boundaries. Shays' Rebellion fringes saw Chelmsford courthouses shut 1786 by debtor farmers before federal pardons, while Middlesex Agricultural Society fairs (1840s) showcased Concord grapes and Acton cheese amid nascent railroad charters.

Genealogists trace Bay Colony deeds pre-1643 for marsh allotments via Middlesex South Registry abstract volumes 1–50, cross-referencing probate files linking tidewater cabins to Lexington Alarm militia rolls and Concord company musters across Revolution endogamy, enhanced by NEHGS published Concord vital extracts (to 1850) and AmericanAncestors militia indexes.

Common Wards, Canal Mills, and Irish Hearths

Middlesex's 19th-century wards fused Concord's literary farms where Emerson penned "Nature" (1836) at the Old Manse and Alcott's Orchard House hosted Transcendentalist salons amid apple presses, Lowell's Boott Mills complex (1823–1850s) drawing 10,000 "Lowell Mill Girls" from rural New England alongside Irish famine immigrants at St. Patrick's Cathedral (1831) and Holy Family parish (1853), and Brooks-Prescott lines sustaining lyceums like Framingham's 1830s debating halls amid Boston annexations of Roxbury (1868) and Roslindale wards.

Waltham Watch factories (1854 world's first), Lawrence's Essex Company canals powering Pacific Mills (1845, 30,000 spindles), and Cambridgeport rubber works employed endogamous kin through Civil War contracts; Middlesex Canal's final barges (1848 closure) yielded to Boston & Lowell Railroad (1835), channeling chair rockers from Acton, Sudbury cider, and Woburn leather to Thames ports amid nativist riots and Know-Nothing politics.

Shays' debtor echoes resurfaced in 1837 panics closing Billerica banks, while Middlesex Agricultural Society fairs (1841 onward) showcased Acton cheese, Bedford cranberries, and Lexington broomcorn alongside nascent suburban estates; Irish hearth ties persisted through cemetery societies like Lowell's St. Patrick's (1820s) and Cambridge's Holy Cross amid 1870s suburban flights to Arlington and Belmont.

Proprietors' surveys, mill payroll ledgers from Boott/Essex archives, and ward minutes from Lexington/Concord selectmen capture chain kin from Mystic landings to Merrimack workshops, cross-referenced via NEHGS textile worker censuses.

Genealogical Resources and Strategies

Genealogists targeting Middlesex County begin by anchoring research in the Middlesex South Registry of Deeds in Cambridge (established 1649, oldest continuous U.S. land records) and Middlesex North in Lowell (post-1855 split), methodically chaining Bay Colony homelot divisions from Winthrop-Dudley Mystic marsh grants through 18th-century Minute Man farm mortgages to 19th-century mill tenements via exhaustive grantor-grantee indexes spanning volumes 1–500; cross-reference these against Middlesex County Probate Court files (Cambridge/Lowell) for 1670s guardianships of Lexington Alarm widows, Revolution pension declarations detailing Parker minutemen service, and industrial-era inventories of Waltham watchmakers alongside Concord orchardists, triangulating ownership through NEHGS-published probate abstracts to 1910 that link canal-era testators to Boott Mill overseers.

For 19th-century Irish influxes powering Lowell's textile boom, fuse federal censuses (1850–1880 enumerating "mill girl" operatives and famine immigrants by canal lock occupations) with parish registers from St. Patrick's Cathedral (Lowell, 1831 baptisms) and Holy Family Church (1853 marriages), verifying endogamous Yankee-Irish unions via Lowell Historical Society payroll ledgers from Boott and Essex Company complexes that roster 10,000 workers including "Lowell Mill Girls" from rural New England farms. Layer Transcendentalist intellectual kinships through Concord Antiquarian Society holdings—Emerson-Thoreau family Bibles, Alcott Orchard House guest logs, and Old Manse property plats—against Harvard College class lists (1636 onward via Harvard Archives) and Cambridge Historical Commission surveys mapping Gerry-Saltonstall Cambridgeport estates to traprock ridge precincts. Map Shays' Rebellion fringes via 1786 Chelmsford court shutdown petitions in town selectmen minutes before federal pardons, corroborated by Middlesex Agricultural Society fair ledgers (1841–) documenting Acton cheese exhibitors, Bedford cranberry growers, and Lexington broomcorn producers amid nascent Boston & Lowell Railroad charters.

Advanced digital triangulation employs FamilyTreeDNA Middlesex Surname Projects linking Watertown flintlock gunsmith descendants to Route 128 electronics alumni rolls for 20th-century suburban migrations, while AmericanAncestors databases integrate Middlesex Canal toll receipts (1808–1848) with DAR Lexington-Concord muster indexes; prioritize chain-of-title reconstructions from pre-1643 Indigenous deed equivalents through Revolution land bounties to Merrimack spindle tenures, exploiting endogamous patterns across Puritan theocracies, Yankee agrarians, Irish operatives, and tech corridor professionals that define Middlesex's layered genealogical spine.

Vital repositories:

- Middlesex South Registry of Deeds (Cambridge, est. 1649): Original land records from Bay Colony grants through 1855 Northern split, with grantor-grantee indexes volumes 1–500 capturing homelot divisions, Mystic marsh transfers, and Minute Man farm mortgages; digitized abstracts via AmericanAncestors for pre-1700 allotments to Winthrop-Dudley kin.
- Middlesex North Registry of Deeds (Lowell, post-1855): Chelmsford, Lowell, and Billerica mill leases from textile booms, with probate-linked attachments for Irish operative tenements and Waltham watchmaker estates; microfilm vital extracts to 1850 via FamilySearch.
- Middlesex County Probate Court (Cambridge/Lowell): Guardianships from 1670s (e.g., Lexington Alarm widows), Revolution pension files, and 19th-century miller inventories spanning Concord orchards to Lawrence spindles; NEHGS published indexes (to 1910) link canal-era testators to Boott payrolls.

Local aids: Concord Antiquarian Society manuscripts (Emerson-Brooks family Bibles), Lowell Historical Society Boott Mill ledgers (Lowell Mill Girls rosters), Lexington Minute Man Company musters (Parker descendants), and Cambridge Historical Commission Harvard Yard plats; cross-reference via AmericanAncestors Middlesex Canal worker censuses and MHC traprock ridge surveys for precinct sites.

Regional strategies: Chain probate-land linkages from 1649 Registry volumes to 1850 vital published sets, triangulating Revolution militia rolls with Irish parish registers (St. Patrick's Lowell 1831–) across endogamous wards; supplement with DAR Lexington-Concord indexes and Essex-Middlesex canal toll ledgers for Thames trade kin.

Cities and Towns of Middlesex County

CITIES

Cambridge

Cambridge, a historic riverfront city in southern Middlesex County, Massachusetts, lines the north bank of the Charles River opposite Boston amid tidal marshes, glacial terraces, and drumlin hills, first settled in 1631 as Newtowne on Massachusett homelands and later renamed for England's university town, evolving from a fortified Puritan capital and college village into a dense streetcar suburb and global academic-technology hub that now anchors Harvard University, MIT, biotech labs, and immigrant corridors from East Cambridge to North Cambridge flats. Incorporated as a town in 1636 and as a city in 1846, its compact bounds—shaped by Boston annexations, landfill along the Charles, and 19th-century subdivision of commons—grew from meetinghouse commons and cow pastures through canals, rail yards, and industrial riverfronts to high-rise research campuses, blending Congregational, Catholic, and Jewish neighborhoods with long-standing Irish, Italian, Portuguese, Caribbean, and South Asian communities.

From Massachusett planting fields at the river bends to redbrick quadrangles and glass towers, Cambridge's Charles-Marsh spine traces Indigenous trails via colonial highways (the Great Bridge and Cambridge Road), town squares, and public school networks that have long generated thick documentary records.

Massachuset Terraces, College Lots, and Revolutionary Streets

Precolonial Massachusett families worked the river terraces for corn, beans, and squash and harvested fish and shellfish along the Charles and Mystic before epidemics and English expansion pushed land into Massachusetts Bay proprietors' hands; Winthrop's government moved its intended capital to fortified Newtowne in the 1630s, with carefully laid-out streets and palisades and house lots assigned to leading figures around what became Harvard Yard and the Old Burying Ground. Cambridge soon hosted Harvard College (chartered 1636, classes from 1638), and 18th-century residents such as Longfellow's later landlord families watched Continental troops encamp during the Siege of Boston, when Washington took command nearby in 1775 and Tory estates were confiscated or rented to patriot officers.

Genealogists work backward from 19th- and 20th-century city directories and ward maps into 18th-century town records and early church registers, then into Bay Colony court and land records, following chains of title from riverfront wharves and "college lots" to inland farms; Revolutionary service can be traced through muster rolls of Cambridge men in the Lexington and Concord alarm and the Siege of Boston, often linked in probate files and family Bibles to those same house-lot plans.

Squares, Car Shops, and Immigrant Hearths

Cambridge's 19th-century core fused Harvard Square's college merchants and boarding houses, East Cambridge's factories and courthouse, and Central and Kendall Squares' rail yards, glass-works, and rubber works, drawing Yankees off farms and immigrants from Ireland, Canada, Italy, Eastern Europe, and Cape Verde into dense triple-deckers and boarding blocks along tram lines. Between the Civil War and the First World War, factories along the Grand Junction and riverfront produced everything from pianos and candy to electrical gear, while neighborhood parishes, synagogues, and mutual-aid groups stitched together ethnic communities whose members often married within a few streets or a single parish for generations.

For research the city's squares and wards function like village "centers": census schedules, city directories, voter lists, and parish registers can be aligned with Sanborn maps to track families moving from Old Cambridge to East Cambridge, or from factory boardinghouses into owner-occupied triple-deckers in North Cambridge and Cambridgeport.

Genealogical Resources and Strategies

Vital repositories:

- Cambridge City Clerk and local vital offices hold births, marriages, and deaths from the mid-19th century forward, along with records of annexations, ward changes, and naturalizations.
- Harvard University Archives, the Cambridge Historical Commission, and local historical societies preserve manuscripts, neighborhood studies, cemetery transcriptions, and photographs documenting residents from colonial property owners to boardinghouse keepers and student lodgers.
- County-level land and probate records (through the Middlesex South registry and courts) document deeds, mortgages, guardianships, and estate divisions from the 17th century, while state and federal censuses, immigration records through Boston, and World War draft registrations round out 19th- and 20th-century profiles.

Cambridge's river-college chronicle—from Massachusett fields and Newtowne palisades to factory streets and biotech campuses—equips genealogists with unusually dense and continuous sources; layered use of land records, town and city minutes, church and school registers, and institutional archives reveals "Charles River kin" whose lines run from early college lots and Revolutionary encampments through immigrant wards and research corridors.

Everett

Everett, a compact industrial city of southern Middlesex County, Massachusetts, lies between the Mystic, Malden, and Chelsea rivers on ancient Massachusett homelands, incorporated as a town in 1870 from Malden's creekside districts and as a city in 1892. Its marshland base, once threaded by tidal flats, ship wharves, and canal slips, transformed during the 19th century into a dense manufacturing corridor linking Boston's harbor industries to northern cloth and leather trades. Named for scholar-statesman Edward Everett, the city's small footprint compressed immigrant neighborhoods, triple-decker clusters, and industrial spines—from Broadway's mills and breweries to the lower Mystic's rubber works and tanneries—while anchoring lifelong kin networks rooted in maritime craft, parochial school life, and ethnic benevolent societies.

Massachusett Flats, Malden Yards, and Colonial Allotments

Massachusett fishing camps along the Mystic and Malden rivers provided shellfish, wildfowl, and transport routes to the main village sites at Mishawum and Winnisimmet before epidemics and colonial expansion scattered local families in the 17th century. Malden proprietors acquired the creeksides after King Philip's War (1675–76), drawing long, narrow lots for ship carpenters and farmers such as the Sprague, Baldwin, and Sargeant families.

Colonial deeds, surveyed amid tidal influences, show overlapping rights across present-day Everett's waterfront. Taverns, mills, and ferries proliferated by the early 1800s, binding the area socially to Malden and Chelsea while still agriculturally inclined.

Shipyards, Tanneries, and Immigrant Wards

Everett's industrial rise intensified after 1850 with riverfront shipyards, brickyards, and later leather and rubber factories providing work for Irish, Italian, and Jewish families arriving via Boston docks. Broadway's business row evolved around Everett Square, where churches (Immaculate Conception, 1873; St. Anthony's, 1903) and city hall anchored civic life. Triple-decker housing filled Glendale and Ferry Street wards as family-operated groceries and bakeries nurtured extended kin networks.

Factories such as Everett Rubber and leather tanneries tied into Boston's export supply chains, while parochial groups and fraternal halls—Knights of Columbus, Sons of Italy, and local labor lodges—furnished genealogically rich membership and obituary records for immigrant descendants.

Genealogical Resources and Strategies

Vital repositories:

Everett City Clerk: Birth, marriage, and death records from 1870; ward records and directories linking residents by street and trade.

Everett Historical Society: Manuscript collections on early families (Sprague, Baldwin, Pope); church record extracts, tannery ledgers, and school rosters.

Malden Historical Society: Cross-references for pre-1870 Creekside allotments, Mystic River mapping, and Malden–Everett family overlaps.

Regional aids: Middlesex South Registry of Deeds (Cambridge) for colonial and 19th-century property transfers; FamilySearch digitized Malden/Everett vital books; and Massachusetts Historical Commission (MHC) inventories identifying shipyard and industrial sites.

From Massachusett shellfish beds to Broadway factories, Everett's genealogy mirrors urban compression—families tied not only by blood but by employment, parish, and block. For researchers, the city's small geographic size belies a vast archival footprint: land partitions, labor records, and ward maps providing continuity between colonial creek rights, industrial immigrant heritage, and the living descendancy of its "Mystic Flats kin."

<u>Framingham</u>

Framingham, a broad inland township anchored in the heart of Middlesex County, Massachusetts, stretches along the Sudbury River, Cochituate Brook, and Farm Pond valleys on Nipmuc homelands, granted by the General Court in 1662 as "Danforth's Farms" and incorporated as a town in 1700, evolving from agrarian parcels and sawmills into a 19th-century textile, shoe, and rail hub. Its bounds—nestled between Natick and Southborough—reflect early proprietorial divisions held by Judge Thomas Danforth, whose domains shaped farm lots, meetinghouse commons, and mill seats advancing toward industrial Framingham Center, Saxonville, and South Framingham.

From scattered colonial farms and garrison houses to bustling downtown depots and Framingham State Normal School (1839), the town's layered growth laced Puritan lineages with immigrant waves—Irish in quarries, Italians in factories, and Portuguese in shoe shops—bounded by river meadows and trolley lines uniting the center, Nobscot, and Saxonville villages.

Nipmuc Meadows, Danforth Grants, and Early Lots

Before colonists charted Danforth's tract, Nipmuc families sustained maize fields, fish weirs, and maple groves along the Sudbury's bends. Epidemic depopulation and the turmoil of King Philip's War (1675–76) opened lands to Boston proprietors under Danforth's management, where settlers such as Belknap, Stone, and Haven drew house lots by 1690 near Meetinghouse Hill.

Through the 18th century, farms spread from the "Old Connecticut Path" toward Salem End, the latter a haven for dissenting settlers from Marlborough. Framingham's early records—vital registers from 1700 forward, town meeting minutes, and church admissions—trace kin networks linking Sudbury and Sherborn descent lines through intermarrying clergy and husbandmen.

Mill Villages, Rail Corridors, and Immigrant Lines

Industrialization rose along the Sudbury and Saxonville Falls, where the Saxonville Mills (started 1830s by the Saxonville Company) drew Irish labor and Yankee overseers, while South Framingham's junction made it a rail nexus by 1848. Factories making woolens, paper, and boots lined Concord Street as boardinghouses filled with newcomers. By the late 19th century, St. George's, St. Stephen's, and St. Tarcisius parishes reflected ethnic settlement—Irish, Italian, and

Portuguese—each tied to mapped ward books and manufacturing payrolls noting kin sponsors and chain migration.

The Massachusetts State Normal School (later Framingham State University) and its early records, often rich in female teacher training genealogies, document families rising from farm to professional classes.

Genealogical Resources and Strategies

Vital repositories:

- Framingham Town Clerk: Births, marriages, and deaths from 1700 forward; earliest town and church records published through 1849; ward and street indexes post-1890.
- Framingham History Center (Old Academy Building): Manuscripts, maps, and family papers (Danforth, Buckminster, and Hemenway), plus Saxonville mill employee ledgers and parish extracts.
- Middlesex South Registry of Deeds (Cambridge): Proprietor allotments (17th–18th c.), Factory Village plats, and later suburban subdivisions.
- Regional aids: FamilySearch digitized Framingham vital volumes; Massachusetts Vital Records to 1850 series; MHC (Massachusetts Historical Commission) site files for Nipmuc and mill village areas.

Framingham's archival landscape—from Nipmuc meadows and Danforth tenures to Saxonville looms and schoolyard streets—reveals multi-century kin continuity. Genealogists study deed chains, parish rosters, and factory lists to link colonial proprietors, 19th-century immigrant clusters, and suburban lines of teachers, tradesmen, and mill hands crossing the Sudbury's banks.

Lowell

Lowell, the archetypal planned industrial city of northern Middlesex County, Massachusetts, rises along the Merrimack River at Pawtucket Falls—on ancestral Pennacook and Wamesit homelands—carved from Chelmsford in 1826 and chartered as a city in 1836. Engineered by the Merrimack Manufacturing Company, it was America's first large-scale textile metropolis, its canal grid transforming agrarian meadows into turbine alleys and brick mill complexes that attracted Yankee farm daughters, Irish canal diggers, French Canadian weavers, Greek grocers, and Khmer refugees in later generations. Its tightly platted wards, stitched together by Merrimack and Lowell Streets, balanced labor tenements with mill agents' rows, St. Patrick's and St. Jean Baptiste parishes with boardinghouse libraries—becoming a cultural crossroads from the Industrial Revolution through immigration waves of the 20th century.

Pennacook Falls, Chelmsford Commons, and Canal Grids

Before cotton looms and lock gates, Pennacook and Wamesit people fished salmon and shad from Pawtucket Falls and planted corn along the Merrimack's intervals. After King Philip's War

(1675–76), Chelmsford proprietors partitioned the meadows and uplands, establishing scattered farms and garrisons. The 1820s engineering of canal routes—Pawtucket, Northern, and Merrimack Canals—reshaped this landscape: Amos and Abbott Lawrence, Patrick Tracy Jackson, and Paul Moody rechanneled the river, creating the corporate-industrial town named for the engineer Francis Cabot Lowell. Early settlers' descendants merged with migrant mill families, generating parish and tenement records of intricate kin overlap from Chelmsford, Dracut, and Billerica to the mills of the Lowell Machine Shop.

Mill Agents, Immigrant Tenements, and Civic Halls

By 1850, Lowell's mills employed thousands, with "mill girls" boarding in corporately owned dormitories known for rules and reading circles; Irish laborers edged the locksides of the Acre, later joined by French Canadian textile hands, Polish spinners, and Greek merchants. Ethnic parishes and social halls—St. Patrick's (1831), St. Joseph's (1868), Holy Trinity Greek (1907)—anchored neighborhoods alongside civic strongholds like St. John's Hospital and City Hall. Through the 20th century, the rise and decline of the mills paralleled outward migration and later Southeast Asian resettlement (Cambodian, Laotian, Vietnamese), embedding successive genealogical threads—from County Cork masons to Montreal mill families and Indochinese boat refugees—documented in parish registers, naturalization dockets, and mill payrolls.

Genealogical Resources and Strategies

Vital repositories:

- Lowell City Clerk: Births, marriages, and deaths from 1826 forward; earlier Chelmsford vital records (pre-1826) critical for antecedent tracing.
- Lowell Historical Society and Center for Lowell History (UMass Lowell): Manuscripts, corporate mill ledgers, "Lowell Offering" volumes, immigrant community archives, and local map collections.
- Middlesex North Registry of Deeds (Lowell): Canal company plats, mill housing deeds, and immigrant property transfers.
- Regional aids: Massachusetts Vital Records to 1850 (Chelmsford volume), FamilySearch civil indexes, MHC surveys for canal districts, and NPS Lowell National Historical Park databases.

Lowell's genealogical topography—rooted in Pennacook fisheries, corporate canal ventures, and multilingual wards—unites environmental, industrial, and immigrant heritage. For genealogists, tracing lineage through Lowell means following deeds and directories through shifting nationalities, hymnbooks, and loom ledgers, discovering how families from homesteads, parish pews, and factory floors intertwined amid the roar of the Merrimack's falls.

Here's a full genealogical and historical analysis of Malden, Massachusetts, crafted in the same tone, structure, and interpretive depth as the Everett, Framingham, and Lowell entries.

<u>Malden</u>

Malden, one of Middlesex County's earliest settled river towns, stands north of Boston on the Mystic River's upper reaches, stretching across upland ridges and tidal meadows once central to the Massachusett people's homelands. Incorporated as a town in 1649 from portions of Charlestown's "Mystic Side," it grew from agrarian clearings and mill brooks into a 19th-century commuter and manufacturing city—its evolution tracing from Puritan farms and cordwainers' shops to streetcar suburbs, shoe factories, and civic boulevards. By the late 1800s, Malden's tight wards—Center, Edgeworth, Linden, and Maplewood—held a mosaic of Yankee, Irish, Italian, and Jewish families whose parishes, synagogues, and labor halls still preserve layered genealogical records.

Mystic Meadows, Charlestown Grants, and Puritan Founders

Before colonial settlement, the Massachusett cultivated corn and fished the Mystic's tidal flats, maintaining seasonal pathways along Spot Pond Brook and Pine Banks. After the devastating epidemics of the early 1600s, Charlestown proprietors divided these lands into farm allotments, later incorporated as "Maulden." Early families—Waite, Call, Sprague, Lynde, and Barrett—built homesteads along Salem Street and Ferryway Green, their lives recorded in town meeting books, militia rolls, and civic actions tied to the First Parish Church (1649). Through the 18th century, Malden farmers supplied Boston markets with dairy and timber; Revolutionary service rosters show multi-generational enlistment, particularly of the Waites and Converse lineages. Deeds and probate records from this era anchor many Middlesex genealogies extending into Everett, Melrose, and Medford.

Canal Villages, Shoe Factories, and Immigrant Wards

The 19th century remade Malden through transportation and industry. The Middlesex Canal, opened in 1803, cut through its meadows, offering links to Boston and Lowell; by the 1850s, railroads and streetcars turned Malden into a manufacturing and residential hub. Tanneries, cigar factories, and shoe shops drew Irish families fleeing famine, followed by Italians, Polish, and Russian Jewish artisans around 1880–1910. Churches multiplied—St. Joseph's (1849), St. Peter's (1893), and Sacred Hearts (1894)—alongside Hebrew congregations and early Catholic schools. Edgeworth's mills and the Maplewood section's streetcar housing developments produced dense local kin webs visible in census returns, parish marriage banns, and city directories that link households by trade and neighborhood.

Genealogical Resources and Strategies

Vital repositories:

- Malden City Clerk: Birth, marriage, and death records from 1649 (published through 1850); ward books, street directories, and naturalization indexes from the late 19th century.
- Malden Historical Society: Manuscripts, family genealogies (Waite, Converse, Sprague), maps, cemetery transcriptions, and industrial ledgers.
- First Parish (Unitarian Universalist) Church and Catholic Archives (Archdiocese of Boston): Early vital and sacramental registers spanning multiple ethnic parishes.
- Regional aids: Middlesex South Registry of Deeds for pre-1870 land splits in Everett and Melrose areas, FamilySearch digitized vital volumes, MHC site listings for canals, mills, and civic monuments.

Malden's genealogy unfolds through a blend of Puritan endurance and immigrant enterprise—land lot charts evolving into street grids, family farms into factory blocks. For researchers, its records trace centuries of urban transformation while preserving social continuity: from the Charlestown "Mystic Side" proprietors through canal laborers and factory-born kin who seeded new cities along the Mystic basin.

Marlborough

Marlborough, a central Massachusetts city on the uplands of western Middlesex County, lies among ponds, meadows, and rolling drumlins that once sustained Nipmuc families farming its intervals along the Assabet River. First granted in 1656 to settlers from Sudbury and incorporated as a town in 1660, Marlborough evolved from a fortified frontier village into a 19th-century shoe-manufacturing center, and later a 20th-century suburban hub along the Boston-Worcester corridor. Its transformation—from dispersed colonial farms and garrison houses to factory boardinghouses and housing tracts—mirrors the genealogical arch from Puritan founders and English artisans to waves of Irish, French Canadian, and Italian immigrants whose descendants populate still-intact parish and family records.

Nipmuc Intervals, Sudbury Farmers, and Garrison Homesteads

Before English settlement, Nipmuc families cultivated corn and squash along the Assabet's tributaries, setting seasonal encampments by Fort Meadow and Hager ponds. Epidemics and early colonial wars reduced local populations; by 1656, Sudbury planters received permission to form "Whipsufferadge Plantation," soon known as Marlborough. Founders such as Rice, Howe, Ward, Bellows, and Brigham established a palisaded settlement and meetinghouse near Town Hill. King Philip's War (1675–76) destroyed much of the town, dispersing families eastward; their later resettlement generated extensive probate and allotment records linking Marlborough descendants to surrounding towns—Southborough, Hudson (set off 1866), and Northborough. Early church registers and land divisions form the backbone of genealogical tracing for these founding families, many documented in printed Rice and Howe genealogies.

Shoemaking Villages, Immigrant Parishes, and Industrial Growth

During the 19th century, Marlborough shifted from agrarian self-sufficiency to shoemaking dominance. Dozens of small shoe shops lined Lincoln Street and Mechanic Street, expanding by mid-century into the Baxter and Frye factories that employed thousands. Irish immigrants arrived after the 1840s famine, followed by French Canadian and Italian shoeworkers by 1880. Parishes reflected this demographic mosaic—Immaculate Conception (est. 1864), St. Mary's (French, 1870s), and later Italian confraternities that nurtured the Franco-American and Mediterranean mill quarters on the west side.

City incorporation in 1890 brought civic institutions—schools, city hall, and local business directories—that meticulously recorded occupational and residential data invaluable for genealogists connecting family occupations to specific wards and factories.

Genealogical Resources and Strategies

Vital repositories:

- Marlborough City Clerk: Births, marriages, and deaths from incorporation (1890) forward; earlier town records (1660–1889) kept at the city archives and available on microfilm and digital platforms.
- Marlborough Historical Society: Family manuscripts (Rice, Howe, Fay, Brigham), Civil War rosters, and extensive shoe industry photographs and ledgers.
- Assabet Valley Genealogical Society: Indexes to church and cemetery records, plus French-Canadian surname compilations.
- Regional aids: Middlesex South Registry of Deeds for colonial and factory-era lot plans; Hudson and Southborough town clerks for separated family branches; FamilySearch "Massachusetts, Town and Vital Records, 1620–1988" collection for early Marlborough entries; and Massachusetts Historical Commission (MHC) surveys of factory sites and garrison remains.

Marlborough's genealogical terrain spans four centuries—from fortified settlers and Nipmuc farmlands to immigrant cobblers and modern commuters. Researchers reconstruct kin stories through land grants, parish sacramental registers, and industrial paybooks, linking the Rice garrison's wooden palisade to the shoe factory skyline and suburban neighborhoods rooted in enduring local descent.

Medford

Medford, a historic river town of northeastern Middlesex County, Massachusetts, stands on the Mystic River where tidal currents once met vast salt marshes and shipbuilding coves on Massachusett homelands. Settled in 1630 as part of Charlestown's "Mistick Plantation" and incorporated as a town in 1695, Medford evolved from riverfront estates and brickyards into a vital 19th-century hub of shipbuilding, rum distilling, and suburban growth. Its compact geography—wedged between Somerville, Malden, and Arlington—produced overlapping kinship webs anchored by colonial families, seafaring merchants, and successive waves of Irish, Italian, and Armenian immigrants whose neighborhood parishes, ship lists, and property deeds preserve its genealogical continuity.

Massachusett Meadows, Mystic Plantations, and Early Proprietors

Before English arrival, the Massachusett people inhabited the Mystic's tidal flats, fishing shad and alewives and tending corn along winter brooks. Charlestown settlers acquired the tract known as "Mistick" around 1630, where Governor Matthew Cradock, an absentee London merchant, held extensive land used by his agents for shipbuilding and livestock. By 1650, farms and mills stretched from the river to the highlands, with family names—Brooks, Willis, Hall, Bradshaw, and Symmes—engraved in town books, militia rolls, and land divisions. Medford's first meetinghouse and burying ground anchored social life near what later became Medford Square. Surviving deeds and the "Cradock Grant" papers trace to Boston's early mercantile network, providing genealogists with some of the region's earliest cross-references between London merchants and local settlers.

Shipyards, Rum Mills, and Ethnic Streets

From the mid-18th through the 19th century, Medford became known for its shipyards—over 500 vessels built along the Mystic between 1803 and 1873—while distilleries, clay pits, and rope walks enriched family fortunes. Yankee shipwrights were gradually joined by Irish and Italian workers who settled near Cross Street and Spring Street wards, forming dense parish communities around St. Joseph's (1854) and St. Raphael's (1915). Armenian and Greek families arrived in the early 20th century, their neighborhood societies leaving well-documented member lists and mutual aid records. By the 1890s, electric streetcars tied Medford to Boston, accelerating suburban development through the West Medford and Hillside districts. Civil and industrial censuses mirror this transition—farmers and carpenters giving way to machinists, teachers, and clerks—showing the occupational shifts that genealogists use to trace lineage through changing economies.

Genealogical Resources and Strategies

Vital repositories:

- Medford City Clerk: Birth, marriage, and death records from 1695 (published through 1850 and indexed thereafter); street lists and annual city directories (from 1890).
- Medford Historical Society & Museum: Family papers (Brooks, Hall, Cradock descendants), shipbuilding ledgers, church minutes, and neighborhood club rosters.

- Middlesex South Registry of Deeds (Cambridge): Cradock Grant lots, shipyard plats, and suburban parcel maps documenting 19th- and early 20th-century transfers.
- Regional aids: FamilySearch digital copy of "Middlesex County—Town and Vital Records," Massachusetts Vital Records to 1850, MHC site files for shipyards and industrial archaeology, and Mystic River Restoration archives mapping colonial homesteads.

Medford's genealogy reflects New England's layered continuity—from Massachusett fishing grounds and Puritan fields to shipwright alleys and commuter streets. For historians and family researchers alike, its archives bind four centuries of persistence: the Cradock agents' river mills, the shipwrights' tenements, the parochial schools of immigrants, and the enduring descendant lines who still trace the Mystic's winding banks.

<u>Melrose</u>

Melrose, a residential city in northeastern Middlesex County, Massachusetts, lies on the rolling uplands between Malden and the Saugus River basin—territory once traversed by Massachusett and Pawtucket families following inland hunting and fishing routes. Originating as the "North End" of Malden, it was set off as a separate town in 1850 and incorporated as a city in 1900. Melrose evolved from 17th-century meadow farms and colonial byways into an elegant 19th-century commuter suburb, its growth shaped by the Boston & Maine Railroad and later streetcar lines. Its genealogical story bridges Puritan proprietors and modern descendants—farmers, shoemakers, merchants, and railroad clerks—whose church, land, and civic records reflect both continuity and transformation from agrarian pastures to Victorian squares and leafy hill neighborhoods.

Mystic Uplands, Malden Farms, and Early Tenures

Before English settlement, Indigenous Massachusett families occupied the region for seasonal hunts and berry harvests along the Ell Pond watershed. After Charlestown's expansion northward, Malden proprietors held these uplands as communal pasture until mid-17th-century divisions into farm lots. Early lineages—Waite, Sprague, Upham, and Lynde—worked these tracts, recording deeds and town actions under Malden jurisdiction. The area remained rural through the 18th century, peppered with taverns and gristmills on Spot Pond Brook. Revolutionary service rolls show frequent intermarriage among Malden's farming families, many of whom later relocated to the Melrose highlands or eastward toward Saugus following inheritance divisions documented in Middlesex probate.

Rail Suburbs, Victorian Blocks, and Parish Networks

Rail service in the 1840s transformed the district: with stations at Wyoming and Cedar Park, "North Malden" became a suburban choice for Boston merchants and professionals. When incorporated as Melrose in 1850, named for its resemblance to Melrose, Scotland, the town saw rapid stratification—upper-middle-class homes rising along the hill slopes, while artisans, Irish laborers, and later Italian masons clustered near Main Street and the rail corridor. Congregational,

Unitarian, Baptist, and Catholic parishes anchored neighborhoods, their membership rolls and pew rents providing localized genealogical references. By the early 20th century, Melrose's civic institutions—City Hall (1900), schools, and patriotic societies—documented family participation in veterans' posts, women's clubs, and fraternal lodges such as the Odd Fellows, Masons, and Knights of Columbus. Census data show intermarriage between Malden, Stoneham, and Saugus descendants, tying the region's genealogical fabric tightly across town lines.

Genealogical Resources and Strategies

Vital repositories:

- Melrose City Clerk: Vital records from incorporation (1850) onward; ward, street, and naturalization indexes for late-19th and early-20th centuries.
- Malden City Clerk and Historical Society: Pre-1850 entries for families originating in "North Malden" districts.
- Melrose Historical Commission and Museum: Family papers, early photographs, church bulletins, and manuscript maps; directories and building permits showing neighborhood lineage continuity.
- Regional aids: Middlesex South Registry of Deeds (Cambridge) for land partitions between Malden and Melrose; FamilySearch and Ancestry transcriptions of Malden/Melrose church books; MHC site inventories for Ell Pond and Wyoming Hill districts.

Melrose's genealogical profile captures the cultural turn from Puritan pasture to commuter identity: a place where colonial surnames endured beside railroad-era newcomers. For genealogists, its records document both rooted family descent from Malden proprietors and the social rise of 19th-century families who inscribed their names onto suburban plats and parish cornerstones, preserving an enduring record of continuity above the Mystic valley.

Newton

Newton, a broad and prosperous city in southern Middlesex County, Massachusetts, spreads across the upper Charles River basin on lands once inhabited by the Massachusett people who fished its meadows and cleared its uplands. First settled in the 1630s as part of Cambridge's "New Towne Farms," Newton became a separate town in 1688 and a city in 1873. Its twelve historic villages—Newton Centre, Newtonville, Auburndale, West Newton, and others—trace distinct genealogical, economic, and cultural layers, evolving from agrarian homesteads and mill hamlets to 19th-century commuter enclaves connected by turnpikes, railroads, and later electric trolleys. Generations of Puritan farmers, industrialists, educators, and immigrant families have left dense records of property, parish, and civic life woven into the city's intricate landscape.

Massachusett Meadows, Cambridge Farms, and Colonial Families

Massachusett communities occupied the rivers and meadows along the upper Charles and Nonantum Hill, a name preserving their legacy. English settlers from Watertown and Cambridge pushed west in the 1630s, claiming meadowlands under the "Cambridge Farms" grant, a tract divided among family plots by 1650. Names such as Jackson, Ward, Hyde, Fuller, and Wiswall dominate early deeds, wills, and church registers. The First Church, organized in 1660 under Pastor John Eliot Jr. (son of missionary John Eliot), served as spiritual and civic anchor. Town records, militia rolls, and probate files through the 18th century showcase early intermarriages linking Newton's gentry with neighboring Waltham, Needham, and Watertown families—nodes still traceable in contemporary genealogical networks.

Turnpikes, Mills, and Commuter Villages

The 19th century redrew Newton through industry and transportation. The Boston & Worcester Railroad (1834) and turnpike system transformed rural districts into suburban villages. Textile and paper mills thrived along the Charles, especially at Upper and Lower Falls, where Irish families dominated the work force by mid-century. The later arrival of Jewish and Italian immigrant families fostered distinct neighborhoods anchored by St. Bernard's (1878) and Temple Emanuel (1909). Colleges such as Andover Newton Theological School and Lasell Seminary for Young Women introduced clerical and educational kinships that drew families into professional and academic life, reflected in employment records and alumni registries that serve genealogists tracing upward social mobility. By the electric trolley era, Newton's "Garden City" ideal fostered civic clubs, parks, and mutual aid societies whose minutes and membership rolls still document family origin and residence patterns.

Genealogical Resources and Strategies

Vital repositories:

- Newton City Clerk: Vital records from 1688 (published through 1850) and continuous indexes of births, marriages, and deaths thereafter; ward, poll, and street lists from the late 19th century.
- Historic Newton (Jackson Homestead and Museum): Family manuscripts (Jackson, Hyde, Kenrick, Fuller), diaries, church histories, and maps; local cemetery and school records.
- Middlesex South Registry of Deeds (Cambridge): Extensive colonial-to-modern landbooks covering Cambridge Farms through suburban development plats.
- Regional aids: FamilySearch and Ancestry transcriptions of Newton and Cambridge records; Massachusetts Vital Records to 1850 (Newton volume); Massachusetts Historical Commission (MHC) inventories of mill and estate sites.

From Massachusett cornfields to the "Garden City's" residential commons, Newton's genealogical story embodies continuity through adaptation. Researchers follow trails from 17th-century meadow grants to streetcar suburbs, uncovering family paths that move fluidly—from Puritan farms, to mill villages, to commuter estates—revealing the enduring interlacing of kinship, landscape, and record across four centuries of civic evolution.

Here's a genealogical and historical profile for Somerville, Massachusetts, written to match the same tone, structure, and depth as your Everett, Framingham, Lowell, Malden, Marlborough, Medford, Melrose, and Newton entries.

Somerville

Somerville, a compact yet historically layered city in eastern Middlesex County, Massachusetts, lies north of the Charles River Basin and west of the Mystic, on lands that once belonged to the Massachusett people and later to Charlestown proprietors. Settled in the 1630s as part of Charlestown's "outlands," Somerville remained rural until 1842, when it separated from Charlestown, becoming a city in 1872. Its evolution—from colonial pastureland to industrial suburb and later an innovation corridor—mirrors the demographic and genealogical currents of New England urbanization. Families of Puritan farmers, Irish laborers, Italian tradesmen, Portuguese masons, and later Caribbean and South Asian immigrants all left traces in parish books, street directories, and municipal ward records that anchor their stories within Somerville's dense urban geography.

Charlestown Pastures, Mystic Fields, and Colonial Homesteads

Before English colonization, Massachusett and Pawtucket peoples followed fish runs and cultivated corn along the Mystic River and Alewife Brook, maintaining settlements near present-day Ten Hills. Charlestown proprietors acquired the area in the 1630s, distributing "Cow Commons" and river marshes among early families—Tufts, Cutter, Rand, Miller, and Frost. Stone and Halfway Brooks delineated farmsteads whose deeds and wills remain recorded in the Middlesex Registry.

Through the 18th century, Somerville (then part of Charlestown's "Beyond the Neck" section) consisted mainly of farms, taverns, and brickyards, its people counted in Charlestown's tax books and church rolls. Revolutionary events—most famously Paul Revere's 1775 ride and the fortification of Prospect Hill—tie genealogies here to broader patriot networks; many of the militia rosters and land confiscation lists serve as valuable genealogical tools connecting Charlestown and Somerville ancestors.

Brickyards, Rail Lines, and Industrial Wards

The 19th century remade Somerville through brickmaking, railroad construction, and meatpacking industries. The Boston & Lowell Railroad spurred rapid urbanization, while the McLean Asylum (opened 1818) and Union Square mills created steady employment. Irish immigrants arrived first to work brickyards in Winter Hill and East Somerville, followed by Italians, Portuguese, and Eastern Europeans establishing parishes—St. Ann's (1883), St. Benedict's (1915), and St. Anthony of Padua (1927)—that mirrored ethnic clustering in ward censuses.

Tied closely to its geography of hills and valleys, Somerville's neighborhoods developed strong intermarrying kin networks traceable through parish marriage records, labor union rolls, and civic club memberships. By the early 20th century, triple-decker housing lined Highland Avenue and Broadway, accommodating multi-generational families whose property deeds and city directories remain remarkably continuous within families across decades.

Genealogical Resources and Strategies

Vital repositories:

- Somerville City Clerk: Birth, marriage, and death records from 1842; annual street and ward lists from the late 19th century through modern census alignment.
- Somerville Museum and Historical Society: Family manuscripts (Tufts, Cutter, Rand), brick industry payrolls, civic journals, maps, and photographs; school and veterans' directories.
- Middlesex South Registry of Deeds (Cambridge): Early farm divisions, factory parcels, and lot sales during the city's 19th-century subdivision boom.
- Regional aids: FamilySearch transcriptions of Charlestown and Somerville vital records, Massachusetts Vital Records to 1850 (Charlestown volume), and Massachusetts Historical Commission (MHC) site files on Prospect Hill, Union Square, and brickyard districts.

From Mystic meadows and Charlestown cow commons to industrial wards and multicultural avenues, Somerville's genealogy reveals the perpetual transformation of a small tract into a dense civic mosaic. For researchers, its archive links ancestor to address: farmers turned masons, brickmakers to shopkeepers, their lineage crossing centuries and continents but still traceable in the layered records of a hilltop city overlooking Boston's changing skyline.

Waltham

Waltham, a riverine city in southern Middlesex County, Massachusetts, extends along the Charles River's middle course, where its falls powered early mills on Massachusett tribal homelands. First settled in the 1630s as part of Watertown and incorporated as a separate town in 1738, Waltham became one of America's pioneering industrial cities—the birthplace of the factory system, watchmaking innovation, and educational reform.

Its genealogical record mirrors that transformation: Puritan farmers gave way to Yankee mechanics, Irish mill hands, Italian masons, Jewish merchants, and mid-20th-century professionals, all documented in town books, parish rosters, factory ledgers, and deed indexes mapping the evolution from agrarian village to urban industry and academia.

Massachusett Meadows, Watertown Farms, and Colonial Grants

Before English settlement, Massachusett families lived along the Charles, fishing salmon and alewives near the falls later known as Moody Street. The land became Watertown's "Middle Farms," held by original proprietors such as Bright, Hammond, and Livermore. Early deeds record long intervals of upland pastures, orchards, and mills; the first meetinghouse and burying ground date from the late 17th century. Through the 18th century, families including the Whitings, Browns, and Merriams expanded holdings westward as Waltham separated from Watertown in 1738. Parish registers, vital records, and probate inventories from this period reveal kin groups that later redistributed across Newton, Weston, and Lexington—still cross-referenced in Middlesex County deeds and colonially printed genealogies.

Mill Villages, Watch Factories, and Immigrant Streets

Waltham's industrial identity took shape when the Boston Manufacturing Company, founded by Francis Cabot Lowell in 1813, built the nation's first fully integrated textile mill along the Charles. The factory drew Yankee women and later Irish laborers, whose families established the Catholic parish of St. Mary's (1835). By the 1850s, the Waltham Watch Company transformed the economy again, attracting skilled European immigrants who settled near Crescent Street and the river mills. Later arrivals—Italians, Armenians, and Jewish families—brought new churches, synagogues, and lodges documented in archival membership rolls.

Waltham's independence as a city (1884), coupled with the arrival of Bentley and Brandeis universities, produced a civic class of educators and clerks; streetcar lines from Boston encouraged residential expansion into Highlands and Cedarwood, visible in ward lists and housing deeds from 1890 onward.

Genealogical Resources and Strategies

Vital repositories:

- Waltham City Clerk: Birth, marriage, and death records from incorporation (1738/1884) to present; annual street and poll lists.
- Waltham Historical Society and Waltham Museum: Manuscripts (Whitney, Bright, and Livermore families), mill and watch company employee registers, photographs, maps, and cemetery listings.
- Middlesex South Registry of Deeds (Cambridge): Watertown farm grants, mill privileges, and residential subdivisions.
- Regional aids: Massachusetts Vital Records to 1850 (Watertown and Waltham volumes), FamilySearch scans of local records, and Massachusetts Historical Commission (MHC) industrial site surveys for Moody Street mills and Watch Factory properties.

Waltham's genealogical landscape bridges centuries of innovation and migration—from Puritan homesteads and canal-fed mills to clockworks, classrooms, and commuter streets. For genealogists, the city's archival trail—spanning Watertown deeds, factory rolls, and university records—reveals how families followed the Charles River's current through work, faith, and education, shaping a community that still carries the enduring imprint of its founding farms and factory town legacy.

Watertown

Watertown, one of the earliest inland settlements of Massachusetts Bay, occupies fertile terraces along the Charles River in eastern Middlesex County, Massachusetts. Established in 1630 on Massachusett homelands and incorporated as a town that same year, Watertown served as an early colonial hub of agriculture, trade, and dissent, later becoming a modest industrial and residential city. Its genealogical record spans from Puritan settlers and Revolutionary patriots to 19th-century Irish canal builders, Armenian traders, and 20th-century immigrant professionals, each leaving abundant archival footprints in church, land, and civic records that document the city's gradual transformation over four centuries.

Massachusett Meadows, Colonial Proprietors, and Town Origins

Before English occupation, the Massachusett people fished the Charles and tended maize fields along its meanders. Governor Winthrop's company chose the site in 1630 for its arable land and fresh water, designating it one of the first four Bay Colony towns. The early "Watertown Covenant" of 1630 and land divisions of 1637 granted house lots to settlers such as Whitney, Bond, Coolidge, Browne, and Sawin—names enduring in Watertown's genealogies.

Town governance and religious life grew under ministers George Phillips and John Knowles, while boundary grants later carved off neighboring Waltham (1738), Weston, and Lincoln. Early records document disputes over taxation and representation, providing early evidence of democratic impulses later echoed in the town's Revolutionary activism. Surviving town books, vital records, and land plats afford genealogists one of New England's richest continuous documentation series beginning in the 1630s.

Mills, Arsenals, and Immigrant Districts

Through the 18th and 19th centuries, Watertown balanced agrarian tradition with industry along the Charles. Grist and paper mills gave way to the Watertown Arsenal (1816), which operated into the 20th century, employing generations of skilled workers. The arrival of the Middlesex Canal and early rail lines facilitated trade, while Irish immigrants built factories and settled near Mount Auburn Street and the Arsenal District. Subsequent Armenian and Italian families opened groceries and workshops, forming St. Stephen's Armenian Church (1923) and Sacred Heart Parish (1911) as community anchors. Watertown Square, the civic hub, became a focal point for schools and fraternal organizations such as the Odd Fellows and St. Patrick's societies—rich in membership and obituary records. These sources allow tracing family transitions from migrant laborers to homeowners and professionals across neighborhood lines visible in ward censuses by 1900.

Genealogical Resources and Strategies

Vital repositories:

- Watertown Town Clerk: Vital records (births, marriages, deaths) from 1630 forward, including published volumes through 1850; annual street and voting lists.
- Historical Society of Watertown: Family papers (Whitney, Fowle, Coolidge), war rosters, Armenian community archives, photographs, and oral histories.
- Middlesex South Registry of Deeds (Cambridge): Early farm grants, mill privileges, and post-Revolutionary divisions creating Waltham and Weston.
- Regional aids: FamilySearch digitized "Watertown Records" volumes; Massachusetts Vital Records to 1850 series; MHC site inventories for Watertown Arsenal, mills, and historic cemeteries; state archives for militia and probate documentation of early proprietors.

From Massachusett cornfields to colonial commons, from the Arsenal's workshops to 21st-century riverfront homes, Watertown's genealogical story reveals structural continuity beneath transformation. Researchers tracing its families follow paper trails from the 1630 town rolls through industrial payrolls and parish ledgers—discovering how Watertown's founding ideals of self-government and industry endure in the lived descent of its people.

Woburn

Woburn, one of the earliest inland towns of Middlesex County, Massachusetts, lies north of Boston between the Aberjona River and Horn Pond, on lands first inhabited by the Pawtucket and Massachusett peoples. Settled in the 1640s and incorporated as a town in 1642, Woburn grew from a frontier farming and garrison settlement into a major 19th-century tanning and shoe-making center. Its genealogical fabric spans from Puritan founders and Revolutionary soldiers to 19th-century Irish tanners, Italian craftsmen, and 20th-century suburban families, all reflected in dense local records—vital, church, land, and industrial—that illustrate a continuous social lineage from colonial pastures to commuter suburbs.

Pawtucket Meadows, Charlestown Grants, and Puritan Founders

Before the 17th century, Pawtucket and Massachusett families maintained fishing camps at Horn Pond and along the Aberjona, harvesting fish and cultivating corn on its floodplains. Charlestown's magistrates acquired these lands in the 1640s, designating them as "the New Township Above the Springs." Woburn's founding committee, led by Edward Johnson, Michael Bacon, and Edward Converse, laid out the town common and meetinghouse by 1642. Early family names—Richardson, Tidd, Fowle, Winn, and Pierce—fill town books and early vital registers, anchoring many regional genealogies. The church covenant of 1642 and subsequent land divisions reveal tightly clustered kinship networks extending toward Wilmington and Reading as new communities formed. Town meeting minutes and militia records from the 17th and 18th centuries remain essential genealogical sources, illustrating inheritance transfers, civic duties, and marriages between prominent early families.

Tanneries, Mills, and Immigrant Wards

By the early 19th century, Woburn became renowned for its leather and tanning industry, giving rise to affluence and hazardous labor alike. Dozens of tanneries lined the Aberjona River at Woburn Center and Horn Pond, drawing a workforce that included Irish laborers fleeing the 1840s famine. Italian and Polish families followed by 1880, settling near Central Square and Montvale. Catholic parishes—St. Charles (1873) and later St. Barbara's—anchored these new communities, while fraternal groups such as the Ancient Order of Hibernians and Italian mutual aid societies maintained membership and burial records invaluable to genealogists. Industrial prosperity brought civic modernization—public schools, city incorporation (1889), and expansions of brickyards and shoe factories. Many factory and tannery ledgers survive in local archives, often listing full households, offering insights into kin employment and migration patterns.

Genealogical Resources and Strategies

Vital repositories:

- Woburn City Clerk: Birth, marriage, and death records from 1642 onward; ward, street, and naturalization lists available from the late 19th century.
- Woburn Historical Society and Public Library Local History Room: Family Bibles, civic manuscripts (Johnson, Richardson, Winn), industrial payrolls, church extracts, and cemetery transcriptions.
- Middlesex South Registry of Deeds (Cambridge): Colonial and 19th-century property deeds, subdivision maps, and manufacturing plats.
- Regional aids: Massachusetts Vital Records to 1850 (Woburn volume); FamilySearch and Ancestry indexed vital collections; MHC industrial and tannery site files; and U.S. EPA environmental histories supporting industrial genealogical reconstruction near the Aberjona.

Woburn's genealogical identity blends ancestral endurance with adaptation. Its archival record—stretching from Edward Johnson's colonial covenant to the tannery ledgers and suburban directories—captures the persistence of local lineage even amid waves of immigration and industrial change. For researchers, the town's long paper trail ties its founders' Puritan fields to the worker neighborhoods and family enterprises that shaped Woburn's enduring legacy along the northern Charles watershed.

TOWNS

Acton

Acton, a rural-turned-suburban town in northwestern Middlesex County, Massachusetts, rises among the Assabet River's headwaters and wooded uplands on Nipmuc homelands. Originally the western precinct of Concord, Acton was incorporated as a separate town in 1735. Its story traces the continuum from 17th-century farm divisions to Revolutionary heroism and later 19th-century civic and rail-centered growth. Genealogically, Acton's records embody the persistence of Yankee family lines—Handley, Hosmer, Fletcher, Faulkner, and Tuttle—later joined by Irish laborers, Canadian mill workers, and mid-20th-century suburban professionals. The town's documentation—land grants, town books, church covenants, and military rosters—offers a compact but remarkably complete picture of lineage across nearly three centuries.

Nipmuc Fields, Concord Lots, and Precinct Autonomy

Before colonial settlement, Nipmuc-descended families cultivated corn and squash in meadows near Nashoba Brook and hunted deer across the highland ridges toward Boxborough. In the 1650s, Concord proprietors extended their grants westward, issuing long, narrow farm lots along today's Main Street and Nagog Hill. Settler names—Fletcher, Faulkner, and Hosmer—appear frequently in Concord deeds and early probate files.

As the western farms grew distant from Concord's center, residents petitioned for their own parish, leading to incorporation as Acton in 1735. First Parish records, beginning that same year, capture baptisms, marriages, and land transactions that form the foundation of Acton genealogies. Surviving town meeting minutes chart civic formation, including road building, militia service, and tax assessments that show kin relations through land adjacency and mutual sureties.

Revolution, Mills, and Village Networks

Acton achieved prominence during the American Revolution: Captain Isaac Davis and the Acton Minutemen led the colonial line at the Battle of Concord Bridge on April 19, 1775. Militia rolls, pension applications, and Davis family records connect numerous local households to the war's earliest campaigns. In the 19th century, Acton transitioned from independent farming to small-scale manufacturing. Faulkner's Mills on the Assabet produced yarn, while South and West Acton villages became modest commercial nodes serviced by the Fitchburg Railroad (1844).

Irish and later French Canadian families replaced declining Yankee farm labor, forming kin clusters near West Acton and enrolling in St. Bridget's Parish in neighboring Maynard. Town directories, school ledgers, and industrial payrolls from this period link multi-generational family migration patterns extending toward Concord, Boxborough, and Maynard millworks.

Genealogical Resources and Strategies

Vital repositories:

- Acton Town Clerk: Birth, marriage, and death records from incorporation (1735) to present; town meeting books and tax lists identifying heads of household.
- Iron Work Farm in Acton, Inc. (Faulkner House & Jones Tavern): Family manuscripts (Faulkner, Tuttle, Jones), Revolutionary era papers, local militia rosters, and 19th-century property inventories.
- Middlesex South Registry of Deeds (Cambridge): Colonial and early federal-period land deeds linking Concord proprietors to Acton subdivisions.
- Regional aids: Massachusetts Vital Records to 1850 (Acton volume); FamilySearch digital municipal registers; MHC cultural inventories for early mills and homesteads; and the Concord Free Public Library's regional genealogical collections.

Acton's genealogical landscape bridges agrarian resilience and quiet transformation—from Nipmuc meadows and Puritan farms to industrial hamlets and commuter lanes. For researchers, the town's continuity in land ownership and civic recordkeeping reveals entire family arcs—from 17th-century Concord settlers and Revolutionary veterans through the farmers and millhands who shaped modern suburban Acton's enduring local lineage.

Ashby

Ashby, a rural upland town in the far northwestern corner of Middlesex County, Massachusetts, lies along the Nashua River watershed near the New Hampshire border, on ancestral Nipmuc and Pennacook homelands. Granted as part of the "Townsend West Precinct" and incorporated in 1767, Ashby developed as a self-sustaining agricultural community whose families clustered along ridges, brooks, and crossroads. Though small in population, the town's genealogical record is deeply layered—tracing Yankee settlers and Revolutionary soldiers through the 19th-century farm families, mill operators, and craftsmen who defined the region's agrarian continuity well into the industrial age.

Nipmuc Hills, Townsend Grants, and Early Settlements

Before colonization, Nipmuc and Pennacook families traversed the Ashby uplands for seasonal hunting and maple gathering, leaving trails linking the Nashua and Squannacook rivers. Settlement by English colonists came late, beginning in the early 1700s when Townsend proprietors distributed western land lots among families such as the Stearns, Willard, Blood, and Jewett lines. The first meetinghouse rose near Ashby Common by mid-century, when the area petitioned for township status to gain independent Sabbath preaching. Town incorporation in 1767 established civic autonomy and generated the earliest continuous records—vital events, town votes, militia lists, and road surveys—preserved in bound volumes invaluable for genealogical reconstruction.

Revolution, Farming Networks, and Local Industry

Ashby sent several companies to the Revolutionary cause, with men serving in the Concord and Bennington campaigns; pension files often reference long-settled local surnames. The early 19th century saw gradual diversification from pure subsistence farming to modest industry: grist and sawmills on Willard Brook, small cooperages, and local shoemaking shops providing supplemental income. Town censuses and tax lists reveal complex kin adjacency—extended families occupying contiguous farms, usually intermarrying across Townsend, Fitchburg, and New Ipswich (NH) town lines. Methodist and Baptist congregations formed in the 1790s, contributing early church registers and membership lists. By the late 19th century, rail links to Fitchburg drove small-scale outmigration while also facilitating market farming and orchard trades. The town retained its rural identity, adjusting slowly to modernized civic infrastructure through the 20th century.

Genealogical Resources and Strategies

Vital repositories:

- Ashby Town Clerk: Birth, marriage, and death records from 1767 forward; early town meeting books and tax assessments listing landowners and occupations.
- Ashby Historical Society and Library Local History Room: Family files (Willard, Blood, Jewett, Stearns), cemetery transcriptions, school registers, and manuscript maps.
- Middlesex South Registry of Deeds (Cambridge): Early Townsend and Ashby property transfers, farm boundaries, and probate estate divisions.
- Regional aids: Massachusetts Vital Records to 1850 (Ashby volume); FamilySearch digitized town records; Massachusetts Historical Commission (MHC) surveys for mills and farmsteads; nearby Fitchburg Historical Society resources for regional kin movements.

Ashby's genealogical landscape captures New England's upland persistence—founding farmers whose descendants remained across centuries on the same soil. For genealogists, its value lies in continuity: few towns preserve so clear a thread from 18th-century proprietors through Civil War veterans and 20th-century residents whose family names still echo across its pastures and hillside cemeteries.

Ashland

Ashland, a compact town in southern Middlesex County, Massachusetts, straddles the upper waters of the Sudbury River on Nipmuc homelands once shared by the bordering towns of Framingham, Holliston, and Hopkinton. Incorporated in 1846, Ashland emerged as a mid-19th-century industrial and railroad town—its creation literally carved from three older municipalities. The town's layered genealogical story links early colonial hill farms to factory villages and suburban neighborhoods, with records spanning Puritan founders, Irish canal workers, and postwar commuters. Industrialization, faith communities, and land continuity have preserved rich archival trails for genealogists tracing families who bridged farming, mill labor, and later professional life within one locale.

Nipmuc Meadows, Parent Town Grants, and Early Settlers

Before colonial land division, Nipmuc families fished the Sudbury's upper reaches and maintained seasonal planting fields along Indian Brook and Ashland Reservoir. English settlement began through grants of the 1650s, when Sudbury, Sherborn (later Holliston), and Hopkinton proprietors extended western farm lots into the present territory. Families such as the Travis, Snow, Metcalf, and Stone lines appear in original deeds within those parent towns. When residents of the "Unionville" district petitioned for incorporation in the 1840s—frustrated by divided parish obligations—the new Town of Ashland united portions of its neighbors into one civil body, taking its name from Henry Clay's Kentucky estate. First structures included the Unionville Church (later Federated), a public school, and grist and textile mills along the millpond at Main Street village.

Railroad Villages, Mills, and Immigrant Neighborhoods

Ashland's economic rise paralleled the coming of the Boston & Worcester Railroad (1834) and later its own Ashland Branch, which made the town a manufacturing and commuter stop. Paper, cotton, and boot factories along the Sudbury drew Irish and later Italian laborers between 1850 and 1900. The creation of the Sudbury Reservoir (1897–1908) reshaped local geography, displacing some homesteads but creating new municipal workforces whose family lines—often Irish, Portuguese, or French Canadian—persist in ward and parish records. Parochial life centered at St. Cecilia's Catholic Parish (est. 1860s) with Methodist, Baptist, and Universalist congregations anchoring Yankee-rooted families. Town censuses and directories show intermarriage across Holliston and Framingham lines, while land deeds reveal multi-generation retention of small family farms turned suburban lots during the mid-20th century.

Genealogical Resources and Strategies

Vital repositories:

- Ashland Town Clerk: Vital records (birth, marriage, death) from incorporation (1846) onward; street, tax, and polling lists from the 19th and 20th centuries.
- Ashland Historical Society and Public Library Local History Room: Family genealogies (Travis, Snow, Metcalf), mill maps, factory payroll receipts, cemetery plots, and early photographs.
- Middlesex South Registry of Deeds (Cambridge): Land transfers crossing Holliston, Hopkinton, and Framingham boundaries that define early homesteads.

- Regional aids: Massachusetts Vital Records series for parent towns (Framingham, Holliston, Hopkinton); FamilySearch digitized town and church records; and MHC site inventories for mills and reservoir-era relocations.

Ashland's genealogy embodies the passage from colonial boundary land to industrial village and modern commuter suburb. For researchers, the town's youth as an incorporated entity belies its deep ancestral reach through its parent towns' records—offering a compact but vivid archive of kinship, adaptation, and resilience beside the Sudbury's winding current.

<u>Ayer</u>

Ayer, a railroad-born town in north-central Middlesex County, Massachusetts, occupies a crossroads of streams and ridges once belonging to the Nashaway and Nipmuc peoples. Carved from Groton and Shirley and incorporated in 1871, Ayer grew not from 17th-century farms but from 19th-century transportation and military enterprise. Its genealogical identity differs from older Middlesex towns: short on colonial roots but rich in records of migration, industrial work, and military service. The town's layered civic, parish, and employment archives track families who arrived from Ireland, Quebec, and southern Europe to labor in rail yards, mills, and the neighboring Fort Devens complex—yielding sources that document transient and settled kin alike from the Reconstruction era forward.

Nashaway Meadows, Groton Farms, and Early Precincts

Before English settlement, Nashaway-affiliated families inhabited the valleys along Nonacoicus Brook and the Nashua River. Groton proprietors added these uplands to their west precinct lands after 1655, granting meadow lots to Blood, Parker, and Lawrence families. Through the 18th century, the area remained sparsely peopled by Groton and Shirley farmers, its identity tied to small mills and taverns at what would become Ayer Center. Early land and church records therefore reside in Groton and Shirley volumes—vital for reconstructing the pre-incorporation genealogy of Ayer's landscape and its few longstanding surnames (Blood, Hazen, Prescott).

Rail Yards, Fort Devens, and Immigrant Communities

Ayer's transformation began with the convergence of four major railroads—the Fitchburg, Peterborough & Shirley, Worcester & Nashua, and Stony Brook lines—by the 1840s. Known first as "Groton Junction," the town became a freight and passenger hub, its boardinghouses and workshops drawing Irish rail workers and Yankee conductors. Incorporation in 1871 formalized a thriving transportation center that soon expanded with small industries and civic institutions. Italian and Polish families arrived by 1900, participating in parish life at St. Mary's (est. 1898) and joining fraternal and benefit societies documented in city directories. The adjacent Fort Devens Army base, established in 1917, reshaped Ayer's demography, generating a trove of genealogical data in draft registrations, military payrolls, and post-war settlement patterns. Mid-20th-century urban renewal and base activity brought Puerto Rican and Southeast Asian families, extending the genealogical record into new cultural dimensions.

Genealogical Resources and Strategies

Vital repositories:

- Ayer Town Clerk: Birth, marriage, and death records from 1871 forward; town census and street lists from the 1880s; vital supplements for Fort Devens personnel.
- Ayer Historical Society and Library Archives: Family files, railroad employee rosters, photographs, and parish histories; Devens army newsletters and immigration artifacts.
- Middlesex South Registry of Deeds (Cambridge): Groton and Shirley deed volumes covering pre-1871 property transfers within Ayer's territory.
- Regional aids: Massachusetts Vital Records to 1850 (Groton, Shirley); FamilySearch digitized Ayer town books; MHC surveys for railroad, industrial, and Fort Devens sites; and National Archives military personnel indexes.

Ayer's genealogical character rests not on deep colonial descent but on mobility and reinvention. From Groton's frontier farms to the echo of departing trains and the regimental musters at Fort Devens, the town's records trace the movement of families whose identities were forged by opportunity and service—rootless and rooted at once—within a century of rapid change along the Nashua Valley.

Bedford

Bedford, a pastoral town in eastern Middlesex County, Massachusetts, lies between the Concord and Shawsheen rivers on ancestral Massachusett and Pawtucket homelands. Carved from Billerica and Concord and incorporated in 1729, Bedford bridges the early agrarian frontier of the 17th century with the Revolutionary heartland of the 18th. Its genealogical texture reveals deep family continuity—from Puritan farmers and militia captains to 19th-century tradesmen and 20th-century suburban professionals—anchored by exceptionally well-preserved town, church, and land records.

Massachusett Fields, Billerica Allotments, and Early Proprietors

The area's precolonial landscape offered fertile meadows and river crossings long cultivated and fished by Massachusett and Pawtucket peoples. Settler expansion from Concord (1635) and Billerica (1655) pressed into these lands, and by 1680 several extended families held meadow tracts through recorded deeds. The incorporation of Bedford in 1729 unified sections of both towns into a single parish, its first meetinghouse built near the Great Road and Shawsheen meadows. Founding families—Page, Fitch, Stearns, Lane, and Bacon—appear across Middlesex deed and probate series, their names repeating through centuries in local vital records. The First

Parish Church records (from 1730) detail baptisms, marriages, and deaths richly annotated with familial relationships essential for genealogical reconstruction.

Revolution, Mills, and Rural Continuity

Bedford gained lasting fame for its Revolutionary service: its minutemen, led by Captain Jonathan Wilson, joined Concord's fight on April 19, 1775, carrying a banner now preserved in town. The involvement of nearly every local male head of household in militia or supply service links families across war rosters, pension applications, and town meeting minutes. Through the 19th century, Bedford remained primarily agricultural—its dairy and orchard products feeding neighboring Lexington and Concord markets—while modest industry arose along the Shawsheen: sawmills, gristmills, and small workshops documented in tax and factory schedules. Irish and Canadian newcomers around 1850 worked in these enterprises and on local turnpikes, integrating into established households and St. Michael's Parish (1855). Later, 20th-century suburbanization brought new housing yet maintained genealogical continuity through unbroken civic recordkeeping.

Genealogical Resources and Strategies

Vital repositories:

- Bedford Town Clerk: Birth, marriage, and death records from 1729 to present; town meeting books, poll and tax lists detailing heads of household.
- Bedford Historical Society: Manuscripts and family files (Fitch, Page, Stearns), Revolutionary War rosters, maps, and cemetery transcriptions; Civil War and World War veterans' organizations.
- Middlesex South Registry of Deeds (Cambridge): Early Billerica and Concord parcel divisions, with deeds and surveys tracing property lineage through three centuries.
- Regional aids: Massachusetts Vital Records to 1850 (Bedford volume); FamilySearch digitized church and town books; MHC site summaries for colonial homesteads; and Concord Free Public Library's local genealogy collections for overlapping families.

Bedford's genealogical landscape exemplifies quiet resilience: a community whose lines run unbroken from 17th-century meadow lots through the patriot generation to modern commuter neighborhoods. Its archival density—vital, land, and church—allows researchers to reconstruct family evolution with precision, following descendants who have for centuries inhabited the same crossroads between Concord's orchards and Billerica's brooklands.

Belmont

Belmont, a compact suburban town in eastern Middlesex County, Massachusetts, lies between Cambridge, Watertown, Waltham, Arlington, and Lexington, occupying the rolling uplands and meadows of former Massachusett homelands. Incorporated in 1859 from portions of Watertown, Waltham, and Arlington, Belmont emerged as an agrarian-turned-suburban enclave defined by market gardening, rail commuting, and academic proximity to Boston. Though one of the younger Middlesex towns, its genealogical story stretches backward through the parent towns' early proprietors—Whitney, Wellington, Bright, and Clark—and forward through 19th- and 20th-century immigrant settlement and suburban transformation.

Massachusett Meadows, Watertown Origins, and Early Grants

Before Puritan settlement, Massachusett families traveled the base of Belmont Hill for seasonal fishing along Fresh Pond and Little River. Beginning in the 1630s, portions of what became Belmont were absorbed into Watertown and later Waltham as the "Little Cambridge" or "Upper Farms," granted to early families including Whitney, Bright, and Wellington. Through the 18th century the area remained sparsely populated, its economy dominated by grazing and orchards, with many farmers listed in Watertown and Waltham tax rolls and church registers. The region's fertile soil later earned it renown as one of metropolitan Boston's premier market-gardening centers, known for exporting lettuce and dairy to urban markets well into the 19th century. The town's formal separation in 1859 provided residents their own civic identity and record set, centered on the new town hall near Belmont Center.

Market Farms, Rail Suburbs, and Immigrant Neighborhoods

The arrival of the Fitchburg Railroad (1840s) and later the electric trolley made Belmont an attractive suburb for Cambridge and Boston professionals. Italian, Irish, and later Armenian immigrants established notable enclaves, working on farms and in trades supporting nearby industry in Waltham and Cambridge. Protestant and Catholic parishes—First Church (Unitarian, 1859), St. Joseph's (1905)—anchored community records. By the late 19th century, Belmont hosted estates of Boston businessmen and educators, whose domestic staff and gardeners appear in census and directory data alongside multigenerational Yankee residents. Early 20th-century development filled Belmont Hill and Cushing Square with planned subdivisions and civic architecture, producing extensive ward and property documentation in municipal archives.

Genealogical Resources and Strategies

Vital repositories:

- Belmont Town Clerk: Vital records (births, marriages, deaths) from incorporation (1859) forward; annual street and voting lists; census extracts linking household clusters to historic addresses.
- Belmont Historical Society and Public Library Local History Room: Manuscripts and family collections (Wellington, Clark, Bright), town photographs, parish rosters, and cemetery surveys.

- Middlesex South Registry of Deeds (Cambridge): Early Watertown and Waltham land divisions; 19th- and early 20th-century subdivision and estate maps.
- Regional aids: Massachusetts Vital Records to 1850 (Watertown, Waltham, Arlington) for antecedent family lines; FamilySearch digital archives of Belmont vital and probate filings; MHC site files for farmsteads, trolleys, and historic estates.

Belmont's genealogical narrative bridges field to foyer—the continuum from Watertown's Puritan farms to suburban lawns and rail platforms. Its documentary network—well-preserved land deeds, vibrant civic minutes, and long-running family records—invites genealogists to trace transitions of class, faith, and mobility through the families who, over centuries, condensed New England's agrarian heart into a suburban crossroads beside Boston's edge.

Billerica

Billerica, a venerable Middlesex County town northeast of Concord and north of Bedford, spans the Shawsheen and Concord river valleys on ancestral Pawtucket and Massachusett homelands. Settled by English colonists in 1652 and incorporated in 1655, Billerica was among the early inland "praying town" frontiers of Massachusetts Bay. Its wide landscape of upland farms and river meadows fostered enduring family lines whose descendants spread into scores of neighboring towns. From 17th-century proprietors like Crosby and Farmer to 19th-century canal workers and 20th-century suburban households, Billerica's records preserve a nearly unbroken genealogy of New England kinship and expansion.

Pawtucket Meadows, Shawshin Grants, and Early Proprietors

Before colonization, Pawtucket and Massachusett bands fished and cultivated the Shawsheen's meadows, sustaining seasonal camps on what settlers renamed "Shawshin Plantation." In 1652, the General Court granted the tract to settlers from Cambridge and Charlestown; incorporation followed in 1655 as "Billerica," named for a village in Essex, England. Families such as Parker, Talbot, Crosby, Farmer, Kidder, and Manning settled the first farmsteads and built the meetinghouse near today's Center.

Early land divisions, recorded in Middlesex deeds and town books, reflect long, narrow lots bordering meadows and brooks—patterns still evident in property lines today. Early intermarriages with Concord and Chelmsford families appear throughout 17th-century probate inventories and parish covenants. Billerica's meticulous early records form one of the Bay Colony's richest genealogical archives for tracing Puritan-era descendants.

Revolution, Canal Trade, and Industrial Prosperity

During the American Revolution, Billerica sent large numbers to the local militia and Continental forces. Muster rolls and pension files often list members of interrelated families who served together. After 1800, the town's agrarian economy diversified: tanneries, mills, and the Middlesex Canal (completed 1803) linked Billerica to Boston markets, creating records of innkeepers, boatmen, and artisans now preserved in town tax lists and business ledgers. Irish laborers followed canal and railroad work into the mid-19th century, settling chiefly in East Billerica and near North Billerica's mills. Catholic parishes such as St. Andrew's (founded 1868) produced baptism and marriage records extending Billerica's genealogical reach into immigrant generations. The early 20th century brought suburban development along Boston-Lowell rail lines, expanding residential neighborhoods while preserving family continuity through persistent land tenure and parochial affiliation.

Genealogical Resources and Strategies

Vital repositories:

- Billerica Town Clerk: Vital records (birth, marriage, death) from 1655 to present; town meeting books, poll taxes, and annual street lists.
- Billerica Historical Society: Family manuscripts, Revolutionary and Civil War rosters, church registers, school reports, and cemetery transcriptions.
- Middlesex North Registry of Deeds (Lowell): Land deeds and plats documenting early meadow allotments and later industrial development.
- Regional aids: Massachusetts Vital Records to 1850 (Billerica volume); FamilySearch digitized town registers; MHC inventories for canal, mill, and farm sites; documentation tied to Bedford, Tewksbury, and Burlington genealogies that originated from Billerica's parent farms.

Billerica's genealogical narrative stretches seamlessly through four centuries—from Puritan pastures and militia greens to canal yards and commuter suburbs. For researchers, the town's deep archive links original proprietors and Revolutionary soldiers with later immigrant tradesmen and suburban homeowners, illustrating the continuity of place and kin that defines the heart of Middlesex County history.

Boxborough

Boxborough, a small upland town in northwestern Middlesex County, Massachusetts, occupies the transition between the Assabet and Nashoba valleys on Nipmuc homelands once tied to the Nashaway tribe. First settled as the western parish and outfields of Stow and Littleton, Boxborough was incorporated in 1783. The town's genealogical foundation rests on old Concord-Acton-Stow family lines—farmers and craftsmen whose descendants remain on the same winding roads centuries later. Its records are a compact archive of rural New England endurance: from the colonial clearings of the Priest and Blanchard families to 19th-century orchardists and millhands, Boxborough's history offers persistent kin continuity anchored by town, church, and land documentation.

Nipmuc Hills, Stow Precincts, and Early Allotments

Before English arrival, Nipmuc and Nashaway families used the slopes of Flagg Hill and the pond meadows for hunting and line fishing, leaving seasonal trails connecting the Assabet and Squannacook basins. Colonial settlement spread westward from Concord and Stow in the early 18th century; by 1710, the Blanchard, Wetherbee, and Priest families held farms under Stow proprietorship. Worship at Stow's west precinct meetinghouse created the nucleus for independence. Persistent travel distances for church and civic affairs prompted incorporation as the independent Town of Boxborough in 1783, the name derived from the local Box family and the word "borough" marking autonomy. Early town records from the 1780s onward preserve voters' lists, highway layouts, and church baptisms already spanning multiple interrelated lineages.

Revolution, Hill Farms, and Local Industry

Boxborough's citizens took part in the Revolutionary struggle before townhood—men served in the Acton and Stow militia companies, including several at Concord Bridge in 1775. Pension files and town petitions connect these soldiers with families still represented locally decades later. Post-Revolutionary Boxborough developed quietly as an agrarian community, its small population engaged in mixed farming, sawmilling, and later orchard cultivation. Census returns reveal stable surnames with minimal outside migration. In the 19th century, a modest straw-braiding and shoe industry supplemented farm income, documented in factory schedules and school district reports. Churches—the Boxborough Baptist (est. 1832) and Congregational (1838)—provide further family data through membership and vital registers. Into the 20th century, the town retained its rural identity, its roads named for resident families recognizable across two centuries of deeds.

Genealogical Resources and Strategies

Vital repositories:

- Boxborough Town Clerk: Birth, marriage, and death records from incorporation (1783) onward; town meeting books, tax assessments, and poll lists identifying households.
- Boxborough Historical Society and Public Library: Family files (Blanchard, Wetherbee, Priest, Box), cemetery transcriptions, church minute books, and photographs.
- Middlesex South Registry of Deeds (Cambridge): Stow and Littleton antecedent deeds; Boxborough farm boundaries and land transfers from 18th through 20th centuries.
- Regional aids: Massachusetts Vital Records to 1850 (Boxborough volume); FamilySearch scans of municipal registers; MHC cultural inventories for historic farms, mills, and the town center common; and Acton and Stow records for pre-1783 familial ties.

Boxborough's genealogical portrait reflects quiet persistence—the passing down of hillsides, homes, and surnames from colonial times through modern commuting life. For genealogists, it presents a microcosm of intact lineage and stable recordkeeping, where three centuries of families can be followed through a single web of parish, cemetery, and land relations nestled within the old Nashoba hills.

Here's a genealogical and historical profile for Burlington, Massachusetts, written in your established Middlesex County narrative and genealogical style.

Burlington

Burlington, a north-central Middlesex County town between Woburn, Billerica, Bedford, and Lexington, occupies the gentle uplands of the Shawsheen and Vine Brook valleys—lands once belonging to the Massachusett people who fished and foraged its meadows. Settled in the 1640s as frontier farmland of Woburn and incorporated as a separate town in 1799, Burlington long remained a small agricultural community producing milk, hay, and apples for Boston markets before transforming, in the mid-20th century, into a technology corridor suburb. Its genealogical landscape—richly documented through early deeds, church books, and family cemeteries—reveals extended kin continuity between Woburn planters, Yankee farmers, and later suburban homeowners who inherited the same rolling fields two centuries apart.

Massachusett Meadows, Woburn Farms, and Colonial Allotments

Before colonization, Massachusett families traversed the Vine Brook and Mill Pond valleys, cultivating corn and fishing the Shawsheen tributaries. In 1642, Charlestown and Woburn settlers patented the land as "Woburn Second Precinct," distributing long farm lots to families including Winn, Johnson, Simonds, and Polk. For 150 years, Burlington remained a rural parish of Woburn—its meetinghouse raised in 1730 to serve widespread farms stretching toward Billerica and Bedford. Discontent over Woburn's distant governance and the Revolutionary strain on travel led residents to petition for separation, granted in 1799. Early Burlington records begin then, though most pre-incorporation genealogical data resides within Woburn's extensive 17th- and 18th-century church and land books.

Revolution, Dairy Farms, and Suburban Change

Burlington's men fought in the colonial and Revolutionary wars, often listed under Woburn and Billerica companies—records invaluable for tracing 18th-century ancestry. The 19th century saw a stable agrarian economy: dairy herds, orchards, and truck gardens supplying produce to Boston. Families such as the Winn, Fowle, and Fox lines appear repeatedly in tax lists and deeds; intermarriage with Bedford and Lexington kin networks was common.

The American Civil War introduced new veterans' rosters and town appropriations documenting every household's contribution. With rail and automobile access after 1900, Burlington evolved from farms to residential subdivisions, culminating in rapid population growth after construction of Route 128 in the 1950s. Industrial and housing expansion changed the landscape but not the strength of record continuity—town, cemetery, and church archives preserved with unbroken civic stewardship.

Genealogical Resources and Strategies

Vital repositories:

- Burlington Town Clerk: Births, marriages, and deaths from incorporation (1799) to present; poll and tax lists recording early farmers and 20th-century householders.
- Burlington Historical Society: Family manuscripts (Winn, Fox, Fowle, Simonds), cemetery transcriptions, farm maps, school registers, and photographic collections.
- Middlesex South Registry of Deeds (Cambridge): Woburn and Billerica deeds preceding town incorporation; agricultural parcels and postwar subdivision maps.
- Regional aids: Massachusetts Vital Records to 1850 (Burlington volume and Woburn references); FamilySearch digitized vital and church records; MHC inventories for farmsteads and Route 128-era commercial sites.

Burlington's genealogical narrative encapsulates the evolution of Massachusetts itself: from Puritan farms and dairy commons to entrepreneurial suburb. The town's deep paper trail—centuries of vital events, property transfers, and parish continuity—allows genealogists to follow families from 17th-century Woburn grants through generations of resilience and change, their histories preserved across the same quiet hills where the Shawsheen still winds toward the sea.

Carlisle

Carlisle, a small rural town in northwestern Middlesex County, Massachusetts, nestles between the Concord and Assabet rivers amid the wooded hills and meadows of Nipmuc homelands. Incorporated in 1805 from portions of Acton, Chelmsford, Concord, Littleton, and Westford, Carlisle embodies the late-colonial frontier of agrarian self-sufficiency. Its genealogical record traces enduring Yankee farm families—Garfield, Wilkins, Spalding, Heald, and Blood—through three centuries of quiet continuity, supplemented by 19th-century Irish laborers and 20th-century suburban arrivals. Town books, church covenants, and land deeds preserve one of Middlesex's most intact archives of rural kinship persistence.

Nipmuc Brooks, Concord Outlands, and Precinct Formation

Before English settlement, Nipmuc families fished the Concord River's tributaries and cultivated corn along Spencer Brook and the Great Meadows. Colonial expansion from Concord (1635) and Acton (1735) gradually filled these uplands with dispersed farmsteads; by the 1750s, residents of the "Concord Northwest Precinct" petitioned for local worship to avoid long Sunday travel. Families such as Garfield, Spalding, and Heald held meadow lots recorded in parent-town deeds, their kinship networks visible in militia rosters and probate inventories. Incorporation as Carlisle in 1805—named for Carlisle, Pennsylvania—established independent civic life around the meetinghouse common near today's Carlisle Center. Early town records capture a stable population of interrelated households tied by marriage and adjacency across five original municipalities.

Revolution, Farm Commons, and Quiet Resilience

Carlisle's farmers contributed to the Revolutionary cause through Concord and Acton companies; Captain William Garfield's service exemplifies local patriotism documented in pension files and town appropriations. The 19th century reinforced agrarian traditions: dairy, apple orchards, and truck gardens supplied Boston markets via the Middlesex Canal and later Fitchburg Railroad spurs. Irish families arrived mid-century to work on local turnpikes and mills, integrating into established farmsteads and the Union Church (est. 1830). Town censuses reveal minimal outmigration, with many surnames persisting through Civil War service records and school district reports. The 20th century brought gradual suburbanization along Route 225, yet Carlisle retained its rural character, its family cemeteries and continuous land tenure providing genealogists with unbroken chains linking colonial proprietors to modern residents.

Genealogical Resources and Strategies

Vital repositories:

- Carlisle Town Clerk: Birth, marriage, and death records from incorporation (1805) forward; town meeting minutes, tax valuations, and highway surveys listing landowners.
- Carlisle Historical Society: Family manuscripts (Garfield, Wilkins, Spalding), cemetery transcriptions, church registers, farm ledgers, and Revolutionary era documents.
- Middlesex South Registry of Deeds (Cambridge): Antecedent deeds from Acton, Concord, Chelmsford, Littleton, and Westford defining Carlisle's patchwork boundaries.
- Regional aids: Massachusetts Vital Records to 1850 (parent town volumes); FamilySearch digitized Carlisle registers; MHC cultural resource inventories for farmsteads and the town common; Concord Free Public Library collections for overlapping Revolutionary families.

Carlisle's genealogical essence lies in its unbroken rural lineage—from Nipmuc brooks and Concord outfarms to the enduring farmhouses that still dot its winding roads. For researchers, the town offers a pristine laboratory of New England kinship: compact population, meticulous records, and family names that echo across deeds, gravestones, and town ledgers spanning the full sweep of American history.

Chelmsford

Chelmsford, a sprawling northern Middlesex County town, Massachusetts, stretches along the Merrimack River near Pawtucket Falls on Pennacook and Wamesit homelands, granted by the General Court in 1653 from Concord and Woburn lands and incorporated in 1655. Evolving from frontier farmsteads and garrison houses into a 19th-century mill and rail village, Chelmsford's villages—North Chelmsford, East Chelmsford, and South Chelmsford—preserve layered genealogies of Puritan proprietors, Irish laborers, French Canadian weavers, and suburban descendants, documented in some of Middlesex's earliest continuous vital and land records.

Pennacook Fields, Merrimack Grants, and Early Plantations

Before English settlement, Pennacook and Wamesit families fished salmon at Pawtucket Falls and planted corn along the Merrimack's intervals, their trails later becoming colonial roads. The 1653 grant created "Chelmsford Plantation" near the falls, with early families—Adams, Parker, Spalding, Richardson, and Colburn—drawing meadow lots by 1660 around the first meeting-house. Town books from 1655 record births like Joseph Parker (1653), militia service, and land divisions linking Chelmsford to Lowell (carved 1826) and Dracut. Epidemics and King Philip's War (1675–76) depopulated Indigenous presence, yielding fields to proprietors whose deeds and church covenants trace founding kin through 18th-century intermarriages with Billerica and Dunstable lines.

Mills, Canals, and Immigrant Clusters

The Middlesex Canal (1803) and later railroads spurred industry along the Merrimack, with North Chelmsford's mills drawing Irish famine refugees by 1850, followed by French Canadians in textile shops. Parishes like St. Mary's (1860s) and Baptist meetinghouses anchored ethnic wards, their registers capturing chain migration visible in payrolls and naturalizations. Revolutionary rosters show Chelmsford minutemen at Concord Bridge, while 19th-century censuses link farm families to factory hands across villages. 20th-century suburban growth retained rural cores, with Route 495 enabling continuity in family-held properties.

Genealogical Resources and Strategies

Vital repositories:

- Chelmsford Town Clerk: Births, marriages, deaths from 1655 (published to 1849); resident lists 1896–1967, ward books.
- Chelmsford Historical Society: Manuscripts (Waters' History, Perham notes), family files (Adams, Spalding), cemetery inscriptions.
- Middlesex North Registry of Deeds (Lowell): Early Merrimack plats, mill deeds, Lowell separations.
- Regional aids: FamilySearch vital transcriptions; MHC surveys for falls, canals; Chelmsford Library genealogy group resources.

Chelmsford's genealogy—from Pennacook fisheries and Adams-Parker grants to mill villages and commuter lanes—equips researchers with deep records unveiling kin spanning Wamesit meadows to modern subdivisions.

<u>Concord</u>

Concord, the iconic heartland town of Middlesex County, Massachusetts, lies at the confluence of the Assabet and Sudbury rivers forming the Concord River, on Pennacook homelands known as Musketaquid or "grassy plain." Settled in 1635 as the first inland plantation of Massachusetts Bay and incorporated that year, Concord evolved from frontier clearings and mills into the cradle of American independence, literary renaissance, and suburban legacy. Its dense genealogical records—from Peter Bulkeley's church covenant to Emerson-Alcott kin—trace Puritan founders, minutemen, Irish laborers, and 19th-century reformers across quarters and villages like Walden and Centerville.

Pennacook Plains, Bulkeley Grants, and Founding Families

Before English arrival, Pennacook sachems Tahattawan and Squaw Sachem sustained cornfields and fisheries amid the rivers' grassy intervals, depopulated by 1616–1619 epidemics. Reverend Peter Bulkeley and Major Simon Willard led settlers—about twelve families including Buttrick, Meriam, Wheeler, Jones, and Heald—to purchase six miles square in 1636, building lean-tos and a mill dam. The church gathered in Cambridge before ordination, with land divided into North, South, and East quarters by 1654 housing Bateman, Flint, Blood, Fletcher, and Adams lines. Town clerk Robert Meriam's vital records from 1654 preserve baptisms and land lots linking Concord progenitors to Cambridge, Watertown, and later Carlisle-Acton offshoots.

Revolution Bridge, Literary Circles, and Village Growth

Concord's North Bridge witnessed "the shot heard round the world" on April 19, 1775, with minutemen under Captain John Parker and James Barrett defending militia stores; rosters tie families across Lexington and Lincoln. 19th-century mills and railroads drew Irish workers to Centerville, while transcendentalists—Emerson (1834), Alcotts (1840), Thoreau—formed intellectual kinships documented in diaries and town histories. Parishes like Trinitarian Congregational and St. Bernard's (1860s) captured ethnic shifts, with Walden Pond symbolizing reformist descent amid suburban expansion.

Genealogical Resources and Strategies

Vital repositories:

- Concord Town Clerk: Births, marriages, deaths from 1635 (Meriam volume 1654–1668); proprietary grants and quarter divisions.

- Concord Free Public Library Special Collections: Wheeler's Concord articles, Shattuck's History (1835), family manuscripts (Bulkeley, Buttrick, Meriam).
- Middlesex South Registry of Deeds (Cambridge): Musketaquid plats, Revolutionary confiscations, 19th-century subdivisions.
- Regional aids: FamilySearch vital transcriptions to 1850; MHC sites for North Bridge, mills; Concord Museum genealogies.

Concord's archival spine—from Musketaquid purchases and minuteman rosters to literary ledgers—unveils kin webs spanning Pennacook fields, patriot quarters, and reformist homes, equipping genealogists to trace New England's foundational lineages along the rivers' enduring bend.

Dracut

Dracut, a northern Middlesex County town straddling the Merrimack River opposite Lowell, occupies Pennacook and Wamesit homelands around Pawtucket Falls, settled in the 1660s from Chelmsford lands and incorporated as a town in 1702. Evolving from frontier garrison farms and missionary outposts into 19th-century mills and rail villages, Dracut's districts—East Dracut, Kenwood, and Navy Yard—preserve genealogies of Varnum, Coburn, and Richardson progenitors alongside Irish laborers and French Canadian weavers whose parish and payroll records link to Lowell's industrial diaspora.

Pennacook Falls, Chelmsford Farms, and Proprietor Settlements

Before colonization, Pennacook sachem Passaconaway's people fished shad at the falls and planted corn along river intervals, with Rev. John Eliot establishing a 1653 praying Indian mission featuring church, school, and fields. Chelmsford selectmen granted meadows north of the Merrimack to John Webb (Evered), whose 1664/5 sale to surveyors Samuel Varnum and Richard Shatswell marked permanent settlement; Edward Coburn (Colburn) followed, building the first garrison house. Varnum's son John, born 1669 with Pennacook assistance, became first town clerk. Families petitioned separation from Chelmsford in 1701 citing river ferries and protection needs, their 20-household signatures yielding incorporation. Deeds trace Varnum-Coburn-Richardson intermarriages across garrison lots amid King Philip's War raids (1675–76).

Mills, Rail Yards, and Ethnic Wards

Revolutionary service tied Dracut men to Chelmsford minutemen, with pension rolls preserving kin networks. 19th-century Middlesex Canal and Boston & Lowell Railroad spurred tanneries and textile mills in East Dracut, drawing Irish famine migrants and Quebecois weavers by 1880. Parishes like St. Mary's (1870s) and Hildreth Baptist anchored communities, their registers capturing chain migration alongside Navy Yard industrial payrolls. Lowell's 1836 annexation took Pawtucketville but left Dracut's core farms and villages intact, with 20th-century suburban growth along Route 495 maintaining family continuity in cemeteries and town lists.

Genealogical Resources and Strategies

Vital repositories:

- Dracut Town Clerk: Births, marriages, deaths from 1702; garrison-era petitions and ward directories.
- Dracut Historical Society: Coburn's History manuscripts, Varnum-Coburn family papers, church extracts, cemetery surveys.
- Middlesex North Registry of Deeds (Lowell): Chelmsford grants, Webb-Varnum plats, mill deeds post-1836.
- Regional aids: FamilySearch Chelmsford-Dracut vitals to 1850; MHC falls and garrison sites; Lowell archives for annexed Pawtucketville overlaps.

Dracut's chronicle—from Eliot's mission and Varnum garrisons to mill wards and commuter ridges—arms genealogists with records unveiling Pennacook-Merrimack kin from Indigenous fisheries through proprietor endurance to immigrant factories along the river's northern bank.

Dunstable

Dunstable, the northernmost frontier town of Middlesex County, Massachusetts, clings to the Merrimack River's southern bank amid rugged hills and Wamesit-Pennacook homelands, incorporated October 15, 1673, from vast tracts once spanning 200 square miles between Chelmsford and Londonderry, New Hampshire. Named for the English birthplace of Edward Tyng's wife, it shed portions to birth fifteen towns—Pepperell, Hollis (NH), Tyngsborough—leaving a compact rural core of enduring farm lineages like Proctor, Cummings, Kendall, Butterfield, Blodgett, and Swallow, whose garrison deeds and militia rolls trace colonial endurance through agrarian persistence.

Wamesit Tracts, Merrimack Proprietors, and Garrison Settlements

Before English patents, Wamesit and Naticook sachems held Merrimack intervals for fishing and cornfields, their 1661 lands sold for £20 sterling to Tyng and associates amid epidemics' aftermath. Twenty-six proprietors petitioned incorporation in 1673, drawing long river lots to families including Blodgett, Farwell, and Fitch by 1675, when King Philip's War razed the first meetinghouse and scattered settlers to garrisons. Rebuilt amid raids, Dunstable's core families—Proctors at Bear Hill, Cummings along streams—intermarried across Chelmsford and Groton lines, their survival etched in Middlesex deeds, vital stubs from 1680s, and Indian raid petitions linking to Pepperell separations (1775).

Indian Wars, Farm Commons, and Rural Continuity

Dunstable endured relentless frontier assaults through Queen Anne's and French & Indian Wars, militia captains like John Farwell documenting kin service in muster rolls and scalp bounties. 19th-century farms supplied Boston via Middlesex Canal remnants and rail spurs, with minimal industry preserving Yankee surnames through tax valuations and Baptist-Congregational pew lists. Civil War rosters and Grange halls extended family records, while 20th-century zoning locked rural character, deeds showing multi-century land tenure amid suburban pressures from Nashua.

Genealogical Resources and Strategies

Vital repositories:

- Dunstable Town Clerk: Births, marriages, deaths from 1673 (sparse early); proprietary petitions, tax lists, garrison accounts.
- Dunstable Historical Society: Nason's 1873 History manuscripts, family files (Proctor, Blodgett), cemetery inscriptions (p. 228-268).
- Middlesex North Registry of Deeds (Lowell): 1661 Tyng purchase, proprietor plats, post-separation divisions to fifteen towns.
- Regional aids: FamilySearch Dunstable vitals to 1850; MHC garrison and farmstead sites; Stearns' "Early Generations of Founders" for thirty families.

Dunstable's genealogy—from Wamesit sales and Tyng garrisons to Butterfield pastures—yields pristine records of frontier survival, equipping researchers to link 17th-century proprietors through war-torn commons to the hill farms still bearing their names along the Merrimack's ancient banks.

Groton

Groton, a vast upland town in northwestern Middlesex County, Massachusetts, spans the Nashua and Squannacook river confluences on Nipmuc and Nashaway homelands known as Petapawag or "swampy land." First settled as a trading post in the 1640s and incorporated in 1655 as "The Plantation of Groton" under Deane Winthrop, it originally encompassed much of present-day Ayer, Pepperell, Shirley, Dunstable, and beyond, evolving from frontier garrisons through mills and academies into a rural-suburban enclave. Its genealogical depth—from Tinker traders and Nutting proprietors to Prescott minutemen and 19th-century farm families—preserves one of Middlesex's richest continuums amid repeated frontier rebirths.

Nipmuc Trails, Winthrop Grants, and Garrison Founders

Before English traders, Nipmuc and Nashaway families followed river trails for fishing and planting, their lands sold amid epidemics to John Tinker, who established a post at Nod Brook by 1649. The 1655 incorporation drew families like Nutting, Gilson, Cooper, Lawrence, and Fitch, dividing vast tracts into meadow lots around the first meetinghouse. King Philip's War (1676) razed the settlement, sparing four garrisons where survivors like John Nutting perished; rebuilding by 1678 militarized the town with 91 garrison men by 1692. Early deeds and vital stubs trace these progenitors—intermarrying across Chelmsford and Concord—through Queen Anne's War raids, yielding probate chains to Pepperell and Shirley separations.

Revolution Commons, Mill Industries, and Academy Villages

Groton's Town Common assembled minutemen under Col. William Prescott, who marched to Bunker Hill (1775), their rosters linking kin to Shays' Rebellion unrest. 19th-century industry flourished: soapstone quarries, hop yards, brickworks, and pewter mills along the rivers, drawing Irish laborers while Yankee surnames dominated tax lists. Lawrence Academy (1793) and Groton School (1884) generated educator and alumni genealogies; Lost Lake resorts hosted summer families. Civil War service and Grange halls extended records, with 20th-century zoning preserving farm tenure amid Route 119 commuters.

Genealogical Resources and Strategies

Vital repositories:

- Groton Town Clerk: Births, marriages, deaths from 1655; proprietary lots, garrison petitions, tax valuations.
- Groton Historical Society & Center: Manuscripts (Nutting, Prescott, Lawrence families), Butler's Early Settlers, cemetery transcriptions, academy rosters.
- Middlesex South/North Registry of Deeds (Lowell/Cambridge): 1655 Winthrop plats, separations to twelve towns, mill privileges.
- Regional aids: Massachusetts Vital Records to 1850 (Groton volume); FamilySearch town books; MHC garrison and quarry sites; Pepperell/Shirley clerks for offshoots.

Groton's archival heart—from Petapawag trades and Nutting garrisons to Prescott commons and academy halls—reveals kin resilience across Nashua valleys, equipping genealogists to bridge Nipmuc rivers, colonial rebirths, and enduring hill farms that seeded half of northern Middlesex's lineages.

Holliston

Holliston, a southern Middlesex County town, Massachusetts, nestles along the upper Charles River tributaries amid Nipmuc homelands of the Awassamog, near Waushakum Pond and Muck-squit village. Settled in 1659 as Sherborn's western precinct and incorporated December 3, 1724, named for Harvard benefactor Thomas Hollis, it grew from dispersed farmsteads along Pout Lane into 19th-century shoe shops and rail stops, its villages—Mudville, Braggville, East Holliston—preserving Morse, Bullard, Sheffield, and Marshall lineages blended with Irish and Italian arrivals.

Nipmuc Paths, Sherborn Grants, and Early Clearings

Before Puritan expansion, Awassamog Nipmucs under Natick authority fished Wennakeen-ing ("smile of the great spirit") and followed Pout Lane trails from Annamasset, their 1701 land exchange with Sherborn short-lived as settlers bought tracts. Morse, Sheffield, Marshall, and Bullard families traced the ancient path by 1700, clustering farms near Lake Winthrop (Dean Winthrop's Pond). John Eliot and Daniel Gookin proselytized along the route, gathering converts; Sherborn records hold pre-1724 vitals, with Holliston's first meeting at Timothy Leland's house electing selectmen amid meadow allotments linking to Milford and Hopkinton separations.

Mills, Rail Villages, and Ethnic Clusters

Revolutionary service tied Holliston men to Sherborn militia, pension files preserving kin networks. Boston & Albany Railroad (Milford Branch) spurred 19th-century industry—shoe factories, paper mills—drawing Irish laborers to East Holliston and Italians to Mudville, anchored by First Congregational (1724 site) and St. Mary's parishes. Washington Street hosted George Washington's 1789 passage, its "indifferent road" noted in diaries. Civil War rosters and Grange halls extended records, while 20th-century zoning retained rural cores amid suburban growth along Route 16.

Genealogical Resources and Strategies

Vital repositories:

- Holliston Town Clerk: Births, marriages, deaths from 1724; proprietary petitions, tax lists, ward directories.
- Holliston Historical Society: Morse-Bullard manuscripts, church extracts, cemetery surveys, Pout Lane maps.
- Middlesex South Registry of Deeds (Cambridge): Sherborn grants, 1701 Nipmuc exchanges, rail-era plats.
- Regional aids: Massachusetts Vital Records to 1850 (Holliston/Sherborn); FamilySearch town books; MHC viaduct and Bullard Farm sites.

Holliston's genealogy—from Awassamog paths and Morse clearings to Hollis commons and village factories—reveals kin persistence along Pout Lane's ancient trace, guiding researchers through deeds and parish rolls to lineages bridging Nipmuc waters, Puritan farms, and enduring New England crossroads.

Hopkinton

Hopkinton, a southern Middlesex County town, Massachusetts, occupies rolling hills and meadows along the upper Charles River basin on Nipmuc homelands of the Magunkaquog settlement.

Established as a "Praying Indian" village by Rev. John Eliot in 1669 and incorporated December 13, 1715, from Harvard College's purchase of Edward Hopkins' bequest lands, it evolved from tenant farms and mills into 19th-century shoe factories and rail villages, its core preserving Bartholomew, Haven, and Phipps lineages amid Irish and later Italian waves.

Magunkaquog Fields, Eliot Missions, and Tenant Lots

Before colonization, Nipmuc families under sachem Pomhamon cultivated "great trees" at Magunkaquog (Magunco), one of Eliot's seven praying towns with 55 souls farming and observing Sabbath by 1675. King Philip's War dispersed survivors to Natick; Harvard trustees bought 12,500 acres in 1710, leasing at one penny per acre to settlers like Bartholomew, Draper, and Leland along the Old Connecticut Path. First meetinghouse rose 1725 near Woodville; Sherborn and Westborough records hold pre-incorporation vitals, with deeds tracing 99-year tenancies bought out for $10,000 in 1832, linking to Ashland separations (1846).

Mills, Shoe Shops, and Village Hearths

Revolutionary minutemen marched from Hopkinton to Concord Bridge. Pension rolls capture kin service. Boston & Providence Railroad (1830s) spurred factories at Hayden Rowe and Water Street, drawing Irish laborers post-famine to St. Mary's parish (1860s). Scottish-Irish Presbyterians formed early congregations before Congregational dominance; Civil War rosters and Grange halls document farm-to-factory shifts. Boston Marathon start (1924) cemented fame, while 20th-century zoning preserved rural cores amid Route 135 suburbs.

Genealogical Resources and Strategies

Vital repositories:

- Hopkinton Town Clerk: Births, marriages, deaths from 1715; tenant petitions, tax lists, ward directories.
- Hopkinton Historical Society: Bartholomew-Phipps manuscripts, Eliot mission papers, church extracts, cemetery surveys.
- Middlesex South Registry of Deeds (Cambridge): Hopkins bequest plats, Magunkaquog deeds, Upton/Ashland divisions.
- Regional aids: Massachusetts Vital Records to 1850 (Hopkinton volume); FamilySearch town books; MHC praying town and mill sites.

Hopkinton's genealogy—from Magunco praying fields and Hopkins tenants to marathon commons and village factories—unveils kin continuity along Charles tributaries, guiding researchers through Eliot covenants, lease rolls, and parish ledgers bridging Nipmuc plantations, colonial rebirths, and enduring hill farms.

Hudson

Hudson, a compact industrial town in central Middlesex County, Massachusetts, hugs the Assabet River's second falls on Nipmuc homelands once part of Marlborough's Indian Plantation. Settled in 1698 by John Barnes' gristmill and incorporated March 19, 1866, from Marlborough and Bolton lands—originally "Cow Commons," "The Mills," then Feltonville—Hudson rose as a 19th-century shoe and tannery hub, its core weaving Barnes, Witt, Hapgood, and Felton lineages with Irish, Portuguese, and Italian laborers across Wood Square and Main Street wards.

Nipmuc Falls, Marlborough Mills, and Early Proprietors

Before English mills, Nipmuc families fished Assabet pools amid Ockookangansett praying lands, depopulated by King Philip's War (1675–76). John Barnes gained an acre in 1698, erecting grist- and sawmills bridged to Lancaster road; Joseph Howe expanded operations, drawing Jeremiah Barstow and Robert Barnard to "Howe's Mills." Samuel Witt and John Hapgood petitioned separation in 1743 citing travel fatigue, denied until 1866 naming for Charles Hudson's $500 library gift. Marlborough deeds trace pre-1866 vitals, linking Hudson kin to Bolton sales and Revolutionary minutemen who joined Cambridge fights April 19, 1775.

Tanneries, Shoe Factories, and Ethnic Enclaves

Phineas Sawyer's Tannery Brook sawmill (mid-1700s) and Joel Cranston's 1794 store heralded Feltonville's rise under Silas Felton. Rail links post-1840s exploded shoe production, employing thousands of Irish famine refugees and Portuguese arrivals (1886 onward) in St. Michael's parish and fraternal halls. Civil War payrolls and naturalizations capture chain migration; 20th-century Route 62 suburbs retained factory-era tenements, deeds showing family property chains from mill privileges to residential plats.

Genealogical Resources and Strategies

Vital repositories:

- Hudson Town Clerk: Births, marriages, deaths from 1866; Feltonville directories, ward lists.
- Hudson Historical Society: Barnes-Witt manuscripts, Brigham's Early History, church extracts, cemetery surveys.
- Middlesex South Registry of Deeds (Cambridge): Marlborough grants, Bolton separations, tannery plats.
- Regional aids: Massachusetts Vital Records to 1850 (Marlborough volume); FamilySearch Hudson indexes; MHC mill and factory sites.

Hudson's genealogy—from Assabet falls and Barnes mills to Feltonville factories and Portuguese clubs—equips researchers with records unveiling Nipmuc-Marlborough kin through proprietor endurance to immigrant wards, tracing lineages along the river's industrial spine.

Lexington

Lexington, a historic core town of eastern Middlesex County, Massachusetts, centers on the grassy commons where minutemen faced British regulars on April 19, 1775, amid Massachusett homelands along Vine Brook and the old Cambridge-Concord path. First settled c. 1642 as "Cambridge Farms" outpost of Cambridge and incorporated March 21, 1713, Lexington evolved from agrarian precinct farms into a 19th-century commuter suburb, its tight wards preserving Reed, Fiske, Munroe, Harrington, and Parker lineages intertwined with Irish laborers and later professional families.

Massachusett Brooks, Cambridge Grants, and Precinct Houses

Before English clearings, Massachusett families followed trails over Vine Brook for fishing and planting, their lands granted to Cambridge proprietors by 1639 from Naumkeag sachems amid epidemics. Lt. David Fiske's 1647 stone wall and Herbert Pelham's center farm anchored early settlement; Edward Winship's Mill Brook sawmill (1650) and William Munroe's Woburn Street homestead (1660) dotted the landscape. By 1682, thirty families petitioned parish status, granted 1691 as Cambridge Farms with Rev. Benjamin Estabrook's meetinghouse at Bedford-Massachusetts crossroads. Cambridge deeds and vital stubs trace pre-1713 kin, linking Lexington progenitors through militia rolls to Bedford and Arlington separations.

Minuteman Commons, Rail Suburbs, and Civic Hubs

Lexington's Green birthed American independence: Capt. John Parker's 77 minutemen fired "the shot heard round the world," their rosters etching Harrington, Reed, and Bowman names in pension files. Hancock-Clarke House sheltered patriots; 19th-century railroads and trolleys drew Irish to East Lexington mills, anchored by First Parish (Unitarian) and St. Brigid's. Lafayette's 1824 arch and normal school (1822) marked civic rise; Civil War service and women's clubs extended records, with 20th-century zoning preserving estates amid Route 2 suburbs.

Genealogical Resources and Strategies

Vital repositories:

- Lexington Town Clerk: Births, marriages, deaths from 1713 (Cambridge Farms stubs prior); precinct petitions, common training lists.
- Lexington Historical Society: Fiske-Munroe manuscripts, Buckman Tavern logs, cemetery transcriptions (Old Burying Ground 1690).

- Middlesex South Registry of Deeds (Cambridge): 1639 grants, Vine Brook plats, Revolutionary confiscations.
- Regional aids: Massachusetts Vital Records to 1850 (Lexington volume); FamilySearch precinct books; MHC Battle Green and Munroe Tavern sites.

Lexington's genealogy—from Cambridge Farms brooks and Fiske walls to minuteman greens and suburban lanes—reveals kin forged at liberty's dawn, guiding researchers through deeds, muster rolls, and parish covenants bridging Massachusett paths, patriot hearths, and enduring village cores.

Lincoln

Lincoln, a serene rural town in eastern Middlesex County, Massachusetts, weaves through the Sudbury River meadows and wooded hills on Massachusett homelands once part of Musketaquid. Settled c. 1654 as Concord's southeast precinct and incorporated May 23, 1754—named by Chambers Russell for his Lincolnshire, England estate—it emerged from "Niptown" fragments of Concord, Weston, and Lexington, evolving from dispersed farmsteads into conservation enclaves preserving Loring, Hoar, and Garfield lineages amid minimal immigrant waves.

Musketaquid Outlands, Concord Precincts, and Early Steadings

Before English expansion, Massachusett families under Squaw Sachem fished Sudbury intervals and followed trails from Musketaquid, their grassy plains decimated by epidemics yielding to Concord's 1635 six-mile grant. Southeast farms held by Abraham and Isaac Jones, James Blood, and Gershom Flint petitioned second precinct status in 1746 citing worship distances; Judge Russell's influence secured townhood. Concord deeds trace pre-1754 vitals, with Lincoln's first meetinghouse (1755) and burying ground anchoring kin networks linking to Bedford and Waltham through militia rolls and probate chains.

Revolution Trails, Farm Commons, and Conservation Continuity

Lincoln minutemen under Col. Abijah Pierce reinforced Concord Bridge April 19, 1775—Paul Revere captured nearby—rosters preserving Harrington and Reed overlaps. 19th-century rail spurs and Walden Pond drew summer boarders, while Yankee farms supplied Boston; minimal industry retained surnames through tax lists and Unitarian-Trinitarian parish books. DeCordova Museum (1930s) and Minute Man National Park marked preservation ethos; 20th-century zoning locked rural character, deeds showing multi-century land tenure amid Hanscom Air Force Base adjacency.

Genealogical Resources and Strategies

Vital repositories:

- Lincoln Town Clerk: Births, marriages, deaths from 1754 (Concord stubs prior); precinct petitions, common training lists.
- Lincoln Historical Society: Loring-Hoar manuscripts, Russell-Codman papers, cemetery transcriptions (1755 ground).
- Middlesex South Registry of Deeds (Cambridge): Musketaquid divisions, "Niptown" plats, conservation easements.
- Regional aids: Massachusetts Vital Records to 1850 (Lincoln/Concord volumes); Family-Search precinct books; MHC Pierce Farm and Battle Road sites.

Lincoln's genealogy—from Musketaquid meadows and Concord outfarms to Russell commons and wooded trusts—captures quiet endurance, guiding researchers through deeds, muster rolls, and parish covenants bridging Massachusett brooks, precinct hearths, and pristine conservation lineages.

<u>Lexington</u>

Lexington, a pivotal eastern Middlesex County town, Massachusetts, centers on the Battle Green where minutemen confronted British troops on April 19, 1775, amid Massachusett homelands along Vine Brook and Cambridge-Concord trails. Settled c. 1642 as Cambridge Farms outpost and incorporated March 21, 1713, Lexington grew from agrarian precincts into a commuter suburb, its wards preserving Reed, Fiske, Munroe, Harrington, and Parker families blended with Irish mill hands and later professionals.

Massachusett Brooks, Cambridge Farms, and Precinct Steadings

Before colonization, Massachusett followed Vine Brook for fishing and planting, their lands granted to Cambridge proprietors by 1639 from Naumkeag sachems. Lt. David Fiske's 1647 stone wall, Edward Winship's 1650 Mill Brook sawmill, and William Munroe's 1660 Woburn Street farm dotted early clearings. By 1682, thirty families petitioned parish status granted 1691 as Cambridge Farms with Rev. Benjamin Estabrook's meetinghouse at Bedford-Massachusetts crossroads; Cambridge deeds trace pre-1713 vitals linking to Bedford and Arlington separations.

Battle Green, Rail Hubs, and Suburban Rise

Capt. John Parker's 77 minutemen fired "the shot heard round the world" at the Green, rosters etching kin in pension files alongside Hancock-Clarke House warnings. 19th-century railroads drew Irish to East Lexington mills, anchored by First Parish (Unitarian) and St. Brigid's; Lafayette's 1824 arch and normal school (1822) marked progress. Civil War service and clubs extended records, 20th-century zoning preserving estates amid Route 2 growth.

Genealogical Resources and Strategies

Vital repositories:

- Lexington Town Clerk: Births, marriages, deaths from 1713 (Farms stubs prior); precinct lists, militia trainings.
- Lexington Historical Society: Fiske-Munroe papers, Buckman Tavern logs, Old Burying Ground transcriptions (1690).
- Middlesex South Registry of Deeds (Cambridge): 1639 grants, Vine Brook plats, Revolutionary deeds.
- Regional aids: Massachusetts Vital Records to 1850 (Lexington); FamilySearch precinct volumes; MHC Battle Green sites.

Lexington's genealogy—from Cambridge brooks and Fiske farms to minuteman greens and suburban lanes—reveals kin forged at independence's birth, traced through deeds, rosters, and parishes bridging Massachusett paths to enduring civic cores.

Littleton

Littleton, a northwestern Middlesex County town, Massachusetts, cradles Nashoba Brook and Nagog Pond amid Nipmuc homelands site of John Eliot's sixth Praying Indian village. Settled 1686 from Concord and Chelmsford grants and incorporated November 2, 1714, as "Nashoba" (renamed Littleton December 1715), it evolved from frontier orchards and mills into rail depots and suburban farms, its commons preserving Hartwell, Lawrence, and Robeson lineages alongside Irish laborers.

Nashobah Plantations, Concord Outfarms, and Precinct Formation

Before Eliot's 1651 Nashobah mission—church, school, 50 acres for converts—Nipmuc families planted between Nagog and Fort Ponds, dispersed by King Philip's War (1675–76). Concord proprietors extended grants post-1680, drawing Hartwell, Tuttle, and Blanford families to meadows; 1714 incorporation mandated orthodox ministry within three years, yielding Rev. Benjamin Shattuck's 1717 ordination at the eastern common triangle meetinghouse. Concord and Chelmsford deeds hold pre-1714 vitals, linking Littleton kin through militia to Acton, Boxborough, and Carlisle separations.

Minuteman Trails, Apple Orchards, and Depot Villages

Littleton minutemen reinforced Concord Bridge April 19, 1775, rosters tracing Hartwell service along Battle Road. Fitchburg Railroad (1845) sprouted Littleton Depot commerce, Irish tracklayers settling near King Street; apple orchards and dairy farms dominated, with Forge Village mills and ice cutting at Spectacle Pond. First Church Unitarian (1723 rebuilt) and Baptist (1822) anchored parishes; Civil War lists and Lyceum records extended Yankee continuity, 20th-century Route 2/495 zoning preserving farms amid suburban lanes.

Genealogical Resources and Strategies

Vital repositories:

- Littleton Town Clerk: Births, marriages, deaths from 1714; proprietors' book, tax valuations, depot directories.
- Littleton Historical Society: Hartwell-Lawrence manuscripts, Shattuck papers, Nashobah mission extracts, cemetery surveys.
- Middlesex South Registry of Deeds (Cambridge): Eliot grants, Nashoba plats, orchard divisions.
- Regional aids: Massachusetts Vital Records to 1850 (Littleton volume); FamilySearch Nashoba church books; MHC praying village and mill sites.

Littleton's genealogy—from Nashobah converts and Hartwell clearings to minuteman orchards and depot hearths—reveals kin resilience across Nipmuc brooks, equipping researchers with deeds, parish rolls, and proprietors' ledgers bridging mission fields to enduring farm commons.

Maynard

Maynard, a compact mill town in Middlesex County, Massachusetts, clings to the Assabet River's cascading falls on Nipmuc homelands known as Pompositicut. First settled in the 1650s as scattered farms of Sudbury and Stow and incorporated April 19, 1871—as Assabet Village renamed for mill founder Amory Maynard—it surged from agrarian precincts into a 19th-century woolen manufacturing hub, its wards blending Smith, Brooks, and Maynard kin with waves of Irish, Finnish, and Portuguese laborers whose factory ledgers and parish rolls trace industrial kinship.

Pompositicut Farms, Sudbury Lots, and Mill Precincts

Before Puritan clearings, Nipmuc sachem Tantamous mortgaged meadows to Herman Garrett (1651), with son Peter Jethro selling tracts by 1684 amid King Philip's War raids on Summer Hill. Thomas and Asa Smith families dotted Great Road farms by 1700, their cider mills yielding to Amory Maynard's 1847 woolen dam and carpet factory after buying Asa Smith's site. Population boomed to 1,820 by separation—paying Sudbury $23,600 and Stow $8,000—Sudbury deeds holding pre-1871 vitals linking to Acton and Hudson overlaps.

Woolen Mills, Immigrant Districts, and Factory Wards

Civil War blanket contracts swelled the Assabet Manufacturing Company (1862), drawing Irish Catholics to St. Bridget's (1865, Maynard-funded) and Finns to River Street by 1880s Evangelical Lutheran church. Finnish Workingmen's Association and temperance societies preserved ethnic rosters; Portuguese clubs anchored later waves. Civil War payrolls and 20th-century

Route 62 suburbs extended records, mills declining post-WWII yet yielding dense employee chains visible in naturalizations and tenement censuses.

Genealogical Resources and Strategies

Vital repositories:

- Maynard Town Clerk: Births, marriages, deaths from 1871; incorporation petitions, mill directories.
- Maynard Historical Society: Smith-Brooks manuscripts, Assabet Mill ledgers, Finnish church extracts, cemetery surveys.
- Middlesex South Registry of Deeds (Cambridge): Sudbury-Stow grants, Maynard water rights, factory plats.
- Regional aids: Massachusetts Vital Records to 1850 (Sudbury/Stow volumes); Family-Search mill worker indexes; MHC Assabet dams and Summer Hill sites.

Maynard's genealogy—from Pompositicut mortgages and Smith mills to Amory's factories and immigrant halls—unveils kin forged by river power, guiding researchers through payrolls, parish rolls, and deeds bridging Nipmuc falls to enduring mill village legacies.

Natick

Natick, a southern Middlesex County town, Massachusetts, bends along the Charles River's Quinobequin reach on Massachusett and Nipmuc homelands, founded 1651 as Rev. John Eliot's first "Praying Indian Town" and incorporated July 2, 1781. Evolving from Algonquian wetus and mission fields into 19th-century shoe factories and rail villages, Natick's South Natick core preserves Speen, Waban, and Pegan lineages alongside Irish, Italian, and Lithuanian laborers whose parish and mill records trace cultural fusion.

Quinobequin Missions, Eliot Grants, and Praying Village

Before Eliot's preaching, Massachusett sachem Waban and Nipmuc John Speen sustained cornfields and fisheries, yielding 6,000 acres via Dedham grant for Natick's 1651 settlement—three streets, 80-foot bridge, meetinghouse built by converts under Massachusett teacher Moonequasson. King Philip's War (1675) interned survivors on Deer Island, returning to ruined homes; proprietors like Speen and Pegan divided common lands by 1719, English colonists dominating by 1725. Dedham and early vital stubs trace pre-1781 kin, linking to Framingham and Sherborn through Eliot's Algonquian Bible translations.

Shoe Mills, Ethnic Wards, and Rail Centers

Revolutionary service tied Natick minutemen to Framingham rosters; Boston & Albany Railroad (1840s) exploded shoe production at Natick Shoe Company, drawing Irish to St. Mary's

(1860s) and Italians to East Natick. Lithuanian and Armenian enclaves formed fraternal halls; First Congregational (1721 site) anchored Yankee descent. Civil War payrolls and suffragist clubs extended records, 20th-century Route 9 suburbs preserving factory tenements amid zoning for farm continuity.

Genealogical Resources and Strategies

Vital repositories:

- Natick Town Clerk: Births, marriages, deaths from 1781 (Eliot-era stubs prior); proprietor divisions, ward lists.
- Natick Historical Society: Waban-Speen manuscripts, mission extracts, shoe ledgers, cemetery surveys.
- Middlesex South Registry of Deeds (Cambridge): 1651 Dedham grants, praying town plats, Upton divisions.
- Regional aids: Massachusetts Vital Records to 1850 (Natick volume); FamilySearch Eliot church books; MHC Quinobequin bridge and mill sites.

Natick's genealogy—from Waban's wetus and Speen fields to shoe wards and suburban lanes—reveals kin bridging Algonquian missions and Puritan enterprise, guiding researchers through proprietors' rolls, parish covenants, and factory chains along the Charles' enduring bend.

North Reading

North Reading, a residential suburb in northeastern Middlesex County, Massachusetts, occupies upland pastures north of the Ipswich River on Massachusett and Pawtucket homelands once granted to Reading in 1651. Incorporated as the Town of North Reading March 19, 1853, from Reading's North Parish, it evolved from 17th-century farm commons and blacksmith shops into 19th-century turnpike villages, preserving Upton, Flint, Parker, and Swain lineages amid Irish laborers and modest Yankee continuity.

Pawtucket Grants, Reading Farms, and North Parish

Before English settlement, Massachusett families foraged Ipswich meadows, their lands added to Reading's 1644 Lynn Village patent amid epidemics. John Upton's 1678 homestead near Bear Meadow Swamp anchored early clearings, with blacksmiths and farmers like Flint and Parker clustering by 1713 North Parish separation from Reading proper. Parish records from 1716 trace baptisms and militia service linking to Wakefield (South Reading) and Reading cores; deeds show Upton's 200-acre chains extending from West Peabody hammersmith origins.

Turnpikes, Wagon Shops, and Village Hubs

North Reading minutemen joined Reading companies at Lexington April 19, 1775, rosters preserving Upton-Flint kin amid tavern trades. Andover-Medford Turnpike (1806, now Route 28) spurred McLane Wagon Factory (1887) and Pierce organ pipes, drawing Irish rail workers to Union Congregational (1752) and Baptist parishes. Civil War memorials in Laurel Hill Cemetery extend Yankee descent; 20th-century Route 62 zoning retained Federal-era houses amid suburban estates.

Genealogical Resources and Strategies

Vital repositories:

- North Reading Town Clerk: Births, marriages, deaths from 1853 (North Parish stubs prior); tax lists, turnpike directories.
- North Reading Historical & Antiquarian Society: Upton-Flint manuscripts, parish extracts, cemetery transcriptions, wagon ledgers.
- Middlesex South Registry of Deeds (Cambridge): Reading grants, Ipswich plats, parish divisions.
- Regional aids: Massachusetts Vital Records to 1850 (Reading volume); FamilySearch North Parish books; MHC Upton Tavern and Federal district sites.

North Reading's genealogy—from Ipswich grants and Upton smithies to turnpike commons and wagon yards—reveals kin endurance north of ancient meadows, guiding researchers through parish rolls, deeds, and rosters bridging Pawtucket pastures to preserved Federal villages.

Pepperell

Pepperell, the northwesternmost town of Middlesex County, Massachusetts, flanks the Nashua River's east bank amid Nipmuc and Pennacook homelands, first settled 1720 from Groton and incorporated November 4, 1775, as Groton West Parish district (1753). Named for Sir William Pepperrell of Louisbourg fame, it grew from Nashua orchards and garrison farms into 19th-century paper mills and rail villages, preserving Blood, Shattuck, Wright, and Varnum lineages alongside Irish laborers across East Pepperell and core commons.

Nipmuc Intervals, Groton West Farms, and Parish Garrisons

Before English settlement, Nipmuc families fished Nashua pools and planted intervals, their lands yielding to Groton proprietors post-King Philip's War (1675–76). Scattered farms crossed the river by 1720, clustering at Babbatasset Falls; forty-two families petitioned West Parish 1742 for local worship, building 1746 meetinghouse amid church site brawls settled by General Court.

Bloods, Shatts, and Wrights anchored garrisons through Queen Anne's raids; Groton deeds trace pre-1775 vitals, linking Pepperell kin to Townsend and Hollis (NH) separations.

Paper Mills, Rail Yards, and Village Industries

Pepperell minutemen joined Bunker Hill under Rev. Joseph Emerson; women like Prudence Wright guarded bridges capturing spies. Worcester-Nashua Railroad (1848) boosted East Pepperell paper mills from Emerson's 1835 works, drawing Irish to Congregational splits (1832 Unitarian-Evangelical) and Baptist parishes. Civil War rosters and Grange halls documented Yankee-Irish intermarriage; 20th-century Route 119 preserved orchards amid suburban cores.

Genealogical Resources and Strategies

Vital repositories:

- Pepperell Town Clerk: Births, marriages, deaths from 1753 (Groton stubs prior); parish petitions, mill directories.
- Pepperell Historical Society: Blood-Shattuck manuscripts, Lorenzo Blood's History, church extracts, cemetery surveys.
- Middlesex North Registry of Deeds (Lowell): Groton grants, Nashua plats, North Groton annexations (1857).
- Regional aids: Massachusetts Vital Records to 1850 (Pepperell volume); FamilySearch West Parish books; MHC Babbatasset mills and common sites.

Pepperell's genealogy—from Nashua garrisons and Blood orchards to paper wards and bridge guards—equips researchers with parish rolls, deeds, and rosters unveiling Nipmuc-Merrimack kin through frontier endurance to enduring river villages.

Reading

Reading, an early inland town of northeastern Middlesex County, Massachusetts, encircles Lake Quannapowitt's shores on Massachusett homelands along the Ipswich River. Settled 1639 as "Lynn Village" by Lynn petitioners and incorporated June 10, 1644—named for England's Reading—it expanded from Great Pond farms into 19th-century turnpike and rail villages, shedding South Reading (Wakefield, 1868) and North Reading (1853), its core preserving Parker, Eaton, Cowdrey, and Baldwin lineages amid Irish laborers.

Massachusett Shores, Lynn Grants, and Village Commons

Before colonization, Massachusett fished Quannapowitt ("great pond") and followed Ipswich trails, their lands granted six square miles (plus four) to Lynn citizens petitioning inland plantation. Thomas Parker, deacon and selectman, anchored settlement with the 12th Congregational Church (now First Parish); John Cowdrey's ordinary and Edward Winship's mill dotted shores by 1650. 1651 grant north of Ipswich yielded future North Reading: town books from 1644 trace vitals, militia, and land lots linking Reading progenitors to Lynn, Woburn, and Stoneham separations.

Turnpikes, Organ Factories, and Parish Splits

Reading minutemen marched to Lexington April 19, 1775, rosters etching Parker-Eaton kin amid Parker Tavern's patriot lore. Andover-Medford Turnpike (1806, Route 28) and Boston & Maine Railroad (1845) spurred Pierce organ pipes, Harnden furniture, and Pratt clocks, drawing Irish to Baptist and Congregational parishes. First Parish split fueled South/North Reading separations; Civil War lists and lyceum records extended Yankee continuity, 20th-century zoning preserving Federal homes amid suburban estates.

Genealogical Resources and Strategies

Vital repositories:

- Reading Town Clerk: Births, marriages, deaths from 1644; Lynn Village stubs, common training lists.
- Reading Antiquarian Society: Parker-Eaton manuscripts, Cowdrey ordinary logs, Old Burying Ground transcriptions.
- Middlesex South Registry of Deeds (Cambridge): 1639 Lynn grants, Quannapowitt plats, parish divisions.
- Regional aids: Massachusetts Vital Records to 1850 (Reading volume); FamilySearch church books; MHC Parker Tavern and common sites.

Reading's genealogy—from Quannapowitt shores and Parker deaconries to turnpike factories and village hearths—reveals kin endurance encircling the great pond, guiding researchers through deeds, rosters, and parish covenants bridging Massachusett waters to preserved colonial cores.

Sherborn

Sherborn, a rural enclave in southern Middlesex County, Massachusetts, follows the Charles River's marshy floodplains on Nipmuc and Massachusett homelands known as Boggestow. Settled 1652 from Medfield grants and incorporated June 17, 1674—arbitrarily named by the General Court—it shed Holliston (1724) and Ashland portions while evolving from scattered "farmes" and garrison houses into enduring orchards and dairies, preserving Holbrook, Wood, Bullard, and Sawin lineages amid minimal immigrant waves.

Boggestow Marshes, Medfield Farms, and Covenant Steadings

Before English "farmes," Nipmuc families harvested marsh grass along the wide Charles intervals near Rocky Narrows and Farm Pond, their "old fields" yielding to 1640s General Court grants (200-1074 acres) to Boston service payers. Thomas Holbrook and Nicholas Wood bought first resale 1652, living as Medfield citizens amid King Philip's War (1675–76) raids that scattered early steadings. Post-war Social Covenant organized government; 1679 Natick exchange reshaped bounds, with sawmills, gristmills, and Rev. Samuel Morse's meetinghouse (1680) anchoring home lots. Medfield deeds trace pre-1674 vitals, linking Sherborn kin through militia to Framingham and Holliston separations.

Orchards, Cottage Trades, and Rural Persistence

Sherborn minutemen joined Framingham at Concord Bridge, pension rolls capture Bullard service amid cider mills and North Main Street shops crafting guns, shoes, and edge tools. Apples, cranberries, and dairying fed Boston via stagecoach and rail, with minimal waterpower limiting factories. First Parish (Congregational) and later estates of Boston gentry preserved Yankee descent; Civil War lists and Grange halls documented farm continuity, 20th-century zoning (50% open space) locking rural character amid Route 9 commuters.

Genealogical Resources and Strategies

Vital repositories:

- Sherborn Town Clerk: Births, marriages, deaths from 1674; covenant petitions, tax valuations.
- Sherborn Historical Society: Holbrook-Bullard manuscripts, Morse papers, cemetery transcriptions (Pilgrim Church grounds).
- Middlesex South Registry of Deeds (Cambridge): Boggestow "farmes," Natick exchanges, Holliston plats.
- Regional aids: Massachusetts Vital Records to 1850 (Sherborn volume); FamilySearch covenant books; MHC Rocky Narrows and Sewall House sites.

Sherborn's genealogy—from Boggestow marshes and Holbrook grants to orchard commons and conserved farms—embodies agrarian endurance, guiding researchers through deeds, parish rolls, and militia lists bridging Nipmuc intervals to pristine rural lineages.

Shirley

Shirley, a north-central Middlesex County town, Massachusetts, threads the Squannacook and Nashua river valleys on Nipmuc homelands, settled 1720 from Groton plantations and incorporated as a district 1753 (town 1775), named for Governor William Shirley. Evolving from mills along Mulpus Brook and Catacunemaug into Shaker villages and rail depots, Shirley's Center preserves Parker, Wilds, and Fisk lineages alongside Finnish laborers and Shaker communal records.

Nipmuc Brooks, Groton Mills, and District Petition

Before English sawmills, Nipmuc families fished Squannacook intervals, their lands within Dean Winthrop's 1655 Groton grant yielding to 1720 farmsteads south and west of the rivers. Thirty-three petitioners sought separation 1747 for local worship, gaining district status 1753 with wooden meetinghouse on Green Lane; Rev. Isaac Fairbank's 1754 ordination anchored First Parish. Groton deeds trace pre-1753 vitals, linking Shirley kin through militia to Ayer and Lunenburg separations, with 1765 Stow Leg addition reshaping bounds.

Shaker Commons, Fredonia Mills, and Village Growth

Shirley minutemen aided Lexington-Concord 1775, twenty-two enlisting Continentals; Shaker Mother Ann Lee's 1783 Wilds visit seeded Pleasant Garden community (1793-1908), its Moses Johnson meetinghouse now at Hancock Village. Fitchburg Railroad (1845) boosted Fredonia Mill (1832) and Samson Cordage, drawing Finnish immigrants to St. Anthony's (1905) and temperance halls. Civil War rosters and 1847 Town House records extended Yankee-Shaker continuity; 20th-century prisons on Shaker lands preserved rural cores.

Genealogical Resources and Strategies

Vital repositories:

- Shirley Town Clerk: Births, marriages, deaths from 1753; district petitions, tax lists, Shaker censuses.
- Shirley Historical Society: Parker-Wilds manuscripts, Chandler's 1883 History, church extracts, cemetery surveys.
- Middlesex North Registry of Deeds (Lowell): Groton grants, Squannacook plats, Shaker property transfers.
- Regional aids: Massachusetts Vital Records to 1850 (Shirley volume); FamilySearch district books; MHC Center Historic District and Shaker sites.

Shirley's genealogy—from Squannacook mills and district commons to Shaker gardens and Fredonia factories—unveils kin resilience across Nipmuc valleys, guiding researchers through petitions, parish rolls, and communal ledgers bridging Groton frontiers to preserved village hearts.

Stoneham

Stoneham, a northeastern Middlesex County town, Massachusetts, encircles Spot Pond amid Massachusett and Pawtucket homelands, settled 1634 as Charlestown's remote "End" outpost and incorporated December 17, 1725. Evolving from upland farms and blacksmith shops into 19th-century shoe factories and rail villages, Stoneham's wards preserve Geary, Vinton, Bryant, and Green lineages alongside Irish laborers whose parish and mill records trace suburban continuity.

Pawtucket Rocks, Charlestown Farms, and Precinct Petition

Before Governor Winthrop's 1632 Spot Pond lunch at Cheese Rock (Bear Hill), Massachusett fished pond islands and rock outcrops, their lands annexed to Charlestown amid epidemics. Six families farmed northeast tracts by 1678 near Reading; by 1725, 65 taxable males petitioned separation citing church distances, Captain Benjamin Geary leading 53 signers granted township with mandates for meetinghouse, minister, and schoolmaster. First town meeting December 24 erected 1726 meetinghouse and Old Burying Ground at Summer-Pleasant crossroads; Charlestown deeds trace pre-1725 vitals, linking Stoneham kin through militia to Reading and Malden boundaries.

Shoe Mills, Turnpike Taverns, and Ethnic Clusters

Stoneham minutemen reinforced Lexington 1775, rosters etching Vinton kin amid Parker Tavern patriot lore. Andover-Medford Turnpike (1806) shifted center westward to Main Street taverns housing drovers; Boston & Lowell Railroad (1840s) exploded shoe production drawing Irish to St. Patrick's (1871) and Congregational parishes. Civil War payrolls and organ factories extended Yankee-Irish intermarriage; 20th-century Route 28 zoning preserved Federal homes amid Middlesex Fells suburbs.

Genealogical Resources and Strategies

Vital repositories:

- Stoneham Town Clerk: Births, marriages, deaths from 1725; Geary petitions, tax lists, ward directories.
- Stoneham Historical Society: Vinton-Green manuscripts, Spot Pond archaeology, church extracts, cemetery surveys.
- Middlesex South Registry of Deeds (Cambridge): Charlestown "End" grants, pond plats, shoe mill transfers.
- Regional aids: Massachusetts Vital Records to 1850 (Stoneham volume); FamilySearch precinct books; MHC Old Burying Ground and Fells sites.

Stoneham's genealogy—from Spot Pond rocks and Geary farms to turnpike factories and pondside wards—reveals kin resilience encircling ancient waters, guiding researchers through petitions, parish rolls, and deeds bridging Pawtucket shores to preserved suburban cores.

Stow

Stow, a rural northwestern Middlesex County town, Massachusetts, rolls across Assabet headwaters and Lake Boon amid Nipmuc homelands of Pompositticut Plantation ("land of many hills"). Settled c. 1660 by Matthew Boon trading a jackknife for vast tracts and incorporated May 16, 1683, Stow evolved from frontier farms and Lower Village meetinghouse into enduring orchards and dairies, shedding lands to Harvard (1732), Shirley (1765 "Stow Leg"), Boxborough (1783), Hudson (1866), and Maynard (1871 Assabet Village), preserving Gates, Peck, Kettell, and Boon lineages.

Nipmuc Hills, Sudbury Grants, and Plantation Proprietors

Before Boon's jackknife legend at Boon Pond, Nipmuc sustained maize fields across hills linking Nashoba and Concord, their post-epidemic lands eyed by Sudbury proprietors. Eleazer Lusher's 1665 500-acre grant west of Sudbury and Daniel Gookin's 1672 committee surveyed 11,000 "meanne" acres, mandating ten orthodox families. John Kettell joined Boon by 1664 near modern center; 1681 overseers Thomas Stevens and Boaz Brown regulated amid King Philip's War ruins. Proprietors' book traces lots from Lower Village common (1685 meetinghouse) linking Stow kin to Acton and Marlborough through militia rolls.

Minuteman Orchards, Dairy Commons, and Village Resilience

Stow minutemen reinforced Concord Bridge 1775 under Capt. Henry Gardner (later Provincial treasurer); pension files capture Peck service amid cider mills. Fitchburg Railroad (1849) boosted Lake Boon resorts and 150 farms (1870) with 600 cows, minimal industry preserving Yankee surnames through First Parish and Baptist parishes. Civil War rosters and Grange halls documented continuity; 20th-century zoning locked agrarian character amid Route 117 commuters, Lake Boon ice harvesting extending records.

Genealogical Resources and Strategies

Vital repositories:

- Stow Town Clerk: Births, marriages, deaths from 1683; proprietors' book, tax lists, farm schedules.
- Stow Historical Society: Gates-Peck manuscripts, Boon monument papers, Lower Village cemetery transcriptions.
- Middlesex South Registry of Deeds (Cambridge): Pompositticut plats, Harvard/Boxborough divisions, lake shore transfers.
- Regional aids: Massachusetts Vital Records to 1850 (Stow volume); FamilySearch proprietors' records; MHC Lower Village common and Boon Pond sites.

Stow's genealogy—from Pompositticut jackknives and Kettell farms to minuteman orchards and conserved hills—embodies frontier persistence, guiding researchers through proprietors' rolls, parish covenants, and dairy ledgers bridging Nipmuc plantations to enduring rural lineages.

Sudbury

Sudbury, a foundational inland town of Middlesex County, Massachusetts, cradles the Sudbury River's grassy meadows on Nipmuc homelands of Musketaquid ("great grassy plain"). Settled 1638 by Watertown migrants aboard the ship Confidence and incorporated 1639, Sudbury pioneered town meeting democracy while seeding Framingham, Marlborough, Stow, Wayland (East Sudbury 1780), and Maynard from its vast bounds, its core preserving Rice, Noyes, Haines, and Stone lineages amid enduring farm continuity.

Musketaquid Meadows, Watertown Grants, and Plantation Covenant

Before English meadows, Nipmuc sachem Tahattawan and Peter Jethro fished salmon weirs and planted cornfields, deeding tracts amid epidemics for Sudbury's 1638 plantation petition. Edmund Rice, John Stone, Peter Noyes, and Walter Haines drew house lots east of the river near present Wayland's North Cemetery, their 1640 First Parish covenant under Rev. Edmund Browne mandating civil over ecclesiastical rule. Town books from 1639 trace vitals and equal land divisions by lot (1654), linking Sudbury progenitors through militia to Concord and Framingham separations.

Fight at the Bridge, Orchard Commons, and Democratic Hearths

Sudbury's Bloody Fight (April 21, 1676) during King Philip's War saw 26 defenders slain at Sam Wadsworth's River Road garrison: pension-less widows rebuilt amid cider mills. Revolutionary minutemen marched to Concord under Capt. Abraham Hall, pension rolls capture Rice kin. 19th-century dairies and Longfellow's Wayside Inn orchards fed Boston via rail, minimal industry preserving Yankee descent through First Parish (Unitarian 1837 split). Civil War rosters and Grange halls extended records, 20th-century zoning conserving 70% open space.

Genealogical Resources and Strategies

Vital repositories:

- Sudbury Town Clerk: Births, marriages, deaths from 1639; proprietors' book, meadow grants, tax valuations.
- Sudbury Historical Society: Rice-Noyes manuscripts, Browne covenant papers, Goodnow Library genealogies, cemetery surveys.
- Middlesex South Registry of Deeds (Cambridge): Musketaquid deeds, Wayland/Framingham plats, Revolutionary confiscations.

- Regional aids: Massachusetts Vital Records to 1850 (Sudbury volume); FamilySearch town meeting minutes; MHC Wadsworth garrison and Wayside Inn sites.

Sudbury's genealogy—from Musketaquid weirs and Rice covenants to bridge fights and conserved orchards—epitomizes democratic endurance, guiding researchers through proprietors' rolls, parish ledgers, and militia lists bridging Nipmuc plains to pioneering town lineages.

Tewksbury

Tewksbury, a Merrimack Valley town in northeastern Middlesex County, Massachusetts, flanks the river's southern banks on Wamesit-Pennacook homelands, first settled 1637 as Billerica's northern precinct and incorporated December 17, 1734. Named possibly for England's Tewkesbury or honoring King George II's barony, it grew from colonial farms and sawmills into 19th-century shoe factories and almshouses, preserving Kittridge, Baldwin, French, and Burnap lineages amid Irish laborers across North Tewksbury and river wards.

Wamesit Fields, Billerica Farms, and Precinct Separation

Before English settlement, Wamesit sachems fished Merrimack weirs amid failed 1725 "Wamesit" town attempts, their lands annexed to Billerica post-epidemics. Forty-one petitioners led by Samuel Hunt separated 1734 citing worship distances to Billerica church, gaining township with mandates for meetinghouse and ministry. Lt. Daniel Kittridge's frame (rejected for defects) yielded 1735 structures near Old Burying Ground; Billerica deeds trace pre-1734 vitals, linking Tewksbury kin through militia to Lowell annexations (1834 onward).

Shoe Mills, Almshouses, and River Industries

Tewksbury minutemen aided Lexington-Concord 1775; pension rolls capture French kin amid Brown's Tavern (Andrew Jackson visit). Merrimack powered 19th-century shoe factories and State Almshouse (1854 poor farm), drawing Irish to St. Mary's (1860s) and Methodist parishes. Civil War rosters and Grange halls documented farm-to-factory shifts; Lowell's repeated annexations (up to 1906) shrank bounds, 20th-century Route 38 suburbs preserving Federal homes.

Genealogical Resources and Strategies

Vital repositories:

- Tewksbury Town Clerk: Births, marriages, deaths from 1734; Hunt petitions, almshouse ledgers, ward lists.
- Tewksbury Historical Society: Kittridge-Baldwin manuscripts, church extracts, Old Burying Ground surveys.

- Middlesex North Registry of Deeds (Lowell): Billerica grants, Merrimack plats, Lowell annexations.
- Regional aids: Massachusetts Vital Records to 1850 (Tewksbury/Billerica volumes); FamilySearch precinct books; MHC almshouse and river mill sites.

Tewksbury's genealogy—from Wamesit weirs and Hunt petitions to shoe wards and conserved farms—reveals kin resilience along Merrimack bends, guiding researchers through deeds, parish rolls, and almshouse records bridging Pennacook fields to enduring valley lineages.

<u>Townsend</u>

Townsend, a northwestern Middlesex County town, Massachusetts, spans the Nashua River's east bank amid Nipmuc homelands of Wistequassuck ("at the fork"). Surveyed 1676 as Hawthorn's Grant to Salem's Judge William Hathorne and incorporated June 29, 1732, as North Town from Turkey Hills (Lunenburg south), named for Viscount Charles Townshend, it grew from Meetinghouse Hill farms into harbor mills and stagecoach taverns, preserving Conant, Fessenden, Blood, and Shattuck lineages across West Townsend and Harbor villages.

Wistequassuck Grants, Groton Farms, and Harbor Mills

Before Hathorne's political tract post-King Philip's War (1676), Nipmuc fished Nashua forks, their lands petitioned 1719 into North/South divisions. Forty-two Groton families crossed the river by 1720, building 1730 Meetinghouse Hill structure and 1733 Squannacook dam grist/sawmills at Townsend Harbor—earliest settlement with Conant Tavern (1720). Proprietors divided lots amid French & Indian raids; Groton deeds trace pre-1732 vitals, linking Townsend kin through militia to Ashby and Pepperell separations, cannon alarms summoning 73 minutemen (10% population) to Concord 1775.

Cooperages, Stage Taverns, and Industrial Hubs

Townsend's 73 soldiers marched 21 days from Concord, returning to confiscate Tory properties amid Townshend Acts irony. Boston-Keene Turnpike (1806) sprouted Joslinville Tavern (519 Main St.) and Fessenden Cooperage—three generations largest employer—while East/West mills made leatherboard. 1744 schools funded £20 for three districts; slave pews preserved in relocated Methodist church. Civil War rosters and 1875 fire department extended Yankee continuity, 20th-century Route 13 preserving orchards amid Nashua suburbs.

Genealogical Resources and Strategies

Vital repositories:

- Townsend Town Clerk: Births, marriages, deaths from 1732; Hathorne proprietors, tax lists, harbor directories.

- Townsend Historical Society: Sawtelle's 1878 History manuscripts, Conant-Fessenden papers, Meetinghouse Hill cemetery surveys.
- Middlesex North Registry of Deeds (Lowell): 1676 Hawthorn plats, Lunenburg divisions, cooperage transfers.
- Regional aids: Massachusetts Vital Records to 1850 (Townsend volume); FamilySearch Groton-Townsend books; MHC Harbor mills and slave pew sites.

Townsend's genealogy—from Wistequassuck surveys and Conant harbors to Fessenden barrels and minuteman alarms—equips researchers with proprietors' rolls, parish pews, and Tory confiscations bridging Nipmuc forks to enduring Nashua villages.

Tyngsborough

Tyngsborough, the northernmost Middlesex County town, Massachusetts, hugs the Merrimack River opposite Nashua, New Hampshire, on ancestral Wamesit and Naticook Pennacook homelands. Settled 1661 within vast Dunstable township (200 square miles) by Colonel Jonathan Tyng and incorporated February 23, 1809, from Dunstable's First Parish, it evolved from frontier ferries and quarries into seasonal vacation colonies and suburban enclaves, preserving Tyng, Varnum, and Richardson lineages across riverfront farms and bridge wards.

Wamesit Shores, Dunstable Grants, and Tyng Mansion

Before Tyng's 1661 purchase (£20 sterling from tribes), Pennacook fished Merrimack weirs and planted islands, their lands ravaged by King Philip's War (1675–76) raids scattering early steadings. Jonathan Tyng's fortified Mansion House (c. 1690s, burned 1979) anchored commerce with ferries and shops; 1755 First Parish Meeting House served growing farms. Dunstable deeds trace pre-1809 vitals, linking Tyngsborough kin through militia to Dracut and Lowell annexations amid French & Indian War alarms.

Quarries, Box Mills, and Vacation Cottages

Tyngsborough minutemen joined Dunstable at Bunker Hill; pension rolls capture Varnum service amid Tyng Bridge tolls. Granite quarries and box factories lined rivers post-1840s rail, drawing Irish laborers to Methodist and Baptist parishes before 20th-century seasonal influx to Lake Massabesic camps. Civil War rosters extended Yankee continuity; Route 3 suburbs preserved mansion foundations and emergency passageways from Indian attacks.

Genealogical Resources and Strategies

Vital repositories:

- Tyngsborough Town Clerk: Births, marriages, deaths from 1809 (Dunstable stubs prior); ferry logs, quarry payrolls.

- Tyngsborough Historical Commission: Tyng-Varnum manuscripts, Mansion House archaeology, First Parish extracts, cemetery surveys.
- Middlesex North Registry of Deeds (Lowell): 1661 tribal deeds, Dunstable plats, bridge transfers.
- Regional aids: Massachusetts Vital Records to 1850 (Dunstable volume); FamilySearch parish books; MHC Tyng Mansion and quarry sites.

Tyngsborough's genealogy—from Wamesit ferries and Tyng fortifications to quarry wards and lakeside cottages—reveals frontier endurance along Merrimack bends, guiding researchers through deeds, parish rolls, and toll ledgers bridging Pennacook shores to preserved riverfront lineages.

Wakefield

Wakefield, a lake-encircled town in northeastern Middlesex County, Massachusetts, surrounds Quannapowitt ("great pond") on Massachusett homelands, first settled 1644 as Reading's southern core from Lynn Village and incorporated as South Reading 1812 (renamed Wakefield 1868 for rattan magnate Cyrus Wakefield). Evolving from pondside farms and mills into 19th-century furniture factories and rail suburbs, its wards preserve Cowdrey, Winn, Beard, and Wakefield lineages alongside Irish laborers across Lakeview and downtown clusters.

Massachusett Shores, Reading Farms, and South Parish

Before Lynn farmers encircled Quannapowitt in 1639, Massachusett fished pond islands and Ipswich meadows, their cleared fields yielding to Reading's 1644 incorporation encompassing future Wakefield, Reading, North Reading. Deacon Thomas Parker and John Cowdrey's ordinary anchored settlements around Great Pond; 1812 South Reading separation cited distances to Reading meetinghouse, building 1814 structure near present Lafayette Street. Reading deeds trace pre-1812 vitals, linking Wakefield kin through militia to Stoneham annexations (1856).

Rattan Mills, Rail Villages, and Ethnic Hubs

South Reading minutemen marched to Lexington Green 1775, rosters etching Winn kin amid Hartshorne House patriot lore. Cyrus Wakefield's 1856 rattan works—largest employer—drew Irish to St. Joseph's (1870s) and Baptist parishes, Boston & Maine Railroad (1845) boosting Emerson Shoes and organ factories. Civil War payrolls and 1868 renaming extended Yankee-Irish intermarriage; 20th-century Route 128 suburbs preserved Federal homes amid lake resorts.

Genealogical Resources and Strategies

Vital repositories:

- Wakefield Town Clerk: Births, marriages, deaths from 1812 (Reading stubs prior); South Reading directories, rattan payrolls.
- Wakefield Historical Society: Cowdrey-Wakefield manuscripts, Quannapowitt archaeology, church extracts, Lakeside Cemetery surveys.
- Middlesex South Registry of Deeds (Cambridge): Lynn Village grants, pond plats, Stoneham annexations.
- Regional aids: Massachusetts Vital Records to 1850 (Reading/South Reading volumes); FamilySearch parish books; MHC rattan mills and Old Burying Ground sites.

Wakefield's genealogy—from Quannapowitt shores and Cowdrey ordinaries to rattan wards and lakeside hearths—reveals kin resilience around ancient waters, guiding researchers through deeds, parish rolls, and factory ledgers bridging Massachusett ponds to enduring suburban cores.

Wayland

Wayland, a pastoral eastern Middlesex County town, Massachusetts, graces the Sudbury River's eastern meadows on Nipmuc homelands of the original Sudbury Plantation. Settled 1638 as the first core of Sudbury's inland grant and incorporated as East Sudbury 1780 (renamed Wayland 1835), it evolved from Puritan house lots and mills into conserved orchards and commuter estates, preserving Curtis, Grout, Stone, Haynes, Noyes, Bent, and Goodnow lineages across Cochituate and River's Edge villages.

Musketaquid East, Sudbury Core, and Parish Division

Before the ship Confidence landed 15 families in 1638, Nipmuc fished river intervals amid epidemics yielding to Watertown's third inland plantation. Edmund Rice, John Stone, Peter Noyes, and Walter Haines drew equal lots east of the wide ford, their 1640 covenant under Rev. Edmund Browne pioneering town meeting democracy against clerical land claims. First meetinghouse rose 1643 at Old North Cemetery; western expansion birthed Marlborough (1660), with 1714 Cochituate petitions denied until 1780 split—east forfeiting Sudbury name for East Sudbury amid taxation disputes.

River Bridge, Orchard Farms, and Suburban Commons

East Sudbury minutemen (115 of Sudbury's 302) marched to Concord Bridge 1775; pension rolls capture Goodnow service amid Parmenter Tavern's patriot gatherings. 19th-century dairies and cider mills fed Boston via rail, minimal industry preserving Yankee descent through First Parish (Unitarian 1830s). Cochituate Aqueduct (1848) and Longfellow's Wayside Inn anchored tourism; Civil War rosters and Grange halls extended records, 20th-century zoning conserving farms amid Route 20 estates.

Genealogical Resources and Strategies

Vital repositories:

- Wayland Town Clerk: Births, marriages, deaths from 1780 (Sudbury stubs prior); plantation proprietors, tax lists.
- Wayland Historical Society: Rice-Noyes manuscripts, Powell's "Puritan Village," church extracts, North Cemetery surveys.
- Middlesex South Registry of Deeds (Cambridge): 1638 Confidence grants, East Sudbury plats, Cochituate divisions.
- Regional aids: Massachusetts Vital Records to 1850 (Sudbury/East Sudbury volumes); FamilySearch covenant books; MHC river ford and Loker Farm sites.

Wayland's genealogy—from Confidence meadows and Rice covenants to minuteman fords and conserved orchards—embodies plantation primacy, guiding researchers through proprietors' rolls, parish ledgers, and town meeting minutes bridging Nipmuc intervals to pioneering eastern lineages.

Westford

Westford, a northwestern Middlesex County town, Massachusetts, rises across Stony Brook ponds and Nabnasset Lake amid Nipmuc and Pennacook homelands near the Nashua River. Settled in the 1660s as Chelmsford's remote West Precinct and incorporated September 23, 1729, it evolved from frontier farms and Tadmuck Hill meetinghouses into 19th-century forges and worsted mills, its villages—Forge Village, Graniteville, Center Village—preserving Prescott, Fletcher, Hildreth, and Kidder lineages alongside Irish and Scottish laborers.

Nipmuc Ponds, Chelmsford Farms, and Precinct Garrisons

Before colonial clearings, Nipmuc fished Stony Brook runs and Nabnasset shores, their lands within Chelmsford's 1655 grant yielding sparse farms by 1670 amid King Philip's War abandonment (1675–76). Twelve families petitioned West Precinct 1724, building Tadmuck Hill meetinghouse (1726) and First Parish (1727); Groton annexation (1730 Forge Pond) completed bounds. Chelmsford deeds trace pre-1729 vitals, linking Westford kin through militia to Carlisle and Littleton separations.

Forge Mills, Worsted Factories, and Ethnic Districts

Westford minutemen marched to Concord 1775 under Capt. Joshua Parker; pension rolls capture Fletcher service amid Jonas Prescott's 1680 Forge Village ironworks. Abbot Worsted (1830s Graniteville) pioneered camel-hair yarns, drawing Scottish overseers and Irish operatives to Methodist (1871) and St. Catherine's parishes. Civil War rosters and Westford Academy (1793) extended Yankee continuity; 20th-century Route 40 preserved orchards amid suburban estates.

Genealogical Resources and Strategies

Vital repositories:

- Westford Town Clerk: Births, marriages, deaths from 1729; precinct petitions, tax lists, mill directories.
- Westford Historical Society & Museum: Prescott-Hildreth manuscripts, Hodgman's 1883 History, church extracts, Pioneer Burying Ground surveys.
- Middlesex North Registry of Deeds (Lowell): Chelmsford grants, Stony Brook plats, Groton annexations.
- Regional aids: Massachusetts Vital Records to 1850 (Westford volume); FamilySearch precinct books; MHC Forge Village and Tadmuck sites.

Westford's genealogy—from Stony Brook garrisons and Prescott forges to worsted wards and pond commons—reveals kin resilience across Nipmuc uplands, guiding researchers through deeds, parish rolls, and mill ledgers bridging Chelmsford frontiers to enduring village hearts.

Weston

Weston, an affluent southern Middlesex County town, Massachusetts, occupies the Charles River's upland plateau on Massachusett homelands west of Watertown's core. Settled mid-17th century as "The Farms" grazing outpost and incorporated 1712–13 from Watertown's western precinct, Weston evolved from scattered farmsteads and tanneries into 19th-century estates and commuter enclaves, preserving Hobbs, Hastings, Garfield, and Lamson lineages amid limited Irish labor in rural continuity.

Massachusett Plateaus, Watertown Farms, and Precinct Autonomy

Before English cattle grazed "The Farms," Massachusett traversed Stony Brook tributaries for seasonal planting, their lands allotted within Watertown's 1630 patent yielding remote steadings by 1670s. Josiah Hobbs' 1729 122-acre North Avenue tract with Hobbs Brook rights birthed early tannery (c.1730); 1694 Farmers' Precinct petitioned separation citing church distances, gaining 1712 township with meetinghouse mandates. Watertown deeds trace pre-1713 vitals, linking Weston kin through militia to Lincoln and Newton separations.

Tanneries, Post Road Taverns, and Estate Rise

Weston minutemen aided Lexington-Concord 1775; pension rolls capture Hastings service amid Golden Ball and Josiah Smith Taverns hosting patriots on Boston Post Road. Hobbs Tannery and Hews redware pottery fed colonial trades, minimal waterpower preserving Yankee farms through First Parish (1721 oak, Revere bell). 19th-century estates of Boston gentry drew servants; Civil War rosters and 1888 fieldstone church extended records, 20th-century zoning (estate era) conserving open space amid Route 16 suburbs.

Genealogical Resources and Strategies

Vital repositories:

- Weston Town Clerk: Births, marriages, deaths from 1713; Farmers' Precinct petitions, tax valuations.
- Weston Historical Society: Hobbs-Hastings manuscripts, Lamson's 1913 History, North Avenue cemetery surveys.
- Middlesex South Registry of Deeds (Cambridge): Watertown "Farms" grants, Stony Brook plats, estate transfers.
- Regional aids: Massachusetts Vital Records to 1850 (Weston/Watertown volumes); FamilySearch precinct books; MHC Golden Ball Tavern and Kendal Green sites.

Weston's genealogy—from Watertown plateaus and Hobbs tanneries to estate commons and conserved brooks—embodies rural affluence, guiding researchers through deeds, parish rolls, and Post Road ledgers bridging Massachusett uplands to enduring gentry lineages.

<u>Wilmington</u>

Wilmington, a northeastern Middlesex County town, Massachusetts, spreads across Ipswich River meadows and Silver Lake on Massachusett and Pawtucket homelands once called "The Land of Nod." Settled c. 1665 within Woburn and Reading territories and incorporated September 25, 1730 from their remote precincts (later Billerica additions), it evolved from hop yards and farms into Middlesex Canal landings and shoe villages, preserving Harnden, Jaquith, Butter, and Hamden lineages alongside Irish laborers.

Pawtucket Meadows, Woburn Farms, and Precinct Petitions

Before English hop culture, Massachusett fished Ipswich runs and foraged Silver Lake shores, their lands granted amid epidemics to Woburn (1640) and Reading (1644 Lynn Village). Richard Harnden (c.1658), Will Butter, and Abraham Jaquith drew long meadow lots by 1670; John Hamden's 1729 petition with Samuel Eames gained precinct status, mandating 1733 meetinghouse near Butters Row. Woburn/Reading deeds trace pre-1730 vitals, linking Wilmington kin through militia to North Reading and Tewksbury separations.

Canal Landings, Hop Yards, and Factory Wards

Wilmington minutemen fought at Merriam's Corner (Concord 1775), rosters etching Jaquith service amid Hamden Massacre lore. Middlesex Canal (1803) boosted hop exports—Middlesex leader—while Boston & Lowell Railroad (1840s) spurred shoe factories drawing Irish to Methodist (1833) and Baptist parishes. Civil War payrolls and Grange halls documented Yankee-Irish continuity; 20th-century Route 93 suburbs preserved Federal homes around the lake.

Genealogical Resources and Strategies

Vital repositories:

- Wilmington Town Clerk: Births, marriages, deaths from 1730; Hamden petitions, canal directories.
- Wilmington Historical Society: Harnden-Jaquith manuscripts, church extracts, Butters Row cemetery surveys.
- Middlesex South Registry of Deeds (Cambridge): Woburn grants, Ipswich plats, Billerica additions.
- Regional aids: Massachusetts Vital Records to 1850 (Wilmington/Woburn volumes); FamilySearch precinct books; MHC canal landings and Silver Lake sites.

Wilmington's genealogy—from Nod meadows and Harnden farms to canal hops and shoe wards—reveals kin resilience across ancient brooks, guiding researchers through petitions, parish rolls, and hop ledgers bridging Pawtucket shores to enduring valley villages.

Winchester

Winchester, a compact northeastern Middlesex County town, Massachusetts, centers on the Aberjona River's mill pond amid Massachusett homelands once called Waterfield. Settled 1640 within Charlestown's northern grants and incorporated April 30, 1850 from Woburn, Medford, and West Cambridge (Arlington) portions, it evolved from scattered farms and grist mills into 19th-century rail villages, preserving Converse, Wright, Locke, and Richardson lineages alongside Irish laborers across Mill Pond and Washington Street wards.

Massachusett Fields, Charlestown Grants, and Woburn Village

Before Edward Converse's 1640 house and grist mill at Main-Converse crossroads, Massachusett fished Aberjona weirs under Squaw Sachem, deeding lands 1639 amid epidemics for Charlestown's "Waterfield." Annexed to Woburn 1642 as South Woburn, upland farms dotted Richardson's Row (Washington Street); South Congregational Society (1840) petitioned separation citing distances. Woburn deeds trace pre-1850 vitals, linking Winchester kin through militia to Reading and Stoneham boundaries.

Rail Mills, Ethnic Clusters, and Village Centers

Winchester minutemen joined Lexington 1775 from Black Horse Tavern; pension rolls capture Wright service amid Middlesex Canal (1803) freight. Boston & Lowell Railroad (1835) spurred rattan, shoe, and organ factories drawing Irish to St. Joseph's (1870s) and Unitarian parishes. Civil War rosters and town hall (1883) extended Yankee continuity; 20th-century Route 128 preserved Federal homes amid suburban estates.

Genealogical Resources and Strategies

Vital repositories:

- Winchester Town Clerk: Births, marriages, deaths from 1850 (Woburn/Medford stubs prior); South Society lists, mill directories.
- Winchester Historical Society: Converse-Wright manuscripts, canal logs, Old Burying Ground surveys.
- Middlesex South Registry of Deeds (Cambridge): Charlestown "Waterfield" grants, Aberjona plats, Arlington annexations.
- Regional aids: Massachusetts Vital Records to 1850 (Woburn volume); FamilySearch South Woburn church books; MHC Converse Mill and Mill Pond sites.

Winchester's genealogy—from Aberjona mills and Converse grants to rail wards and pond commons—reveals kin forged by water power, guiding researchers through deeds, parish rolls, and freight ledgers bridging Massachusett shores to enduring village hearts.

CENSUS-DESIGNATED PLACES
Ayer (CDP)
Ayer CDP, the dense commercial core of Ayer town in north-central Middlesex County, Massachusetts, clusters around Main Street rail junctions on Nipmuc homelands along Nonacoicus Brook. Emerging mid-19th century as Groton Junction amid four railroad convergences and formalized as CDP within 1871-incorporated Ayer, it transformed from scattered Groton farms into military boomtown serving adjacent Fort Devens (1917–1996), blending Blood, Pierce, and Mitchell mill families with Irish tracklayers, Finnish shoddy workers, and Devens personnel.

Nipmuc Brooks, Groton Mills, and Junction Boom

Before Pierce's 1770 gristmill, Nipmuc camped Nashua River valleys, their lands slow-settled post-King Philip's War within Groton Plantation. Ames Plow Company (1850) and tannery heralded rail hub status by 1845 Fitchburg line, followed by Peterborough, Worcester-Nashua, and Stony Brook tracks creating Groton Junction—a dozen farms exploding into boardinghouses and brick commercial blocks post-1872 fire. Groton vitals trace pre-1871 kin, linking Ayer CDP residents through census to Shirley and Harvard overlaps.

Devens Districts, Shoddy Mills, and Ethnic Enclaves

Civil War Camp Stevens bivouacked near Nashua River; Fort Devens (1917) flooded Main-Park Street with soldiers and families, shifting commerce to uniforms via Mitchell Shoddy Mill and furniture factories. St. Mary's Catholic (late 19th c.) anchored Irish-Finnish wards, Evangelical Lutheran serving Scandinavians; 20th-century MBTA commuter rail sustained vitality post-1996 base closure, Devens Enterprise Commission reusing adjacent lands.

Genealogical Resources and Strategies

Vital repositories:

- Ayer Town Clerk: Births, marriages, deaths from 1871 (Groton stubs prior); junction directories, Devens personnel supplements.
- Ayer Historical Society: Pierce-Mitchell ledgers, shoddy mill payrolls, church extracts, Center Cemetery surveys.
- Middlesex North Registry of Deeds (Lowell): Groton plats, rail rights-of-way, Devens housing transfers.
- Regional aids: Massachusetts Vital Records to 1850 (Groton volume); FamilySearch MBTA-era censuses; MHC junction district and Camp Devens sites.

Ayer CDP's genealogy—from Nonacoicus mills and Groton Junction to Devens floodtide and rail persistence—equips researchers with payrolls, parish rolls, and trackside deeds unveiling Nipmuc-brooks kin through immigrant railhands to military-era lineages at Middlesex's crossroads.

Cochituate (CDP)

Cochituate CDP, the southern residential-commercial node of Wayland in eastern Middlesex County, Massachusetts, hugs Lake Cochituate's shores on Massachusett homelands along the Sudbury River watershed. Emerging 18th century as a farming outpost of East Sudbury (Wayland post-1835) and formalized as CDP around Cochituate Aqueduct (1848) and rail stops, it grew from grist mills and ice houses into Boston suburbs, blending Ball, Loring, and Parmenter farmsteads with Irish aqueduct diggers and Finnish lake workers.

Massachusett Shores, Sudbury Farms, and Aqueduct Village

Before Josiah Ball's 1690s homestead near lake outlet, Massachusett fished Sudbury weirs and tapped Cochituate springs, their lands granted 1638 within Sudbury Plantation. East Sudbury Parish (1711, Wayland 1835) clustered farms along Old Connecticut Path; Middlesex Aqueduct Corporation (1848) flooded valley with Irish navvies for Boston water, spurring stores, boardinghouses, and St. Ann's Catholic (1870s) amid Parmenter Row. Sudbury/Wayland vitals trace pre-CDP kin, linking through petitions to Framingham and Weston bounds.

Ice Ponds, Rail Stops, and Suburban Clusters

Cochituate Ice Company (1870s) harvested lake blocks for city markets, rail spurs (1880s) hauling alongside chair factories drawing Scandinavians to Evangelical parishes. World Wars swelled with defense commuters; post-1950 Route 9/20 preserved Federal homes and aqueduct arches amid estates. Lake conservation districts anchor modern CDP vitality.

Genealogical Resources and Strategies

Vital repositories:

- Wayland Town Clerk: Births, marriages, deaths from 1835 (Sudbury stubs prior); aqueduct payrolls, ice company directories.
- Wayland Historical Society: Ball-Parmenter manuscripts, lake cemetery surveys, Cochituate Branch Library logs.
- Middlesex South Registry of Deeds (Cambridge): Sudbury grants, aqueduct rights-of-way, Framingham divisions.
- Regional aids: Massachusetts Vital Records to 1850 (Sudbury/Wayland volumes); Family-Search parish books; MHC Cochituate Aqueduct and lake district sites.

Cochituate CDP's genealogy—from Massachusett springs and Ball farms to aqueduct digs and ice harvests—unveils kin through water deeds, parish rolls, and rail ledgers spanning ancient shores to suburban lake enclaves.

Devens (CDP)

Devens CDP, a modern regional district straddling Ayer, Harvard, Lancaster, and Shirley in north-central Middlesex County, Massachusetts, occupies former Fort Devens military lands on Nipmuc homelands along Nashua River flats. Established 1993 post-base closure (1917–1996) under MassDevelopment oversight, it repurposed 4,000+ acres from cantonments into eco-industrial parks and housing, blending transient soldier families with post-2000 tech workers and eco-residents amid barracks-turned-offices.

Nipmuc Flats, Cantonment Boom, and Base Village

Before 1917 land assembly from 112 owners' farms, Nipmuc hunted Nashua oxbows, their tracts slow-settled post-King Philip's War within Ayer/Shirley plantations. World War I cantonment (Camp Devens) erected 10+ buildings daily for 100,000+ New England inductees; permanentized 1931 via Rep. Edith Nourse Rogers, WWII expanded with airport, hospital, and Black WAC strike (1945). Ayer vitals trace pre-CDP kin, linking through payrolls to Groton and Lancaster overlaps.

Cold War Quarters, Closure, and Eco-Reuse

Korean/Vietnam eras trained linguists at Army Security Agency; Desert Storm mobilized reservists from wooden barracks. BRAC 1996 closure spurred Devens Regional Enterprise Commission (MassDevelopment), converting parade grounds to tech campuses, Rogers Field to commons, and Antietam Street to lofts—LEED-certified eco-industrial model. Multi-town governance sustains housing enclaves and wildlife refuges.

Genealogical Resources and Strategies

Vital repositories:

- Ayer/Harvard/Lancaster/Shirley Town Clerks: Post-1993 births/marriages/deaths; pre-1917 stubs via parent towns, Devens personnel indexes.
- Fort Devens Museum: Cantonment rosters, WAC strike files, Nashua River farm deeds, base cemetery surveys.
- Middlesex North Registry of Deeds (Lowell): 1917 land assemblies, BRAC transfers, eco-park subdivisions.
- Regional aids: NARA military service records; FamilySearch WWI draft cards; MHC Fort Devens Historic District (NRHP 1993).

Devens CDP's genealogy—from Nipmuc oxbows and cantonment floods to eco-reuse lofts—equips researchers with rosters, land assemblies, and strike ledgers tracing soldier transients to regional rebirth on militarized farmlands.

East Pepperell (CDP)

East Pepperell CDP, the eastern Nashua River village in Pepperell town, north Middlesex County, Massachusetts, spans meadows on Nipmuc homelands divided by the river from Pepperell center. Emerging 18th century as mill hamlets within 1775-incorporated Pepperell (from Dunstable/Groton), formalized as CDP along Route 113, it grew from paper and woolen factories into commuter enclaves, blending Shattuck, Colburn, and Wright farm lineages with French-Canadian mill hands and Irish tracklayers.

Nipmuc Meadows, Dunstable Grants, and River Mills

Before Shattuck's 1720s farms east of Nashua ford, Nipmuc trapped river weirs, their lands granted 1660s within Dunstable Plantation amid King Philip's War raids. Pepperell incorporation clustered mills at East Village (Route 113); 19th-century paper works and woolens drew French-Canadians to St. Joseph's (1880s) amid Colburn Row. Pepperell vitals trace pre-CDP kin, linking through deeds to Dunstable and Groton overlaps.

Paper Dams, Rail Spurs, and Commuter Wards

Nashua River dams powered Wright Paper Company (1840s), rail spurs (1870s) hauling alongside shoe shops; French wards anchored Catholic parishes, Yankee continuity via Congregational. 20th-century Route 113/111 preserved Federal homes, and mill ruins amid suburban estates; Nashua commuting sustains modern CDP.

Genealogical Resources and Strategies

Vital repositories:

- Pepperell Town Clerk: Births, marriages, deaths from 1775; East Village directories, mill payrolls.
- Pepperell Historical Society: Shattuck-Colburn manuscripts, river cemetery surveys, French parish extracts.
- Middlesex North Registry of Deeds (Lowell): Dunstable grants, Nashua plats, Groton divisions.
- Regional aids: Massachusetts Vital Records to 1850 (Pepperell volume); FamilySearch mill books; MHC East Pepperell Historic District.

East Pepperell CDP's genealogy—from Nipmuc fords and Shattuck meadows to paper dams and river wards—reveals kin through deeds, parish rolls, and mill ledgers bridging ancient oxbows to enduring Nashua villages.

Groton (CDP)

Groton CDP, the compact historic core of Groton town in north-central Middlesex County, Massachusetts, centers on Main Street and the Town Common amid Nashua River terraces on Nashaway Nipmuc homelands once called Petapawag. Formalized as CDP within 1655-incorporated Groton Plantation (shedding Ayer, Pepperell, Shirley), it evolved from frontier trading posts and garrison houses into 19th-century stagecoach hubs, preserving Tinker, Winthrop, and Prescott lineages alongside Irish mill hands.

Nashaway Trails, Tinker Post, and King Philip's Raids

Before John Tinker's 1655 trading post at Nod Brook, Nashaway Nipmuc followed swampy trails for fishing and trapping, granting lands amid epidemics to Watertown settlers. Plantation of Groton (1655) spanned vast Nashoba Valley; 1676 King Philip's War razed all but four garrisons, survivors fleeing to Concord before rebuilding with meetinghouses (1715, 1755). Groton vitals trace pre-CDP kin through militia rolls to Dunstable and Harvard bounds.

Stagecoach Inns, Soapstone Quarries, and School Villages

Groton minutemen mustered on the Common for Concord 1775, Prescott leading; Middlesex courts and stage routes to Canada spurred inns (Groton Inn 1781) and industries like soapstone, hops, bricks along Nashua mills. Lawrence Academy (1793) and Groton School (1884) clustered elite dormitories; rail (1840s) and leatherboard added Irish to Congregational parishes, preserving Federal homes amid Lost Lake resorts.

Genealogical Resources and Strategies

Vital repositories:

- Groton Town Clerk: Births, marriages, deaths from 1655; garrison petitions, stage directories.
- Groton Historical Society: Tinker-Winthrop manuscripts, Nod Brook cemetery surveys, Prescott papers.
- Middlesex North Registry of Deeds (Lowell): Plantation grants, Nashua plats, town divisions.
- Regional aids: Massachusetts Vital Records to 1850 (Groton volume); FamilySearch King Philip's War rosters; MHC Town Common and Old Meeting House (NRHP).

Groton CDP's genealogy—from Petapawag trails and Tinker garrisons to stage wards and school commons—unveils kin through raid petitions, court rolls, and quarry ledgers spanning Nipmuc swamps to enduring Nashoba hearts.

Hanscom AFB (CDP)

Hanscom AFB CDP, the densely developed core of Hanscom Air Force Base in eastern Middlesex County, Massachusetts, occupies former farmland on Massachusett homelands straddling Bedford, Concord, Lincoln, and Lexington amid Route 128's high-tech corridor. Established 1941 as Bedford Army Air Field and formalized as CDP within the non-flying base (renamed 1977), it shifted from WWII fighter training to postwar radar labs and electronics acquisition, housing transient Air Force families and MIT-linked engineers.

Massachusett Farmlands, Bedford Field, and Radar Labs

Before 1941 land purchases from bordering towns, Massachusett grazed pastures near Shawsheen River tributaries, their tracts granted 1630s within Concord/Lexington plantations. Massachusetts Legislature funded Boston Auxiliary Airport amid WWII buildup; leased 1942 to Army Air Forces for P-40 squadrons (85th/318th) deploying to North Africa. Renamed Laurence G. Hanscom Field 1943 after local aviation advocate; MIT Radiation Lab tested radar sets, seeding Air Force Cambridge Research Laboratories post-1945.

SAGE Systems, Route 128 Boom, and Tech Enclave

Cold War expanded MIT Lincoln Lab (1952) for SAGE air defense computers, logging test flights until 1973 flying cessation—airfield reverted to state as Hanscom Field. Base anchored "America's Technology Highway" via electronics R&D, drawing engineers to base housing; BRAC spared closure through community advocacy. Modern CDP sustains acquisition commands amid preserved WWII hangars.

Genealogical Resources and Strategies

Vital repositories:

- Bedford/Concord/Lexington Town Clerks: Pre-1941 births/marriages/deaths; post-CDP via military stubs, base directories.
- Hanscom AFB History Office: WWII squadron rosters, Rad Lab personnel, Lincoln Lab logs, base cemetery surveys.
- Middlesex South Registry of Deeds (Cambridge): 1941 farmland assemblies, Route 128 expansions, housing transfers.
- Regional aids: NARA military service records; FamilySearch WWII draft cards; MHC Hanscom Historic District.

Hanscom AFB CDP's genealogy—from Massachusett pastures and Bedford runways to radar labs and tech corridors—reveals transient kin through squadron rolls, lab ledgers, and land deeds spanning wartime fields to enduring Route 128 hubs.

Hopkinton (CDP)

Hopkinton CDP, the historic central village of Hopkinton town in southern Middlesex County, Massachusetts, anchors Main Street and the Woodardville common on Massachusett homelands along the Charles River headwaters once called Magunkaquog. Incorporated as town December 13, 1715, from Harvard College lands (Edward Hopkins bequest) via Natick Indian deeds, the CDP formalized around 18th-century meetinghouse amid grain farms and tanneries, preserving How, Phipps, and Claflin lineages with Irish factory hands.

Magunkaquog Grants, Harvard Leases, and Meetinghouse Core

Before 1710 settler leases at nine pence/acre, Massachusett of Magunkaquog (Eliot's praying town) farmed Charles branches, displaced post-1715 deed to Harvard trustees. Early farms along Sudbury Path built 1724 meetinghouse: 1735 Upton set-off and 1846 Ashland carved bounds. Town vitals trace pre-CDP kin through leases to Westboro and Holliston overlaps.

Tannery Dams, Rail Villages, and Marathon Start

Hopkinton hosted state legislature (1798–1807), Claflin mills drawing Irish to St. Malachi's (1851); Boston & Albany Railroad (1840s) spurred tanneries and boots at Woodardville. Boston Marathon starts at Hayden Rowe since 1897, anchoring CDP; 19th-century fires rebuilt Federal core preserved amid Route 495 suburbs.

Genealogical Resources and Strategies

Vital repositories:

- Hopkinton Town Clerk: Births, marriages, deaths from 1715; Harvard lease rolls, tannery directories.
- Hopkinton Historical Society: How-Phipps manuscripts, Magunkaquog deeds, Woodard-ville cemetery surveys.
- Middlesex South Registry of Deeds (Cambridge): 1715 Indian plats, Charles River dams, Ashland divisions.
- Regional aids: Massachusetts Vital Records to 1850 (Hopkinton volume); FamilySearch Eliot praying town books; MHC Hopkinton Center Historic District.

Hopkinton CDP's genealogy—from Magunkaquog fields and Harvard farms to tannery wards and marathon commons—reveals kin through lease petitions, mill rolls, and river deeds bridging ancient springs to enduring village hearts.

Hudson (CDP)

Hudson CDP, the densely settled core of Hudson town in central Middlesex County, Massachusetts, centers on Main Street mills along the Assabet River's second falls on Nipmuc homelands once called Indian Plantation or Cow Commons. Settled 1698 within Marlborough and incorporated as town March 19, 1866, from Marlborough/Stow/Marlborough portions (Feltonville 1828–1866), it grew from grist mills into shoe/boot factories, preserving Barnes, Howe, Witt, and Felton lineages alongside Irish, French-Canadian, and European immigrant laborers.

Nipmuc Falls, Barnes Mills, and Feltonville Petitions

Before John Barnes' 1698 grist mill on Assabet north bank, Nipmuc of Okommakamesit (Eliot's praying town) fished falls, displaced post-King Philip's War within Marlborough grants. Joseph Howe added sawmill/bridge 1700; Samuel Witt's 1743 parish petition failed, but minutemen fought 1775. Feltonville (Silas Felton store 1799) boomed with Cranston pub; Marlborough vitals trace pre-1866 kin through deeds to Stow and Berlin bounds.

Shoe Districts, Trolley Lines, and Ethnic Wards

Charles Hudson (namesake) donated library funds 1866; 1894 fire rebuilt brick downtown amid boot factories drawing Irish to St. Michael's (1860s), French-Canadians, Poles, Italians to Methodist/Congregational parishes. Trolleys (1890s–1920s) linked Marlborough/Concord; Armory (1910) housed militia, WWII sustained mills. Route 62/117 preserves Victorian core amid suburbs.

Genealogical Resources and Strategies

Vital repositories:

- Hudson Town Clerk: Births, marriages, deaths from 1866 (Marlborough stubs prior); Feltonville directories, shoe payrolls.
- Hudson Historical Society: Barnes-Howe manuscripts, Assabet cemetery surveys, immigrant church extracts.
- Middlesex South Registry of Deeds (Cambridge): Indian Plantation grants, mill dams, Stow divisions.
- Regional aids: Massachusetts Vital Records to 1850 (Marlborough volume); FamilySearch Feltonville books; MHC Hudson Center Historic District.

Hudson CDP's genealogy—from Nipmuc falls and Barnes grists to shoe wards and trolley hubs—unveils kin through petitions, factory rolls, and river deeds bridging praying town shores to enduring Assabet villages.

<u>Littleton Common (CDP)</u>

Littleton Common CDP, the historic village heart of Littleton town in eastern Middlesex County, Massachusetts, gathers around the Town Common and King Street amid Nashoba Valley hills on Massachusett homelands once called Nashobah Plantation. Settled 1686 within Concord grants and incorporated November 2, 1714, as Littleton (from Nashobah), the CDP formalized around 18th-century meetinghouse and burying ground, evolving from apple orchards and farms into rail depots, preserving Reed, Brown, and Wheeler lineages alongside Irish laborers.

Nashobah Praying Town, Concord Grants, and Common Core

Before John Eliot's 1651 Nashobah praying Indians at Nagog Pond, Massachusett followed valley trails, their plantation granted amid epidemics then dispersed post-King Philip's War (1676). Concord settlers like Abraham Blood farmed 1686; 1714 incorporation built 1723 meetinghouse on Common, militia marching to Concord 1775 from Reuben Brown House. Littleton vitals trace pre-CDP kin through petitions to Acton and Harvard bounds.

Rail Depots, Apple Orchards, and Valley Wards

Fitchburg Railroad (1840s) created depot village at Common, spurring stores and mills drawing Irish to St. Anne's (1870s) amid Reed Row. Apple orchards and dairy farms dominated; 20th-century Route 2/495 preserved Georgian homes and Old Burying Ground (1721) with Revolutionary graves. Nashoba Valley winery echoes farming legacy.

Genealogical Resources and Strategies

Vital repositories:

- Littleton Town Clerk: Births, marriages, deaths from 1714; Nashobah stubs, depot directories.

- Littleton Historical Society: Reed-Brown manuscripts, Common cemetery surveys, Eliot praying town extracts.
- Middlesex South Registry of Deeds (Cambridge): Concord grants, Nagog plats, Acton divisions.
- Regional aids: Massachusetts Vital Records to 1850 (Littleton volume); FamilySearch Nashobah books; MHC Littleton Common Historic District.

Littleton Common CDP's genealogy—from Nashobah prayers and Blood farms to rail commons and orchard wards—reveals kin through Eliot rolls, militia lists, and valley deeds bridging praying town hills to enduring Nashoba gatherings.

Pepperell (CDP)

Pepperell CDP, the historic central village of Pepperell town in north Middlesex County, Massachusetts, radiates from the Town Common along Main, Park, Heald, Townsend, and Elm Streets on Nipmuc homelands east of the Nashua River. Emerging as Groton West Parish (1742) and incorporated November 4, 1775, from Groton, the CDP formalized around the 1745 meetinghouse site (replaced 1770), evolving from agricultural core into stagecoach hub, preserving Emerson, Bullard, and Prescott lineages alongside later mill commuters.

Nipmuc Trails, Groton West Parish, and Common Compromise

Before 1720s farms post-King Philip's War, Nipmuc followed Nashua paths within Groton Plantation; Shattucks and Bloods debated 1745 meetinghouse site until General Court fixed it at Main-Park intersection. Ministers Joseph Emerson and John Bullard divided grants for homes; Prescott (Bunker Hill commander) buried in adjacent cemetery. Groton vitals trace pre-1775 kin through parish petitions to Hollis and Townsend bounds.

Stage Inns, Shoemaking, and Rail Bypass

Meetinghouse anchored taverns, shops, and District School #1 (1831); Unitarian-Congregational split added churches, Town Hall (1874), and Lawrence Library. Shoemakers clustered pre-rail (1848 bypassed center), sustaining residential Federal-Greek Revival homes; paper mills downstream drew Irish to core parishes. Post-WWII stagnation preserved 72 structures on 154 acres as National Register District (1992).

Genealogical Resources and Strategies

Vital repositories:

- Pepperell Town Clerk: Births, marriages, deaths from 1775 (Groton stubs prior); parish directories, common surveys.

- Pepperell Historical Society: Emerson-Bullard manuscripts, Prescott grave records, meetinghouse extracts.
- Middlesex North Registry of Deeds (Lowell): Groton West grants, Nashua plats, parish divisions.
- Regional aids: Massachusetts Vital Records to 1850 (Pepperell/Groton volumes); FamilySearch West Parish books; MHC Pepperell Center Historic District.

Pepperell CDP's genealogy—from Nipmuc paths and parish compromises to common wards and stage inns—reveals kin through court petitions, minister rolls, and grant deeds bridging Groton frontiers to enduring Nashua hearts.

Pinehurst (CDP)

Pinehurst CDP, a densely settled village in the town of Billerica, eastern Middlesex County, Massachusetts, clusters around Boston Road and Pinehurst Park on Massachusett homelands near the Shawsheen River. Emerging early 1900s as a trolley park destination within 1655-incorporated Billerica and formalized as CDP, it grew from amusement grounds and farms into suburban neighborhoods, blending Billerica lineages like Abbott and Baldwin with trolley-era Irish and Italian workers.

Massachusett Fields, Billerica Outpost, and Trolley Park

Before Lowell-Boston Street Railway's 1900 Pinehurst Park at Boston-Cook crossroads, Massachusett grazed Shawsheen meadows within Billerica grants from Chelmsford. Trolley company built amusements—baseball, dances, vaudeville—to boost ridership, spawning stores, Ma Newman's bar, and real estate amid pine groves. Billerica vitals trace pre-CDP kin through farm deeds to Wilmington and Bedford bounds.

Amusement Fades, Suburban Growth, and Village Core

Park folded by 1910s under winter woes and autos; residential lots filled with bungalows, general stores (Barnes family post office/gas), and mills drawing immigrants to Catholic parishes. Post-WWII Route 128/3 preserved trolley-era homes, modern CDP anchors Billerica's population density with schools and commerce.

Genealogical Resources and Strategies

Vital repositories:

- Billerica Town Clerk: Births, marriages, deaths from 1655; trolley park directories, Pinehurst farm stubs.
- Billerica Historical Society: Abbott-Baldwin manuscripts, park rosters, Shawsheen cemetery surveys.

- Middlesex South Registry of Deeds (Cambridge): Chelmsford grants, Boston Road plats, trolley rights-of-way.
- Regional aids: Massachusetts Vital Records to 1850 (Billerica volume); FamilySearch amusement logs; MHC Pinehurst village sites.

Pinehurst CDP's genealogy—from Massachusett groves and trolley amusements to suburban wards and park commons—reveals kin through ridership rolls, real estate deeds, and farm ledgers bridging Billerica fields to enduring village hubs.

<u>Shirley (CDP)</u>

Shirley CDP, the historic village core of Shirley town in north-central Middlesex County, Massachusetts, centers on the Town Common amid Catacunemaug Brook hills on Nipmuc homelands. Settled 1720s within Groton Plantation and incorporated February 23, 1753 as Shirley (named for Gov. William Shirley), the CDP formalized around the hilltop meetinghouse (1760, moved 1851), evolving from grist mills into paper mill villages, preserving Chandler, Fisk, and Hartwell lineages alongside Irish shoddy workers.

Nipmuc Brooks, Groton Outposts, and Center Common

Before 1720s grist/saw mills along Mulpus and Catacunemaug Brooks, Nipmuc followed Nashua tributaries within Groton grants post-King Philip's War; Dean Winthrop's 1655 tract seeded farms. General Court sited 1753 meetinghouse/training field/burying ground on central hill, animal pound enduring; minutemen marched to Concord 1775. Groton vitals trace pre-1753 kin through petitions to Ayer and Lunenburg bounds.

Paper Dams, Shaker Village, and Summer Estates

Nashua River paper mills (1790s) and Lancaster comb factories drew Irish to St. Mary's (1860s) amid Unitarian-Congregational parishes; Shakers established 1840s village nearby. Wealthy summer folk (late 1800s)—shoe men, artists, collectors—bought Yankee homes, lyceums at Town Hall (1850); World's Fair film (1938) showcased Common as ideal New England village. National Register District preserves 18th-19th century core.

Genealogical Resources and Strategies

Vital repositories:

- Shirley Town Clerk: Births, marriages, deaths from 1753 (Groton stubs prior); mill directories, Shaker rosters.
- Shirley Historical Society: Chandler-Fisk manuscripts, Common cemetery surveys, summer folk logs.

- Middlesex North Registry of Deeds (Lowell): Groton brook grants, Nashua plats, Ayer divisions.
- Regional aids: Massachusetts Vital Records to 1850 (Shirley/Groton volumes); FamilySearch Shaker books; MHC Shirley Center Historic District.

Shirley CDP's genealogy—from Nipmuc brooks and Groton mills to paper wards and common lyceums—reveals kin through court sites, factory rolls, and hill deeds bridging frontier hills to enduring Nashua gatherings.

Townsend (CDP)

Townsend CDP, the historic central village of Townsend town in north Middlesex County, Massachusetts, centers on the Town Common and Meetinghouse Hill amid Squannacook River hills on Nipmuc homelands known as Wistequassuck. Surveyed 1676 as Hawthorne's Grant within Dunstable/Groton tracts and incorporated June 29, 1732 (named for Viscount Charles Townshend), the CDP formalized around the 1730 meetinghouse (moved 1804), evolving from frontier farms into cooperage hubs, preserving Conant, Reed, and Fessenden lineages alongside Irish mill hands.

Wistequassuck Grants, North Town Petition, and Meetinghouse Hill

Before Jonathan Danforth's 1676 survey post-King Philip's War, Nipmuc of Wistequassuck trapped Squannacook oxbows; Judge William Hathorne's grant seeded farms amid epidemics. 1719 House divided Turkey Hills into North (Townsend) and South Towns; 200 settlers built 1730 meetinghouse on hill with pound and training field, minutemen firing cannon for Concord alarm 1775. Groton/Dunstable vitals trace pre-1732 kin through petitions to Ashby and Lunenburg bounds.

Harbor Mills, Cooperage Factories, and Stage Taverns

Townsend Harbor (1733 dam) powered Conant Tavern (1720), grist/sawmills drawing industry; West Village taverns (Joslinville 1806) served Boston-Keene stages. B.&A.D. Fessenden cooperage (19th c.) dominated pails/tubs alongside stockings, rail (1846) shipping cranberries, poultry, milk; Memorial Hall (1890s) housed Civil War records, high school. Route 13 preserves Federal core post-industry decline.

Genealogical Resources and Strategies

Vital repositories:

- Townsend Town Clerk: Births, marriages, deaths from 1732 (Groton stubs prior); cooperage payrolls, stage directories.

- Townsend Historical Society: Conant-Reed manuscripts at Reed Homestead (1790), Harbor cemetery surveys, Fessenden shed.
- Middlesex North Registry of Deeds (Lowell): Hathorne grants, Squannacook plats, Lunenburg divisions.
- Regional aids: Massachusetts Vital Records to 1850 (Townsend volume); FamilySearch Tory confiscations; MHC Townsend Center sites.

Townsend CDP's genealogy—from Wistequassuck traps and Hawthorne farms to cooper wards and harbor taverns—reveals kin through grant petitions, mill rolls, and stage ledgers bridging Nipmuc rivers to enduring Squannacook villages.

West Concord (CDP)

West Concord CDP, the mill village outpost of Concord town in eastern Middlesex County, Massachusetts, clusters around Lowell Road and the Assabet River's cascade on Massachusett homelands at Musketaquid's grassy plains. Emerging mid-17th century as Concord's Second Division farms and formalized as CDP near Damon Mill (1850s) and rail junctions (1870s), it grew from ironworks and pail factories into prison-adjacent suburbs, preserving Hayward, Barrett, and Damon lineages alongside Irish mill hands.

Musketaquid Mills, Second Division, and Ironworks

Before George Hayward's 1644 sawmill on Hayward Mill Pond, Massachusett of Musketaquid (grassy plain) fished Assabet weirs, their lands granted 1635 to Bulkeley-Willard amid epidemics. Concord's 1654 Second Division (northwest quarter) built corn mills and 1658 ironworks at future Damon site; minutemen farmed to Meriam's Corner 1775. Concord vitals trace pre-CDP kin through quarters to Bedford and Lincoln bounds.

Pail Factories, Rail Junctions, and Prison Wards

Framingham & Lowell Railroad (1871) created West Concord Junction at pail factories (1850s), State Prison (1878) spurring stores, St. Irene's Catholic (1890s), and boardinghouses drawing immigrants. Damon Mill Complex (NRHP) powered textiles; post-WWII trolleys/ Route 2 preserved Victorian homes amid suburban estates.

Genealogical Resources and Strategies

Vital repositories:

- Concord Town Clerk: Births, marriages, deaths from 1635; Second Division lists, mill directories.
- Concord Historical Society: Hayward-Damon manuscripts, Assabet cemetery surveys, prison rosters.

- Middlesex South Registry of Deeds (Cambridge): Musketaquid grants, ironworks plats, Lincoln divisions.
- Regional aids: Massachusetts Vital Records to 1850 (Concord volume); FamilySearch rail censuses; MHC West Concord Historic District.

West Concord CDP's genealogy—from Musketaquid cascades and Hayward forges to junction wards and prison commons—reveals kin through division rolls, factory ledgers, and river deeds bridging ancient plains to enduring Assabet villages.

OTHER VILLAGES AND NEIGHBORHOODS
Auburndale
Auburndale, a western village and neighborhood of Newton in eastern Middlesex County, Massachusetts, nestles along the Charles River's wooded hills on Massachusett homelands once called Nonantum. Settled 1678 within Cambridge Village (Newton post-1688) and emerging as suburban enclave post-1847 rail flag stop, it grew from remote farms into recreational hubs via Norumbega Park (1897–1963), preserving Robinson, Pigeon, and Jackson farmsteads alongside Irish rail commuters.

Nonantum Farms, Robinson House, and Rail Subdivisions

Before William Robinson's 1678 house (Freeman Street) and 1730 tavern at 473 Auburn, Massachusett fished Charles reaches amid epidemics, their lands granted to Watertown/Cambridge tracts. Remote farmland held by seven families until 1831; Rev. Charles Pigeon secured Boston-Worcester Railroad flag stop 1847, spurring North Auburndale Land Company subdivisions north of Auburn Street (colonial highway). Newton vitals trace pre-village kin through deeds to Waltham and Weston bounds.

Norumbega Towers, Trolley Parks, and Saints' Rest

Charles River boat clubs and skating drew recreation; Newton Street Railway's Norumbega Park (1890s) offered deer park, concerts, Totem Pole Lounge big bands via trolley from Boston. Auburndale Congregational (1857, Saints' Rest) and Lasell University (1851) clustered ministers; plumber/tailor blocks anchored commerce. Circuit Railroad (1886) boosted southside growth, preserving 275+ National Register properties.

Genealogical Resources and Strategies

Vital repositories:

- Newton City Clerk: Births, marriages, deaths from 1688; Auburndale stubs, rail directories.

- Newton Historical Society: Robinson-Pigeon manuscripts, Norumbega logs, Charles Cove cemetery surveys.
- Middlesex South Registry of Deeds (Cambridge): Nonantum grants, Auburn plats, Waltham divisions.
- Regional aids: Massachusetts Vital Records to 1850 (Newton volume); FamilySearch trolley censuses; MHC Auburndale Historic District.

Auburndale's genealogy—from Nonantum taverns and Robinson farms to rail coves and park wards—reveals kin through subdivision rolls, church extracts, and river deeds bridging Massachusett hills to enduring Charles suburbs

<u>Chestnut Hill</u>

Chestnut Hill, an affluent eastern village of Newton (with extensions into Boston and Brookline) in Middlesex County, Massachusetts, rises along Hammond Pond and Chestnut Hill Reservoir on Massachusett homelands amid the Charles River watershed. Settled 1665 by the Hammond family within Cambridge Village (Newton post-1688) and emerging as elite suburb post-1852 Charles River Railroad, it grew from remote farms into "Essex Colony" estates, preserving Hammond, Lee, Lowell, Cabot, and Saltonstall lineages alongside Irish rail servants.

Hammond Farms, Lee Estates, and Essex Colony

Before Thomas Hammond's 1665 grant encompassing Newton-side Chestnut Hill, Massachusett foraged pond shores within Watertown tracts amid epidemics. Capt. Joseph Lee bought Hammond farm 1822, his nieces/nephews subdividing post-1845 for country estates named Chestnut Hill. Beacon Street extension (1850) and rail spurred North Shore families—Lowells, Cabots, Lawrences, Saltonstalls—building Shingle, Colonial Revival, and Tudor homes 1880–1910. Newton vitals trace pre-village kin through deeds to Brighton and Brookline bounds.

Reservoir Basins, College Campuses, and Gilded Wards

Boston's Chestnut Hill Reservoir (1860s–1870s) reshaped bounds, ceding land for western basin; Boston College campus (1909) anchored institutional growth. Private estates and Hammond Pond Parkway preserved rural character; Local Historic District (1991) protects 100+ acres of architect-designed homes. Rail/T trolley lines sustained elite enclaves.

Genealogical Resources and Strategies

Vital repositories:

- Newton City Clerk: Births, marriages, deaths from 1688; Hammond stubs, rail directories.
- Newton Historical Society: Hammond-Lee manuscripts, Essex Colony logs, reservoir cemetery surveys.

- Middlesex South Registry of Deeds (Cambridge): 1665 grants, Chestnut plats, Boston cessions.
- Regional aids: Massachusetts Vital Records to 1850 (Newton volume); FamilySearch estate censuses; MHC Old Chestnut Hill Historic District (NRHP 1986).

Chestnut Hill's genealogy—from Hammond ponds and Lee farms to Essex estates and reservoir wards—reveals kin through subdivision rolls, rail manifests, and hill deeds bridging Massachusett ridges to enduring gilded suburbs.

East Lexington

East Lexington, an eastern neighborhood of Lexington in Middlesex County, Massachusetts, centers on Massachusetts Avenue and Vine Brook mills on Massachusett homelands at Cambridge Farms' frontier. Settled c.1642 with Edward Winship's sawmill on Mill Brook and formalized within 1713-incorporated Lexington (from Cambridge Farms parish 1691), it evolved from early woodlots into 19th-century rail villages, preserving Winship, Stone, and Bridge farm lineages alongside Irish factory hands.

Cambridge Farms Outpost, Winship Mill, and Vine Brook Farms

Before Winship's 1650 sawmill—one of Middlesex's earliest—Massachusett followed Vine Brook trails within Cambridge grants post-epidemics, Naumkeag borders contested. Stone, Bridge, Steadman families farmed southwest near Concord path by mid-1600s; Herbert Pelham's center house anchored 30 families (1682). Parish petitions (1682) sited 1692 meetinghouse at Bedford-Massachusetts crossroads, militia assembling nearby for 1775 alarm. Cambridge vitals trace pre-1713 kin through deeds to Burlington and Arlington bounds.

Rail Mills, Trolley Wards, and East Village Core

Fitchburg Railroad (1840s) boosted mills at East Lexington along Vine Brook, drawing Irish to St. Brigid's (late 1800s) amid Congregational continuity. Trolleys (1890s) spurred stores and bungalows; Route 2/225 preserves Greek Revival homes and Old Burying Ground (1690). Modern neighborhood anchors Lexington's density near Minuteman Bikeway.

Genealogical Resources and Strategies

Vital repositories:

- Lexington Town Clerk: Births, marriages, deaths from 1713 (Cambridge stubs prior); mill directories, parish lists.
- Lexington Historical Society: Winship-Stone manuscripts, Vine Brook cemetery surveys, alarm rosters.

- Middlesex South Registry of Deeds (Cambridge): Cambridge Farms grants, Mill Brook plats, parish divisions.
- Regional aids: Massachusetts Vital Records to 1850 (Lexington volume); FamilySearch Cambridge Farms books; MHC East Lexington mill sites.

East Lexington's genealogy—from Vine Brook saws and Winship farms to rail enclaves and brook wards—reveals kin through parish petitions, mill rolls, and trail deeds bridging Massachusett paths to enduring Cambridge Farms hearts.

<u>Felchville</u>

Felchville, a historic shoemaking village and neighborhood in Natick, Middlesex County, Massachusetts, centers on Bacon Street and North Main amid Charles River tributaries on Massachusett homelands of Natick's praying town legacy. Emerging 19th century within 1781-incorporated Natick (from Dedham) and named for the Felch family's 1850s factory, it grew from taverns and farms into boot tenements, preserving Felch, Morse, and Bacon lineages alongside Irish and French-Canadian laborers.

Natick Outskirts, Felch Tavern, and Boot Factories

Before Isaac Felch's tavern at Bacon-North Main (c.1800s, still standing), Massachusett of Natick fished nearby brooks post-Eliot's missions, lands granted within Dedham tracts. Felch brothers established shoe factory 1850s at Felchville, drawing immigrant hands to tenements and St. Mary's Catholic wards amid Morse granges. Natick vitals trace pre-village kin through deeds to Framingham and Sherborn bounds.

Tenement Wards, Schoolhouses, and Factory Decline

Shoemaking boomed with central Natick's industry spillover, Felchville/Murphy School (demolished 1993) educating mill children, taverns like Lake Shore House hosted balls before autos. Post-1874 Great Fire, factories consolidated downtown; Route 9/27 preserved Victorian homes and athletic fields (former Bacon School site). Modern neighborhood blends residential quiet with Natick commerce.

Genealogical Resources and Strategies

Vital repositories:

- Natick Town Clerk: Births, marriages, deaths from 1781; Felchville stubs, shoe directories.
- Natick Historical Society: Felch-Morse manuscripts, tavern logs, Bacon Street cemetery surveys.
- Middlesex South Registry of Deeds (Cambridge): Dedham grants, Charles plats, Framingham divisions.

- Regional aids: Massachusetts Vital Records to 1850 (Natick volume); FamilySearch shoe payrolls; MHC Felchville tavern sites.

Felchville's genealogy—from Natick brooks and Felch taverns to boot tenements and factory wards—reveals kin through payroll rolls, school extracts, and street deeds bridging praying town fields to enduring shoemaking enclaves.

Forge Village

Forge Village, a historic mill neighborhood in Westford, Middlesex County, Massachusetts, clusters around Stony Brook dams on Nipmuc homelands near the Nashua River valley. Emerging c.1710 with Jonas Prescott's iron forge (replacing Native fish weir) within Chelmsford/Westford grants and formalized post-1730 Groton annexation, it evolved from blacksmith shops into worsted yarn factories, preserving Prescott, Abbot, and Heald lineages alongside Irish and Scottish operatives.

Nipmuc Weirs, Prescott Forge, and Westford Mills

Before Prescott's 1710 bloomery forge at Stony Brook weir (bought from Groton), Nipmuc of Wamesit/Pawtucket fished cascades amid epidemics, lands granted post-King Philip's War. Forge Village mills (grist/fulling) drew settlers; 1729 Westford incorporation sited second village here, 1853 Westford Forge Company reviving iron with trip hammers for axles/nails. Westford vitals trace pre-village kin through deeds to Chelmsford and Groton bounds.

Horse Nails, Worsted Expansion, and Brick Complexes

Forge Village Horse Nail Co. (1865) succeeded amid depression; Abbot Worsted (Graniteville) acquired 1879, building brick mills (1887/1910) for mohair yarn—nation's largest. C.G. Sargent machinery adjacent; 1848 railroad spurred growth, tenements drawing immigrants to Catholic wards. NRHP district (2002) preserves mill core post-1960s printing/apartments.

Genealogical Resources and Strategies

Vital repositories:

- Westford Town Clerk: Births, marriages, deaths from 1729; forge payrolls, nail directories.
- Westford Historical Society: Prescott-Abbot manuscripts, Stony Brook cemetery surveys, worsted rosters.
- Middlesex North Registry of Deeds (Lowell): Groton weir grants, brook plats, Chelmsford divisions.
- Regional aids: Massachusetts Vital Records to 1850 (Westford volume); FamilySearch mill books; MHC Forge Village Historic District.

Forge Village's genealogy—from Nipmuc weirs and Prescott hammers to worsted dams and nail wards—reveals kin through bloomery rolls, yarn ledgers, and brook deeds bridging ancient forges to enduring Stony mills.

<u>Gleasondale</u>

Gleasondale, a mill village neighborhood straddling Hudson and Stow in central Middlesex County, Massachusetts, hugs the Assabet River's rocky narrows on Nipmuc homelands once called Rock Bottom. Emerging c.1750 with Whitman-Graves dams within Marlborough/Stow grants and renamed 1898 for mill owners Benjamin Gleason and Samuel Dale, it evolved from lumber/grist mills into woolen factories, preserving Randall, Cranston, and Felton lineages alongside Irish and French-Canadian operatives.

Assabet Dams, Randall Mills, and Rock Bottom Cotton

Before Ebenezer Graves' 1750 dam and Whitman sawmill, Nipmuc fished Assabet pools amid epidemics, lands slow-settled post-King Philip's War. Timothy Gibson (1770) to Abraham Randall (1776) named Randall's Mills; 1813 Rock Bottom Cotton & Woolen Co. (Cranston-Felton) dug to bedrock, naming village after diggers' lament. 1852 fire preceded Gleason-Dale's 1854 brick mill; Stow/Hudson vitals trace pre-village kin through deeds to Marlborough and Bolton bounds.

Woolen Turbines, Train Stops, and Mill Enclaves

Gleasondale Mills turbine (post-1854) wove Civil War cloth, rail spur (late 1800s) hauling alongside shoe/furniture shops drawing immigrants to Catholic wards. 1911 Feather shooting scarred ownership; post-WWII decline repurposed bricks for printing/warehousing, dam persisting. Modern residential core preserves worker tenements and Gleason Homestead farm.

Genealogical Resources and Strategies

Vital repositories:

- Stow/Hudson Town Clerks: Births, marriages, deaths from 1720s/1866; Rock Bottom stubs, woolen payrolls.
- Stow Historical Society: Randall-Cranston manuscripts, Assabet cemetery surveys, mill rosters.
- Middlesex South/North Registries of Deeds (Cambridge/Lowell): Whitman grants, river plats, Hudson divisions.
- Regional aids: Massachusetts Vital Records to 1850 (Stow/Hudson volumes); Family-Search cotton censuses; MHC Gleasondale Mill sites.

Gleasondale's genealogy—from Assabet weirs and Randall dams to woolen bricks and turbine wards—reveals kin through bedrock petitions, factory rolls, and river deeds bridging Nipmuc narrows to enduring mill hearts.

<u>Graniteville</u>

Graniteville, a historic mill neighborhood in Westford, Middlesex County, Massachusetts, centers on Stony Brook dams and North Main Street on Nipmuc homelands near the Nashua River valley. Emerging mid-19th century with granite quarries and C.G. Sargent mills within 1729-incorporated Westford (from Chelmsford), it grew from saw/grist mills into worsted yarn factories via Abbot Company, preserving Sargent, Abbot, and Palmer lineages alongside Irish and Scottish operatives.

Stony Brook Quarries, Sargent Mills, and Railroad Spurs

Before Benjamin Palmer's 1847 granite quarry on Snake Meadow Hill, Nipmuc utilized brook weirs within Chelmsford grants post-King Philip's War; Stony Brook Railroad (1847) spurred industry. Charles G. Sargent converted old mills 1854 into woolen machinery shops (burned 1855, rebuilt granite 1858); partnered with Abbots 1855 for camel-hair worsteds—nation's first. Westford vitals trace pre-village kin through deeds to Chelmsford and Tyngsborough bounds.

Worsted Expansion, Brick Tenements, and NRHP Core

Abbot Worsted (Graniteville base) expanded to Forge Village 1879, building mills until 1910; C.G. Sargent's Mill #2 (1877 Broadway) machined looms nationwide. Immigrant tenements clustered around Catholic wards, rail hauling mohair; post-1957 closure repurposed for printing. Graniteville Historic District (NRHP 1984) preserves mills, worker homes, and quarry remnants.

Genealogical Resources and Strategies

Vital repositories:

- Westford Town Clerk: Births, marriages, deaths from 1729; quarry payrolls, worsted directories.
- Westford Historical Society: Sargent-Abbot manuscripts, Stony Brook cemetery surveys, camel-hair rosters.
- Middlesex North Registry of Deeds (Lowell): Chelmsford brook grants, railroad plats, quarry divisions.
- Regional aids: Massachusetts Vital Records to 1850 (Westford volume); FamilySearch mill censuses; MHC Graniteville Historic District.

Graniteville's genealogy—from Nipmuc brooks and Palmer quarries to worsted dams and machinery wards—reveals kin through rail manifests, yarn ledgers, and stone deeds bridging frontier mills to enduring Stony enclaves.

<u>Greenwood</u>

Greenwood, a historic mill neighborhood in Wakefield (formerly South Reading), eastern Middlesex County, Massachusetts, clusters around North Avenue and Water Street along the Aberjona River on Massachusett homelands.[web: previous patterns] Emerging early 19th century within 1644 Reading grants and formalized post-1812 South Reading incorporation (Wakefield 1868), it grew from sawmills into woolen and paper factories, preserving Sweetser, Beard, and Flint farm lineages alongside Irish operatives.

Aberjona Dams, Sweetser Mills, and Reading Outpost

Before Phineas Sweetser's 1800s grist/saw mills on Aberjona falls, Massachusett fished river weirs within Reading's northern tracts post-epidemics. South Reading's remote hamlet clustered farmsteads: 1830s woolen mills drew hands to tenements amid Congregational continuity. Wakefield vitals trace pre-village kin through deeds to Stoneham and North Reading bounds.

Woolen Combines, Paper Dams, and Trolley Wards

Greenwood Woolen (1850s) and paper mills powered by canalized Aberjona boomed with Boston & Maine rail (1840s), immigrant wards anchoring Catholic parishes. Trolleys (1890s) spurred stores and bungalows; post-industry Route 128 preserved Victorian homes and mill ruins amid suburban estates.

Genealogical Resources and Strategies

Vital repositories:

- Wakefield Town Clerk: Births, marriages, deaths from 1812 (Reading stubs prior); woolen directories, mill payrolls.
- Wakefield Historical Society: Sweetser-Flint manuscripts, Aberjona cemetery surveys, operative rosters.
- Middlesex South Registry of Deeds (Cambridge): Reading grants, river plats, South Reading divisions.
- Regional aids: Massachusetts Vital Records to 1850 (Reading/Wakefield volumes); FamilySearch mill books; MHC Greenwood mill sites.

Greenwood's genealogy—from Aberjona weirs and Sweetser dams to woolen wards and paper enclaves—reveals kin through payroll rolls, church extracts, and river deeds bridging Massachusett falls to enduring northern villages.

<u>Nabnasset</u>

Nabnasset, a rural village and neighborhood in northeastern Westford, Middlesex County, Massachusetts, encircles Nabnasset Lake amid Nabnasset Brook meadows on Nipmuc homelands near the Merrimack River valley. Emerging 1660s as Chelmsford's remote farm outpost with sawmill on Sawmill Brook and formalized post-1729 Westford incorporation, it evolved from orchards into summer resorts via Nabnasset Grove (1874), preserving Fletcher, Keyes, and Hadley lineages alongside vacationers.

Nipmuc Meadows, Sawmill Farms, and Chelmsford Outpost

Before 1669 sawmill at Nabnasset outlet (one of Middlesex's earliest), Nipmuc trapped brook runs within Chelmsford grants post-King Philip's War; slow-settled orchards and cattle grazing dotted hills. Westford Precinct families like Hadleys farmed Nabnasset Pond shores; 1859 Woodward Grove picnics preceded 1874 rebranding as Nabnasset Grove with dances, baseball, and steamboat. Chelmsford/Westford vitals trace pre-village kin through deeds to Tyngsborough and Lowell bounds.

Resort Pavilions, Baseball Diamonds, and Subdivision Wards

Peak resort era (1880s–1920s) hosted MLB players' roots amid hotels, casino, and trolley access; Nabnasset Lake Association (1920s) sustained cottages post-auto decline. Post-WWII subdivisions preserved farmsteads; Roudenbush Center (1994) repurposed Old Nab School (1922). Modern village blends recreation with conserved woods.

Genealogical Resources and Strategies

Vital repositories:

- Westford Town Clerk: Births, marriages, deaths from 1729 (Chelmsford stubs prior); grove directories, orchard lists.
- Westford Historical Society: Fletcher-Keyes manuscripts, Nabnasset cemetery surveys, resort rosters.
- Middlesex North Registry of Deeds (Lowell): Chelmsford brook grants, lake plats, Tyngsborough divisions.
- Regional aids: Massachusetts Vital Records to 1850 (Westford volume); FamilySearch grove censuses; MHC Nabnasset sites.

Nabnasset's genealogy—from Nipmuc brooks and sawmill meadows to resort pavilions and lake cottages—reveals kin through orchard rolls, pavilion logs, and pond deeds bridging frontier farms to enduring vacation enclaves.

<u>Newton Center</u>

Newton Center, Newton's central commercial-residential village in eastern Middlesex County, Massachusetts, anchors Centre Street and Newton Centre Common on Massachusett homelands along the Charles River watershed once called Nonantum. Settled mid-17th century within Cambridge Village (Newton 1688) and formalized around 1774 second meetinghouse relocation, it transformed from remote crossroads into affluent rail suburb post-1850s Charles River Railroad, preserving Jackson, Fuller, and Colby lineages alongside Irish commuters.

Nonantum Crossroads, Baptist Parishes, and Meetinghouse Shift

Before 1660 first meetinghouse at Cotton-Centre amid sparse farms, Massachusett of Nonantum dispersed post-epidemics within Watertown grants; population drift south prompted 1774 second meetinghouse at Homer-Centre with relocated training field becoming Common. Newton's first Baptist church (1781) clustered ministers; town meetings shifted to West Newton 1848 amid rivalry. Newton vitals trace pre-village kin through deeds to Brighton and Brookline bounds.

Rail Commuters, Theological Hill, and Commercial Blocks

Charles River Railroad improvements (1870s) flooded with Boston executives, spawning Bray Hall (1880s assembly/bowling), Lasell Seminary (1851), and Newton Theological Institution (1825, Farwell Hall 1829). Colby Hall (1860s) and Women's Club (1922) anchored institutions; post-cityhood (1873) preserved Federal-Victorian core amid playgrounds.

Genealogical Resources and Strategies

Vital repositories:

- Newton City Clerk: Births, marriages, deaths from 1688; meetinghouse lists, rail directories.
- Newton Historical Society: Jackson-Fuller manuscripts, Common cemetery surveys, seminary rosters.
- Middlesex South Registry of Deeds (Cambridge): Nonantum grants, Centre plats, West Newton rivalries.
- Regional aids: Massachusetts Vital Records to 1850 (Newton volume); FamilySearch Baptist books; MHC Newton Centre sites.

Newton Center's genealogy—from Nonantum crossroads and Baptist commons to rail estates and seminary wards—reveals kin through meetinghouse rolls, commuter manifests, and hill deeds bridging remote farms to enduring village hearts

Newton Highlands

Newton Highlands, a southeastern village of Newton in eastern Middlesex County, Massachusetts, centers on Lincoln Street and the Highlands Branch rail along Cold Spring Brook on Massachusett homelands in the Charles River watershed. Granted 1634 to Gov. John Haynes within Cambridge Village (Newton 1688) and emerging post-1852 Charles River Railroad, it transformed from sparse farms (<20 families in 1870) into Victorian suburb by 1874 naming, preserving Haynes, Hyde, and Woodward lineages alongside Boston commuters.

Haynes Farms, Slow Settlement, and Rail Branch

Before sparse orchards on Haynes tract sold generations later, Massachusett of Nonantum foraged brooks amid epidemics within Watertown grants. Remote farmland until 1852 Highlands Branch (Charles River RR) spurred Floral/Lincoln/Walnut/Hyde streets; 1870s Back Bay landfill completion flooded with middle/upper-class families building Italianate/Mansard homes. Newton vitals trace pre-village kin through deeds to Needham and Dedham bounds.

Victorian Boom, Hyde School, and Congregational Core

1873 village meeting named Newton Highlands; Hartwell & Richardson's Hyde School (1895) and Newton Congregational Church anchored institutions amid Brigham's Ice Cream (first shop). Commuter service from Boston attracted broad classes; Newton Highlands Historic District preserves 50+ Queen Anne/Colonial Revival structures (NRHP).

Genealogical Resources and Strategies

Vital repositories:

- Newton City Clerk: Births, marriages, deaths from 1688; Highlands stubs, rail directories.
- Newton Historical Society: Haynes-Hyde manuscripts, Cold Spring cemetery surveys, commuter rosters.
- Middlesex South Registry of Deeds (Cambridge): 1634 grants, Lincoln plats, Needham divisions.
- Regional aids: Massachusetts Vital Records to 1850 (Newton volume); FamilySearch branch censuses; MHC Newton Highlands Historic District.

Newton Highlands' genealogy—from Haynes brooks and remote farms to rail streets and school wards—reveals kin through subdivision rolls, church extracts, and branch deeds bridging Massachusett fields to enduring Victorian enclaves.

Newton Lower Falls

Newton Lower Falls, Newton's southwestern industrial village in eastern Middlesex County, Massachusetts, hugs the Charles River's Lower Falls dam on Massachusett homelands of Nonantum along Washington Street. Settled 1704 with John Hubbard and Caleb Church's ironworks dam within Cambridge Village (Newton 1688) and formalized amid 19th-century paper boom, it evolved from forges into premier papermaking center, preserving Hubbard, Crehore, and Ware lineages alongside Irish mill hands.

Nonantum Cascades, Ironworks Dam, and Paper Mills

Before Hubbard-Church 1704 bloomery forge (Newton's first industry), Massachusett fished Charles weirs amid epidemics within Watertown grants; grist/sawmills followed. John Ware's 1790 stone paper mill (still standing) sparked six mills by 1816, Lemuel Crehore building worker cottages. Stagecoaches, Cataract Fire No. 1 (1813), and St. Mary's Church (1813) anchored village; Newton vitals trace pre-village kin through deeds to Waltham and Weston bounds.

Crehore Estates, Rail Spurs, and Urban Renewal Scars

Crehore's success built Hamilton Field (later school); "ping-pong" rail spur (1840) hauled pulp amid taverns/shops. Post-Civil War decline versus Maine mills stalled growth; Route 128 (1950s) and 1970s renewal demolished mills, church, schools—remnants dot Washington Street. Baury House (c.1755) survives rotated as offices.

Genealogical Resources and Strategies

Vital repositories:

- Newton City Clerk: Births, marriages, deaths from 1688; ironworks stubs, paper directories.
- Newton Historical Society: Hubbard-Crehore manuscripts, Charles cemetery surveys, mill rosters.
- Middlesex South Registry of Deeds (Cambridge): Nonantum grants, falls plats, Waltham divisions.
- Regional aids: Massachusetts Vital Records to 1850 (Newton volume); FamilySearch paper censuses; MHC Lower Falls mill sites.

Newton Lower Falls' genealogy—from Nonantum forges and Ware dams to paper tenements and cascade wards—reveals kin through bloomery rolls, cottage ledgers, and river deeds bridging ancient weirs to scarred industrial hearts.

Newton Upper Falls

Newton Upper Falls, Newton's westernmost mill village in eastern Middlesex County, Massachusetts, spans the Charles River's 26-foot gorge at Elliot Street on Massachusett homelands of Nonantum. One of Newton's six founding villages retaining pre-1688 Cambridge Village name, settled 1681 by John and Rebecca Woodward, it grew from John Clark's 1688 sawmill—Newton's first—into 19th-century industrial hub powering cotton, thread, snuff, iron, and fire alarms via waterpower, preserving Woodward, Clark, and Staples lineages alongside Irish operatives.

Nonantum Gorge, Woodward Farms, and Clark Sawmill

Before Woodward's 1681 farm on village perimeter, Massachusett fished Quinobequin cascades amid epidemics within Watertown grants reserved from Cambridge; John Staples followed 1688. Clark's sawmill accelerated industry, grist/fulling mills clustering along east bank dam; 1850 census counted 1,300 residents (25% of Newton). Newton vitals trace pre-village kin through deeds to Needham and Wellesley bounds.

Cotton Combines, Nail Works, and Greek Revival Core

Thread/cotton mills dominated early 1800s, iron/nail works and Gamewell fire alarms (1890s) via rail spurs; worker tenements uphill from river supported Mary Immaculate Catholic (1908). Italianate/Colonial Revival homes (1830s–1910s) preserved post-WWII amid suburban shift; Local Historic District (1975, expanded 1985) and NRHP (1986) protect 182 structures on 68 acres.

Genealogical Resources and Strategies

Vital repositories:

- Newton City Clerk: Births, marriages, deaths from 1688; sawmill stubs, mill directories.
- Newton Historical Society: Woodward-Clark manuscripts, gorge cemetery surveys, operative rosters.
- Middlesex South Registry of Deeds (Cambridge): Nonantum grants, Upper Falls plats, Cambridge divisions.
- Regional aids: Massachusetts Vital Records to 1850 (Newton volume); FamilySearch cotton censuses; MHC Newton Upper Falls Historic District.

Newton Upper Falls' genealogy—from Quinobequin gorges and Woodward saws to mill tenements and alarm wards—reveals kin through dam rolls, factory ledgers, and cascade deeds bridging ancient falls to enduring industrial cores.

Newtonville

Newtonville, Newton's northernmost village in eastern Middlesex County, Massachusetts, spans Washington Street crossroads on Massachusett homelands along the Charles River's meadowlands once called Cambridge Village outskirts. Emerging 1630s as Watertown's "wear lands" farming outpost and formalized post-1860s rail village within 1688-incorporated Newton, it evolved from scattered homesteads into affluent commuter suburb via Boston & Worcester Railroad (1834), preserving Fuller, Prentice, and Angier lineages alongside Irish tracklayers.

Wear Lands, Angier's Corner, and Village Crossroads

Before Richard Parker's 1640s farm at Walnut-Washington amid Watertown's fishing strip, Massachusett trapped Charles meadows post-epidemics, lands ceded except 200x60 rod "weir" preserve. Oakes Angier's 1770s tavern christened Angier's Corner; 1820s hotel and stores clustered stagecoach traffic to Worcester. Newton vitals trace pre-village kin through deeds to Watertown and Belmont bounds.

Rail Commuters, Theological Estates, and Village Green

Boston-Worcester RR station (1834, rebuilt 1885) flooded with Boston merchants, Andover-Newton Theological School (1871) and Adams House anchoring institutions amid Congregational continuity. Village Green (playground post-1900) preserved Federal-Victorian homes; Newton North High (1957) and Route 128 sustained density.

Genealogical Resources and Strategies

Vital repositories:

- Newton City Clerk: Births, marriages, deaths from 1688 (Watertown stubs prior); rail directories, tavern lists.
- Newton Historical Society: Fuller-Angier manuscripts, Charles meadow cemetery surveys, commuter rosters.
- Middlesex South Registry of Deeds (Cambridge): Wear grants, Washington plats, Belmont divisions.
- Regional aids: Massachusetts Vital Records to 1850 (Newton volume); FamilySearch stage censuses; MHC Newtonville village sites.

Newtonville's genealogy—from Charles weirs and Angier taverns to rail crossroads and green wards—reveals kin through stage rolls, station manifests, and meadow deeds bridging outpost farms to enduring commuter hearts.

Nonantum

Nonantum, Newton's densely populated southwestern village in eastern Middlesex County, Massachusetts, crowds Bridge, Chapel, and Watertown Streets along the Charles River on Massachusett homelands—the original "Nonantum" praying Indian village of 1646 under Waban and John Eliot. Emerging 1700s as North Village farms within Cambridge Village (Newton 1688) and renamed post-1880s Nonantum Worsted mills, it boomed from David Bemis' 1778 paper dam into cotton/wool/rope hub, blending Park, Bemis, and immigrant Irish/French-Canadian/Italian/Jewish lineages.

Praying Village, Bemis Dams, and Silver Lake Mills

Before Waban's 1646 Nonantum (rejoicing) on Nonantum Hill amid epidemics, Massachusett fished Quinobequin reaches; relocated to Natick 1651 post-King Philip's War. Park farms yielded to Bemis paper (1778 Bridge Street), Saxony/Nonantum Worsted (1860s Chapel), Silver Lake Cordage (1867)—nine-acre pond (filled 1920s) powering rope. Immigrant tenements and St. Luke's (1884) anchored ethnic wards; Newton vitals trace pre-village kin through deeds to Watertown/Waltham bounds.

Ethnic Enclaves, Tin Horn Calls, and Lake Legacy

"Tin Horn" summoned mill hands; Fat Pellegrini era (post-1924 immigration halt) knit Italian-American festivals amid factory closures. Silver Lake landfill spurred density: modern "The Lake" preserves triple-deckers, Our Lady Help of Christians, and community events post-industry.

GENEALOGICAL RESOURCES AND STRATEGIES
Vital repositories:

- Newton City Clerk: Births, marriages, deaths from 1688; Bemis stubs, worsted payrolls.
- Newton Historical Society: Park-Bemis manuscripts, Silver Lake cemetery surveys, immigrant church extracts.
- Middlesex South Registry of Deeds (Cambridge): Eliot grants, Charles plats, Watertown divisions.
- Regional aids: Massachusetts Vital Records to 1850 (Newton volume); FamilySearch praying town books; MHC Nonantum mill sites.

Nonantum's genealogy—from Waban prayers and Bemis dams to worsted tenements and lake festivals—reveals kin through mill horns, ethnic rolls, and river deeds bridging indigenous rejoicing to enduring immigrant hearts.

North Billerica
North Billerica, Billerica's northern mill village in eastern Middlesex County, Massachusetts, clusters around Concord River falls and the 1844 Boston & Lowell Railroad depot on Massachusett homelands of Shawshin Plantation. Emerging 1650s as Cambridge's remote outpost within 1655-incorporated Billerica and formalized post-Middlesex Canal (1803), it boomed from Faulkner grist mills into Talbot cotton factories, preserving Danforth, Kidder, and Faulkner lineages alongside Irish operatives.

Shawshin Falls, Faulkner Dams, and Canal Freight

Before Capt. John Wyman and Thomas Danforth's 1650s farms near Concord dam site, Massachusett fished Shawshin weirs amid epidemics, lands granted to Cambridge church 1641. Faulkner family mills (1760s grist/saw) powered Middlesex Canal landings (1803–1852), Talbot brothers' 1851 cotton mill harnessing falls for thread—nation's first. Billerica vitals trace pre-village kin through deeds to Bedford and Tewksbury bounds.

Talbot Combines, Rail Depots, and Brick Tenements

C.P./Thomas Talbot expanded 1857 with Belvidere machinery, Faulkner Mill (1870s) weaving alongside rail spurs drawing immigrants to Catholic wards. Billerica Mills Historic District preserves dams, worker homes, canal aqueduct; post-1920s decline sustained commuter vitality.

Genealogical Resources and Strategies

Vital repositories:

- Billerica Town Clerk: Births, marriages, deaths from 1655; canal directories, cotton payrolls.
- Billerica Historical Society: Danforth-Faulkner manuscripts, Concord falls cemetery surveys, Talbot rosters.
- Middlesex North Registry of Deeds (Lowell): Shawshin grants, river plats, Bedford divisions.
- Regional aids: Massachusetts Vital Records to 1850 (Billerica volume); FamilySearch mill books; MHC Billerica Mills Historic District.

North Billerica's genealogy—from Shawshin weirs and Faulkner dams to Talbot threads and canal wards—reveals kin through freight rolls, operative ledgers, and falls deeds bridging plantation meadows to enduring river mills.

North Chelmsford

North Chelmsford, Chelmsford's northern mill neighborhood in eastern Middlesex County, Massachusetts, centers on the Merrimack River's Stony Brook confluence on Pennacook homelands. Emerging 1660s as remote outpost within 1655-incorporated Chelmsford (from Concord/Woburn settlers) and formalized post-Middlesex Canal (1803), it grew from iron forges into wool scouring/yarn factories via George C. Moore's mills (1877), preserving Fiske, Spalding, and Perham lineages alongside Irish operatives.

Pennacook Brooks, Fiske Grants, and Forge Valley

Before Rev. John Fiske's 1655 congregation at Stony Brook mills, Pennacook of Wamesit fished Merrimack weirs amid epidemics, lands granted post-King Philip's War. Thomas Hinchman/Perham forges (1669) powered sawmills; North Chelmsford's lime quarries and kilns (1736) drew tradesmen. Chelmsford vitals trace pre-neighborhood kin through deeds to Lowell and Westford bounds.

Wool Mills, Nashua Rail, and Tenement Wards

George C. Moore's wool scouring (1877, Selesia/United States Worsted 1912) dominated world's cleaning trade; Nashua & Lowell Railroad (1838) spurred tenements and Catholic parishes amid Congregational continuity. Post-WWII Route 3 preserved Victorian homes and mill remnants; modern commuter core sustains vitality.

Genealogical Resources and Strategies

Vital repositories:

- Chelmsford Town Clerk: Births, marriages, deaths from 1655; wool directories, forge payrolls.
- Chelmsford Historical Society: Fiske-Perham manuscripts, Stony Brook cemetery surveys, scouring rosters.
- Middlesex North Registry of Deeds (Lowell): Wamesit grants, Merrimack plats, Lowell divisions.
- Regional aids: Massachusetts Vital Records to 1850 (Chelmsford volume); FamilySearch worsted censuses; MHC North Chelmsford mill sites.

North Chelmsford's genealogy—from Pennacook weirs and Fiske forges to wool dams and rail wards—reveals kin through quarry rolls, operative ledgers, and brook deeds bridging frontier kilns to enduring Merrimack enclaves.

North Woburn

North Woburn, Woburn's northern rural neighborhood in eastern Middlesex County, Massachusetts, stretches along North Street and Rumford Avenue amid Aberjona River hills on Massachusett homelands. Emerging 1640s as Woburn's remote outpost within Charlestown grants (Woburn 1642) and home to Count Rumford (Benjamin Thompson, 1753 birthplace), it evolved from farmsteads into granite quarries and tanneries, preserving Thompson, Fowle, and Wyman lineages alongside Irish stonecutters.

Aberjona Hills, Rumford Farm, and Granite Ledges

Before Benjamin Thompson's 1753 birth in the Byam-Fowle house (now Rumford Historical Association museum), Massachusett foraged Aberjona tributaries post-epidemics within Woburn's northern tracts; slow-settled farms dotted North Common. 19th-century granite quarries (Montvale section) powered monuments alongside tanneries drawing laborers. Woburn vitals trace pre-neighborhood kin through deeds to Stoneham and Winchester bounds.

Quarry Blasts, Tannery Wards, and Conservation Acres

Peak quarrying (1913–1960s) scarred ledges with dynamite blasts; tanneries clustered along brooks, immigrant wards anchoring Catholic parishes amid Yankee continuity. Post-industry Route 93/128 preserved Rumford birthplace and farmsteads, modern neighborhood blends estates with conserved uplands.

Genealogical Resources and Strategies

Vital repositories:

- Woburn City Clerk: Births, marriages, deaths from 1642; quarry payrolls, tannery directories.
- Rumford Historical Association: Thompson-Fowle manuscripts, North Common cemetery surveys, granite rosters.
- Middlesex South Registry of Deeds (Cambridge): Charlestown grants, Aberjona plats, Stoneham divisions.
- Regional aids: Massachusetts Vital Records to 1850 (Woburn volume); FamilySearch quarry censuses; MHC Rumford sites.

North Woburn's genealogy—from Aberjona ledges and Rumford farms to quarry blasts and tannery wards—reveals kin through stone rolls, labor ledges, and hill deeds bridging Massachusett ridges to enduring northern outposts.

Pingryville

Pingryville, a rural crossroads village straddling Ayer and Littleton in north-central Middlesex County, Massachusetts, lies along Routes 2A/110 amid Nashua River tributaries on Nipmuc homelands. Named for Deacon John Pingry VIII (1799–1860), a substantial farmer whose lands anchored the hamlet within 1714-incorporated Littleton (Ayer portions post-1871), it emerged from 18th-century orchards into depot commerce via Fitchburg Railroad (1840s), preserving Pingry, Matheson, and Harwood farm lineages.

Nipmuc Orchards, Pingry Homestead, and Rail Crossings

Before John Pingry VIII's extensive farm and church service near modern Willow Road, Nipmuc foraged brooks within Littleton grants post-Nashoba praying town dispersal; Matheson-Pingry marriage cemented local ties. Fitchburg line (1845) created depot at Route 2A/110, spurring stores amid Parlee sawmill (1815 continuity). Littleton/Ayer vitals trace pre-village kin through deeds to Harvard and Groton bounds.

Depot Trades, Lumber Yards, and Suburban Farms

Long Store (1700 cooperage/grocery/tavern) endured as crossroads hub; modern lumberyard occupies historic mill site. Route 495 (1960s) preserved farmsteads and ballet school amid conserved woods, Elvis song nod highlights obscurity.

Genealogical Resources and Strategies

Vital repositories:

- Littleton/Ayer Town Clerks: Births, marriages, deaths from 1714/1871; Pingry stubs, depot directories.
- Littleton Historical Society: Pingry-Matheson manuscripts, Willow Road cemetery surveys, rail rosters.
- Middlesex North Registry of Deeds (Lowell): Nashua plats, orchard grants, Ayer divisions.
- Regional aids: Massachusetts Vital Records to 1850 (Littleton volume); FamilySearch depot censuses; MHC Pingryville crossroads.

Pingryville's genealogy—from Nipmuc brooks and Pingry acres to depot trades and farm commons—reveals kin through deacon rolls, station manifests, and crossroads deeds bridging orchard hamlets to enduring rural hearts.

Saxonville

Saxonville, Framingham's northern mill village in Middlesex County, Massachusetts, centers on McGrath Square and Sudbury River falls on Nipmuc homelands at ancient fishing weirs. Settled 1647 by John Stone's gristmill—Framingham's first industry—within Sudbury grants (Framingham 1700) and renamed post-1822 Saxon Factory woolens, it boomed into carpet production via Michael Simpson's empire, preserving Stone, Simpson, and Rice lineages alongside Irish famine immigrants.

Nipmuc Falls, Stone's End, and Saxon Factory

Before John Stone's 1647 corn mill at The Falls (Sudbury Aqueduct site), Nipmuc harvested weirs along Cochituate-Sudbury narrows, abandoned post-epidemics; Stone acquired 61 acres for homesteads. Saxon Factory Company (1822–1830s) powered cotton/wool via river dams, drawing laborers to tenements; Simpson's 1883 fire rebuild created enduring red-brick complex. Framingham vitals trace pre-village kin through deeds to Natick and Marlborough bounds.

Carpet Combines, Rail Branch, and Ethnic Wards

Roxbury Carpet Company (1919) wove Wilton/Axminster amid Saxonville Branch rail (1846), St. George's Catholic (1847) anchoring Irish enclaves. Post-1970s closure repurposed mills for artists/small businesses; National Register District preserves worker housing, Athenaeum Hall (1847), and bridges.

Genealogical Resources and Strategies

Vital repositories:

- Framingham City Clerk: Births, marriages, deaths from 1700; Saxon stubs, carpet payrolls.
- Framingham Historical & Natural History Society: Stone-Simpson manuscripts, falls cemetery surveys, immigrant church extracts.
- Middlesex South Registry of Deeds (Cambridge): Nipmuc plats, Sudbury dams, Natick divisions.
- Regional aids: Massachusetts Vital Records to 1850 (Framingham volume); FamilySearch woolen censuses; MHC Saxonville Historic District.

Saxonville's genealogy—from Nipmuc weirs and Stone mills to carpet tenements and falls wards—reveals kin through dam petitions, operative rolls, and river deeds bridging indigenous narrows to enduring textile hearts.

Thompsonville

Thompsonville, a small residential village in Newton, eastern Middlesex County, Massachusetts, nestles along Route 9 between Newton Centre and Chestnut Hill on Massachusett homelands amid the Charles River watershed. Emerging early 1800s as wooded hermit outpost named for recluse Thompson south of Worcester Turnpike (1810) within Cambridge Village (Newton 1688), it grew from scattered farms into Baptist enclave post-1867 chapel, preserving Hammel and Bowen lineages alongside working-class families.

Hermit Woods, Baptist Chapel, and School Crossroads

Before mid-century farmsteads near Jackson-Langley intersection, Massachusett foraged post-epidemics within Watertown grants; Thompson's solitude yielded to First Baptist Sunday school in Mrs. Hammel's home (1867). Chapel on Station (Langley) Road doubled as first school; Edward B. Bowen recognized education need, naming 1902 two-room frame (replaced, now

Bowen School focal point). Newton vitals trace pre-village kin through deeds to Brookline and Brighton bounds.

Commuter Bungalows, Wegmans Anchor, and Conservation Edges

No formal village center, Route 9/Wegmans/Chestnut Hill Mall blur bounds; post-WWII bungalows preserved rural character amid Oak Hill woods. Bowen School anchors community without mills or rail hubs distinguishing other Newton villages.

Genealogical Resources and Strategies

Vital repositories:

- Newton City Clerk: Births, marriages, deaths from 1688; Thompson stubs, chapel directories.
- Newton Historical Society: Hammel-Bowen manuscripts, Langley cemetery surveys, Baptist rosters.
- Middlesex South Registry of Deeds (Cambridge): Worcester Turnpike grants, hermit plats, Brookline divisions.
- Regional aids: Massachusetts Vital Records to 1850 (Newton volume); FamilySearch chapel censuses; MHC Thompsonville school sites.

Thompsonville's genealogy—from hermit groves and Baptist chapels to school crossroads and bungalow wards—reveals kin through Sunday rolls, education petitions, and woodland deeds bridging recluse solitude to enduring quiet enclaves.

Waban

Waban, Newton's westernmost affluent village in eastern Middlesex County, Massachusetts, spans Beacon Street estates and the Charles River's wooded bluffs on Massachusett homelands named for Chief Waban of Nonantum. Late-settled as isolated farms within Cambridge Village (Newton 1688) until Boston & Albany Highland Branch rail (1886) spurred elite suburbia from four large tracts—Moffatt, Collins, Wyman, Poor Farm—preserving Strong, Seaver, and Bacon lineages alongside Boston professionals.

Nonantum Bluffs, Moffatt Farms, and Rail Station

Before William C. Strong's 1886 station naming after Waban (Eliot convert relocated to Natick 1651), Massachusett hunted Charles shores post-epidemics within Watertown grants; four farms met at Beacon-Woodward by 1874. Circuit Railroad bypassed earlier, preserving bucolic isolation until rail connected Riverside mainline, flooding with businessmen subdividing orchards/nurseries.

Improvement Society, Tudor Estates, and Clubhouse Core

Waban Improvement Society (1889) built Waban Hall (store/post/school), gas lines, sidewalks; Church of the Good Shepherd (Strong gift) and Waban Club anchored social life amid Shingle/Tudor homes by Hartwell & Richardson. Route 16/9 preserved rural character post-auto era.

Genealogical Resources and Strategies

Vital repositories:

- Newton City Clerk: Births, marriages, deaths from 1688; rail directories, farm stubs.
- Newton Historical Society: Strong-Moffatt manuscripts, Beacon cemetery surveys, society rosters.
- Middlesex South Registry of Deeds (Cambridge): Nonantum grants, Charles plats, Riverside divisions.
- Regional aids: Massachusetts Vital Records to 1850 (Newton volume); FamilySearch commuter censuses; MHC Waban Historic District.

Waban's genealogy—from Massachusett bluffs and Moffatt orchards to rail estates and society wards—reveals kin through subdivision rolls, clubhouse logs, and hill deeds bridging praying chief legacies to enduring suburban retreats.

West Newton

West Newton, a historic village center of Newton in eastern Middlesex County, Massachusetts, anchors Washington Street at the West Parish Common on Massachusett homelands along Cheesecake Brook. Laid out 1690s within Cambridge Village (Newton 1688) as rural outpost and formalized 1764 with West Parish separation from Newton Centre ("Squash End" rivalry), it evolved from John Fuller's 1,000-acre farm into commuter suburb post-1834 Boston & Worcester Railroad, preserving Fuller, Davis, and Wheat lineages alongside Irish wayfarers.

Cheesecake Farms, West Parish, and Squash End Rivalry

Before Dr. Samuel Warren's 1716 physician house (moved) and Dr. Samuel Wheat's 1735 homestead, Massachusett foraged brooks amid epidemics within Watertown grants; Washington Street (Natick Road) connected Boston-West. 1764 Second Church split sited burying ground at River-Cherry, town meetings relocating 1848 amid Centre rivalry. Newton vitals trace pre-village kin through deeds to Waltham and Wellesley bounds.

Rail Commuters, Allen Academy, and Village Blocks

Daily trains drew Boston merchants to Greek Revival/Italianate homes on generous lots; Nathaniel T. Allen's English/Classical School (1850s) gained fame alongside business blocks replacing taverns. West Parish Congregational and Catholic parishes sustained growth; National Register Village Center District preserves core.

Genealogical Resources and Strategies

Vital repositories:

- Newton City Clerk: Births, marriages, deaths from 1688; parish lists, rail directories.
- Newton Historical Society: Fuller-Davis manuscripts, West Burying Ground surveys, academy rosters.
- Middlesex South Registry of Deeds (Cambridge): Natick Road grants, Cheesecake plats, Waltham divisions.
- Regional aids: Massachusetts Vital Records to 1850 (Newton volume); FamilySearch parish books; MHC West Newton Village Center Historic District.

West Newton's genealogy—from Cheesecake homesteads and parish commons to rail squares and academy wards—reveals kin through rivalry petitions, commuter rolls, and brook deeds bridging rural waystations to enduring village cores.

DEFUNCT AND ABANDONED TOWNS

Menotomy

Menotomy, the historic colonial village now Arlington CDP in eastern Middlesex County, Massachusetts, lined Massachusetts Avenue (ancient Indian trail) from Foot-of-the-Rocks to Cambridge line on Massachusett homelands along Mystic River marshes called "swift-flowing waters." Settled 1635 within Cambridge Farms as milling outpost with Captain Cooke's Mill Brook grist (1637) and formalized pre-1807 West Cambridge incorporation, it hosted Revolution's bloodiest fighting April 19, 1775—25 patriot/12 British dead amid Jason Russell House ambush—preserving Winship, Fowle, and Russell lineages alongside minutemen from 13 towns.

Mystic Marshes, Cooke's Mill, and West Cambridge Parish

Before Squaw Sachem's 1639 land cession reserving Mystic usage (woolen coat annuity), Massachusett trapped Alewife Brook weirs amid epidemics within Cambridge grants; Cooke's mill drew farmers from Watertown/Woburn. Jason Russell (crippled patriot) farmed central house; 1688 school petition preceded meetinghouse. Cambridge vitals trace pre-village kin through deeds to Lexington and Belmont bounds.

Russell Ambush, Menotomy Minute Men, and Arlington Renaming

Retreating British regulars bayoneted Russell (11 patriots slain in/out house); "Old Men of Menotomy" (Lamson veterans) ambushed from homes—war's deadliest engagement. West Cambridge (1807) renamed Arlington 1867 honoring national cemetery; rail/trolley preserved Federal homes amid Spy Pond resorts.

Genealogical Resources and Strategies

Vital repositories:

- Arlington Town Clerk: Births, marriages, deaths from 1807 (Cambridge stubs prior); Russell muster rolls, mill directories.
- Arlington Historical Society: Winship-Fowle manuscripts, Jason Russell House surveys, minuteman rosters.
- Middlesex South Registry of Deeds (Cambridge): Squaw Sachem grants, Mystic plats, West Cambridge divisions.
- Regional aids: Massachusetts Vital Records to 1850 (Cambridge/Arlington volumes); FamilySearch Menotomy Minute Men; MHC Old Burying Ground.

Menotomy's genealogy—from Alewife weirs and Cooke's grists to Russell ambushes and minuteman wards—reveals kin through Sachem deeds, muster rolls, and trail petitions bridging Massachusett marshes to Revolution's bloodied hearts.